— Simon & Schuster —

HANDBOOK *for* WRITERS

SIXTH CANADIAN EDITION

LYNN QUITMAN TROYKA

DOUGLAS HESSE

with the assistance of Cy Strom

PEARSON

Toronto

Vice-President, Editorial Director:
  Gary Bennett
Editor-in-Chief: Michelle Sartor
Acquisitions Editor: David S. Le Gallais
Sponsoring Editor: Carolin Sweig
Marketing Manager: Jennifer Sutton
Developmental Editor: Megan Burns
Project Manager: Richard di Santo
Manufacturing Manager: Susan
  Johnson
Production Editor: Doug Bell,
  PreMediaGlobal

Copy Editor: Cy Strom
Proofreaders: Lisa Berland, Trish
  O'Reilly
Compositor: PreMediaGlobal
Permissions Researcher:
  Mary Rose MacLachlan
Art Director: Julia Hall
Interior and Cover Designer:
  Miriam Blier
Cover Image: Vincent van Gogh,
  The Yellow Books, 1887 (oil on canvas) /
  Getty Images

Credits and acknowledgments borrowed from other sources and reproduced, with permission, in this textbook appear on the appropriate page within the text, and on pages 727–730.

Original edition published by Pearson Education, Inc., Upper Saddle River, New Jersey, USA. Copyright © 2009 Lynn Quitman Troyka. This edition is authorized for sale only in Canada.

If you purchased this book outside the United States or Canada, you should be aware that it has been imported without the approval of the publisher or the author.

2   16

Library and Archives Canada Cataloguing in Publication

Troyka, Lynn Quitman, 1938–
  Simon & Schuster handbook for writers / Lynn Quitman Troyka, Douglas Hesse.—6th Canadian ed.
  Includes bibliographical references and index.
  ISBN 978-0-13-266599-5
  1. English language—Rhetoric—Handbooks, manuals, etc.   2. English language—Grammar—Handbooks, manuals, etc.   3. Report writing—Handbooks, manuals, etc.
I. Hesse, Douglas   II. Title.   III. Title: Handbook for writers.   IV. Title: Simon and Schuster handbook for writers.

PE1408.T76 2012   808'.042   C2011-907247-5

ISBN 978-0-13-266599-5

Personal Message to Students

FROM LYNN QUITMAN TROYKA AND DOUG HESSE

As writers, many of you have much in common with both of us. Sure, we've been at it longer, so we've had more practice, and most rules have become cemented in our heads. However, we share with you a common goal: to put ideas into words worthy of someone else's reading time.

We also share the constant desire to become better writers. Given our extensive teaching experience, this probably sounds odd. However, writing is a lifelong enterprise. Just as we did, you'll write not only in composition classes, but also in other courses throughout college. Writing will likely be an important part of your career, of your role as a public citizen, and even of your personal life. It has certainly been central to ours. Whenever we get stuck in an unfamiliar writing situation or while learning new writing technology, we rummage through strategies we've developed over time. We talk to friends and colleagues, in person, by phone, and by e-mail, and they consult us, too.

We offer this book to you, then, as our partners in the process of writing. We hope that its pages help you give voice to your thoughts—now and years from now. We trust you'll find our advice useful in the wide range of writing situations you're bound to encounter in college and in life. You're always welcome to write us at <troykalq@nyc.rr.com> or <ddhesse@du.edu> to share your reactions to this book and your experiences as writers. We promise to answer.

Each of us would like to end this message with a personal story.

From Doug: I first glimpsed the power of writing in high school, when I wrote sappy—but apparently successful—love poems. Still, when I went to college, I was surprised to discover all I didn't know about writing. Fortunately, I had good teachers and developed lots of patience. I needed it. I continue to learn from my colleagues, my students, and my coauthor, Lynn.

From Lynn: When I was an undergraduate, handbooks for writers weren't common. Questions about writing nagged at me. One day, browsing in the library, I found an incorrectly shelved, dust-covered book whose title included the words *handbook* and *writing*. I read it hungrily and kept checking it out from the library. Back then, I could never have imagined that someday I might write such a book myself. Now that we've completed the ninth edition of the *Simon & Schuster Handbook for Writers,* I'm amazed that I ever had the nerve to begin. This proves to me—and I hope to you—that anyone can write. Students don't always believe that. I hope you will.

With cordial regards,

Lynn Quitman Troyka   *Doug Hesse*

How to Use the Simon & Schuster Handbook for Writers

The *Simon & Schuster Handbook for Writers* is designed to help you find what you need to become a better writer. You will find many features to highlight key concepts and develop your skills. We are confident you will find the *Simon & Schuster Handbook for Writers* to be a useful tool in your academic life and beyond.

- **The detailed Overview of Contents** starting on the inside front cover lists all parts and chapters in the book. Locate the specific topic you need to reference and then turn to the page indicated.

- **An access code** packaged with every new copy of the text gives you access to MyCanadianCompLab, which includes an electronic version of the book and many more online resources. More information about MyCanadianCompLab can be found on page xvi of the *Simon & Schuster Handbook for Writers*. You can register for access at www.mycanadiancomplab.ca.

- **A list of supplementary material** available with this book can be found in the Preface.

- **NEW Quick Reference Boxes** throughout the book offer easy access to some of the most common and important issues that will come up as you write. You will also find a List of Quick Reference Features at the end of the book.

- **Documentation Source Maps** are designed to clearly illustrate the process for citing different types of sources.

Annotated replications of original sources are presented along with step-by-step guidelines. Visual tools throughout the research and documentation sections simplify the research writing process.

- **The Terms Glossary** is an easy way to find the definitions for common writing-related terms. Words and phrases called out in SMALL CAPITAL LETTERS throughout the book can be found in the Terms Glossary.

- **Two Indexes** provide quick and convenient navigation by topic. The ESL Index puts a list of topics for multilingual students in one convenient place. An easy-to-reference and comprehensive Subject Index covers virtually everything found in the book.

- **A list of Proofreading Marks and Response Symbols** is at the back of the book. Consult this list if your instructor uses revision and proofreading symbols when commenting on your writing.

The following sample page illustrates features that help you navigate the *Simon & Schuster Handbook for Writers*. ➤

Elements on the Pages of This Handbook

Box title

Indicates the last section on the page

Chapter number

How can I write about quantitative data or information?   **3g**

Quick Reference Box

QUICK REFERENCE   **3.5**

Transitional expressions and the relationships they signal

ADDITION	also, in addition, too, moreover, and, besides, furthermore, equally important, then, finally
EXAMPLE	for example, for instance, thus, as an illustration, namely, specifically
CONTRAST	but, yet, however, nevertheless, nonetheless, conversely, in contrast, still, at the same time, on the one hand, on the other hand

ESL icons call out information that may be of particular use for ESL or multilingual students.

ESL TIP: For information about using articles with COUNT and NONCOUNT NOUNS, and about articles with PROPER NOUNS and GERUNDS, see Chapter 54.

Indicates new section of a chapter

3g   How can I write about quantitative data or information?

Quantitative information or data come in the form of numbers. Such information can be an important source of detail and evidence in almost any kind of writing. However, some writings especially require writers to translate numbers into words and to explain what they mean.

Boys and Girls: Understanding the Rhetoric of Audience

Plug It In: Understanding the Rhetoric of Proof

Icons point you to relevant resources on MyCanadianCompLab. In the eText version of the book, these icons become live links.

ALERT: Use *a* when the word following it starts with a consonant: *a carrot, a broken egg.* Also, use *a* when the word following starts with an *h* that is sounded: *a hip, a home.* Use *an* when the word following starts with a vowel sound: *an honour, an old bag, an egg.*

Take care to keep clear distinctions among these sections. Lab reports and empirical studies frequently include two other parts. One is an ABSTRACT, a short overview of the entire report, which appears directly after your title. The other is a list of REFERENCES, which is crucial if you discuss other published research. We provide more information about writing lab reports, as well as an example, in Chapter 41.

Alerts highlight important rules and best practices.

Bet this is a fragment. Check Chapter 8.

Whereas
While Canadians and Americans considered animation entertainment for
mainly
children. The Japanese viewed it as entertaining primarily for adults. Since the
beginning of print, cartooning in Japan has been aimed at adults, so anime was a
in this tradition
natural step. It's interesting how graphic novels were important in Japan long before

Small capitals call out Glossary key terms.

Hand-edited examples illustrate editing and revision strategies.

EXERCISE 3-2   Working individually or with a group, look at each list of words and divide the words among three headings: "Positive" (good connotations); "Negative" (bad connotations); and "Neutral" (no connotations). If you think that a word belongs under more than one heading, you can assign it more than once, but be ready to explain your thinking. For help, consult a good dictionary and 12d.2.

Exercise

193

Page number

MyCanadianCompLab

Save Time. Improve Results.

More than 6 million students have used a Pearson MyLab product to get a better grade.

MyCanadianCompLab is an all-in-one learning and testing environment for introductory English. The easy-to-navigate site provides a variety of resources including

- An interactive Pearson eText
- A "composing" space with all the tools you need to improve your writing skills
- Audio and video material to view or listen to, whatever your learning style
- Personalized learning opportunities—YOU choose what, where, and when you want to study
- Self-assessment tests to guide you on making the most efficient use of study time

In the printed text, you will find icons (described in the Preface) that link you to related content on MyCanadianCompLab. In the eText, these icons are hyperlinked to the online resources.

If you do not already have an access code, you can buy one online at www. mycanadiancomplab.ca.

You will have access to a number of resources to help you become a better writer!

Composing at the Centre

At the heart of MyCanadianCompLab is an easy-to-use online composing space. This unique application allows you to compose an essay and submit it to your instructor all in one place!

Resources at Your Fingertips

As you research, draft, and revise, resources are available at your fingertips. By clicking on the Writer's Toolkit, you can get the help you need when you need it.

Access to Tutor Services

You can easily and directly link to Pearson Tutor Services, powered by Smarthinking. The Smarthinking tutor provides feedback on your submitted paper within 24 hours and the feedback appears right in the composing space.

MyCanadianCompLab helps you focus your efforts where they are needed. Know your strengths and weaknesses before your first in-class exam.

Go to www.mycanadiancomplab.ca and follow the simple registration instructions on the Student Access Code Card found with this text. Your unique access code is hidden there. If your text does not come with a code, you can purchase one at www.mycanadiancomplab.ca.

Preface

This sixth Canadian edition of the *Simon & Schuster Handbook for Writers* gives you comprehensive access to the information you need about the writing process, from mastering grammar to using correct punctuation, from writing research papers to documenting sources, and from writing for the Web to writing using visuals. The **organizational structure** corresponds to the way that writers actually use the topics and strategies. The *Simon & Schuster Handbook* is carefully designed for usability in college or university and beyond, as illustrated in this preface.

Supportive, friendly tone The authors make topics easy to understand, to welcome you into conversations about becoming better writers. In the *Simon & Schuster Handbook for Writers*, all information suits a wide variety of student needs.

NEW coverage of academic writing New Chapters 2 and 7, "Essential Processes for Academic Writing" and "Strategies for Writing Typical Kinds of Papers," not only guide you through the writing process but also offer specific instruction for the most common types of academic writing in any of your college or university courses.

Emphasis on critical thinking Chapter 4, "Thinking Critically About Ideas and Images," explicitly connects critical thinking with the kinds of strategies and habits that writers practise, including how to view images critically.

DOCUMENTATION COVERAGE WITH THE MOST CURRENT STANDARDS ACROSS THE DISCIPLINES.

- **MLA documentation** reflects 2009 updates in the seventh edition of the *MLA Handbook for Writers of Research Papers*.
- **NEW updated APA documentation** reflects 2009 updates in the sixth edition of the *Publication Manual of the American Psychological Association*.
- **NEW updated *Chicago Manual* (CM) documentation** reflects 2010 updates in the sixteenth edition of the *Chicago Manual of Style*.
- **Council of Science Editors (CSE) documentation** reflects the 2006 seventh edition of *Scientific Style and Format: The CSE Manual for Authors, Editors, and Publishers*.
- **IEEE (formerly Institute of Electrical and Electronics Engineers) documentation** reflects the 2009 *IEEE Standards Style Manual*.

Easy access to common errors integrated throughout the text Common errors that most writers make are called out as **Alerts** or in **Quick Reference Boxes** throughout the text.

NEW coverage of writing outside the classroom New Chapters 43 and 44, "Business and Professional Writing" and "Writing for the Public," give you essential guidance for resumés and cover letters, memos, and reports.

NEW coverage of writing with new media Chapter 42, "Making Presentations and Using Multimedia," explains how and why to use tools like PowerPoint for presentations, and Chapter 46, "Multimodal Texts and Writing for the Web," teaches you how to create websites, blogs, and other digital texts that incorporate not only images but also sound and video.

Comprehensive coverage of argument. Chapter 5, "Writing Arguments," reflects current theory, research, and practice.

Information for multilingual writers throughout, as well as in a separate section Whether English is your only language or you are multilingual, the *Simon & Schuster Handbook for Writers* gives you clear answers to your questions about standard Canadian English grammar, punctuation, sentence correctness, and style. Look for this symbol ⬤ to find ESL tips. In addition, an entire section, Part 7, "Writing When English Is Not Your First Language," is devoted to issues of special concern to multilingual students.

Student and professional writing samples The *Simon & Schuster Handbook for Writers* contains a number of complete samples of student writing and professional writing on topics of interest.

Extensive coverage of Writing Across the Curriculum Part 6, "Writing Across the Curriculum—and Beyond," is designed to connect writing in the composition classroom to writing in other disciplines and in the world beyond.

- Chapter 39, "Comparing the Disciplines," connects the writing students do in other classes, thereby providing a resource for students throughout their college or university years.
- Chapter 40, "Writing About the Humanities and Literature," which includes a sample student literature paper, explains the types of writing that students do in the humanities.
- Chapter 41, "Writing in the Social Sciences and Natural Sciences," reflects the current range of practices and theories for teaching and writing in these disciplines.

A contemporary visual and functional design The visual and functional design makes navigation quick and easy (see the elements of the pages of this handbook on page xv for an illustrated walk-through of the design).

- The **Overview of Contents** starting on the inside front cover provides a comprehensive list of parts, chapters, and sections. To find a specific topic, use the **List of Quick-Reference Features**, the **ESL Index**, and the **Subject Index** at the end of the book.
- **Seven Parts** separate major topics into sections. Each part opener contains a list of contents for that specific part. Numbered chapters contain uncomplicated discussions in small "chunks" of information. Every chunk has a chapter number plus a letter in alphabetical order within the chapter.
- **Major headings are worded to resemble Frequently Asked Questions (FAQs)** you're likely to be asking when you consult the *Simon & Schuster Handbook for Writers*. Look for the FAQ repeated in a "running head" at the top of each right-hand page to help you navigate smoothly through the book. You can also use the coloured rectangle at the top outside corner of each page to check which chapter you're using.
- **Exercises** give you the chance to practise the skills described in each chapter. In the sixth edition of the *Simon & Schuster Handbook for Writers, the design* of this feature has been improved in order to make navigation between text and exercise even easier.
- **NEW Quick Reference Boxes** offer a quick way to find important information. If you ever need to locate a box by topic, you can turn to the **List of Quick-Reference Features** at the end of the book. Also, you will find **Alerts** throughout the book to remind you about a rule or other relevant information. For example, in a sentence discussion, an Alert might remind you of a comma rule that applies.

Integrated online resources in MyCanadianCompLab An online version of the *Simon & Schuster Handbook for Writers* activates the Watch, Listen, and Explore icons in the text to link to additional resources. (More information on MyCanadianCompLab is provided on page xvi and in the section about supplements below.)

Supplements

The following supplements accompany the sixth Canadian edition to aid in teaching and learning:

FOR STUDENTS

MyCanadianCompLab (www.mycanadiancomplab.ca)

The moment you know.
Educators know it. Students know it. It's that inspired moment when something that was difficult to understand suddenly makes perfect sense. Our MyLab products have been designed and refined with a single purpose in mind—to help educators create that moment of understanding with their students.

MyCanadianCompLab delivers **proven results** in helping individual students succeed. It provides **engaging experiences** that personalize, stimulate, and measure learning for each student. And, it comes from a **trusted partner** with educational expertise and an eye on the future.

MyCanadianCompLab can be used by itself or linked to any learning management system. To learn more about how MyCanadianCompLab combines proven learning applications with powerful assessment, visit www.mycanadiancomplab.ca.

MyCanadianCompLab—the moment you know.

You can use the access code packaged with every new copy of the *Simon & Schuster Handbook for Writers,* Sixth Canadian Edition, to access diverse resources for writing in one easy place:

- Sections on writing, research, and grammar cover all the key topics in the text, providing additional instruction, examples, and practice.
- A Pearson eText, an electronic version of this textbook, allows you to review material easily as you work online.
- An online composing space includes tools such as writing tips and editing FAQs, so that you can get help as you need it, without ever leaving your writing environment.
- The portfolio feature helps you create an ePortfolio of your work that you can easily share with your instructor and peers.

Access to MyCanadianCompLab can also be purchased separately from your bookstore or from Pearson Education Canada.

Throughout the printed text, you will find the following icons that link you to related content on MyCanadianCompLab. In the Pearson eText, these icons are hyperlinked directly to the online resources:

Watch icons link to videos that illustrate aspects of the writing process, plus grammar and editing tutorials that use video prompts.

Listen icons link to instruction and practice questions that you can download and listen to on an MP3 player.

Explore icons link to writing samples that provide good models of writing, many with annotations that highlight key aspects or stimulate reflection and discussion.

CourseSmart for Students. CourseSmart goes beyond traditional expectations—providing instant online access to the textbooks and course materials you need at an average savings of 60%. With instant access from any computer and the ability to search your text, you'll find the content you need quickly, no matter where you are. And with online tools like highlighting and note-taking, you can save time and study efficiently. See all the benefits at www.coursesmart.com/students.

FOR INSTRUCTORS

Instructor's Manual. This manual offers instructors and teaching assistants teaching tips, background notes, thought-provoking quotations about writing, and answers to the in-text exercises. It is available for download from a password-protected section of Pearson Canada's online catalogue (www.pearsoned.ca/highered). Navigate to your book's catalogue page to view a list of supplements. See your local sales representative for details and access.

MyCanadianCompLab. (www.mycanadiancomplab.ca) MyCanadianCompLab empowers student writers and facilitates writing instruction by integrating a composing space and ePortfolio with proven resources and tools, such as practice exercises, diagnostics, and multimedia assets. Instructor functions include the following:

- The To Do section enables instructors to create and deliver assignments online and helps keep students on track by listing due dates and assignment details in one place.
- A range of Grammar Diagnostics are available, allowing instructors to evaluate students' progress at different stages throughout a course.
- The Gradebook captures both student grades from self-grading exercises on the site and grades given to writing assignments by the instructor, allowing instructors to easily assess student and class progress.
- Instructors can integrate MyCanadianCompLab into their traditional or online courses to whatever degree they'd like: from simply using exercises in the Resource section for homework or extra help to delivering their entire course online. Students can also use MyCanadianCompLab on their own, benefiting from the composing space and its integrated resources, tools, and services with no involvement from the instructor.

See your local sales representative for further information and access.

PEARSON CUSTOM LIBRARY

For enrollments of at least 25 students, you can create your own textbook by choosing the chapters that best suit your own course needs. To begin building your custom text, visit www.pearsoncustomlibrary.com. You may also work with a dedicated Pearson Custom editor to create your ideal text—publishing your own original content or mixing and matching Pearson content. Contact your local Pearson representative to get started.

CourseSmart for Instructors. CourseSmart goes beyond traditional expectations—providing instant online access to the textbooks and course materials you need at a lower cost for students. And even as students save money, you can save time and hassle with a digital eTextbook that allows you to search for the most relevant content at the very moment you need it. Whether it's evaluating textbooks or creating lecture notes to help students with difficult concepts, CourseSmart can make life a little easier. See how when you visit www.coursesmart.com/instructors.

Technology Specialists. Pearson's Technology Specialists work with faculty and campus course designers to ensure that Pearson technology products, assessment tools, and online course materials are tailored to meet your specific needs. This highly qualified team is dedicated to helping schools take full advantage of a wide range of educational resources, by assisting in the integration of a variety of instructional materials and media formats. Your local Pearson Canada sales representative can provide you with more details on this service program.

Acknowledgments

We heartily thank all those students who, to our great luck, have landed in our writing courses. We admire how they and their counterparts in classrooms around the world strive to write skilfully, think critically, and communicate successfully, in college or in university and beyond. We especially thank the individual students who have given us permission to make them "published authors" by including their exemplary writing in this handbook.

Hundreds of students have contacted us by e-mail or letter with their reactions to, and questions about, the *Simon & Schuster Handbook for Writers* or related matters. We deeply appreciate these messages. We take your comments seriously and use them to improve our teaching and this book. Any student now using the *Simon & Schuster Handbook for Writers* is welcome to get in touch with us at <troykalq@nyc.rr.com>, at <dhesse@du.edu>, or c/o English Editor, Higher Education Division, Pearson Education Canada, 26 Prince Andrew Place, Toronto, ON M3C 2T8. We promise to answer.

Along with our colleagues at Pearson Education, we'd like to call special attention to an expert team of advisers and contributors who helped us shape and polish this edition to be a truly great resource for instructors and students alike. We could not have completed this challenging task without the meaningful contributions of this team:

Cy Strom of Colborne Communications in Toronto, Ontario, continues his critically important role as adapter of our Canadian editions and adviser to our overall work on handbooks.

Melinda Reichelt, University of Toledo, helped write new chapters and integrated content for multilingual writers.

Dorothy Minor, Tulsa Community College, and Leslie Leach, College of the Redwoods, skilfully revised and added to the exercises throughout the book and the answers in the AIE.

Georgia Newman, Polk Community College, a colleague and dear friend, meticulously updated the AIE to be relevant for today's instructors.

Plentiful appreciation goes to members of Pearson Education's Advisory Board for this text, who continue to share perspectives on teaching writing.

Many thanks are due to all those instructors who have provided valuable comments over the various editions of this book, including the reviewers for the sixth Canadian edition:

Stephen Ahern, Acadia University; Karen Inglis, Kwantlen Polytechnic University; Sue Laver, The McGill Writing Centre; Karen McCrindle, University of Toronto Scarborough; Melanie Fahlman Reid, Capilano University; Shannon Smyrl, Thompson Rivers University; and Andrea Westcott, Capilano University.

A project as complicated as the *Simon & Schuster Handbook for Writers* cannot be undertaken without the expertise and dedication of many professionals. We would like to thank the exceptional people at Pearson Education who facilitated our work on the ninth American edition. For the sixth Canadian edition, Cy Strom was supported by Carolin Sweig (Sponsoring Editor), Megan Burns (Developmental Editor), Suzanne Schaan

(Supervising Developmental Editor), Richard di Santo (Project Manager), and proofreaders Lisa Berland and Trish O'Reilly. Sonia Tan, as Media Content Editor, was responsible for MyCanadianCompLab.

Doug values Lynn Troyka's vast knowledge, skill, dedication to teaching, and patience with a greenhorn. He appreciates the support of the Honors Program staff at Illinois State University, the insights of his longtime colleagues Jan Neuleib, Ron Fortune, Ron Strickland, and Jim Kalmbach, and the energies of his Illinois State students. He further states, "Carol Rutz, Erika Lindeman and, foremost and always, Kathi Yancey, have been exemplary professional and personal friends. Dan Graybill, Michelle Staley, Susan Bellas, and Lawrence Bellas are constant sources of support and friendship. My children, Monica, Andrew, and Paige, amaze me with their creativity, as does the best writer I know: Becky Bradway, my wife."

Lynn especially appreciates her coauthor Doug Hesse for his gentle friendship and invaluable participation in revising the *Simon & Schuster Handbook for Writers*. Lynn thanks Ida Morea, her administrative assistant, for her loving friendship; Kristen Black, the treasured child of Lynn's heart, if not her womb; Dan Black, Kristen's multi-talented, loving son-in-law; Lynn's precious grandchildren Lindsey and Ryan Black; Lynn's loyal sister Edith Klausner; and David and Lynn's hardy brother-in law Hy Cohen. With a rejoicing heart, Lynn welcomes into her family the wise, loving Bernice Joseph, David's caregiver and Lynn's personal assistant, along with Bernice's family: Rachael and Eric Thomas, Nickyla, Nicholas, and Nehemiah, as well as Mauricia Joseph. Lynn also thanks her special friends for being irreplaceably woven into the texture of her life: Avery Ryan, Esq.; Rose Dulude, PhD; Melanie Mejia, MS; Susan Bartelstone; Jimmy, Gavin, and Ian Ryan, Douglas Young III and his wife Anna; and Joseph W. Thweatt. Above all, Lynn thanks her beloved husband David, her sweetheart and eternal companion.

Lynn Quitman Troyka
Doug Hesse

About the Authors

LYNN QUITMAN TROYKA, Adjunct Professor in the Graduate Program in Language and Literature at the City College (CCNY) of the City University of New York (CUNY), has also taught at Queensborough Community College. Former editor of the *Journal of Basic Writing,* she has had her writing and research published in major journals and various scholarly collections. She also conducts workshops in the teaching of writing. Dr. Troyka is coauthor of *Quick Access Reference for Writers,* Sixth Edition, Pearson Prentice Hall; *QA Compact,* Second Edition, Pearson Prentice Hall; the Canadian editions of her *Simon & Schuster Handbook for Writers* and *Quick Access Reference for Writers; Structured Reading,* Seventh Edition, Prentice Hall; and *Steps in Composition,* Eighth Edition, Prentice Hall.

Dr. Troyka is a past chair of the Conference on College Composition and Communication (CCCC); the Two-Year College Association (TYCA) of the National Council of Teachers (NCTE); the College Section of NCTE; and the Writing Division of the Modern Language Association (MLA). She received the 2001 CCCC Exemplar Award, the highest CCCC award for scholarship, teaching, and service; the Rhetorician of the Year Award; and the TYCA Pickett Award for Service.

"This information," says Dr. Troyka, "tells what I've done, not who I am. I am a teacher. Teaching is my life's work, and I love it."

DOUG HESSE, Professor of English and Director of Writing at the University of Denver, previously held several positions at Illinois State University, including Director of the Honors and Writing Programs and also Director of the Center for the Advancement of Teaching. Dr. Hesse earned his PhD from the University of Iowa. He has also taught at the University of Findlay, Miami University (as Wiepking Distinguished Visiting Professor), and Michigan Tech.

Dr. Hesse is a past chair of the Conference on College Composition and Communication (CCCC), the nation's largest professional association of college writing instructors. A past president, as well, of the Council of Writing Program Administrators (WPA), Dr. Hesse edited that organization's journal, *Writing Program Administration.* He has been a member of the executive committee of the National Council of Teachers of English (NCTE) and chaired the Modern Language Association (MLA) Division on Teaching as a Profession.

He is the author of over fifty articles and book chapters in such journals as *College Composition and Communication, College English, JAC, Rhetoric Review,* and the *Journal of Teaching Writing* and in such books as *Essays on the Essay; Writing Theory and Critical Theory; The Writing Program Administrator's Sourcebook; Literary Nonfiction;*

The Private, the Public, and the Published; and *Passions, Pedagogies, and 21st Century Technologies.* He is also coauthor with Lynn Quitman Troyka of *Quick Access Reference for Writers,* Sixth Edition, Pearson Prentice Hall and *QA Compact,* Second Edition, Pearson Prentice Hall. He has consulted at over forty colleges and universities.

The writing program he directs at the University of Denver is only one of twenty-five internationally to receive the CCCC Certificate of Excellence. "Of all these accomplishments," says Dr. Hesse, "the one that matters most to me was being named Distinguished Humanities Teacher. That one came from my students and suggests that, in however small a way, I've mattered in their education and lives."

To David, the love of my life

LYNN QUITMAN TROYKA

To Don and Coral Hesse

DOUG HESSE

Writing Situations and Processes

MyCanadianCompLab

Visit MyCanadianCompLab at
mycanadiancomplab.ca for

- Writing exercises
- Help with analyzing visuals
- Video tutorials
- Other resources, including an eText version of this book

Chapter 1

UNDERSTANDING ACADEMIC AND OTHER WRITING SITUATIONS

((◦•
AUDIO
LESSON
Section 1:
Big Ideas—
Writing Well
in College

1a   What is the current scene for writers?

Writing well improves your success in your courses. That plain fact has been true for decades. However, writing plays an equally key role in your career and your life beyond the classroom. We wrote this book to help you achieve success in all of these settings. As writers and writing teachers, we find it fascinating—and heartening—to witness the current explosion of writing. You might be among the millions of people who regularly compose e-mails and text messages, keep journals or **blogs**, craft stories or poems, create websites, or use Facebook or MySpace to connect with others—all without anyone asking you to do so. Ordinary people write about their favourite television programs, analyze politics, or simply share their experiences and thoughts. The internet and wireless devices have made it easier for people to share writing, and digital technologies allow them to mix words, images, sounds, and videos. We live in an age when people do more writing than at any other time in history (see Figure 1.1).

If you're someone who chooses to write out of personal interest, we offer this book to help you stretch into new types of writing. If you don't very much like to write, we hope that you might discover the satisfaction of putting your thoughts into words—and we hope this book helps ease your way. We've composed these pages because we repeatedly see in your classes that everyone can make the concentrated effort needed to become an effective writer. Certainly, if you spend time and energy working on your writing skills, your efforts can bring you academic, professional, and personal rewards.

The writing that people choose to do on their own complements the kind of writing that they do for school and work. As a student, you can expect to write in a variety of courses across the curriculum, not just in English. Writing is also vital in your career. The Conference Board of Canada's *Employability Skills 2000+* lists the communication skills needed by a high-quality workforce. Prominent among them is the ability to "write and speak so others pay attention and understand."* Recent surveys of people in a variety of jobs and professional fields say that they spend an average of 30 percent of each day writing.

1b   What is a writing situation?

((◦•
AUDIO
LESSON
Section 1:
Big Ideas—
Writing
Successfully
Beyond
College

Think of the following situations: writing a text message to a friend; a research paper for a history class; a job application letter; a website for a museum. These situations result in texts widely different in length, format, content, organization, and style. A **writing situation** is the combination of several elements: your topic, your purpose, your audience, your role as a writer, and the context and special requirements. For a list of the elements of the writing situation, see Quick Reference 1.1.

*Employability Skills 2000+ Brochure 2000E/F (Ottawa: The Conference Board of Canada, 2000), 11 April 2008. Web. 7 May 2009.

Figure 1.1 Different varieties and styles of writing

We explain the important concepts of **purpose** and **audience** in sections 1c and 1d, but first we'll define some other elements of the writing situation. You'll often be assigned a topic, the subject you need to write about and, perhaps, the sources (7b) that you'll need to use. Topics can be general or very specific; you'll be more successful if you narrow broad topics (2b.3).

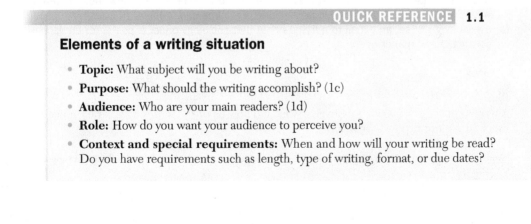

QUICK REFERENCE 1.1

Elements of a writing situation

- **Topic:** What subject will you be writing about?
- **Purpose:** What should the writing accomplish? (1c)
- **Audience:** Who are your main readers? (1d)
- **Role:** How do you want your audience to perceive you?
- **Context and special requirements:** When and how will your writing be read? Do you have requirements such as length, type of writing, format, or due dates?

3

It may surprise you to learn that you can take on different **roles** (personalities or identities) for different writing situations. For example, suppose you're trying to persuade readers to save energy. You might emphasize your concerns as a prospective parent who is personally worried about the future, or you might instead present yourself as an objective and impersonal analyst.

The **context** can affect the writing situation. Context refers to the circumstances in which your readers will encounter your writing. For example, persuading people to buy fuel-efficient cars when gas is cheap is very different from when its cost has been rising constantly.

Special requirements are practical matters such as how much time you're given to complete the assignment and how long it should be. For example, your reading audience expects more from an assignment that you had a week to complete than from one due overnight. In the second case, your readers realize you had to write in relative haste, though no one ever accepts sloppy or careless work. Your audience expects most from assignments that call for reading or other research, so be sure to build enough time for that process early into your schedule.

Understanding a writing situation guides your writing process and shapes your final draft. A writing process that might be effective in one situation might not be appropriate for another, and the final drafts would have different characteristics. For example consider the following task: "In a five page paper for a political science course, describe government restrictions on cigarette advertising." Your INFORMATIVE* purpose would require careful research and an objective, serious style, complete with a list of works cited or references. In contrast, if you were asked to write a 300-word newspaper editorial arguing that smoking should (or should not) be banned in all public places, your writing would reflect your PERSUASIVE purpose for a public audience, explain positions more quickly, probably have a more energetic style, and include no list of references. Consider other examples. Writing a history paper in the short, informal style of a text message definitely won't impress a professor. Similarly, texting your friends in long paragraphs will make them impatient (and perhaps wonder who's using your cell phone).

As the above examples show, your writing situation also helps determine the TONE of your writing. Tone refers to the attitude conveyed in writing, mostly by the writer's word choice. A tone can be formal, informal, laid back, pompous, sarcastic, concerned, judgmental, sympathetic, and so on. The tone you use greatly affects your reader's sense of the ROLE you've chosen. If you want to come across as a serious, thoughtful writer in an academic situation, but your tone is sarcastic and biting, your readers won't take you seriously. We discuss tone at greater length in section 8d.

EXERCISE 1-1   Either in a class discussion or in a short paper, explain how these different situations would result in different kinds of writing: a resumé and cover letter, a research paper for a sociology course, an e-mail to a friend about that sociology paper, a poster for an upcoming concert, a newspaper editorial.

1c   What does "purpose" mean for writing?

A writer's purpose for writing motivates what and how he or she writes. Quick Reference 1.2 lists four major purposes for writing.

---

*Words printed in SMALL CAPITAL LETTERS are discussed elsewhere in the text and are defined in the Terms Glossary at the back of this book.

Purposes for writing

- To express yourself or build connections with others
- To inform a reader
- To persuade a reader
- To create a literary work

In this handbook, we concentrate on the two major purposes for most academic writing: to **inform** and to **persuade.** The two remaining purposes listed here are important for contributing to human thought and culture, but they relate less to what most academic writing involves.

1c.1 What is expressive writing?

Expressive writing is writing to express your personal thoughts and feelings. Much expressive writing is for the writer's eyes only, such as that in diaries, personal journals, or exploratory drafts. Other people, however, express themselves in e-mails to friends and colleagues or in blogs for all the world to see. A crucial reason for much of this kind of writing is to make connections with others. (For example, Figure 1.2 shows a blog by a Canadian group that does volunteer work in Africa.) Social networking sites like Facebook establish and deepen human contact this way.

Some expressive writing for public audiences falls into the category of literary writing. The excerpt here comes from a student's memoir.

> When we lived in Manitoba, the fall and winter holidays were my touchstones—the calendar moved along in comforting sequence. I wrapped the snow and foods and celebrations around me like a soft blanket. I burrowed in. Now that we live in Victoria, I don't need that blanket. But I surely do miss it.
>
> —Daniel Casey, student

1c.2 What is informative writing?

Informative writing seeks to give information to readers and usually to explain it. Another name for this type of writing is *expository writing* because it expounds on—sets forth in detail—observations, ideas, facts, scientific data, and statistics. You can find informative writing in textbooks, encyclopedias, technical and business reports, nonfiction books, newspapers, and many magazines.

The essential goal of informative academic writing is to educate your readers about something. Like all good educators, therefore, you want to present your information clearly, accurately, completely, and fairly. In Chapter 3 of this handbook, we show you many strategies that writers use for informative writing. These strategies can help you deliver your message, but above all, your success depends on whether your readers can verify your information as accurate. Quick Reference 1.3 gives you a checklist to assess your informative writing. But first, here's a paragraph written to inform.

> "Diamonds in the rough" are usually round and greasy looking. But diamond miners are in no need of dark glasses to shield them from the dazzling brilliance of the mines for quite

Blogs may have profile sections in which bloggers can tell others about themselves and their interests.

Blogs often include photographs.

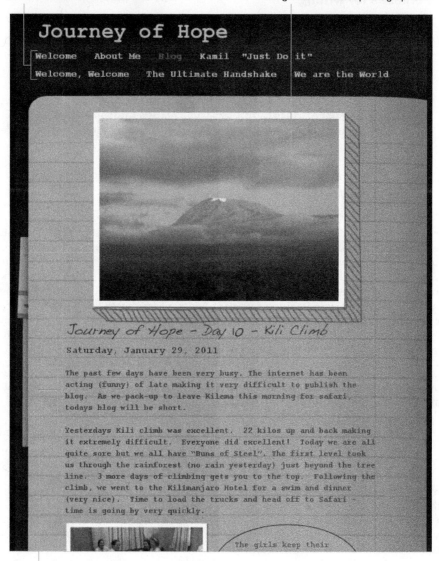

Bloggers can freely write down thoughts in the same way they might write in a print journal.

Figure 1.2 A blog for a community service group

another reason: even in a diamond pipe, there is only one part diamond per 14 million parts of worthless rock. Approximately 46,000 pounds of earth must be mined and sifted to produce the half-carat gem you might be wearing. No wonder diamonds are expensive!

—Richard B. Manchester, "Diamonds"

As informative writing, this paragraph works because it focuses clearly on its TOPIC (diamonds in the rough), presents facts that can be verified (who, what, when, where), and is written in a reasonable tone.

QUICK REFERENCE 1.3

Informative writing

- Is its information clear?
- Does it present facts, ideas, and observations that can be verified?
- Does its information seem complete and accurate?
- Is the writer's tone reasonable and free of distortions? (8d)

1c.3   What is persuasive writing?

Persuasive writing, also called *argumentative writing*, seeks to persuade readers to support a particular opinion. When you write to persuade, you deal with debatable topics, those that people can consider from more than one point of view. Your goal is to change your readers' minds about the topic—or at least to bring your readers' opinions closer to your point of view. To succeed, you want to evoke a reaction in your audience so that they think beyond their present position or take action. Examples of persuasive writing include newspaper editorials, letters to the editor, opinion essays in newspapers and magazines, reviews, sermons, books that argue a point of view, and business proposals. Chapter 5 of this handbook discusses ways to write effective arguments.

In general terms, persuasive writing means you need to move beyond merely stating your opinion. You need to give the basis for that opinion. You support your opinion by using specific, illustrative details to back up your **generalizations**, which are usually very broad statements. The first sentences of sections 1c.1, 1c.2, and 1c.3 in this chapter are examples of generalizations.

Quick Reference 1.4 gives you a checklist to assess your persuasive writing. But first, here's a paragraph written to persuade.

> Even when efficiency is restricted properly to means, it is often used incorrectly in public discussion. Particularly in an age of fiscal austerity, efficiency is at times twisted by political leaders to mean cost-cutting or cost-containment. The error should be obvious: neither cost-cutting nor cost-containment is inherently efficient if the quality or the quantity of the public goods governments provide is reduced more than the costs. Distorting efficiency this way often masks a distrust of government as the custodian of the public interest and political preference for markets as the providers of public as well as private goods. That is much of what we have heard lately in Canada, for example, in the testimony over the safety of our water.
>
> —Janice Gross Stein, *The Cult of Efficiency*

As persuasive writing, this paragraph works because it makes a point about the common misuse of the term *efficiency* and develops this point with sound reasoning (efficiency in

AUDIO LESSON Section 1: Big Ideas—Constructing an Argument

AUDIO LESSON Section 2: Practice Questions—Constructing an Argument

AUDIO LESSON Section 3: Rapid Review—Constructing an Argument

providing public goods can't be separated from the quality and quantity of the goods provided). The appeal to the reader's agreement includes an analysis that the writer supports with evidence from a recent event.

Persuasive writing

- Does it present a point of view about which opinions vary?
- Does it support its point of view with specifics?
- Does it base its point of view on sound reasoning and logic?
- Are the parts of its argument clear?
- Does it intend to evoke a reaction from the reader?

EXERCISE 1-2 For each paragraph, decide if the dominant purpose is *informative*, *persuasive*, or *expressive*. Then, use the information in section 1c to explain your answers.

A. Trees are living archives, carrying within their structure a record not only of their age but also of precipitation and temperature for each year in which a ring was formed. The record might also include the marks of forest fires, early frosts and, incorporated into the wood itself, chemical elements the tree removed from its environment. Thus, if we only knew how to unlock its secrets, a tree could tell us a great deal about what was happening in its neighborhood from the time of its beginning. Trees can tell us what was happening before written records became available. They also have a great deal to tell us about our future. The records of past climate that they contain can help us to understand the natural forces that produce our weather, and this, in turn, can help us plan.
—James S. Trefil, "Concentric Clues from Growth Rings Unlock the Past"

B. Much of how the people live in rural Saskatchewan today continues to stem from the value system and the exigencies of pioneer life. The first settlers here almost immediately had to become self-sufficient, since the governmental system of land division ensured large distances between families at a time when transportation was always slow and uncertain, and in a climate where the weather was frequently too severe to allow travel. (That this system also ensured loneliness for the women who were always less mobile than the men is an underlying, but not fully articulated, theme in western Canadian life.) In most respects farm life at least has changed a great deal since those early days, and these changes have left the society in a general way still operating within a value system that does not always make sense in the new conditions.
—Sharon Butala, "Rural Saskatchewan: Creating the Garden"

C. Although Littleman, my eleven-year-old poodle, has never been separated from his thirteen-year-old mother, Simone, they are remarkably different. Simone weighs in at about five kilograms with very delicate, sophisticated features and coarse, curly hair. Slightly shorter, Littleman tops the scale at no more than three kilograms and is quite handsome with his teddy-bear features and soft wavy hair. Simone was the first dog in the family and is a pedigreed poodle. In many ways she is the picture of a thoroughbred, with her snobby attitude and nonchalant manners. On the other hand, Littleman came into the family a year later with four other puppies of pure breeding, but they were never registered. Unlike his mother, Littleman is very friendly, almost to the point of being pesty at times.
—Linda Neal, student

EXERCISE 1-3 Consulting section 1c, write on each of these topics twice, once to inform and once to persuade your reader: diets, tastes in music, reality television, part-time jobs, road rage. Be prepared to discuss how your two treatments of each topic differ.

1d   What does "audience" mean for writing?

Your **audience** consists of everyone who will read your writing. Thinking like a writer about audience means figuring out how to successfully reach your audience in various kinds of situations. For example, papers that you write for a history course differ in form and style from lab reports that you write in biology, and both differ from memos that you write on the job, letters that you write to a newspaper editor, or e-mails that you write to a friend. Effective writers know they need to adjust their writing for different tasks and audiences.

After you graduate, your audiences are likely to be readers of your business, professional, and public writing (Chapters 43–44). In college or university, you'll surely address a mix of audience types that expect to read ACADEMIC WRITING. Here's a list of categories of those audiences, each of which is detailed in the section listed in parentheses.

- General educated audiences (1d.1)
- Specialist audiences (1d.2)
- Your instructor (who represents your general or specialized readers) (1d.3)
- Your peers (classmates, co-workers, friends, or others like yourself) (6a)

The more specifics you can assume about each of your audiences for your academic writing, the better your chances of communicating with it successfully.

ESL TIPS: (1) If you do not share a cultural background with your readers, it may be difficult for you to estimate how much your readers know about your topic. Discussing your topic with friends or classmates might help you decide what background information you need to include in your paper.

(2) If you come from outside North America, you may be surprised by the directness with which people speak and write in Canada. If so, we hope you'll read our open letter to multilingual students about honouring one's own culture. (It introduces Part Seven of this handbook.) Your own tradition may expect elaborate or ceremonial written language that does not introduce the central point immediately, preferring tactful, indirect discussion. In contrast, Canadian writing contains language and style that are direct, straightforward, and without digressive embellishments. Instructors here expect academic writing to contain a thesis statement (usually at the end of the introductory paragraph); to demonstrate a tightly organized presentation of information from one paragraph to the next; to back up generalizations with supporting details; and to end with a paragraph that presents a logical conclusion to the discussion. In addition, you are expected to use standard English grammar that follows the rules used by educated speakers. ●

To analyze your audience, you might ask yourself whatever questions in Quick Reference 1.5 you think will be useful in each situation.

1d.1   What is a general educated audience?

A **general educated audience** is composed of experienced readers who regularly read newspapers, magazines, and books. These readers, with general knowledge of many subjects, are likely to know something about your topic, but may not possess specialized knowledge on that particular subject. Consequently, avoid specialized or technical terms, although you can use a few as long as you include everyday definitions.

AUDIO LESSON Section 1: Big Ideas—Using Language Well and Addressing Your Audience

AUDIO LESSON Section 2: Practice Questions—Using Language Well and Addressing Your Audience

AUDIO LESSON Section 3: Rapid Review—Using Language Well and Addressing Your Audience

QUICK REFERENCE 1.5

Ways to analyze your audience

WHAT SETTING ARE THEY READING IN?

- Academic setting? Specifically, what subject?
- Workplace setting? Specifically, what business area?
- Public setting? Specifically, what form of communication (newspaper? blog? poster?)

WHO ARE THEY?

- Age, gender, economic situation
- Ethnic or linguistic backgrounds, political philosophies, religious beliefs
- Roles (student, parent, voter, wage earner, property owner, and others)
- Interests, hobbies

WHAT DO THEY KNOW?

- Level of education
- Level of knowledge: Do they know less than you about the subject? as much as you about the subject? more than you about the subject?
- Beliefs: Is the audience likely to agree with your point of view? disagree with your point of view? have no opinion about the topic?
- Interests: Is the audience eager to read about the topic? open to the topic? resistant to or not interested in the topic?

WHAT IS THEIR RELATIONSHIP TO YOU?

- Distance and formality: Do you know each other personally or not? Does your audience consist of friends, family, or close peers, or are they more remote?
- Authority: Does your reader have the authority to judge or evaluate you (a supervisor at work, a teacher)? Do you have the authority to evaluate your reader?

General readers usually approach a piece of writing expecting to become interested in it. They hope to learn about a new topic, to add to their store of knowledge about a subject, and, often, to see a subject from a perspective other than their own. (Of course, there are also readers who are not particularly well-read or open to new ideas.) As a writer, you need to fulfill the expectations of your interested and curious general readers.

1d.2 What is a specialist audience?

A **specialist audience** is composed of readers who have expert knowledge of specific subjects or who are particularly committed to those subjects. Many people are experts in their occupational fields, and some become experts in areas that simply interest them. People from a particular group background (for example, religious, linguistic, geographic, or occupational) may be knowledgeable in those areas.

Specialist readers may also share assumptions and beliefs. You will want to take these into account and treat them respectfully. Additionally, whenever you introduce a concept that's probably new to a specialist audience, explain the concept thoroughly rather than assuming that the audience will understand it right away.

1d.3   What is my instructor's role as audience?

As your audience, your instructor functions in three ways. First, your instructor assumes the role of your target audience, either as a general reader or a specialist reader. Second, your instructor acts as a coach committed to helping you improve your writing. Third, your instructor evaluates your final drafts.

Instructors know that few students are experienced writers or experts on the subjects they write about. Still, they expect your writing to reflect your having taken the time to learn something worthwhile about a topic and then to write about it clearly. Instructors are experienced readers who can recognize a minimal effort almost at once.

As important, instructors are people whose professional lives centre on intellectual endeavours. You need, therefore, to write on topics that contain intrinsic intellectual interest and to discuss them according to the expectations for academic writing.

Don't assume that your instructor can mentally fill in what you leave out of your writing. Instructors—indeed, all readers—can't be mind readers, so they expect students to write on a topic fully. If you think you might be saying too little, ask your peers to read your writing and tell you if you've developed your topic sufficiently.

1e   What should I know about writing in a digital age?

Computers are important tools for creating documents, finding resources, managing work, and communicating with others. Almost all writing projects, whether in school or beyond, require them. Some instructors make allowances when getting to a computer is impossible, but the clear preference is for word-processed final drafts. If you don't own a computer you can use computers on most campuses (often in libraries and student centres), in public libraries, and in Internet cafés.

1e.1   Creating documents

A computer's word-processing software (for example, Microsoft Word or OpenOffice) offers invaluable help at various stages of the WRITING PROCESS. Word processing allows you easily to add, delete, revise, or move material, even from one document to another. Some writers prefer to print their drafts to revise or edit them by hand and then enter the changes in the computer; other writers do almost all their revising and editing on the screen.

Word processing also allows you to make quick format changes. You can easily shift between single-spacing and double-spacing or put a WORKS CITED page into the correct DOCUMENTATION STYLE (Chapters 36–38). The toolbar at the top of the word-processing window contains numerous formatting options, and exploring how they work can save you time in the long run.

Be careful using the special aids for writers that are built into word-processing software, as they have limitations.

- **Spell-check tools** show you words that don't match the dictionary in the software. These programs are a big help for spotting a misspelling or mistyping (*typo*), but they won't call your attention to your having typed *form* when you intended to type *from*. Therefore, always remember to read your work carefully after you use a spell-checker.
- **Thesaurus tools** give you SYNONYMS for words. They can't, however, tell you which ones fit well into your particular sentences. Whenever a synonym is unfamiliar or hazy, look it up in your dictionary. You don't want to use words that strike you as attractive options but then

AUDIO LESSON Section 1: Big Ideas— Electronic Rhetoric

AUDIO LESSON Section 2: Practice Questions— Electronic Rhetoric

AUDIO LESSON Section 3: Rapid Review— Electronic Rhetoric

11

turn out to distort your communication. For example, a synonym for *friend* is *acquaintance*, but these words have different senses.

- **Grammar- or style-check tools** check your writing against the software's strict interpretations of rules of grammar, word use, punctuation, and other conventions. Can you always rely on those standards? No. These signals call attention to a possible error. The decision to change the usage, however, is yours. Consult this handbook when you're not sure what a program is suggesting or whether you're justified in deviating from the program's rules.

1e.2 Finding resources

In addition to helping you produce and revise writing, computers help you find sources. Most library catalogues and databases are searchable with computers, both from within the library and remotely, through the Internet. Catalogues and databases are large collections of references that experts have gathered and organized. Often they lead to sources that are available online. Many companies also subscribe to database and information services. Chapter 34 explains how to use catalogues and databases.

Sources on the World Wide Web, which you find using search engines like Google and Yahoo, usually aren't in databases compiled by experts. Chapter 34 explains how to use the Web—and how to avoid misusing it. Especially keep in mind that anyone can post anything online. Some of what you find is plain wrong.

Online sources present particular challenges to writers, including the possibility of PLAGIARISM, a serious academic offence that involves representing someone else's words or ideas as your own. Chapter 35 describes effective and ethical ways of using sources and avoiding plagiarism.

1e.3 Managing your work

Computers allow you to save drafts of your papers or to organize your work into various folders. For example, you might create a folder for each document you write and also keep all notes, drafts, and ideas related to that project in the folder. Figure 1.3 shows how one student has started a folder for all the projects in her writing course. In the subfolder for project 2, she has ideas, notes, peer comments, and drafts. She created this folder in the "My Documents" directory in Microsoft Windows.

Computers and associated technologies also allow you to store vast quantities of your own writing and research. Storage devices such as flash drives (also called thumb/jump/keychain drives) or even MP3 players allow you to store cheaply hundreds or thousands of megabytes of information in something small enough to keep in your pocket. Not only can you potentially keep every word you ever write (as a lifelong portfolio), but you can store photos and other images that you might need for a certain writing project, and you can download vast quantities of source materials from databases.

1e.4 Communicating with others

E-mail, instant messaging, and similar technologies not only help you communicate with friends but also help you prepare formal writing projects. For example, discussing a topic online with others can generate ideas. Some instructors organize such discussions in Web-based programs such as WebCT or Blackboard. People in all walks of life often exchange ideas on discussion boards, listservs, and "blogs."

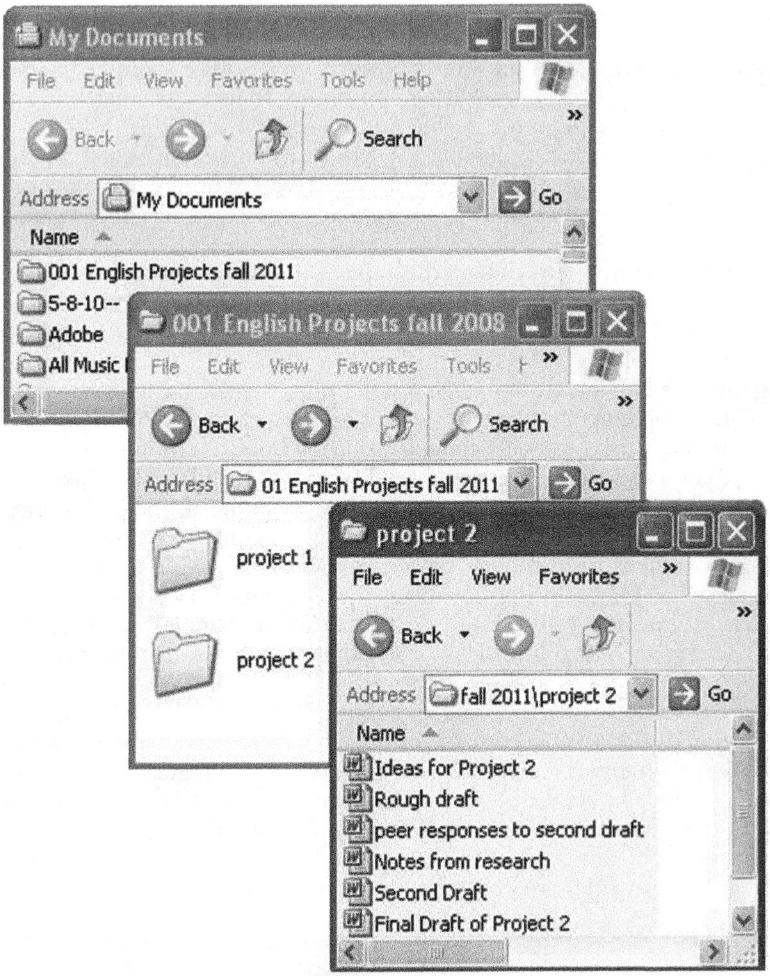

My Documents

File   Edit   View   Favorites   Tools   Help

Back   •   ➔   •   🗁   🔍 Search

Address 🗁 My Documents   ✔ ➔ Go

Name ▲

🗁 001 English Projects fall 2011
🗁 5-8-10--
🗁 Adobe
🗁 All Music

001 English Projects fall 2008

File   Edit   View   Favorites   Tools   »

Back   •   ➔   •   🗁   🔍 Search

Address 🗁 01 English Projects fall 2011   ✔ ➔ Go

🗁 project 1

🗁 project 2

project 2

File   Edit   View   Favorites   »

Back   •   ➔   •   🗁

Address 🗁 fall 2011\project 2   ✔ ➔ Go

Name ▲

Ideas for Project 2
Rough draft
peer responses to second draft
Notes from research
Second Draft
Final Draft of Project 2

Figure 1.3 Using the computer to manage writing projects

Computers allow you to share drafts of your work without physically meeting with others. You can send a draft as an e-mail attachment or save it on a community server or website. That way, classmates or colleagues—or even instructors or supervisors—have access to it and can offer suggestions for revision. Certainly, if you're working on a collaborative project, the ability to share drafts and to discuss revisions online has many advantages. Chapter 6 explains how to work effectively with others.

🛈 **ALERT:** Some instructors never allow students to receive feedback on their writing outside of class. Clarify each instructor's rules about such matters. Pleading ignorance of a law is rarely a sufficient defence. ●

1f What forms of writing do computers enable?

For decades, formal writing has consisted of essays and reports containing only words, with occasional tables and figures. These forms will always remain essential, and you need to master them. However, computers enable different kinds of writing. You can place photographs or illustrations into documents. You can easily create tables and graphs, and you can use different fonts and graphical elements. As a result, writers can more easily produce brochures, pamphlets, or other documents that, in the past, required a graphic artist (see Chapter 45).

Other forms of writing are designed to appear on computers rather than on paper. Sometimes they contain audio or video files, or they connect to other documents and websites. Some writing situations may call for you to make a webpage rather than write a traditional paper.

A **blog** (or Web log) lets a writer post a series of messages that anyone can read on the Internet. Some people create blogs to serve as a diary of their daily experiences; others offer sites geared toward comments about a particular hobby or interest. Blogs can be very personal, written to an audience of friends and family. Other blogs have taken on an international readership, as is the case with particular news, political, and author blogs.

A **wiki** is a website that allows readers to change its content. Several people can work on the same document from remote places around the globe. One popular wiki site is Wikipedia, an online encyclopedia; anyone can post an article to this site, and anyone can revise an article already posted there. For this reason, use caution when considering any Wikipedia content, and ask your instructor whether he or she will permit you to use it for scholarly research. Try to confirm the information you find in Wikipedia in other reliable sources. For more information on using and citing Web resources, see Chapters 36–38.

A **digital portfolio** is a collection of several texts in electronic format that you've chosen to represent the range of your skills and abilities. Unlike regular paper portfolios, digital versions contain links between—and within—individual texts; they can be modified and shared easily and cheaply; and they can be put online for wide reading. Figure 1.4 shows the opening screen of one student's digital portfolio for a first-semester writing course. Note that all the paper titles are links to the papers themselves.

Figure 1.4 Opening screen of a student's digital portfolio

Presentations, using software such as PowerPoint, allow you to create slides to project while you speak, providing visuals to accompany your oral remarks. PowerPoint slides can incorporate words, images, and sounds. Chapter 42 provides more advice on creating presentations.

Podcasts are sound files that are shared over the Internet. Their name comes from Apple's familiar iPod player. What do podcasts have to do with writing? A good number of podcasts are miniature essays or commentaries that their writers have carefully polished and then read, as a script. Podcasts are the oral form of blogs. Many podcast directories are available on the Internet.

Videos are motion image files or clips. People are increasingly conveying ideas or information through short videos filmed with a camera, edited with computer software, and uploaded to the Internet. Video clips may enhance some presentations. Websites like YouTube demonstrate the ease with which people can produce and upload videos, some of them amazingly good, many of them plain awful. Mainstream professional, educational, and commercial websites also frequently contain videos. Some blogs actually take the form of video logs or "vlogs."

What is a discussion of videos doing in a handbook of writing? Effective videos are often built around carefully written and narrated scripts, which may contain titles or captions. We discuss visuals in multimedia in Chapter 42. Always check with instructors before integrating audiovisual elements into your writing. And don't worry if your knowledge about producing any of these types of writing is limited. Instructors who require such projects can tell you how to proceed.

1g What resources can help me with writing?

Every writer needs access to four essential resources: a dictionary, a thesaurus, a handbook for writers, and a library. The first three are each generally available in electronic form as well as in traditional print, although you may find the book versions more convenient.

A **dictionary** is indispensable. Most university and college bookstores offer a variety of hardback "college dictionaries." Before buying one, browse through a few definitions, check the format and accessories (information in the front and back), and choose the book you like best. Keeping a lightweight paperback abridged dictionary in your book bag can be handy for checking unknown words on the spot. Many dictionaries and other reference books can be downloaded onto a mobile device.

Unabridged dictionaries list all recognized words in standard use in English. The reference section of every library usually stocks one. Some libraries may also maintain an unabridged dictionary online.

Another valuable resource for writers is a **thesaurus**, which is a collection of *synonyms*. The alphabetically arranged ones are the easiest to use.

A **handbook for writers** is also vital for you to own. A handbook—such as the one you're reading—gives you detailed information about rules of grammar and punctuation and about other writing conventions. (Note that this handbook also exists in an online version that can be accessed through a code you received if you bought the book new.) It also offers extensive advice about how to write successfully, whether for college or university, business, or the public. It shows you step by step how to write and document research papers. Some handbooks, including this one, contain guidance on how to write for a variety of courses other than English. This resource is an invaluable writing tool in courses other than English, as well as in your career, and it will serve you well for years.

College or university libraries, sometimes called *learning resource centres*, are essential for writers. Libraries are fully stocked with all manner of reference books, circulating books, resources for online access, and more. Some resources are available online through the library's website. It's helpful to know what resources are available at your library so that you can dive right in when you need to get information. Chapter 34 provides advice on using the library.

Finally, you need two other, less tangible resources as a writer: time and confidence. We know that people live incredibly busy lives, juggling work, school, and personal responsibilities. While it may seem obvious (or insensitive) to say that you need time to write effectively, we're simply encouraging you to create and protect time for yourself as a writer. It helps to think of writing as a series of processes that take time to pursue. Confidence may seem just as elusive, especially when you face challenging new writing situations. It might help to remember that countless people like you are steadily developing their writing skills each day. We see them in our classes all the time. We have confidence that your efforts will also bring rewards.

Chapter 2

ESSENTIAL PROCESSES FOR ACADEMIC WRITING

2a **What processes do academic writers use?**

Office Hours: Prewriting

Many people think that professional writers can sit down at their computers, think of ideas, and magically produce a finished draft, word by perfect word. Experienced writers know better. They know that writing is a process, a series of activities that starts the moment they begin thinking about a subject and ends with proofreading the final draft. Experienced writers also know that good writing is rewriting, again and yet again. Their drafts are filled with additions, deletions, rewordings, and rearrangements.

For example, see in Figure 2.1 how Lynn revised the paragraph you just read. Lynn didn't make all the changes at the same time, even though it looks that way on the example. She went through the paragraph four times before she was satisfied with it. Notice that she deleted and added text, and changed wording throughout. Doug's revisions to the opening of Chapter 1—believe it or not—were even more thorough and convoluted.

Writing is an ongoing process of considering alternatives and making choices. Knowing and practising a few general processes will help you with almost every writing situation. Different assignments may emphasize some techniques more than others, and we'll discuss them in Chapter 7. Here, however, we focus on processes that are essential for nearly all writing.

> ~~Chapter One discusses what writing is. This chapter explains~~
> ~~how writing happens~~ Many people think that professional writers
>   *magically*
> can sit down at their computers, think of ideas, and produce a
> finished draft, word by perfect word. Experienced writers know
> better. They know that writing is a process. ~~The writing process is~~
>   *they begin*
> a series of activities that starts the moment thinking about a subject
>   *proofreading*
> begins and ends with the final draft. Experienced writers also know
> that good writing is rewriting, again and yet again. *Their drafts*
> *are filled with additions, deletions, rewordings, and rearrangements.*

Figure 2.1 Draft and revision of Lynn Troyka's first paragraph in Chapter 2

In this chapter, we discuss each part of the writing process separately. In real life, the steps overlap. They loop back and forth, which is why writing is called a recursive process. Quick Reference 2.1 lists the steps.

QUICK REFERENCE   **2.1**

Steps in the writing process

- **Planning** means discovering and compiling ideas for your writing.
- **Shaping** means organizing your material.
- **Drafting** means writing your material into sentences and paragraphs.
- **Revising** means evaluating your draft and then rewriting it by adding, deleting, rewording, and rearranging.
- **Editing** means checking for correct grammar, spelling, punctuation, and mechanics.
- **Proofreading** means reading your final copy to eliminate typing or handwriting errors.

Do you like, as we do, to visualize a process? If so, see the drawing in Figure 2.2. The arrows show movement. You might move back before going ahead (perhaps as you revise, you realize you need to plan some more); or you might skip a step and come back to it later (perhaps in the middle of revising, you jump into editing for a few minutes because a punctuation or grammar rule affects how you express your point); and so on.

As you work with the writing process, allow yourself to move freely through each step to see what's involved. Notice what works best for you. As you develop a sense of your preferred writing methods, adapt the process to fit each writing situation. No single way exists for applying the writing process.

Our personal advice from one writer to another is this: Most writers struggle some of the time with ideas that are difficult to express, sentences that won't take shape, and words that aren't precise. Be patient with yourself. Don't get discouraged. Writing takes time. The more you write, the easier it will become—though writing never happens magically.

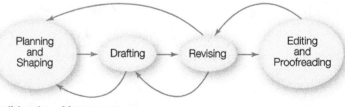

Figure 2.2 Visualizing the writing process

((• **2b** **How do I begin an academic writing project?**

About the
Audio
Lessons for
Before You
Write,
Organize
Begin every writing assignment by carefully analyzing the writing situation you're given. Some assignments are very specific. For example, here's an assignment that leaves no room for choice: "In a 500-word article for a high school audience, explain how oxygen is absorbed in the lungs." Students need to do precisely what's asked, taking care not to wander off the topic. More often, however, writing-class assignments aren't nearly as specific

as that one. Often, you'll be expected to select your own topic (2b.1) or even your own purpose and audience.

AUDIO LESSON Section 1: Big Ideas— Before You Write, Organize

AUDIO LESSON Section 2: Practice Questions— Before You Write, Organize

AUDIO LESSON Section 3: Rapid Review— Before You Write, Organize

2b.1   Selecting your own topic or purpose

If you have to choose a topic, don't rush. Take time to think through your ideas. Avoid getting so deeply involved in one topic that you cannot change to a more suitable topic in the time allotted.

Not all topics are suitable for ACADEMIC WRITING. Your topic needs to have inherent intellectual interest: ideas and issues meaty enough to demonstrate your thinking and writing abilities. Think through potential topics by breaking each into its logical subsections. Then, make sure you can supply sufficiently specific details to back up each general statement. Conversely, make sure you aren't bogged down in so many details you can't figure out what GENERALIZATIONS they support.

Work toward balance by finding a middle ground. Beware of topics so broad that they lead to well-meaning but vague generalizations and of topics so narrow that they lead nowhere after a few sentences.

Suppose your assignment doesn't indicate a writing purpose—for example, "Write an essay on smoking," Here, you're expected to choose a purpose and think about what you intend to write on the topic. Will you try to explain to a general educated audience why people smoke? Will you try to persuade a specialized audience of smoking parents to quit? Will you summarize the current literature on the costs of smoking in order to inform an audience of economists? Considering different audiences and purposes can help you find a topic angle that engages you.

Most instructors put each assignment in writing in a handout, on a website, or perhaps on the board. But some instructors give assignments orally during class, expecting you to write them down. Try to record every word. Don't hesitate to ask question if you don't catch all the words or if something isn't clear—and be sure to write down the answers because they often tend to slip from memory. Listen, too, to questions other students ask.

In the rest of this chapter, we present the writing processes of two students, Sara Cardini and Alex Garcia, as they plan and shape their material. You'll see Cardini's essay evolving through three separate, complete drafts. Later, in Chapter 5, you'll see how Garcia's essay developed. To start, here are the written assignments each student received.

Sara Cardini received this assignment:

Addressing an educated audience, write an essay of 900 to 1300 words discussing something you learned outside of a classroom. Your writing purpose can be informative or persuasive. Expect to write three drafts. (1) Your first draft, typed double-spaced, is due two classes from today. (2) Your clean second draft, typed double-spaced, without notes or comments, is due two classes later. Clip to it your first draft showing all notes you made to yourself or took from comments your peer-response group made; you can handwrite notes and comments. I'll read your second draft as an "essay in progress" and will make comments to help you toward a third (and final) draft. (3) The third draft, typed double-spaced, is due one week after I return your second draft with my comments.

Alex Garcia was given this assignment:

Write an essay of 1000 to 1500 words that argues for a particular action on an issue that interests you. Your final draft is due in two weeks.

Cardini's first step was to analyze her writing situation (Quick Reference 1.1). She looked at the very general topic—explain to an educated audience something you learned outside of a classroom—and she saw that she needed to narrow it considerably. She tentatively decided her purpose would be informative, though she thought she might have to switch to a persuasive purpose as she went along. She knew that she would share her first draft with her PEER-RESPONSE GROUP to help her toward her second draft. She also understood that her instructor would be her final audience. She was aware of the requirements for time and length.

Garcia also read his assignment and analyzed his writing situation. Because the topic was very broad, he knew he would have to spend a good deal of time deciding what he wanted to write about. On the other hand, he understood that his assigned purpose was persuasive. The audience was not specified; he knew that his instructor would be the main audience, but he also decided to write in a way that would address a broader public audience. He kept in mind the requirements for time and length.

2b.2   Broadening a narrow topic

You know a topic is too narrow when you realize there's little to say after a few sentences. When faced with a too-narrow topic, think about underlying concepts. For example, suppose you want to write about Wilfrid Laurier. If you chose "Wilfrid Laurier was the first French-speaking prime minister of Canada," you would be working with a single fact rather than a topic. To expand beyond such a narrow thought, you could think about the general area that your fact fits into—Canadian political history. Although that is too broad to be a useful topic, you are headed in the right direction. Next, you might think of a topic that relates to Laurier's political impact, such as "What effect did Wilfrid Laurier's francophone origins have on the success of the Liberal Party?" Depending on your WRITING SITUATION (1b), you might need to narrow your idea further by focusing on Laurier's impact in a single area such as the question of national unity or the debate over religious education.

2b.3   Narrowing a broad topic

Narrowing a broad topic calls for you to break the topic down into subtopics. Most broad subjects can be broken down in hundreds of ways, but you need not think of all of them. Settle on a topic that interests you, one narrowed enough—but not too much—from a broad topic. For example, if you're assigned "relationships" as the topic for a 1000-word essay, "What kinds of relationships are there?" is too broad. "Alexandra and Gavin have dated for two years" is too narrow. You'd probably be on target with a subtopic such as "In successful relationships, people learn to accept each other's faults." You could use 1000 words to explain and give concrete examples of typical faults and discuss why accepting them is important. Here are two more examples.

SUBJECT	*music*
WRITING SITUATION	first-year composition class
	informative purpose
	instructor as audience
	500 words; one week
POSSIBLE TOPICS	"How music affects moods"
	"The main characteristics of country music"
	"The relationships between plots of Puccini's operas"

SUBJECT	*cities*
WRITING SITUATION	sociology course
	persuasive purpose
	peers and then instructor as audience
	950 to 1000 words; ten days
POSSIBLE TOPICS	"Comforts of city living"
	"Discomforts of city living"
	"Importance of the writings of Jane Jacobs on city planning"

Sara Cardini, the student whose essay appears in this chapter, knew that her very general assigned topic—"Explain to an educated audience something you learned outside of a classroom"—was too broad. To narrow it, she used the following structured techniques for discovering and compiling ideas: browsing her journal (2c.1), FREEWRITING (2c.2), and MAPPING (2c.5). They helped her decide that she wanted to discuss how she learned about a culture other than her own. She realized that even her narrower topic "Japanese culture" would still be too broad. She considered "Japanese music" or "Japanese schools." In the end, she chose "Japanese videos" and, even more specifically, a kind of Japanese animation called "anime" (commonly pronounced AN-a-may). Extensive experience had taught her about the topic, and she could think of both generalizations and specific details to use in her essay. In addition, Cardini knew that if she needed to do research, she could find sources in books and magazines and on the Internet.

Alex Garcia also needed to narrow his topic to suit a 1000- to 1500-word essay. To explore several possible topics, he used BRAINSTORMING (2c.3). Once he had chosen a topic (whether buying organic food is worthwhile), he used the "journalist's questions" (2c.4) to compile more ideas and then a subject tree (2e) to check whether he was ready to begin drafting.

2c How can I come up with ideas and information?

If you've ever felt you'll never think of anything to write about, don't despair. Instead, use structured techniques, sometimes called *prewriting strategies* or *invention techniques*, for discovering and compiling ideas. Professional writers use them to uncover hidden resources in their minds. For a list of the techniques, see Quick Reference 2.2.

((•
AUDIO
LESSON
Section 1:
Big Ideas—
Finding a
Research
Topic

QUICK REFERENCE 2.2

Ways to discover and compile ideas for writing

- Keep an idea log and a journal (2c.1)
- Freewrite (2c.2)
- Brainstorm (2c.3)
- Ask the "journalist's questions" (2c.4)
- Map (2c.5)
- Talk it over (2c.6)
- Read, browse, or search (2c.7)
- Incubate (2c.8)

Try out each one. Experiment to find out which techniques suit your style of thinking. Even if one technique produces good ideas, try another to see what additional possibilities might turn up.

Save all of the ideas you generate as you explore possible topics. You never know when something you have initially rejected might become useful from another point of view. Computers make it easy to keep a folder labelled, for example, "explorations," in which you can store your ideas.

ESL TIP: The structured techniques discussed here aim to let your ideas flow out of you without your judging them right away. If it's difficult for you to implement these techniques using English, consider doing several in your primary language. Then, choose one that seems to have potential for your writing and do it over again in English. ●

2c.1   Using an idea log or journal

As you develop the habits of mind and behaviour of a writer, your ease with writing will grow. One such habit is keeping an idea log. Professional writers are always on the lookout for ideas to write about and details to develop their ideas. They listen, watch, talk with people, and generally keep an open mind. Because they know that good ideas can evaporate as quickly as they spring to mind, they're always ready to jot down their thoughts and observations. Some carry a pocket-size notepad, while others use a mobile device or a laptop. If you use an idea log throughout your college or university years, you'll see your powers of observation increase dramatically.

Additionally, many professional writers keep a daily writing **journal**. Doing this will allow you to have a conversation in writing with yourself. Your audience is you, so the content and tone can be as personal and informal as you wish. Even fifteen minutes a day can be enough. If you don't have that chunk of time, write in your journal before you go to bed, between classes, on a bus. Some people find that the feel of pen on paper, perhaps in a bound blank journal, is important to this kind of writing. Others keep journals in computer files. Several people even put their journals online as blogs. For examples of blogs (or to start one of your own), go to <http://www.blogger.com>.

Unlike a diary, a journal isn't a record of what you do each day. A journal is for your thoughts from your reading, your observations, even your dreams. You can respond to quotations, react to movies or plays, or reflect on your opinions, beliefs, and tastes. Keeping a journal can help you in three ways. First, writing every day gives you the habit of productivity; the more you write and the more you feel words pouring out of you onto paper, the more easily you'll write in all situations. Second, a journal promotes close observation and discovery, two habits of mind that good writers cultivate. Third, a journal is an excellent source of ideas for assignments.

Figure 2.3 shows an excerpt of a journal entry Sara Cardini had made before she got the assignment to write about something she had learned outside the classroom. Even though she hadn't thought of her entry as a potential subject for an essay, when she read through her journal for ideas, she realized that she could bring one of her great interests into the classroom.

2c.2   Freewriting

Freewriting is writing non-stop. You write down whatever comes into your mind without stopping to wonder whether the ideas are good or the spelling is correct. When you freewrite, don't do anything to interrupt the flow. Don't censor any thoughts or flashes of insight. Don't go back and review. Don't delete.

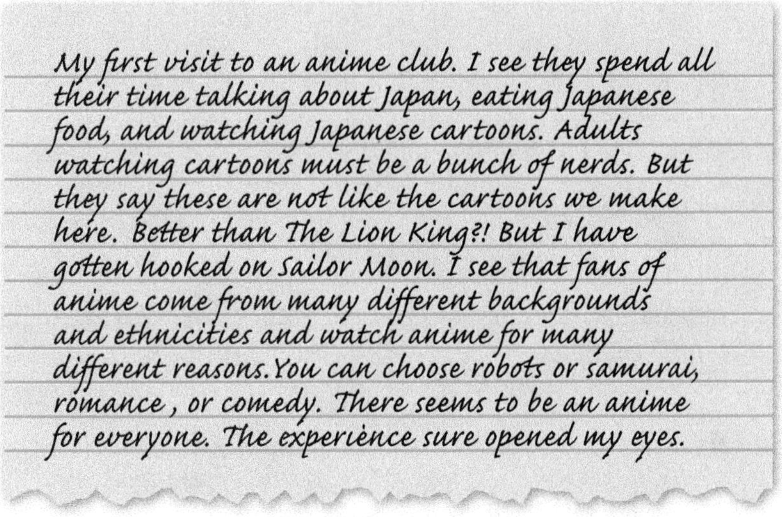

> *My first visit to an anime club. I see they spend all their time talking about Japan, eating Japanese food, and watching Japanese cartoons. Adults watching cartoons must be a bunch of nerds. But they say these are not like the cartoons we make here. Better than The Lion King?! But I have gotten hooked on Sailor Moon. I see that fans of anime come from many different backgrounds and ethnicities and watch anime for many different reasons. You can choose robots or samurai, romance, or comedy. There seems to be an anime for everyone. The experience sure opened my eyes.*

Figure 2.3 Excerpt from Sara Cardini's journal

Freewriting helps get you used to the "feel" of your fingers rapidly hitting computer keys or your pen moving across paper. Freewriting works best if you set a goal—perhaps writing for fifteen minutes or filling one or two pages. Keep going until you reach that goal, even if you have to write one word repeatedly until a new word comes to mind. Some days when you read over your freewriting, it might seem mindless, but other days your interesting ideas may startle you.

In **focused freewriting**, you write from a specific starting point—a sentence from your general freewriting, an idea, a quotation, or anything else you choose. Except for this initial focal point, focused freewriting is the same as regular freewriting. Write until you meet your time or page limit, and don't censor yourself. If you go off the topic, that's fine: See where your thoughts take you. Just keep moving forward.

Like a journal, freewriting is a good source of ideas and details. When Sara Cardini thought her growing interest in Japanese animation might qualify for her assignment, she explored the topic through focused freewriting on watching anime (Figure 2.4).

2c.3 Brainstorming

Brainstorming means listing everything you can think of about a topic. Let your mind roam freely, generating quantities of ideas. Write words, phrases, or sentence fragments— whatever comes to you. If you run out of ideas, ask yourself questions such as *What is it? What is it the same as? How is it different? Why or how does it happen? How is it done? What causes it or results from it? What does it look, smell, sound, feel, or taste like?*

After you've compiled a list, go to step two: Look for patterns, ways to group the ideas into categories. You'll probably find several categories. Set aside any items that don't fit into a group. If a category interests you but has only a few items, brainstorm that category alone.

You can brainstorm in one concentrated session or over several days, depending on how much time you have for an assignment. Brainstorming with other writers can be especially fruitful: One person's ideas bounce off the next person's, and collectively more ideas come to mind.

> *In watching anime, my eyes were opened to a world I would never have known otherwise. I learned not to be so judgmental about animation (which I always thought was for kids). While anime seemed strange and confusing to me at first, before long I realized the importance of studying art from another country. The more I watched and understood anime, the less strange it seemed, and the more I realized that I had just been judging from my limited Canadian point of view. Somewhere in Japan, there is probably some university student who is learning about North America from our movies. Now, if the Japanese student and I ever meet, we will be closer to understanding each other.*

Figure 2.4 Excerpt from Sara Cardini's freewriting

When brainstorming or FREEWRITING on a computer, try "invisible writing." Temporarily darken your computer monitor. A blank screen can help you focus on getting the words out without the temptation to stop and criticize, but the computer will still be recording your words. When you can write no more, turn on the monitor to see what you have.

Brainstorming was a technique Alex Garcia used to find his topic about the benefits of organic foods. It helped him think through several topics and generate some ideas about the one that most appealed to him (Figure 2.5).

- women on TV commercials; realistic?
- health care funding–don't know much on that
- possibilities for wind energy: argue or explain
- the North American diet
- the effects of fast food–do I have anything to add?
- organic foods: worth it? benefits? costs?

Figure 2.5 Alex Garcia's brainstorming

EXERCISE 2-1 Here's a list brainstormed for a writing assignment. The topic was "Ways to promote a new movie." Working individually or in a peer-response group, look over the list and group the ideas. You'll find that some ideas don't fit into a group. Then, add any other ideas you have to the list.

coming attractions	suspense
TV ads	book the movie was based on
provocative	locations
movie reviews	Internet trailers
how movie was made	adventure
sneak previews	newspaper ads
word of mouth	stars
director	dialogue
topical subject	excitement
special effects	photography

2c.4 The "journalist's questions"

When journalists report a story, they gather and write about information by asking who did what, when it happened, where it happened, and why and how it happened. The same questions come in handy for writers exploring a topic. The **journalist's questions** are *Who? What? When? Where? Why?* and *How?*

Alex Garcia used the journalist's questions to expand his thinking on the value of eating organic foods. His answers, listed below, showed him that he had enough material for a good essay.

WHO?	**Who** benefits from the organic food industry?
WHAT?	**What** kinds of organic foods are available?
WHEN?	**When** did organic foods become popular?
WHERE?	**Where** can I find evidence that organic foods are healthier?
WHY?	**Why** do some people doubt the value of organic foods?
HOW?	**How** exactly should someone evaluate the evidence?

2c.5 Mapping

Mapping, also called *clustering*, is a visual form of brainstorming. When some writers actually see ways that their ideas connect, they begin to think more creatively. Other writers like mapping to help them check the logical relationships between ideas.

To map, write your topic in the middle of a sheet of paper and draw a circle around it. Now, moving out from the centre, use lines and circles to show ideas that are subtopics of the topic in the centre circle. Continue to subdivide and add details. At any time, you can move to a blank space on your map and start a new subtopic. Try to keep going without censoring yourself.

Sara Cardini used mapping to prompt herself to discover ideas about Japanese animation. When she finished, she was satisfied that she'd have enough to say in her essay. Figure 2.6 shows part of Sara Cardini's clustering for the second paragraph of her essay about Japanese anime.

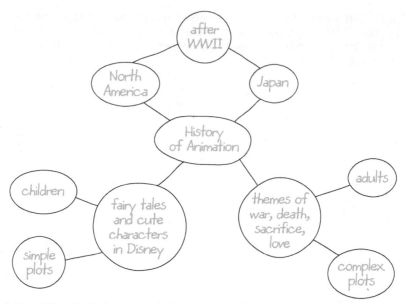

Figure 2.6 Part of Sara Cardini's mapping for her essay on anime

2c.6   Talking it over

Talking it over is based on the notion that two heads are better than one. When you discuss a topic with someone interested in listening and making suggestions, you often think of new ideas. You can even play roles, having other people pretend they disagree with you. Answering their questions or challenges can spur new thinking.

People you trust can serve as "sounding boards" and tell you if your ideas are complete and reasonable. If your instructor sets up PEER-RESPONSE GROUPS in your class, you might ask the other members to serve as sounding boards. Otherwise, talk with a good friend or another adult.

Chatting online through instant messaging, e-mail, and so on, lets you exchange ideas, which not only stimulates your thinking but also acts as a writing warm-up.

((•

AUDIO
LESSON
Section 2:
Practice
Questions—
Finding a
Research
Topic

2c.7   Reading and browsing

Reading newspapers, magazines, and books can provide a constant source of ideas. Academic writers do this all the time. Spending time in the PERIODICALS or new books section of a library or browsing a good bookstore can alert you to fresh topics. Just looking at magazine covers, images, or a table of contents is often productive. If browsing generates a topic, systematic searches will yield more information (Chapter 34).

((•

AUDIO
LESSON
Section 1:
Big Ideas—
Becoming a
Critical Reader
and a Better
Writer

Internet searches help you find topics and locate specific information. Internet searches scan the WORLD WIDE WEB using **search engines**, which are software programs that rapidly search and find online information sources.

Chapter 34 provides extensive guidelines for searching the Internet. Briefly, however, try the Open Directory <http://www.dmoz.org> to see a list of broad subject areas.

Next, click on "Society" to see a number of slightly more specific topics, including "Relationships." Note that each of them would be much too broad to write about. However, if you keep clicking on topic headings, you'll move to more and more specific subjects. Browsing through the layers of topics can help you think of several ideas for your writing. If you know a general topic area, you can type it in the search window of the program and then click on more specific subcategories. Figure 2.7 illustrates this process.

EXERCISE 2-2   Go to <http://www.dmoz.org>. Choose one of the headings in the Open Directory project. Continue to click on topics under that heading to create a path to a specific topic. Be ready to explain the path you used, what you found, and what you think the strengths and weaknesses of the topics you identified would be. Finally, go back to the opening page of the directory and repeat the process with a different heading.

EXERCISE 2-3   Explore some of the following topics by typing them into the search window of a search engine. Be ready to explain the sequence of topics you discover.

1. mobile devices
2. intelligence
3. sustainability
4. world music
5. disability

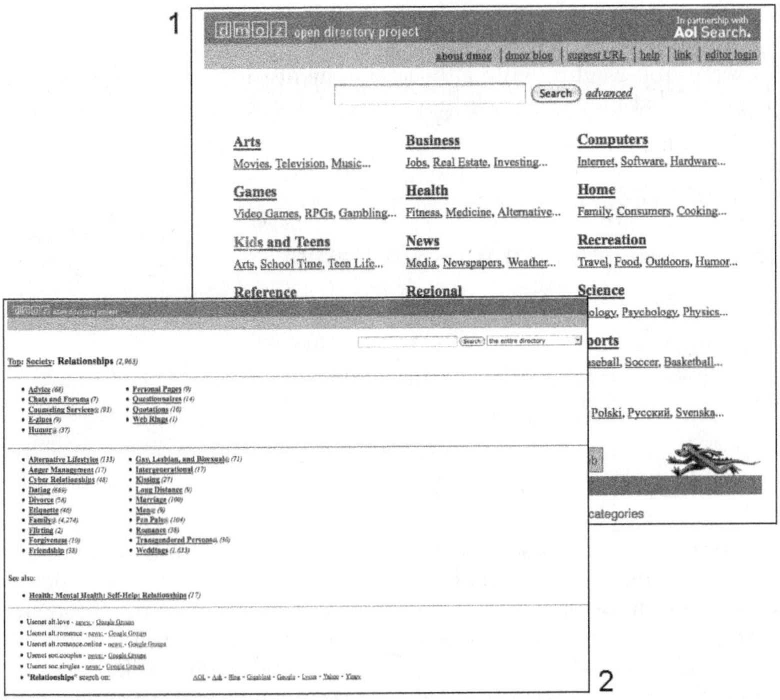

Figure 2.7 Screen shot of the Open Directory

27

AUDIO
LESSON
Section 3:
Rapid
Review—
Finding a
Research
Topic
Incubation refers to giving your ideas time to grow and develop. This technique works especially well when you need to step back and evaluate what you've discovered and compiled for your writing. For example, you might not see how your material can be pulled together at first, but if you let it incubate, you might discover connections you didn't see originally. Conversely, if some parts of your essay seem too thin in content, incubation gives you distance from your material so that you can decide what works. Ideally, incubate your ideas overnight or for a couple of days—but even a few hours can help.

If you don't have the luxury of a lengthy incubation period, some strategies may help you jump-start your writing. One method is to turn your attention to something entirely unrelated. Concentrate hard on that other matter so that you give your conscious mind over to it totally. After a while, relax and guide your mind back to your writing. Often, you'll see what you've discovered and compiled for writing in a different way.

EXERCISE 2-4   Try each structured technique for discovering and compiling ideas discussed in 2c.1 through 2c.8. Use your own topics or select from the suggestions below.

1. professions and job prospects
2. an important personal decision
3. professional sports

4. advertisements on television
5. what you want in a life partner

2d   What is a thesis statement?

A **thesis statement** is the central message of an essay. The thesis statement presents the TOPIC of your essay, your particular focus on that topic, and your PURPOSE for writing about that topic. You want to write a thesis statement with great care so that it prepares your readers for what follows. Quick Reference 2.3 lists the basic requirements for a thesis statement.

QUICK REFERENCE 2.3

Basic requirements for a thesis statement

- It states the essay's subject—the topic that you discuss.
- It conveys the essay's purpose—either informative or persuasive.
- It indicates your focus—the assertion that presents your point of view.
- It uses specific language, not vague words.
- It may briefly state the major subdivisions of the essay's topic.

Some instructors add to these basic requirements. You might, for example, be asked to put your thesis statement at the end of your introductory paragraph (as in the final draft of Sara Cardini's essay, in section 2l.3). Some instructors require that the thesis statement be contained in one sentence; other instructors permit two sentences if the topic is complex. All requirements, basic and additional, are designed to help you develop a thesis statement that will guide the writing of your essay and help you communicate clearly with your reader. By the way, never confuse the role of a thesis statement with the role of an essay's title (2i.3).

ESL TIP: A thesis statement, especially in the introductory paragraph, is commonly found in the ACADEMIC WRITING of North American and some other cultures. Readers and writers from some cultures prefer not to state their main idea so bluntly at the beginning of a piece of writing. Because Canadian readers of academic writing generally expect such a statement, using one will probably help your readers better understand your writing. ●

Most writers find that their thesis statement changes somewhat with each successive draft of an essay. Still, when you revise its language, be sure to stick to the essential idea you want to communicate. A thesis statement is a guide; it helps you stay on the topic and develop your ideas in an essay. To start, make an **assertion**—a sentence stating your topic and the point you want to make about it. This assertion focuses your thinking as you develop a preliminary thesis statement. Next, move toward a final thesis statement that most accurately reflects the content of your essay.

Following is the evolution of Sara Cardini's thesis statement from a simple assertion to the final version in her essay on anime. The final version fulfills all the requirements described in Quick Reference 2.3.

NO   I think Japanese animation is the most interesting current cartoon form. [This assertion is a start, but simply proclaiming something "interesting" is dull.]

NO   Most people think cartoons are simple entertainments for kids, but there are exceptions to that rule. [This statement draws readers in by promising to show them how their expectations may be inadequate and that there really isn't a "rule" involved.]

NO   Anime films are sophisticated Japanese cartoons. [This statement is closer to a thesis statement because it's more specific. It promises to show that anime is sophisticated. However, the concept that anime contrasts with North American cartoons is an important part of Sara's paper, and that concept is missing here.]

NO   The purpose of this paper is to explain Japanese anime and how anime films differ from North American cartoons. [This version clearly states a main point of the paper, but it's inappropriate because it announces what the writer is going to do.]

YES   Anime has traditions and features that distinguish it from Canadian and American cartoons and make it sophisticated enough to appeal to adults. [The final version serves as Cardini's thesis statement by effectively conveying the main ideas and point of her essay.]

THESIS STATEMENTS FOR INFORMATIVE ESSAYS

For essays with an informative purpose (1c.2), here are more examples of thesis statements for 900- to 1300-word essays. The NO versions are assertions or preliminary thesis statements. The YES versions fulfill the requirements in Quick Reference 2.3.

TOPIC *reality television*

NO   There are many kinds of reality television shows.

YES   A common feature of reality television shows is a villain, a contestant that viewers love to hate.

TOPIC *women artists*

NO   Paintings by women express gender issues.

YES   The biblical paintings of Artemisia Gentileschi highlight acts of revenge by women against men.

THESIS STATEMENTS FOR PERSUASIVE ESSAYS

For essays written with a persuasive purpose (1c.3), here are examples of thesis statements written for 900- to 1300-word essays. Again, the NO versions are assertions or preliminary thesis statements. The YES versions fulfill the requirements in Quick Reference 2.3.

TOPIC *urban sprawl*

NO Large North American cities and their suburbs are expanding into the countryside uncontrollably.

YES Despite their stated concerns about urban sprawl, municipal politicians actually facilitate it through zoning, transportation, and infrastructure policies.

TOPIC *deceptive advertising*

NO Deceptive advertising is not adequately prosecuted.

YES Political contributions and the nomination of ex-politicians to their boards effectively exempt large corporations from laws against deceptive advertising.

EXERCISE 2-5 Each set of sentences below offers several versions of a thesis statement. Within each set, the thesis statements progress from weak to strong. The fourth thesis statement in each set is the best. Referring to requirements listed in Quick Reference 2.3, work individually or with a group to explain why the first three choices in each set are weak and the last is best.

A. 1. Advertising is complex.
   2. Magazine advertisements appeal to readers.
   3. Magazine advertisements must be creative and appealing to all readers.
   4. To appeal to readers, magazine advertisements must skilfully use language, colour, and design.
B. 1. Tennis is a popular sport.
   2. Playing tennis is fun.
   3. Tennis requires various skills.
   4. Changes in racquet technology and serving styles call for a different set of skills from the one that champion players needed in the past.
C. 1. Tom Thomson painted in Algonquin Park.
   2. Tom Thomson studied art and worked in an advertising studio.
   3. The Tom Thomson "myth" portrays him as an untaught phenomenon.
   4. The influence of Tom Thomson's art education and professional background shows in the painting techniques he explored.
D. 1. We should pay attention to the environment.
   2. We should worry about air pollution.
   3. Automobile emissions cause air pollution.
   4. Governments should raise emissions standards for passenger cars and SUVs.
E. 1. Many people aren't interested in politics.
   2. Citizens have become increasingly dissatisfied with the political process.
   3. Many postsecondary students are cynical about the political process.
   4. Lowering the voting age would involve students constructively in the political process, harness their idealism, and increase their voting turnout.

EXERCISE 2-6   Here are writing assignments, narrowed topics, and tentative thesis statements. Alone or with a peer-response group, evaluate each thesis statement according to the basic requirements in Quick Reference 2.3.

1. *Marketing assignment:* 700- to 800-word persuasive report on a local restaurant. *Audience:* the instructor and the restaurant's manager. *Topic:* increasing business. *Thesis:* The restaurant could attract more customers if it improved the quality of its food, its appearance, and the friendliness of its staff.

2. *Art assignment:* 300- to 500-word analysis of an Inuit print. *Audience:* the instructor and other students in the class. *Topic:* Pitseolak Ashoona's *Perils of the Sea Travellers*. *Thesis: Perils of the Sea Travellers* is one of the most moving images of traditional Inuit life.

3. *Biology assignment:* 800- to 1000-word informative report about DNA sequencing. *Audience:* the instructor and visiting students and instructors attending a seminar. *Topic:* medical uses of DNA sequencing. *Thesis:* Any medical facility using DNA sequencing should have a permanent ethical oversight committee.

4. *Journalism assignment:* 200- to 300-word article about campus diversity. *Audience:* the instructor, the student body, and the administration. *Topic:* international students. *Thesis:* This province is a leader in attracting international students.

5. *Nursing assignment:* 400- to 500-word persuasive report about technology changes in nursing. *Audience:* nursing students and professionals. *Topic:* using handheld computers to track patient information. *Thesis:* More hospitals require nurses to use handheld computers to enter patient data instead of using traditional charts.

2e   How do I plan and organize my ideas?

After you've generated ideas and information, you need to decide the best way to organize it. A plan helps you start drafting. Like a story, an essay needs a beginning, a middle, and an end: a shape. The essay's introduction sets the stage; the essay's body paragraphs provide the substance of your message in a sequence that makes sense; and the concluding paragraph ends the essay logically. Each paragraph's length in an informative essay needs to be in proportion to its function. Introductory and concluding paragraphs are usually shorter than body paragraphs. Body paragraphs are usually approximately equal to each other in length. If one body paragraph becomes overly long in relation to the others, consider breaking it into two paragraphs. (We discuss paragraph writing in Chapter 3.) The major elements in an informative essay are listed in Quick Reference 2.4. (For the major elements in a persuasive essay using classical argument, see Quick Reference 5.1 in 5e.)

Shaping an essay takes place on two levels. One is grouping individual ideas or pieces of information into paragraphs. The other is arranging those paragraphs into the best possible order and relationship to each other.

To group your information, look for topics that are related to each other and, within them, search for layers of generality. Which ideas or information can fit under which topics? For example, suppose you're writing a paper about how social networking has changed people's lives. Among the ideas that you've brainstormed are the following:

Social networking lets friends stay in constant touch.

Texting distracts from other activities.

The use of social networking exposes a gap between older and younger people.

Social networks have played a role in some political movements.

Everyone I know from school has a Facebook account.

Some people say they intend to close their Facebook accounts.

Being "friends" no longer means what it used to.

Elements in an informative essay

1. **Introductory paragraph:** Leads into the topic of the essay and tries to capture the reader's interest (3c).

2. **Thesis statement:** States the central message of the writing. The thesis statement usually appears at the end of the introductory paragraph (2d).

3. **Background information:** Provides a context for understanding the points that a writer wants to make. You can integrate background information into the introductory paragraph. More complex information may require a separate paragraph (as in the second paragraph in Sara Cardini's essay, in section 2l).

4. **Points of discussion:** Support the essay's thesis statement. They're the essential content of the body paragraphs in an essay (3d). Each point of discussion consists of a general statement backed up by specific details.

5. **Concluding paragraph:** Ends the essay smoothly, flowing logically from the rest of the essay (3k).

Although the list seems somewhat random, you can see that several of the ideas are about personal matters, and some are about social and political effects. You can group the ideas under those generalizations, and you can generate even more specific ideas about each one. For example, more specific details about texting could include the thought that it encourages people to observe themselves coldly as actors in the events they encounter; specific political examples of social networking could include popular revolutions in North Africa and the Middle East. Keep in mind that what separates most good writing from bad is the writer's ability to move back and forth between general statements and specific details.

A **subject tree** shows you visually whether you have sufficient content, at varying **levels of generality** or **specificity,** to start a first draft of your writing. A subject tree also visually demonstrates whether you have a good balance of general ideas and specific details. If what you have are mostly general ideas—or, the other way around, mostly specific details—go back to techniques for discovering and compiling ideas (2c) so that you can come up with what is missing.

Alex Garcia created a subject tree, shown in Figure 2.8, using software tools to help him shape the fifth paragraph in his essay (5n).

Once you've sorted your ideas and information into groups organized by generalizations, you're ready to shape your work at another level. You need to figure out the best order for the sections and paragraphs that you've planned. Of course, like all elements of the writing process, organizing is recursive: it loops back to its earlier stages as you go on. Although an initial plan might change considerably as you revise your work, a plan is still helpful for writing your first draft.

2f   What is outlining?

An **outline** lays out the relationships among ideas in a piece of writing. Outlines can lead writers to see how well their writing is organized. Many instructors require outlines to be submitted either before or with an essay.

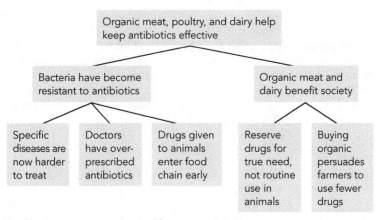

Figure 2.8 Alex Garcia's subject tree for the fifth paragraph in his essay

Some writers like to outline; others don't. If you don't, but you're required to write an outline, tackle the job with an open mind. You may be pleasantly surprised at what the rigour of outline writing does to your perception of your essay.

An outline can be *informal* or *formal*. Try outlining at various steps of the WRITING PROCESS: before drafting, to arrange ideas; while you draft, to keep track of your material; while you revise, to check the logical flow of thought or to reveal what information is missing, repeated, or off the topic; or in whatever other ways you find helpful.

INFORMAL OUTLINES

An **informal outline** is a working plan that lays out the major points of an essay. Because it's informal, it doesn't need to use the numbering and lettering conventions of a formal outline. Complete sentences aren't required; words and phrases are acceptable. Sara Cardini used an informal outline for planning her essay. Here is part of an informal outline for the third paragraph of her essay.

SARA CARDINI'S INFORMAL OUTLINE

Thesis statement: Anime has traditions and features that distinguish it from Canadian and American cartoons and make it sophisticated enough to appeal to adults.

qualities of anime
    quick movements
    jazz and rock music
    large eyes for characters
    complicated drawings
    Samurai X as an example

FORMAL OUTLINES

A traditional **formal outline** follows long-established conventions for using numbers and letters to show relationships among ideas. MLA STYLE doesn't officially endorse using an outline or any one outline style. However, many instructors do assign outlines, and they prefer the traditional format shown here. Increasingly, some instructors prefer a less traditional format for a formal outline, one which includes the content of the introductory paragraph and the concluding paragraphs. An example of such an outline appears in section 36e. Either of these styles of formal outline—the traditional or the less traditional—can be a sentence outline, composed entirely of complete sentences, or a topic outline, composed only of words and phrases. So that you can compare the two styles of outlines, both examples below outline the third paragraph of Sara Cardini's essay on Japanese anime. Never mix the two styles in one outline.

Writers who use formal outlines say that a sentence outline brings them closer to drafting than a topic outline does. This makes sense because topic outlines carry less information. But you have to find out which type works better for you.

TOPIC OUTLINE

Thesis statement: Anime has traditions and features that distinguish it from Canadian and American cartoons and make it sophisticated enough to appeal to adults.

I. Anime qualities
  A. Quick images
  B. Jazz and rock soundtracks
  C. Character eyes and features
  D. Colourful, complicated art
      1. *Samurai X* as example
      2. *Samurai X* about nineteenth-century warrior
      3. *Samurai X* art like old Japanese prints

SENTENCE OUTLINE

Thesis statement: Anime has traditions and features that distinguish it from Canadian and American cartoons and make it sophisticated enough to appeal to adults.

I. Complex plots are but one of the distinctive features of anime.
  A. Anime images move quickly, with a style often more frantic than in North American cartoons.
  B. Anime soundtracks frequently use jazz and rock music rather than symphonic music.
  C. Most striking are the large eyes and sharp features of the characters.
  D. The drawing is more colourful, more complicated, and often more abstract than that in most North American cartoons.
      1. A TV series called *Samurai X* is one of the most popular anime series with both North American and Japanese audiences.
      2. *Samurai X* is set in the nineteenth century and tells the story of one warrior's life.
      3. *Samurai X* art is drawn beautifully to look both like older Japanese art prints and like more contemporary movies such as *Crouching Tiger, Hidden Dragon.*

EXERCISE 2-7   Here is a sentence outline. Individually or with your peer-response group, revise it into a topic outline. Then, be ready to explain why you prefer using a topic outline or a sentence outline as a guide to writing.

Thesis statement: Taxpayers should demand more investment in public transportion.

I. The current level of public transportation is inadequate everywhere.
  A. Cities need the ability to move lots of residents.
      1. Increased population in large cities causes transportation pressures.

2. Some cities have responded well.
3. Most cities have responded poorly.
   B. People need to move easily and cheaply between cities and towns.
      1. Cars are the only way to reach many cities and towns.
      2. It is easier and less expensive to travel in Europe.
II. The lack of public transportation causes many problems.
   A. Driving individual cars increases pollution.
   B. Space for building new roads and highways is limited.
   C. Congestion on city streets limits productivity.
   D. Many people aren't able to drive themselves.
      1. Young or elderly people may not drive.
      2. Many people cannot afford cars.
III. Improving public transportation is possible.
   A. Cities can expand bus services and light rail services.
   B. Parts of Canada can develop a wider rail service.
   C. Although improvements are costly, we can afford them.
      1. We can reallocate money from building new roads.
      2. Building and running transportation creates jobs and adds to our tax base.
      3. Individual savings will offset any tax increase.

2g What can help me write a first draft?

Office Hours: Drafting

Drafting means getting ideas onto paper or into a computer file in sentences and paragraphs. In everyday conversation, people use the word *writing* to talk about drafting, but writing is too broad a term here. The word *drafting* more accurately describes what you do when you write your first attempt—your first *draft*—to generate words.

A **first draft** is the initial version of a piece of writing. Before you begin a first draft, seek out places and times of the day that encourage you to write. You might write best in a quiet corner of the library, or at 4:30 a.m. at the kitchen table before anyone else is awake, or outside alone with nature, or with a steady flow of people walking by. Most experienced writers find they concentrate best when they're alone and writing where they won't be interrupted. But individuals differ, and you may prefer background noise—a crowded cafeteria, with the low hum of conversation at the next table, for example.

A caution: Don't mislead yourself. You can't produce a useful first draft while talking to friends and stopping only now and then to jot down a sentence. You won't draft smoothly while watching television or being constantly interrupted.

Finally, resist delaying tactics. While you certainly need a computer or a pad of paper and a pen or pencil, you don't need fifteen perfectly sharpened pencils neatly lined up on your desk.

Quick Reference 2.5 offers suggestions for ways to move from planning and shaping into drafting. Experiment to see what works best for you. And be ready to adjust what works according to each WRITING SITUATION.

Now, dive in. Using the planning and shaping you've done as a basis, start writing. The direction of drafting is forward: Keep pressing ahead. If you wonder about the spelling of a word or a point of grammar, don't stop. Use a symbol or other signal to alert you to revisit later. Use whatever you like: boldface, underlining, a question mark before and after, an asterisk, or all capital letters. If the exact word you want escapes you while you're drafting, substitute an easy synonym and mark it to go back to later. If you question your sentence style or the order in which you present supporting details, boldface or underline the passage or insert a symbol or the word *Style?* or *Order?* nearby so that you can return to it later. If you begin to run out of ideas, reread what you have written—not to start revising prematurely, but only to propel yourself to keep moving ahead with your first draft. Once you finish your draft, search for the boldfaces, underlines, symbols, or words that you've used to alert yourself to reconsider something. If it's a word, you can use the "Edit>Find" function on your word-processing program toolbar.

When drafting on the computer, use your "Save" function often to protect your work, at least every five minutes. (This can be set up as an automatic function.) To prevent losing what you've written, back up your files diligently. Also, print your work regularly—very definitely at the end of each work session—so that you always have a hard copy in case your computer develops problems (a not unusual occurrence).

A first draft is a preliminary or *rough draft*. Its purpose is to get your ideas onto disk or into computer memory or on paper. Never are first drafts meant to be perfect.

QUICK REFERENCE 2.5

Ways to start drafting

- **Write a discovery draft.** Put aside all your notes from planning and shaping, and write a discovery draft. This means using FOCUSED FREEWRITING to get ideas on paper or onto your computer screen so that you can make connections that spring to mind as you write. Your discovery draft can serve as a first draft or as one more part of your notes when you write a more structured first draft.

- **Work from your notes.** Sort your notes from planning and shaping into groups of subtopics. When you start writing, you can systematically concentrate on each subtopic without having to search repeatedly through your pile of notes. Arrange the subtopics in what seems to be a sensible sequence, knowing you can always go back later and re-sequence the subtopics. Now, write a first draft by working through your notes on each subtopic. Draft either the entire essay or chunks of a few paragraphs at one time.

- **Use a combination of approaches.** When you know the shape of your material, write according to that structure. When you feel "stuck" and don't know what to say next, switch to writing as you would for a discovery draft.

2h How can I overcome writer's block?

If you're afraid or otherwise feel unable to start writing, perhaps you're being stopped by **writer's block**. You want to get started but somehow can't. Often, writer's block occurs because the writer harbours a fear of being wrong. To overcome that fear, or any other cause of your block, first admit it to yourself. Face it honestly so that you can understand whatever is holding you back. Writer's block can strike professional as well as student writers, and a variety of techniques to overcome it have become popular.

The most common cause of writer's block involves a writer's belief in myths about writing.

MYTH   Writers are born, not made.

TRUTH   Everyone can write. Writers don't expect to "get it right" the first time. Being a good writer means being a patient rewriter.

MYTH   Writers have to be "in the mood" to write.

TRUTH   If writers always waited for "the mood" to occur, few would write at all. News reporters and other professional writers have deadlines to meet, whether or not they're in the mood to write.

MYTH   Writers have to be really good at grammar and spelling.

TRUTH   Writers don't let spelling and grammar block them. They write, and when they hear that quiet inner voice saying that a word or sentence isn't quite right, they mark the spot with a symbol or word in all capitals. After they're finished drafting, they return to these and work on them, perhaps using this handbook or a dictionary or thesaurus to check themselves.

MYTH   Writers don't have to revise.

TRUTH   Writers expect to revise—several times. Once words are on paper, writers can see what readers will see. This "revision" helps writers revise.

MYTH   Writing can be done at the last minute.

TRUTH   Drafting and revising take time. Ideas don't leap onto paper in final, polished form.

Quick Reference 2.6 lists reliable strategies writers have developed to overcome writer's block. If you feel blocked, experiment to discover which works best for you. Also, add your own ideas about how to get started. As you use the list in Quick Reference 2.6, suspend judgment of your writing. Let things flow. Don't find fault with what you're keying or writing. Your goal is to get yourself under way. You can evaluate and improve your writing when you're revising it. According to research, premature revision stops many writers cold—and leads to writer's block. Your reward for waiting to revise until after you finish your first draft is the comfort of having a springboard for the revision work in front of you.

QUICK REFERENCE **2.6**

Ways to overcome writer's block

- **Check that one of the myths about writing discussed in section 2h, or one of your own, isn't stopping you.**

- **Avoid staring at a blank page.** Relax and move your hand across the keyboard or page. Write words, scribble, or draw while you think about your topic. The physical act of getting anything on paper can stir up ideas and lead you to begin drafting.

- **Visualize yourself writing.** Many professional writers say that they write more easily if they first picture themselves doing it. Before getting out of bed in the

continued ➤

morning or while waiting for a bus or walking to classes, mentally construct a visual image of yourself in the place where you usually write, with the materials you need, busy at work.

- **Picture an image or a scene, or imagine a sound that relates to your topic.** Start writing by describing what you see or hear.

- **Write about your topic in a letter or e-mail to a friend.** This technique helps you relax and makes drafting nothing more than a chat on paper with someone you feel comfortable with.

- **Try writing your material as if you were someone else.** When they take on a role, many writers feel less inhibited about writing.

- **Start by writing the middle of your essay.** Skip the introduction and begin with a body paragraph, and write from the centre of your essay out, instead of from beginning to end.

- **Use FREEWRITING or FOCUSED FREEWRITING.**

- **Change your method of writing.** If you usually use a computer, try writing by hand. When you write by hand, switch between pencil and pen or ink colours and treat yourself to good-quality paper so that you can enjoy the pleasure of writing on smooth, strong paper. Often that pleasure propels you to keep going.

- **Switch temporarily to writing about a topic that you care about passionately.** Write freely about that topic. Once writing starts to pour out of you, you can often use the momentum to switch back to the topic of your assignment.

Office
Hours:
Revising

2i   How do I revise?

Revising is rewriting. When you see the word *revision,* break it down to *re-vision,* which means "to see again with fresh eyes." To revise, you evaluate, change, and re-evaluate your draft to figure out ways to improve it. To do this, you need to read your writing honestly, without losing confidence or becoming defensive. After all, what's on the page is ink, not ego. As you work, look at whatever you change and evaluate the revision first on its own and then in the context of the surrounding material. Continue until you're satisfied that your essay is the best you can make it, in light of your specific WRITING SITUATION.

Whenever possible within your time frame, distance yourself from each draft. The best way is to leave a chunk of time between finishing a first draft and starting to revise. Doing so helps you develop an objective sense of your work. Student writers often want to hold on to their every word, especially if they had trouble getting started on a first draft. Resist such a feeling vigorously. Put away your draft and allow the rosy glow of authorial pride to dim a bit. The classical writer Horace recommended waiting nine years before revising! You might try to wait a few hours or even thirty minutes. Better yet, take a day or two before going back to look at your work with fresh eyes.

Also, as you're revising, don't start EDITING too soon. Editing comes after revising. Research shows that premature editing distracts writers from dealing with the larger issues that revision involves.

2i.1　Goals and activities during revision

Your goal during revision is to improve your draft at three levels: content, organization, and ideas.

To revise successfully, you need to understand that writing is revising. The myth that good writers never have to revise is nonsense. Final drafts evolve from first drafts. Here's how to prepare your mind for revising:

- Shift mentally from suspending judgment (during idea gathering and drafting) to making judgments. Read your draft objectively with "a cold eye" to evaluate it.
- Decide whether to write an entirely new draft or to revise the one you have. Be critical as you evaluate your first draft, but don't be overly harsh. Many early drafts provide sufficient raw material for revision to get under way.
- Be systematic. Most writers work best when they concentrate on each element sequentially. Start with your draft's overall organization; next, move to its paragraphs, then to its sentences, and finally to its word choice. If you need practice in being systematic, try using a revision checklist, either one supplied by your instructor or the one in this handbook.

You can engage in the activities of revision, listed in Quick Reference 2.7, by hand or on the computer, which allows you to make both large and small changes easily. Use "Cut" and "Paste" to reorder sentences or rearrange paragraphs. You might, for example, split up a paragraph, join two paragraphs, or otherwise shuffle them. Similarly, you might reorder the sequence of some sentences or interchange sentences between paragraphs. Sometimes, these experiments won't yield anything useful, but they might reveal a few surprises that help you "re-vision" your work.

((•

AUDIO LESSON
Section 1:
Big Ideas—
Revising,
Editing, and
Proofreading

((•

AUDIO LESSON
Section 2:
Practice
Questions—
Revising,
Editing, and
Proofreading

QUICK REFERENCE　2.7

Major activities during revision

- **Add:** Insert needed words, sentences, and paragraphs. If your additions require new content, return to the structured techniques shown in section 2b.
- **Cut:** Get rid of whatever goes off the topic or repeats what has already been said.
- **Replace:** As needed, substitute new words, sentences, and paragraphs for what you have cut.
- **Move:** Change the sequence of paragraphs if the material isn't presented in logical order. Move sentences within paragraphs or to other paragraphs when your PARAGRAPH ARRANGEMENT does not allow the material to flow.

As you try various revisions, use the "Save As" function (or the equivalent) on your computer to save drafts under slightly different names, such as "Animation Draft 1," "Animation Draft 2," and so on. By saving several drafts of your paper, you can always return to earlier versions if you later decide you prefer something in one of them. If you want to drop material, resist deleting it instantly. As handbook authors, we save almost everything. Doug, for instance, typically keeps a file named "Junk" for just this purpose. Lynn names her folder of discarded drafts of sentences, paragraphs, and whole essays "Discarded Stuff."

Beware of two temptations when writing with the computer. Because you can rearrange and otherwise revise endlessly, you may need to set limits, or you'll never finish the assignment. The opposite seduction is also possible: A neatly printed page may look like a final draft, but it definitely isn't one.

2i.2   The role of a thesis statement in revision

The THESIS STATEMENT of your essay has great organizing power because it controls and limits what your essay can cover. Therefore, as you revise, keep checking the accuracy of your thesis statement. Use the thesis statement's controlling power to bring it and your essay into line with each other. When your essay is finished, the thesis statement and what you say in your essay should match. If they don't, you need to revise either the thesis statement or the essay—or sometimes both.

Every writer's experience with revising a thesis statement varies from essay to essay. Sara Cardini, the student you met earlier in this chapter as she did her planning and shaping, wrote several versions of her thesis statement (shown in 2d) for her drafts. You can read Cardini's three complete drafts, along with comments, at the end of this chapter.

2i.3   The role of a title in revision

Your **title** can also show you what needs revising because it clarifies the overall point of the essay. An effective title sets you on your course and tells your readers what to expect. Some writers like to begin their first drafts with a title at the top of the page to focus their thinking. Then, as they revise drafts, they revise the title. If, however, no title springs to mind, don't be concerned. Often, a good title doesn't surface until after drafting, revising, and even editing. It can take that long to come up with one. Whatever you do, never tack on a title as an afterthought right before handing in your essay. A suitable title is essential for readers to think about as they begin focusing on your essay.

Titles can be direct or indirect. A **direct title** tells exactly what the essay will be about: for example, "The Characteristics of Japanese Animation." A direct title contains key words under which the essay could be catalogued in a library or an online database. The title shouldn't be too broad. For example, Cardini's first and second drafts of a title were "Japanese Videos" and "Japanese Anime" (2l.1 and 2l.2). By her final draft, Cardini had revised the title to "The Appeal of Japanese Animation for Adults" (2l.3). Conversely, a direct title should not be too narrow. "The Graphics of Anime" is too narrow a title for Cardini's essay, given what she discusses in it.

An **indirect title** only hints at the essay's topic. It tries to catch the reader's interest by presenting a puzzle that can be solved by reading the essay. When writing an indirect title, you don't want to be overly obscure or cute. For example, a satisfactory indirect title for Cardini's final draft might be "More Than Simple Cartoons?" In contrast, the indirect title "Imagining That Walt Disney Had Been Japanese" wouldn't work because it's only remotely related to the point of the essay. Also, "Thanks, *Sailor Moon*" would probably be seen as overly cute for academic writing.

🛈   **ALERT:** When you write the title at the top of the page or on a title page, never enclose it in quotation marks or underline it. Let your title stand on its own, without decoration. Where you place it will depend on which DOCUMENTATION STYLE you're using. ●

Whether direct or indirect, your essay title stands on its own. It's never continued in the opening sentence of your essay. For example, Cardini's essay, titled "The Appeal of Japanese

Animation for Adults," would suffer a major blow if the first sentence were "It certainly does" or "I am the proof." Similarly, never does the first sentence of an essay refer to the essay's title. Rather, the first sentence starts the flow of the essay's content.

2i.4 The role of unity and coherence

Chapter 3 shows you many techniques for achieving unity and coherence in an essay, but here we need to preview the concepts because they're central concerns as you revise.

An essay has **unity** when all of its parts relate to the THESIS STATEMENT and to one another. Does each paragraph—especially each body paragraph—contain examples, reasons, facts, and details that relate directly to your thesis and the essay's purpose? As you revise, do you notice that anything in the essay is off the topic? An essay achieves **coherence** through closely built relationships among ideas and details that are built on word choice, use of TRANSITIONAL EXPRESSIONS, clear use of PRONOUNS, and effective PARALLELISM.

2i.5 Using a revision checklist

A revision checklist can focus your attention as you evaluate and revise your writing. Use such a checklist, either one provided by your instructor or one that you compile on your own, based on Quick Reference 2.8.

QUICK REFERENCE 2.8

Revision

Your goal is to answer *yes* to each question. If you answer *no*, you need to revise. The section numbers in parentheses tell you where to look in this handbook for help.

1. Is your essay topic suitable and sufficiently narrow? (2b.3)
2. Does your thesis statement communicate your topic, focus, and purpose? (2d, Quick Reference 2.3)
3. Does your essay show that you are aware of your audience? (Quick Reference 1.5)
4. Have you checked for places where your reader would be confused or need more information? (4a–e, 4h)
5. Have you checked for places where a skeptical reader would object to your argument or not be convinced? (4i, Chapter 5)
6. Is your essay arranged effectively? (3a–b)
7. Have you checked for material that strays off the topic? (3d, 3f)
8. Does your introduction prepare your reader for the rest of the essay? (3c)
9. Do your body paragraphs express main ideas in topic sentences as needed? (3e) Are your main ideas clearly related to your thesis statement? (2d)
10. Do you provide specific, concrete support for each main idea? (3f)
11. Do you use transitions and other techniques to connect ideas within and between paragraphs? (3j)
12. Does your conclusion give your essay a sense of completion? (3k)

ESL TIP: If you'd like information about issues of English grammar that often affect ESL students, consult Part Seven in this handbook. Topics include those related to culture and education, as well as linguistic concerns, such as ARTICLES (Chapter 51); WORD ORDER (Chapter 52); PREPOSITIONS (Chapter 53); VERBALS (Chapter 54); and MODAL AUXILIARY VERBS (Chapter 55). ●

2j   How do I edit?

Editing means checking the technical correctness of your writing. You carefully examine your writing for correct grammar, spelling, punctuation, capitalization, and use of numbers, italics, and abbreviations. Some people use the terms *editing* and *revising* interchangeably, but these terms refer to very different steps in the writing process. In contrast to revising, editing involves looking at each word for its technical correctness. By editing, you fine-tune the surface features of your writing.

Editing is crucial in writing. No matter how much attention you've paid to planning, shaping, drafting, and revising, you need to edit carefully. Slapdash editing distracts and annoys your reader; lowers that reader's opinion of you and what you say in your essay; and, in a course assignment, usually earns a lower grade.

Our best advice to you about editing is this: Don't rush. Editing takes time. Inexperienced writers sometimes rush editing, eager to "get it over with." Resist any impulse to hurry. Be systematic and patient. Checking grammar and punctuation takes your full concentration, along with time to look up and apply the rules in this handbook.

When do you know you've finished revising and are ready to edit? Ask yourself, "Is there anything else I can do to improve the content, organization, development, and sentence structure of this draft?" If the answer is no, you're ready to edit.

Word-processing programs include editing tools such as a spell-checker, style-checker, thesaurus, and readability analyzer. As we explained in Chapter 1, each tool has shortcomings serious enough to create new errors. Yet, if you use the tools intelligently with their shortcomings in mind, they can be useful.

Whenever possible, edit on a paper copy of your writing. It's much easier to spot editing errors on a printed page than on a computer screen. Double-space your paper before printing it for revising or editing. The extra space gives you room to write in your changes clearly so that you can read them easily later. After you finish editing, you can transfer your corrections to the computer. If you must edit onscreen, highlight every two or three sentences and read each slowly. By working in small segments, you reduce the tendency to read too quickly and miss errors.

Using an editing checklist, either one provided by your instructor or one based on Quick Reference 2.9 that you tailor to your particular needs, can help you move through editing systematically.

A time-saving method for editing is to create a personal file of editing errors you tend to make repeatedly. For example, if the difference between *its* and *it's* always escapes you, or if you tend to misuse the colon, your personal file of editing errors can remind you to look over your draft for those problems.

Editing

Your goal is to answer *yes* to each below. If you answer *no,* you need to edit. The numbers in parentheses tell you which chapters in this handbook to go to for more information.

1. Are your sentences concise? (Chapter 11)

2. Are your sentences interesting? Do you use parallelism, variety, and emphasis correctly and to increase the impact of your writing? (Chapters 9–10)

3. Have you used exact words? (Chapter 12)

4. Is your usage correct and your language appropriate? (Chapter 13)

5. Have you avoided sexist or stereotypical language? (Chapter 12)

6. Is your grammar correct? (Chapters 14–22)

7. Is your spelling correct? (Chapter 31)

8. Have you used commas correctly? (Chapter 24)

9. Have you used all other punctuation correctly? (Chapter 23 and 25–29)

10. Have you used capital letters, italics, abbreviations, and numbers correctly? (Chapter 30)

11. Have you used the appropriate citation and documentation formats? (Chapters 36–38)

2k   How do I proofread?

((•●
AUDIO LESSON Section 3: Rapid Review— Revising, Editing, and Proofreading

To **proofread**, check your final draft for accuracy and neatness before handing it in. In contrast to editing, which is a check for technical correctness, proofreading is typographical. This is your last chance to catch typing (or handwriting) errors and to make sure what you hand in is a clean transcription of your final draft.

When proofreading, read your work carefully line by line, looking for typing errors, such as letters or words accidentally omitted, words typed twice in a row, wrong indents to start each paragraph, and similar typos or slips. Then, print out a complete fresh copy. Reprinting just one page is often difficult because of reflowing text. Never expect your instructor to make allowances for handwritten corrections.

Some techniques for proofreading include (1) using a ruler under each line as you read it to prevent yourself from looking beyond that line; (2) reading backwards, sentence by sentence, to prevent yourself from being distracted by the content of the paper; and (3) proofreading your final draft aloud, to yourself or to a friend, so that you can hear errors that have slipped past your eyes. As with revising and editing, whenever possible, print and proofread a double-spaced paper copy of your writing. Again, it's much easier to spot errors on a printed page than onscreen. If you must proofread onscreen, highlight every two or three sentences and read each slowly. Enlarging the type onscreen is another helpful trick to help you focus word by word.

2I A student essay in three drafts

The following sections observe Sara Cardini, a student, planning to write on the topic of Japanese animation. Earlier in this chapter, you'll find her writing assignment (2b), how she used an entry in her journal (2c.1), mapped her ideas (2c.5), wrote her THESIS STATEMENT (2d), and outlined (2f).

2I.1 The first draft of a student essay

Here's Sara's first draft (Figure 2.9) showing her own notes to herself about revisions to make in the second draft. The notes resulted from comments of her PEER-RESPONSE GROUP and from her personal rereading of her draft.

Sara Cardini

Mr. Bantham

English 101 *I know. It's not specific enough*

10 April 2013

Japanese Videos *Oops. The opening sentence shouldn't continue the title*

There certainly are many reasons to like it. Like most people, I watched

Italicize titles in final draft; underline them as a reminder cartoons as a child, consuming daily doses of Hey, Arnold and Doug and watching The Lion King over and over again. Then, I discovered Sailor Moon and an entirely

different approach to animation. Sailor Moon is just one of hundreds of

I'd better show pronunciation animated television series to come from the creative minds of Japan. These

series and thousands of films are called anime. Because much anime is

created for adults, I have continued to watch it as I have gotten older.

in my interest I am not alone. In recent years, anime rocks. Still, people who are unfamiliar *Tone appropriate?*

with anime may wonder why adults would waste their time watching cartoons.

(Some careful analysis makes the answer clear.) Anime is a sophisticated

Japanese cartoon style. *Need to add thesis concept that anime differs from North American cartoons.*

Figure 2.9 Sara Cardini's first draft, with notes

Someone watching (animes) for the first time notices several distinctive qualities:

Check plural

~~The most obvious difference between Japanese and North American cartoons is, of~~

I think I'm going off track here. Are these points important to my comparison?

course, the language. Most anime will let you choose between a dubbed version

(with actors speaking English) and a subtitled version (in which the English is

written at the bottom of the screen). True anime fans will never watch the dubbed

version. As a result, North American viewers are barraged with Japanese voices that

seem to use a high-pitched, very fast speaking style. Of course, the film depicts

Japanese houses, trees, rooms, and such in a way that shows the contrasts between

~~their country and ours.~~ Anime images move quickly, with a style often more frantic

Keep verb tenses consistent.

Too itsy bitsy. Make into one sentence

than in North American cartoons. Their soundtracks frequently (used) jazz and

rock rather than ~~traditional~~ *symphonic* music. People in anime are very stylized, not

realistic. The drawing is colourful. It is more complicated. It is often more abstract

"take" isn't the right verb—fix

than most cartoons produced here. ~~E.G.~~ *For example,* (take) a TV series called Samurai X, the

most popular anime cartoons with both North American and Japanese audiences.

Samurai X is set in the nineteenth century and tells the story of one warrior's life. It is

wordy

drawn beautifully in a way that looks both like older Japanese art prints and like

more contemporary movies such as Crouching Tiger, Hidden Dragon.

Bet this is a fragment. Check Chapter 4.

Whereas

~~While~~ Canadians and Americans considered animation entertainment for

mainly

children. The Japanese viewed it as ~~entertaining~~ primarily for adults. Since the

beginning of print, cartooning in Japan has been aimed at adults, so anime was a

in this tradition

natural step. It's interesting how graphic novels were important in Japan long before

they were here, but lately you see more and more graphic novels. In North America,

Used same word twice. Get out my thesaurus.

aside from editorial cartoons and newspaper funny pages, comics were (aimed)

adolescent males

primarily at ~~boys~~. Hollywood animation in the 1940s and 1950s was different.

Think of Walt Disney. Japanese cartoons were developed for both kids and

continued ➤

old people, male and female audiences. In Japan, animated cartoons take on

adult subjects often absent from North American cartoons. ← *Examples needed*

There must be a better word The special style of anime comes largely from the films being produced for *Right word?*

narrow audiences. The animators were creating works only for a Japanese market,

at least until quite recently. Therefore, it did not take into account the traditions

of other cultures. Indeed, Hollywood animation was produced for an international

audience, which called for recognizable themes that came out of familiar European

uninitiated   *an Eastern*

traditions. For rookie viewers, then, anime provides a crash course in a culture quite

different from their own. Nearly all serious anime fans own guides that explain *Add more detail here*

such things as Japanese social hierarchies. For instance, several anime feature

a *hagoromo* or feathered cloak worn by a mythological figure known as the *tennyo*.

symbolic

Knowing that this figure has a certain meaning for a Japanese viewer and is not just

a random decoration or character adds to the depth of a scene in which it appears.

Decoding some of these cultural references is undoubtedly some of the fun and

challenge for the true *otakon*, or anime fan.

Japanese television has many daily animated series that vary in terms of

complex

sophistication and audience. Some of these have extremely complicated scripts,

while others are bad by nearly any standard. Several of these television series now

Add examples appear in North America. A wide range of anime feature films is readily available

on DVD, and many have even found their way into theatres. For instance, Akira is a

film about life thirty years after a nuclear war. Probably the most famous theatrical

Better look at this sentence again!

anime in North America is Spirited Away. Directed by Hayao Miyasaki, in

which a young girl, Chihiro, is able to free her parents from a spell after many

probably

magical adventures. The movie will become a probably classic. Anime appears

in all kinds of types and genres, from childish works like Pokémon to dark science

fiction like Ghost in the Shell. *I think I should move this up as the topic sentence for this paragraph.*

Verb tense ok?

Best word? One reason grown-ups enjoy anime is because they missed a form they loved

continued ➤

of design, creativity, sophistication, and content

as children. Anime gives them animated art but adds an adult level. While there have

been a few North American cartoons aimed at adults (The Simpsons, South Park),

the animation is less detailed and the tone is usually satiric. There are no such

barriers in anime.

By studying anime, I also learned more about Japan. I met people who took

Japanese language classes and had travelled to cities such as Tokyo and Osaka.

I found out about Japanese popular culture and how much fashion, music, etc., the

Japanese borrow from the West and how much we borrow from them. I discovered

that while the Japanese are very different in some traditions, they are very much

like us in terms of their love of movies, TV, and music. For the first time, I *Does this para relate directly to my thesis?*

became very interested in how people in another country live. Now I am

considering travelling to Japan.

As Americans, Canadians, and Europeans come to embrace anime, the form

watered down

may change. Some fans fear that the art of anime will be ~~wasted~~ in the bid for

popularity and profits. Others celebrate the combination of styles as some

Western animators borrow from the Japanese. In this essay I have explained

Japanese animation. ← —— *I shouldn't declare what I have done. My ending needs work.*

21.2 The second draft of a student essay

For her second draft, Sara Cardini revised by working systematically through the notes she had written on the draft. The notes came from her own thinking as well as from the comments of the peer-response group with which she had shared her paper.

From the assignment (2b), Sara knew that her instructor would consider this second draft an "essay in progress." Her instructor's responses would help her write a final draft. She expected two types of comments: questions to help her clarify and expand on some of her ideas, and references to some of this handbook's section codes (number-letter combinations) to point out errors. Here is her second draft (Figure 2.10).

Sara Cardini

Mr. Bantham

English 101

14 April 2013

[handwritten note: Think about the title as you clarify the overall point of your essay.]

Japanese Anime

[handwritten note: What might be an attention-catching opening line?]

Like most people, I watched cartoons as a child, consuming daily doses of

Hey, Arnold and *Doug* and watching *The Lion King* over and over again.

[handwritten note: When?]

Then, I discovered *Sailor Moon* and an entirely different approach

to animation. *Sailor Moon* is just one of hundreds of animated television

series to come from the creative minds of Japan. These series and

thousands of films are called anime (commonly pronounced AN-ah-may).

[handwritten note: What personal background do you have in this area?]

Because much anime is created for adults, I have continued to watch it

[handwritten note: For comma use, see 24c]

as I have gotten older. I am not alone in my interest. In recent years,

anime has become hugely popular in North America. Still, people who are

[handwritten note: If this sentence is necessary, why put it in parentheses?]

unfamiliar with anime may wonder why adults waste their time watching

[handwritten note: Indicate the purpose of your paper without announcing it.]

cartoons. (Some careful analysis makes the answer clear.) The purpose

of this paper is to explain Japanese anime and how it differs from the style

of North American cartoons.

[handwritten note: Should this para come after the background information?]

[handwritten note: Think about a stronger link between paragraphs.]

Someone watching anime for the first time notices several distinctive qualities.

Anime images move quickly, with a style often more frantic than in North American

cartoons. Their soundtracks frequently use jazz and rock rather than

[handwritten note: Interesting, but I'd like to know more detail]

symphonic music. People in anime are very stylized, not realistic. The

[handwritten note: Since this para gives background information, does it belong here?]

drawing is more colourful, more complicated, and often more abstract than in most

cartoons produced here. For example, a TV series called *Samurai X* is one of the most

popular anime cartoons with both North American and Japanese audiences. *Samurai X*

is set in the nineteenth century and tells the story of one warrior's life.

[handwritten note: Why is it popular?]

Figure 2.10 Sara Cardini's second draft, with her instructor's responses.

Whereas Canadians and Americans considered animation entertainment for

children, the Japanese viewed it as mainly for adults. Since the beginning of print,

This para needs a stronger topic sentence.

cartooning in Japan has targeted adults, so anime was a natural step in this tradition.

It's interesting how graphic novels were important in Japan long before they

Off topic?

were here, but lately you see more and more graphic novels. In North America, aside

from editorial cartoons and newspaper funny pages, comics were aimed

A little more guidance, please.

From what?

primarily at adolescent males. Hollywood animation in the 1940s and 1950s

was different. Think of Walt Disney. Japanese cartoons were developed for

Off topic?

both kids and old people, male and female audiences. In Japan, animated cartoons

take on adult subjects often absent from North American cartoons. These subjects

include war, death, sacrifice, love, Japan's historical past and future, and

A link to the next para would be welcome here.

even occasionally sex and violence.

The unique style of anime comes largely from the films being

Right word?

produced for narrow audiences. The animators were creating works only for

What does it refer to? See 16p.

a Japanese market, at least until quite recently. Therefore, it did not take

into account the traditions of other cultures. Indeed, Hollywood animation

Right word?

was produced for an international audience, which called for recognizable

themes that came out of familiar European traditions. For uninitiated viewers, then,

anime provides a crash course in an Eastern culture quite different from their own.

Nearly all serious anime fans own guides that explain such things as Japanese

social hierarchies, clothing, dining habits, traditions, rituals, and mythology.

See next page.

For instance, several anime feature a *hagoromo*, or feathered cloak, worn by a

mythological figure known as the *tennyo*. Knowing that this figure has a symbolic

continued ➤

[Excellent point!]

meaning for a Japanese viewer and is not just a random decoration or character adds to the depth of a scene in which it appears. Decoding some of these cultural references is undoubtedly some of the fun and challenge for the true *otakon*, or anime fan.

Anime appears in all kinds of types and genres, from childish works like

[Do you really mean childish?]

Pokémon to dark science fiction like *Ghost in the Shell*. Japanese televison has many daily animated series that vary in terms of sophistication and audience. Some of these have extremely complex scripts, while others are bad by nearly any

[Meaning what?]

standard. Several of these television series now appear in North America, with some of the best known including *Inuyasha* and *Evangelion*. A wide range of anime feature films are readily available on DVD, and many have even found their

[See previous page.]

way into theatres. For instance, *Akira* is a film about life thirty years after a

[More detail would make this vivid.]

nuclear war. Probably the most famous theatrical anime video in North America is *Spirited Away*, directed by Hayao Miyasaki, in which a young girl, Chihiro, is able to free her parents from a spell after many magical adventures. The movie will probably become a classic.

One reason North American adults enjoy anime is because they miss a form they loved as children. Anime gives them animated art but adds an adult level of design, creativity, sophistication, and content. While there have been a few North American cartoons aimed at adults (*The Simpsons*, *South Park*), the animation is less detailed and the tone is usually satiric. There are no such barriers in anime.

[Interesting concluding thoughts]

As Americans, Canadians, and Europeans come to embrace anime,

[Bringing in your voice again makes for an effective ending.]

the form may change. Some fans fear that the art of anime will be watered down in the bid for popularity and profits. Others celebrate the combination of styles as some Western animators borrow from the Japanese. In this essay I have proved that anime deserves our attention.

[But avoid making an absolute claim like this.]

50

continued ➤

Dear Sara,
 You've done yourself proud. And you've inspired me to look up the fascinating subject of Japanese anime.
 As you revise for your final draft, I'd urge you to acquire a little more personal voice. Think about how you feel on this subject and put that in words. Also, think about my questions and the codes that refer you to sections of the Troyka handbook.
 I will enjoy reading your final draft.

RB

21.3   A student's final draft

For her final draft, Sara Cardini worked systematically through her second draft with an eye on her instructor's responses. Also, she revised in places where her instructor hadn't commented. As another check, Sara referred to the revision checklist (Quick Reference 2.8).

Next, to edit her final draft, Sara looked up the handbook codes (number-letter combinations) her instructor wrote on her second draft. She also consulted the editing checklist (Quick Reference 2.9). Then, before she started to proofread, she took a break from writing so she could refresh her ability to see typing errors. Distance from her work, she knew, would also help her see it more objectively.

Sara's final draft appears on the following pages with notes in the margins to point out elements that help the essay succeed. These notes are for you only; don't write any notes on your final drafts.

Sara Cardin's final draft

Cardini 1

Header at top right has name and page number

Sara Cardini
Mr. Bantham
English 101
28 April 2013

Includes name, course information, and date, double-spaced and flush left

Centres title

The Appeal of Japanese Animation for Adults

Includes attention-getting first line

I confess that I am an animation addict. Like most people, I watched cartoons as a child, consuming daily doses of *Hey, Arnold* and *Doug* and watching *The Lion King* over and over again. Then in junior

continued ➤   51

high, just about the time I was getting tired of cartoons, I discovered *Sailor Moon* and an entirely different approach to animation. *Sailor Moon* is just one of hundreds of animated television series to come from the creative minds of Japan. These series and thousands of films are called *anime* (commonly pronounced AN-ah-may). Because much anime is created for adults, I have continued to watch it as I have gotten older. In fact, my interest has grown so strong that I have studied Japanese, have attended anime conferences, and am now studying filmmaking. I am not alone in my interest. In recent years, anime has become hugely popular in North America. Still, people who are unfamiliar with anime may wonder why adults would waste their time watching cartoons. Some careful analysis makes the answer clear. Anime has traditions and features that distinguish it from Canadian and American cartoons and make it sophisticated enough to appeal to adults.

Animation developed differently here and in Japan after World War II. Whereas Canadians and Americans considered animation entertainment for children, the Japanese viewed it as mainly for adults. Since the beginning of print, cartooning in Japan has targeted adults, so anime was a natural step in this tradition. In North America, aside from editorial cartoons and newspaper funny pages, comics were aimed primarily at adolescent males. Therefore, Hollywood animation in the 1940s and 1950s was different from the type developed in Japan. The early work of Walt Disney, for example, came from fairy tales, or it featured cute animal characters. In Japan, animated cartoons take on adult subjects often absent from North American cartoons. These subjects include war, death, sacrifice, love, Japan's historical past and future, and even occasionally sex and violence. The plot lines are often extremely complex. Stories that would be kept simple in a Disney film to avoid viewer confusion have no such restrictions in Japan.

Complex plots are but one of the distinctive features of anime. Anime images move quickly, with a style often more frantic than in

Marginal annotations:

- Provides her credentials on this topic
- Introduces a question
- Offers a thesis
- Provides background on topic
- Uses comparison and contrast to develop paragraph
- Uses specific details to explain anime

(Proportions shown in this paper are adjusted to fit space limitations of this book. Follow actual dimensions shown in this book and your instructor's directions.)

continued ➤

Cardini 3

North American cartoons. Their soundtracks frequently use jazz and rock rather than symphonic music. However, perhaps most striking are the large eyes and sharp features of the characters. People in anime are very stylized, not realistic. The drawing is more colourful, more complicated, and often more abstract than most cartoons produced here. For example, a TV series called *Samurai X* is one of the most popular anime cartoons with both North American and Japanese audiences. *Samurai X* is set in the nineteenth century and tells the story of one warrior's life. It is drawn beautifully in a way that looks both like older Japanese art prints and like more contemporary movies such as *Crouching Tiger, Hidden Dragon*.

Provides a concrete example

The unique style of anime comes largely from the films being produced for specific audiences. The animators were creating works only for a Japanese market, at least until quite recently. Therefore, they did not take into account the traditions of other cultures. In contrast, Hollywood animation was produced for an international audience, which called for recognizable themes that came out of familiar European traditions. For uninitiated viewers, then, anime provides a crash course in an Eastern culture quite different from their own. Nearly all serious anime fans own guides that explain such things as Japanese social hierarchies, clothing, dining habits, traditions, rituals, and mythology. To cite one small example, several anime feature a *hagoromo*, or feathered cloak, worn by a mythological figure known as the *tennyo*. Knowing that this figure has a symbolic meaning for a Japanese viewer and is not just a random decoration or character adds to the depth of a scene in which it appears. Decoding some of these cultural references is undoubtedly some of the fun and challenge for the true *otakon*, or anime fan.

Uses cause and effect to explain differences

Cites a very specific example

Anime appears in all kinds of types and genres, from children's works like *Pokémon* to dark science fiction like *Ghost in the Shell*. Japanese television has many daily animated series that vary in terms of sophistication and audience. Some of these have extremely complex scripts, while others are painfully simplistic. Several of these television series now appear in North America, with some of the best known including *Inuyasha* and *Evangelion*. A wide range of anime feature films are readily available on DVD, and many have even found their way into theatres.

Uses classification to explain types

Provides a specific titles as examples

continued ➤   53

Cardini 4

Focuses at length on one prominent example

For example, *Akira* is a film about life thirty years after a nuclear war. A misfit boy, Tetsuo, accidentally discovers the government experiments that led to that war and then learns that scientists are starting similar experiments once again. Probably the most famous theatrical anime film in North America is *Spirited Away*, directed by Hayao Miyasaki, in which a young girl, Chihiro, is able to free her parents from a spell after many magical adventures. The movie will probably become a classic.

States a reason in the topic sentence

Contrasts North American cartoons with anime

One reason North American adults enjoy anime is because they miss a form they loved as children. Anime gives them animated art but adds an adult level of design, creativity, sophistication, and content. While there have been a few North American cartoons aimed at adults (*The Simpsons, South Park*), the animation is not very detailed and the tone is usually satiric. There are no such barriers in anime.

Speculates about the future in concluding strategy

Uses final comment to return to her opening idea

As Americans, Canadians, and Europeans come to embrace anime, the form may change. Some fans fear that the art of anime will be watered down in the bid for popularity and profits. Others celebrate the combination of styles as some Western animators borrow from the Japanese. As an animation addict, I welcome more North American animation for adults. Still, I would be disappointed if the distinctive qualities of anime disappeared. I fervently hope the Japanese animators will maintain their exotic creativity.

Chapter 3

WRITING PARAGRAPHS, SHAPING ESSAYS

3a   How do I shape essays?

A good essay has an effective beginning, middle, and end. The key word is *effective*. Beginnings interest your reader and create expectations for the rest of the essays, usually through a THESIS STATEMENT, your main point. Middles explain or provide arguments for the thesis, usually through a series of statements and supporting details or evidence. Writers organize their main ideas to build a logical and engaging sequence. What separates most good writing from bad is the writer's ability to move back and forth between main ideas and specific details. Endings provide closure. They make readers feel that the writing achieved its purpose and that the writer had a skilled sense of his or her audience to the very end. One key to shaping essays is understanding how paragraphs work.

((•
AUDIO
LESSON
Section 1: Big
Ideas—
Becoming a
Critical Reader
and a Better
Writer

((•
AUDIO
LESSON
Section 2:
Practice
Questions—
Becoming a
Critical Reader
and a Better
Writer

3b   How do paragraphs work?

A **paragraph** is a group of sentences that work together to develop a unit of thought. Paragraphing permits writers to divide material into manageable parts. When a group of paragraphs works together in logical sequence, the result is a complete essay or other whole piece of writing.

Paragraphs function differently in different types of writing. In many academic papers, each paragraph is a logical unit that develops a single idea, often expressed as a topic sentence (3e), with each topic sentence contributing to the paper's thesis. You might think of these paragraphs as bricks that form a wall, or as rooms that together form a building. In writing that tells a story or explains a process, there are often few topic sentences. In newspaper or journalistic writing, paragraph breaks frequently occur more for dramatic effect than for logic.

To signal the start of a new paragraph, indent the first line about one-half inch, or 1.25 cm. Skip no extra lines between paragraphs. Business writing (Chapter 43) is an exception: It calls for BLOCK STYLE for paragraphs, which means you do not indent the first line but rather leave a double space between paragraphs.

We explain later in this chapter the rich variety of paragraph arrangements (3h) and rhetorical strategies (3i) at your disposal for writing paragraphs. But first, let's look at characteristics of paragraphs in general. We start by discussing introductory paragraphs (3c); then, body paragraphs (3d through 3i); and last, concluding paragraphs (3k).

3c   How can I write effective introductory paragraphs?

👁
Finding a
Topic for
Argument

An **introductory paragraph** leads the reader to sense what's ahead. It sets the stage. It also, if possible, attempts to arouse a reader's interest in the topic.

A THESIS STATEMENT can be an important component in an introduction. Many instructors require students to place the thesis statement at the end of the opening paragraph. By

55

doing this, students learn to state the central point of the essay early on. If an introduction points in one direction and the rest of the essay goes off in another, the essay isn't communicating a clear message. Professional writers don't necessarily include a thesis statement in their introductory paragraphs. Most have the skill to maintain a line of thought without overtly stating a main idea. Introductory paragraphs, as well as concluding paragraphs (3k), are usually shorter than body paragraphs (3d).

Be careful not to tack on a sloppy introduction at the last minute. The introductory paragraph is too important to be tossed off with merely a few shallow lines. While many writers prefer to write only a thesis statement as an introduction in an early draft, they always return to write a complete introductory paragraph after the body—the main part—of the writing is finished. For a list of specific strategies to use and pitfalls to avoid for introductory paragraphs, see Quick Reference 3.1.

QUICK REFERENCE 3.1

Introductory paragraphs

STRATEGIES TO USE

- Providing relevant background information
- Relating briefly an interesting story or anecdote
- Giving one or more pertinent—perhaps surprising—statistics
- Asking one or more provocative questions
- Using an appropriate quotation
- Defining a KEY TERM
- Presenting one or more brief examples (3i)
- Drawing an ANALOGY (3i)

STRATEGIES TO AVOID

- Don't write statements about your purpose, such as "I am going to discuss the causes of falling oil prices."
- Don't apologize, as in "I am not sure this is right, but this is my opinion."
- Don't use overworked expressions, such as "Haste makes waste, as I recently discovered" or "Love is grand."

Always integrate an introductory device into the paragraph so that it leads smoothly into the thesis statement. Some examples follow. In this chapter, each example paragraph has a number to its left for your easy reference. Here's an introductory paragraph that uses two brief examples to lead into the thesis statement at the end of the paragraph.

1 On seeing another child fall and hurt himself, Hope, just nine months old, stared, tears welling up in her eyes, and crawled to her mother to be comforted—as though she had been hurt, not her friend. When 15-month-old Michael saw his friend Paul crying, Michael fetched his own teddy bear and offered it to Paul; when that didn't stop Paul's tears, Michael brought Paul's security blanket from another room. Such small acts of sympathy and caring, observed in scientific studies, are leading researchers to trace the roots of empathy—the ability to share another's emotions—to infancy, contradicting a long-standing assumption that infants and toddlers were incapable of these feelings.

—Daniel Goleman, "Researchers Trace Empathy's Roots to Infancy"

In paragraph 2, the opening quotation sets up a dramatic contrast with the thesis statement.

2 "Alone one is never lonely," says May Sarton in her essay "The Rewards of Living a Solitary Life." Most people, however, don't share Sarton's opinion: They're terrified of living alone. They're used to living with others—children with parents, roommates with roommates, friends with friends, spouses with spouses. When the statistics catch up with them, therefore, they're rarely prepared. Chances are high that most adult men and women will need to know how to live alone, briefly or longer, at some time in their lives.

—Tara Foster, student

In paragraph 3, the writer asks a direct question, and next puts the reader in a dramatic situation to arouse interest in the topic.

3 What should you do? You're out riding your bike, playing golf, or in the middle of a long run when you look up and suddenly see a jagged streak of light shoot across the sky, followed by a deafening clap of thunder. Unfortunately, most outdoor exercisers don't know whether to stay put or make a dash for shelter when a thunderstorm approaches, and sometimes the consequences are tragic.

—Gerald Secor Couzens, "If Lightning Strikes"

EXERCISE 3-1   Write an introduction for each of the three essays informally outlined below. Then, for more practice, write one alternative introduction for each. If you have a peer-response group, share the various written introductions and decide which are most effective. For help, see 3b.

1. Surfing the Web

   Thesis statement: The contents of the World Wide Web reveal people's obsessions in the twenty-first century.

   Body paragraph 1: sites with offensive content
   Body paragraph 2: chats, blogs, and hobbies
   Body paragraph 3: financial investments and auctions

2. Cell phones

   Thesis statement: Cell phones have changed how some people behave in public.

   Body paragraph 1: driving
   Body paragraph 2: restaurants
   Body paragraph 3: movies and concerts
   Body paragraph 4: sidewalks, parks, and other casual spaces

3. Personal privacy

   Thesis statement: We have given up much of the right to privacy that we once valued.

   Body paragraph 1: surveillance cameras
   Body paragraph 2: miniaturized photographic and recording devices
   Body paragraph 3: social networking sites, video sharing sites
   Body paragraph 4: blogs

3d What are body paragraphs?

In most academic writing, each **body paragraph**, the paragraphs between an introductory paragraph (3c) and a concluding paragraph (3k), consists of a main idea and support for that idea. To be effective, a body paragraph needs three characteristics: development (3f), unity (3g), and coherence (3g). Quick Reference 3.2 gives an overview of all three characteristics.

QUICK REFERENCE **3.2**

Characteristics of effective body paragraphs

- **Development:** Have you included detailed and sufficient support for the main idea of the paragraph? (3f)
- **Unity**: Have you made a clear connection between the main idea of the paragraph and the sentences that support, develop, or illustrate the main idea? (3g)
- **Coherence**: Have you progressed from one sentence to the next in the paragraph smoothly and logically? (3g)

Paragraph 4 is an example of an effective body paragraph.

4   The Miss Plastic Surgery contest, trumpeted by Chinese promoters as "the world's first pageant for artificial beauties," shows the power of cosmetic surgery in a country that has swung from one extreme to another when it comes to the feminine ideal. In the 10th century, Emperor Li Yu ordered his consort to bind her feet; women practiced the painful ritual for more than 900 years in the belief that small feet were more alluring. In contrast, at the height of the Cultural Revolution in the 1960s and 1970s, Maoist officials condemned any form of personal grooming or beautification as "unrevolutionary" and regularly beat women for owning hairbrushes, wearing blush, or painting their nails.

—Abigail Haworth, "Nothing About These Women Is Real"

Paragraph 4 has UNITY (3g) in that the main idea—the feminine ideal in China has swung from one extreme to another—stated in the TOPIC SENTENCE (3e) is supported by detailed examples. It has COHERENCE (3g) in that the content of every sentence ties into the content of the other sentences. Also, the paragraph *coheres*—sticks together—because of the use of transitional phrases ("In the 10th century" and "In contrast," for example). It has PARAGRAPH DEVELOPMENT (3f) in that the details provide support for the main idea.

3e What are topic sentences?

A **topic sentence** contains the main idea of a paragraph and controls its content. Often, the topic sentence comes at the beginning of a paragraph, though not always. Professional essay writers, because they have the skill to carry the reader along without explicit signposts, sometimes decide not to use topic sentences. However, instructors often require students to use topic sentences. As apprentice writers, students might have more difficulty writing unified paragraphs.

TOPIC SENTENCE STARTING A PARAGRAPH

In ACADEMIC WRITING, most paragraphs begin with a topic sentence so that readers know immediately what to expect. Paragraph 5 is an example.

> Music patronage was at a turning point when Mozart went to Vienna in the last part of the eighteenth century. Many patrons of music continued to be wealthy aristocrats. Haydn's entire career was funded by a rich prince. Mozart's father and, for a time, Mozart himself were in the employ of another prince. But when Mozart went to Vienna in 1781, he contrived to make a living from a variety of sources. In addition to performances at aristocratic houses and commissions for particular works, Mozart gave piano and composition lessons, put on operas, and gave many public concerts of his own music.
>
> —Jeremy Yudkin, "Composers and Patrons in the Classic Era"

5

Sometimes, a topic sentence both starts a paragraph and, in different wording, ends the paragraph. Paragraph 6 is an example.

> Modern science cannot explain why the laws of physics are exactly balanced for animal life to exist. For example, if the big bang had been one-part-in-a-billion more powerful, it would have rushed out too fast for the galaxies to form and for life to begin. If the strong nuclear force were decreased by two percent, atomic nuclei wouldn't hold together. Hydrogen would be the only atom in the universe. If the gravitational force were decreased, stars (including the sun) would not ignite. These are just three of more than 200 physical parameters within the solar system and universe so exact that they cannot be random. Indeed, the lack of a scientific explanation has allowed these facts to be hijacked as a defense of intelligent design.
>
> —Robert Lanza, "A New Theory of the Universe"

6

TOPIC SENTENCE ENDING A PARAGRAPH

Some paragraphs give supporting details first and wait to state the topic sentence at the paragraph's end. This approach is particularly effective for building suspense or for creating a bit of drama. Paragraph 7 is an example.

> Once the Romans had left, the political situation in Britain deteriorated rapidly. Softened by their dependence on the Roman legions, the Romanized Britons were ill-equipped to defend themselves from renewed attacks by the Picts in the north. Then, even as the Britons were trying to cope with their fiercer northern neighbors, a much more calamitous series of events took place: waves of Germanic-speaking people from the Continent began to invade the island. The "English" were coming to England.
>
> —C. M. Millward, "The Arrival of the English"

7

TOPIC SENTENCE IMPLIED, NOT STATED

Some paragraphs are a unified whole even without a single sentence that readers can point to as the topic sentence. They are constructed so that most readers can catch the main idea. Paragraph 8 is an example. What do you think might be a straightforward topic sentence for it?

> It is easy to identify with the quest for a secret document, somewhat harder to do so with a heroine whose goal is identifying and understanding the element radium, which is why in dramatic biography writers and directors end up reverting to fiction. To be effective, the dramatic elements must, and finally will, take precedence over any "real" biographical facts. We viewers do not care—if we wanted to know about the element radium, we would read a book on the element radium. When we go to the movies to see *The Story of Marie Curie* we want to find out how her little dog Skipper died.
>
> —David Mamet, *Three Uses of the Knife: On the Nature and Purpose of Drama*

8

EXERCISE 3-2   Working individually or with a group, identify the topic sentences in the following paragraphs. If the topic sentence is implied, write the point the paragraph conveys. If a paragraph appears to have a topic sentence that repeats in different words later in the paragraph, identify both versions. For help, consult section 3e.

A. A good college program should stress the development of high-level reading, writing, and mathematical skills and should provide you with a broad historical, social, and cultural perspective, no matter what subject you choose as your major. The program should teach you not only the most current knowledge in your field but also—just as important— **9** prepare you to keep learning throughout your life. After all, you'll probably change jobs, and possibly even careers, at least six times, and you'll have other responsibilities, too— perhaps as a spouse and as a parent and certainly as a member of a community whose bounds extend beyond the workplace.

—Frank T. Rhodes, "Let the Student Decide"

B. You've already assessed your site and been introduced to soil composition. You know that light and shade are important. All these conditions and more are important. There's another I haven't discussed yet: hardiness. Hardiness refers to the ability of a plant to withstand cold temperatures, the kind of cold we get in a Canadian winter. **10** Beginning gardeners—just as anyone starting out in a chosen field—need positive reinforcement. Although our friends and relations will laud our efforts, the true critics will be the plants and their feedback can be ruthless: "I'm dying! You failed me!" So if you're starting out, make life easy and happy for yourself. Choose plants for your conditions to ensure success.

—Wendy Thomas, *Getting Started on a Great Canadian Garden*

C. Let me begin with an admission. I am a designer, which means I cannot afford the luxury of cynicism. Designers are called upon to come up with solutions to problems of every imaginable description, from designing a machine to provide kidney dialysis at home to **11** creating an interface for complex critical systems like air-traffic control. No matter what the specific nature of a project—whether it's a park or a product, a book or a business— optimism is always central to my work. It's as important to what I do as research tools, computer systems, or a sense of colour.

—Bruce Mau, "Imagining the Future"

((•
About the
Audio Lessons
for Before You
Write, Organize

((•
AUDIO
LESSON
Section 1: Big
Ideas—Before
You Write,
Organize

((•
AUDIO
LESSON
Section 2:
Practice
Questions—
Before You
Write, Organize

3f   **How can I develop my body paragraphs?**

You develop a **body paragraph** by supplying detailed support for the main idea of the paragraph communicated by your TOPIC SENTENCE (3e), whether stated or implied. **Paragraph development** is not merely a repetition, using other words, of the main idea. When this happens, you're merely going around in circles. We've deliberately manipulated paragraph 4 (in 3d) to create paragraph 12. It is an example of a poorly developed paragraph. It goes nowhere; rather, it restates one idea three times in different words.

NO   **12**   The Miss Plastic Surgery contest, trumpeted by Chinese promoters as "the world's first pageant for artificial beauties," shows the power of cosmetic surgery in a country that has swung from one extreme to another when it comes to the feminine ideal. In past decades, China did not promote personal grooming. Beautification is a recent development.

To check whether you are providing sufficient detail in a body paragraph, use the RENNS Test. Each letter in this acronym cues you to remember a different kind of supporting detail at your disposal, as listed in Quick Reference 3.3.

AUDIO LESSON
Section 3:
Rapid Review—
Before You
Write, Organize

QUICK REFERENCE **3.3**

The RENNS Test: Checking for supporting details

R = **Reasons** provide support.

E = **Examples** provide support.

N = **Names** provide support.

N = **Numbers** provide support.

S = **Senses**—sight, sound, smell, taste, touch—provide support.

Use the RENNS Test to check the quality of your paragraph development. Of course, not every paragraph needs all five kinds of RENNS details, nor do the supporting details need to occur in the order of the letters in *RENNS*. Paragraph 13 contains three of the five types of RENNS details. Identify the topic sentence and as many RENNS as you can before reading the analysis that follows the paragraph.

13   A dramatic increase in the grizzly bear sightings in Alberta has touched off a heated dispute among wildlife experts that centres on a seemingly simple issue: Are there really more grizzlies or merely more observers? More than 400 sightings were reported in Alberta in 1992, almost 10 times the number reported 10 years ago. The province's Department of Environmental Protection now estimates that 800 to 850 grizzly bears live in Alberta and that their number will reach 1000 by the turn of the century. Wildlife-conservation groups say the jump in sightings is mainly fuelled by greater activity by recreational users in the remote backcountry where grizzlies live. "My guess is, there are only 300 to 400 bears, and more likely, it's closer to the lower end," says Brian Horejsi, a conservation biologist with the group Speak Up For Wildlife.
    —Terry Bullick, "When Is a Grizzly Not a Grizzly?"

Paragraph 13 succeeds because it does more than merely repeat its topic sentence, which is its first sentence. It develops the topic sentence to support the claim that grizzlies have not actually increased in number. It uses numbers to document the apparent increase in sightings of grizzlies, but it uses reasons to discount the claim that the rise in numbers means more actual bears. It has names, such as Speak Up for Wildlife and the Department of Environmental Protection, that support the claim.

EXERCISE 3-3   Working individually or with a peer-response group, look again at the paragraphs in Exercise 3-2. Identify the RENNS in each paragraph. For help, consult 3f.

3g   How can I create unity and coherence in paragraphs?

A paragraph has **unity** when the connection between the main idea and its supporting sentences is clear. A paragraph has **coherence** when its sentences relate to each other not only in content but also in choice of words and grammatical structures. Unity emphasizes meaning; coherence emphasizes structure.

Writing in
Action:
Achieving
Paragraph
Unity

Unity is ruined when any sentence in a paragraph "goes off the topic," which means its content doesn't relate to the main idea or to the other sentences in the paragraph. To show you broken unity, in paragraph 14 we've deliberately inserted two sentences (the fourth and the next to last) that go off the topic and ruin a perfectly good paragraph, shown as paragraph 15. (Neither a personal complaint about stress nor hormones produced by men and women during exercise belong in a paragraph defining different kinds of stress.)

NO

14 Stress has long been the subject of psychological and physiological speculation. In fact, more often than not, the word itself is ill defined and overused, meaning different things to different people. Emotional stress, for example, can come about as the result of a family argument or the death of a loved one. Everyone says, "Don't get stressed," but I have no idea how to do that. Environmental stress, such as exposure to excessive heat or cold, is an entirely different phenomenon. Physiologic stress has been described as the outpouring of the steroid hormones from the adrenal glands. During exercise, such as weightlifting, males and females produce different hormones. Whatever its guise, a lack of a firm definition of stress has seriously impeded past research.

YES

15 Stress has long been the subject of psychological and physiological speculation. In fact, more often than not, the word itself is ill defined and overused, meaning different things to different people. Emotional stress, for example, can come about as the result of a family argument or the death of a loved one. Environmental stress, such as exposure to excessive heat or cold, is an entirely different phenomenon. Physiologic stress has been described as the outpouring of the steroid hormones from the adrenal glands. Whatever its guise, a lack of a firm definition of stress has seriously impeded past research.

—Herbert Benson, MD, *The Relaxation Response*

In a coherent paragraph, the sentences follow naturally from one to the next. Techniques for achieving coherence are listed in Quick Reference 3.4; refer to the sections shown in parentheses for complete explanations.

QUICK REFERENCE 3.4

Techniques for achieving coherence

- Using appropriate transitional expressions (3g.1)
- Using pronouns when possible (3g.2)
- Using deliberate repetition of a key word (3g.3)
- Using parallel structures (3g.4)
- Using coherence techniques to create connections among paragraphs (3g.5)

3g.1 Using transitional expressions for coherence

Transitional expressions are words and phrases that signal connections among ideas. **Transitions** are bridges that lead your reader along your line of thought. They offer cues about what follows. Commonly used transitional expressions are listed in Quick Reference 3.5.

QUICK REFERENCE 3.5

Transitional expressions and the relationships they signal

ADDITION	also, in addition, too, moreover, and, besides, furthermore, equally important, then, finally
EXAMPLE	for example, for instance, thus, as an illustration, namely, specifically
CONTRAST	but, yet, however, nevertheless, nonetheless, conversely, in contrast, still, at the same time, on the one hand, on the other hand
COMPARISON	similarly, likewise, in the same way
CONCESSION	of course, to be sure, certainly, granted
RESULT	therefore, thus, as a result, so, accordingly, consequently
SUMMARY	hence, in short, in brief, in summary, in conclusion, finally
TIME	first, second, third, next, then, finally, afterward, before, soon, later, meanwhile, subsequently, immediately, eventually, currently
PLACE	in the front, in the foreground, in the back, in the background, at the side, adjacent, nearby in the distance, here, there

ALERT: In ACADEMIC WRITING, set off a transitional expression with a comma, unless the expression is one short word (24c and 24g). ●

Vary your choices of transitional words. For example, instead of always using *for example,* try *for instance.* Also, when choosing a transitional word, make sure it correctly says what you mean. For instance, don't use *however* if you mean *therefore.* The three brief examples below demonstrate how to use transitional expressions for each context.

COHERENCE BY ADDITION

Woodpeckers use their beaks to find food and to chisel out nests. *In addition,* they claim their territory and signal their desire to mate by using their beaks to drum on trees.

COHERENCE BY CONTRAST

Most birds communicate by singing. Woodpeckers, *however,* communicate by the duration and rhythm of the drumming of their beaks.

COHERENCE BY RESULT

The woodpecker's strong beak enables it to communicate by drumming on dry branches and tree trunks. *As a result,* woodpeckers can communicate across greater distances than songbirds can.

Paragraph 16 demonstrates how transitional expressions (shown in bold) enhance a paragraph's COHERENCE.

16 Certain aspects of Canadian cultural activity bear the stamp of this nation's rough, windswept, wilderness origins: ice hockey, wildlife prints, Farley Mowat, cottage-going, curling, toques. **To this list** we propose adding cuisine. **How else to account for** the enduring Canadian fondness for heavy, bland and non-nutritious fare than by noting that decades after there was any compelling reason to do so, Canadians still seem to eat purely for ballast: to bulk up to keep from being blown away. **Indeed**, it must be considered a providential accident of history that no less a pioneer of high-calorie, comfort-and-convenience cuisine than James Lewis Kraft, founding father of processed cheese and namesake of the unstoppable Kraft Dinner, was born in 1875 in Stevensville, Ontario. **Moreover**, a Canuck invented that handy, fattening favourite—the chocolate bar. **Yes**, in 1910, Arthur Ganong, a St. Stephen, New Brunswick, mogul with a sweet tooth, decided he'd had enough of messing up his pockets with sticky, individual chocolates. **Within months**, the world's first bars of chocolate (conveniently wrapped in tin foil) were rolling off Ganong's factory's line.

—Geoff Pevere and Greig Dymond, *Mondo Canuck*

3g.2   Using pronouns for coherence

Pronouns—words that refer to nouns or other pronouns—allow readers to follow your train of thought from one sentence to the next without boring repetition. Without pronouns, you would have to repeat nouns over and over. For example, this sentence uses no pronouns and therefore has needless repetition: *The woodpecker scratched the woodpecker's head with the woodpecker's foot.* In contrast, with pronouns the sentence can be *The woodpecker scratched **its** head with **its** foot.* Paragraph 17 illustrates how pronouns (shown in bold) contribute to COHERENCE.

17 After Gary Hanson, now 56, got laid off from **his** corporate position in 2003, **he**, **his** wife, Susan, and **his** son, John, now 54 and 27, respectively, wanted to do a spot of cleaning. Though **they** are hard at work, **they** are not scrubbing floors or washing windows. **They** are running **their** very own house-cleaning franchise, *The Maids Home Services*, which **they** opened in February.

—Sara Wilson, "Clean House: Getting Laid Off from His Corporate Job Gave This Franchisee a Fresh Start"

3g.3   Using deliberate repetition for coherence

A key word or phrase is central to the main idea of the paragraph. **Repetition** of key words or phrases is a useful way to achieve COHERENCE in a paragraph. The word or phrase usually appears first in the paragraph's TOPIC SENTENCE (3e) and then again throughout the paragraph. The idea of repetition is to keep a concept in front of the reader.

Use this technique sparingly to avoid being monotonous. Paragraph 18 contains repeated words and phrases (shown in bold) closely tied to the concept of anthropology that make the paragraph more coherent.

18 **Anthropology**, broadly defined, is the study of **humanity**, from its evolutionary origins millions of years ago to its present great numbers and worldwide diversity. Many other disciplines, of course, share with **anthropology** a focus on one aspect or another of **humanity**. **Like** sociology, economics, political science, psychology, and other behavioral and social sciences, **anthropology** is concerned with the way people organize their lives and relate to one another in interacting, interconnected groups—societies—that share basic beliefs and practices. **Like** economists, **anthropologists are interested in** society's material foundations—in how people produce and distribute food and other valued goods. **Like** sociologists, **anthropologists are interested in** the way people structure their relations in society—in families, at work, in institutions. **Like** political scientists,

anthropologists are interested in power and authority: who has them and how they are allocated. And, **like** psychologists, **anthropologists are interested in** individual development and the interaction between society and individual people.

—Nancy Bonvillain, "The Study of Humanity"

3g.4 Using parallel structures for coherence

Parallel structures are created when grammatically equivalent forms are used in series, usually of three or more items, but sometimes only two (see PARALLELISM, Chapter 10). Using parallel structures helps to give a paragraph coherence. The repeated parallel structures reinforce connections among ideas, and they add both tempo and sound to the sentence.

Writing in Action: Achieving Parallelism

In paragraph 19, the authors use several parallel structures (shown in bold): a parallel series of words (*the sacred, the secular, the scientific*); parallel phrases (*sometimes smiled at, sometimes frowned upon*); and six parallel clauses (the first being *banish danger with a gesture*).

19 Superstitions are **sometimes smiled at** and **sometimes frowned upon** as observances characteristic of **the old-fashioned**, **the unenlightened**, children, peasants, servants, immigrants, foreigners, or backwoods people. Nevertheless, they give all of us ways of moving back and forth among the different worlds in which we live—**the sacred, the secular**, and **the scientific**. They allow us to keep a private world also, where, smiling a little, we can **banish danger with a gesture** and **summon luck with a rhyme**, **make the sun shine in spite of storm clouds**, **force the stranger to do our bidding**, **keep an enemy at bay**, and **straighten the paths of those we love**.

—Margaret Mead and Rhoda Metraux, "New Superstitions for Old"

3g.5 Creating coherence among paragraphs

The same techniques for achieving coherence in a paragraph apply to showing connections among paragraphs in a piece of writing. All four techniques help: transitional expressions (3g.1), pronouns (3g.2), deliberate repetition (3g.3), and parallel structures (3g.4).

Passage 20 shows two paragraphs and the start of a third. Repeated words connecting these paragraphs include *nation, nationalism, history, historical,* and *Canadian(s).* The "From that year on" sentence tightly links the first and second paragraphs: A reader does not know what year is meant or what important events made it a turning point without reading the first paragraph. The opening sentence of the third paragraph creates another strong link by repeating the term *nationalism,* the word that concludes the second paragraph. This concept, introduced in the first two paragraphs, is qualified and nuanced in the final paragraph.

20 As a nation, Canada was born again in 1957. The year lies across our history like a faultline: Diefenbaker won his first election; Pearson won his Nobel Peace Prize; Walter Gordon brought down his report on foreign ownership; and the Canada Council was established. These events, along with Quebec's Quiet Revolution, which began three years later, created the Canada of today, a society that seems to contain only a few trace elements of what Earle Birney called in the 1940s "a highschool land / deadset in adolescence."

From that year on, Canadian-American relations were redefined by a force for which there was no historical antecedent. This was the force, at first tentative and apologetic, then increasingly vocal, then rancorous, then celebratory, of Canadian nationalism.

This nationalism was always firmly rooted in pragmatism. Whenever times got tough or the price of flag-waving seemed likely to be too high, Canadians lowered their banners. This was predictable. Far more interesting was the way the minimum acceptable low-water mark of nationalist expression demanded by Canadians of their governments kept getting raised.

—Richard Gwyn, *The 49th Paradox*

EXERCISE 3-4 Working individually or with a peer-response group, locate the coherence techniques in each paragraph. Look for transitional expressions, pronouns, deliberate repetition, and parallel structures. For help, consult 3g.

A. Bridges are nowhere, always spanning disparate places, themselves placeless, suspended. To stand on the Bathurst Street Bridge after a rain, smelling the wet concrete first poured into its flanking sidewalks in 1916, caught up with looking at its top-chorded columns, cross-stitched with metal bars, makes a place amid the transit, rumbling across and below it,

21 like stopping in a stream. Once, walking south across the bridge to get to Fort York, I found five brightly coloured plastic raspberries clustered together on one of its broad iron shoulders, as if it had borne fruit overnight. False fruit from a no place, but also, I thought, a gift, wrought from something that has borne so much of the city, beside it, below it, above.

—Ward McBurney, "Bathurst Sreet Bridge"

B. Newton's law may have wider application than just the physical world. In the social world, racism, once set into motion, will remain in motion unless acted upon by an outside force. The collective "we" must be the outside force. We must fight racism through education.

22 We must make sure every school has the resources to do its job. We must present to our children a culturally diverse curriculum that reflects our pluralistic society. This can help students understand that prejudice is learned through contact with prejudiced people, rather than with the people toward whom the prejudice is directed.

—Randolph H. Manning, "Fighting Racism with Inclusion"

C. The snow geese are first, rising off the ponds to breakfast in the sorghum fields up the river. Twenty thousand of them, perhaps more, great white birds with black wing tips rising out of the darkness into the rosy reflected light of dawn. They make a sweeping turn, a cloud of wings rising above the cottonwoods. But cloud is the wrong word. They don't form

23 a disorderly blackbird rabble but a kaleidoscope of goose formations, always shifting, but always orderly. The light catches them—white against the tan velvet of the hills. Then they're overhead, line after line, layer above layer of formations, and the sky is filled with the clamor of an infinity of geese.

—Tony Hillerman, *Hillerman Country*

EXERCISE 3-5 Working individually or with a peer-response group, use RENNS (3f) and techniques for achieving coherence (3g) to develop three of the following topic sentences into paragraphs. When finished, list the RENNS and the coherence techniques you used in each paragraph.

1. It is important to read the newspaper with a critical, and even skeptical, eye.
2. There is a huge difference between how older and younger people use the World Wide Web.
3. What we throw out in our trash says a great deal about Canadian culture.
4. Learning to cook involves more than just learning to follow recipes.
5. The friends we make at college (or university) will remain important in our later lives and careers.

3h How can I arrange a paragraph?

During DRAFTING, you concentrate on getting ideas onto the page or screen. Later, during REVISION, you can experiment to see how else your sentences might be arranged for greatest impact. You may find sometimes that only one possible arrangement can work. For example, if you're explaining how to bake a cake, you want to give the directions in a particular order. At other times, you may find that more than one arrangement is possible. Quick Reference 3.6 lists the most common ways to arrange a paragraph. More about each arrangement follows in this section.

QUICK REFERENCE   3.6

Ways to arrange sentences in a paragraph

- By time
- By location
- From general to specific
- From specific to general
- From least to most important
- From problem to solution

ARRANGING BY TIME

In a paragraph arranged according to time, or **chronological order**, events are presented in whatever order they took place. Narratives often follow this arrangement. Using a time sequence is a very natural and easy way to organize a paragraph. Paragraph 24 is an example.

> **24** Reading comes first. The reading of tracks and weather signs is a fundamental mammalian occupation, practised before primates started walking on their hind legs, much less using their hands to write. And writing, in a sense, is always on the verge of being born. All of us who speak by means of gesture, or who gesture as we talk, are gesturing toward writing. But it is a rare event for instincts such as these to crystallize into a system that can capture and preserve the subtleties of speech in graphic form. Such a system can only mature within a culture prepared to sustain it. Starting from scratch, with no imported models, people have made the shift from oral to literate culture at least three times but perhaps not many more than that. In Mesopotamia about 5,000 years ago, in northern China about 4,500 years ago, and in Guatemala and southern Mexico about 3,500 years ago, humans created a script and a scribal culture, apparently without imported models of any kind.
>
> —Robert Bringhurst, *The Solid Form of Language*

ARRANGING BY LOCATION

A paragraph arranged according to location, or **spatial order**, leads the reader's attention from one place to another. The movement can be in any direction—from top to bottom, left to right, inside to outside, and so on. Paragraph 25 moves the reader through an interior.

> **25** The old store, lighted only by three fifty-watt bulbs, smelled of coal oil and baking bread. In the middle of the rectangular room, where the oak floor sagged a little, stood an iron stove. To the right was a wooden table with an unfinished game of checkers and a stool

made from an apple-tree stump. On shelves around the walls sat earthen jugs with corncob stoppers, a few canned goods, and some of the two thousand old clocks and clockworks Thurmond Watts owned. Only one was ticking; the others he just looked at.

—William Least Heat-Moon, *Blue Highways*

ARRANGING FROM GENERAL TO SPECIFIC

The most common pattern for arranging information is from **general to specific**. Typically, the general statement is the TOPIC SENTENCE, and the supporting details (see RENNS, 3f) explain the specifics. Paragraph 26 is an example.

26 The problem with vitamin D in Canada is one of geography and climate. Because the sun is low on the horizon during winter, it passes through more of the Earth's atmosphere; the atmosphere acts as a filter and shuts out most of the low-wavelength UV rays that we need to make vitamin D. That, plus shorter day length and our tendency to cover our bodies with clothing, means that from October to April we don't get nearly enough sunlight to produce natural vitamin D. If we don't take large doses of artificial vitamin D, in the form of fish oils (halibut and cod livers are best, but there are no more cod, and any fatty fish will do) and egg yolk, then we get poor bone development and repair. Dark or tanned skin is also a poorer producer of vitamin D than fair or untanned skin.

—Wayne Grady, *Chasing the Chinook*

ARRANGING FROM SPECIFIC TO GENERAL

A less common paragraph arrangement moves from **specific to general**. Paragraph 27 is an example. To achieve the greatest impact, the paragraph starts with details that support the topic sentence, which ends the paragraph.

27 Replacing the spark plugs is probably the first thing most home auto mechanics do. But too often, the problem lies elsewhere. In the ignition system, the plug wires, distributor unit, coil, and ignition control unit play just as vital a role as the spark plugs. Moreover, performance problems are by no means limited to the ignition system. The fuel system and emissions control system also contain several components that equal the spark plug in importance. The do-it-yourself mechanic who wants to provide basic care for a car must be able to do more than change the spark plugs.

—Danny Witt, student

ARRANGING FROM LEAST TO MOST IMPORTANT

A paragraph arranged from **least to most important** uses **climactic order**, which means that the high point—the climax—comes at the end. For a paragraph to be arranged from least to most important, it has to have at least three items: least, more, most. And remember that the last item always packs the greatest impact and is the most memorable. Paragraph 28 is an example. ("The Department" in the paragraph is Canada's Department of External Affairs.)

28 The significance of General de Gaulle's famous *"Vive le Québec libre"* spoken from a balcony in Montreal in 1967 was debated in the Department as it was throughout the country. Mr. Pearson declared the general's utterance to be unacceptable, and de Gaulle promptly left the country without completing his visit. Although there were some dissenting voices, particularly to the effect that the government had overreacted, there was general agreement that the General's statement was not a slip of the tongue. After General de Gaulle's visitation, the government could no longer assume that the influence of France would always be benign so far as Canada was concerned. Now one thing had become clear: Canada's relations with France had become a matter of prime concern not just within the Department, but at all its diplomatic posts.

—Arthur Andrew, *The Rise and Fall of a Middle Power*
(James Lorimer & Company Ltd.)

ARRANGING FROM PROBLEM TO SOLUTION

In some cases, an effective arrangement for a paragraph is **problem to solution**. Usually, the topic sentence presents the problem. The very next sentence presents the main idea of the solution. Then, the rest of the paragraph covers the specifics of the solution. Paragraph 29 is an example.

29 When I first met them, Sara and Michael were a two-career couple with a home of their own, and a large boat bought with a large loan. What interested them in a concept called voluntary simplicity was the birth of their daughter and a powerful desire to raise her themselves. Neither one of them, it turned out, was willing to restrict what they considered their "real life" into the brief time before work and the tired hours afterward. "A lot of people think that as they have children and things get more expensive, the only answer is to work harder in order to earn more money. It's not the only answer," insists Michael. The couple's decision was to trade two full-time careers for two half-time careers, and to curtail consumption. They decided to spend their money only on things that contributed to their major goal, the construction of a world where family and friendship, work and play, were all of a piece, a world, moreover, which did not make wasteful use of the earth's resources.

—Linda Weltner, "Stripping Down to Bare Happiness"

EXERCISE 3-6   Working individually or with a peer-response group, rearrange the sentences in each paragraph below so that it flows logically. To begin, identify the topic sentence, use it as the paragraph's first sentence, and continue from there. For help, consult 3h.

PARAGRAPH A

1. Remember, many people who worry about offending others wind up living according to other people's priorities.
2. Learn to decline, tactfully but firmly, every request that doesn't contribute to your goals.
3. Of all the timesaving techniques ever developed, perhaps the most effective is the frequent use of the word *no*.
4. If you point out that your motivation isn't to get out of work but to save your time to do a better job on the really important things, you'll have a good chance of avoiding unproductive tasks.
   —Edwin Bliss, "Getting Things Done: The ABC's of Time Management"

PARAGRAPH B

1. After a busy day, lens wearers often don't feel like taking time out to clean and disinfect their lenses, and many wearers skip the chore.
2. When buying a pair of glasses, a person deals with just the expense of the glasses themselves.
3. Although contact lenses make the wearer more attractive, glasses are easier and less expensive to care for.

4. However, in addition to the cost of the lenses themselves, contact lens wearers must shoulder the extra expense of cleaning supplies.

5. This inattention creates a danger of infection.

6. In contrast, contact lenses require daily cleaning and weekly enzyming that inconvenience lens wearers.

7. Glasses can be cleaned quickly with water and tissue at the wearer's convenience.

—Heather Martin, student

PARAGRAPH C

1. The researchers found that the participation of women in sport was a significant indicator of the health and living standards of a country.

2. Today, gradually, women have begun to enter sport with more social acceptance and individual pride.

3. In 1952, researchers from the Finnish Institute of Occupational Health who conducted an intensive study of the athletes participating in the Olympics in Helsinki predicted, "Women are able to shake off civil disabilities which millennia of prejudice and ignorance have imposed upon them."

4. Myths die hard, but they do die.

—Marie Hart, "Sport: Women Sit in the Back of the Bus"

EXERCISE 3-7   Working individually or with a peer-response group, determine the arrangements in these paragraphs. Choose from time, location, general to specific, specific to general, least to most important, and problem to solution. For help, consult 3h.

A. A combination of cries from exotic animals and laughter and gasps from children fills the air along with the aroma of popcorn and peanuts. A hungry lion bellows for dinner, his roar breaking through the confusing chatter of other animals. Birds of all kinds chirp endlessly at curious children. Monkeys swing from limb to limb, performing gymnastics for gawking
30 onlookers. A comedy routine by orangutans employing old shoes and garments incites squeals of amusement. Reptiles sleep peacefully behind glass windows, yet they send shivers down the spines of those who remember the quick death many of these reptiles can induce. The sights and sounds and smells of the zoo inform and entertain children of all ages.

—Deborah Harris, student

B. No one even agrees anymore on what "old" is. Not long ago, 30 was middle-aged and 60 was old. Now, more and more people are living into their 70s, 80s and beyond—and many
31 of them are living well, without any incapacitating mental or physical decline. Today, old age is defined not simply by chronological years, but by degree of health and well-being.

—Carol Tavris, "Old Age Isn't What It Used to Be"

C. Lately, bee researchers have been distracted by a new challenge from abroad. It's, of course, the so-called "killer bee" that was imported into Brazil from Africa in the mid-1950s and has been heading our way ever since. The Africanized bee looks like the Italian bee but
32 is more defensive and more inclined to attack in force. It consumes much of the honey that it produces, leaving relatively little for anyone who attempts to work with it. It travels fast, competes with local bees and, worse, mates with them. It has ruined the honey industry in Venezuela and now the big question is: Will the same thing happen here?

—Jim Doherty, "The Hobby That Challenges You to Think Like a Bee"

EXERCISE 3-8   Working individually or collaborating with others, decide what would be the best arrangement for a paragraph on each topic listed here. Choose one or a combination of time, location, general to specific, specific to general, least to most important, and problem to solution. For help, consult 3h.

1. characteristics of annoying people

2. romantic comedies

3. how to deliver bad news

4. teaching someone a new job

3i   How can rhetorical patterns help me write paragraphs?

Rhetorical patterns (sometimes called *rhetorical strategies*) are techniques for presenting ideas clearly and effectively. You choose a specific rhetorical pattern according to what you want to accomplish. Quick Reference 3.7 lists the common rhetorical patterns at your disposal.

Into the Wind: Understanding the Rhetoric of Arrangement

QUICK REFERENCE 3.7

Common rhetorical patterns of thought (strategies) for paragraphs

- Narrative
- Description
- Process
- Examples
- Definition

- Analysis
- Classification
- Comparison and contrast
- Analogy
- Cause-and-effect analysis

Often, your TOPIC SENTENCE will steer you toward a particular pattern. For example, if a topic sentence is "Grilling a great hot dog is easy," the implied pattern is to explain the process of how to grill a hot dog. Or if a topic sentence is "To see what kinds of videos people are watching, look at YouTube's featured categories," the implied pattern—or rhetorical strategy—is to give examples.

Sometimes, you need to use a combination of rhetorical strategies. For example, a paragraph explaining why one brand of paint is superior to another might call for comparison and contrast combined with description—and, perhaps, also definition and examples. Many of the rhetorical patterns discussed in this chapter are used in writing ARGUMENTS. See Chapter 5 and especially section 5g for a broader discussion of argument (or persuasive writing).

All in the Family: Understanding the Rhetoric of Subject

It's All About the Food: Understanding the Rhetoric of Argument

Plug It In: Understanding the Rhetoric of Proof

NARRATIVE

Narrative writing is a rhetorical strategy that tells a story. A *narration* relates what is happening or what has happened. Paragraph 33 is an example.

33   There were ten major gold company analysts waching Bre-X stock in October 1995, when the price blew through $30 on October 20, a level that meant investors valued the company at more than $700 million. Normally, analysts move up their target price for a $30 stock by a few dollars at a time. Not with Bre-X. Targets rose in leaps and bounds.

By October 23, 1995, Bre-X was changing hands at $43 and Lévesque's Fowler, still en-thralled by his "visual inspection," set out a one-year target of $62, which would rank Bre-X as one of the five largest gold companies in Canada. In Indonesia, the geologists stayed true to form. Rather than verifying the existing deposit, Felderhof and de Guzman continued to do step-out drilling. Three new holes were drilled that extended the size of the deposit to a strip 2.75 kilometres long. All three found gold. The stock soared on the news.

—Douglas Goold and Andrew Willis, *The Bre-X Fraud*

DESCRIPTION

Writing a **description** is a rhetorical strategy that appeals to a reader's senses—sight, sound, smell, taste, and touch. *Descriptive writing* paints a picture in words. Paragraph 34 is an example.

34 Walking to the ranch house from the shed, we saw the Northern Lights. They looked like talcum powder fallen from a woman's face. Rouge and blue eye shadow streaked the spires of a white light which exploded, then pulsated, shaking the colors down—like lives—until they faded from sight.

—Gretel Ehrlich, "Other Lives"

PROCESS

Writing about a **process** is a rhetorical strategy that reports a sequence of actions by which something is done or made. A process usually proceeds chronologically—first do this, then do that. A process's complexity dictates the level of detail in the writing. For example, para-graph 35 provides an overview of a complicated process. Paragraph 36, on the other hand, gives explicit step-by-step directions.

35 Making chocolate isn't as simple as grinding a bag of beans. The machinery in a choco-late factory towers over you, rumbling and whirring. A huge cleaner first blows the beans away from their accompanying debris—sticks and stones, coins and even bullets can fall among cocoa beans being bagged. Then they go into another machine for roasting. Next comes separation in a winnower, shells sliding out one side, beans falling from the other. Grinding follows, resulting in chocolate liquor. Fermentation, roasting, and "conching" all influence the flavor of chocolate. Chocolate is "conched"—rolled over and over against it-self like pebbles in the sea—in enormous circular machines named conches for the shells they once resembled. Climbing a flight of steps to peer into this huge, slow-moving glacier, I was expecting something like molten mud but found myself forced to conclude it resem-bled nothing so much as chocolate.

—Ruth Mehrtens Galvin, "Sybaritic to Some, Sinful to Others"

36 Traditionally, oil was extracted by pressing the olives between granite millstones. Many non-industrial mills now use a modern continuous-cycle system. The olives are conveyed up a belt, washed, and cut into pulp. The resulting paste is kneaded and centrifugally "decanted" to separate it into solids, water, and oil.

—Lori de Mori, "Making Olive Oil"

EXAMPLES

A paragraph developed by **examples** presents particular instances of a larger category. For instance, examples of the category "endangered animals" could include the black rhinoc-eros, South China tiger, Bulmer's fruit bat, and silvery gibbon. Paragraph 37 is an example of this strategy. On the other hand, sometimes one **extended example**, often called an *illustration*, is useful. Paragraph 38 is an example of this technique.

> What meaning can we give to the symbols chosen to represent different countries? Ever since the Middle Ages, England has had its regal lion, whose image needs no explanation. France still uses "Marianne," a beautiful woman symbolizing the French Revolution, and
> **37** the American revolutionaries chose for their country's totem the fierce, independent bald eagle. Canadians used to display the beaver, an animal that was seen as an industrious lumberjack—maybe early Canadians recognized themselves in that image. Now we prefer the maple leaf, to which we can give whatever meaning we want.
>
> —Sivan Chand, student

> He was one of the greatest scientists the world has ever known, yet if I had to convey the essence of Albert Einstein in a single word, I would choose *simplicity*. Perhaps an anecdote
> **38** will help. Once, caught in a downpour, he took off his hat and held it under his coat. Asked why, he explained, with admirable logic, that the rain would damage the hat, but his hair would be none the worse for its wetting. This knack of going instinctively to the heart of the matter was the secret of his major scientific discoveries—this and his extraordinary feeling for beauty.
>
> —Banesh Hoffman, "My Friend, Albert Einstein"

DEFINITION

When you define something, you give its meaning. **Definition** is often used together with other rhetorical strategies. If, for example, you were explaining how to organize a seashell collection, you'd probably want to define the two main types of shells: bivalve and univalve. You can also develop an entire paragraph by definition, called an **extended definition**. An extended definition discusses the meaning of a word or concept in more detail than a dictionary definition. If the topic is very abstract, the writer tries to put the definition in concrete terms. Sometimes a definition tells what something is not, as well as what it is, as in paragraph 39.

> Chemistry is that branch of science that has the task of investigating the materials out of which the universe is made. It is not concerned with the forms into which they may be fashioned. Such objects as chairs, tables, vases, bottles, or wires are of no significance in chem-
> **39** istry; but such substances as glass, wool, iron, sulfur, and clay, as the materials out of which they are made, are what it studies. Chemistry is concerned not only with the composition of such substances, but also with their inner structure.
>
> —John Arrend Timm, *General Chemistry*

ANALYSIS

Analysis, sometimes called *division,* divides things up into their parts. It usually starts, often in its topic sentence, by identifying one subject and continues by explaining the subject's distinct parts, as in paragraph 40.

> Jazz is by its very nature inexact, and thus difficult to define with much precision: humble in its roots, yet an avenue to wealth and fame for its stars; improvised anew with each performance, but following a handful of tried-and-true formulas; done by everybody but
> **40** mastered by an elite few; made by African Americans, but made the definition of its age by white bands—and predominantly white audiences. Jazz is primarily an instrumental idiom, but nearly all jazz is based on songs with words, and there are great jazz singers. "If you have to ask what jazz is," said Louis Armstrong, "you'll never know."
>
> —D. Kern Holoman, "Jazz"

CLASSIFICATION

Classification groups items according to a shared characteristic. Paragraph 41 groups— classifies—languages into different families.

41   This paragraph is written in one of the many languages that belong to the vast Indo-European language family. The earliest languages belonging to this family were spoken across a broad geographical zone extending from the Indian Subcontinent through Iran and Asia Minor (Turkey), and up into Europe as far east as the Black Sea and as far west as the Atlantic. Imagine a tree with a huge network of branches extending from its trunk. The trunk is an extinct language presumed to be the ancestor of all the surviving members of the family. Several big branches stretch up into Europe. The biggest branches include important modern-day subfamilies: the Slavic languages (with Russian, Czech, Polish, etc., reaching out from the main branch); the Germanic languages (with English, German, Swedish, etc., branching out); and the Romance languages, which derive from Latin (with French, Italian, Spanish, etc., reaching out). Smaller European subfamilies include a few other important languages.

COMPARISON AND CONTRAST

A paragraph developed by *comparison* deals with similarities; a paragraph developed by *contrast* deals with differences. **Comparison and contrast** writing is usually organized one of two ways: You can use *point-by-point organization,* which moves back and forth between the items being compared; or you can use *block organization,* which discusses one item completely before discussing the other. Quick Reference 3.8 lays out the two patterns visually.

QUICK REFERENCE **3.8**

Comparison and contrast

POINT-BY-POINT STRUCTURE

   Student body: college A, university B
   Curriculam: college A, university B
   Location: college A, university B

BLOCK STRUCTURE

   College A: student body, curriculum, location
   University B: student body, curriculum, location

Paragraph 42 is structured point by point, going back and forth between the two children (whose names are in boldface) being compared.

42   My husband and I constantly marvel at the fact that our two sons, born of the same parents and only two years apart in age, are such completely different human beings. The most obvious differences became apparent at their births. Our firstborn, **Mark**, was big and bold—his intense, already wise eyes, broad shoulders, huge and heavy hands, and powerful, chunky legs gave us the impression he could have walked out of the delivery room on his own. Our second son, **Wayne**, was delightfully different. Rather than having the football physique that **Mark** was born with, **Wayne** came into the world with a long, slim, wiry body more suited to running, jumping, and contorting. **Wayne's** eyes, rather than being intense like **Mark's**, were impish and innocent. When **Mark** was delivered, he cried only momentarily, and then seemed to settle into a state of intense concentration, as if trying to absorb everything he could about the strange, new environment he found himself in. Conversely, **Wayne** screamed from the moment he first appeared. There was nothing helpless or pathetic about his cry either—he was darn angry!

—Rosanne Labonte, student

Paragraph 43 uses the block pattern for comparison and contrast. The writer first discusses games and then business (each key word is in boldface).

> **Games** are of limited duration, take place on or in fixed and finite sites, and are governed by openly promulgated rules that are enforced on the spot by neutral professionals. Moreover, they're performed by relatively evenly matched teams that are counseled and led through every move by seasoned hands. Scores are kept, and at the end of the game, a winner
> **43** is declared. **Business** is usually a little different. In fact, if there is anyone out there who can say that the business is of limited duration, takes place on a fixed site, is governed by openly promulgated rules that are enforced on the spot by neutral professionals, competes only on relatively even terms, and performs in a way that can be measured in runs or points, then that person is either extraordinarily lucky or seriously deluded.

—Warren Bennis, "Time to Hang Up the Old Sports Clichés"

ANALOGY

An **analogy** is an extended comparison between objects or ideas from different classes—things not normally associated. Analogy is particularly effective in explaining unfamiliar or abstract concepts because a comparison can be drawn between what is familiar and what is not. An analogy often begins with a SIMILE or METAPHOR (12c), as in paragraph 44.

> Casual dress, like casual speech, tends to be loose, relaxed, and colorful. It often contains what might be called "slang words": blue jeans, sneakers, baseball caps, aprons, flowered cotton housedresses, and the like. These garments could not be worn on a formal occasion without causing disapproval, but in ordinary circumstances, they pass without remark. "Vulgar
> **44** words" in dress, on the other hand, give emphasis and get immediate attention in almost any circumstances, just as they do in speech. Only the skillful can employ them without some loss of face, and even then, they must be used in the right way. A torn, unbuttoned shirt or wildly uncombed hair can signify strong emotions: passion, grief, rage, despair. They're most effective if people already think of you as being neatly dressed, just as the curses of well-spoken persons count for more than those of the customarily foul-mouthed do.

—Alison Lurie, *The Language of Clothes*

CAUSE-AND-EFFECT ANALYSIS

Cause-and-effect analysis examines outcomes and the reasons for those outcomes. Causes lead to an event or an effect, and effects result from causes. (For a discussion of correct logic for assessing CAUSE AND EFFECT, see 4h.) Paragraph 45 discusses how developments in science, combined with market pressures (the cause), led to the development of new flavour compounds to use with potato chips (the effect).

> Once upon a time, flavor research was a matter of asking housewives to munch a few potato
> **45** chips in the hopes that the company had stumbled on the perfect formula for reconstituting potatoes. But as the science became more sophisticated, and market pressures demanded more novelty and authenticity, flavor scientists had to create new varieties like "Mesquite

BBQ" chips to sit alongside regular barbecue flavor. To fill that hungry maw, Dewis and his colleagues work to analyze hundreds of thousands of substances and develop compounds that will please the buying public in four ways—through smell, taste, sensation and emotion. To do so flavor scientists are homing in on molecules, receptors, brain structures and genetic code that will enable them to create flavors tailored to consumers' palates, health condition, demographics, even genotype. The industry doesn't just talk about things tasting good any-more. Now it's about providing an exceptional "flavor experience."

—Tamara Holt, "The Science of Yummy"

EXERCISE 3-9   Working individually or with a peer-response group, decide what rhetorical strategies are used in each paragraph. Choose from any one or a combination of narrative, description, process, examples, definition, analysis, classification, comparison and contrast, analogy, and cause and effect. For help, consult 3i.

A. Another way to think about metamessages is that they frame a conversation, much as a picture frame provides a context for the images in the picture. Metamessages let you
   46 know how to interpret what someone is saying by identifying the activity that is going on. Is this an argument or a chat? Is it helping, advising, or scolding? At the same time, they let you know what position the speaker is assuming in the activity, and what position you are being assigned.

—Deborah Tannen, *You Just Don't Understand*

B. The contrast between English Canadian and Quebecois attitudes to the United States is striking. In English Canada there has been an anguished debate for generations as to whether Canadian culture can preserve its distinctiveness amid the nightly electronic deluge of up to sixty cable TV stations in most Canadian homes. At Videotron, Quebec's largest
   47 cable TV company, they beam all the American soaps into Quebec homes, but they know that the most popular shows—the ones that get up to 80 percent of the Quebec population staying home at night—are the ones written and acted in Quebec. As long as they can see what they want in their own language, Quebecois believe their culture will be secure.

—Michael Ignatieff, *Blood and Belonging*

C. In the case of wool, very hot water can actually cause some structural changes within the fiber, but the resulting shrinkage is minor. The fundamental cause of shrinkage in wool is felting, in which the fibers scrunch together in a tighter bunch, and the yarn, fabric, and
   48 garment follow suit. Wool fibers are curly and rough-surfaced, and when squished together under the lubricating influence of water, the fibers wind around each other, like two springs interlocking. Because of their rough surfaces, they stick together and can't be pulled apart.

—James Gorman, "Gadgets"

D. Buctouche is a small town at the mouth of the Buctouche River in New Brunswick. It is also the summer home of Antonine Maillet. I had just translated Maillet's short novel *Christophe Cartier de la noisette, dit Nounours*, and was about to embark on her monumental allegory *Le huitiéme jour*, and I wanted to get the lay of the Acadian landscape. I had a literary sense of the Buctouche area, but I wanted to see it and hear it
   49 for myself. I stopped outside a low brick building, one of those five-and-dime stores that sell cheap clothes and expensive souvenirs, including small Acadian flags—the French *tricolore* with a yellow *Stella maris* in one corner. When I went up to the cash, I asked, in my best French, which house belonged to Antonine and received a long, friendly reply. To my complete astonishment I could not understand a word of it. I had entered a private realm, a kind of hidden valley that had its own customs, its own flag and its own language.

Some call this place the Republic of Madawaska, but for more than 350 years it has been known as the land of Acadia.

—Wayne Grady, *Chasing the Chinook*

E. Lacking access to a year-round supermarket, the many species—from ants to wolves—that in the course of evolution have learned the advantages of hoarding must devote a lot of energy and ingenuity to protecting their stashes from marauders. Creatures like beavers and honeybees, for example, hoard food to get them through cold winters. Others, like
50 desert rodents that face food scarcities throughout the year, must take advantage of the short-lived harvests that follow occasional rains. For animals like burying beetles that dine on mice hundreds of times their size, a habit of biting off more than they can chew at the moment forces them to store their leftovers. Still others, like the male MacGregor's bowerbird, stockpile goodies during mating season so they can concentrate on wooing females and defending their arena d'amour.

—Jane Brody, "A Hoarder's Life: Filling the Cache—and Finding It"

EXERCISE 3-10 Working individually or with a peer-response group, reread the paragraphs in Exercise 3-7 and determine the rhetorical strategy (or strategies) being used in each.

3j What is a transitional paragraph?

Transitional paragraphs are found in long essays. These paragraphs form a bridge between one long discussion on a single topic that requires a number of paragraphs and another discussion, usually lengthy, of another topic. Paragraph 51 is an example of a transitional paragraph that allows the writer to move from a long discussion of the extent and sources of anger in our society to a long discussion of possible remedies.

So is there any hope for you and your anger? Is there any reason to believe that you will
51 be able to survive the afternoon commute without screaming or tailgating or displaying choice fingers?

—Andrew Santella, "All the Rage"

3k What are effective concluding paragraphs?

A **concluding paragraph** ends the discussion smoothly by following logically from the essay's introductory paragraph (3c) and the essay's body paragraphs (3d). Always integrate a concluding device into the final paragraph so that the discussion does not end abruptly. A conclusion that is hurriedly tacked on is a missed opportunity to provide a sense of completion and a finishing touch that adds to the whole essay. Quick Reference 3.9 lists strategies for concluding your essay as well as strategies to avoid.

The same writers who wait to write their introductory paragraph until they've drafted their body paragraphs often also wait to write their concluding paragraph until they've drafted their introduction. They do this to coordinate the beginning and end so that they can make sure they don't repeat the same strategy in both places.

Paragraph 52 concludes an essay on the media use and misuse of "experts," and how the battles between self-assured pundits have only left us with an "authority vacuum." The brief paragraph sums up the essays points.

And then, when we have finally flattened out the notion of expertise, when everyone's claim is superficially as good as everyone else's—when, in short, everyone is a pundit—we can get
52 down to the real work of citizenship: making sense of arguments on their own merits, not on the basis of who offers them. Maybe then, as we go along, some genuine experts will emerge.

—Mark Kingwell, "The Voice of The Pundit Is Heard in the Land"

Strategies for concluding paragraphs

STRATEGIES TO TRY

- A strategy adapted from those used for introductory paragraphs (3c)—but be careful to choose a different strategy for your introduction and conclusion:
  - Relating a brief concluding interesting story or anecdote
  - Giving one or more pertinent—perhaps surprising—concluding statistics
  - Asking one or more provocative questions for further thought
  - Using an appropriate quotation to sum up the THESIS STATEMENT
  - Redefining a key term for emphasis
- An ANALOGY that summarizes the thesis statement
- A SUMMARY of the main points, but only if the piece of writing is longer than three to four pages
- A statement that urges awareness on the part of readers
- A statement that looks ahead to the future
- A call to readers

STRATEGIES TO AVOID

- Introducing new ideas or facts that belong in the body of the essay
- Rewording your introduction
- Announcing what you've discussed, as in "In this paper, I have explained why oil prices have dropped."
- Making absolute claims, as in "I have proved that oil prices don't always affect gasoline prices."
- Apologizing, as in "Even though I'm not an expert, I feel my position is correct."

Paragraph 53 concludes an essay that argues for the recognition of First Nations governments in Canada. It reinforces the essay's message with a call for justice and cooperation.

53 What we are looking for is not just power to deal with the social problems we face but reconciliation with Canada. We are trying to find a way of creating harmony in the country. The way you achieve that is to produce justice; our people have to feel justice, not just think about it. We have to experience it before we can believe it. There is absolutely no way that First Nations governments can meet the needs of the First Nations peoples without the help of the provinces or the federal government. What we are asking is to become partners working towards the same future.

—Ovide Mercredi, "Self-Government as a Way to Heal"

EXERCISE 3-11 Working individually or in a peer-response group, return to Exercise 3-1, in which you wrote introductory paragraphs for three informally outlined essays. Now, write a concluding paragraph for each.

Chapter 4

THINKING CRITICALLY ABOUT IDEAS AND IMAGES

4a What is critical thinking?

Thinking isn't something you choose to do, any more than a fish chooses to live in water. To be human is to think. But while thinking may come naturally, awareness of how you think doesn't.

Critical thinking means taking control of your conscious thought processes. If you don't take control of those processes, you risk being controlled by the ideas of others. In fact, critical thinking is an attitude as much as an activity. If you face life with curiosity and a desire to dig beneath the surface, you're a critical thinker. The essence of critical thinking is thinking beyond the obvious—beyond the flash of visual images on a television screen, the alluring promises of glossy advertisements, the evasive statements by some people in the news, the half-truths of propaganda, the manipulations of SLANTED LANGUAGE and faulty reasoning.

The word *critical* here has a neutral meaning. It doesn't mean taking a negative view or finding fault, as when someone criticizes another person for doing something incorrectly. Rather, the term means examining ideas thoroughly and deeply.

As an example of how critical thinking works, consider how the various elements of Figure 4.1 shape our response to the image. A look at the surface content of the photograph simply shows three people standing by a car. A closer look may uncover the deeper content that leads readers to a "close reading" of the scene.

The car in the photograph is a small model—almost certainly not a typical family vehicle. It even looks as if it may have been used a little roughly. One door is partly open, while two of the three figures in the photograph stand next to the empty driver's seat. Something is probably about to happen, some rapidly evolving action that has been frozen by the photographer's lens.

The three figures appear to be teenagers or young adults, all wearing "hoodies." Their body language may tell us something about their interaction. Two who are wearing nearly identical light-coloured sweaters stand slouched against the car, facing the third. One of these two, however, is leaning forward with his head and is engaged with the third, who is facing him head on. This third youth, dressed in a zipped "hoodie" with a pattern that differs from the others, tilts his head slightly as if to reinforce a point he is making, and points his finger directly at his counterpart's chest. In fact, he is holding his hand only centimetres away from the other's chin.

When we follow the pointing finger, we see that the middle youth is drawing his upper body back to recoil from the other's gesture.

What kind of interaction is this? Is a challenge being issued? An order being given? The youths may be gang members. Perhaps they are working out a plan before they get into the car.

Figure 4.1 An image for critical analysis

The setting of the image is hard to define. We see an untended lawn and a rough-looking fence. What looks like a road sign next to a gravel path or driveway appears to set the scene by a small road. This may be a suburb or the outskirts of a town. The open and nearly featureless scene suggests that the action is about to move on and pick up again in another location.

Reread the analysis of Figure 4.1. Do you think the fact that the youth who is pointing his finger is also wearing a contrasting sweater is too obvious to be part of a real-life scene? Do the elements in the image (and observations in the analysis) combine too neatly in making their point? In fact, the photograph was staged—it's not a scene from life. Pat yourself on the back if you suspected that. We'll return to analyzing images in section 4j.

((•●
AUDIO
LESSON
Section 1: Big
Ideas—
Becoming a
Critical
Reader and a
Better Writer

4b   What are the elements of critical thinking?

Quick Reference 4.1 describes the general process of critical thinking and critical reading. It is just as fluid as the WRITING PROCESS. Expect sometimes to combine steps, reverse their order, and return to parts of the process you thought you had completed.

((•●
AUDIO
LESSON
Section 2:
Practice
Questions—
Becoming a
Critical
Reader and a
Better Writer

4c   How do I read to comprehend?

When you read to comprehend, you try to understand the basic, literal meaning of a text. Your goal is to discover the main ideas, the supporting details, or, in a work of fiction, the central details of plot and character.

Steps in the critical thinking and critical reading process

1. **Comprehend** or **summarize.** Understand the literal meaning: the "plain" meaning on the surface of the material. Be able to extract and restate its main message or central point or to accurately and objectively describe an image, event, or situation. Add nothing. Read "on the lines."

2. **Analyze.** Examine the material by breaking it into its component parts. Ask about the nature or meaning of each part and how it contributes to the overall meaning or effect.

3. **Infer.** Read "between the lines" to see what's not stated but implied.

4. **Synthesize.** Connect what you've summarized, analyzed, and inferred with your prior knowledge or experiences, with other ideas or perspectives, or with other readings, texts, or situations.

5. **Evaluate.** Read "beyond the lines." Judge the quality of the material or form your own informed opinion about it. Answer such questions as "Is it reasonable? Fair? Accurate? Convincing? Ethical? Useful? Comprehensive? Important?"

4c.1   Reading closely and actively

Reading is an active process—a dynamic, meaning-making interaction between the page and your brain. The secret to **reading closely and actively** is to annotate as you read, writing notes in a book or article's margins and using asterisks and other codes to alert yourself to special material. Some readers start annotating right away, while others wait to annotate after they've previewed the material and read it once. Experiment to determine what works best for you. We recommend using two different ink colours, one for close reading and one for active reading (see Figure 4.2).

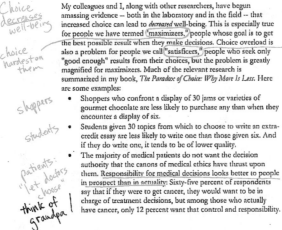

Figure 4.2 A sample of annotated reading (close reading in green, active reading in black)

Close reading means annotating for content. You might, for example, number and briefly list the steps in a process or summarize major points in the margin. When you review, your marginal notes help you glance over the material and quickly recall what it's about.

Active reading means annotating to make connections between the material and your own knowledge or experiences. This is your chance to converse on paper with the writer. Consider yourself a partner in the making of meaning, a full participant in the exchange of ideas. Active reading is a key to ANALYSIS (section 4d), INFERENCE (4e), SYNTHESIS (4f), and EVALUATION (4g).

If you feel uncomfortable writing in a book, create a *double-entry notebook*. Draw a line down the centre of your notebook page. On one side, write content notes (close reading). On the other, write synthesis notes (active reading). Be sure to write down exactly where in the reading you're referring to. Illustrated in Figure 4.3 is a short example from a double-entry notebook.

EXERCISE 4-1   Annotate the rest of the essay by Barry Schwartz, titled "The Tyranny of Choice," In section 7f. Depending on your instructor's directions, follow the annotation example in Figure 4.2, adapt the double-entry example in Figure 4.3, or try both.

4c.2   Reading systematically

To **read systematically** is to use a structured plan: **Preview, Read,** and **Review.**

1. **Preview:** Before you begin reading, start making predictions. When your mind is reading actively, it is guessing what's coming next, either confirming or revising its prediction, and moving on to new predictions. For example, suppose you're glancing through a magazine and come across the title "The Heartbeat." Your mind begins guessing: Is this a love story? Is this about how the heart pumps blood? Maybe, you say to yourself, it's a story about some-one who had a heart attack. Then, as you read the first few sentenes, your mind confirms

Content Notes	Synthesis Notes
--increased wealth and choice haven't made people happier	
--fewer people than in 1974 report being "very happy"	I wonder if people define happiness different today than they did 30-40 years ago
--depression and suicide have increased, especially among young people	Scary. There could be lots of causes, and I wonder if wealth and choice are the most important
--demand for counselling has increased at colleges and universities	Could it be that more students seek counselling? Maybe need was there before but people didn't act.

Figure 4.3 A double-entry notebook

which guess was correct. If you see words like *electrical impulse, muscle fibres,* and *contraction,* you know instantly that you're in the realm of physiology.

- To preview a book, first look at the table of contents. What topics are included? What seems to be the main emphasis? Which sections will be most important? If there's an introduction or preface, skim it.
- To preview a particular reading (for example, a chapter or an article), read all the headings, large and small. Note the boldfaced words and all visuals and their captions, including photographs, drawings, figures, tables, and boxes.
- Check for introductory notes about the author and head notes, which often precede individual works in collections of essays or short stories. Read pivotal paragraphs, such as the opening and (unless you're reading for suspense) closing.
- Jot a few questions that you expect—or hope—the reading will answer.

2. **Read:** Read the material closely and actively (see section 4c.1). Identify the main points and start thinking about how the writer supports them.

3. **Review:** Go back to questions you jotted during previewing. Did the reading answer them? (If not, your predictions could have been wrong or you may not have read carefully; reread to determine which.) Also, look at the annotations you made through close and active reading. What do these add up to? Where are places you need to go back? Keep in mind that collaborative learning can reinforce what you learn from reading. Ask a friend or classmate to discuss the material with you and quiz you.

ALERT: The speed at which you read depends on your purpose for reading. When you're hunting for a particular fact, you can skin the page until you find what you want. When you read about a subject you know well, you might read somewhat rapidly, slowing down when you come to new material. When you're unfamiliar with the subject, you need to work slowly to give your mind time to absorb the new material. ●

QUICK REFERENCE **4.2**

More ways to help your reading comprehension

- **Make associations.** Link new material to what you already know, especially when you're reading about an unfamiliar subject. You may even find it helpful to read an encyclopedia article or an easier book on the subject first in order to build your knowledge base.
- **Simplify tough sentences.** If the author's writing style is complex, "unpack" the sentences: Break them into smaller units or reword them in a simpler style.
- **Make it easy to focus.** If your mind wanders, do whatever it takes to concentrate. Arrange for silence or music, for being alone or in the library with others who are studying. Try to read at your best time of day.
- **Allot the time you need.** To comprehend new material, you must allow sufficient time to read, reflect, reread, and study. Discipline yourself to balance classes, working, socializing, and family activities. Reading for comprehension takes time.
- **Master the vocabulary.** If you don't understand key terms in your reading, you can't fully understand the concepts. As you encounter new words, try to figure out their meanings from context clues. Also, many textbooks list key terms and their definitions in a *glossary* at the end of each chapter or of the book. Of course, nothing replaces having a good dictionary at hand.

To analyze something is to break it into parts, just as a chemist does, for example, in order to figure out the compounds in a particular mixture. However, it's easier to define analysis than to understand and apply it to reading. The key is knowing what parts to examine and how.

QUICK REFERENCE 4.3

Elements of analysis

1. Separate facts from opinions (4d.1).
2. Identify the evidence (4d.2).
3. Identify cause and effect (4d.3).
4. Describe the tone (4d.4; 8d).

4d.1   Separating facts from opinions

A helpful step in analyzing a reading is to distinguish **fact** from **opinion**. *Facts* are statements that can be verified. *Opinions* are statements of personal beliefs. Facts can be verified by observation, research, or experimentation, but opinions are open to debate. Problems arise when a writer blurs the distinction between fact and opinion. Critical readers will know the difference.

For example, here are two statements, one a fact, the other an opinion.

1. Women can never make good mathematicians.
2. Although fear of math isn't purely a female phenomenon, girls tend to drop out of math classes sooner than boys, and some adult women have an aversion to math and math-related activity that is akin to anxiety.

Reading inferentially, you can see that statement 1 is clearly an opinion. Is it worthy of consideration? Perhaps it could be open to debate, but the word *never* implies that the writer is unwilling to allow for even one exception. Conversely, statement 2 at least seems to be factual, though research would be necessary to confirm or deny the position.

You may find it practical to label key sentences "facts" or "opinions" as part of your analysis.

EXERCISE 4-2   Working individually or with a peer response group, decide which statements are facts and which are opinions. When the author and source are provided, explain how that information influenced your judgment. For help, consult 4d.1.

1. Our cities tend to be functional but nondescript, anchored against the wind, with nothing to please the eye. Quebec City is an exception.
   —Mordecai Richler, *Oh Canada! Oh Quebec!*

2. Advertisements for synthetic sports clothing frequently claim that it insulates better and dries more quickly than cotton.

3. Grief, when it comes, is nothing we expect it to be.
   —Joan Didion, *The Year of Living Dangerously*

4. The vested interests of acquired knowledge and conventional wisdom have always been by-passed and engulfed by new media.

—Marshall McLuhan, *Understanding Media*

5. History is the branch of knowledge that deals systematically with the past.

—*Webster's New World College Dictionary,* Fourth Edition

6. In 1927, F. E. Tylcote, an English physician, reported in the medical journal *Lancet* that in almost every case of lung cancer he had seen or known about, the patient smoked.

—William Ecenbarger, "The Strange History of Tobacco"

7. Journalist Jeffrey Simpson wrote a column in the *Globe and Mail* in November 2010, in which he commented that Canadians have not given enough consideration to more efficient health-care models.

8. David Suzuki and Naomi Klein are essential reading for anyone who wants to gain an understanding of globalization.

9. Since the mid-1960s, hepatitis—meaning, simply, the inflammation of the liver—has become a major health problem. As many as 500 million people carry hepatitis B or C, the most serious forms. Up to 500,000 of them live in Canada.

—Anita Elash, *Maclean's*

10. A critical task for all of the world's religions and spiritual traditions is to enrich the vision—and the reality—of the sense of community among us.

—Joel D. Beversluis, *A Sourcebook for Earth's Community of Religions*

4d.2   Identifying the evidence

For any opinions or claims, you next need to identify and analyze the evidence that the writer provides. **Evidence** consists of facts, examples, the results of formal studies, and the opinions of experts. A helpful step in analysis is to identify the kind of evidence used (or what evidence is missing).

RECOGNIZING PRIMARY VERSUS SECONDARY SOURCES

Primary sources are firsthand evidence based on your own or someone else's original work or direct observation. Primary sources can take the form of experiments, surveys, interviews, memoirs, observations, and original creative works (for example, poems, novels, paintings and other visual art, plays, films, or musical compositions).

Secondary sources report, describe, comment on, or analyze the experiences or work of others. Quick Reference 4.4 illustrates the difference.

Primary sources have the advantage of being "closer" to the subject matter or phenomenon. Of course, that doesn't make them perfect. For example, you can't interview only three undergraduates and make claims about all students everywhere. Furthermore, not all eyewitnesses are reliable, so you must judge which ones to believe. Still, readers often find enhanced credibility in primary research. With secondary sources, there's always a risk that the writer isn't reporting the original material accurately, whether intentionally or not.

For example, suppose a primary source author concluded, "It would be a mistake to assume that people's poverty level reflects their intelligence," but a secondary source author represents this as "poverty level is connected to intelligence." Problem! The value of a second-hand account hinges on the reliability of the reporter, which depends on the specificity, accuracy, and authority of his or her observations, as well as where he or she published them. Quick Reference 4.5 provides a checklist for evaluating sources.

Examples of differences between primary and secondary evidence

Primary Source	Secondary Source
Results published in Statistics Canada's *Canadian Health Measures Survey* indicating a decline in fitness levels between 1981 and 2009	*Maclean's* magazine article on childhood and youth obesity citing Statistics Canada survey figures
Nega Mezlekia's memoir of Africa and Canada, *Notes from the Hyena's Belly* (winner of the Governor General's Literary Award for non-fiction)	Blog written by Professor Lawrence Douglass discussing the immigrant experience as portrayed in three personal memoirs, including *Notes from the Hyena's Belly*
Brian Eno's computer-generated sound and image installation, *77 Million Paintings,* exhibited in the Glenbow Museum, Calgary	Panel discussion on Eno's installation by Gemma L. Day (art critic), Luis Ocampo (musicologist), and Franceline Joyal (computer scientist)

Evaluating sources

- **Is the source authoritative?** Did an expert or a person you can expect to write credibly on the subject write it? If it's a memoir or eyewitness account, does it have the kind of detail and perspective that makes the writer credible?

- **Is the source published in a reliable place?** Does the material appear in a reputable publication—a book published by an established publisher, a respected journal or magazine—or on a reliable Internet site?

- **Is the source well known?** Is the source cited elsewhere as you read about the subject? (If so, the authority of the source is probably widely accepted.)

- **Is the tone balanced?** Is the language relatively objective (and therefore more likely to be reliable), or is it slanted (probably not reliable)?

- **Is the source current?** Is the material up-to-date and therefore more likely to be reliable, or has later authoritative and reliable research made it outdated? ("Old" isn't necessarily unreliable. In many fields, classic works of research remain authoritative for decades or even centuries.)

- **Are its findings valid (if a primary source)?** Did the experiment, survey, interview, or study seem to be conducted rigorously? Are the conclusions justified by the data?

- **Is it accurate and complete (if a secondary source)?** Does it accurately summarize and interpret the primary resource? Does it leave out anything important?

EXERCISE 4-3   Individually or with a group, choose one of the following thesis statements and list the kinds of primary and secondary sources you might consult to support the thesis (you can guess intelligently, rather than checking to make sure that the sources exist). Then, decide which sources in your list would be primary and which secondary.

> **THESIS STATEMENT 1:**   People who regularly perform volunteer work lead happier lives than those who don't.
>
> **THESIS STATEMENT 2:**   Whether someone regularly performs volunteer work or not ultimately has no effect on that person's happiness.

EVALUATING EVIDENCE

You can evaluate evidence by asking the following questions to guide your judgment.

- **Is the evidence sufficient?** To be sufficient, evidence can't be skimpy. As a rule, the more evidence, the better. Readers have more confidence in the results of a survey that draws on a hundred respondents than one that draws on ten. As a writer, you may convince your reader that violence is a serious problem in high schools on the basis of only two examples, but you'll be more convincing with additional examples.

- **Is the evidence representative?** Evidence is representative if it is typical. As a reader, assess the objectivity and fairness of evidence. Don't trust a claim or conclusion about a group based on only a few members rather than on a truly typical sample. A pollster survey-ing national political views would not get representative evidence by interviewing people only in Calgary because that group doesn't represent the regional, racial, political, and ethnic makeup of the entire electorate. As a writer, the evidence you offer should represent your claim fairly; don't base your point on an exception.

- **Is the evidence relevant?** Relevant evidence is directly related to the conclusion you're drawing. Determining relevance often demands subtle thinking. Suppose you read that one hundred students who had watched television for more than two hours a day throughout high school earned significantly lower scores on a college entrance exam than one hundred students who had not. Can you conclude that students who watch less television perform better on college entrance exams? Not necessarily. Other differences between the two groups could account for the different scores: geographical region, family background, socioeconomic group, or the quality of schools attended.

- **Is the evidence accurate?** Accurate evidence is correct and complete. Inaccurate evidence is useless. Evidence must come from a reliable source, whether it is primary or secondary. Equally important, evidence must be presented honestly, not misrepresented or distorted.

- **Is the evidence qualified?** Reasonable evidence doesn't make extreme claims. Claims that use words such as *all, always, never,* and *certainly* are disqualified if even one exception is found. Conclusions are more sensible and believable when qualified with words such as *some, many, may, possibly, often,* and *usually.* Remember that today's "facts" may be revised as time passes and knowledge grows.

4d.3   Identifying cause and effect

Cause and effect describes the relationship between one event (cause) and another re-sulting event (effect). The relationship also works in reverse: One event (effect) results from another event (cause). Whether you begin with a cause or with an effect, you're using the same basic pattern.

Cause A ──────▶ produces ──────▶ effect B

You may seek to understand the effects of a known cause:

More studying ———→ produces ———→ ?

Or you may seek to determine the cause or causes of a known effect:

? ———→ produces ———→ recurrent headaches

When you're analyzing a reading, look for any claims of cause and effect. For any that you find, think carefully through the relationship between cause A and effect B. Just because A happened before B or because A and B are associated with each other doesn't mean A caused B. Consult the guidelines in Quick Reference 4.6.

QUICK REFERENCE **4.6**

Assessing cause and effect

- **Is there a clear relationship between events?** Related causes and effects happen in sequence: A cause occurs before an effect. First the wind blows; then a door slams; then a pane of glass in the door breaks. But CHRONOLOGICAL ORDER merely implies a cause-and-effect relationship. Perhaps someone slammed the door shut. Perhaps someone threw a baseball through the glass pane. A cause-and-effect relationship must be linked by more than chronological sequence. The fact that B happens after A doesn't prove that A causes B.

- **Is there a pattern of repetition?** Scientific proof depends on a pattern of repetition. To establish that A causes B, every time A is present, B must occur. Or, put another way, B never occurs unless A is present. The need for repetition explains why Health Canada sponsors or runs many clinical trials before approving a new medicine.

- **Are there multiple causes and/or effects?** Avoid oversimplification. The basic pattern of cause and effect—single cause, single effect (A causes B)—rarely represents the full picture. Multiple causes and/or effects are more typical of real life. For example, it would be oversimplification to assume that a lower crime rate is strictly due to high employment rates. Similarly, one cause can produce multiple effects. For example, advertisements for a liquid diet drink focus on the drink's most appealing effect, rapid weight loss, ignoring less desirable effects such as lost nutrients and a tendency to regain the weight.

EXERCISE 4-4 For each of the sentences below, explain how the effect might not be a result of the cause given.

EXAMPLE The number of shoppers downtown increased because the city planted more trees there.

Planting trees might have made the downtown more attractive and drawn more shoppers. However, there may be other reasons: new stores opening, more parking, a suburban mall closed down, and so on.

1. Attendance at baseball games declined because the team raised prices.
2. Test scores improved because the school instituted a dress code.
3. Because of the Internet, people are reading fewer books than they did twenty years ago.

4d.4 Describing tone

Tone refers to the attitude conveyed in writing, mostly by the writer's word choice. A tone can be formal, informal, laid back, pompous, sarcastic, concerned, judgmental, sympathetic, and so on. We discuss tone at greater length in section 8d.

For now, however, as a critical reader, be suspicious of a highly emotional tone in writing. if you find it, chances are the writer is trying to manipulate the audience. As a writer, if you find your tone growing emotional, step back and rethink the situation. No matter what point you want to make, your chance of communicating successfully to an audience depends on your using a moderate, reasonable tone. For instance, the exaggerations below in the NO example (*robbing treasures, politicians are murderers*) might hint at the truth of a few cases, but they're too extreme to be taken seriously. The language of the YES version is far more likely to deliver its intended message.

> NO Urban renewal must be stopped. Urban redevelopment is ruining this country, and money-hungry capitalists are robbing treasures from law-abiding citizens. Corrupt politicians are murderers, caring nothing about people being thrown out of their homes into the streets.

> YES Urban renewal is revitalizing our cities, but it has caused some serious problems. While investors are trying to replace slums with decent housing, they must also remember that they're displacing people who don't want to leave their familiar neighbourhoods. Surely, a cooperative effort between government and the private sector can lead to creative solutions.

4e How do I draw inferences?

When you read for **inferences**, you're reading to understand what's suggested or implied but not explicitly stated. Here's an example.

> If you enroll in Urban Geography 011, you may want to ask for the independent study option. That gives you an hour or two of face time with the professor every week. You won't even *see* a TA until midterms, when five or six of them proctor the exam in the big gym.

On the literal level, this short paragraph advises the reader to take the independent study option in a certain class. But there's clearly more going on. Among the inferential meanings are (1) most students have little access to the professor; (2) it is worthwhile to meet with this professor; (3) the writer doesn't respect the class's teaching assistants; and (4) many students take this class, since it has at least five or six teaching assistants and uses the big gym for its midterm exam. The writer doesn't say these things directly, but the reader can understand them nevertheless.

Drawing inferences takes practice. Quick Reference 4.7 lists questions to help you read "between the lines." A discussion of each point follows.

QUICK REFERENCE 4.7

Drawing inferences during reading

- What is the point, even if the writer doesn't state it outright?
- How might the writer's position influence his or her perspective?
- Can I detect **bias** in the material?
- What are the implications of the reading?

4e.1   The writer's position

As a reader, when you can "consider the source"—that is, find out exactly who made a statement—you can open up new perspectives. For example, you would probably read an essay for or against capital punishment differently if you knew the writer came from a country that still had the death penalty rather than from Canada.

Although considering the source can help you draw inferences, take care that you don't fall prey to argument to the person (4i). Just because someone you don't respect voices an opinion doesn't mean that the position is necessarily wrong.

4e.2   Bias

For inferential reading, you want to detect **bias**, also known as **prejudice**. When writing is distorted by hatred or distrust of individuals, groups of people, or ideas, you as a critical reader want to suspect the accuracy and fairness of the material. Bias can be worded in positive language, but critical readers aren't deceived by such tactics. Similarly, writers can merely imply their bias rather than state it outright. For example, suppose you read, "Poor people like living in crowded conditions because they're used to such surroundings" or "Women are so wonderfully nurturing that they can't succeed in business." As a critical reader, you will immediately detect the bias. Therefore, always question material that rests on a weak foundation of discrimination and narrow-mindedness.

4e.3   What are implications of the reading?

An **implication** takes the form, "If this is true (or if this happens), then that might also be true (or that might be the consequence.)" One way to consider implications, especially for readings that contain a proposal, is to ask, "Who might benefit from an action, and who might lose?" For example, consider the following short argument.

> Because parking downtown is so limited, we should require anyone putting up a new building to construct a parking lot or contribute to parking garages.

It doesn't take much to infer who might benefit: people driving downtown who are looking for places to park. With a little more thought, you can see how store owners could benefit if shoppers have an easier time finding parking. Who might lose? Well, having to provide parking will add to building costs, and these may be passed to customers. More room for parking means less room for building, so the downtown could sprawl into neighbourhoods. More parking can encourage more driving, which contributes to congestion and pollution.

Now, benefits may outweigh losses—or the other way around. The point is that if you think about the implications of ideas in a reading, you can generate some inferences.

EXERCISE 4-5   Consider the implications of the following short argument, focusing on who might gain and lose from the following proposal:

In an effort to attract more foreign students to its universities and increase the skill level of the work force, one province intends to give foreign students with PhD degrees granted in that province a fast track to permanent residency status in Canada. This will let students who wish to remain in this country start working in their fields and gain Canadian citizenship quickly.

EXERCISE 4-6   Read the following passages, then (1) list all literal information, (2) list all implied information, and (3) list the opinions stated. Refer to sections 4b–4d.1 for help.

EXAMPLE   The study found many complaints against the lawyers were not investigated, seemingly out of a "desire to avoid difficult cases."

—Normal F. Dacey

Literal information: Few complaints against lawyers are investigated.

Implied information: The term *difficult* cases implies a cover-up: Lawyers, or others in power, hesitate to criticize lawyers for fear of being sued or for fear of a public outcry if the truth about abuses and errors were revealed.

Opinions: No opinions. It reports on a study.

A. I remember a weekend in Ottawa in the 1970s, when I helped to organize a meeting with men in prison: a group of ex-inmates and offenders, prison guards, policemen, prison chaplains, prison directors, and psychologists. We shared together, ate together, slept in dormitories. Nobody carried any label or sign showing to which group they belonged. We were together as persons, not as representatives of a group. It was, if you like, an image for me of how we actually behave towards each other when we have no "markers" to tell us what we are supposed to feel towards someone. It was also a small indication of what society might look like, and how it might function, if we could overcome our prejudices.

—Jean Vanier, *Becoming Human*

B. In the misty past, before Bill Gates joined the company of the world's richest men, before the mass-marketed personal computer, before the metaphor of an information superhighway had been worn down to a cliché, I heard Roger Schank interviewed on National Public Radio. Then a computer science professor at Yale, Schank was already well known in artificial intelligence circles. Because those circles did not include me, a new programmer at Sperry Univac, I hadn't heard of him. Though I've forgotten the details of the conversation, I have never forgotten Schank's insistence that most people do not need to own computers.

That view, of course, has not prevailed. Either we own a personal computer and fret about upgrades, or we are scheming to own one and fret about the technical marvel yet to come that will render our purchase obsolete. Well, there are worse ways to spend money, I suppose. For all I know, even Schank owns a personal computer. They're fiendishly clever machines, after all, and they've helped keep the wolf from my door for a long time.

—Paul De Palma,
<http://www.when_is_enough_enough?.com>

4f   **How do I synthesize?**

To **synthesize** is to put things together. When analysis and inference generate specific ideas, try to put them together with things you know from your experience or previous learning or from other readings. For example, suppose you read an opinion that reminds you of a similar opinion by an expert you respect. Making that connection is an act of critical thinking. It takes you beyond the reading itself. Or suppose that someone provides evidence for a claim, but further reading shows you that the facts cited are incomplete or even inaccurate. This synthesis allows you to read the first source more critically.

Synthesis also happens between a reading and your own experience. Take the following example.

> Probably no time in life is as liberating or stimulating as the undergraduate years. Freed from the drudgery of a career and the obligations of family life, students have the luxury to explore new ideas and pursue new paths of knowledge. These years are a joyful time of endless possibility.

If you're single parent taking classes at night or someone who is working a couple of jobs and worrying about paying back loans, your perspective probably differs from the author's. Synthesizing the reading and your experience would result in a critical evaluation. We discuss synthesis with additional examples in section 7f.4.

4g   How do I evaluate?

When you read to evaluate, you're judging the writer's work. **Evaluative reading** comes after you've summarized, analyzed, and synthesized the material (see Quick Reference 4.1). Reading "between the lines" is usually concerned with recognizing tone, detecting bias, differentiating fact from opinion, and determining the writer's position. Reading to evaluate "beyond the lines" requires an overall assessment of the soundness of the writer's reasoning, evidence, or observations, and the fairness and perceptiveness the writer shows, from accuracy of word choice and tone to the writer's respect for the reader.

Evaluating is the step where you make judgments. Ultimately, should we trust the author or not? Should we accept his or her conclusions and recommendations? An important additional strategy for answering questions like these is assessing reasoning processes.

4h   How do I assess reasoning processes critically?

AUDIO
LESSON
Section 3:
Rapid
Review—
Becoming a
Critical Reader
and a Better
Writer

To think, read, and write critically, you need to distinguish *sound reasoning* from *faulty reasoning*. **Induction** and **deduction** are two basic reasoning processes, natural thought patterns people use every day to help them think through ideas and make decisions.

4h.1   Inductive Reasoning

About the
Audio
Lessons for
Constructing
an Argument

AUDIO
LESSON
Section 1: Big
Ideas—
Constructing
an Argument

Inductive reasoning moves from particular facts or instances to general principles. Suppose you go to the Motor Vehicle Licence Agency to renew your driver's licence and have to stand in line for two hours. A few months later you return to get new licence plates, and once again you have to stand in line for two hours. You mention your annoyance to a couple of friends who say they had exactly the same experience. You conclude that the registry is inefficient and indifferent to the needs of its patrons. You've arrived at this conclusion by means of induction. Quick Reference 4.8 shows the features of inductive reasoning.

4h.2   Deductive Reasoning

Deductive reasoning is the process of reasoning from general claims to a specific instance. Suppose you know that students who don't take a literature option can't major in business communication. If your friend tells you she isn't taking any literature courses, you

Inductive reasoning

- **Inductive reasoning moves from the specific to the general.** It begins with specific evidence—facts, observations, or experiences—and moves to a general conclusion.
- **Inductive conclusions are considered reliable or unreliable, not true or false.** Because inductive thinking is based on a sampling of facts, an inductive conclusion indicates probability—the degree to which the conclusion is likely to be true—not certainty.
- **An inductive conclusion is held to be reliable or unreliable in relation to the quantity and quality of the evidence** (4d) on which it's based.
- **Induction leads to new "truths."** It can support statements about the unknown based on what's known.

can make a reasonable conclusion about her major. Your reasoning might go something like this:

PREMISE 1   Students who don't take a literature option can't major in business communication.

PREMISE 2   My friend isn't taking any literature courses.

CONCLUSION   Therefore, my friend isn't majoring in business communication.

Deductive arguments have three parts: two **premises** and a conclusion. This three-part structure is known as a **syllogism**. The first and second premises of a deductive argument may be statements of fact or assumptions. They lead to a conclusion, which is the point at which you want to think as precisely as possible because you're into the realm of *validity*.

Whether or not an argument is **valid** has to do with its form or structure. Here, the word *valid* isn't the general term people use in conversation to mean "acceptable" or "well grounded." In the context of reading and writing logical arguments, the word *valid* has a very specific meaning. A deductive argument is *valid* when the conclusion logically follows from the premises; otherwise, it is *invalid*. For example:

VALID DEDUCTIVE ARGUMENT

PREMISE 1   When it snows, the streets get wet. [fact]

PREMISE 2   It is snowing. [fact]

CONCLUSION   Therefore, the streets are getting wet.

INVALID DEDUCTIVE ARGUMENT

PREMISE 1   When it snows, the streets get wet. [fact]

PREMISE 2   The streets are getting wet. [fact]

CONCLUSION   Therefore, it is snowing.

Here's the problem with the invalid deductive argument: It has acceptable premises because they are facts. However, the argument's conclusion does not follow because it ignores other reasons the streets might be wet. For example, the streets could be wet from rain, from street-cleaning trucks that spray water, or from people washing their cars. Because the conclusion doesn't follow logically from the premises, the argument is invalid.

Another problem in a deductive argument can occur when the premises are implied but not stated—called **unstated assumptions**. An argument can be logically valid even though it is based on wrong assumptions. To show that such an argument is invalid, you need to attack the assumptions, not the conclusion, as wrong. For example, suppose a corporation argues that it can't install pollution-control devices because the cost would cut deeply into its profits. This argument rests on the unstated assumption that no corporation should do something that would lower its profits. That assumption is wrong, and so is the argument. To show that both are wrong, you need to challenge the assumptions.

Similarly, if a person says that certain information is correct because it's written in the newspaper, that person's deductive reasoning is flawed. The unstated assumption is that everything in a newspaper is correct—which isn't true. Whenever there's an unstated assumption, you need to state it outright and then check that it's true. Quick Reference 4.9 summarizes deductive reasoning.

QUICK REFERENCE 4.9

Deductive reasoning

- **Deductive reasoning moves from the general to the specific.** The three-part structure that makes up a deductive argument, or SYLLOGISM, includes two premises and a conclusion drawn from them.
- **A deductive argument is valid if the conclusion logically follows from the premises.**
- **A deductive conclusion may be judged true or false.** If both premises are true, the conclusion is true. If the argument contains an assumption, the writer must prove the truth of the assumption to establish the truth of the argument.
- **Deductive reasoning applies what the writer already knows.** Though it doesn't yield new information, it builds stronger arguments than inductive reasoning because it offers the certainty that a conclusion is either true or false.

EXERCISE 4-7 Working individually or with a peer-response group, determine whether each conclusion here is valid or invalid. Be ready to explain your answers. For help, consult 4h.

1. All required reading for my course is accessible on the Internet.
   My professor assigned her thesis as required reading.
   My professor's thesis is accessible on the Internet.

2. You should not believe everything you read on the Internet.
   Your professor's thesis is posted on the Internet.
   You should not believe your professor's thesis.

3. The Prairies produced politicians who were charismatic speakers.
   John Diefenbaker and Tommy Douglas were Prairie politicians.
   Therefore, John Diefenbaker and Tommy Douglas were charismatic speakers.

4. Mosquitoes are a problem in tropical climates.
   Mosquitoes are a problem in Winnipeg.
   Therefore, Winnipeg has a tropical climate.

5. All great chefs are men.
   Madame Benoît was a great chef.
   Madame Benoît was a man.

4i How can I recognize and avoid logical fallacies?

Logical fallacies are flaws in reasoning that lead to illogical statements. Though logical fallacies tend to occur when ideas are argued, they can be found in all types of writing. Interestingly, most logical fallacies masquerade as reasonable statements, but in fact, they're attempts to manipulate readers by appealing to their emotions instead of their intellects, their hearts rather than their heads. The name for each logical fallacy indicates the way that thinking has gone wrong.

*((•***

AUDIO
LESSON
Section 2:
Practice
Questions—
Constructing
an Argument

*((•***

AUDIO
LESSON
Section 3:
Rapid
Review—
Constructing
an Argument

HASTY GENERALIZATION

A **hasty generalization** draws conclusions from inadequate evidence. Suppose someone says, "My hometown is the best place in the province to live," and gives only two examples to support the opinion. That's not enough. And others might not feel the same way, perhaps for many reasons. Therefore, the person who makes such a statement is indulging in a hasty generalization. **Stereotyping** is another kind of hasty generalization. It happens, for example, when someone says, "Everyone from country X is dishonest." Such a sweeping claim about all members of a particular ethnic, religious, racial, or political group is stereotyping. Yet another kind of stereotyping is **sexism**, and another is **ageism**.

FALSE ANALOGY

A **false analogy** draws a comparison in which the differences outweigh the similarities or the similarities are irrelevant. For example, "Old Joe Smith would never make a good prime minister because an old dog can't learn new tricks" is a false analogy. Joe Smith doesn't learn political skills the way a dog learns tricks. Homespun analogies like this have an air of wisdom about them, but they tend to fall apart when examined closely.

BEGGING THE QUESTION

Begging the question, also called *circular reasoning,* tries to offer proof by simply using another version of the argument itself. For example, the statement "Wrestling is a dangerous sport because it is unsafe" begs the question. Because *unsafe* is a synonym for *dangerous,* the statement goes around in a circle, getting nowhere. Here's another example of circular reasoning but with a different twist: "Wrestling is a dangerous sport; otherwise, those powerful wrestlers would not get injured." Here, the support for the second part of the statement is the argument made in the first part of the statement. Yet the second part is presented as if it supports the first part.

IRRELEVANT ARGUMENT

An **irrelevant argument** reaches a conclusion that doesn't follow from the premises. Irrelevant argument is also called *non sequitur* (Latin for "it does not follow"). An argument is irrelevant when a conclusion doesn't follow from the premises. Here's an example: "Marie Trudel is a forceful speaker, so she'll make a good mayor." You'd be on target if you asked, "What does speaking ability have to do with being a good mayor?"

FALSE CAUSE

A **false cause** assumes that because two events are related in time, the first caused the second. False cause is also known as *post hoc, ergo propter hoc* (Latin for "after this, therefore because of this"). For example, if someone claims that a new weather satellite launched last week has caused the rain that's been falling ever since, that person is connecting two events that, while related in time, have no causal relationship to each other. The launching didn't cause the rain.

SELF-CONTRADICTION

Self-contradiction uses two premises that can't both be true at the same time. Here's an example: "Only when nuclear weapons have finally destroyed us will we be convinced of the need to control them." This is self-contradictory because no one would be around to be convinced if everyone has been destroyed.

RED HERRING

A **red herring**, also called *ignoring the question,* tries to distract attention from one issue by introducing a second that's unrelated to the first. Here's an example: "Why worry about pandas becoming extinct when we haven't solved the plight of the homeless?" You'd be on target if you asked, "What do homeless people have to do with pandas?" If the argument were to focus on proposing that the money spent to prevent the extinction of pandas should go instead to the homeless, the argument would be logical; however, the original statement is a fallacy. By using an irrelevant issue, a person hopes to distract the audience, just as putting a herring in the path of a bloodhound would distract it from the scent it's been following.

ARGUMENT TO THE PERSON

An **argument to the person** means attacking the person making the argument rather than the argument itself. It's also known as the *ad hominem* (Latin for "to the man") attack. When someone criticizes a person's appearance, habits, or character instead of the merits of that person's argument, the attack is a fallacy. Here's an example: "We'd take her position on child abuse seriously if she were not so nasty to her husband." You'd be on target if you were to ask, "What does nastiness to an adult, though not at all nice, have to do with an opinion on child abuse?"

GUILT BY ASSOCIATION

Guilt by association means that a person's arguments, ideas, or opinions lack merit because of that person's activities, interests, or companions. Here's an example: "Jack belongs to the International Hill Climbers Association, which declared bankruptcy last month. This makes him unfit to be mayor of our city." That Jack is a member of a group that declared bankruptcy has nothing to do with Jack's ability to be mayor.

JUMPING ON THE BANDWAGON

Jumping on the bandwagon means something is right or permissible because "everyone does it." It's also called *ad populum* (Latin for "to the people"). This fallacy operates in a statement such as "How could off-track snow boarding be risky if thousands of people have done it?" Following the crowd doesn't work where research and careful reasoning indicate otherwise.

FALSE OR IRRELEVANT AUTHORITY

Using **false** or **irrelevant authority** means citing the opinion of someone who has no expertise in the subject at hand. This fallacy attempts to transfer prestige from one area to another. Many television commercials rely on this tactic—a famous golf player praising a brand of energy drink or a movie star lauding a wireless phone service provider.

CARD-STACKING

Card-stacking, also known as *special pleading,* ignores evidence on the other side of a question. From all available facts, people choose only those facts that show the best (or worst) possible case. Many ads use this strategy. When three slim, happy consumers praise a diet plan, only at the very end of the ad does the announcer say—in a very low and speedy voice—that results vary. Indeed, even that statement is vague and uninformative.

THE EITHER-OR FALLACY

The **either-or fallacy**, also called *false dilemma*, offers only two alternatives when more exist. Such fallacies tend to touch on emotional issues, so many people accept them until they analyze the statement. Here's an example: "Either go to college or forget about getting a job." This rigid, two-sided statement ignores the truth that many jobs don't require a college education.

TAKING SOMETHING OUT OF CONTEXT

Taking something out of context deliberately distorts an idea or a fact by removing it from the material surrounding it. Suppose that a newspaper movie critic writes, "The plot was predictable and boring, but the music was sparkling." The next day, an advertisement for the movie claims "critics call it 'sparkling.'" Clearly, the ad has taken the critic's words out of context (only the music was called "sparkling") and thereby distorts the original.

APPEAL TO IGNORANCE

Appeal to ignorance tries to make an incorrect argument based on something never having been shown to be false—or, the reverse, never having been shown to be true. Here's an example: "Because it hasn't been proven that eating food X doesn't cause cancer, we can assume that it does." The statement is a fallacy because the absence of opposing evidence proves nothing. Such appeals can be very persuasive because they prey on people's superstitions or lack of knowledge. Often, they're stated in the fuzzy language of DOUBLE NEGATIVES.

AMBIGUITY AND EQUIVOCATION

Ambiguity and **equivocation** are statements open to more than one interpretation, thus concealing the truth. Here's an example: "Because of the Opposition's rowdy and impertinent behaviour during Question Period, the Prime Minister had no duty to give pertinent answers." The argument contains a fallacy because it takes "pertinent," meaning "relevant to the question," as the counterpart of "impertinent," which in this sentence means "ill-mannered."

EXERCISE 4-8   Following are letters to the editor of a newspaper. Working alone or with a peer-response group, do a critical analysis of each, paying special attention to logical fallacies.

1. To the Editor:

   I am writing to oppose the plan to convert the abandoned railroad tracks into a bicycle trail. Everyone knows that the only reason the mayor wants to do this is so that she and her wealthy friends can have a new place to play. No one I know likes this plan, and if they did, it would probably be because they're part of the wine and cheese set, too. The next thing you know, the mayor will be proposing that we turn the schools into art museums or the park into a golf course. If you're working hard to support a family, you don't have time for this bike trail nonsense. And if you're not working hard, I don't have time for you.

   Jan Gonesh

2. To the Editor:

   I encourage everyone to support the bicycle trail project. Good recreation facilities are the key to the success of any community. Since the bike trail will add more recreation opportunities, it will guarantee the success of our town. Remember that several years ago our neighbours over in Douglas Lake decided not to build a new park, and look what happened to their economy, especially that city's high unemployment rate. We can't afford to let the same thing happen to us. People who oppose this plan are narrow-minded, selfish, and unmindful of Canada's multicultural mosaic and the "Just Society" that Pierre Trudeau fought for.

Susan Thompson

3. To the Editor:

I'm tired of all this nonsense about pollution and global warming. We had plenty of cold days last winter, and as my dentist said, "If this is global warming, then I'd sure hate to see global cooling." Plus, there were lots of days this summer when I haven't had to turn on my air conditioner. I know there are statistics that some people say show the climate is changing, but you can't trust numbers, especially when they come from overpaid scientists. These people just aren't happy unless they're giving us something to feel guilty about, whether it's smoking, drinking, or driving SUVs. Maybe if they stopped wasting their time worrying about pollution, they could do something useful, like find a cure for cancer.

Mario Dubé

4j   How can I view images with a critical eye?

iPod
Advertisement

"The Scream"

Our digital age surrounds us with images in publications, on computers, on television, on cell phones. These images shape attitudes and beliefs, often in subtle ways. Consider, for example, how our notions of beauty have been shaped through the years by countless pictures of people of certain shapes and sizes. As a result—and as we suggested at the start of this chapter—you need to use critical thinking to analyze images as well as words. Doing so heightens your sensitivity to how others use images and equips you to use them effectively yourself.

You can view images critically in the same way that you can read texts critically by using summary, analysis, synthesis, and evaluation (Quick Reference 4.1) and by using literal, analytic, inferential, and evaluative reading (see sections 4.c–g). For example, look at Figure 4.4 with a critical eye.

- *Summarizing* the picture, as well as viewing it literally, you can see—at a minimum—a street full of older buildings with modern skyscrapers in the distance.

Figure 4.4 A streetscape

- *Analyzing* the picture, as well as viewing it inferentially, you can "read between the lines" to see that it's fairly rich with layers of meaning. You can think about the meanings conveyed by the contrast between these buildings and the modern skyscrapers or about the lives of the people who live and work in each place. You can focus on the message of the comparative sizes of the buildings and skyscrapers; on the contrast between this street and those you imagine at the base of the skyscrapers; on why the photographer chose this perspective; on how different captions might give the picture different meanings. For example, consider the differences among three different captions: "Progress," "Inequality," or "The Neighbourhood." Many possible ideas can come to mind as you study the picture critically.

- *Synthesizing* the picture, you can connect what you've analyzed and inferred to ideas you've learned from various life experiences, readings, and other images.

- *Evaluating* the picture is the last step in viewing it critically. Resist evaluating prematurely, to allow your evaluation to be informed by the results of the earlier steps—thinking and reading critically. In evaluating a visual critically, instead of being satisfied with a reaction such as "I do/don't like the picture," you can speak of how the visual "struck" you at first glance; how it did or didn't gain depth of meaning as you analyzed it, looking at what could be inferred and/or imagined; and how it lent itself to synthesis within the realms of your personal experience and education.

EXERCISE 4-9 Working individually or with a peer-response group, use critical thinking to consider one or both of the following photographs: Figure 4.5 and Figure 4.6. Write either informal notes or a mini-essay, according to what your instructor requires. Use the questions in Quick Reference 4.10 to generate your summary, analysis, synthesis, and evaluation of the photograph(s).

QUICK REFERENCE 4.10

Some helpful questions for analyzing visual images

- What does the image show?
- What are its parts? Do the parts belong together (a lake, trees, and mountains), or do they contrast with one another (a woman in a fancy dress sitting on a tractor)? What might be the significance of the relationships among the parts?
- If there is a foreground and a background in the image, what is in each and why?
- If the image is a scene, what seems to be going on? What might be its message? If the image seems to be part of a story, what might have happened before or after?
- How do the people, if any, seem to be related? For example, do they appear to be friends, acquaintances, or strangers?
- If the image has a variety of shadings, colourings, and focuses, what's sharply in focus, blurry, bright, in shadows, colourful, or drab? How do such differences, or lack of them, call attention to various parts of the image?
- Can you think of any connections between the image and things you've experienced or learned from school, work, or reading; visits to museums or other cultural sites; watching movies, plays, and television; or other aspects of your life?
- From your observations, what is your evaluation of the image?

Figure 4.5 An image to analyze (Exercise 4-9)

Figure 4.6 An image to analyze (Exercise 4-9)

❊   **4k**   How can images persuade?

Greenpeace
Photograph

❊

Venezuelan Mural

Because they convey much information instantly, and because they can generate powerful emotional responses (*pathos*), images play a strong role in persuasion. (Just think about advertising!) Sometimes persuasion comes through a single well-chosen image: a picture of a

Figure 4.7 **A landscape with barrels**

bruised child's face demonstrates the cruelty of child abuse; a picture of a grateful civilian hugging a soldier seeks to show that a military action is just and good. In their campaign ads, politicians frequently choose highly unflattering photographs of their opponents, hoping to make them look foolish, incompetent, or unpleasant.

Figure 4.7 is a photograph of a pile of rusted barrels in a beautiful natural setting. The contrast between the barrels and the snow-covered mountains in the background, the lake, and the clear sky is stark and alarming. The barrels stand between viewers and the stunning scenery; people can't ignore or look around them. The photographer has created this contrastive image to persuade you—but to what purpose? Perhaps this photo is an argument against pollution. Perhaps it's an argument against industrial development. Perhaps it is arguing that people can act carelessly. While images can be powerful, they're often more ambiguous than words; images can't state what they mean, although they can move viewers in certain fairly predictable directions. In Figure 4.7, you know that the photographer intends to disturb you.

Frequently, people use a series of images to persuade. Some magazines use photo essays, two or more pictures meant to be viewed in a specific order to achieve a desired effect. An editorial cartoon might include two or more panels to make its point. More often than not, photo essays and editorials include captions or other text along with the images themselves.

4I   How can I analyze words combined with images?

Many texts—from webpages to advertisements, posters, brochures, and so on—are **multimodal** in that they combine words and images. (See section 46a for a discussion of multimodal texts.) These texts can take advantage of *logos* and *ethos*, in addition to the *pathos* (5g) readily created by pictures alone. Critically analyzing multimodal texts means considering the images (Quick Reference 4.10) and the words separately, and then analyzing how the two elements combine to create a single effect.

Ask yourself, "What is the relationship between the words and the image(s)?" and 'Why did the writer choose this particular image for these particular words?"

- Sometimes words and images reinforce one another. A poster with several sentences about poverty, for example, may have a picture of an obviously malnourished person.
- Other times, words and images contrast with one another for effect. Think of a picture of a belching smokestack accompanied by a caption that says, "Everyone deserves fresh air."
- Occasionally, a text might contain images simply to add visual interest. A little decoration is sometimes fine, but always be on your guard for images that seem simply to be thrown in for the sake of including an image. If there isn't a good reason for a particular combination of words and images, the images may be there to compensate for a weak message.

Document design is the name given to the overall arrangement of words and visuals in a text. Chapter 45 explains several principles of document design.

EXERCISE 4-10 Working individually or with a peer-response group, use critical thinking to analyze the visual argument in Figure 4.8. Write either informal notes or a mini-essay, according to what your instructor requires.

Figure 4.8 An advertisement from Greenpeace

4m   What can images add to my writing?

Occasionally, you might be tempted to add images to your writing because you want to add visual interest. In some contexts that is a laudable goal, as long as the images support or enhance the message your writing is trying to deliver. Always, however, be wary of throwing in images for no good reason. Your readers will rightly assume your images are there to communicate a message related to the text, and if none emerges, your entire document loses credibility. The best rule for inserting a photograph or other type of illustration into your writing is "When in doubt, leave it out."

There are four basic relationships between an image and a text. The image can simply illustrate or reinforce the text, as when an advertisement for apples contains a picture of an apple. The image can extend the text, as when a text about dangers of pollution, for example, shows a dead animal, even if the text doesn't refer to animals. The image can contrast with the text, creating irony. For example, suppose you see a picture of starving children, and the caption says, "What a great time to be alive!" Finally, the image can simply decorate the text, bearing none of the previous four relationships to the words but simply existing to draw attention.

Of course, some types of writing almost require images. Some posters, advertisements and websites, for example, would have far less impact if they contained words alone. For example, Figure 4.9 is a public service advertisement by the World Wildlife Fund, an organization dedicated to conservation and sustainable development. You'll notice that the image not only calls stunning attention to the ad, it reinforces the message in the bottom right corner. The text reads, "A single tin of paint can pollute millions of litres of water." The impact of improperly disposed waste is clearly illustrated by the striking image of a skyscraper-sized paint can as the source of an urban river.

However, sometimes the use of words alone as stylized design elements can emphasize the message the writer is trying to convey. For example, Figure 4.10 is a poster that simply includes some words in various colours and sizes. The result is a powerful visual message about climate change.

✱
Finding a New
Power Source
(Research
Paper with
Visuals)

✱
Into the Wind:
Understanding
the Rhetoric of
Arrangement

Figure 4.9 An advertisement from the World Wildlife Fund

Figure 4.10 A poster about global warming

As you think about whether to include images in your papers, consult Chapter 45, which discusses DOCUMENT DESIGN, the overall, well-planned arrangement of words and visuals in a text. Also, you may want to consult Chapter 46, which gives advice about MULTIMODAL texts—compositions that extensively combine words, images, and perhaps even more.

Chapter 5

WRITING ARGUMENTS

5a What is a written argument?

Writing in Action: Investigating Assumptions

When you write an **argument**, you attempt to convince a reader to agree with you on a topic open to debate. You support your position, proposal, or interpretation with EVIDENCE, reasons, and examples. Some people use the terms *argument* and *persuasive writing* interchangeably. When people distinguish between them, *persuasive writing* is the broader term. It includes advertisements, letters to editors, and emotional speeches and writing, as well as formal written arguments.

A written argument consists of two main elements:

* The **claim** states the issue and then takes a position on a debatable topic (the position can be written as a THESIS STATEMENT).
* Facts and logical reasoning provide **support** for the claim (the support needs to be in the form of evidence, reasons, and examples).

In daily life, you might think of an argument as a personal conflict or disagreement, begun in anger and involving emotional confrontations. Many radio programs, websites, and BLOGS reinforce this impression by featuring people who seem more interested in pushing their own agendas than in trying to persuade reasonably. For academic writing, as well as business and public writing, however, arguments are ways of demonstrating CRITICAL THINKING, calmly and respectfully. On difficult issues, your goal is to persuade an audience to consider your ideas with an open mind, which means that your audience's viewpoints and values need to influence your decisions about content, organization, and style. The passion that underlies a writer's position comes not from angry words but from the force of a balanced, well-developed, clearly written presentation.

In this chapter, you'll learn how to develop an effective claim, or thesis, how to generate support, and how to organize your argument using two strategies: the classical pattern and the Rogerian pattern. In addition, you'll find information about how to analyze and refute opposing arguments.

5b What are common types of arguments?

Many people believe that all writing contains an element of argument. In this view, even seemingly informative pieces like summaries, reports, and analyses attempt to convince readers that the author has done a skilful job and that the result is worth their time and attention. Even if we just concentrate on those writings in which writers are explicitly trying to persuade readers, there are several different types of arguments.

Definition arguments persuade readers to interpret a term in a particular way. You might think it strange that definitions are a matter for argument; after all, doesn't the dictionary solve all those questions? But consider how people contest terms like "sexual harassment," "success," or even "happiness." What some people might label a work of art, others might term pornography. Is assisted suicide "murder" or "a medical procedure"? What are the characteristics a film must have to be called a romantic comedy?

Evaluation arguments persuade readers that something is good or bad, worthwhile or a waste of time, better or worse than other things like it, and so on. Common examples are movie, music, or television reviews, but every time we judge a politician or new model of car, we're also evaluating. Evaluation arguments have two elements. They argue that a particular set of criteria are important for measuring a particular class of things (for example, "mysteries must keep the audience guessing until the end"), and they argue that the thing being evaluated meets or doesn't meet those criteria ("because you could figure out very early who was the thief, it was a bad film").

Cause-and-effect arguments take one of two different forms. One is to argue that an existing situation results from a particular cause or set of causes. For example, you might take the situation of homelessness and argue that certain causes are most responsible (such as mental illness or minimum wages that are too low). Another is to argue that something will cause a certain effect. For example, you might argue that if we built more nuclear power plants, we would reduce global warming. You can see how cause-and-effect arguments are important in making policy decisions.

Proposal arguments convince readers that a particular solution to a problem or a particular way of addressing a need is best. Such arguments need to do two things. First, they must prove the existence of a need or problem that is important enough to require attention. Second, they must offer a solution and demonstrate how it will work and will be more feasible and effective than other possibilities. Suppose you want to convince city council to provide better bus service to your campus. You'd be writing a proposal argument.

Finding a
Topic for
Argument

5c How do I choose a topic for an argument?

When you choose a topic for written argument, be sure that it's open to debate. Don't confuse matters of information (facts) with matters of debate. An essay becomes an argument when it makes a claim—that is, *takes a position*—about a debatable topic. An effective way to develop a position is to ask two (or more) opposing questions about a topic.

FACT	First-year students here must take an English credit.
DEBATABLE	Should first-year students here be required to take an English credit?
ONE SIDE	First-year students here should not be required to take an English credit.
OTHER SIDE	First-year students here should be required to take an English credit.

Though you need to select one side of a debatable question to defend in your essay, always keep the other side (or sides) in mind. Devoting some space to state and counter the opposing viewpoint shows readers that you're well informed and fair-minded. This effect is even stronger if you always maintain a respectful tone by avoiding insults, abstaining from exaggerations, and resisting sarcasm. If you neglect to mention opposing views, your readers could justifiably assume you're not well informed, fair-minded, or disciplined as a thinker. When multiple alternative viewpoints exist, choose the major opposing one, unless otherwise directed by your instructor.

Instructors sometimes assign students a topic and even the position to take. In such cases, you need to fulfill the assignment even if you disagree with the point of view.

Readers expect you to reason logically about the assigned position. Indeed, experienced debate teams practise arguing all sides of an issue. Being assigned topics or positions is also common in work settings. Perhaps a manager asks you to develop a persuasive marketing campaign or to negotiate a price break from a supplier. Perhaps you'll be told to convince other workers that a new process will save them time and effort.

If you choose your own topic and position, select one that has sufficient substance for academic writing. Readers expect you to take an intelligent, defensible position and to support it reasonably and convincingly. For example, "Book censorship in public libraries" is worthy of a college or university essay; "The colour of baseball caps" is not. Also, so that you choose a claim sufficiently narrow to be practical, consider the length and time specified in your assignment.

Even if you think that all sides of a debatable topic have merit, you need to choose one of them anyway. Don't become paralyzed from indecision. Concentrate on the merits of one position, and argue that position as effectively as possible, reserving some space to counter objections. Of course, the more thoroughly you think through all sides of the topic, the broader the perspective you'll bring to your writing, and the more likely it is that your writing will be effective. Finally, however, you'll need to take a position.

5d How do I develop a claim and a thesis statement for my argument?

A CLAIM is a statement that expresses a point of view on a debatable topic. It can be supported by evidence, reasons, and examples (including facts, statistics, names, experiences, and expert testimony). The exact wording of the claim rarely finds its way into the essay, but the claim serves as a focus for your thinking. Later, it serves as the basis for developing your THESIS STATEMENT.

TOPIC	The price of organic foods
CLAIM	The benefits of organic foods outweigh their extra costs.
CLAIM	The benefits of organic foods do not outweigh their extra costs.

To stimulate your thinking about the topic and decide the claim you'll argue, work with the PLANNING techniques discussed in Chapter 2. Another well-favoured strategy is to create a two-column list, labelling one column *Pro* or *For*, the other *Con* or *Against*. If there are more than two opposing sides, label the columns accordingly. The columned list displays the quantity and quality of your material so that you can decide whether you're ready to start DRAFTING.

Alex Garcia, the student who wrote the argument essay that appears in section 5n, chose his own topic for a written argument in a first-year writing class. Alex was a biology major who was fascinated with genetic engineering, especially of food. While exploring this topic, he became interested in the broader issue of organic food. As a consumer himself, he had a direct stake in this matter. When he began reading articles he found through library research, he thought they would all come out clearly in favour of organic foods. When he found that not all of them did, he knew that the controversy would make a good topic for his argument. Here's how Alex progressed from topic to claim to thesis statement.

TOPIC	Whether organic foods are better than regular ones
MY POSITION	I think people should buy organic foods when they can.

107

THESIS STATEMENT (FIRST DRAFT)	It is good for people to buy organic foods. [This is a preliminary thesis statement. It clearly states the writer's position, but the word *good* is vague.]
THESIS STATEMENT (SECOND DRAFT)	In order to achieve health benefits and to improve the quality of the environment, organic foods should be purchased by consumers. [This revised thesis statement is better because it states not only the writer's claim but also a reason for the claim. However, it suffers from a lack of conciseness and from the unnecessary passive construction "should be purchased."]
THESIS STATEMENT (FINAL DRAFT)	Research shows that the health and environmental benefits of organic foods outweigh their extra costs. [This final version works well because it states the writer's claim clearly and concisely, with verbs all in the active voice. The writer now has a thesis statement suitable for the time and length given in his assignment. Also, it meets the requirements for a thesis statement given in Quick Reference 2.3.]

EXERCISE 5-1   Working individually or with a peer-response group, develop a claim and a thesis statement for each of the topics listed at the end of the exercise. You may choose any defensible position. For help, consult 5a through 5d.

> **EXAMPLE**   TOPIC: Book censorship in high school
>
> CLAIM: Books should not be censored in high school.
>
> THESIS STATEMENT: When books are taken off high school library shelves or are dropped from high school curricula because they are considered inappropriate to read, students are denied an open exchange of ideas.

1. commercials for alcoholic beverages on television
2. the relationship of reason to belief
3. athletes' use of performance-enhancing drugs and supplements.
4. requiring students to undertake volunteer or community service

((•
AUDIO LESSON
Section 1:
Big Ideas–
Constructing
an Argument

((•
AUDIO LESSON
Section 2:
Practice
Questions–
Constructing
an Argument

((•
AUDIO LESSON
Section 3:
Rapid
Review–
Constructing
an Argument

5e   What is the structure of a classical argument?

No single method is best for organizing all arguments, but a frequently used structure is the **classical argument**. The ancient Greeks and Romans developed the six-part structure described in Quick Reference 5.1.

5f   How do I support my argument?

Use reasons, examples, and evidence to support an argument's claim. (See RENNS, 3f.) One good method of developing reasons for an argument is to ask yourself *why* you believe your claim. When you respond "Because ...," you offer reasons for your claim. Another method is to list the pros and cons of your claim. The lists usually contain reasons. Evidence needs to be sufficient, representative, relevant, accurate, reasonable, and

The structure of a classical argument

1. **Introductory paragraph:** Sets the stage for the position argued in the essay. It gains the reader's interest and respect (3c).

2. **Thesis statement:** States the topic and position you want to argue (2d).

3. **Background information:** Gives readers the basic information they need for understanding your thesis and its support. As appropriate, you might include definitions of key terms, historical or social context, prior scholarship, and other related material. You can include this as part of your introductory paragraph, or it can appear in its own paragraph placed immediately after the introduction.

4. **Evidence and reasons:** Supports the position you're arguing on the topic. This is the core of the essay. Each reason or piece of evidence usually consists of a general statement backed up with specific details, including examples and other RENNS (3f): reasons, examples, names, numbers, and senses. Evidence needs to meet the standards for critical thinking (Chapter 4). Depending on the length of the essay, you might devote one or two paragraphs to each reason or type of evidence. For organization, you might choose to present the most familiar reasons and evidence first. Alternatively, you might proceed from the least important to the most important point so that your essay builds to a climax.

5. **Response to opposing position:** Sometimes referred to as the *rebuttal* or *refutation*. This material mentions and defends against an opposite point of view. Often this refutation, which can be lengthy or brief according to the overall length of the essay, appears in its own paragraph or paragraphs, usually immediately before the concluding paragraph or immediately following the introductory paragraph, as a bridge to the rest of the essay. If you use the latter structure, you can choose to place your thesis statement either at the end of the introductory paragraph or at the end of the rebuttal paragraph. Yet another choice for structures has each paragraph present one type of evidence or reason and then immediately state and respond to the opposing position. (See 5l for advice on handling opposing arguments.)

6. **Concluding paragraph:** Ends the essay logically and gracefully—never abruptly. It often summarizes the argument, elaborates its significance, or calls readers to action (3k).

current. Specifically, evidence consists of facts, statistics, expert testimony, personal experience, and so on.

> It's All About the Food: Understanding the Rhetoric of Argument

If you consult SOURCES to find supporting evidence, reasons, or examples, be sure to use correct DOCUMENTATION within the text of your essay and in the WORKS CITED or REFERENCES list at the end of your paper (Chapters 36–38). By doing this, you avoid engaging in PLAGIARISM, adopting someone else's ideas and trying to pass them off as your own. Plagiarism is a serious offence that can result in your failing a course or even being dismissed from your academic institution (Chapter 35).

5g What types of appeals can provide support?

An effective argument relies on three types of **persuasive appeals**: logical appeals, emotional appeals, and ethical appeals. The ancient Greeks called these appeals *logos, pathos,* and *ethos*. Quick Reference 5.2 summarizes how to use the appeals.

The Slee
Reasonir
(PowerPo
Presenta

QUICK REFERENCE 5.2

Guidelines for persuasive appeals

- **Be logical:** Use sound reasoning (*logos*).
- **Enlist the emotions of the reader:** Appeal to the values and beliefs of the reader by arousing the reader's "better self" (*pathos*).
- **Establish credibility:** Show that you as the writer can be relied on as a knowledgeable person with good sense (*ethos*).

The **logical appeal** (*logos*) is the most widely used and intellectually solid and sound appeal in arguments. Sound reasoning involves using effective evidence and reasons. When the student writer Alex Garcia argues that some foods carry health risks, he cites research pointing to specific diseases (5n). Logical writers analyze CAUSE AND EFFECT correctly. They use appropriate patterns of INDUCTIVE REASONING and DEDUCTIVE REASONING, and they distinguish clearly between fact and opinion. Finally, sound reasoning means avoiding LOGICAL FALLACIES. One strategy for generating logical appeals is the **Toulmin model**, developed by the philosopher Stephen Toulmin, discussed in 5h.

When you use **emotional appeals** (*pathos*), you try to persuade your readers by appealing to their hearts more than their minds. Such appeals are generally more effective when you combine them with logical appeals. If an employee asks for a raise and gives a reason like "I have a family to support," that person probably won't get very far. The employee needs in addition to prove how his or her contributions have gone well beyond the job description, dramatically increased sales, or created other advantages.

Emotional appeals can use descriptive language and concrete details or examples to create a mental picture for readers, which is an approach that leads them to feel or understand the importance of your claim. Figure 5.1 provides an example of emotional appeals. You want to appeal to your audience's values and beliefs through honest examples and descriptions that add a sense of humanity and reality to the issue you're arguing. However, avoid manipulating your readers with biased, SLANTED LANGUAGE. Readers see through such tactics and resent them.

When you use **ethical appeals**, or *ethos,* you establish your personal credibility with your audience. Audiences don't trust a writer who states opinions as fact, distorts evidence, or makes claims that can't be supported. They do trust a writer who comes across as honest, knowledgeable, and fair. Ethical appeals can't take the place of logical appeals, but the two work well together. One effective way to make an ethical appeal is to draw on your personal experience. (Some instructors don't want students to write in the first person, so check with your instructor before you try this technique.) Be sure that any personal experience relates directly to the generalization you're supporting. Considering a variety of perspectives, reasonably and fairly addressing opposing viewpoints (Quick Reference 5.1), using reliable SOURCES, and using a reasonable TONE communicate that you're being fair-minded.

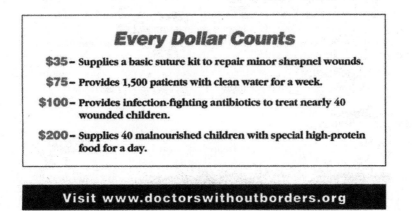

Sleeping Sickness
Untreated, It Inevitably Kills

Spread by tsetse flies, this dreaded tropical disease claims more than 66,000 lives a year in 36 African nations. Doctors Without Borders volunteer Rebecca Golden returned from Angola, where a desperate battle against sleeping sickness is being waged after years of war have wrecked that nation's health care system.

"The treatment is a form of arsenic and is extremely painful," says Rebecca. "I was visiting some children receiving their medicine and was amazed at their courage and strength. **When the arsenic entered their bloodstream, they curled their toes, turned their heads, and closed their eyes tightly.** Their choice was to die or take the treatment. They accepted it with such calm. After 20 years of war and lost family members, they seem to accept this as just another part of the survival process."

Your support helps Doctors Without Borders save lives. **In our battle against sleeping sickness and other diseases, your gift can make a vital difference.**

Every Dollar Counts

$35 – Supplies a basic suture kit to repair minor shrapnel wounds.

$75 – Provides 1,500 patients with clean water for a week.

$100 – Provides infection-fighting antibiotics to treat nearly 40 wounded children.

$200 – Supplies 40 malnourished children with special high-protein food for a day.

Visit www.doctorswithoutborders.org

Figure 5.1 An argument that appeals to emotions

5h   What is the Toulmin model for argument?

One powerful method for generating logical appeals and for analyzing the arguments of others is the Toulmin model. It defines three essential elements in an effective argument: the claim, the support, and the warrants. They describe concepts that you've encountered before, as Quick Reference 5.3 explains. For example, identifying the **warrants** (assumptions that are often unstated) is a good critical thinking strategy.

The concept of *warrant* is similar to the concept of *inferences,* a key component of critical thinking (4a). Inferences are not stated outright but are implied "between the lines" of the writing. Similarly, warrants are unspoken underlying assumptions in an argument. Consider the following simple argument: "Johnson should not be elected mayor. She was recently divorced." The *claim* is that Johnson shouldn't be elected. The *support* is that Johnson has been divorced. The unstated *warrant* is "divorced people are not qualified to be mayor." Before they can accept the claim that Johnson shouldn't be elected, readers have to accept this warrant. Of course, a majority of readers would reject the warrant. Thus, this argument is weak. To identify the warrants in an argument, ask "What do I need to assume so that the support is sufficient for establishing each claim?"

The Toulmin model for argument

- **Claim:** A variation of a thesis statement. If needed, the claim is qualified or limited.

  Alex Garcia makes the following claim in his argument: Health and environmental benefits of organic foods outweigh their extra costs.

- **Support:** Reasons and EVIDENCE, moving from broad reasons to specific data and details, support the claim.

  Alex offers three main reasons: (1) Organic produce is safer for individuals. (2) Organic meats and dairy products are safer for society as a whole. (3) Organic farming is better for the environment. He then provides evidence for each of those reasons, drawing on source materials.

- **Warrants:** The writer's underlying assumptions, which are often implied rather than stated. Warrants may also need support (also called *backing*).

  Alex's essay has several warrants, among them: (1) We should always make choices that increase our safety; and (2) preserving the environment enhances our quality of life. (Notice that these warrants are debatable. For example, we routinely make choices that are less safe than their alternatives; going skiing is more dangerous than staying at home, for instance. Quality of life is determined by many factors.)

The concepts in the Toulmin model can help you write arguments with a critical eye. They can be quite useful on their own as well as when applied to the CLASSICAL ARGUMENT structure (Quick Reference 5.1). As you read and revise your own arguments, identify the claim, support, and warrants. If you don't have a clear claim or support, you'll probably have to assume that your argument is weak. Furthermore, make sure that all of your warrants will be convincing to readers. If they aren't, you need to support the warrants with logical reasons.

EXERCISE 5-2 Individually or with a peer-response group, discuss these simple arguments. Identify the claim, support, and warrants for each.

> **EXAMPLE** The department should establish an honour code. Last year more than fifty students were caught cheating on exams.
> **Claim:** The department should establish an honour code.
> **Support:** Last year, more than fifty students were caught cheating on exams.
> **Warrants:**
> A. Enough students cheat on exams that the department should address the problem.
> B. Cheating should be prevented.
> C. Students would not have cheated if there had been an honour code.

1. The student council should raise student activity fees. It is planning an expensive campaign to lobby the education minister.

2. Buy only locally produced goods. Several factories have closed in our region in the past decade.

3. The university should require all students to own laptop computers. Most students will have to use computers in their jobs after graduation.

5i What part does audience play in my argument?

((●

AUDIO
LESSON
Section 1:
Big Ideas–
Using
Language
Well and
Addressing
Your
Audience

The PURPOSE of written argument is to convince your AUDIENCE either to agree with you or to be open to your position. In writing an argument, you want to consider what your readers already know or believe about your topic. Will the audience be hostile or open-minded to your position? Will it resist or adopt your point of view? What values, viewpoints, and assumptions will your audience hold?

Unfortunately, some people can be persuaded by purely sensational or one-sided claims. Witness the effects on some readers of highly charged advertising or of narrowly one-sided political positions. Critical thinking quickly reveals the weaknesses of such arguments, including a frequent use of LOGICAL FALLACIES (4i). That's why academic audiences expect a higher standard and value, above all, logical appeals and appropriate, adequate support.

In many instances, of course, you can't expect to change your reader's mind, which means that your goal is to demonstrate that your point of view has merit. If you think that your audience is likely to read your point of view with hostility, you might consider using Rogerian argument.

5j How can Rogerian argument help me reach opposing audiences?

Rogerian argument seeks common ground between points of view. The Rogerian approach is based on the principles of communication developed by the psychologist Carl Rogers. According to Rogers, communication is eased when people find common ground in their points of view. Quick Reference 5.4 explains the structure of a Rogerian argument, which can be an effective alternative to CLASSICAL ARGUMENT structure.

QUICK REFERENCE 5.4

The structure of a Rogerian argument

1. **Introduction:** Sets the stage for the position that is argued in the essay. It gains the reader's interest and respect (3c).

2. **Thesis statement:** States the topic and position you want to argue (5c–d).

3. **Common ground:** Explains the issue, acknowledging that your readers probably don't agree with you. Speculates about and respectfully gives attention to the points of agreement you and your readers might share, especially concerning underlying problems or issues. You might even acknowledge situations in which your reader's position may be desirable. This may take one paragraph or several, depending on the complexity of the issue.

4. **Discussion of your position:** Gives evidence and reasons for your stand on the topic, as in classical argument (Quick Reference 5.1).

5. **Concluding paragraph:** Summarizes why your position is preferable to your opponent's (3k).

When it comes to argument, people often "agree to disagree" in the best spirit of intellectual exchange. As you write a Rogerian argument, remember that your audience wants to see how effectively you've reasoned and presented your position. This stance approaches that of a formal oral debate in which all sides are explored with similar intellectual rigour.

A reasonable TONE tells your audience that you're being fair-minded. When you anticipate opposing positions and refute them with balanced language and emphasis, you demonstrate that you respect the other side. No matter how strongly you disagree with opposing arguments, never insult the other side. Name-calling reflects poor judgment and a lack of self-control. Avoid exaggerating, and never show anger. The more emotionally loaded a topic (for example, abortion or capital punishment), the more tempted you might be to use careless, harsh words. For instance, calling the opposing position "stupid" would say more about you as the writer than it would about the issue.

EXERCISE 5-3   Here is the text of a notorious e-mail fraud that has been sent to many people. Hundreds of variations of this e-mail exist, but usually the writer claims to have a large amount of money that he or she wants to transfer to a Canadian or American bank. The writer wants the recipient's help in making the transfer. This is a complete lie. The writer has no money and is trying to trick people into revealing their bank account numbers to steal their money.

Either alone or in a small group, examine the ways this writer tries to establish emotional and ethical appeals. *Note:* We've reproduced the e-mail with the often incorrect original wording, grammar, and punctuation.

Good day,

It is my humble pleasure to write this letter irrespective of the fact that you do not know me. However, I came to know of you in my private search for a reliable and trustworthy person that can handle a confidential transaction of this nature in respect of this, I got your contact through an uprooted search on the internet. Though I know that a transaction of this magnitude will make any one apprehensive and worried, but I am assuring you that all will be well at the end of the day.

I am Ruth Malcasa, daughter of late Mr James Malcasa, who was killed by rebel forces on the 24th of December, 1999 in my country. When he was still alive, he deposited one trunk box containing the sum of USD$10 million dollars in cash (Ten Million dollars). with a private security and safe deposit company here. This money was made from the sell of Gold and Diamond by my mother and she has already decided to use this money for future investment of the family.

My father instructed me that in the case of his death, that I should look for a trusted foreigner who can assist me to move out this money from my country immediately for investment. Based on this, I solicit for your assistance to transfer this fund into your Account, but I will demand for the following requirement: (1) Could you provide for me a safe Bank Account where this fund will be transferred to in your country after retrieving the box containing the money from the custody of the security company. (2) Could you be able to introduce me to a profitable business venture that would not require much technical expertise in your country where part of this fund will be invested?

I am a Christian and I want you to handle this transaction based on the trust I have established on you. For your assistance in this transaction, I have decided to compensate you with 10 percent of the total amount at the end of this business. The security of this business is very important to me and as such, I would like you to keep this business very confidential. I shall expect an early response from you. Thank you and God bless. Yours sincerely, Ruth Malcasa.

51   How do I handle opposing arguments?

Dealing with opposing positions is crucial to writing an effective argument. If you don't acknowledge arguments that your opponents might raise, and explain why they are faulty or inferior, you create doubts that you have thoroughly explored the issue. You risk seeming narrow-minded.

The next-to-last paragraph in Alex Garcia's paper (5n), which summarizes opposing arguments, strengthens both his *ethos* (credibility) and his *logos* (logic). He's so confident in his own position that he can point out research that contradicts his position and even concede that this research is reasonably solid. Alex does suggest some promising new research that may eventually support him, but the most important thing he does is explain why, even if organic food is not more nutritious, the other reasons he has argued are strong enough to carry his thesis. He had found this counter-argument when doing his research. When you do research for your own arguments, look for opinions that oppose your position, not only ones that agree with yours.

If your research doesn't generate opposing arguments, develop them yourself. Imagine that you're debating someone who disagrees with you; what positions would that person take and why? You can ask a classmate or friend to perform this role. Another strategy is to take the opposite side of the argument and try to develop the best reasons you can for that position. (In some formal debating situations, people are expected to prepare both sides of an issue and only learn immediately before the debate which position they are to argue.)

Once you have generated opposing arguments, you need to refute them, which means you want to show why they're weak or undesirable. Imagine that you're writing about national security and individual rights. You believe that the government shouldn't be allowed to monitor a private citizen's e-mail without a court order, and you have developed a number of reasons for your position. To strengthen your paper, you also generate some opposing arguments, including "People will be safer from terrorism if police can monitor e-mail" and "Only people who have something to hide have anything to fear." How might you refute these claims? Following are some suggestions.

- **Examine the evidence for each opposing argument** (4d–h). Look especially for missing or contradictory facts. In the given example, you might question the evidence that people would be safer from terrorism if police could monitor e-mail.

- **Use the Toulmin model to analyze the opposing argument** (5h). What are the claims, support, and warrants? Often, it's possible to show that the warrants are questionable or weak. For example, a warrant in the counter-arguments above is that the promise of increased safety is worth the price of privacy or individual rights. You might show why this warrant is undesirable.

- **Demonstrate that an opposing argument depends on emotion rather than reasoning.** An argument that relies on fear of terrorism may be open to the charge that it manipulates emotions.

- **Redefine key terms.** The expression *something to hide* is intended to make readers think of criminal activities, but it may also extend to our own innocent secrets.

- **Explain the negative consequences of the opposing position.** Imagine that the opposing position actually won out, and explain how the results would be damaging. For example, if everyone knew that government officials might monitor their computer use, consider how this might affect free speech.

- **Concede an opposing point, but explain that doing so doesn't destroy your own argument.** You might decide to concede that monitoring of e-mail by the police may be more efficient than monitoring governed by the courts. However, you could argue that police procedures are carried out more conscientiously and thus with more real effectiveness when subject to court scrutiny.
- **Explain that the costs of the other position are not worth the benefits.**

EXERCISE 5-4   Individually or with a peer-response group, practise developing objections to specific arguments and responses to those objections. To do this, choose a debatable topic and brainstorm a list of points on that topic, some on one side of the topic, some on another. Following are some arguments to get you started. If you're part of a group, work together to assign the different positions for each topic to different sets of students. Then, conduct a brief debate on which side has more merit, with each side taking turns. At the end, your group can vote for the side that is more convincing.

1. It should be legal/illegal to ride motorcycles without a helmet.
2. Women should/should not expect pay equal to men's for the same work.
3. Students should/should not be required to take certain courses in order to graduate.

5m   How did one student draft and revise his argument essay?

In his first draft, Alex focused on how organic farming would benefit the environment, and he found lots of studies of how traditional farming practices affect water and soil quality. However, he realized that this argument alone might seem remote to many readers, so he explored how agricultural chemicals affect consumers. Extensive research resulted in a second draft that included concerns for individuals and society at large. Alex was surprised to encounter evidence that organic foods weren't necessarily more nutritious. Initially, he wanted just to ignore it, but then he decided his paper would be stronger if he dealt with this opposing viewpoint. His third draft, where he included it, was where he developed his introductory paragraph, which until this point he had just sketched generally. Throughout the process, he checked facts and sources in library databases. Before completing the paper, he looked carefully at his use *of pathos* and *ethos* and consulted the revision checklist (see Quick Reference 2.8). Finally, he referred to the special checklist for revising written arguments in Quick Reference 5.5.

QUICK REFERENCE   5.5

Revising written arguments

- Is the thesis statement about a debatable topic? (5c–d)
- Do the reasons or evidence support the thesis statement? Are the generalizations supported by specific details? (5d)
- Does the argument deal with readers' assumptions, needs, and concerns? (5i)
- Does the argument appeal chiefly to reason? Is it supported by an ethical appeal? If it uses an emotional appeal, is the appeal restrained? (5g)
- Is the tone reasonable? (5k)
- Is the opposing position stated and refuted? (5l)

EXERCISE 5-5   Working individually or with a peer-response group, choose a topic from this list. Then, plan an essay that argues a debatable position on the topic. Apply all the principles you've learned in this chapter.

1. animal experimentation
2. cloning of human beings
3. genetically modified foods
4. value of space exploration
5. French immersion

5n   Final draft of a student's argument essay in MLA style

Garcia 1

Alex Garcia

Professor Brosnahan

WRIT 1122

4 May 2013

Why Organic Foods Are Worth the Extra Money

A small decision confronts me every time I walk into the grocery store. I see a display of enticing apples for around $1.79 per pound. Next to them is a similar display of the same kind of apples, perhaps just a little smaller and just a little less perfect. These sell for $2.29 per pound. The difference between the two is the tiny sticker that reads "organic." Are those apples worth the extra money, especially when my budget is tight and the other ones appear just fine? Millions of shoppers face this same decision whenever they decide whether to buy organic food, and the right answer seems complicated, especially when the Canadian government makes no "specific claims about the health, safety and nutrition of such organic products" that meet its standards for labelling as organic (Canadian General Standards Board iv). However, current research shows that the health and environmental benefits of organic foods outweigh their extra costs.

Organic foods are produced without using most chemical pesticides, without artificial fertilizers, without genetic engineering, and without radiation. In the case of organic meat, poultry, eggs, and dairy products, the animals are normally raised without antibiotics and are not given growth hormones (Canadian General Standards Board 1-2, 12). As a result, people sometimes use the term "natural" instead of "organic," but "natural" is less precise. Until recently, people could never be quite

continued ➤   117

Garcia 2

sure what they were getting when they bought supposedly organic food, unless they bought it directly from a farmer they knew personally. The Canadian federal standards that food must meet in order to be labelled and sold as organic were established in 2006 and then amended in 2008.

According to environmental scientist Craig Minowa, organic foods tend to cost about 15% more than non-organic, mainly because they are currently more difficult to mass-produce. Farmers who apply pesticides often get larger crops from the same amount of land because there is less insect damage. Artificial fertilizers tend to increase the yield, size, and uniformity of fruits and vegetables, and herbicides kill weeds that compete with desirable crops for sun, nutrients, and moisture. Animals that routinely receive antibiotics and growth hormones tend to grow more quickly and produce more milk and eggs. In contrast, organic farmers have lower yields and, therefore, higher costs. These get passed along as higher prices to consumers.

Still, the extra cost is certainly worthwhile in terms of health benefits. Numerous studies have shown the dangers of pesticides for humans. An extensive review of research by the Ontario College of Family physicians concludes that "Exposure to all the commonly used pesticides . . . has shown positive associations with adverse health effects" (Sanborn et al. 173). The risks include cancer, psychiatric effects, difficulties becoming pregnant, miscarriages, and dermatitis. Carefully washing fruits and vegetables can remove some of these dangerous chemicals, but according to the prestigious journal *Nature*, even this does not remove all of them (Giles 797). Certainly, if there's a way to prevent these poisons from entering our bodies, we should take advantage of it. The few cents saved on cheaper food can quickly disappear in medical expenses for treating conditions caused or worsened by chemicals.

Organic meat, poultry, and dairy products can address another health concern: the diminishing effectiveness of antibiotics. In the past decades, many kinds of bacteria have become resistant to drugs, making it extremely difficult to treat some kinds of tuberculosis, pneumonia, staphylococcus infections, and less serious diseases ("Dangerous" 1). True, this has happened mainly because doctors have over-prescribed antibiotics to patients who expect a pill for every illness. However,

continued ➤

routinely giving antibiotics to all cows and chickens means that these drugs enter our food chain early, giving bacteria lots of chances to develop resistance. A person who switches to organic meats won't suddenly experience better results from antibiotics; the benefit is a more gradual one for society as a whole. However, if we want to be able to fight infections with effective drugs, we need to reserve antibiotics for true cases of need and discourage their routine use in animals raised for food. Buying organic is a way to persuade more farmers to adopt this practice.

Another benefit of organic foods is also a societal one: Organic farming is better for the environment. In his review of several studies, Colin Macilwain concluded that organic farms nurture more and diverse plants and animals than regular farms (797). Organic farms also don't release pesticides and herbicides that can harm wildlife and run into our water supply, with implications for people's health, too. Macilwain notes that those farms also can generate less carbon dioxide, which will help with global warming; also, many scientists believe that organic farming is more sustainable because it results in better soil quality (798). Once again, these benefits are not ones that you will personally experience right away. However, a better natural environment means a better quality of living for everyone and for future generations.

Some critics point out that organic products aren't more nutritious than regular ones. Physician Sanjay Gupta, for example, finds the medical evidence for nutritional advantages is "thin" (60). The *Tutts University Health and Nutrition Letter* also reports that the research on nutritional benefits is mixed, with one important study showing "no overall differences" ("Is Organic" 8). Nutritional value, which includes qualities such as vitamins and other beneficial substances, is a different measure than food safety. At this point, it seems that nutrition alone is not a sufficient reason to buy organic foods. Perhaps future research will prove otherwise; a 2007 study, for example, showed that organically raised tomatoes have higher levels of flavonoids, nutrients that appear to have many health benefits (Mitchell et al.). In the meantime, however, environmental quality and, most importantly, avoiding chemicals remain convincing reasons to purchase organic food, even if the same cannot yet be claimed for nutrition.

continued ➤   119

Garcia 4

Despite the considerable benefits for purchasing organic products, there remains each consumer's decision in the grocery store. Are the more expensive apples ultimately worth their extra cost to me? It's true that there are no easily measurable one-to-one benefits, no way to ensure that spending fifty cents more on this produce will directly improve my quality of life by fifty cents. However, countless people are rightly concerned these days about our personal health and the health of the world in which we live, and I am one of them. It's nearly impossible to put a value on a sustainable, diverse natural environment and having the physical health to enjoy it.

The long-term benefits of buying organic, for anyone who can reasonably afford to, far outweigh the short-term saving in the checkout line.

Garcia 5

Works Cited

Canada. Canadian General Standards Board. *Organic Production Systems—General Principles and Management Standards.* Gatineau: Canadian General Standards Board, Sept. 2006 (amended Oct. 2008). Web. 20 Jan. 2013.

"Dangerous Bacterial Infections Are on the Rise." *Consumer Reports on Health* Nov. 2007: 1-4. Print.

Giles, Jim. "Is Organic Food Better for Us?" *Nature* 428.6985 (2004): 796-97. Print.

Gupta, Sanjay, and Shahreen Abedin. "Rethinking Organics." *Time* 20 Aug. 2007: 60. Print.

"Is Organic Food Really More Nutritious?" *Tufts University Health and Nutrition Letter.* Tufts University, Sept. 2007: 8. Web. 25 Nov. 2012.

Macilwain, Colin. "Is Organic Farming Better for the Environment?" *Nature* 428.6985 (2004): 797-98. Print.

Minowa, Craig. Interview by Louise Druce. *FYI on Organics: Organic Q & A.* Organic Consumers Assn., 29 June 2004. Web. 30 June, 2013.

Mitchell, Alyson E., et al. "Ten-Year Comparison of the Influence of Organic and Conventional Crop Management Practices on the Content of Flavonoids in Tomatoes." *Journal of Agricultural Food Chemistry* 55.15 (2007): 6154-59. Web. 5 Feb. 2013.

Sanborn, Margaret, et al. *Pesticides Literature Review: Systematic Review of Pesticide Human Health Effects.* Toronto: Ontario College of Family Physicians, 2004. Web. 28 Nov. 2012.

Chapter 6

WRITING WITH OTHERS

6a What is writing with others?

A surprising amount of writing depends on two or more people working together. The other person could be a friend, a classmate, a co-worker, a writing tutor (in a campus writing centre), or an instructor whose comments on a draft guide your revision. In the professional world, a project manager or supervisor will frequently read your reports and proposals and ask you to make changes. Of course, you'll be making suggestions about other people's writings, too. Sections 6c and 6d explain how to give and receive help effectively.

A more direct kind of writing with others happens when two or more people **collaborate** to complete a single project. This handbook is a prime example. Lynn wrote some sections, and then Doug revised them—and vice versa. We planned the book over e-mail, in telephone calls, and in person. Drafts flew back and forth over the Internet. We also worked with editors who suggested—and sometimes required—revisions. Each of us brought different knowledge, experience, and talents.

Collaborative writing projects are extremely common in the business and professional world. Marketing managers, for example, lead teams who conduct consumer research and then—as a group—write up their findings. Often, the size or complexity of a project means that only a team of people can accomplish it. Different team members bring different skills and expertise. In these professional settings, group members must reach general agreement on how to proceed and contribute equally.

Collaborative writing assignments are increasingly popular in academic courses across the curriculum, especially in business, the sciences, and the social sciences (Figure 6.1). Even if they aren't required to write full papers, small groups are commonly asked to brainstorm a

Figure 6.1 A collaborative group at work

topic together before individual writing tasks, to discuss various sides of a debatable topic, or to share reactions to an essay or piece of literature the class reads, and so on.

Writing collaboratively enhances confidence when writers support one another. Experience in collaborative writing has benefits beyond your college or university years because working well with others is a skill that employers value.

ALERT: Some instructors and students use the terms *peer-response group* and *collaborative writing* to mean the same thing. In this handbook, we use *collaborative writing* (6b) for students writing an essay, a research paper, or a report together in a group. We use *peer-response group* (6c) for students getting together in small groups to help one another write and revise. ●

6b   How can I collaborate with other writers?

Three qualities are essential to collaborative writing. The first is careful planning. Your group needs to decide when and how it will meet; what steps it will follow and what the due dates will be; what software you'll use; and who will be responsible for what. Everyone in the group needs to commit to the plan, making changes only after deliberation by everyone.

The second essential quality is a fair division of labour. Almost nothing causes bad feelings more quickly than when some group members think they're doing more than their share. During early planning meetings, the group should figure out the tasks involved in the project and estimate how much time and effort each will take. (You can rebalance things during later meetings, if necessary.)

One basic way a group can divide tasks is according to the different steps in the writing process. One or more people can be in charge of generating ideas or conducting research; one or more can be in charge of writing the first draft; one or more can be in charge of revising; and one or more may be in charge of editing, proofreading, and formatting the final draft. It's hard to separate these tasks cleanly, however, and we warn that writing the first draft often requires more effort than any other element. This approach also means that some group members will be waiting for others to complete their parts.

A second way to divide tasks is to assign part of the project to each person. Many projects can be broken into sections, and using an outline (2f) can help you see what those sections are. Each person can then plan, write, revise, and edit a section, and the other members can serve as a peer-response group to make suggestions for revision. This approach can have the advantage of distributing the work more cleanly at the outset, but it often takes a lot of work at the end to stitch the parts together and to complete the final editing.

You'll probably find your group using a combination of these two approaches. You'll also probably find it useful to assign people basic roles such as leader (or facilitator) and recorder (or secretary). These roles can change during the project, but in our experience, groups find it efficient when someone takes responsibility for calling and leading meetings.

The third essential element of collaborative projects is clear communication. Open and honest communication is vital, and people need to put aside their own egos to build a productive and trusting atmosphere. Keep notes for every meeting so that the group has a clear record of what was decided; one way to do this is to have someone send an e-mail summarizing each meeting. The group should resolve any disagreements before moving on. You'll also find it effective to ask for regular reports from each group member. These don't have to be long—a few sentences will do it—but they keep everyone informed about others' progress, and they keep you on track, too.

Guidelines for collaborative writing

STARTING

1. Learn each other's names and exchange e-mail addresses and phone numbers so that everyone can stay in touch outside of class.

2. Participate actively in the group process. During discussions, help set a tone that encourages everyone to participate by including people who don't like to interrupt, who want time to think before they talk, or who are shy. Conversely, help the group set limits if someone dominates the discussions or makes all the decisions. If you lack experience contributing in a group setting, think about how you can take an active role.

3. As a group, assign everyone work to be done between meetings. Distribute the responsibilities as fairly as possible. Also, decide whether to choose one discussion leader or to rotate leadership, unless your instructor assigns a particular procedure.

4. Make decisions regarding the technology you'll use. If everyone can use the same word-processing program, for example, that will make sharing drafts or parts of drafts much easier. If not, you can use the "Save As" function in major word-processing programs to save files in a common format. Decide if you'll share materials via e-mail attachments, CDs, flash drives, a server, or even through a WIKI (46f). If any group members are unfamiliar with these processes, others need to help them learn. (Different areas and levels of expertise are an advantage of working in groups.)

5. Set a timeline and deadlines for the project. Agree on what to do in the event that someone misses a deadline.

PLANNING

6. After discussing the project, brainstorm as a group or use structured techniques for discovering and compiling ideas.

7. Together, agree on the ideas that seem best and allow for a period of INCUBATION, if time permits. Then, discuss your group choices again.

8. As a group, divide the project into parts and distribute assignments fairly. For example, if the project requires research, decide who will do it and how they'll share their findings with others. If one person is going to be responsible for preparing drafts from pieces that others have written, make sure his or her other responsibilities are balanced.

9. As a group, OUTLINE or otherwise sketch an overview of the project to get a preliminary idea of how best to use material contributed by individuals.

10. As you work on your part of the project, take notes in preparation for giving your group a progress report.

continued ➤

DRAFTING

11. Draft a THESIS STATEMENT that sets the direction for that the rest of the paper. The group needs to agree on one version before getting too far into the draft. Your group might revise the thesis statement after the whole paper has been drafted, but using a preliminary version gets everyone started in the same direction.

12. Draft the rest of the paper. Decide whether each member of the group should write a complete draft or one part of the whole. For example, each group member might take one main idea and be responsible for drafting that section. Share draft materials among the group members electronically (see step 4). If this is impossible, make photocopies. For most group meetings, it will be important to have a paper copy of group materials, so print (or photocopy) copies for everyone.

REVISING

13. Read over the drafts. Are all the important points included?

14. Use the revision checklist (Quick Reference 2.8) and work either as a group or by assigning portions to subgroups. If different people have drafted different sections, COHERENCE and UNITY should receive special attention in revision, as should the introduction and the conclusion.

15. Agree on a final version. Either work as a group, or assign someone to prepare the final draft and make sure every group member has a copy.

EDITING AND PROOFREADING THE WRITING

16. Use the editing checklist (Quick Reference 2.9) to double-check for errors. If you find errors, correct them and print out the page or the whole draft again. No matter how well the group has worked collaboratively and written the paper, a sloppy final version reflects negatively on the entire group.

17. As a group, review printouts or photocopies of the final draft. Don't leave the last stages to a subgroup. Draw on everyone's knowledge of grammar, spelling, and punctuation. Use everyone's eyes for proofreading.

18. If your instructor asks, be prepared to describe your personal contribution to the project and to describe or evaluate the contributions of others.

EXERCISE 6-1   Working in a small group, plan how your group would proceed on one or more of the following collaborative projects, satisfying each of the three essential criteria for group work. (*Note:* You don't actually have to complete the project; the purpose of this exercise is to develop your planning skills.)

*   A report for a public audience in which you evaluate smartphones.
*   A research project in which you analyze the political views of students on your campus.
*   A persuasive paper in which you argue whether Canada should pass laws to make it harder for Canadian companies to move jobs to other countries.

Be prepared to explain your thoughtful and thorough planning to your instructor or to class members.

6c How can I give useful feedback to others?

There are two main ways to give feedback to other writers. One is in a small group, usually three to five people, who together discuss each group member's draft out loud. Another way is to work in pairs, providing oral or, more often, written comments for each other.

Office Hours: Peer Review, Part 1

Office Hours: Peer Review, Part 2

6c.1 Working in peer-response groups

In some writing classes, instructors divide students into PEER-RESPONSE GROUPS. A peer is an "equal": another writer like you. Participating in a peer-response group makes you part of a respected tradition of colleagues helping colleagues. Professional writers often seek comments from other writers to improve their rough drafts. As a member of a peer-response group, you're not expected to be a writing expert. Rather, you're expected to offer responses as a practised reader and as a fellow student writer who understands what writers go through.

ALERT: Some instructors use the term *workshopping* for peer response. The term comes from creative-writing programs, sometimes called "writers' workshops," where the main learning strategy is to have students discuss each others' work in progress. ●

The role of peer-response group members is to react and discuss, not to do the work for someone. Hearing or reading comments from your peers might be a new experience, one you may find surprising, as well as informative and helpful. When peers share their writing, group members get the added advantage of learning other students' approaches to writing the same assignment.

Peer-response groups are set up in different ways. One arrangement calls for students to pass around and read one another's drafts silently, writing down reactions or questions in the margins or on a response form created by the instructor. Figure 6.2 shows an example of a response form. In another arrangement, students read their drafts aloud, and then each peer responds either orally or in writing on a response form. Yet another arrangement asks for focused responses to only one or two features of each draft (perhaps each member's thesis statement, or topic sentences and supporting details, or use of transitional words, for example).

Whatever the arrangement of your group, you want to be clear about exactly what you are expected to do, both as a peer-responder and as a writer. If your instructor gives you guidelines for working in a group, follow them carefully. If you've never before participated in a peer-response group, or in the particular kind of group that your instructor forms, consult the guidelines in Quick Reference 6.2; watch what experienced peers do; and ask your instructor questions (your interest shows a positive, cooperative attitude). Otherwise, just dive in knowing that you'll learn as you go.

6c.2 Giving a peer response as an individual

Often an instructor will have two people exchange drafts and provide responses and suggestions to each other. All of the general guidelines for peer response in groups apply to situations when you're the only person giving feedback, especially being helpful, specific, and polite.

You might find it useful to play a role if you feel awkward about making suggestions to a classmate—especially if you think that some critical comments will help revision.

Peer Response Questions and Directions

Reviewer's name: _____

Writer's name: _____

*Directions to **Writer**: Please choose three questions you'd like the reviewer to address. Circle them.*

*Directions to **Reviewer**: Please read the work and provide clear and detailed answers to each of the THREE questions to which the writer has asked you to respond. Continue on the back, if needed. After you've completed this, talk about your answers with the writer. Then write up a half-page synthesis and suggested plan for further action.*

1. **How can this writer make the central argument of this essay stronger, clearer, or more easily accessible to readers?**

2. **Identify any paragraphs whose purpose is unclear or that seem to be working at cross purposes, and explain how the writer can revise them to make the purpose clear.**

3. **Does the sequence of the argument build successfully? If not, suggest a way to reorder it and identify transitions that may need clarifying.**

4. Writers can offer their readers guidance in a number of ways, (clearly defining their terms, explaining exactly how the evidence supports their claims, etc.). **Identify places in this essay where these forms of guidance could be stronger, and explain specifically how the writer can strengthen them.**

5. **Are there places in which you feel the textures or structures of language are serving the writer's purpose effectively? Are there places in which the language could be modified?**

Figure 6.2 A peer-response form

(Instructors sometimes even assign such roles.) For example, instead of responding as yourself, pretend that you're a skeptical member of the writer's target audience. Respond as that person would, even in his or her voice. Separating your own personality from your responses can provide useful distance. Of course, you could also take the opposite role, responding as a friendly audience member who agrees with the writer; assuming that role can be particularly helpful if you personally disagree with a draft's position. If you're playing a role as you respond, you should make that clear to the writer by explaining, for example, that you're "playing devil's advocate," a person who is disagreeing on purpose in order to test and, ultimately, strengthen the writer's position.

Guidelines for participating in peer-response groups

One major principle needs to guide your participation in a peer-response group: Always take an upbeat, constructive attitude, whether you're responding to someone else's writing or receiving responses from others.

- Think of yourself as a coach, not a judge.
- Consider all writing by your peers as "works in progress."
- After hearing or reading a peer's writing, briefly summarize it to check that you and your peer agree on what the peer said or meant to say.
- Start with what you think is well done. No one likes to hear only negative comments.
- Be honest in your suggestions for improvement.
- Base your responses on an understanding of the writing process, and remember that you're reading drafts, not finished products. All writing can be revised.
- Give concrete and specific responses. General comments such as "This is good" or "This is weak" don't offer much help. Describe specifically what is good or weak.
- Follow your instructor's system for putting your comments in writing so that your fellow writer can recall what you said. If one member of your group is supposed to take notes, speak clearly so that the person can take accurate notes. If you're the note taker, be accurate and ask the speaker to repeat what he or she said if the comment went by too quickly.

As with group peer response, your instructor may have you use a response form or follow a set of questions. (See Figure 6.2.) Here are some other questions you might find useful:

- What part of the paper was most interesting or effective?
- If you had to remove one paragraph, which would you sacrifice and why?
- If you had to rearrange two parts of the paper, which would you change and why?
- What one additional fact, argument, or piece of information might improve the paper?

Another good strategy is for the writer to generate a couple of questions that he or she would particularly like the reviewer to answer. Avoid questions that require only a *yes* or *no* response. Instead of answering specific questions, the instructor might ask you simply to write a letter to the author about the strengths and weaknesses of the draft. Peer response can take practice to do well. Our students have found that if they're thoughtful while writing open responses to others, they get useful responses in return. Figure 6.3 on p. 128 shows an example of one student's peer response to another.

EXERCISE 6-2

1. Choose a paper that you're writing (or have written). Create a set of questions that you would ask a peer reviewer to answer.
2. Show your questions to someone else in your class. Ask that person to comment on how effective those questions would be for generating constructive comments; let your reviewer know that he or she may also suggest additional questions.

Directions. I'll pair you up with another student. Your task is to write a letter in which you play the role of someone who disagrees with the author of the paper; explain as carefully as you can why you disagree. State your own arguments and explain why they lead to a different conclusion. Now, I want you to be polite about this; don't indulge in the extreme language we looked at earlier in the course. However, to be helpful to the author you should be as persuasive as possible—even if you're playing a role that you actually disagree with. Send this letter by e-mail, with a copy to me (dhesse@du.edu).

Dear Leslie,

    To begin with I thought your paper was very thorough and well thought out. It was lengthy and covered all the important things you needed to. But as I've been asked to take the role of someone who disagrees, then offer constructive criticism, there are some things that I think would help clarify and convince your readers who are on the fence about your position.

    Your argument is that sex education in schools needs to be complete and that "abstinence only" education is inadequate. You use a lot of statistics and surveys. This is good, it added credibility and scientific reasoning, but when I see these, I wonder where you found these studies and whether they are themselves factual. You reiterated multiple times that abstinence-only educators use statistics that are untrue or slanted to favour their position. How does the reader know that you haven't made your own facts up or slanted them in your favour? My suggestion would be to label your studies and discuss where they came from and why they're credible. If one of them is from a government agency, you can include the address so the reader could verify the facts. I'm not accusing you of doing this, but it would only make your paper more believable.

    Because I am a strong believer in no sex before marriage, I worry about giving students too much information. I think that sex before marriage causes more problems than it solves. I do believe that giving out specific advice about contraception can encourage people to engage in sex before they are ready. Instead we should encourage students to wait. Can you prove to me that having information doesn't lead to early sexual activity?

    You stated on page two that a study found that consensual sex between two teenagers had no mental health effects on them. I disagree with this finding. Regardless of age and relationship status of the two parties involved, someone often gets hurt by casual sex. If there was a relationship before, it has the potential to be destroyed due to the new baggage. If one of the parties involved uses it as a one night stand and the other person really liked the other, he or she suffers emotional distress that could be extreme. Actually, I'm not sure this point belongs in your paper; because it's controversial, I wonder if your paper would be stronger without it.

                        Sincerely,
                        Stephen

Figure 6.3   An example of one student's peer response

6d   How can I benefit from others' help?

Turning to the sometimes sticky issue of how to accept criticism of your writing, we offer you two pieces of personal advice from our own experience.

First, keep in mind that most students don't like to criticize their peers. They worry about being impolite or inaccurate, or losing someone's friendship. Try, therefore, to cultivate an attitude that encourages your peers to respond as freely and as helpfully as possible. It's important to show that you can listen without getting angry or feeling intruded on.

Second, realize that most people tend to be at least a little defensive about even the best-intentioned and most tactful criticism. Of course, if a comment is purposely mean or sarcastic, you and all the others in your peer-response group have every right to say so, and to not tolerate such comments.

ESL TIP: Students from cultures other than those in Canada or the United States might feel uncomfortable in the role of critic. Please know, however, that peer-response groups are fairly common in schools and at jobs because people usually think that "two heads are better than one." Sharing and questioning others' ideas—as well as how they are expressed in writing—is an honourable tradition in Canada and the United States. Peer-response groups help writers politely but firmly explore concepts and language, so please feel free to participate fully. In fact, some instructors grade you on your open participation in such activities. ●

Making good use of peers' comments

Adopt an attitude that encourages your peers to respond freely. Listen and resist any urge to interrupt during a comment. A common rule in many writing workshops is that the paper's author must remain silent until the group has finished its discussion. (It's actually useful to hear people misinterpreting what you thought you said or meant.)

Remain open-minded. Your peers' comments can help you see your writing in a fresh way, which can help you improve your next draft.

Ask for clarification if a comment isn't clear. If a comment is too general, ask for specifics.

Finally, no matter what anyone says about your writing, it remains yours alone. You retain "ownership" of your writing always, and you don't have to make every suggested change. Use only the comments that you think can move you closer to reaching your intended audience and purpose. Of course, if a comment from your instructor points out a definite problem, and you choose to ignore it, that could have an impact on your grade—though many instructors are open to an explanation of your rationale for deciding to ignore what they said.

6e How can I participate effectively in online discussions?

You might take a course that happens entirely online, where discussion happens through typed remarks via e-mail or a program like Blackboard. However, even courses that meet in traditional classrooms often have an online written component. Contributing to the discussion between class meetings makes you an active learner, allows the instructor to gauge the level of your understanding, and enriches the class by circulating a diversity of opinions.

There are two kinds of online discussions. In **synchronous** discussions, all the participants are online at the same time. The discussions are scheduled in advance and everyone meets online in "real time" for a specific amount of time. Instant messaging is an example of synchronous discussion. In **asynchronous** discussions, participants are online at different times. The discussion is usually open for hours or days, and there may be long periods of time between individual messages.

Whether you're in a completely online course environment or in an enhanced traditional classroom, being prepared for a few key things will help you participate effectively. First, your instructor may post a question and require everyone to respond to it, at least once. Also, your instructor may provide additional directions about the length or content of your posting or about its timing. (For example, he or she might say, "By midnight on Tuesday, post your answer to the discussion question.") Finally, your instructor might give directions about responding to something that others have posted in the discussion. Quick Reference 6.4 contains some additional guidelines about online discussions.

((•
AUDIO LESSON
Section 1:
Big Ideas–
Electronic
Rhetoric

((•
AUDIO LESSON
Section 2:
Practice
Questions–
Electronic
Rhetoric

((•
AUDIO LESSON
Section 3:
Rapid
Review–
Electronic
Rhetoric

Guidelines for online discussions

- Unless specifically instructed to do otherwise, write in complete sentences and paragraphs. Academic discussions are more formal than e-mails or text messages between friends, so don't use the kind of shorthand you might use in those situations.

- Provide a context for your remarks. You might begin your message by summarizing a point from a reading before giving your opinion. Your contribution should be able to stand on its own; otherwise, it should clearly connect to the rest of the conversation.

- Respond to other writers. If someone makes a particularly good point, say so—and explain why. If you disagree with someone, politely explain why you disagree and be sure to support your reasoning. Discussions work better when people are actually discussing, and not just speaking while ignoring their audience.

- Be polite and work for the good of the discussion. When people aren't meeting face to face, they can be rude—sometimes even when they don't mean to be. You have to work extra hard to make sure that your TONE is constructive and helpful.

Chapter 7

STRATEGIES FOR WRITING TYPICAL KINDS OF ACADEMIC PAPERS

7a What are typical kinds of papers I'll write in my courses?

Arguments and research papers are two of the most common types of academic writing. In a written argument you try to persuade readers to take an action, adopt a position, or see a viewpoint as legitimate. Research papers (sometimes called term papers or seminar papers) involve gathering information from several sources, which you then summarize, analyze, and synthesize. We devote all of Chapter 5 to arguments. In addition, since there are many elements in writing a research paper, we devote Chapters 32 through 38 to this kind of writing.

Expecting one set of guidelines to be perfect for every single variety of writing would be unrealistic. Analyzing the WRITING SITUATION (Chapter 1) and understanding the WRITING PROCESS (Chapter 2) are important and useful for all writing. But we've found that general advice is even more helpful when combined with strategies for writing particular types of papers. Explaining the most common ones is our purpose in this chapter.

Consider the following writing assignments you might get:

- A lengthy library research paper
- A summary of a reading
- A report on a laboratory experiment
- A proposal
- A personal essay
- An essay exam
- A critical response to a reading

These types of writing obviously differ in terms of length, PURPOSE, CONTEXT, and special considerations. But notice how each type also uses different SOURCES, how the writer's ROLE changes (for example, from an impartial observer to the centre of attention whose experience and personality are explored), and how format and style can vary. Knowing a few strategies will help you with different kinds of writing.

🔊 **ALERT:** Terms that describe different types of writing are often used interchangeably. Most instructors attach specific meanings to each one. If your instructor's use of terms isn't clear, ask for clarification. For example, the words *essay, theme,* and *composition* usually—but not always—refer to written works of about 500 to 1500 words. *Essay* is probably the most common. Similarly, the word *paper* can mean anything from a few paragraphs to a complex research project; it often refers to longer works. ●

((•
AUDIO LESSON
Section 1:
Big Ideas–
Writing
Successfully
in Other
Courses

((•
AUDIO LESSON
Section 2:
Practice
Questions–
Writing
Successfully
in Other
Courses

((•
AUDIO LESSON
Section 3:
Rapid
Review–
Writing
Successfully
in Other
Courses

((•

AUDIO
LESSON
Section 1:
Big Ideas–
Researching
Your Topic

((•

AUDIO
LESSON
Section 2:
Practice
Questions–
Researching
Your Topic

((•

AUDIO
LESSON
Section 3:
Rapid
Review–
Researching
Your Topic

7b What sources will I use in academic writing?

A **source** is any form of information that provides ideas, examples, information, or evidence. Commonly, people think of readings (books, articles, websites, and so on) when they think of sources. We devote most of Chapter 32 to finding and using written sources, and we spend all of Chapters 36 through 38 explaining how to document them. Section 7f provides strategies for making thorough use of readings.

There are other kinds of sources, too. Your own memories and experiences are a source, even though you may not think of them that way. Some academic situations allow or even require personal experiences. As with every assignment, check with your instructor. You'll find more about writing from experiences in 7c.

Another kind of source is direct observation. For example, you might be asked to observe people in a particular setting, take notes on their behaviour, and write a paper that explains what you've seen. You might be asked to attend a lecture and summarize what the speaker had to say or, additionally, to write a reaction to it. You might be asked to gather instances of a particular social or cultural phenomenon and explore the meaning of that phenomenon. For example, an assignment that asks you to analyze how adolescents are portrayed in current television programs would require you carefully to observe several television shows, take notes, and explain your findings. We explain some types of writing about observations in 7d.

Statistical or quantitative information is another kind of source. Statistical or quantitative information comes to us in the form of raw numbers ("217 people admitted to jaywalking"), percentages ("14 percent admitted to jaywalking"), or other statistics. You might find this information in a published written source: a table of information that reports results from a survey or measurements from a laboratory study. Alternatively, you may be collecting the data yourself. Laboratory courses typically have students perform experiments, make careful measurements, and report their findings. Business, education, or social science courses often have students conduct surveys or interviews. We discuss writing about statistical or quantitative information in 7e.

Finally, we note that many assignments mix sources. You might be asked to relate one of your experiences to a written account of someone else's. You might do a study (for example, of public displays of affection) that combines direct observations with a survey. We've explained these types separately to make them clearer.

EXERCISE 7-1 Working alone or in a group, discuss the kinds of sources you might use in each of the following writing questions.

1. Scholar Kyung Kim offers three suggestions for improving high schools. Would her suggestions have worked at the high school you attended?

2. Are most students at your school liberal or conservative? What about students around the country?

3. What qualities generally seem true of romantic comedy movies that have been released in the past year?

7c How can I write about experiences?

Some writing assignments may ask you to write about your memories or experiences. Generally, such writings will involve telling a story, often accompanied by reflection or analysis.

7c.1 Memoirs and personal essays

In *memoirs,* writers tell what they remember about something that happened to them. While memoirs, like autobiographies, can cover most of a person's life, they often focus on a particular incident or a few related incidents.

Students often think that, unless something important has happened to them, their lives aren't worth writing about. Nothing could be further from the truth. What makes a memoir good is less *what* it's about than *how* the writer writes about it. Consider the following short example.

> I can remember my father driving our car through the Alberta Badlands one summer. The hood of the car baked in the hot sun as we looked out the window at the sandy hills and cliff formations.

There's nothing very interesting here, just some facts and a bare description. But consider this version:

> After a brief pause, my father carefully unfolded his sunglasses and wrapped them around his ears. The white Ford growled on the gravel shoulder and the air-conditioning unit began to whine. Soon both the tires and the air-conditioner were humming quietly as we picked up speed on the smooth pavement. Dead ahead of us, a crack opened in the flat prairie. The road swerved as we dipped into the gorge that the river had made, with sun and shade playing along the sides. The Badlands! Hills and crazy cliffs stood layered in browns and sun-drenched yellows like a chocolate mocha cake made out of sand. I shaded my eyes with my hand when we took a sudden turn, because the Ford's hood was now reflecting the white-hot sun through the windshield. As I turned my head to escape the glare, I saw the dark ribbon of the Red Deer River at the bottom of the valley. We'd soon be in Drumheller.

The basic information is no more dramatic than the first version we shared. However, the careful description makes it interesting. The main purpose of a memoir is to create a vivid sense of the experience for its readers. Memoirs have an expressive or literary purpose.

Personal essays are closely related to memoirs (in fact, your instructor may use the terms interchangeably). Once again, you'll want to tell about an experience. Personal essays tend to contain more reflection and to make their points more explicitly. They answer the question, "What does this experience mean?" or "How does my experience illustrate a particular idea?"

Important Elements of Memoirs and Personal Essays

- A well-told story. Your readers will want to know what happened. They will also want enough background information and context to understand and appreciate what happened and why it made an impression.
- Lively details. Help your readers see and hear, perhaps even smell, taste, and feel what you were experiencing. Recreate the place and time, the people who were involved. Give readers reason to like (or dislike) the places or people involved by the way you characterize them.
- Reflective or analytic paragraphs or passages. In addition to telling readers what happened, also tell them what you were thinking (take us inside your head at the time) or what you make of it now, looking backward.
- An effective use of style and TONE (Chapter 8).

AUDIO LESSON Section 1: Big Ideas– Using Language Well and Addressing Your Audience

Office Hours: Prewriting

Advice on Process

1. Generating
   - In your first draft, concentrate on getting the basic story down. Pretend you're writing to a friend who is interested in what you're saying.
   - Try creating some detailed scenes, describing the physical setting and including some dialogue so readers will get a sense of being there.
   - Do some FREEWRITING or use other invention strategies to explore the significance of your story. What did you learn at the time? How about looking back now? How does the experience connect to other experiences, readings, or things you've noticed in the world around you (in movies or books, for example, or at work, in school, or in family life)?

2. Shaping
   - The basic shape of a memoir is a story; however, it will also likely have some commentary or reflection (when you step back and explain what it all means). You can put that reflection at the beginning, in the middle, or at the end, or you can scatter it throughout the piece. Choose the strategy that seems most effective.
   - You can begin at the beginning of the story, but you can also begin with some exciting or interesting part from the middle or the end, then go back to the beginning to tell how it all started. You've probably seen movies that have flashbacks, which are examples of this technique.
   - Try to have places in your story where you slow down, creating a scene in detail, as well as where you speed up, covering events quickly so you can get to the interesting stuff.

3. Revising
   - Do your story and its details convey your impression of the experience? A common piece of advice is to "show, not tell." Try this experiment. Temporarily leave out any explicit statements about the story and what it means, and show the draft to a friend or peer. Let that person tell you the point or meaning. If the reader can't—or if the interpretation differs significantly from yours—you need to revise. Put the explicit statements back in for your final draft.
   - Are there places where you need more specific detail?
   - Are there places where the writing drags and needs to be cut?
   - Are the reflective or analytic parts thoughtful and interesting, or are they formulaic or obvious?

7c.2 Literacy narratives

A literacy narrative is a specific kind of memoir in which you tell the story of how you developed as a reader and writer. Generally, these stories stretch from your earliest memories to the present day. First-year writing instructors sometimes assign literacy narratives, as do some education or social sciences instructors.

Important Elements of Literacy Narratives

- The same elements that are important to memoirs and personal essays: a good story, lively details, and reflection.
- Examples of your previous reading, writing, or other language experiences. These may include book titles, papers you have written, people important in your development as a reader and writer, scenes from school or home, and so on.

Advice on Process

1. Generating and drafting (questions to help you generate ideas)
   - What are the earliest books or stories you can remember someone reading to you? The earliest you can remember reading yourself? Can you tell us about more than the titles? Why do you think you remember them?
   - If people read to you, what do you remember about them? Can you create a word picture of them?
   - Where did you read or write at different points in your life? Can you describe the settings vividly?
   - What were your favourite books? What topics did you like to read about? What particular works do you remember?
   - What were your worst experiences reading or writing? What made them bad?
   - Who or what were the strongest influences on your reading or writing—either for good or ill?
   - How did reading and writing fit in (or not) with other activities in your life?
   - Why do you think you became the type of reader and writer you are today?

2. Shaping
   The strategies for shaping literacy narratives are the same as those for shaping memoirs and personal essays.

3. Revising and editing (questions to ask yourself, or to have a peer-response group ask [6c.1], when you revise)
   - Do all the incidents contribute effectively to the whole narrative? Are there any that need to be cut or shortened?
   - Are there places that would be stronger if you created a more vivid scene?
   - Are there smooth connections and transitions between the different elements?
   - Have you reflected on the meaning of the experiences? Have you included general observations on what your experiences add up to and tell about yourself as a reader and writer?

EXERCISE 7-2

1. Write a memoir about a trip you took, whether it was across town or across the country. The quality of your writing is more important than how unusual the trip was.

2. Write a section of a literacy narrative focusing on one of three periods in your life: birth to age 9; age 10 to 15; age 16 to the present.

7d How can I write about observations?

Writing about observations means writing about things you directly and intentionally see or experience. *Intentionally* is the important word. Sometimes you write about things that you just happened to notice or experience. However, in academic writing situations, observations are almost always purposeful and deliberate. You observe as a writer with a specific goal.

AUDIO
LESSON
Section 1:
Big Ideas–
Becoming a
Critical
Reader and a
Better Writer

7d.1 Reports of observations

Sometimes your assignment is to report about an event. You're asked to attend a presentation or lecture and summarize the talk. You go to a concert, play, or sporting event with the goal of explaining what happened. In these writing situations, your purpose is to inform,

((•
AUDIO
LESSON
Section 2:
Practice
Questions–
Becoming a
Critical
Reader and a
Better Writer

and your role is to be an objective reporter, much like a journalist. Other times you may be asked to describe a scene (a landscape, a theatre set, a classroom), a person, a process, an object (a sculpture, a building, a machine), or an image. We devote a separate section (4j) to viewing and analyzing images.

Important Elements of a Report

- A clear description of what you observed, complete and appropriately detailed—but not excessively detailed.
- Objectivity.
- The proper format that your instructor requires.

Advice on Process

1. Generating and drafting
   - Take careful notes. The quality of your report will depend on its clear and complete details.
   - If you're writing about an event, gather information needed to answer the JOURNALIST'S QUESTIONS (see 2c.4). Write your first draft as soon after the event as possible, while your notes are still fresh.
   - Ask questions, if possible, not only of speakers or performers but also of other people attending the event. Ask what they observed.
   - Be precise with descriptions, noting both major and seemingly minor details.

2. Shaping
   - Orient your readers in the first paragraph. Provide all of the general information (who, what, when, where, how, and why) in your opening.
   - Provide details in body paragraphs. You can organize events or processes either by chronological order (the sequence in which things happened) or by categories or topics.
   - Organize reports about objects by giving a big picture, and then moving either spatially (left to right, top to bottom, centre to edge) or by features to enhance the description.

3. Revising (questions to ask yourself or to have peers answer)
   - Have you maintained objectivity throughout? Would your report agree with the report of someone else writing about the same thing?
   - Did you write an introduction that gives readers a good overall picture?
   - Would everything be clear to an audience who hadn't observed what you did?
   - Are there any places where you either need more detail or need to make the report more concise?
   - Have you fulfilled all of the assignment's special considerations?

7d.2 Reviews or evaluations

A *review* is a report plus an evaluation: a reasoned judgment of whether something is good or bad, fair or unfair, true or false, effective or useless. You're familiar with movie, music, and product reviews, which are designed to help you decide whether to invest your time, attention, or money. Reviews in academic situations show how thoughtfully you can evaluate a presentation, performance, product, event, artwork, or some other object.

Important Elements of Reviews

- Both a summary or description and one or more evaluations of the source's quality or significance. Your thesis takes the form of an evaluation.
- Reasons for your evaluation and evidence for those reasons.
- Answers to any specific questions your instructor asks. Be sure to follow any special considerations of the assignment.

Advice on Process

1. Generating and drafting
   - The advice for reporting applies. In addition, you need to generate an assessment. This involves critical thinking (Chapter 4).
   - Analyze the source, using strategies in 4d. Pay attention to both content and style.
   - Synthesize, if appropriate. How does the source relate to others like it?
2. Shaping
   - Provide an overview of the event and your thesis in the opening paragraph.
   - Summarize the source in the early part of the paper (a paragraph or two after your opening) so your audience understands it. Depending on the type of source you're writing about, this could include a summary of the plot, a description of the setting, a list of songs performed, a physical description of an image or object, or so on.
   - In each of your remaining body paragraphs, start with a topic sentence that makes an assertion about some feature, followed by an explanation or evidence. You may want to save details from your summary/description to include when you discuss particular features.
3. Revising and editing
   - Is the basic information clear?
   - Have you made judgments?
   - Have you provided enough details and evidence to make your judgments convincing?

7d.3   Interpretations

An interpretation makes an argument about what something means or why it's significant. You might be familiar with interpretations from studying fiction or poetry; we talk more about that kind of writing in 7f and Chapter 40. However, interpretation is hardly restricted to readings. Consider the following different assignment questions:

- In the painting *Guernica*, what do you think Picasso wants his viewers to feel and understand?
- What is the atmosphere of a particular place (a coffee shop, a shopping mall, a club)?
- How are doctors and nurses portrayed on television?

Each of these examples involves both description and interpretation. When you're doing an interpretation, don't feel like you have to guess the "right answer," as if there's one and only one right meaning. Instead, the quality of your work will depend on generating interesting insights that you then support with reasons. Analysis (4d) and inference (4e) are especially important for interpretation.

Important Elements of an Interpretation

- A clear explanation of the event, phenomenon, or object that you're interpreting.
- Statements about what the subject of your interpretation means or why it's significant.
- Convincing support, including reasoning, to show why your interpretive statements are convincing.

Advice on Process

1. Generating
   - Summarize and describe very carefully; the act of paying close attention can generate insights.
   - Use strategies of analysis. In particular, see the strategies in 4d.
   - Use strategies of inference. In particular, see the strategies in 4e.
   - Don't be afraid to explore. Brainstorm as many possible interpretations as you can; many of them might be outlandish, but it's better to choose from several possible interpretations than to be stuck with the first thing that comes to mind.
   - Play "the believing game." Believe that you have the authority and expertise to generate an interpretation and boldly put it on paper.

2. Shaping
   - Good interpretations have a thesis that states the meaning or significance that your paper will then go on to explain.
   - Body paragraphs will each offer an explanation for your interpretation, with support and reasoning showing readers why it is plausible.

3. Revising
   - Play "the doubting game." Assume (for the purpose of thinking critically) that your interpretation is flawed. State the flaws. Then revise to address them.
   - Ask whether the balance of summary and interpretation is effective. Are there places where you need more reasoning or support?

7d.4   Case Studies

Some **case studies** are careful descriptions and interpretations of individuals, usually focusing on some set of features in relation to a specific situation or issue (for example, "students who work in fast food" or "parents coping with divorce"). The word *case* might suggest a hospital case to be solved, and indeed medical journals publish these kinds of cases; however, *case* also has a more neutral sense of an "instance," and people in case studies usually don't have anything wrong with them, physically or otherwise.

Case studies are important in psychology, social work, education, medicine, and similar fields in which it's useful to form a comprehensive portrait of people in order to understand them and, in some cases, to help them. In some fields, such as education, people do case studies in order to understand or test theories and practices.

Case studies can also lead to theories or other kinds of research. For example, if you wondered about what factors make people happy at their jobs, you might do a case study (or two or three) of individual workers to generate possible criteria. People about whom you write case studies are called **subjects**. A kind of writing related to a case study is a **profile**, in which you create a portrait in words of a person.

Important Elements of Case Studies of Individuals

- A combination of observation, interview, and discussion of any artifacts you might have from your subject (writings, test results, creative works, and so on).
- A focus on particular traits important to the purpose of the study.
- A combination of report and interpretation or analysis.
- Depending on the type of case study and its purpose, recommendations for a course of action, a discussion of implications, or a commentary on a theory. (For this last, also see 7f.5.)

Advice on Process

1. Generating
   - Arrange to meet or observe the subject of your case study or profile. Take notes about the meeting, focusing on characteristics, mannerisms, and perhaps interactions with others.
   - Conduct one or more interviews, following our guidelines in Quick Reference 32.1.
   - Look for patterns in your notes. Use mapping (clustering) to group similar ideas (2c.5). Give each idea a paragraph or two, stating the idea as a topic sentence, and then using details from your notes to support your observations.

2. Shaping
   - Learn whether you're to follow a standard report format (see, e.g., 7e.3).
   - Use the opening to introduce your subject, explain your purpose for studying him or her, and present a thesis that states your main finding, interpretation, or impression.
   - Organize the following paragraphs by qualities you recognized in your subject, for example, by aspects of her or his personality, behaviour, attitudes, or interactions. In each case try to explain why your subject has those qualities.

3. Revising
   - Will your readers get a complete and accurate sense of this person?
   - Are there any places where your information is "thin," where you made an interpretation but didn't back it up?
   - Have you included interpretation, explaining the reasons for what you observed? If so, have you fully justified your conclusions?
   - Is your tone respectful and fair?

7d.5   Ethnographies

The term *case studies* also refers to a kind of research about a particular group of people or situation (consider studies of online video game players, of varsity hockey players and their study habits, of a store's marketing strategy, and so forth). They are closely related to **ethnographies**, another form of FIELD RESEARCH (32c), in that both generally are comprehensive studies of people interacting in a particular situation. Situational case studies and ethnographies are common in courses in business, education, or the social sciences, particularly anthropology and sociology. Someone might do an ethnography of a classroom in order to understand the interactions and relationships among students. Or someone might do a situational case study of an office, a club or social organization, a church, and so on.

Important Elements of Situational Case Studies or Ethnographies

- Thick description. The anthropologist Clifford Geertz coined the term *thick description* to explain the kinds of details needed in ethnographies. Pay attention to everything, from the setting, to interactions, to what people say.
- Interpretation. The purpose of an ethnography is to offer an explanation of what the situation means in context.

Advice on Process

1. Generating
   - Schedule ample time to observe the situation you're writing about; visit more than once if at all possible.
   - Follow the strategies for field research (32c).
   - Take extensive notes. Double-column field research notes (Figure 32.1) are particularly effective.
   - Interview people who are involved (Quick Reference 32.2), if possible, or have them complete questionnaires that you can analyze (Quick Reference 32.1).
   - Look for patterns in your notes. Group similar information or ideas and analyze each group; this forms the basis for paragraphs.

2. Shaping
   - Some formal case studies and ethnographies take forms similar to lab reports and other empirical studies (7e.3) and have the following sections: Introduction (explaining the issue and perhaps reviewing other literature); Procedures (describing how you chose the setting or people to study, how you gathered information, and so on); Findings (the longest part of the paper, usually, in which you relate what you learned; and Discussion or Conclusions (in which you explain what is significant about what you learned).
   - Other case studies put less emphasis on the structure above; instead, they contain more narrative, letting the finding unfold like a story, or they are organized according to topics and support materials.

3. Revising (the questions for revising case studies of individuals apply)
   - Would a participant in the scene you're describing share your interpretation? Ethnographers frequently let their subjects read a draft and comment on it.
   - What alternative interpretations are available? What conclusions could someone else draw from your notes?

EXERCISE 7-3

1. Write a short report that explains a concert, lecture, or other event to an audience of people who didn't attend it.

2. Write a review of one of the following: a new electronic device, a current movie, a class that you attended, a place where you worked. Your audience is other people who are deciding whether to purchase the device, attend the movie or class, or accept a job at that place.

3. Write a case study of one of your classmates, focusing on that student's educational experiences, hobbies or entertainment interests, and career hopes.

4. Working either alone or with others, write a case study of one of the following situations: people with an activity in common (a team, a musical group, a gathering of video game players); a workplace; a class; a coffee shop.

5. Write an interpretation for a general educated audience of a representation of certain types of people on a particular type of television show. Choose one of the following types of people: adolescents; university students; single parents; white-collar professionals; blue-collar workers; gays or lesbians. Then choose one of the following types of shows: sitcoms, crime dramas, medical dramas, reality shows, game shows.

7e How can I write about quantitative data or information?

Quantitative information or data come in the form of numbers. Such information can be an important source of detail and evidence in almost any kind of writing. However, some writings especially require writers to translate numbers into words and to explain what they mean.

Boys and Girls: Understanding the Rhetoric of Audience

7e.1 Reports of data

Reporting data is parallel to summarizing; you need to present information clearly and objectively. The challenge with these types of assignments is that the numbers seem to "speak for themselves." In other words, if you have a table of information it might seem pointless to write about it. A table is an efficient way to present information, and converting absolutely everything into words would be a waste of time. As a result, reports usually combine words and numbers. To illustrate how this kind of writing works, we've included part of a student paper below. In it, Sam Varma reports information from Statistics Canada on the levels of university degrees awarded men and women in Canada between 2005 and 2008.

Plug It In: Understanding the Rhetoric of Proof

Sample Student Report of Quantitative Data

Varma 1

Sam Varma
Political Science 1121
Professor Bateman
24 May 2013

University Degrees Awarded to Men and Women in Canada

A recent Statistics Canada survey (2010) compares Canadian men and women according to their fields of study and the levels of university degrees they earned between 2005 and 2008. The picture it gives of male-female differences in fields of study chosen is complex and beyond the scope of this report. The survey's findings as to the levels of the degrees earned, however, are clear-cut. They indicate important changes taking place in Canadian society. Over the coming years, the patterns of change in educational attainment shown in Table 1 should have an enormous impact on men's and women's employment and earnings prospects.

continued ➤

141

Varma 2

Table 1   University qualifications awarded by program level and gender

	2005[r]	2006[r]	2007[r]	2008	2007 to 2008
	number				% change
Total[1,2]	216,240	227,085	242,787	244,380	0.7
Male	86,970	90,102	95,367	97,620	2.4
Female	129,255	136,941	147,381	146,721	−0.4
Undergraduate level[1]	173,541	182,478	196,125	191,340	−2.4
Male	66,279	68,985	73,812	73,557	−0.3
Female	107,250	113,460	122,280	117,765	−3.7
Bachelor's, first professional and applied degree[1]	152,028	161,766	176,025	171,882	−2.4
Male	58,644	61,809	66,900	66,819	−0.1
Female	93,372	99,933	109,095	105,048	−3.7
Other undergraduate qualifications awarded[1]	21,516	20,715	20,100	19,455	−3.2
Male	7,635	7,176	6,915	6,735	−2.6
Female	13,878	13,527	13,188	12,717	−3.6
Graduate level[1]	41,445	42,777	44,823	46,794	4.4
Male	20,109	20,322	20,814	21,582	3.7
Female	21,336	22,449	24,003	25,206	5.0
Master's degree[1]	33,012	34,152	34,971	36,423	4.2
Male	15,936	16,068	16,140	16,536	2.5
Female	17,079	18,081	18,828	19,881	5.6
Earned doctorate	4,191	4,446	5,010	5,421	8.2
Male	2,349	2,517	2,772	3,027	9.2
Female	1,842	1,926	2,238	2,397	7.1
Other graduate qualifications awarded[1]	4,239	4,179	4,842	4,950	2.2
Male	1,824	1,737	1,905	2,019	6.0
Female	2,415	2,442	2,940	2,928	−0.4

Source: Statistics Canada. "University Degrees, Diplomas and Certificates Awarded."
The Daily. 14 July 2010. Table 1. Web. 12 May 2013.
[r]revised.
1. Includes sex unknown.
2. Includes the other types of programs offered in universities.
Note(s): Qualifications awarded figures may not add up because of rounding to a multiple of 3.
Qualifications awarded figures do not include the University of Regina.

continued ➤

Varma 3

The survey uses the term "university qualifications awarded" to refer to degrees earned as well as the small number of other undergraduate and graduate diplomas and certificates that universities award. The survey breaks down the qualifications awarded at the undergraduate level and at the graduate level as follows.

Undergraduate level:

- bachelor's degrees (e.g., BA, BSc)
- first professional and applied degrees (e.g., BEng—bachelor of engineering)
- a small number of other undergraduate qualifications

Graduate level:

- master's degrees (e.g., MA, MSc)
- doctorates (PhD)
- a small number of other graduate qualifications

This report will concentrate on the two main program levels defined by the survey: the undergraduate and graduate levels.

The first important observation we can make using the data in Table 1 is that through all four years, in all undergraduate and all graduate qualifications awarded, women outnumber men by more than 40,000 individuals per year. By 2008, this gender gap increased to nearly 50,000. Of a total of 244,380 men and women awarded qualifications that year, the number of women was 146,721, while the number of men was 97,620. In other words, in 2008, women, who amount to approximately 50% of the population, earned 60% of the degrees, diplomas, and certificates awarded by Canadian universities. . . .

Varma 6

Work Cited

Statistics Canada. "University Degrees, Diplomas and Certificates Awarded." *The Daily*, 14 July 2010. Web. 12 May 2013.

In his report, Sam opens with a brief overview of the survey and then describes what parts of it he will and will not be discussing. He states the importance of the data and briefly explains the terminology that the survey uses. When he starts summarizing its findings, he begins with what he sees as the most important information. He takes the biggest category, all degrees awarded, over all four years, and then moves on to the trend he sees developing over time and a detailed description of the latest year's figures. Most important for this type of writing, he remains objective, adding nothing to the information that anyone else wouldn't.

Important Elements of Reporting Data

- Clear and accurate translation of numbers into language.
- Judicious selection and summary of data to report.
- Objective reporting, unless your task is to go a step further to analyze or interpret (7e.2).

Advice on Process

1. Generating
   - Ask yourself what the key information is, and what readers most need to see or recognize in the data.
   - If you're stuck, begin by trying to put everything into sentences. You probably won't want to keep all of these sentences in your final draft; however, you should start writing rather than stare at a blank page.

2. Shaping
   - In the first paragraph, provide a summary or overview of the data you're reporting. Tell its source, how it was gathered, and its purpose. Your thesis will generally forecast the kind of information that follows.
   - Group pieces of related information. Each grouping will potentially become a paragraph.
   - Create or reproduce any charts or tables that would be too wordy to translate into language.

3. Revising
   - Do your words accurately report the main information?
   - Will your readers better understand the information through your language, or has your language contributed little?
   - Have you made the writing as interesting as you can, given the limitation of maintaining objectivity?
   - Have you documented the source(s) accurately?

7e.2   Analyses of data

Most papers that emphasize quantitative information go beyond reporting and into analysis or synthesis: drawing conclusions about what the information means or connecting it to other pieces of information or ideas. When you analyze data, you interpret it, going beyond translating numbers into language.

Sam Varma's paper in section 7e.1 reports on a comparison of men and women in Canada in terms of the university degrees they are awarded. Here is how a paragraph analyzing the data might begin:

> The steady pattern according to which women far outnumber men in completing their university studies deserves serious attention. As we have seen, the gender gap over the four years studied remained about 20%, while the actual raw number of students has usually increased. That means that every year, a disproportionate number of men have been entering the work force without the qualifications they need to succeed in a technological economy.

Notice that the analysis reports findings, but it does so in the context of what they might mean and provides reasons for that interpretation.

Important Elements of Analyses

- A clear report of the data, as explained in 7e.1.
- Statements that make interpretations, inferences, or evaluations of the data.
- Reasoning and support that convince readers that your statements are justified.

Advice on Process

1. Generating
   - Follow strategies for generating reports of data.
   - Use techniques for analysis (4d) and making inference (4e).
   - Brainstorm. For example, try to write ten different statements about what the information means or what its implications might be. Many of them will be invalid, but don't let that stop you. At least one or two will probably be worthwhile.

2. Shaping
   - Your basic organization will be a summary of the data (report) followed by analysis. However, don't summarize everything up front—just the most important materials. During your analysis, you'll want to quote or cite some of the data, and you don't want to repeat yourself.

3. Revising
   - Have you been fair and accurate in the way you've represented the information?
   - Have you considered alternative interpretations?
   - Have you provided clear and convincing explanations for any analytic, interpretive, or evaluative comments?
   - Have you documented your paper appropriately?

7e.3   Lab reports and empirical studies

Report 8:
Lab Report
(interactive)

A **lab report** is a specific way of presenting and discussing the results of experiments or laboratory measurements, in chemistry, biology, physics, engineering, and other sciences. Lab experiments are one kind of **empirical research,** a name that generally refers to attempts to measure something (from physical substances to behaviours) in order to prove or disprove a theory or hypothesis. Other disciplines that use experiments are psychology and other social sciences, some areas of education, economics, and so on. However, those disciplines also use sources like surveys or very specific observations to collect data. Both lab reports and other kinds of empirical research studies tend to have the same standard elements.

Important Sections of Lab Reports and Similar Empirical Studies

- **Introduction.** State your purpose, present background materials (for example, a review of previous studies) and your hypothesis.
- **Methods and materials.** Describe the equipment and procedures.
- **Results.** Accurately and objectively provide information that you acquired through your study.
- **Discussion.** Interpret and evaluate your results, including whether they supported your hypothesis and why or why not.
- **Conclusion.** Discuss the implications of your work, along with any limitations. Suggest further studies.

Take care to keep clear distinctions among these sections. Lab reports and empirical studies frequently include two other parts. One is an ABSTRACT, a short overview of the entire report, which appears directly after your title. The other is a list of REFERENCES, which is crucial if you discuss other published research. We provide more information about writing lab reports, as well as an example, in Chapter 41.

EXERCISE 7-4 Following is part of a table from Statistics Canada's 1995 General Social Survey reporting on attitudes toward women's work outside the home. Write a 100–300 word analysis of the findings.

Table 2 Attitudes of people aged 15 and over, by sex, 1995

	Very important	Important	Not important	Not at all important	Don't know	Total
Man and woman should contribute to household income						
			%			
Men	12	56	19	0	11	100
Women	15	58	15	1	9	100
Total	13	57	17	1	10	100
A job is all right, but what most women really want is a home and children						
			%			
Men	4	42	32	2	18	100
Women	6	40	37	4	11	100
Total	5	41	35	3	15	100

Source: Statistics Canada, 1995 General Social Survey

7f How can I write about readings?

Nearly all types of writing about observations have counterparts in writing about reading. You may be asked to write summaries, critical responses, analyses or interpretations, and syntheses. To illustrate some of these types and strategies for doing them, we'll refer to the following part of an essay by Barry Schwartz, titled "The Tyranny of Choice."

Does increased affluence and increased choice mean we have more happy people? Not at all. Three recently published books—by the psychologist David Myers, the political scientist Robert E. Lane, and the journalist Gregg Easterbrook—point out how the growth of material affluence has not brought with it an increase in subjective well-being. Indeed, they argue that we are actually experiencing a *decrease* in well-being. . . . And, as a recent study published in *The Journal of the American Medical Association* indicates, the rate of serious clinical depression has more than tripled over the last two generations, and increased by perhaps a factor of 10 from 1900 to 2000. Suicide rates are also up . . . in almost every developed country. And both serious depression and suicide are occurring among people younger than ever before. . . .

Why are people increasingly unhappy even as they experience greater material abundance and freedom of choice? Recent psychological research suggests that increased choice may itself be part of the problem. . . .

My colleagues and I, along with other researchers, have begun amassing evidence—both in the laboratory and in the field—that increased choice can lead to *decreased* well-being. This is especially true for people we have termed "maximizers," people whose goal is to get the best possible result when they make decisions. . . . Much of the relevant research is summarized in my book, *The Paradox of Choice: Why More Is Less.* Here are some examples:

- Shoppers who confront a display of 30 jams or varieties of gourmet chocolate are less likely to purchase *any* than when they encounter a display of six.

- Students given 30 topics from which to choose to write an extra-credit essay are less likely to write one than those given six. And if they do write one, it tends to be of lower quality.
- The majority of medical patients do not want the decision authority that the canons of medical ethics have thrust upon them. Responsibility for medical decisions looks better to people in prospect than in actuality: Sixty-five percent of respondents say that if they were to get cancer, they would want to be in charge of treatment decisions, but among those who actually have cancer, only 12 percent want that control and responsibility. . . .

> These examples paint a common picture: Increasing options does not increase well-being, especially for maximizers, even when it enables choosers to do better by some objective standard. We have identified several processes that help explain why increased choice decreases satisfaction. Greater choice

- Increases the burden of gathering information to make a wise decision.
- Increases the likelihood that people will regret the decisions they make.
- Increases the likelihood that people will *anticipate* regretting the decision they make, with the result that they can't make a decision at all.
- Increases the feeling of missed opportunities, as people encounter the attractive features of one option after another that they are rejecting.

7f.1   Summaries

((•
AUDIO
LESSON
Section 1:
Big Ideas—
Working with
Sources and
Avoiding
Plagiarism

To *summarize* is to extract the main messages or central points of a reading and restate them in a much briefer fashion. A summary doesn't include supporting evidence or details. It's the gist of what the author is saying. Also, it isn't your personal reaction to what the author says. How you summarize depends on your situation and assignment. For example, you can summarize an entire 500-page book in a single sentence, in a single page, or in five or six pages. Most of the time when you get an assignment to write a summary, your instructor will tell you how long it needs to be; if he or she doesn't, it's reasonable for you to ask.

Following are examples of two different levels of summary based on "The Tyranny of Choice" passage above.

Summary in a Single Sentence

Research finds that people with large numbers of choices are actually less happy than people with fewer choices (Schwartz).

Summary in 50 to 100 Words

Boshoven 1

Kristin Boshoven
English 101
Professor Lequire
5 April 2013

Summary of "The Tyranny of Choice"

Research finds that people with large numbers of choices are actually less happy than people with fewer choices. Although the amount of wealth and choice has increased during the past thirty years, fewer

continued ➤

people report themselves as being happy, and depression, suicide, and mental health problems have increased. While some choice is good, too many choices hinder decision making, especially among "maximizers," who try to make the best possible choices. Research in shopping, education, and medical settings shows that even when people eventually decide, they experience regret, worrying that the options they didn't choose might have been better (Schwartz).

Boshoven 2

Work Cited

Schwartz, Barry. "The Tyranny of Choice." *Chronicle of Higher Education* 23 Jan. 2004: B6. Print.

Both summaries put ideas in the author's own words and capture only the main idea. Notice that the longer summary begins with the same sentence as the short one, leading with the reading's main idea.

One decision to make is whether to refer to the author during your summary or to leave him or her out. Check to see whether your instructor has a preference. The second example above could be rewritten (the three dots are ellipses, showing material left out):

In "The Tyranny of "Choice" Barry Schwartz summarizes research that finds . . . while some choice is good, too many choices. . . .

Important Elements of Summaries

- Inclusion of only the source's main ideas.
- Proportional summary of the source. This means that longer and more important aspects of the original need to get more space and attention in your summary.
- Use of your own words. If there are particular key terms or phrases, include them in quotation marks, but otherwise put everything into your own words.
- Accurate DOCUMENTATION of the original source.

Advice on Process

Note: For more help in writing a summary, see 35j.

1. Generating
   - Identify TOPIC SENTENCES or main ideas, separating them from examples or illustrations. Focus on the main ideas.
   - Take notes in your own words; then put the source away. Write from your notes, going back to check the original only after you've written a first draft.
2. Shaping
   - Begin with a sentence that summarizes the entire reading, unless you're writing a particularly long summary.

- Follow the order of the original.
- Include a Works Cited page (Chapter 36) or References (Chapter 37), depending on the required style.

3. Revising
- Have you maintained objectivity throughout?
- Have you put things into your own words?
- Have you been proportional?
- Have you accurately documented?
- Is there an even more CONCISE (see Chapter 11) way to state certain things?

7f.2   Critical responses

A **critical response** essay has two missions: to provide a SUMMARY of a source's main idea and to respond to that idea.

A well-written critical response accomplishes these two missions with style and grace. That is, it doesn't say, "My summary is . . ." or "Now, here's what I think. . . ." Instead, you want the two missions to blend together as seamlessly as possible. A critical response essay may be short or somewhat long, depending on whether you're asked to respond to a single passage or to an entire work.

Here's student Kristin Boshoven's short critical response to Barry Schwartz's essay, "The Tyranny of Choice," which we reprinted above. Note that it incorporates the summary she wrote for a previous assignment.

AUDIO LESSON Section 1: Big Ideas— Becoming a Critical Reader and a Better Writer

AUDIO LESSON Section 2: Practice Questions— Becoming a Critical Reader and a Better Writer

Boshoven 1

Kristin Boshoven

English 101

Professor Lequire

7 April 2013

Too Much Choice: Disturbing but not Destructive

Barry Schwartz argues that people with large numbers of choices are actually less happy than people with fewer choices. Although the amount of wealth and choice has increased during the past thirty years, studies show that fewer people report themselves as being happy. Depression, suicide, and mental health problems have increased. While some choice is good, too many choices hinder decision making, especially among people whom Schwartz calls "maximizers," who try to make the best possible choices. Research in shopping, education, and medical settings shows that even when people eventually decide, they experience regret, worrying that the options they didn't choose might have been better.

Although Schwartz cites convincing evidence for his claims, he ultimately goes too far in his conclusions. Excessive choice does seem to

continued ➤

Boshoven 2

make life harder, not easier, but it alone can't be blamed for whatever unhappiness exists in our society.

My own experience supports Schwartz's finding that people who have thirty choices of jam as opposed to six (B6) often don't purchase any. About a month ago my husband and I decided to buy an inexpensive global positioning (GPS) device to use in our car. When we went to the store, we were confronted with twenty different models, and even though a helpful salesperson explained the various features to me, we couldn't make up our minds. We decided to do more research, which was a mistake. After weeks of reading reviews and product reports, we are close to making a decision. However, I have a sinking feeling that as soon as we buy something, we'll learn that another choice would have been better, or ours will drop $50 in price. In the meantime, we could have been enjoying the use of a GPS for the past month, if we had not worried so much. I could relate similar experiences trying to choose which movie to see, which dentist to visit, and so on. I suspect others could, too, which is why I find Schwartz's argument convincing at this level.

However, when he suggests that the increase of choice is a source of things like depression and suicide, he goes too far. Our society has undergone tremendous changes in the past forty or fifty years, and many of those changes are more likely to cause problems than the existence of too much choice. For example, workers in the 1950s through the 1970s could generally count on holding jobs with one company as long as they wanted, even through retirement. A 1950s autoworker, for example, might not have been thrilled in his job (and these were jobs held almost exclusively by men), but at least he could count on it, and it paid enough to buy a house and education for his family. The economic uncertainties of the past twenty years, and especially since 2001, have meant that workers—and now women as well as men—do not have the same job stability as decades ago.

Although I agree that too many choices can lead to anxiety and even unhappiness, there are larger factors. If people report more depression and suicide than they once did, a more likely candidate is economic and social uncertainty, not having too many kinds of cereal on the grocery store shelves.

continued ➢

Boshoven 3

Work Cited

Schwartz, Barry. "The Tyranny of Choice." *Chronicle of Higher Education*
    23 Jan. 2004: B6. Print.

Important Elements of Critical Responses

- A clear and concise representation of the source.
- Statements of agreement, disagreement, or qualified agreement (you accept some points but not others), accompanied by reasons and evidence for your statements.

Advice on Process

1. Generating
    - Use active reading and CRITICAL READING to identify the main points and generate reactions to the article.
    - Use techniques for ANALYZING (4d), drawing INFERENCES (4e), and ASSESSING REASONING PROCESSES (4h).
2. Shaping
    - Write a summary of the main idea or central point of the material you're responding to.
    - Write a smooth TRANSITION between the summary and your response. This transitional statement, which bridges the two parts, need not be a formal THESIS STATEMENT, but it needs to signal clearly the beginning of your response.
    - Respond to the source using your prior knowledge and experience.
3. Revising
    - Have you combined summary and response? Have you explained your response in a way that readers will find thoughtful and convincing?
    - Have you fulfilled all documentation requirements? See Chapters 36 through 38 for coverage of DOCUMENTATION STYLES. Ask your instructor which style to use.

7f.3   Interpretations and analyses

Interpretations and analyses resemble critical responses in that they make claims about a reading. Critical responses ask whether a source is "good," but interpretations and analyses ask what a source means. You might be most familiar with this kind of writing from previous English or literature courses in which a teacher asked you to interpret a poem, play, or story. In fact, we've devoted much of Chapter 40 to writing about literature.

7f.4   Syntheses

To *synthesize* is to weave together material from several sources. Unsynthesized ideas and information are like separate spools of thread, neatly lined up. Synthesized ideas and information are threads woven into a tapestry. By synthesizing, you show evidence of your ability to bring ideas together. Synthesis goes beyond summary and comes after it in the critical thinking process (4b).

   One common synthesizing task is to connect two or more readings or source materials into a single piece of writing. You complete this synthesis after you have summarized, analyzed, and evaluated each of the source materials. Another common type of synthesis is to connect material to what you already know, creating a new final product that is your own.

SYNTHESIZING MULTIPLE SOURCES

Your goal in synthesizing multiple sources is to join two or more texts together into a single writing. The resulting text needs to be more than just a succession of summaries. That is, avoid merely listing who said what about a topic. Such a list isn't a synthesis. It does not create new connections among ideas.

The following example shows how student Tom Mentzer synthesized two sources. First read Source 1 and Source 2, and then read Tom's synthesis.

SOURCE 1

In Shishmaref, calamity has already arrived. The village of 600 Inupiaq lies on the fragile barrier island of Sarichef, where sea ice forms later each year, exposing the land to autumn storms that carve away 50 feet or more of shoreline a season. Two houses have slipped into the sea; 18 others have been moved back from the encroaching ocean; others buckle from the melting permafrost. Ten million dollars has been spent on seawalls, to no avail. Residents have concluded permanent resettlement is their only option.

—Julia Whitty and Robert Knoth, "Sea Change"

SOURCE 2

Global temperatures have risen by about 0.6 degrees Celsius since the nineteenth century. Other measures of climate bolster the theory that the world is getting warmer: satellite measurements suggest that spring arrives about a week earlier now than in the late 1970s, for example, and records show that migratory birds fly to higher latitudes earlier in the season and stay later.

—John Browne, "Beyond Kyoto"

Now read Tom's synthesis. Notice how he used SUMMARY and PARAPHRASE to synthesize the two sources. Also notice how the first sentence in his synthesis weaves the sources together with a new concept.

EXAMPLE OF A SYNTHESIS OF TWO SOURCES

Global warming is affecting both the natural and artificial worlds. Rising temperatures have accelerated spring's arrival and changed the migration patterns of birds (Browne 20). They have also changed life for residents of Arctic regions. For example, eighteen families in Shishmaref, Alaska, had to move their houses away from the coast because the permafrost under the beaches had thawed (Whitty and Knoth).

—Tom Mentzer, student

Notice how Tom's synthesis uses in-text citations (MLA style) to signal to the reader which information he has borrowed from the two sources. In the Works Cited list at the end of his paper, Tom listed full source information for both sources. To learn how to document your sources, see Chapters 36 (MLA), 37 (APA), or 38 (CM, CSE, IEEE).

SOURCES LISTED IN TOM'S WORKS CITED PAGE

Browne, John. "Beyond Kyoto." *Foreign Affairs* 83.4 (2004): 20–32. Print.

Whitty, Julia, and Robert Knoth. "Sea Change." *Mother Jones.* Foundation for National Progress, Sept.–Oct. 2007. Web. 2 Jan. 2013.

Process Advice

- Make comparisons with—or contrasts between—concepts, ideas, and information. Do the sources generally agree or disagree? What are the bases of their agreement or disagreement? Are there subtle differences or shades of meaning or emphasis?

- Create definitions that combine and extend definitions you encounter in the separate sources.
- Use examples or descriptions from one source to illustrate ideas in another. See the related discussion in section 7f.5.
- Use processes described in one source to explain those in others.
- In revising, ask, "Have I truly synthesized the sources, or have I just written about one and then the other?"

EXERCISE 7-5   Write a one-paragraph synthesis of the passage by Barry Schwartz (printed on pages 146 and 147) and the following opening to a short article by Ronni Sandroff, editor of *Consumer Reports on Health:*

> Last time I dropped by my pharmacy in search of a decongestant, I was stopped cold by the wall-sized display of remedies. The brands I had used in the past had multiplied into extended families of products. Yes, I saw *Contac, Excedrin, Tylenol,* and *Vicks,* but each brand came in multiple versions. Products for severe colds, coughs and colds, and headache and flu abounded, and there were further choices: gels, tablets, capsules, extended release, extra strength. I was eager to just grab a product and go, but to find the right one I had to dig out my reading glasses and examine the fine print.
>
> —Ronni Sandroff, "Too Many Choices"

SYNTHESIZING WITH ONE SOURCE

If you're working with only one source, you need to make connections between the source and your prior knowledge, whether from experience, films or television, classes or conversations, or previous readings. Don't be afraid to synthesize. We're always surprised when we find that some students assume that what they think has no value. Nothing could be further from the truth.

In the following example of a synthesis with one source (Source 2 above), student Mikayla Stoller connected her reading to her previous knowledge, in this case a movie she had seen. Her first sentence links the two with a new idea.

EXAMPLE OF A SYNTHESIS WITH ONE SOURCE

Even if the existence of global warming is well established, the consequences of it may not be. A 0.6 degrees Celsius rise in temperature over the past century has caused spring to arrive earlier and migrating birds to change their habits (Browne 20). However, some believe that global warming could have the unexpected effect of causing a new ice age. The 2004 movie *The Day after Tomorrow* portrayed New York City as suddenly frozen over with ice because of climate changes. Although most scientists criticized the science in that movie, it seems clear that global warming will alter the world as we know it.

—Mikayla Stoller, student

Mikayla used parenthetical citations in the body of her paragraph and included the full citation in her Works Cited list at the end of her paper.

SOURCE AS LISTED IN MIKAYLA'S WORKS CITED PAGE

Browne, John. "Beyond Kyoto." *Foreign Affairs* 83.4 (2004): 20–32. Print.

Advice on Process

- Use your powers of play. Toss ideas around, even if you make connections that seem outrageous. Try opposites (for example, read about athletes and think about the most nonathletic person you know). Try turning an idea upside down (for example, if you have read about the value of being a good sport, list the benefits of being a bad sport).
- Use the technique of mapping (clustering) (2c.5) to lay out visually the relationships among elements in your source and other ideas that come to mind.
- Discuss the source with another person. Summarize its content and elicit the other person's opinion or ideas. Deliberately debate that opinion or challenge those ideas.
- Write your personal response to the material. Explain whether you agree or disagree and also the reasons why you respond as you do.

7f.5 Essays that apply theories or concepts (essays of application)

Essays that apply theories or concepts (**essays of application**) take general information from one source (usually a reading but perhaps a lecture) and apply it to another, usually for the purpose of interpretation or evaluation. Three example assignments will make this clearer.

1. How does Smith's theory of social deviance explain the behaviours of the criminals who are portrayed in Jones's book?
2. Based on your own experiences, are Beaudoin's categories of high school cliques accurate and sufficient?
3. Which symptoms of depression, as explained by Kho, does the narrator of *The Bell Jar* seem to display? Which does she not?

Assignments like these require a form of synthesis, in that they combine two or more sources into a single piece of writing. However, the sources have characteristics that distinguish essays of application from other syntheses, which is why we explain them separately. One source explains a theory, concept, or definition; even if it's based on details from formal research or study, its purpose is to offer a generalization about something. The other source is more specific, consisting of stories, experiences, scenarios, observations, quantitative data, or reports of events (perhaps even fictional situations, as in example 3 above), with little or no analysis or interpretation.

Instructors sometime assign essays of application to test how well you grasp concepts; being able to apply an idea to a new situation demonstrates your deeper understanding of it. They may also assign such essays to help you analyze or interpret a situation or body of information in ways you might not have considered. For example, suppose you're asked to read an article that claims that, from a very early age, gender determines the roles assumed by children playing in mixed groups, and then to apply the article to your own observations of children at play. You would pay attention to that situation differently if you were asked to apply a different theory (for example, that physical size determines play roles). Finally, you might apply a theory to a situation in order to test it. Suppose you observe play situations and find that boys and girls all play the same kinds of roles. A paper resulting from this application will explain why the theory may be invalid.

Important Elements of Essays of Application

- A clear and accurate summary of the theory or concept you're applying.

Advice on Process

1. Generating
   - Use strategies for summary or report (whichever is appropriate) to explain each source.
   - Brainstorm a list of all the possible ways the specific source illustrates the concept or theory. Use analysis and inference.
   - Brainstorm a list of all the possible ways the specific source disproves or complicates the concept or theory. Use analysis and inference.
   - Use other generating strategies.

2. Shaping
   - Begin your essay in one of two ways: (A) Start with a brief summary of the theory or concept, leading to a thesis that states how it applies to the specific source (situation, reading, or information) you're discussing. (B) Start with a brief summary of the specific source (situation, reading, or information), leading to a thesis that states how it demonstrates, disproves, or complicates the theory or concept.
   - If you follow opening strategy A, your next paragraph(s) will need to summarize the specific source. If you follow strategy B, your next paragraph(s) will need to summarize the theory or concept.
   - Follow these paragraphs with paragraphs that support your thesis, giving reasons (and support) for your assertion.
   - (Optional). Discuss any facts or observations that seem not to fit your thesis. Explain why they, nonetheless, don't mean you're wrong.

3. Revising
   - Have you explained both sources accurately and efficiently, using summary, QUOTATION, or paraphrase?
   - Have you written a strong thesis that relates one source to the other?
   - Have you provided reasons to support your thesis and developed your paragraphs to provide details showing that those reasons are solid?
   - Have you used complete and accurate documentation of sources, using the style required by your instructor?

7f.6   Annotated bibliographies

An annotated bibliography is a list of sources that includes publishing information, a brief summary, and usually your commentary on the content of each. Such commentary often describes how the sources in the bibliography relate to one another (33j).

7f.7   Essay exams

Essay exam is a broadly used term for questions that require you to answer in paragraphs, usually in a timed situation. Prepare for essay exams by rereading your class material and by doing some writing. Making up a few possible questions is an excellent way of studying, and having yourself answer those practice questions under pressure is good preparation for the real thing. When you receive an essay question, resist the urge to start writing immediately. Use a margin or scratch paper to jot an informal outline or series of points you want to make. Take care to understand the question and respond directly to it. For example, if the question asks you to RESPOND, ANALYZE, SYNTHESIZE, or apply, you don't just want to SUMMARIZE. Most of the time, an essay exam will ask you to perform a very specific task. After you've drafted your answer, save some time to proofread. It's easy to introduce errors when you're writing under pressure.

Writing Effectively, Writing with Style

MyCanadianCompLab

Visit MyCanadianCompLab at
mycanadiancomplab.ca for

- More information on writing essays
- Chapter exercises
- Other resources, including an eText version of this book

Chapter 8

STYLE AND TONE IN WRITING

((•
AUDIO
LESSON
Section 1:
Big Ideas—
Writing Well
in College

8a What do style and tone in writing involve?

Style and tone both refer to *how* you say something, in contrast with *what* you're saying. Style and tone are not rule bound, as grammar is. The sentence structures you shape, from simple to complex, contribute to the style of your writing. The words you choose create the tone in your sentences. They work in concert. After we discuss how they operate together, we address style and tone separately (8c and 8d) to differentiate the larger elements of crafting sentences from the smaller elements of skilful word choice.

((•
AUDIO
LESSON
Section 1:
Big Ideas—
Using
Language
Well and
Addressing
Your Audience

8b How do style and tone operate in writing?

Style and tone operate together through a combination of formality and personality. The level of **formality** in writing can be roughly divided into three categories. Formal writing belongs in the language of ceremonies, contracts, policies, and some literary writing. "Formal writing," by the way, doesn't mean dull and drab. Lively language always enhances such material. **Informal writing** is casual, colloquial, and sometimes playful, usually found in e-mails, text messages, Facebook postings, and certain BLOGS.* Semiformal writing, which sits between these poles, is the style and tone found in academic writing, as well as in much business and public writing. Its style is clear and efficient, and its tone is reasonable and evenhanded.

((•
AUDIO
LESSON
Section 2:
Practice
Questions—
Using
Language
Well and
Addressing
Your Audience

Generally, when you write for an audience about whom you know little, a somewhat more formal style and tone is appropriate. If informal writings are T-shirts and jeans, and formal writings are tuxedos and evening gowns, then semiformal writings are business-casual attire. Here are examples of writing in the three levels of formality.

((•
AUDIO
LESSON
Section 3:
Rapid
Review—
Using
Language
Well and
Addressing
Your Audience

INFORMAL	It's totally sweet how gas makes stars.
SEMIFORMAL	Gas clouds slowly transform into stars.
FORMAL	The condensations of gas spun their slow gravitational pirouettes, slowly transmogrifying gas cloud into star.

—Carl Sagan, "Starfolk: A Fable"

Informal language tends to date quickly; consider how old-fashioned "groovy" sounds today. That's a persuasive reason to avoid it in writings that intend to stand the test of time.

Personality refers to how much the writer reveals about him- or herself with patterns of sentence structure and choice of words. An intimate style and tone, which treats the reader as a close friend, includes specific personal experiences and opinions.

---

*Words printed in SMALL CAPITAL LETTERS are discussed elsewhere in the text and are defined in the Terms Glossary at the back of this book.

A familiar or polite style and tone includes some experiences or personal thoughts, but only of a kind you might share in a professional relationship with an instructor, supervisor, or colleague. In such writing, the reader can glimpse the writer behind the language, but not as fully as in intimate writing because the emphasis is on the ideas or subject matter. An impersonal style reveals nothing about the writer, so that the content is all that the reader is aware of.

INTIMATE When our grade ten teacher assigned *In the Skin of a Lion* by Michael Ondaatje, I got cranky right away. Why did he lay something so hard on us? I couldn't figure out the story or what was up with the characters.

FAMILIAR/POLITE The next day in class, I was relieved to discover that most other students had run into the same problems as I had reading the novel.

IMPERSONAL Our teacher explicated the story line and clarified how to decode the character development, which enabled the class to appreciate the narrative.

Quick Reference 8.1 lays out the levels of formality and of personality as conveyed by the style and tone you insert into your writing.

QUICK REFERENCE 8.1

Major elements that create style and tone in writing

Elements	Levels		
Formality	Informal	Semiformal	Formal
Personality	Intimate	Familiar/Polite	Impersonal

EXERCISE 8-1 Working individually or in a group, describe the style of each of the following paragraphs in terms of formality and personality.

1. Google has yet to hit upon a strategy that combines the innovation it is known for with an appeal to the self-interest that is the currency of the capital's power brokers. One reason AT&T and Microsoft have succeeded in stoking antitrust interest against Google—quite ironic, given that both companies have been subject to large government antitrust actions—is that they're better versed in the fine points of lobbying. Both companies, for example, hold sway over many lawmakers by frequently reminding them how many employees live in their districts ("jobs" is a metric lawmakers respond to).
   —Joshua Green, "Google's Tar Pit"

2. Prices are rising for the black sludge that helps make the world's gears turn. If you think we're talking about oil, think again. Petroleum prices have tumbled from their record highs. No sooner was there relief at the pump, however, than came a squeeze at the pot. That jolt of coffee . . . has gotten more expensive and could go even higher this year. . . .
   —*New York Times,* "Joe Economics"

3. Studies of home-based telework by women yield mixed results regarding the usefulness of telework in facilitating work-life balance. Most research on the social impacts of home-based telework focuses on workers—employees or self-employed—who deliberately choose that alternative work arrangement. Labour force analysts, however, predict an

increase in employer-initiated teleworking. As a case study of the workforce of one large, financial-sector firm in Canada, this article considers the conditions of employment of involuntary teleworkers, those required by their employer to work full-time from a home office. In-depth interviews were conducted with a sample of 18 female teleworkers working for the case study firm in a professional occupation.

—Laura C. Johnson, Jean Andrey, and Susan M. Shaw,
"Mr. Dithers Comes to Dinner"

4. I remember vividly the moment that I entered the world of literacy, education, institutional "correctness," and, consequently, identity. I was demonstrating to my older sister how I wrote my name. The memory comes after I had been literally taught how to do it—which strokes of the pencil to use to create the symbols that equate to my name.

—Elise Geraghty, "In the Name of the Father"

8c How do I write with style?

Writing with **style** comes with lots of practice. It rarely shows up on most first drafts. The pleasure of creating a graceful, engaging style in your writing results from experimenting with different structures. And every so often, writers surprise themselves with sentences and passages of enormous power and impact that emerge almost unbidden on the page. Those are magical moments. To write with style, refer to Quick Reference 8.2; as you do, add your own personal hints so that you can make the material your own.

QUICK REFERENCE 8.2

How to create good writing style

- Try out different sentence types to maintain readers' interest (9a, 9n, 9r).
- Use sentence coordination and subordination to vary the pace (9d–m).
- Vary sentence length to keep your readers' attention (9c).
- Experiment with diction or word choice (12d–e, 12h).
- Use figurative language (12c).
- Employ the gracefulness of parallelism in sentences and larger sections for the pleasure of your readers (Chapter 10).
- Be consistent in your level of formality and personality (8b).

👁 **8d How do I write with appropriate tone?**

Writing in
Action:
Exploring
Appropriate
Language

Tone in writing involves choosing the right words to deliver your meaning. Tone operates like tone of voice, except that you can't rely on facial expressions and voice intonations to communicate your written message. The language you choose in your writing creates the tone you relay to your readers.

Your choice of words, or **diction** (12d), determines the degree to which your readers notice the language itself along with the content that the language is conveying. Well-written figurative language (12c) can create pleasant surprises for readers. However, if you draw too much attention to your language without communicating a clear message, your writing suffers. Conversely, if you use only simple, monotonous words, you may create a dull drone.

Your word choice can result in a wide range of possible tones, some desirable and some not. We list several in Quick Reference 8.3.

QUICK REFERENCE 8.3

Some examples of desirable and undesirable tone

SERIOUS	The advent of space travel supported the predictions of science fiction, especially those of the nineteenth-century novelist Jules Verne.
LIGHT OR BREEZY	What a trip to flip through Verne's *From the Earth to the Moon* and find spaceships taking off from Tampa, Florida, near Cape Canaveral.
SARCASTIC	Some poor slobs probably think Verne is worth worshipping like a god.
MEAN	Verne also made some dumb forecasts.
CONDESCENDING	Although most people struggle to read Jules Verne's sometimes complex books, those who succeed can consider themselves at least reasonably competent readers.
WHINING	Why should Jules Verne be the third most translated writer in the world? He's no big deal. I could write as well as he did.

Achieving the tone you want in each piece of writing calls for experimenting with words. If you consult a thesaurus, be sure to check the definition of any synonym that's new to you. Lynn once had an excellent student who used the word "profound" instead of "deep," without looking it up in a dictionary. The result was this sentence: "The trenches beneath some parts of that sea were dangerously profound." That misuse ruined an otherwise intelligent passage.

As with style in writing, appropriate tone results from your private trials, rejections, and explorations. Good tone rarely shows up on most first drafts. Quick Reference 8.4 offers you some suggestions for achieving an appropriate tone in your writing. Add your own advice to the list to personalize it.

QUICK REFERENCE 8.4

How to use appropriate tone in writing

- Reserve a highly informal tone for conversational writing.
- Use a semiformal tone in your academic writing and when you write for supervisors, professionals, and other people you know only from a distance.
- Avoid an overly formal, ceremonious tone.
- Choose a tone that suits your topic and your readers.
- Whatever tone you choose, be consistent in each piece of your writing.

EXERCISE 8-2 Revise each of the sentences to create a different tone. The sentences in Quick Reference 8.3 provide some examples. For a further challenge, see how many different tones you can create.

1. Many Canadians spend much of their leisure time watching professional sports.
2. If you want to waste your money buying organic foods, who am I to stop you?
3. When considering the purchase of clothing in order to possess a serviceable wardrobe, it is imperative to select items in which the colour combinations are harmonious and pleasing.

Chapter 9

SENTENCE VARIETY AND STYLE

9a How do sentences affect style?

AUDIO LESSON Section 1: Big Ideas—Using Language Well and Addressing Your Audience

Sentences affect style through their length (9c), structures like COORDINATION and SUBORDINATION (9k), and types. The main sentence types in English are SIMPLE, COMPOUND, COMPLEX, and COMPOUND-COMPLEX (14q). When any one type dominates a piece of writing, it affects the style, especially if the sentences are also generally the same length. A flurry of short, simple sentences creates a blunt, direct style. Such a style often gains in clarity but loses in interest. A series of long, involved sentences creates a lofty, sometimes even stuffy, style. It may achieve sophistication but sacrifice clarity.

9b What are variety and emphasis in writing?

AUDIO LESSON Section 2: Practice Questions—Using Language Well and Addressing Your Audience

When you write sentences of different lengths and types within a piece of writing, you create **sentence variety.** Working in concert with sentence variety, **emphasis** allows you to add weight to ideas of special importance.

Using techniques of variety and emphasis adds style and clarity to your writing. When readers see variety in your writing, they see you as versatile and in control of language. Usually, the best time to apply the principles of variety and emphasis is while you are REVISING.

9c How do different sentence lengths create variety and emphasis?

AUDIO LESSON Section 3: Rapid Review—Using Language Well and Addressing Your Audience

To emphasize one idea among many others, you can express it in a sentence noticeably different in length from the sentences surrounding it. In the following example, a four-word sentence between two longer sentences carries the key message of the passage (boldface added).

Writing in Action: Achieving Variety

> Today is one of those excellent January partly cloudies in which light chooses an unexpected landscape to trick out in gilt, and then shadow sweeps it away. **You know you're alive.** You take huge steps, trying to feel the planet's roundness arc between your feet.
> —Annie Dillard, *Pilgrim at Tinker Creek*

Writing in Action: Combining Sentences

Sometimes a string of short sentences creates impact and emphasis. Yet, at other times, a string of short sentences can be dull to read.

EXERCISE 9-1 The following paragraph is dull because it has only short sentences. Combine some of the sentences to make a paragraph that has a variety of sentence lengths.

There is a problem. It is widely known as sick-building syndrome. It comes from indoor air pollution. It causes office workers to suffer. They have trouble breathing. They have painful rashes. Their heads ache. Their eyes burn.

Similarly, a string of COMPOUND SENTENCES can be monotonous to read and may fail to communicate relationships among ideas.

EXERCISE 9-2   The following paragraph is dull because it has only compound sentences. Revise it to provide more variety.

Science fiction writers are often thinkers, **and** they are often dreamers, **and** they let their imaginations wander. Jules Verne was such a writer, **and** he predicted spaceships, **and** he forecast atomic submarines, **but** most people did not believe airplanes were possible.

9d   What are coordination and subordination?

Two important sentence structuring methods are **coordination** and **subordination**, which reflect relationships between ideas that you seek to express. Coordination shows the equality of ideas, while subordination shows that one idea is more important than others. Using these structures effectively creates variety and emphasis. We explain each of them in sections 9e and 9i, but an example will help you see the basic principle:

TWO SENTENCES	The sky turned dark grey. The wind died down.
USING COORDINATION	The sky turned dark grey, **and** the wind died down.
USING SUBORDINATION 1	**As** the sky turned dark grey, the wind died down. [Here, the wind is the focus.]
USING SUBORDINATION 2	**As** the wind died down, the sky turned dark grey. [Here, the sky is the focus.]

9e   What is coordination of sentences?

Coordination of sentences is a grammatical strategy to communicate that the ideas in two or more INDEPENDENT CLAUSES are equivalent or balanced. Coordination can produce harmony by bringing related elements together. Whenever you use the technique of coordination of sentences, make sure that it works well with the meaning you want to communicate.

The sky turned **brighter, and** people emerged happily from buildings.
The sky turned **brighter;** people emerged happily from buildings.

9f   What is the structure of a coordinate sentence?

A **coordinate sentence,** also known as a *compound sentence* (14q), consists of two or more INDEPENDENT CLAUSES joined either by a semicolon or by a comma working in concert with a COORDINATING CONJUNCTION (*and, but, for, or, nor, yet, so*). Here, you can see the pattern for coordination of sentences.

$$\text{Independent clause} \left\{ \begin{array}{l} \text{, and} \\ \text{, but} \\ \text{, for} \\ \text{, or} \\ \text{, nor} \\ \text{, yet} \\ \text{, so} \\ \text{;} \end{array} \right\} \text{independent clause.}$$

Each COORDINATING CONJUNCTION has its own meaning. When you choose one, be sure that its meaning accurately expresses the relationship between the equivalent ideas that you want to convey.

- **and** means addition
- **but** and **yet** mean contrast
- **for** means reason or choice
- **or** means choice
- **nor** means negative choice
- **so** means result or effect

ALERT: Always use a comma before a coordinating conjunction that joins two INDEPENDENT CLAUSES (24b). ●

9h How can I use coordination effectively?

COORDINATION is effective when each INDEPENDENT CLAUSE is related or equivalent. If they aren't, the result looks like a coordinated sentence, but the ideas are unrelated.

> NO   Computers came into common use in the 1970s, and they sometimes make costly errors. [The statement in each independent clause is true, but the ideas are not related or equivalent.]

> YES   Computers came into common use in the 1970s, and now they are indispensable business tools.

Coordination is also most effective when it's not overused. Simply stringing sentences together with COORDINATING CONJUNCTIONS makes relationships among ideas unclear—and the resulting sentence lacks style.

> NO   Dinosaurs could have disappeared for many reasons, **and** one theory holds that a sudden shower of meteors and asteroids hit the earth, **so** the impact created a huge dust cloud that caused a false winter. The winter lasted for years, **and** the dinosaurs died.

> YES   Dinosaurs could have disappeared for many reasons. One theory holds that a sudden shower of meteors and asteroids hit the earth. The impact created a huge dust cloud that caused a false winter. The winter lasted for years, killing the dinosaurs.

EXERCISE 9-3 Working individually or with a group, revise these sentences to eliminate illogical or overused coordination. If you think a sentence needs no revision, explain why. For help, consult sections 9e through 9h.

> **EXAMPLE** Fencing, once a form of combat, has become a competitive sport worldwide, and today's fencers disapprove of those who identify fencing with fighting.

> Fencing, once a form of combat, has become a competitive sport worldwide, *but* today's fencers disapprove of those who identify fencing with fighting.

1. As depicted in movies, fencing sometimes appears to be reckless swordplay, and fencing requires precision, coordination, and strategy.
2. In the 1800s, fencing became very popular, and it was one of the few sports included in the first modern Olympic Games in 1896, and fencing has been part of the Olympics ever since.
3. Fencing equipment includes a mask, a padded jacket, a glove, and one of three weapons—a foil, épée, or sabre—and a fencer's technique and targets differ depending on the weapon used and the fencer's experience.
4. Generally, a fencer specializes in one of the three weapons, but some competitors are equally skilled with all three.
5. The object of fencing is to be the first to touch the opponent five times, and a "president," who is sometimes assisted by a number of judges, officiates at competitions.

9i What is subordination in sentences?

Subordination is a grammatical strategy to communicate that one idea in a sentence is more important than another idea in the same sentence. To use subordination, you place the more important idea in an INDEPENDENT CLAUSE and the less important—the subordinate—idea in a DEPENDENT CLAUSE. The information you choose to subordinate depends on the meaning you want to deliver.

INDEPENDENT CLAUSE

Two cowboys fought a dangerous Alberta snowstorm **while they**

DEPENDENT CLAUSE   DEPENDENT CLAUSE

were looking for cattle. When they came to a canyon,

INDEPENDENT CLAUSE

they saw outlines of buildings through the blizzard.

To illustrate the difference in writing style when you use subordination, here's a passage with the same message as the example above, but without subordination.

> Two cowboys fought a dangerous Alberta snowstorm. They were looking for cattle. They came to a canyon. They saw outlines of buildings through the blizzard.

9j What sentence structures express subordination?

A sentence that uses subordination contains a DEPENDENT CLAUSE starting with a SUBORDINATING CONJUNCTION, a RELATIVE PRONOUN, or a RELATIVE ADVERB.

> **If** they are very lucky, the passengers may glimpse dolphins breaking water playfully near the ship. [Subordinating conjunction *if*]
>
> —Elizabeth Gray, student

We stood on the deck of the ferry **that** was taking us to the Gulf Islands. [relative pronoun *that*]

It was one of those mornings **when** a salty breeze blows in from the Pacific. [relative adverb *when*]

An independent clause can stand on its own as a sentence. A dependent clause cannot, because it doesn't express a complete thought. As you can see from these three sample sentences, the information in each dependent clause can be understood only in relation to other information contained in the same sentence (see also 14p).

! **ALERT:** Any clause that expresses subordination is called a dependent clause. You will often see the term *subordinate clause* used as a synonym.

You will sometimes find the term *subordinate clause* reserved for the type of dependent clause that always starts with a subordinating conjunction—that is, sometimes the term is used to refer to only *adverb clauses.* The term *relative clause* may refer to any dependent clause that starts with a relative pronoun or a relative adverb; this includes *adjective clauses* and those dependent *noun clauses* that start with relative pronouns (14p). ●

For patterns of subordination with dependent clauses, see Quick Reference 9.1. The three types of dependent clauses are ADVERB CLAUSES, ADJECTIVE CLAUSES, and dependent NOUN CLAUSES (14p).

- An adverb clause functions as an ADVERB and starts with a subordinating conjunction (9k).
- An adjective clause functions as an ADJECTIVE and starts with either a relative pronoun (Quick Reference 14.2) or a relative adverb (14g).
- A dependent noun clause clause functions as a NOUN and starts with either a relative pronoun (Quick Reference 14.2) or a subordinating conjunction (9k).

A sentence that contains one or more dependent clauses is called a complex sentence (14q).

QUICK REFERENCE **9.1**

Subordination

SENTENCES WITH ADVERB CLAUSES

- **Adverb clause,** independent clause.

    After the sky grew dark, the wind died suddenly.
- Independent clause, **adverb clause.**

    Birds stopped singing, **as they do during an eclipse.**
- Independent clause **adverb clause.**

    The stores closed **before the storm began.**

SENTENCES WITH ADJECTIVE CLAUSES

- Independent clause **restrictive (essential)[*] adjective clause.**

    Weather forecasts warned of a storm **that might bring a 45-centimetre snowfall.**
- Independent clause, **nonrestrictive (nonessential)[*] adjective clause.**

    Spring is the season for tornadoes, **which may have wind speeds over 350 km/h.**
- Beginning of independent clause **nonrestrictive (essential)[*] adjective clause** end of independent clause.

    Anyone **who lives through a tornado** remembers its power.

[*]For an explanation of RESTRICTIVE and NONRESTRICTIVE ELEMENTS, see section 24f.

QUICK REFERENCE **9.1** *continued*

- Beginning of independent clause, **nonrestrictive (nonessential)*** **adjective clause,** end of independent clause.

  The sky, **which had been clear,** turned greenish black.

SENTENCES WITH NOUN CLAUSES

- Independent clause **dependent noun clause**.

  People in the affected area heard **that a storm was on its way**.

- Independent clause **dependent noun clause**.

  You all know **where to take shelter during a tornado**.

9k   What meaning does each subordinating conjunction convey?

Each SUBORDINATING CONJUNCTION has its own meaning. When you choose one, be sure that its meaning accurately expresses the relationship between the ideas that you want to convey. Quick Reference 9.2 lists subordinating conjunctions according to their different meanings.

QUICK REFERENCE **9.2**

Subordinating conjunctions and their meanings

TIME

after, before, once, since, until, when, whenever, while

     After you have handed in your report, you cannot revise it.

REASON OR CAUSE

as, because, since

     Because you have handed in your report, you cannot revise it.

PURPOSE OR RESULT

in order that, so that, that

     I want to read your report **so that** I can evaluate it.

CONDITION

even if, if, provided that, unless

     Unless you have handed in your report, you can revise it.

CONTRAST

although, even though, though, whereas, while

     Although you have handed in your report, you can ask to revise it.

CHOICE

than, whether

     You took more time to revise **than** I did before the lab report deadline.

PLACE OR LOCATION

where, wherever

     Wherever you say, I'll come to hand in my report.

EXERCISE 9-4   Working individually or with a group, combine each pair of sentences, using an adverb clause to subordinate one idea. Then, revise each sentence so that the adverb clause becomes the independent clause. For help, see 9i through 9k, especially Quick Reference 9.2.

> **EXAMPLE** Some people think of their bodies as a blank canvas. They feel free to transform themselves into strange and unique works of art.
>
> > a. Because some people think of their bodies as a blank canvas, they feel free to transform themselves into strange and unique works of art.
> >
> > b. Some people feel free to transform themselves into strange and unique works of art, for they think of their bodies as a blank canvas.

1. Body modification has become astonishingly popular. No one can walk the streets of a Canadian city without seeing a parade of piercings and tattoos.
2. Unusual trends and rituals emerge in the urban subculture. Scholars rush in with their theories.
3. One theory sees body decorations and mutilations as an initiation into a symbolic community. A sociologist named David Le Breton focuses instead on their ability to promote individual self-expression.
4. Le Breton thinks that people use nose rings and tongue piercings, implants, and vivid tattoos to construct their own identity in a consumer society. Some people ask if our society is developing a whole new approach to the human body.
5. Not long ago, a man with a simple earring was considered outré. Our perceptions must have changed along with our customs.

EXERCISE 9-5   Working individually or with a group, combine each pair of sentences, using an adjective clause to subordinate one idea to the other. Then, revise each sentence so that the adjective clause becomes the independent clause. Use the relative pronoun given in parentheses. For help, consult 9i through 9k, especially Quick Reference 9.1.

> **EXAMPLE** Aristides was an ancient Greek politician famous for his honesty and judgment. He was known as Aristides the Just. (who)
>
> > a. Aristides, *who* was an ancient Greek politician famous for his honesty and judgment, was known as Aristides the Just.
> >
> > b. Aristides, *who* was known as Aristides the Just, was an ancient Greek politician famous for his honesty and judgment.

1. An ancient Athenian law allowed voters to banish politicians from their city. It asked citizens to write the name of an unpopular politician on their ballots. (that)
2. A voter was filling out a ballot when Aristides the Just walked by. The voter needed help in spelling *Aristides*. (who)
3. Aristides knew the voter did not recognize him. He asked why the voter wanted to banish that particular politician. (who)
4. The voter said he resented hearing someone called "the Just" all the time. He handed Aristides his ballot. (who)
5. Aristides' reaction demonstrated that the nickname "the Just" was well deserved. His reaction was to write his own name on the voter's ballot even though that person's vote helped banish Aristides. (which)

9l   How can I use subordination effectively?

To be effective, a SUBORDINATING CONJUNCTION must communicate a sensible relationship between the INDEPENDENT CLAUSE and the DEPENDENT CLAUSE. See Quick Reference 9.2 for a list of subordinating conjunctions and their different meanings.

> **NO**   **Because** Beethoven was deaf when he wrote them, his final symphonies were masterpieces. [*Because* is illogical here; it says the masterpieces resulted from the deafness.]

> **YES**   **Although** Beethoven was deaf when he wrote them, his final symphonies were masterpieces. [*Although* is logical here; it says Beethoven wrote masterpieces in spite of his being deaf.]

Subordination is also most effective when you avoid overusing it and crowding too many images or ideas together in one sentence. This causes readers to lose track of the message. Whenever you write a sentence with two or more dependent clauses, check that your message is clear.

> **NO**   A new technique for eye surgery, **which is supposed to correct nearsightedness, which previously could be corrected only by glasses,** has been developed, **although many eye doctors do not approve of the new technique because it can create unstable vision, which includes intense glare from headlights on cars and many other light sources.** [The base sentence *A new technique for eye surgery has been developed* is crowded with five dependent clauses attached to it.]

> **YES**   A new technique for eye surgery, **which is supposed to correct nearsightedness,** has been developed. Previously, only glasses could correct nearsightedness. Many doctors do not approve of the new technique **because it can create unstable vision.** The problems include intense glare from car headlights and many other sources of light. [In this revision, one long sentence has been broken into four sentences, which makes the material easier to read and the relationships among ideas clearer. Two dependent clauses remain, which balance well with the other sentence constructions. Some words have been moved to new positions.]

ESL TIP: If your instructor, manager, or peer reviewers advise that your sentences are too long and complex, limit the number of words in each sentence. Many ESL instructors recommend that you revise any sentence that contains more than three independent and dependent clauses in any combination. ●

EXERCISE 9-6   Working individually or with a group, correct illogical or excessive subordination in this paragraph. As you revise according to the message you want to deliver, use some dependent clauses as well as some short sentences. (Also, if you wish, apply the principles of coordination discussed in sections 9d through 9h.) For help, consult 9l.

    When the independent recording label Arts&Crafts set up shop, it chose a modest office building, which is on the edge of Toronto's Chinatown. The building has well-maintained wooden floors, although a close look reveals scars in the wood and even a few sewing needles caught between the planks, because the building once held hundreds of sewing machines and work tables. Until the situation changed in the 1970s, Spadina Avenue, which is only steps away, was at the centre of the city's garment district, where immigrants from the south and east of Europe filled its workshops. Even though today, the artwork from a Broken Social Scene CD cover decorates Arts&Crafts' office, a platinum disc by Feist leans against a wall, while boxes of CDs crowd the floor, two floors down a clothing industry trade union has its headquarters, although now it represents other workers, too. If visitors to Arts&Crafts look to one side as they turn the corner at Spadina, they can see a commemorative sculpture standing on the sidewalk, since it is made of half a dozen giant buttons and a towering sewing thimble.

9m How can I effectively use coordination and subordination together?

Your writing style improves when you use a logical and pleasing variety of SENTENCE TYPES, utilizing COORDINATION and SUBORDINATION to improve the flow of ideas. Here's a paragraph that demonstrates a good balance in the use of coordination and subordination.

> When I was growing up, I lived on a farm just across the field from my grandmother. My parents were busy trying to raise six children and to establish their struggling dairy farm. It was nice to have Grandma so close. While my parents were providing the necessities of life, my patient grandmother gave her time to her shy, young granddaughter. I always enjoyed going with Grandma and collecting the eggs that her chickens had just laid. Usually, she knew which chickens would peck, and she was careful to let me gather the eggs from the less hostile ones.
>
> —Patricia Mapes, student

When you use both coordination and subordination, never use both a COORDINATING CONJUNCTION and a SUBORDINATING CONJUNCTION to express one relationship in one sentence.

NO   **Although** the story was well written, **but** it was too illogical. [The subordinating conjunction *although* expresses the contrast, so also using *but* is incorrect.]

YES   **Although** the story was well written, it was too illogical.

YES   The story was well written, **but** it was too illogical.

EXERCISE 9-7   Working individually or in a group, use subordination and coordination to combine these sets of short, choppy sentences. For help, consult 9d through 9l.

EXAMPLE   Owls cannot digest the bones and fur of the mice and birds they eat. They cough up a furry pellet every day.

Because owls cannot digest the bones and fur of the mice and birds they eat, *they* cough up a furry pellet every day.

1. Owl pellets are the latest teaching tool in biology classrooms. The pellets provide an alternative to dissecting frogs and other animals.
2. Inside the pellet are the remains of the owl's nightly meal. They include beautifully cleaned hummingbird skulls, rat skeletons, and lots of bird feathers.
3. The owl-pellet market has been cornered by companies in the United States. These companies distribute pellets to thousands of biology classrooms all over the world.

4. Company workers scour barns and the ground under trees where owls nest to pick up the pellets. The pellets sell for $1 each.

5. The owl-pellet business may have a short future. The rural areas of the United States are vanishing. Old barns are being bulldozed. All the barns are torn down. The owls will be gone, too.

EXERCISE 9-8   Working individually or with a group, revise this paragraph to make it more effective by using coordination and subordination. For help, consult sections 9d through 9l.

The de Havilland aircraft company built the first Twin Otter bush plane in 1965. A bush plane is a small propeller craft. It is adapted to rugged conditions. The wheels can be replaced with skis to land on snow. They can be switched for hollow floats to land on water. Bush pilots love the Twin Otter. The Twin Otter has proven its reliability everywhere from Canada's Arctic to the world's jungles and deserts. The plane's powerful turboprop engines let it take off and land in difficult terrain. Turboprop engines use a gas turbine to drive the propellers. From 1965 through 1988, de Havilland built more than 800 Twin Otters in its Downsview, Ontario, plant. Seattle-based Boeing ended production of the small Twin Otter two years after it bought de Havilland. Boeing specializes in large aircraft. In 2006, Viking Air, a Canadian firm, bought the rights to the airplane. Viking is now manufacturing a new generation of Twin Otters in Calgary.

9n   How do occasional questions, commands, or exclamations create variety and emphasis?

The majority of sentences in English are DECLARATIVE—they tell something by making a statement. Declarative sentences offer an almost infinite variety of structures and patterns. For variety and emphasis, you might want to use three alternative types of sentences occasionally.

A sentence that asks a question is called INTERROGATIVE. Occasional questions, placed appropriately, tend to involve readers. A sentence that issues a command is called IMPERATIVE. Occasional mild commands, appropriately used, gently urge a reader to think along with you. A sentence that makes an exclamation is called EXCLAMATORY. An occasional exclamatory sentence can enliven writing, but you should use this sentence type only rarely in ACADEMIC WRITING.

ALERT: A declarative statement ends with a period (Chapter 23)—or semicolon (Chapter 25) or colon (Chapter 26). A mild command ends with a period. A strong command and an exclamation end with an exclamation mark (Chapter 23). •

Here's a paragraph with declarative, interrogative, and imperative sentences.

Does anyone look in the Yellow Pages any longer? Search engines are the new master reference. Just think of the last time you used the Yellow Pages—chances are good that you used the online version. In fact, it was the way people searched the online Yellow Pages that alerted executives in the company that produces this commercial directory to take another look at their product. To be precise, they examined the directory's user friendliness. They came up with a plan to revise the directory to match people's online search behaviour, and to match the search categories to the products and services people really look for these days. Out went categories like carbon paper, buttonhole makers, and typesetting machines; in came sushi and graffiti removal. Take a look in YellowPages.ca now. Even its home page now looks and behaves like a search engine.

9o What are cumulative and periodic sentences?

The **cumulative sentence** is the most common sentence structure in English. Its name reflects the way information accumulates in the sentence until it reaches a period. Its structure starts with a SUBJECT and VERB and continues with modifiers. Another term for a cumulative sentence is *loose sentence* because it lacks a tightly planned structure.

For greater impact, you might occasionally use a **periodic sentence**, also called a *climactic sentence*, which reserves the main idea for the end of the sentence. This structure tends to draw in the reader as it moves toward the period. If overused, however, periodic sentences lose their punch.

CUMULATIVE   We act as if we expect them all to thank us for it, after we have frightened our own people, disregarded our friends, and intimidated those we should be trying to win over to our side.

PERIODIC   We have frightened our own people, disregarded our friends, and intimidated those we should be trying to win over to our side, and now we expect them all to thank us for it.

You can build both cumulative and periodic sentences to dramatic lengths.

9p How can modifiers create variety and emphasis?

MODIFIERS can expand sentences to add richness to your writing and create a pleasing mixture of variety and emphasis. Your choice of where to place modifiers to expand your sentences depends on the focus you want each sentence to communicate, either on its own or in concert with surrounding sentences. Be careful where you place modifiers because you don't want to introduce the error known as a MISPLACED MODIFIER.

BASIC SENTENCE   The river rose.

ADJECTIVE   The **swollen** river rose.

ADVERB   The river rose **dangerously.**

PREPOSITIONAL PHRASE   The river rose **above its banks.**

PARTICIPIAL PHRASE   **Swelled by melting snow,** the river rose.

ABSOLUTE PHRASE   **Uprooted trees swirling away in the current,** the river rose.

ADVERB CLAUSE   **Because the snows had been heavy that winter,** the river rose.

ADJECTIVE CLAUSE   The river, **which runs through vital farmland,** rose.

EXERCISE 9-9   Working individually or with a group, expand each sentence by adding each kind of modifier illustrated in 9p.

1. We bought a house.
2. The roof leaked.
3. I remodelled the kitchen.
4. Neighbours brought food.
5. Everyone enjoyed the barbecue.

9q **How does repetition affect style?**

You can repeat one or more words that express a main idea when your message is suitable. This technique creates a rhythm that focuses attention on the main idea. Here's an example that uses deliberate repetition.

> The **knowledge** that you can have is inexhaustible, and what is inexhaustible is benevolent. The **knowledge** that you cannot have is of the riddles of birth and death, of our future destiny and the purposes of God. Here there is no **knowledge**, but illusions that restrict freedom and limit hope. Accept the mystery behind **knowledge**. It is not darkness but shadow.
>
> —Northrop Frye, Convocation Address, 1988

Frye repeats the word *knowledge* in different contexts to distinguish between the kinds of knowledge available to humans. His repetition of *inexhaustible*, his use of the parallel phrases *The knowledge that you can have . . . The knowledge that you cannot have*, and his linking of important concepts with the conjunctions *and* and *but* set up a series of rhythms that give this passage an almost prophetic power.

At the same time, don't confuse deliberate repetition with a lack of vocabulary variety.

> NO   An insurance agent can be an excellent adviser when you want to buy a car. An insurance agent has complete records on most cars. An insurance agent knows which car models are prone to have accidents. An insurance agent can tell you which car models are the most expensive to repair if they are in a collision. An insurance agent can tell you which models are most likely to be stolen. [Although only a few synonyms exist for *insurance agent, car,* and *model*, some do and should be used. Also, the sentence structure here lacks variety.]

> YES   If you are thinking of buying a new car, an insurance agent, who usually has complete records on most cars, can be an excellent adviser. Any professional insurance broker knows which automobile models are prone to have accidents. Did you know that some cars suffer more damage than others in a collision? If you want to know which vehicles crumple more than others and which are the most expensive to repair, ask an insurance agent. Similarly, some car models are more likely to be stolen, so find out from the person who specializes in dealing with car insurance claims.

9r **How else can I create variety and emphasis?**

CHANGING WORD ORDER

Standard word order in English places the SUBJECT before the VERB.

> The **mayor** *walked* into the room. [*Mayor*, the subject, comes before the verb *walked*.]

Any variation from standard word order creates emphasis. For example, **inverted word order** places the verb before the subject.

> Into the room *walked* the **mayor.** [*Mayor*, the subject, comes after the verb *walked*.]

CHANGING A SENTENCE'S SUBJECT

The subject of a sentence establishes the focus for that sentence. To create the emphasis you want, you can vary each sentence's subject. All of the sample sentences below express the same information, but the focus changes in each.

Our study *showed* that 25 percent of undergraduates' time is spent eating or sleeping. [Focus is on the study.]

Undergraduates *eat or sleep* 25 percent of the time, according to our study. [Focus is on the undergraduates.]

Eating or sleeping *occupies* 25 percent of undergraduates' time, according to our study. [Focus is on eating and sleeping.]

Twenty-five percent of undergraduates' time *is spent* eating or sleeping, according to our study. [Focus is on the percentage of time.]

EXERCISE 9-10 Working individually or with a group, revise the sentences in each paragraph to change the passage's style. For help, consult the advice in all sections of this chapter.

1. Thirst is the body's way of surviving. Every cell in the body needs water. People can die by losing as little as 15 to 20 percent of their water requirements. Blood contains 83 percent water. Blood provides indispensable nutrients for the cells. Blood carries water to the cells. Blood carries waste away from the cells. Insufficient water means cells cannot be fuelled or cleaned. The body becomes sluggish. The body can survive eleven days without water. Bodily functions are seriously disrupted by a lack of water for more than one day. The body loses water. The blood thickens. The heart must pump harder. Thickened blood is harder to pump through the heart. Some drinks replace the body's need for fluids. Alcohol or caffeine in drinks leads to dehydration. People know they should drink water often. They can become moderately dehydrated before they even begin to develop a thirst.

2. June is the wet season in Ghana. Here in Accra, the capital, the morning rain has ceased. The sun heats the humid air. Pillars of black smoke begin to rise above the vast Agbobgloshie Market. I follow one plume toward its source. I pass lettuce and plantain vendors. I pass stalls of used tires. I walk through a clanging scrap market. In the market hunched men bash on old alternators and engine blocks.

   —Based on a paragraph by Chris Carroll in "High Tech Trash"

3. Because of the development of new economies around the world, with resulting demands for new construction and goods, especially in places like China, there is a high demand for steel, and a new breed of Western entrepreneurs is making money in meeting this opportunity. For much of industrial history, steel was made from iron ore and coke, a process that resulted in what might be called "new steel." However, it has now become even more profitable to make recycled steel, melting down junk and recasting it, a process made possible because steel, unlike paper and plastic, can be recycled indefinitely. Because the process saves energy and helps the environment by saving on the amount of ore that has to be mined, manufacturing recycled steel has benefits beyond profitability.

Chapter 10

PARALLELISM

Common
Grammar
Errors:
17. Lack of
Parallel
Structure

10a What is parallelism?

When you write words, PHRASES, or CLAUSES within a sentence to match in their grammatical forms, the result is **parallelism**. Parallelism emphasizes information or ideas in writing. The technique relates to the concept of parallel lines in geometry. Parallelism delivers grace, rhythm, and impact.

> They come like foxes through the woods. They attack like lions. They take flight like birds, disappearing before they really appear.
>
> —Jérôme Lalemant, *The Jesuit Relations*

The Jesuit missionary and martyr conveys the sense of stealth, courage, and speed of the Iroquois by using parallel sets of similes from the natural world. The images gather force relentlessly.

You gain several advantages in using parallel structures:

* You can express ideas of equal weight in your writing.
* You can emphasize important information or ideas.
* You can add rhythm and grace to your writing style.

Many writers attend to parallelism when they are REVISING. If you think while you're DRAFTING that your parallelism is faulty or that you can enhance your writing style by using parallelism, underline or highlight the material and keep moving forward. When you revise, you can return to the places you've marked.

A **balanced sentence** is a type of parallelism in which contrasting content is delivered. The two parallel structures are usually, but not always, INDEPENDENT CLAUSES. A balanced sentence uses COORDINATION. The two coordinate structures are characterized by opposites in meaning, sometimes with one structure cast in the negative.

> By night, the litter and desperation disappeared as the city's glittering lights came on; by day, the filth and despair reappeared as the sun rose.
>
> —Jennifer Kirk, student

ALERT: Authorities differ about using a comma, a semicolon, or nothing between the parts of a short balanced sentence. In ACADEMIC WRITING, to avoid appearing to make the error of a COMMA SPLICE, use a semicolon (or revise in some other way), as in the following sentence.

> Mosquitoes don't bite; they stab. ●

10b How do words, phrases, and clauses work in parallel form?

When you put words, PHRASES, and CLAUSES into parallel form, you enhance your writing style with balance and grace.

PARALLEL WORDS Recommended exercise includes running, swimming, and cycling.

PARALLEL PHRASES Exercise helps people maintain healthy bodies and handle mental pressures.

PARALLEL CLAUSES Many people exercise because they want to look healthy, because they need to increase stamina, and because they hope to live longer.

10c How does parallelism deliver impact?

Writing in Action: Achieving Parallelism

Parallel structures serve to emphasize the meaning that sentences deliver. Deliberate, rhythmic repetition of parallel forms creates an effect of balance, reinforcing the impact of a message.

> Travel a thousand miles by train and you are a brute; pedal five hundred on a bicycle and you remain basically a bourgeois; paddle a hundred in a canoe and you are already a child of nature.
>
> —Pierre Elliott Trudeau, "The Ascetic in a Canoe"

Here's a longer passage in which parallel structures, concepts, and rhythms operate. Together, they echo the intensity of the writer's message.

> **It is a good country for** the honest, industrious artisan. **It is a fine country for** the poor labourer who, after a few years of hard toil, can sit down in his own log-house and look abroad on his own land and see his children well settled in life as independent freeholders. **It is a good country for** the rich speculator who can afford to lay out a large sum in purchasing land in eligible situations; for it he has any judgement he will make a hundred per cents as interest for his money after waiting a few years. But **it is a hard country for** the poor gentleman whose habits have rendered him unfit for manual labour.
>
> —Catharine Parr Trail, *The Backwoods of Canada*

EXERCISE 10-1 Working individually or with a group, highlight all parallel elements of the Catharine Pair Traill passage above in addition to those shown in boldface.

10d How can I avoid faulty parallelism?

AUDIO LESSON
Section 1:
Big Ideas—
Correcting
Common
Errors:
Subject-Verb
Agreement
and Parallel
Structure

Faulty parallelism usually results when you join nonmatching grammatical forms.

PARALLELISM WITH COORDINATING CONJUNCTIONS

The coordinating conjunctions are *and, but, for, or, nor, yet,* and *so.* To avoid faulty parallelism, write the words that accompany coordinating conjunctions in matching grammatical forms.

((‿•
AUDIO
LESSON
Section 2:
Practice
Questions—
Correcting
Common
Errors:
Subject-Verb
Agreement
and Parallel
Structure

NO	**Love *and* being married** go together.
YES	**Love *and* marriage** go together.
YES	**Being in love *and* being married** go together.

PARALLELISM WITH CORRELATIVE CONJUNCTIONS

Correlative conjunctions are paired words such as *not only . . . but (also), either . . . or,* and *both . . . and.* To avoid faulty parallelism, write the words joined by correlative conjunctions in matching grammatical forms.

((‿•
AUDIO
LESSON
Section 3:
Key Terms—
Correcting
Common
Errors:
Subject-Verb
Agreement
and Parallel
Structure

NO	Differing expectations for marriage ***not only*** **can lead to disappointment *but also* makes the couple angry.**
YES	Differing expectations for marriage ***not only*** **can lead to disappointment *but also* can make the couple angry.**

PARALLELISM WITH *THAN* AND *AS*

To avoid faulty parallelism when you use *than* and *as* for comparisons, write the elements of comparison in matching grammatical forms.

NO	**Having a solid marriage** can be more satisfying ***than* the acquisition of wealth.**
YES	**Having a solid marriage** can be more satisfying ***than* acquiring wealth.**
YES	**A solid marriage** can be more satisfying ***than* wealth.**

PARALLELISM WITH FUNCTION WORDS

Function words include ARTICLES (*the, a, an*); the *to* of the INFINITIVE (*to* love); PREPOSITIONS (for example, *of, in, about*); and sometimes RELATIVE PRONOUNS. When you write a series of parallel structures, be consistent in the second and successive structures about either repeating or omitting a function word. Generally, repeat function words only if you think that the repetition clarifies your meaning or highlights the parallelism that you intend.

NO	**To assign** unanswered letters their proper weight, **free** us from the expectations of others, **to give** us back to ourselves—here lies the great, the singular power of self-respect.
YES	**To assign** unanswered letters their proper weight, **to free** us from the expectations of others, **to give** us back to ourselves—here lies the great, the singular power of self-respect.

—Joan Didion, "On Self-Respect"

I have in my own life a precious friend, a woman of 65 **who has** lived very hard, **who is** wise, **who listens** well, **who has been** where I am and can help me understand it, and **who represents** not only an ultimate ideal mother to me but also the person I'd like to be when I grow up.

—Judith Viorst, "Friends, Good Friends—and Such Good Friends"

We looked into the bus, which **was** painted blue with orange daisies, **had** picnic benches instead of seats, and **showed** yellow curtains billowing out its windows.

—Kerrie Falk, student

EXERCISE 10-2 Working individually or with a group, revise these sentences by putting appropriate information in parallel structures. For help, consult 10a through 10d.

> **EXAMPLE** Difficult bosses affect not only their employees' performances but their private lives are affected as well.
>
> Difficult bosses affect not only their employees' performances *but their private lives as well.*

1. According to the psychologist Harry Levinson, the five main types of bad boss are the workaholic, the kind of person you would describe as bullying, a person who communicates badly, the jellyfish type, and someone who insists on perfection.

2. As a way of getting ahead, to keep their self-respect, and for survival purposes, wise employees handle problem bosses with a variety of strategies.

3. To cope with a bad-tempered employer, workers can both stand up for themselves and reasoning with a bullying boss.

4. Often, bad bosses communicate poorly or fail to calculate the impact of their personality on others; being a careful listener and sensitivity to others' responses are qualities that good bosses possess.

5. Employees who take the trouble to understand what makes their bosses tick, engage in some self-analysis, and staying flexible are better prepared to cope with a difficult job environment than suffering in silence like some employees.

EXERCISE 10-3 Working individually or with a group, combine the sentences in each numbered item, using techniques of parallelism. For help, consult 10a through 10d.

> **EXAMPLE** A few years ago Canadians witnessed a renaissance of skateboarding. Skateboarding inspired its own clothing styles. In fact, a skateboard culture also was developed.
>
> A few years ago Canadians witnessed a renaissance of skateboarding, *which not only inspired its own clothing styles but also developed its own culture.*

1. Cities became filled with whirling skateboarders; they flew on their skateboards. These skateboarders hopped curbs and would leap boldly up and down stairs. They also careened unsteadily down railings.

2. Not long afterward began the reign of in-line skates. They were built for speed. Young adults adopted them to commute and also in order to show off their style.

3. Skateboarders, who had a preference for gymnastic feats, were unlike the people who used in-like skates. These people favoured a graceful, undulating style marked by sweeping strides.

4. Late in the 1990s, small-wheeled scooters became popular. Adults liked them. They also became popular with young children.

5. Any town that has a sidewalk has certainly seen children wobbling on these scooters. If a town is big enough to have a rush hour, people there probably have seen business people on motorized versions, trying to beat the traffic.

EXERCISE 10-4   Working individually or with a group, underline the parallel elements in these three passages. Next, imitate the parallelism in the examples, using a different topic of your choice for each.

1. From books I learned that I am congenitally a fantastically skilful liar, an indefatigable gossip, a cunning weaver of superbly successful plots, a consummate manipulator, a subtle mistress of innuendo, that I am gifted with a fabulous imagination. I discovered that I am a compulsive rumour-monger, a capricious maker and breaker of reputations, so talented in the arts of persuasion that I can out-talk and out-argue any man and convince him of anything.
    —Adele Wiseman, "Word Power: Women and Prose in Canada Today"

2. It was the 18th of October, 1830, in the morning, when my feet first touched the Canadian shore. I threw myself on the ground, rolled in the sand, seized handfuls of it and kissed them, and danced around, till, in the eyes of several who were present, I passed for a madman.
    —Josiah Henson (an escaped slave and the model for Harriet Beecher Stowe's Uncle Tom), *An Autobiography*

3. It was Sunday morning at 11 o'clock and David Suzuki was on the radio, warning of the environmental catastrophe looming around his listeners. A generation ago most of us would have been in church at this time; and here we were in church again. Dr. Suzuki's programme, with its visions of Armageddon and its call to repentance and conversion, was surely a sermon.
    —David Cayley, "The Beer Can or the Highway?"

10e How does parallelism work in outlines and lists?

All items in formal OUTLINES and lists must be parallel in grammar and structure. (For more about outline format and outline development, see section 2f.)

OUTLINES

NO   Reducing Traffic Fatalities

    I. Stricter laws
       A. Top speed should be 80 km/h on highways.
       B. Higher fines
       C. Requiring jail sentences for repeat offenders
   II. The use of safety devices should be mandated by law.

YES   Reducing Traffic Fatalities

    I. Passing stricter speed laws
       A. Making 80 km/h the top speed on highways
       B. Raising fines for speeding
       C. Requiring jail sentences for repeat offenders
   II. Mandating by law the use of safety devices

LISTS

NO Workaholics share these characteristics:

1. They are intense and driven.
2. Strong self-doubters
3. Labor is preferred to leisure by workaholics.

YES Workaholics share these characteristics:

1. They are intense and driven.
2. They have strong self-doubts.
3. They prefer labor to leisure.

EXERCISE 10-5 Working individually or with a group, revise this outline so that all lines are complete sentences in parallel form. For help, consult 2f and 10e.

Improving Health

I. Exercise
   A. Aerobics
   B. Stretching and strength training
   C. Vary routine
II. Better Eating Habits
   A. Healthy food
   B. Eat less
   C. Eat more often

Chapter 11

CONCISENESS

11a What is conciseness?

Conciseness requires you to craft sentences that are direct and to the point. Its opposite, **wordiness**, means that you are filling sentences with empty words and phrases that contribute nothing to meaning. Wordy writing is padded with deadwood, forcing readers to clear away the branches and overgrowth—an annoying waste of time that implies the writer isn't skilled. Usually, the best time to work on making your writing more concise is while you're REVISING.*

WORDY ~~As a matter of fact,~~ the [T] [local] television station ~~which is situated~~

~~in the local area~~ wins ~~a great~~ many awards ~~in the final~~

~~analysis because of~~ its ~~type of~~ [for] coverage of ~~all kinds of~~ controversial issues.

CONCISE The local television station wins many awards for its coverage of controversial issues.

Common Grammar Errors: 19. Wordiness and Redundancy

11b What common expressions are not concise?

Many common expressions we use in informal speech are not concise. Quick Reference 11.1 lists some and shows you how to eliminate them.

EXERCISE 11-1 Working individually or with a group, revise these sentences in two steps. First, underline all words that interfere with conciseness. Second, revise each sentence to make it more concise. (You'll need to drop words and replace or rearrange others.)

> **EXAMPLE** It seems that most North Americans think of motor scooters as vehicles that exist only in European countries.
>
> <u>It seems that</u> most North Americans think of motor scooters as <u>vehicles that exist</u> only in European countries.
>
> Most North Americans think of motor scooters as only European vehicles.

1. As a matter of fact, in the popular imagination, motor scooters are the very essence of European style.

---

*Words printed in SMALL CAPITAL LETTERS are discussed elsewhere in the text and are defined in the Terms Glossary at the back of the book.

QUICK REFERENCE 11.1

Cutting unnecessary words and phrases

EMPTY WORD OR PHRASE	WORDY EXAMPLE REVISED
as a matter of fact	Many marriages, ~~as a matter of fact,~~ end in divorce.
at the present time	The revised proposal for outdoor lighting angers many villagers ~~at the present time.~~ _now_
because of the fact that, in light of the fact that, due to the fact that	~~Because of the fact that~~ the museum has a special exhibit, it stays open late.
by means of	We travelled by ~~means of~~ a car.
factor	The project's final cost was the essential ~~factor~~ to consider.
for the purpose of	Work crews arrived ~~for the purpose~~ of fixing the potholes. _to_
have a tendency to	The team ~~has a tendency~~ to lose home games. _tends_
in a very real sense	~~In a very real sense,~~ all firefighters are heroes.
in the case of	~~In the case of~~ the election, ~~the~~ result will be close.
in the event that	~~In the event that~~ you're late, I will buy our tickets. _If_
in the final analysis	~~In the final analysis, no~~ two eyewitnesses agreed on what they saw. _N_
in the process of	We are in ~~the process of~~ reviewing the proposal.
it seems that	~~It seems that~~ the union went on strike over health benefits. _T_
manner	The child spoke in ~~a reluctant manner.~~ _reluctantly_
nature	The movie review was ~~of a sarcastic nature.~~
that exists	The crime rate ~~that exists~~ is unacceptable.
the point I am trying to make	~~The point I am trying to make is~~ television reporters invade our privacy. _T_
type of, kind of, sort of	Gordon took a relaxing ~~type of~~ vacation.
what I mean to say is	~~What I mean to say~~ is I love you.

2. Today, over one million scooters are purchased by people in Europe each year, compared with a number that amounts to only a few thousand buyers in Canada.

3. In fact, Europeans have long used fuel-efficient, clean-running scooters for the purpose of getting around in a manner that is relatively easy in congested cities.

4. The use of these brightly coloured, manoeuvrable scooters allows city dwellers to zip through traffic jams and thereby to save time as well as to save gas.

5. However, sales of scooters, it might interest you to know, are in the process of increasing in North America.

6. What I am trying to say is that motor scooters use much less gasoline than cars, and that as a matter of fact the cost factor is about one-fourth that of an inexpensive new car.

7. In addition, some motor scooters, it is pleasing to note, now run on electricity, which in fact makes them noise and emission free.

8. A scooter running by means of electrical power amounts to a cost in the neighbourhood of 50 cents to travel 180 kilometres at 50 km/h.

9. Members of many different population groups, from students to retired persons, have begun to be finding this type of vehicle to be of a useful nature in a very real sense.

10. Travelling by means of an agile, snappy scooter makes getting around campus or doing errands in a city neighbourhood quick and easy.

11c What sentence structures usually work against conciseness?

Two sentence structures, although appropriate in some contexts, often work against conciseness because they can lead to wordiness: writing EXPLETIVE constructions and writing in the PASSIVE VOICE.

AVOIDING EXPLETIVE CONSTRUCTIONS

An expletive construction starts with *it* or *there* followed by a form of the VERB *be*. When you cut the expletive construction and revise, the sentence becomes more direct.

~~It is necessary for~~ students ~~to~~ ^S ^{must} fill in both questionnaires.

~~There are~~ eight instructors ~~who~~ teach in the Computer Science Department.

ESL TIPS: (1) *It* in an expletive construction is not a PRONOUN referring to a specific ANTECEDENT. *It* is an "empty" word that fills the SUBJECT position in the sentence but does not function as the subject. The actual subject appears after the expletive construction: ***It was the teacher*** *who answered the question.* If put concisely, the sentence would be *The teacher answered the question.* (2) *There* in an expletive construction does not indicate a place. Rather, *there* is an "empty" word that fills the subject position in the sentence but does not function as the subject. The actual subject appears after the expletive construction: ***There are many teachers*** *who can answer the question.* If concise, the sentence would be *Many teachers can answer the question.* ●

AVOIDING THE PASSIVE VOICE

In general, the passive voice is less concise—as well as less lively—than the ACTIVE VOICE. In the active voice, the subject of a sentence does the action named by the verb.

ACTIVE   Professor Horvath teaches public speaking. [*Professor Horvath* is the subject, and
           he does the action: He *teaches*.]

In the passive voice, the subject of a sentence receives the action named by the verb.

PASSIVE   Public speaking is taught by Professor Horvath. [*Public speaking* is the subject,
            and it receives the action *taught*.]

Unless your meaning justifies using the passive voice, choose the active voice. (For more
information, see 15n through 15p.)

PASSIVE   Volunteer work was done by students for credit in sociology. [The passive
            phrase *was done by students* is unnecessary for the intended meaning. *Students* are doing
            the action and should get the action of the verb.]

ACTIVE   **The students did** volunteer work for credit in sociology.

ACTIVE   **Volunteer work earned** students credit in sociology. [Since the verb has
           changed to *earned*, *volunteer work* performs the action of the verb.]

In mistakenly believing the passive voice sounds "mature" or "academic," student writers sometimes use it deliberately. Wordy, overblown sentences suggest that a writer hasn't
revised carefully.

NO   One very important quality developed during a first job is self-reliance. This
       strength was gained by me when I was allowed by my supervisor to set up
       and conduct a survey project on my own.

YES   Many individuals develop the important quality of self-reliance during their
        first job. I gained this strength when my supervisor allowed me to set up and
        conduct my own survey project.

YES   During their first job, many people develop self-reliance, as I did when my
        supervisor let me set up and conduct my own survey project.

11d How else can I revise for conciseness?

Four other techniques can help you achieve conciseness: eliminating unplanned repetition
(11d.1); combining sentences (11d.2); shortening CLAUSES (11d.3); and shortening
PHRASES and cutting words (11d.4). These techniques involve matters of judgment.

Writing in
Action:
Combining
Sentences

11d.1 Eliminating unplanned repetition

Unplanned repetition, or redundancy, delivers the same message more than once, usually
in slightly different words. Redundancy implies that the writer lacks focus and judgment.
The opposite—planned repetition—reflects both focus and judgment, as it creates a powerful rhythmic effect; see 10c. As you revise, check that every word is necessary for delivering your message.

NO   Bringing **the project** to **final completion** three weeks early, the supervisor
       of **the project** earned our **respectful regard**. [*Completion* implies *bringing to
       final*; *project* is used twice in one sentence; and *regard* implies *respect*.]

YES   Completing the project three weeks early, the supervisor earned our respect.
        [eighteen words reduced to eleven by cutting all redundancies]

NO **Astonished**, the architect **circled around** the building **in amazement**.
[*Circled* means "went around," and *astonished* and in *amazement* have the same meaning.]

YES **Astonished,** the architect **circled** the building. [nine words reduced to six]

YES The architect **circled** the building **in amazement**. [nine words reduced to seven]

ESL TIP: In all languages, words often carry an unspoken message that is assumed by native speakers of the language. In English, some implied meanings can cause redundancy in writing. For example, *I nodded vigorously to indicate enthusiastic agreement* is redundant. Most native speakers of English expect that nodding vigorously implies enthusiastic agreement. ●

11d.2 Combining sentences

Look at sets of sentences in your writing to see if you can fit information contained in one sentence into another sentence. (For more about combining sentences, see Chapter 9, particularly 9c, 9e, 9j and 9m.)

TWO SENTENCES The *Titanic* hit an iceberg and sank. Seventy-three years later, a team of French and American scientists located the ship's resting site.

SENTENCES COMBINED Seventy-three years after the *Titanic* hit an iceberg and sank, a team of French and American scientists located the ship's resting site.

TWO SENTENCES Cameras revealed that the stern of the ship was missing and showed external damage to the ship's hull. Otherwise, the *Titanic* was in excellent condition.

SENTENCES COMBINED Cameras revealed that, aside from a missing stern and external damage to the ship's hull, the *Titanic* was in excellent condition.

11d.3 Shortening clauses

Look at clauses in your writing to see if you can more concisely convey the same information. For example, sometimes you can cut a RELATIVE PRONOUN and its verb.

WORDY The *Titanic,* **which was** a huge ocean liner, sank in 1912.

CONCISE The *Titanic,* a huge ocean liner, sank in 1912.

Sometimes you can reduce a clause to a word.

WORDY The scientists held a memorial service for the passengers and crew **who had drowned**.

CONCISE The scientists held a memorial service for the **drowned** passengers and crew.

Sometimes an ELLIPTICAL CONSTRUCTION (14p and 22h) can shorten a clause. If you use this technique, be sure that any omitted word is implied clearly.

WORDY	**When they were** confronted with disaster, some passengers behaved heroically, **while** others **behaved** selfishly.
CONCISE	Confronted with disaster, some passengers behaved heroically, others selfishly.

11d.4 Shortening phrases and cutting words

Sometimes you can reduce a phrase or redundant word pair to a single word. Redundant word pairs and phrases include *each and every, one and only, forever and ever, final and conclusive, perfectly clear, few* (or *many*) *in number, consensus of opinion,* and *reason . . . is because.*

NO	**Each and every** person was hungry after the movie.
YES	**Every** person was hungry after the movie.
YES	**Each** person was hungry after the movie.

NO	The **consensus of opinion** was that the movie was disappointing
YES	The **consensus** was that the movie was disappointing.
YES	**Everyone agreed** that the movie was disappointing.

WORDY	More than fifteen hundred **travellers on that voyage** died in the shipwreck.
CONCISE	More than fifteen hundred **passengers** died in the shipwreck.

Sometimes you can rearrange words so that others can be deleted.

WORDY	Objects **found** inside the ship included **unbroken** bottles of wine and expensive **undamaged** china.
CONCISE	**Found undamaged** inside the ship were bottles of wine and expensive china.

11e How do verbs affect conciseness?

ACTION VERBS are strong verbs. *Be* and *have* are weak verbs that often lead to wordy sentences. When you revise weak verbs to strong ones, you can both increase the impact of your writing and reduce the number of words in your sentences. Strong verbs come into play when you revise your writing to reduce PHRASES and to change NOUNS to verbs.

WEAK VERB	The plan before the city council **has to do with** tax rebates.
STRONG VERB	The plan before the city council **proposes** tax rebates.

WEAK VERBS	The board members **were of the opinion** that the changes in the rules **were changes they would not accept**.
STRONG VERBS	The board members **said** that **they would not accept** the changes in the rules.

((•
AUDIO LESSON
Section 1:
Big Ideas—
Verbs

((•
AUDIO LESSON
Section 2:
Practice Questions—
Verbs

REPLACING A PHRASE WITH A VERB

Phrases such as *be aware of, be capable of, be supportive of* can often be replaced with one-word verbs.

I **envy** [not *am envious of*] your mathematical ability.

I **appreciate** [not *am appreciative of*] your modesty.

Your skill **illustrates** [not *is illustrative of*] how hard you studied.

REVISING NOUNS INTO VERBS

Many nouns are derived from verbs, including nouns that end in *-ance, -ment,* and *-tion* (*tolerance, enforcement, narration*). When you turn such wordy nouns back into verbs, your writing is more concise.

NO   The **accumulation of** paper lasted thirty years.

YES   The paper **accumulated** for thirty years.

NO   We **arranged for the establishment of** a student advisory committee.

YES   We **established** a student advisory committee.

NO   The building **had the appearance of** having been neglected.

YES   The building **appeared** to have been neglected.

EXERCISE 11-2   Working individually or with a group, combine each set of sentences to elimi-nate wordy constructions. For help, consult 11c through 11e.

EXAMPLE   In recent years, ranchers have tried to raise and market many exotic meats. These meats have included emu, ostrich, and bison. These attempts have failed.

In recent years, ranchers have tried but failed to raise and market many exotic meats, such as emu, ostrich, and bison.

1. Each new attempt of ranchers to raise exotic animals like emu, ostrich, and bison for the commercial value of their meat follows a pattern. There is a similar pattern to each new attempt. Each new attempt begins when a few people make the claim that some exotic animal tastes better than beef and is more nutritious.

2. Emus were discovered by ranchers. Emus are birds that look like small ostriches. Emus quickly became unprofitable to raise. Only a few consumers found emu meat tasty.

3. It was found by ostrich ranchers that there was an early, strong demand for the meat of ostriches. That strong demand soon fizzled out quite a bit, the ranchers found.

4. There is the American Ostrich Association. The membership of the American Ostrich Association once used to be 3000. Today, the membership of the American Ostrich Association now has only 500 people belonging to it.

5. Bison, also known as buffalo, were a longer-lasting craze. Ranchers had a strong desire to own the mighty animals; however, the price of bison was increased greatly by the demand. It became uneconomical for ranchers to purchase young animals.

6. Also, bison are difficult to raise. They tend to need strong fences to hold them in. They cannot find enough food to eat. They eat by grazing. The land of some buffalo ranches consists of poor pasture land or is in mountainous terrain.

7. Recently, the yak has been discovered by ranchers. The yak is an animal from Central Asia. It is from rugged mountainous areas. For centuries, the yak has supported the people of the Himalayan region.

8. Yaks have the ability to forage more efficiently compared with bison or cows. Yaks are easier to care for than bison or cows. Yaks possess a better resistance to many diseases.

9. Chefs in a few gourmet restaurants are beginning to serve yak meat. They are devising fancy recipes for it. They are featuring it on their menus. The meat is mild-tasting and succulent. The meat is also low in fat.

10. Even though yaks are easy to raise and even are environmentally friendly, there is a problem. The ranchers must overcome that problem before they can raise yaks profitably. That problem is the fact that consumers lack familiarity with yaks. Consumers have a reluctance to try yak meat.

EXERCISE 11-3 Working individually or with a group, revise this paragraph in two steps. First, underline all words that interfere with conciseness. Second, revise the paragraph to make it more concise. (You'll need to drop words and replace or rearrange others.)

EXAMPLE Within a matter of minutes after the completion of a championship game, the winning team's players are enabled to put on caps that have been embroidered with their team's name, the year, as well as the word "champions."

Minutes after completing a championship game, the winning team's players receive caps embroidered with their team's name, the year, and the word "champions."

(1) At the present time, caps for sports teams are manufactured in factories located primarily in Asian countries such as China, Korea, and Taiwan. (2) Championship caps are quickly produced and shipped by factories wherever they are needed for both of the two teams playing in a final game or series. (3) The very moment the game ends, a trucking company delivers the caps to the winning team's locker room, and it then immediately and instantly burns the losing team's caps so as to prevent embarrassing anyone. (4) Companies that produce all types of sports apparel know that in most cases there is only a short period of time available for making and earning high profits from merchandise connected to a winning team. (5) Within barely a day or two, they flood the market with all sorts of every kind of T-shirts, jackets, caps, coffee mugs, in addition to banners showing and presenting the winning team's championship information.

Chapter 12

THE IMPACT OF WORDS

12a What is Canadian English?

North American English, evolving over centuries into a rich language, reflects the contributions of many cultures. Food names, for example, show how other languages and cultures loaned words to English. Africans brought the word *okra;* Spanish and Latin American peoples contributed *tortilla* and *taco.* From German we got *hamburger;* Italian supplied *spaghetti* and *antipasto;* Yiddish is responsible for *bagel;* and Japanese gave us *sushi.*

French language and culture have especially influenced the Canadian variety of North American English. The most characteristic borrowings are words such as *portage, voyageur, lacrosse, francophone, Métis,* and *concession* road. The languages of the Aboriginal peoples of Canada have also enriched the English spoken here with words such as *kayak, pemmican, chinook,* and *caribou.* Yet what most distinguishes Canadian English from other North American speech is the mark left on it by waves of nineteenth-century immigrants from the British Isles. Their varieties of English merged with the English that the Loyalists, who had fled the American Revolution, had brought to Canada decades earlier.

In all languages, the meanings of some words change with time. For example, W. Nelson Francis points out in *The English Language* (New York: Norton, 1965) that the word *nice* "has been used at one time or another in its 700-year history to mean . . . foolish, wanton, strange, lazy, coy, modest, fastidious, refined, precise, subtle, slender, critical, attentive, minutely accurate, dainty, appetizing, agreeable."

12b What is edited Canadian English?

AUDIO LESSON Section 1: Big Ideas—Using Language Well and Addressing Your Audience

AUDIO LESSON Section 2: Practice Questions— Using Language Well and Addressing Your Audience

ACADEMIC WRITING in Canada uses **edited Canadian English**, a medium or formal level of language that conforms to established standards of grammar, sentence structure, punctuation, and spelling. The same standards apply in textbooks (including this one), serious magazines and newspapers, and most nonfiction books. Edited Canadian English is one of the varieties of STANDARD ENGLISH, which is spoken and written in a number of countries and used by educated people to standardize communication throughout the world.

Nonstandard English is legitimately spoken in some regions and by some groups. As well, different forms of colloquial language and slang are used among friends or in specific social settings. With their own grammar and usage, these forms of speech (and, sometimes, writing) communicate clearly to other speakers of the same varieties of English. Yet employment and academic situations normally require the ability to write in one of the forms of standard English, at a medium or formal level (8b).

Advertising language and other popular forms have their own uses and their own appeal, but are not models of the standard English that academic writing uses to treat sophisticated subjects.

12c What is figurative language?

AUDIO LESSON Section 3: Rapid Review—Using Language Well and Addressing Your Audience

Figurative language uses words for more than their literal meanings. Such words aren't merely decorative or pretentious (12g). Figurative language greatly enhances meaning. It makes comparisons and connections that draw on one idea or image to explain another. Quick Reference 12.1 explains the different types of figurative language and describes one type you should avoid, the **mixed metaphor**.

QUICK REFERENCE   **12.1**

Types of figurative language

- **Analogy:** Comparing similar traits shared by dissimilar things or ideas. Its length can vary from one sentence (which often takes the form of a simile or metaphor) to a paragraph.

    To understand the workings of a **ball and socket joint,** you can look at the movements of **your own shoulder;** the tool that you saw yesterday in the robotics laboratory was moved by a **mechanical shoulder.**

- **Irony:** Using words to suggest the opposite of their usual sense.

    Told that a minor repair on her home would cost $2000 and take two weeks, she said, **"Oh, how nice!"**

- **Metaphor:** Comparing otherwise dissimilar things. A metaphor doesn't use the word *like* or *as* to make a comparison.

    Rush-hour **traffic** in the city **bled out through major arteries** to the suburbs.

- **Personification:** Assigning a human trait to something not human.

    The **book begged** to be read.

- **Overstatement** (also called *hyperbole*)**:** Exaggerating deliberately for emphasis.

    If this paper is late, the professor will **kill** me.

- **Simile:** Comparing dissimilar things. A simile uses the word *like* or *as*.

    Langston Hughes observes that a deferred **dream dries up "like a raisin in the sun."**

- **Understatement:** Emphasizing by using deliberate restraint.

    It feels **warm** when the temperature reaches **35 degrees.**

- **Mixed metaphor:** Combining two or more inconsistent images in one sentence or expression. Never use a mixed metaphor.

    NO   Quick-witted John Crosbie was skilled at stickhandling his way through the shoals of Question Period. [*Stickhandling* is a hockey manoeuvre; *shoals* are submerged sandbanks and rocks that endanger ships.]

    YES   Quick-witted John Crosbie was skilled at stickhandling his way through the challenges of Question Period.

EXERCISE 12-1 Working individually or with a group, identify each type of figurative language or figure of speech. Also revise any mixed metaphors. For help, consult 12c.

1. Good manners are the grease for the wheels of human interaction.
2. Without manners, people would be meaner than junkyard dogs.
3. Being rude is like tracking mud on a freshly mopped floor.
4. If you can't mind your business, at least mind your manners.
5. Good manners are the icing on the cake of human behaviour.
6. Being rude should be a criminal offence.
7. Compliments are magicians wielding great power.
8. When you're rude to people, you're playing with fire and getting in over your head.
9. Being polite when you're frustrated, irritated, and exasperated is as difficult as staying awake while driving when you haven't had enough sleep.
10. He's so tactless that if speech were a weapon, his would be a blunt instrument.

Writing in
Action:
Exploring
Appropriate
Language

12d How can using exact diction enhance my writing?

Diction, the term for choice of words, affects the clarity and impact of any writing you do. Your best chance of delivering your intended message to your readers is to choose words that fit exactly with each piece of writing. To choose words correctly—that is, to have good diction—you need to understand the concepts of *denotation* and *connotation*.

12d.1 What is denotation?

The **denotation** of a word is its exact, literal meaning. It's the meaning you find when you look up the word in a dictionary. A dictionary is your ultimate authority for a word's denotation.

- An **unabridged dictionary** contains the most extensive, complete, and scholarly entries. Such dictionaries include all infrequently used words that abridged dictionaries often omit. The most comprehensive, authoritative unabridged dictionary of English is the *Oxford English Dictionary* (*OED*), which traces each word's history and gives quotations to illustrate changes in meaning and spelling over the life of the word.
- An **abridged dictionary** contains most commonly used words. Many of these dictionaries are referred to as "college editions." Two dictionaries intended for Canadian users are the *Gage Canadian Dictionary* (revised and expanded, 2000), and the *Canadian Oxford Dictionary* (second edition, 2004). For British style, Canadians usually consult the *Concise Oxford Dictionary*; some prefer an American dictionary such as *Merriam-Webster's Collegiate Dictionary*. Many dictionaries are available online.
- A **specialized dictionary** focuses on a single area of language. You can find dictionaries of slang (for example, *Dictionary of Slang and Unconventional English*, ed. Eric Partridge); word origins (for example, *Dictionary of Word and Phrase Origins*, ed. William Morris and Mary Morris); synonyms (for example, *Gage Canadian Thesaurus*; *Roget's 21st Century Thesaurus*); usage (for example, *Guide to Canadian English Usage*, by Margery Fee and Janice McAlpine); idioms (for example, *Dictionary of Canadianisms on Historical Principles*, ed. Walter S. Avis et al.; *Longman Dictionary of English Idioms*); regionalisms (for example, *Dictionary of Newfoundland English*, ed. G. M. Story et al.; *Dictionary of American Regional English*, ed. Frederic Cassidy); and many others.

ESL TIP: For students whose native language is not English, recommended dictionaries include the *American Heritage English as a Second Language Dictionary,* the *Oxford ESL Dictionary,* and the *Longman Dictionary of Contemporary English.* Each dictionary's introductory pages describe the types of information found in word entries. ●

12d.2   What is connotation?

Connotation refers to ideas implied by a word. Connotations are never completely fixed, for they can vary in differing contexts. They involve associations and emotional overtones that go beyond a word's definition. For example, *home* usually evokes more emotion than its denotation "a dwelling place" or its synonym *house. Home* carries the connotation, for some, of the pleasures of warmth, security, and love of family. For others, however, *home* may carry unpleasant connotations, such as abusive experiences or the impersonal atmosphere of an institution to house the elderly.

USING A THESAURUS

Sometimes a good college dictionary explains the differences among synonyms; a thesaurus is devoted entirely to providing synonyms for words. In distinguishing among **synonyms**— the other words close in meaning to a word—a thesaurus demonstrates connotation in operation. As you use a thesaurus, remain very alert to the subtle shades of meaning that create distinctions among words. For instance, using *notorious* to describe a person famous for praiseworthy achievements in public life is wrong. Although *notorious* means "well-known" and "publicly discussed"—which is true of famous people—the connotation of the word is "unfavourably known or talked about." Sports hero Gordie Howe is famous, not notorious. Murderer Paul Bernardo, by contrast, is notorious.

Here's another example, with the word *obdurate,* which means "not easily moved to pity or sympathy." Its synonyms include *inflexible, obstinate, stubborn,* and *hardened.*

> NO   Footprints showed in the **obdurate** concrete.
> YES   The supervisor remained **obdurate** in refusing to accept excuses.
> YES   My **obdurate** roommates won't let my pet boa constrictor live in the bathtub.

ALERT: Most word-processing programs include a thesaurus. Be cautious in using it. Unless you know the exact meaning of a synonym, as well as its part of speech, you may choose a wrong word or introduce a grammatical error into your writing. For example, one word-processing program's thesaurus offers these synonyms for *deep* in the sense of "low (down, inside)": *low, below, beneath,* and *subterranean.* None of these words could replace *deep* in a sentence such as *The crater is too deep* [not too low, too below, too beneath, or too subterranean] *to be filled with sand or rocks.* ●

EXERCISE 12-2   Working individually or with a group, look at each list of words and divide the words among three headings: "Positive" (good connotations); "Negative" (bad connotations); and "Neutral" (no connotations). If you think that a word belongs under more than one heading, you can assign it more than once, but be ready to explain your thinking. For help, consult a good dictionary and 12d.2.

> **EXAMPLE** grand, big, bulky, significant, oversized
>
> > *Positive:* grand, significant; *Negative:* bulky, oversized; *Neutral:* big

1. harmony, sound, racket, shriek, melody, music, noise, pitch, voice
2. talkative, articulate, chattering, eloquent, vocal, verbose, gossipy, fluent, gabby
3. decorative, beautiful, modern, ornate, overelaborate, dazzling, flashy, elegant, sparkling
4. long, lingering, enduring, continued, drawn-out, stretched, never-ending, unbreakable, incessant
5. calculating, shrewd, crafty, ingenious, keen, sensible, sly, smooth, underhanded

12e How can using specific words enhance my writing?

The Use of Imagery in Writing (PowerPoint Presentation)

Specific words identify individual items in a group (*Ford, Honda*). **General words** relate to an overall group (*car*). **Concrete words** identify what can be perceived by the senses, by being seen, heard, tasted, felt, smelled (*padded black leather dashboard*), and convey specific images and details. **Abstract words** denote qualities (*kind*), concepts (*speed*), relationships (*friends*), acts (*cooking*), conditions (*bad weather*), and ideas (*transportation*), and are more general.

Usually, specific and concrete words bring life to general and abstract words. Therefore, whenever you use general and abstract words, try to supply enough specific, concrete details and examples to illustrate them.

GENERAL His car gets good gas mileage.

SPECIFIC His Miser Hybrid uses about 7 litres per 100 kilometres on the highway and 8 litres per 100 kilometres in the city.

GENERAL Her car is comfortable and easy to drive.

SPECIFIC When she drives her new Cushia on a five-hour trip, she arrives refreshed and does not need a long nap to recover, as she did when she drove her ten-year-old Upushme.

What separates most good writing from bad is the writer's ability to move back and forth between the general and abstract and the specific and concrete. Consider these sentences that effectively use a combination of general and specific words to compare cars:

GENERAL CONCRETE ┌──── SPECIFIC ────┐ ABSTRACT ┌── SPECIFIC ──┐
My car, a midnight-black Corvette LS1 convertible, has a powerful 5.7-litre V8 engine
GENERAL SPECIFIC GENERAL SPECIFIC ┌── CONCRETE ──┐
with ride controls, the Tour for regular driving, and the Sport for a close-to the-road feel.
GENERAL CONCRETE ┌──── SPECIFIC ────┐
In contrast, Harvey's automobile, a bright red Dodge Viper SRT-10 convertible, has a
ABSTRACT┌──────── SPECIFIC ────────┐
mighty 8.3-litre V10 engine with 6-speed manual transmission.

EXERCISE 12-3 Revise this paragraph by providing specific and concrete words and phrases to explain and enliven the ideas presented here in general and abstract language. You may revise the sentences to accommodate your changes in language. For help, consult 12e.

I hope to get a job as an administrative assistant in the company. At the interview, the person who would be my supervisor was pleasant. We seemed to get along well. The other assistants in the division appeared to be nice. My courses clearly have prepared me for the position. I think the job would teach me a great deal more. The salary is a bit less than I had hoped for, but the Human Resources representative promised me raises at regular intervals if my work is good. Also, my trip to work would not take too much time for me. If my interviewer calls to offer me the job, I will accept it.

12f What is gender-neutral language?

Biased and Sexist Language

Gender-neutral language, also referred to as *gender-free* or *nonsexist language,* relies on terms that don't communicate whether the person is male or female (for example, in replacing *policeman* with *police officer* or *doctors' wives* with *doctors' spouses*).

Sexist language assigns roles or characteristics to people on the basis of their sex and gender. Many people today feel that sexist language unfairly discriminates against both sexes. It inaccurately assumes that every nurse and homemaker is female (and therefore referred to as "she"), and that every physician and stockbroker is male (and therefore referred to as "he"). One common instance of sexist language occurs when the pronoun *he* is used to refer to someone whose sex is unknown or irrelevant. Although tradition holds that *he* is correct in such situations, many people find it offensive. They feel that using masculine pronouns to represent all humans excludes women and thereby distorts reality.

Nearly all businesses and professional organizations require gender-neutral language in written communications. It is accurate and fair, and it is sound business practice to be inclusive of potential clients.

Gender-neutral language rejects demeaning STEREOTYPES or outdated assumptions, such as "women are bad drivers" and "men can't cook." In your writing, never describe women's looks, clothes, or age unless you do the same for men or doing so is important to the context. Never use a title for one spouse and the first name for the other spouse: *Phil Miller* (not *Mr. Miller*) and *his wife, Jeannette,* travel on separate planes; or *Jeannette and Phil Miller* live in Regina. Quick Reference 12.2 gives you guidelines for using gender-neutral language.

QUICK REFERENCE **12.2**

How to avoid sexist language

- Avoid using only the masculine pronoun to refer to males and females together. The *he or she* and *his or hers* constructions act as singular PRONOUNS, and they therefore call for singular VERBS. Try to avoid overusing *he or she* constructions. A better solution is revising to the plural. You can also revise to omit the gender-specific pronoun.

  NO   A **doctor** has little time to read outside **his** specialty.

  YES   A **doctor** has little time to read outside **his or her** specialty.

  NO   A successful **stockbroker** knows **he** has to work long hours.

  YES   Successful **stockbrokers** know **they** have to work long hours.

  NO   **Everyone** hopes that **he or she** will win the scholarship.

  YES   **Everyone** hopes to win the scholarship.

- Avoid using *man* when referring to both men and women.

  NO   **Man** is a social animal.

  YES   **People** are social animals.

continued ➤

NO	The history of **mankind** is predominantly violent.
YES	**Human** history is predominantly violent.

NO	Dogs are **men's** best friends.
YES	Dogs are **people's** best friends.

- Avoid stereotyping jobs and roles by gender when referring to both men and women.

NO	YES
chairman	chair, chairperson
policeman	police officer
businessman	businessperson, business executive
statesman	statesperson, diplomat
teacher . . . she	teachers . . . they
principal . . . he	principals . . . they

- Avoid expressions that seem to exclude one sex.

NO	YES
the common man	the average person
man-sized sandwich	huge sandwich
old wives' tale	superstition

- Avoid using demeaning and patronizing labels.

NO	YES
male nurse	nurse
gal Friday	assistant
coed	student
My girl can help.	My secretary can help. (*Or, better still,* Ida Morea can help.)

EXERCISE 12-4 Working individually or with a group, revise these sentences by changing sexist language to gender-neutral language. For help, consult 12f.

1. Dogs were one of the first animals to be domesticated by mankind.

2. Traditionally, certain breeds of dogs have helped men in their work.

3. On their long shifts, firemen often kept Dalmatians as mascots and companions, whereas policemen preferred highly intelligent and easily trained German shepherds.

4. Another breed, the Newfoundland, accompanied many fishermen on their ocean voyages, and the Newfoundland has been credited with rescuing many a man overboard.

5. Breeds known as hunting dogs have served as the helpers and companions of sportsmen.

6. Maids and cleaning women didn't need dogs, so no breed of dog is associated with women's work.

7. Another group that dogs have not helped is postmen.

8. Everyone who owns a dog should be sure to spend some time exercising his dog and making sure his dog is in good health.

9. No man-made inventions, such as televisions or computers, can take the place of having a dog.

10. Now even though most dogs do not work, they are still man's best friend.

12g   What other types of language do I want to avoid?

Language that distorts or tries to manipulate a reader needs to be avoided in ACADEMIC WRITING. These and other types of language to avoid in an academic LEVEL OF FORMALITY are listed, with examples, in Quick Reference 12.3.

QUICK REFERENCE   **12.3**

Language to avoid in academic writing

- Never use **slanted language**, also called *loaded language;* readers feel manipulated by the overly emotional TONE and DICTION.

    NO   Our MP is a deceitful, crooked thug.

    YES   Our MP lies to the public and demands bribes.

    NO   Why do labs employ Frankensteins to maim helpless kittens and puppies?

    YES   Why do labs employ uncaring technicians who harm kittens and puppies?

- Never use **pretentious language**; readers realize you're showing off.

    NO   As I alighted from my vehicle, my clothing became besmirched with filth.

    YES   My coat got muddy as I got out of my car.

    NO   He has a penchant for ostentatiously flaunting recently acquired haberdashery accoutrements.

    YES   He tends to show off his new clothes shamelessly.

- Never use **sarcastic language**; readers realize you're being nasty.

    NO   He was a regular Albert Einstein with my questions. [This is sarcastic if you mean the opposite.]

    YES   He had trouble understanding my questions.

- Never use **colloquial language**; readers sense you're being overly casual and conversational.

    NO   Christina flunked chemistry.

    YES   Christina failed chemistry.

- Never use **euphemisms**, also called *doublespeak;* readers realize you're hiding the truth (more in 12k).

    NO   Our company will **downsize** to meet efficiency standards.

    YES   Our company has to cut jobs to maintain its profits.

continued ➤

> NO   We consider our hostages as **foreign guests** being guarded by **hosts**.
>
> YES   We consider our hostages as enemies to be guarded closely.

- Never use NONSTANDARD ENGLISH (12b).
- Never use MIXED METAPHORS (12c).
- Never use SEXIST LANGUAGE or STEREOTYPES (12f).
- Never use REGIONAL LANGUAGE (12h).
- Never use CLICHÉS (12i).
- Never use unnecessary JARGON (12j).
- Never use BUREAUCRATIC LANGUAGE (12l).

12h   What is regional language?

Regional language, also called *dialectal language,* is specific to certain geographical areas. A small grocery store or corner store, for example, is called a *dépanneur* in Quebec, even by English speakers. In the Atlantic provinces, a *tickle* is a narrow sea channel. Using a dialect in writing for the general reading public tends to shut some people out of the communication. Except when dialect is the topic of the writing, ACADEMIC WRITING rarely accommodates dialect well. Avoid it in academic assignments.

12i   What are clichés?

A **cliché** is a worn-out expression that has lost its capacity to communicate effectively because of overuse. Many clichés are SIMILES or METAPHORS, once clever but now flat. For example, these are clichés: *dead as a doornail, gentle as a lamb,* and *straight as an arrow.*

    If you've heard certain expressions repeatedly, so has your reader. Instead of a cliché, use descriptive language that isn't worn out. If you can't think of a way to rephrase a cliché, drop the words entirely.

    Interestingly, however, English is full of frequently used word groups that aren't clichés: for example, *up and down* and *from place to place.* These common word groups aren't considered clichés, so you can use them freely. If you're not sure of how to tell the difference between a cliché and a common word group, remember that a cliché often—but not always—contains an image (*busy as a bee* and *strong as an ox*).

EXERCISE 12-5   Working individually or with a group, revise these clichés. Use the idea in each cliché to write a sentence of your own in plain, clear English. For help, consult 12i.

1. The bottom line is that Carl either raises his grade point average or finds himself in hot water.
2. Carl's grandfather says, "When the going gets tough, the tough get going."
3. Carl may not be the most brilliant engineering major who ever came down the pike, but he has plenty of get-up-and-go.
4. When they were handing out persistence, Carl was first in line.
5. The $64 000 question is, Will Carl make it safe and sound, or will the school drop him like a hot potato?

12j   When is jargon unnecessary?

Jargon is the specialized vocabulary of a particular group. Jargon uses words that people outside that group might not understand. Specialized language exists in every field: professions, academic disciplines, business, various industries, government departments, hobbies, and so on.

Reserve jargon for a specialist AUDIENCE. As you write, keep your audience in mind as you decide whether a word is jargon in the context of your material. For example, a hockey fan easily understands a sportswriter's use of words such as *offside, icing,* and *crosscheck,* but they are jargon words to people unfamiliar with the rules of hockey. Avoid using jargon unnecessarily. When you must use jargon for a nonspecialist audience, be sure to explain any special meanings.

The example below shows specialized language used appropriately; it's taken from an undergraduate textbook. The authors can assume that students know the meaning of *eutrophicates, terrestrial,* and *eutrophic.*

> As the lake eutrophicates, it gradually fills until the entire lake will be converted into a terrestrial community. Eutrophic changes (or eutrophication) are the nutritional enrichment of the water, promoting the growth of aquatic plants.
>
> —Davis and Solomon, *The World of Biology*

12k   What are euphemisms?

Euphemisms attempt to avoid the harsh reality of truth by using more pleasant, "tactful" words. Good manners dictate that euphemisms sometimes be used in social situations: For example, *passed away* is, in some situations, thought to be gentler than *died.* Such uses of euphemisms are acceptable.

In other situations, however, euphemisms drain meaning from truthful writing. Unnecessary euphemisms might describe socially unacceptable behaviour (for example, *Johnny has a vivid imagination* instead of *Johnny lies*). They also might try to hide unpleasant facts (for example, *She is between assignments* instead of *She's lost her job*). Avoid unnecessary euphemisms, especially in academic and business writing: You want to express yourself directly and deliver a clear message.

12l   What is bureaucratic language?

Bureaucratic language uses words that are stuffy and overblown. Bureaucratic language (or *bureaucratese,* a word created to describe the style) is marked by unnecessary complexity. This kind of language can take on a formality that complicates the message and makes readers feel left out.

> NO   In reference to the above captioned, you can include a page that additionally contains an Include instruction under the herein stated circumstances. The page including the Include instruction is included when you paginate the document, but the included text referred to in its Include instruction is not included. [This message is meaningless, but the writer seems to understand the message. Anyone who doesn't is clearly uninformed or unable to read intelligently!]
>
> —From instructions for compiling a user's manual

In response to earlier editions of this handbook, we've been asked to give a YES alternative for this example. We regret that we can't understand enough of the NO example to do that. If you can, please contact us at <doug.hesse@gmail.com> or <troykalq@nyc.rr.com>.

EXERCISE 12-6   Working individually or with a group, revise these examples of pretentious language, jargon, euphemisms, and bureaucratic language. For help, consult 12g and 12i through 12l.

1. Allow me to express my humble gratitude to you two benefactors for your generous pledge of indispensable support on behalf of the activities of our fair city's youngsters.

2. No lateral transfer applications will be processed before an employee's six-month probation period terminates.

3. She gave up the ghost shortly after her husband kicked the bucket.

4. Creating nouns in positions meant for verbs is to utter ostentatious verbalizations that will lead inexorably to further obfuscations of meaning.

5. After his operation, he would list to port when he stood up and list to starboard when he sat down.

6. The precious youths were joy riding in a temporarily displaced vehicle.

7. The forwarding of all electronic communiqués must be approved by a staff member in the upper echelon.

8. Coming to a parting of the ways is not as easy as pie.

Chapter 13

USAGE GLOSSARY

A usage glossary presents the customary manner of using particular words and phrases. "Customary manner," however, is not as firm in practice as the term implies. Usage standards change. If you think a word's usage might differ from what you read here, consult a dictionary published more recently than the current edition of this handbook.

Informal or *colloquial* in a definition means that the word or phrase is found in everyday or conversational speech, but it needs to be avoided in ACADEMIC WRITING. *Nonstandard* indicates that the word or phrase, although widely understood in speech and dialect writing, isn't suitable in standard spoken or written English.

Terms of grammar and writing in this Usage Glossary are defined in the Terms Glossary, which follows the last chapter.

a, an Use *a* before words that begin with a consonant (*a dog, a grade, a hole*) or a consonant sound (*a one-day sale, a European*). Use *an* before words or acronyms that begin with a vowel sound or a silent *h* (*an owl; an hour; an MRI*). Most writers of North American English use *a*, not *an*, before words starting with a pronounced *h: a* (not *an*) *historical event.*

accept, except The verb *accept* means "agree to; receive." As a preposition, *except* means "excluding." As a verb, *except* means "exclude; leave out."

> The workers wanted to **accept** [verb] management's offer **except** [preposition] for one detail: They wanted the limit on overtime **excepted** [verb] from the contract.

advice, advise *Advice*, a noun, means "recommendation." *Advise*, a verb, means "recommend; give advice."

> I **advise** [verb] you to follow your car mechanic's **advice** [noun].

affect, effect As a verb, *affect* means "cause a change in; influence." (*Affect* is a noun in psychology.) As a noun, *effect* means "result or conclusion"; as a verb, *effect* means "bring about."

> Loud music **affects** people's hearing for life, so some bands have **effected** changes to lower the volume. Many fans, however, don't care about the harmful **effects** of high decibel levels.

aggravate, irritate *Aggravate* is used colloquially to mean "irritate." In academic writing, use *aggravate* only to mean "intensify; make worse." Use *irritate* to mean "annoy; make impatient."

> The coach was **irritated** by reduced time for practice, which **aggravated** the team's difficulties with concentration.

ain't *Ain't* is a nonstandard contraction. Use *am not, is not,* or *are not* for standard spoken and written English.

all ready, already *All ready* means "completely prepared." *Already* means "before; by this time."

> The team was **all ready** to play, but it had **already** begun to rain

all right *All right* is always written as two words, never one (never *alright*).

all together, altogether *All together* means "in a group; in unison." *Altogether* means "entirely; thoroughly."

> The three cousins and six nephews said that it was **altogether** absurd for them to stay **all together** in a single hotel room.

allude, elude *Allude* means "refer to indirectly." *Elude* means "escape notice."

> The detectives **alluded** to budget cuts by saying, "Conditions beyond our control allowed the suspect to **elude** us."

allusion, illusion An *allusion* is an indirect reference to something. An *illusion* is a false impression or idea.

> The couple's casual **allusions** to European tourist sites created the **illusion** that they had visited them.

a lot *A lot* is informal for *a great deal* or *a great many*. Avoid using it in academic writing. If you must use it, write it as two words (never *alot*).

a.m., p.m. Use these abbreviations only with numbers, not as substitutes for the words *morning*, *afternoon*, and *evening*. Use *midnight* and *noon* in preference to 12:00 a.m. and 12:00 p.m. Many editors and dictionaries use capital letters for these abbreviations. Whichever style you choose, be consistent in each piece of writing.

> We will arrive in the **evening** [not *p.m.*], and we must leave by **8:00 a.m.**

among, amongst, between Use *among* for three or more items. Use *between* for two items. (A few exceptions are allowable; consult a good dictionary.) North American English prefers *among* to *amongst*.

> My three housemates discussed **among** [not *between* or *amongst*] themselves the choice **between** staying in school and getting full-time jobs.

amoral, immoral *Amoral* means "neither moral nor immoral." *Amoral* also means "without any sense of what's moral or immoral." *Immoral* means "morally wrong."

> Although many people consider birth control an **amoral** issue, some religions consider using birth control **immoral**.

amount, number Use *amount* for noncountable things (wealth, work, happiness). Use *number* for countable items.

> The **amount** of rice to cook depends on the **number** of guests.

an See *a, an*.

and/or This term is appropriate in business and legal writing when either or both of the two items can apply:

> We are planning to open additional offices in Montreal and/or Moncton.

In the humanities, writers usually express the alternatives in words:

> We are planning to open additional offices in Montreal, Moncton, or both.

anymore Use *anymore* with the meaning "now, any longer" only in negations or questions. In positive statements, instead of *anymore,* use an adverb such as *now.*

No one wants to live without air conditioning **anymore**. Summers are so hot **now** [not *anymore*] that more people than ever suffer from heatstroke.

anyone, any one *Anyone* is a singular indefinite pronoun meaning "any person at all." *Any one* (two words), an adjective that modifies a pronoun, means "a member of a group."

Anyone could test-drive **any one** of the display vehicles.

anyplace *Anyplace* is informal. Use *any place* or *anywhere* instead.

anyways, anywheres *Anyways* and *anywheres* are nonstandard for *anyway* and *anywhere.*

apt, likely, liable *Apt* and *likely* are used interchangeably. Strictly, *apt* indicates a tendency or inclination. *Likely* indicates a reasonable expectation or greater certainty than *apt* does. *Liable* usually denotes legal responsibility or implies unpleasant consequences, but usage today allows it to mean *likely.*

Evander is **apt** to run stop signs, so he is **likely** to get a ticket. That means he's **liable** for any consequences. [Some authorities in Canada also permit *likely* to be used as an adverb: *He'll likely get a ticket.* Many do not.]

as, as if, as though, like Use *as, as if,* or *as though,* but not *like,* to introduce a clause.

This hamburger tastes good, **as** [not *like*] a hamburger should. It tastes **as if** [or *as though,* not *like*] it were barbecued over charcoal, not gas.

Both *as* and *like* can function as prepositions in comparisons. However, use *as* to indicate equivalence between two nouns or pronouns, and use *like* to indicate similarity but not equivalence.

My friend Roger served **as** [not *like*] mediator in a dispute about my neighbour's tree that dripped sap on my driveway **like** [not *as*] a leaky tap.

assure, ensure, insure *Assure* means "promise; convince." *Ensure* and *insure* both mean "make certain or secure," but *insure* is reserved for financial or legal matters.

The insurance agent **assured** me that he could **insure** my car, but only I could **ensure** that I would drive safely.

as to *As to* is nonstandard for *about.*

awful, awfully *Awful* is an adjective meaning "inspiring awe" and "creating fear." *Awfully* is an adverb meaning "in a way to inspire awe" and "terrifying." Only colloquially are *awful* and *awfully* used to mean "very" or "extremely."

a while, awhile As two words, *a while* (an article and a noun) can function as a subject or object. As one word, *awhile* is an adverb. In a prepositional phrase, the correct form is *for a while, in a while,* or *after a while.*

It took **a while** [article and noun] to drive to the zoo, where we saw the seals bask **awhile** [adverb modifying verb *bask*] in the sun after romping **for a while** [prepositional phrase] in the water.

backup, back up As a noun, *backup* means "a replacement, fill-in, surrogate; a copy of computer files." As an adjective, *backup* means "alternative." As a verb, *back up* (two words) means "to serve as a substitute or support"; "to accumulate, as from a stoppage"; and "to make a backup copy of a computer disk or hard drive."

I'll need a **backup** [noun] of your hard drive if I'm going to serve as your **backup** [adjective] computer consultant. I **back up** [verb] all computer disks and drives when I work with them.

bad, badly   *Bad* is an adjective only after linking verbs (*look, feel, smell, taste, sound;* these verbs can function as either linking verbs or action verbs depending on the context). *Badly* is an adverb.

Farmers feel **bad** [feel is a linking verb, so bad is the adjective] because a **bad** [adjective] drought is **badly** [adverb] damaging their crops.

been, being   *Been* and *being* cannot stand alone as main verbs. They work only with auxiliary verbs.

You **are being** [not being] honest to admit that you **have been** [not been] tempted to eat the whole pie.

being as, being that   *Being as* and *being that* are nonstandard for *because* or *since.*

We had to forfeit the game **because** [not being as or being that] our goalie was badly injured.

beside, besides   As prepositions, *beside* means "next to, by the side of," and *besides* means "other than, in addition to." As an adverb, *besides* means "also, moreover."

She stood **beside** the new car, insisting that she would drive. No one **besides** her had a driver's licence. **Besides**, she owned the car.

better, had better   *Better* is informal for *had better*

We **had better** [not better alone] be careful of the ice.

between   See *among, amongst, between.*

bias, biased   As a noun, *bias* means "a mental leaning for or against something or someone." As an adjective, *biased* means "prejudiced." As a verb, *bias* means "create prejudice." The past tense of this verb is *biased.*

Horace's **bias** [noun] against some politicians grew from his disapproval of their **biased** [adjective] attitudes toward the unemployed. Eventually, Horace **biased** [verb] his wife against politicians as well.

breath, breathe   *Breath* is a noun; *breathe* is a verb.

Take a deep **breath** [noun] before you start so that you can **breathe** [verb] normally afterward.

bring, take   *Bring* indicates movement from a distant place to a near place. *Take* indicates movement from a near to a distant place.

If you **bring** over sandwiches, we'll have time to **take** [not bring] the dog to the vet.

but, however, yet   Use *but, however,* or *yet* alone, not in combination with each other.

The economy is strong, **but** [not but yet or but however] unemployment is high.

calculate, figure   These are colloquial terms for *estimate, imagine, expect, think,* and the like.

can, may   *Can* signifies ability or capacity. *May* requests or grants permission. In negative expressions, *can* is acceptable for *may.*

> When you **can** [not *may*] get here on time, you **may** [not *can*] be excused early. However, if you are *not* on time, you **cannot** [or *may not*] expect privileges.

can't hardly, can't scarcely   These double negatives are nonstandard for *can hardly* and *can scarcely.*

capitol, capital   *Capital* means a city in which government sits (Winnipeg, *capital* of Manitoba) or that takes first place in some respect (Leamington, tomato *capital* of Canada); it is also used to mean wealth or, as an adjective, "most important." *Capitol,* in the United States, means "a building that houses the legislature."

> If our group raises enough **capital,** we will send a delegation to Oregon's state **capitol** to lobby against softwood tariffs.

censor, censure   The verb *censor* means "delete objectionable material; judge." The verb *censure* means "condemn or reprimand officially."

> The town council **censured** the mayor for trying to **censor** a report.

chairman, chairperson, chair   Many writers and speakers prefer the gender-neutral terms *chairperson* and *chair* to *chairman.* In general, *chair* is used more than *chairperson.*

choose, chose   *Choose* is the simple form of the verb. *Chose* is the past-tense form of the verb.

> I **chose** a movie last week, so you **choose** one tonight.

cite, site, sight   The verb *cite* means "quote by way of example, authority, or proof." The noun *site* means "a particular place or location" and is not to be confused with *sight.*

> The private investigator **cited** evidence from the crime **site** and the defendant's web**site.**

> We are planning a visit to the historic **sites** near Quebec City, and then we will rent a car to see the **sights** of the Gaspé.

cloth, clothe   *Cloth* is a noun meaning "fabric." *Clothe* is a verb meaning "dress with garments or fabric."

> "**Clothe** me in red velvet," proclaimed the king, and the royal tailors ran to gather samples of **cloth** to show him.

complement, compliment   As a noun, *complement* means "something that goes well with or completes." As a noun, *compliment* means "praise, flattery." As a verb, *complement* means "bring to perfection; go well with, complete." As a verb, *compliment* means "praise, flatter."

> The dean's **compliment** was a perfect **complement** to the thrill of my graduating. My parents felt proud when she **complimented** me publicly, an honour that **complemented** their joy.

comprise, include   See *include, comprise.*

conscience, conscious The noun *conscience* means "a sense of right and wrong." The adjective *conscious* means "being aware or awake."

Always be **conscious** of what your **conscience** is telling you.

consensus of opinion This phrase is redundant; use *consensus* only.

Parliament reached **consensus** on the issue of campaign reform.

continual(ly), continuous(ly) *Continual* means "occurring repeatedly." *Continuous* means "going on without interruption."

Larry needed intravenous fluids **continuously** for days, so the nurses **continually** monitored him.

could care less *Could care less* is nonstandard for *could not care less.*

could of *Could of* is nonstandard for *could have.*

couple, a couple of *Couple* means "two," but it can also be nonstandard for *a few* or *several.*

Rest here for **a few** [not *a couple* or *a couple of*] minutes.

criteria, criterion A *criterion* is "a standard of judgment." *Criteria* is the plural of *criterion.*

A sense of history is an important **criterion** for judging political candidates, but voters must consider other **criteria** as well.

data *Data* is the plural of *datum,* a word rarely used today. Informally, *data* is used as a singular noun that takes a singular verb. In academic or professional writing, *data* is considered plural and takes a plural verb (although this usage is currently viewed as overly formal by some).

The **data** suggest [not *suggests*] some people are addicted to e-mail.

different from, different than Some authorities prefer *different from* to *different than* in all circumstances, although *different than* is usually considered acceptable to introduce a clause.

Please advise us if your research yields data **different from** past results; your last report was far **different than** we expected it to be.

disinterested, uninterested *Disinterested* means "impartial, unbiased." *Uninterested* is used for "not interested, indifferent."

Jurors need to be **disinterested** in hearing evidence, but never **uninterested.**

don't *Don't* is a contraction for *do not,* never for *does not* (its contraction is *doesn't*).

She **doesn't** [not *don't*] like crowds.

effect See *affect, effect.*

elicit, illicit The verb *elicit* means "draw forth or bring out." The adjective *illicit* means "illegal."

The MP's **illicit** conduct **elicited** a mass outcry from her constituents.

elude See *allude, elude.*

emigrate (from), immigrate (to)   *Emigrate* means "leave one country to live in another." *Immigrate* means "enter a country to live there."

>   My great-grandmother **emigrated** from Kiev to London, England, in 1890. Then, she **immigrated** to Toronto in 1892.

enclose, inclose; enclosure, inclosure   In North American English, *enclose* and *enclosure* are the preferred spellings.

ensure   See *assure, ensure, insure.*

enthused   *Enthused* is nonstandard for *enthusiastic.*

>   Adam was **enthusiastic** [not *enthused*] about the course he chose.

etc.   *Etc.* is the abbreviation for the Latin *et cetera,* meaning "and the rest." For writing in the humanities, avoid using *etc.* Acceptable substitutes are *and the like, and so on,* or *and so forth.*

everyday, every day   The adjective *everyday* means "daily." *Every day* (two words) is an adjective with a noun.

>   Being late for work has become an **everyday** [adjective] occurrence for me. **Every day** [subject] brings me closer to being fired. I worry about it **every day.**

everyone, every one   *Everyone* is a singular, indefinite pronoun. *Every one* (two words) is an adjective and a pronoun, meaning "each member in a group."

>   **Everyone** enjoyed **every one** of the comedy skits.

everywheres   *Everywheres* is nonstandard for *everywhere.*

except   See *accept, except.*

explicit, implicit   *Explicit* means "directly stated or expressed." *Implicit* means "implied, suggested."

>   The warning on cigarette packs is **explicit**: "Smoking can kill you." The **implicit** message is "Don't smoke."

farther, further   Many writers reserve *farther* for geographical distances and *further* for all other cases.

fewer, less   Use *fewer* for anything that can be counted (that is, with count nouns): *fewer* dollars, *fewer* fleas, *fewer* haircuts. Use *less* with collective nouns (or other noncount nouns): *less* money, *less* scratching, *less* hair.

flaunt, flout   Flaunt means "show off; display." Flout means "disregard; disobey."

>   Those who **flout** the rules of good usage are simply **flaunting** their ignorance.

former, latter   When two items are referred to, *former* signifies the first item and *latter* signifies the second item. Never use *former* and *latter* when referring to more than two items.

>   Brazil and Ecuador are South American countries. Portuguese is the official language in the **former**, Spanish in the **latter**.

go, say   All forms of *go* are nonstandard when used in place of all forms of *say.*

>   While stepping on my hand, Frank **says** [not *goes*], "Your hand is in my way."

gone, went   *Gone* is the past participle of *go; went* is the past tense of *go.*

They **went** [not *gone*] to the concert after Ira **had gone** [not *had went*] home.

good, well   *Good* is an adjective. As an adverb, *good* is nonstandard. Instead, use *well.*

Good [adjective] maintenance helps cars run **well** [adverb; not *good*].

good and   *Good and* is a nonstandard intensifier. Instead, use more precise words.

They were **exhausted** [not *good and tired*].

got, have   *Got* is nonstandard for *have.*

What do we **have** [not *got*] for supper?

hardly   Use *hardly* with *can,* never with *can't.*

have, of   Use *have,* not *of,* after such verbs as *could, should, would, might,* and *must.*

You ***should* have** [not *should of*] called first.

have got, have to, have got to   Avoid using *have got* when *have* alone delivers your meaning. Also, avoid using *have to* or *have got to* for *must.*

he/she, s/he, his/her   When using gender-neutral language, write out *he or she* or *his or her* instead of using and/or constructions. To be more concise, switch to plural pronouns and antecedents. (For more about gender-neutral language, see 12f.)

Everyone bowed *his or her* head. [**Everyone** bowed **his** head is considered sexist language if women were present when the heads were bowed.]

The **people** bowed **their** heads.

historic, historical   The adjective *historic* means "important in history" or "highly memorable." The adjective *historical* means "relating to history." Most writers in North America use *a,* not *an,* before these words.

hopefully   *Hopefully* is an adverb meaning "with hope, in a hopeful manner," so as an adverb, it can modify a verb, an adjective, or another adverb. However, *hopefully* is often considered nonstandard as a sentence modifier meaning "we hope"; in academic writing, avoid this usage.

They waited **hopefully** [adverb] for the crippled airplane to land. **We hope** [not *Hopefully,*] it will land safely.

humanity, humankind, humans, mankind   To use gender-neutral language, choose *humanity, humankind,* or *humans* instead of *mankind.*

Some think that the computer has helped **humanity** more than any other twentieth-century invention.

if, whether   At the start of a noun clause that expresses speculation or unknown conditions, you can use either *if* or *whether.* However, in such conditional clauses use only *whether* (or *whether or not*) when alternatives are expressed or implied. In a conditional clause that does not express or imply alternatives, use only *if.*

If [not *whether*] you promise not to step on my feet, I might dance with you. Still, I'm not sure **if** [or *whether*] I want to dance with you. Once I decide, I'll dance with you **whether** [not *if*] I like the music or **whether** [not *if*] the next song is fast or slow.

illicit   See *elicit, illicit.*

illusion   See *allusion, illusion.*

immigrate   See *emigrate, immigrate.*

immoral   See *amoral, immoral.*

imply, infer   *Imply* means "hint at or suggest." *Infer* means "draw a conclusion." A writer or speaker *implies;* a reader or listener *infers.*

> When the cabinet minister **implied** that she would be taking French lessons, reporters **inferred** that she was planning to run for her party's leadership.

include, comprise   The verb *include* means "contain or regard as part of a whole." The verb *comprise* means "consist of or be composed of."

incredible, incredulous   *Incredible* means "extraordinary; not believable." *Incredulous* means "unable or unwilling to believe."

> Listeners were **incredulous** as the freed hostages described the **incredible** hardships they had experienced.

in regard to, with regard to, as regards, regarding   Use *about, concerning,* and *for* in place of these wordy phrases. Also, avoid the nonstandard *as regards to.*

> **Concerning** [not in *regard to,* with *regard to, as regards,* or *regarding*] your question, we can now confirm that your payment was received.

inside of, outside of   These phrases are nonstandard when used to mean *inside* or *outside.* When writing about time, never use *inside of* to mean "in less than."

> She waited **outside** [not *outside* of] the apartment house. He changed to clothes that were more informal in **less than** [not *inside of*] ten minutes.

insure   See *assure, ensure, insure.*

irregardless   *Irregardless* is nonstandard for *regardless.*

is when, is where   Never use these constructions when you define something. Instead, use active verbs.

> Defensive driving **involves staying** [not *is when you stay*] alert.

its, it's   *Its* is a personal pronoun in the possessive case. *It's* is a contraction of *it is* or *it has.*

> The dog buried **its** bone today. **It's** hot today, which makes the dog restless. **It's** been hotter than usual this week.

kind, sort   Combine *kind* and *sort* with *this* or *that* when referring to singular nouns. Combine *kinds* and *sorts* with *these* or *those* when referring to plural nouns. Also, never use *a* or *an* after *kind of* or *sort of.*

> To stay cool, drink **these kinds** of fluids [not *this kind*] for **this sort of** day [not *this sort of a*].

kind of, sort of   These phrases are colloquial adverbs. In academic writing, use *somewhat.*

> The campers were **somewhat** [not *kind of*] dehydrated after the hike.

later, latter   *Later* means "after some time; subsequently." *Latter* refers to the second of two items.

> The college library stays open **later** than the town library; also, the **latter** is closed on weekends.

lay, lie   The verb *lay* (***lay***, *laid, laid, laying*) means "place or put something, usually on something else" and needs a direct object. The verb *lie* (***lie***, *lay, lain, lying*), meaning "recline," doesn't need a direct object. Substituting *lay* for *lie*, or the opposite, is nonstandard.

> **Lay** [not *lie*] down the blanket [direct object], and then place the baby to **lie** [not *lay*] in the shade.

leave, let   *Leave* means "depart." *Leave* is nonstandard for *let*. *Let* means "allow, permit."

> Could you **let** [not *leave*] me use your car tonight?

less   See *fewer, less.*

lie   See *lay, lie.*

like   See *as, as if, as though, like.*

likely   See *apt, likely, liable.*

lots, lots of, a lot of   These are colloquial constructions. Instead, use *many, much,* or *a great deal.*

mankind   See *humanity, humankind, humans, mankind.*

may   See *can, may.*

maybe, may be   *Maybe* is an adverb; *may be* (two words) is a verb phrase.

> **Maybe** [adverb] we can win, but our team **may be** [verb phrase] too tired.

may of, might of   *May of* and *might of* are nonstandard for *may have* and *might have.*

media   *Media* is the plural of *medium,* yet colloquial usage now pairs it with a singular verb (for example, *The **media saturates** us with information about every fire*).

morale, moral   *Morale* is a noun meaning "a mental state relating to courage, confidence, or enthusiasm." As a noun, *moral* means an "ethical lesson implied or taught by a story or event." As an adjective, *moral* means "ethical."

> One **moral** [noun] of the story is that many people who suffer from low **morale** [noun] still abide by high **moral** [adjective] standards.

most   *Most* is nonstandard for *almost.* Also, *most* is the superlative form of an adjective (*some* words, *more* words, ***most*** words) and of adverbs (***most*** suddenly).

> **Almost** [not *Most*] all writers agree that Shakespeare penned the **most** [adjective] brilliant plays ever written.

Ms.   *Ms.* is a woman's title free of reference to marital status, equivalent to *Mr.* for men. Generally, use *Ms.* unless a woman requests *Miss* or *Mrs.*

must of   *Must of* is nonstandard for *must have.*

number   See *amount, number.*

of   Use *have*, not *of*, after modal auxiliary verbs (*could, may, might, must, should, would*). See also *could of; may of, might of; must of; should of; would of.*

off of   *Off of* is nonstandard for *off.*

>   Don't fall **off** [not *off of*] the stage.

OK, O.K., okay   These three forms are informal. In academic writing, choose words that express more specific meanings. If you must use the term, choose the full word *okay.*

>   The weather was **suitable** [not *okay*] for a picnic.

on account of, owing to the fact that   Use *because* or *because of* in place of these wordy phrases.

>   **Because of the rain** [not *On account of the rain* or *Owing to the fact that it rained*], the picnic was cancelled.

oral, verbal   The adjective *oral* means "spoken or being done by the mouth." The adjective *verbal* means "relating to language" (*verbal* skill) or to words rather than actions, facts, or ideas.

outside of   See *inside of, outside of.*

percent, percentage   Use *percent* with specific numbers: 2 *percent*, 95 *percent*. Use *percentage* to refer to portions of a whole in general terms.

>   Less than **6 percent** of Canada's land is legally protected as wilderness, a smaller **percentage** [not *percent*] than is commonly believed.

pixel, pixellation, pixillated   *Pixel*, a relatively new word created from "picture/pix" and "element," is the name for a small dot on a video screen. *Pixellation* (with an *e*, as in *pixel*) is a noun meaning "a film technique that makes people appear to move faster than they are." *Pixillated* (with an *i*), a verb unrelated to *pixels*, derives from *pixie*, meaning "a mischievous elf," and now describes someone who is slightly drunk.

plus   *Plus* is nonstandard for *and, also, in addition*, and *moreover.*

>   The band booked three concerts in Hungary, **and** [not *plus*] it will tour Poland for a month.

>   **In addition,** [not *Plus,*] it may perform once in Austria.

practice, practise   In Canada, *practice* is the noun; *practise* is the verb.

precede, proceed   *Precede* is a verb that means "go before." *Proceed* is a verb that means "advance, go on, undertake, carry on."

>   **Preceded** by elephants and music, the ringmaster **proceeded** into the main tent.

pretty   *Pretty* is informal for *rather, quite, somewhat*, or *very.*

>   The flu epidemic was **quite** [not *pretty*] severe.

principal, principle   As a noun, *principal* means "chief person; main or original amount." As an adjective, *principal* means "most important." *Principle* is a noun that means "a basic truth or rule."

>   During the assembly, the **principal** [noun] said, "A **principal** [adjective] value in our democracy is the **principle** [noun] of free speech."

proceed   See *precede, proceed.*

quotation, quote   *Quotation* is a noun, and *quote* is a verb. Don't use *quote* as a noun.

One newspaper reporter **quoted** [verb] the candidate, and soon the **quotations** [noun—not *quotes*, which is a verb] were widely broadcast.

raise, rise   *Raise* is a verb (*raise, raised, raised, raising*) that means "lift" or "construct" and needs a direct object. *Rise* (*rise, rose, risen, rising*) means "get up," "go upward," or "revolt," and doesn't need a direct object.

If the citizens **rise** [not *raise*], they will **raise** [not *rise* or *rise up*] the flag of liberty.

real, really   These words are nonstandard for *very* and *extremely.*

reason is because   This phrase is redundant. To be concise and correct, use *reason is that.*

One **reason** we moved **is that** [not is *because*] our factory was relocated.

reason why   This phrase is redundant. To be concise and correct, use *reason* or *why.*

I don't know **why** [not *the reason why*] they left home.

regarding   See *in regard to, with regard to, as regards, regarding.*

regardless   See *irregardless.*

respectful, respectfully   As an adjective, *respectful* means "marked by respect, showing regard or honour." *Respectfully* is the adverb form of *respectful.* Be careful not to confuse these words with *respective* and *respectively* (see next entry).

The child listened **respectfully** [adverb] to the lecture about **respectful** [adjective] behaviour.

respective, respectively   *Respective,* an adjective, refers to two or more individual persons or things. *Respectively,* an adverb, refers back to two or more individuals or things in the same sequence in which they were originally mentioned.

After the fire drill, Dr. Daniel Eagle and Dr. Jessica Chess returned to their **respective** offices [that is, he returned to his office, and she returned to her office] on the second and third floors, **respectively** [his office is on the second floor, and her office is on the third floor].

rise   See *raise, rise.*

scarcely   Use *scarcely* with *can,* never with *can't.*

seen   *Seen* is the past participle of the verb *see* (*see, saw, seen, seeing*). *Seen* is nonstandard for *saw,* a verb in the past tense. Always use *seen* with an auxiliary verb.

Last night, **I saw** [not *seen*] the movie that you **had seen** [not *seen*] last week.

set, sit   The verb *set* (*set, set, setting*) means "put in place, position, put down" and needs a direct object. The verb *sit* (*sit, sat, sitting*) means "be seated" and usually doesn't take a direct object. Substituting *set* for *sit,* or the opposite, is nonstandard.

Susan **set** [not *sat*] the sandwiches beside the salad, made Spot **sit** [not *set*] down, and then **sat** [not *set*] on the sofa.

shall, will, should *Shall* was once used with *I* and *we* for future-tense verbs, and *will* was used for all other persons. Today, *shall* is considered formal, and *will* is more widely used. In questions, *should* and *shall* are often used synonymously.

> We **will** [or *shall*] depart on Monday, but he **will** [never *shall*] wait until Thursday to depart.

> **Should** [or *Shall*] I telephone ahead to reserve a suite at the hotel?

should of *Should of* is nonstandard for *should have.*

sit See *set, sit.*

site See *cite, site, sight.*

sometime, sometimes, some time The adverb *sometime* means "at an unspecified time." The adverb *sometimes* means "now and then." *Some time* (two words) is an adjective with a noun that means "an amount or span of time."

> **Sometime** [adverb for "at an unspecified time"] next year, I must take my qualifying exams. I **sometimes** [adverb for "now and then"] worry whether I'll find **some time** [adjective with a noun] to study for them.

sort of See *kind of, sort of.*

stationary, stationery *Stationary* means "not moving; unchanging." *Stationery* refers to paper and related writing products.

> Using our firm's **stationery**, I wrote to city officials about a **stationary** light pole that had been knocked over in a car accident.

such *Such* is informal for intensifiers such as *very* and *extremely.* However, *such* is acceptable to mean "of the same or similar kind."

> The play got **very** [not *such*] bad reviews. The playwright was embarrassed by **such** strong criticism.

supposed to, used to The final *-d* is essential in both phrases.

> We were **supposed** to [not *suppose to*] leave early. I **used** to [not *use to*] wake up before the alarm rang.

sure *Sure* is nonstandard for *surely* or *certainly.*

> I was **certainly** [not *sure*] surprised at the results.

sure and, try and Both phrases are nonstandard for *sure to* and *try to.*

> Please **try to** [not *try and*] reach my doctor.

than, then *Than* indicates comparison; *then* relates to time.

> Please put on your gloves, and **then** your hat. It's colder outside **than** you think.

that, which Use *that* with restrictive (essential) clauses only. You can use *which* with both restrictive and nonrestrictive (nonessential) clauses; however, many people reserve *which* to use only with nonrestrictive clauses.

> The house **that** [or *which*] Jack built is on Beanstalk Street, **which** [not *that*] runs past the reservoir.

their, there, they're   *Their* is a possessive pronoun. *There* means "in that place" or is part of an expletive construction. *They're* is a contraction of *they are.*

> **They're** going to **their** accounting class in the building over **there** near the library. Do you know that **there** are twelve sections of Accounting 101?

theirself, theirselves, themself   These words are nonstandard for *themselves.*

them   Use *them* as an object pronoun only. Do not use *them* in place of the adjectives *these* and *those.*

> Let's buy **those** [not *them*] delicious looking strawberries.

then   See *than, then.*

thusly   *Thusly* is nonstandard for *thus.*

till, until   Both are acceptable, although *until* is preferred for academic writing.

to, too, two   *To* is a preposition; it also is part of an infinitive verb. *Too* is an adverb meaning "also; more than enough." *Two* is a number.

> When you go **to** Prince Edward Island, visit Green Gables. Try **to** find a seaside restaurant for dinner, **too.** It won't be **too** expensive because **two** people can share a lobster.

toward, towards   Although both are acceptable, *toward* is somewhat more common in North America.

try and, sure and   See *sure and, try and.*

type   *Type* is nonstandard when used to mean *type of.*

> I recommend that you use only that **type of** [not *type*] glue on plastic.

unique   Never combine *unique* with *more, most,* or other qualifiers.

> A **unique** [not *very unique*] heating system in one Quebec home uses hydrogen for fuel.

uninterested   See *disinterested, uninterested.*

used to   See *supposed to, used to.*

utilize   *Utilize* is considered an overblown word for *use.*

> The team **used** [not *utilized*] all its players to win the game.

verbal, oral   See *oral, verbal.*

wait on   *Wait on* is an informal substitute for *wait for. Wait on* is appropriate only when people give service to others.

> I had to **wait for** [not *wait on*] half an hour for the hotel desk clerk to **wait on** me.

way, ways   When referring to distance, use *way* rather than *ways.*

> He is a long **way** [not *ways*] from home.

well   See *good, well.*

where   *Where* is nonstandard for *that* when *where* is used as a subordinating conjunction.

> I read **that** [not *where*] salt raises blood pressure.

where . . . at   This phrase is redundant; use only *where.*

> **Where** is your house? [not *Where is your house at?*]

whether   See *if, whether.*

which   See *that, which.*

who, whom   Use *who* as a subject or a subject complement; use *whom* as an object (see 16g).

who's, whose   *Who's* is the contraction of *who is,*or sometimes, *who has. Whose* is a possessive pronoun.

> **Who's** willing to drive? **Whose** truck should we take? **Who's** seen my car keys?

will   See *shall, will, should.*

-wise   The suffix *-wise* means "in a manner, direction, or position" (*lengthwise, clockwise*). Never attach *-wise* indiscriminately to create new words. When in doubt, consult a dictionary to see if the *-wise* word you have in mind is acceptable.

World Wide Web   Written out, the three words start with a capital W. Its abbreviation only in URLs is *www.* When you use only the word *Web,* start it with a capital W.

would of   *Would of* is nonstandard for *would have.*

your, you're   *Your* is a possessive. *You're* is the contraction of *you are.*

> **You're** kind to volunteer **your** time at the seniors' centre.

Understanding Grammar and Writing Correct Sentences

MyCanadianCompLab

Visit MyCanadianCompLab at
mycanadiancomplab.ca for

- Diagnostic tests
- Grammar exercises
- Grammar video tutorials
- Other resources, including an eText version of this book

Chapter 14

PARTS OF SPEECH AND SENTENCE STRUCTURES

PARTS OF SPEECH

14a   Why learn the parts of speech?

Knowing the names and definitions of parts of speech gives you a vocabulary for identifying words and understanding how language works to create meaning. No part of speech exists in a vacuum. To identify a word's part of speech correctly, you need to see how the word functions in a sentence. Sometimes the same word functions differently in different sentences, so check the part of speech used in each instance.

> We ate **fish**. [*Fish* is a noun. It names a thing.]

> We **fish** on weekends. [*Fish* is a verb. It names an action.]

14b   What is a noun?

A **noun** names a person, place, thing, or idea: *student, college, textbook, education.* Quick Reference 14.1 lists different kinds of nouns.

ESL TIPS: Here are some useful tips for working with nouns. ●

- Nouns often appear with words that tell how much or how many, whose, which one, and similar information. These words include ARTICLES* (*a, an, the*) and other determiners or limiting adjectives; see 14f and Chapter 51.
- Nouns sometimes serve as ADJECTIVES. For example, in the term *police officer,* the word *police* serves as an adjective to describe *officer.*
- Nouns in many languages other than English are inflected. This means they change form, usually with a special ending, to communicate gender (male, female, neuter); number (singular, plural); and case (see 16a through 16k).
- Words with these suffixes (word endings) are usually nouns: *-ness, -ence, -ance, -ty,* and *-ment.*

---

*Words printed in SMALL CAPITAL LETTERS are discussed elsewhere in the text and are defined in the Terms Glossary at the back of this book.

QUICK REFERENCE **14.1**

Nouns

PROPER	name specific people, places, or things (first letter is always capitalized)	*Rick Mercer, Moose Jaw, Toyota*
COMMON	name general groups, places, people, or things	*comedian, city, automobile*
CONCRETE	name things experienced through the senses: sight, hearing, taste, smell, and touch	*landscape, pizza, thunder*
ABSTRACT	name things not knowable through the senses	*freedom, shyness*
COLLECTIVE	name groups	*family, team*
NONCOUNT OR MASS	name "uncountable" things	*water, time*
COUNT	name countable items	*lake, minute*

Note: Some nouns fit into more than one category. For example, *family* is both a common noun and a collective noun.

14c   What is a pronoun?

A pronoun takes the place of a NOUN. The words or word that a pronoun replaces is called the pronoun's ANTECEDENT. See Quick Reference 14.2 for a list of different kinds of pronouns. For information on how to use pronouns correctly, see Chapters 16 and 17.

⊙ Writing in Action: Learning What Pronouns to Use

David is an accountant. [The noun *David* names a person.]

He is an accountant. [The pronoun *he* refers to its antecedent, *David*.]

The finance committee needs to consult **him**. [The pronoun *him* refers to its antecedent, *David*.]

⊙ Writing in Action: Recognizing Antecedents

QUICK REFERENCE **14.2**

Pronouns

PERSONAL *I, you, its, her, they, ours,* and others	refer to people or things	*I saw **her** take a book to **them**.*
RELATIVE *who, which, that*	introduce certain NOUN CLAUSES and ADJECTIVE CLAUSES	*The book **that** I lost was valuable.*
INTERROGATIVE *which, who, whose,* and others	introduce a question	***Who** called?*

continued ➤

Pronouns

DEMONSTRATIVE *this, that, these, those*	point out the antecedent	*Whose books are **these**?*
REFLEXIVE OR INTENSIVE *myself, themselves,* and other *-self* or *-selves* words	reflect back to the antecedent; intensify the antecedent	*They claim to support **themselves**. **I myself** doubt it.*
RECIPROCAL *each other, one another*	refer to individual parts of a plural antecedent	*We respect **each other**.*
INDEFINITE *all, anyone, each* and others	refer to nonspecific persons or things	***Everyone** is welcome here.*

EXERCISE 14-1   Underline and label all nouns (N) and pronouns (P). Refer to 14a through 14c for help.

           P   N   P   N   N
EXAMPLE   My mother celebrated her eightieth birthday this summer with
           P   N   N   P   N
           her family and friends; she greatly enjoyed the festivities.

1. More and more people live into their eighties and nineties because they get better health care and they take better care of themselves.
2. Many elderly people now live busy lives, continuing in businesses or volunteering at various agencies.
3. My mother, Elizabeth, for example, spends four hours each morning as a volunteer for the Red Cross, where she takes histories from blood donors.
4. My neighbours, George and Sandra, who are eighty-six years old, still own and run a card and candy shop.
5. Age has become no obstacle for active seniors as evidenced by the activities they pursue today.

((•
AUDIO
LESSON
Section 1:
Big Ideas—
Verbs

14d   What is a verb?

Main verbs express action, occurrence, or state of being. For information on how to use verbs correctly, see Chapter 15.

((•
AUDIO
LESSON
Section 2:
Practice
Questions—
Verbs

     I **dance**. [action]

     The audience **became** silent. [occurrence]

     Your dancing **was** excellent. [state of being]

   ALERT: If you're not sure whether a word is a verb, try substituting a different TENSE for the word. If the sentence still makes sense, the word is a verb.

NO	He is a **changed** man. He is a **will change** man. [*Changed* isn't a verb because the sentence doesn't make sense when *will change* is substituted.]
YES	The man **changed** his profession. The man **will change** his profession. [*Changed* is a verb because the sentence makes sense when the verb *will change* is substituted.] ●

AUDIO
LESSON
Section 3:
Rapid Review
—Verbs

EXERCISE 14-2   Underline all main verbs. Refer to 14d for help.

> **EXAMPLE** A distinctive group of self-published magazines <u>is called</u> simply "zines."

1. Many young writers found regular mass-market magazines boring and irrelevant.
2. Some of them created their own small magazines, or "zines," for readers with the same interests and tastes.
3. Most zines contain cartoons, short stories, and personal essays.
4. Typically, zines are given odd names like *Ottawa's Plague* and *I Hate My Generation*.
5. Their creators shock their small group of readers with satire, bizarre fantasies, and wild rumours about popular rock bands.

14e   What is a verbal?

Verbals are verb parts functioning as NOUNS, ADJECTIVES, or ADVERBS. Quick Reference 14.3 lists the three different kinds of verbals.

QUICK REFERENCE   **14.3**

Verbals and their functions

INFINITIVE *to* + verb	1. noun 2. adjective or adverb	*To eat now is inconvenient. Still, we have far to go.*
PAST PARTICIPLE *-ed* form of REGULAR VERB or equivalent in IRREGULAR VERB	adjective	*Boiled, filtered water is safe.*
PRESENT PARTICIPLE *-ing* form of verb*	1. adjective 2. verb (PROGRESSIVE FORM)	*Running* water may not be safe. He was **thinking** of the danger.
GERUND *-ing* form of verb	noun	*Eating in diners on the road is an adventure.*

*A present participle has the same *-ing* form as a **gerund**, and sometimes the gerund is included as a type of present participle.

ESL TIP: For information about correctly using *infinitives* and *gerunds* as objects, see Chapter 54. ●

14f   What is an adjective?

Common
Grammar
Errors: 12.
Adjective-
Adverb
Confusion

Adjectives modify—that is, they describe or limit—NOUNS, PRONOUNS, and word groups that function as nouns. For information on how to use adjectives correctly, see Chapter 18.

> I saw a **green** tree. [*Green* modifies the noun *tree*.]
> It was **leafy**. [*Leafy* modifies the pronoun *it*.]
> The flowering trees were **beautiful**. [*Beautiful* modifies the noun phrase *the flowering trees*.]

Descriptive adjectives such as *green, leafy,* and *beautiful* describe the condition or the properties of a noun or a pronoun.

ESL TIP: You can identify some kinds of adjectives by looking at their endings. Usually, words with the suffixes *-ful, -ish, -less,* and *-like* are adjectives. •

Determiners, frequently called **limiting adjectives,** tell whether a noun is general (*a* tree) or specific (*the* tree). Determiners also tell which one (*this* tree), how many (*twelve* trees), whose (*our* tree), and similar information.

The determiners *a, an,* and *the* are almost always called **articles.** *The* is a **definite article.** Before a noun, *the* conveys that the noun refers to a specific item (*the* plan). *A* and *an* are **indefinite articles.** They convey that a noun refers to an item in a nonspecific or general way (*a* plan).

ALERT: Use *a* when the word following it starts with a consonant: *a carrot, a broken egg.* Also, use *a* when the word following starts with an *h* that is sounded: *a hip, a home.* Use *an* when the word following starts with a vowel sound: *an honour, an old bag, an egg.* •

ESL TIP: For information about using articles with COUNT and NONCOUNT NOUNS, and about articles with PROPER NOUNS and GERUNDS, see Chapter 54. •

Quick Reference 14.4 lists kinds of determiners. Notice, however, that some of the words function also as pronouns. To identify a word's part of speech, always check to see how it functions in each particular sentence.

That car belongs to Harold. [*That* is a limiting adjective.]

That is Harold's car. [*That* is a demonstrative pronoun.]

QUICK REFERENCE **14.4**

Determiners (or limiting adjectives)

ARTICLES *a, an, the*	*The news reporter used a cell phone to report an assignment.*
DEMONSTRATIVE *this, these, that, those*	*Those students rent **that** house.*
INDEFINITE *any, each, few, other,* *some,* and others	*Few films today have complex plots.*
INTERROGATIVE *what, which, whose*	*What answer did you give?*
NUMERICAL *one, first, two, second,* and others	*The **fifth** question was tricky.*
POSSESSIVE *my, your, their,* and others	*My violin is older than **your** cello.*
RELATIVE *what, which, whose,* *whatever,* and others	*We do not know **which** road to take.*

14g What is an adverb?

Common
Grammar
Errors: 12.
Adjective-
Adverb
Confusion

Adverbs modify—that is, adverbs describe or limit—VERBS, ADJECTIVES, other adverbs, and CLAUSES. For information on how to use adverbs correctly, see Chapter 18.

Chefs plan meals **carefully**. [*Carefully* modifies the verb *plan*.]

Vegetables provide **very** important vitamins. [*Very* modifies the adjective *important*.]

Those potato chips are **too** heavily salted. [*Too* modifies the adverb *heavily*.]

Fortunately, people are learning that overuse of salt is harmful. [*Fortunately* modifies the rest of the sentence, an independent clause.]

Descriptive adverbs show levels of intensity, usually by adding *more* (or *less*) and *most* (or *least*): *more* happily, *least* clearly (18e). Many descriptive adverbs are formed by adding *-ly* to adjectives: *sadly, loudly, normally*. But many adverbs do not end in *-ly: very, always, not, yesterday*, and *well* are a few. Some adjectives look like adverbs but are not: *brotherly, lonely, lovely*.

Relative adverbs are words such as *where, why,* and *when*. They are used to introduce ADJECTIVE CLAUSES.

Conjunctive adverbs create logical connections between sentences or clauses. Although a conjunctive adverb modifies an idea contained in the preceding sentence or clause, it does not have to appear at the start of its own. For example, you can follow the sentence "Isaac Newton's rival Robert Hooke was an important scientist" with any of the following:

However, we consider Newton even more important.

We consider Newton, **however**, even more important.

We consider Newton even more important, **however**.

Quick Reference 14.5 lists the kinds of relationships that conjunctive adverbs can show.

QUICK REFERENCE **14.5**

Conjunctive adverbs and relationships they express

RELATIONSHIP	ADVERBS
ADDITION	*also, furthermore, moreover, besides*
CONTRAST	*however, still, nevertheless, conversely, nonetheless, instead, otherwise*
COMPARISON	*similarly, likewise*
RESULT OR SUMMARY	*therefore, thus, consequently, accordingly, hence, then*
TIME	*next, then, meanwhile, finally, subsequently*
EMPHASIS	*indeed, certainly*

EXERCISE 14-3   Underline and label all adjectives (ADJ) and adverbs (ADV). For help, consult 14e through 14g.

 ADJ ADV ADJ ADJ

EXAMPLE Creative scientists and scientifically minded designers are developing new

 ADJ

kinds of experimental robots.

1. Getting mechanical inventions to interact easily with humans in their homes and workplaces remains a major challenge.

2. Some engineers think that we should design robots to evolve into their own final shapes, instead of trying to predict the most efficient robotic shapes and movements.

3. Accordingly, these engineers remind us that our big computers have developed into sleek handheld devices without a master plan to guide this evolution.

4. A student at UBC has recently examined how nonverbal gestures can build friendly interactions between humans and robots.

5. She compares her research to studying two people who reach for the last piece of chocolate on a plate and analyzing what their hand movements, which may be hesitant and polite or quick and aggressive, tell us about their relationship.

Prepositions and Prepositional Phrases

Common Grammar Errors: 20. Preposition Problems

14h   What is a preposition?

Prepositions are words that convey relationships, usually in time or space. Common prepositions include *in, under, by, after, to, on, over,* and *since.* a PREPOSITIONAL PHRASE consists of a preposition and the words it modifies. For information about prepositions and commas, see 24k.2.

> **In the fall**, we will hear a concert **by our favourite tenor**.
>
> **After the concert,** he will fly **to San Francisco**.

ESL TIP: For a list of prepositions and the IDIOMS they create, see Chapter 53. ●

14i   What is a conjunction?

A **conjunction** connects words, PHRASES, or CLAUSES. **Coordinating conjunctions** join two or more grammatically equal words, phrases, or clauses. Quick Reference 14.6 lists the coordinating conjunctions and the relationships they express.

> We hike **and** camp every summer. [*And* joins two words.]
>
> We hike along scenic trails **or** in the wilderness. [*Or* joins two phrases.]
>
> I love the outdoors, **but** my family does **not**. [*But* joins two independent clauses.]

QUICK REFERENCE   **14.6**

Coordinating conjunctions and relationships they express

RELATIONSHIP	WORDS
ADDITION	*and*
CONTRAST	*but, yet*
RESULT OR EFFECT	*so*
REASON OR CAUSE	*for*
CHOICE	*or*
NEGATIVE CHOICE	*nor*

Correlative conjunctions are two conjunctions that work as a pair: *both . . . and; either . . . or; neither. . . nor; not only. . . but (also); whether. . . or;* and *not. . . so much as.*

Both English **and** French are spoken in many homes in Canada.

Not only students **but also** business people should study a second language.

Subordinating conjunctions introduce DEPENDENT CLAUSES and show that the dependent clause in a sentence is grammatically less important than the INDEPENDENT CLAUSE. Quick Reference 14.7 lists the most common subordinating conjunctions. For information about how to use them correctly, see 9d through 9m.

Because of the ice storm, school was cancelled.

Many people were happy **after** they heard the news.

QUICK REFERENCE 14.7

Subordinating conjunctions and relationships they express

RELATIONSHIP	WORDS
TIME	*after, before, once, since, until, when, whenever, while*
REASON OR CAUSE	*as, because, since*
RESULT OR EFFECT	*in order that, so, so that, that*
CONDITION	*if, even if, provided that, unless*
CONTRAST	*although, even though, though, whereas*
LOCATION	*where, wherever*
CHOICE	*than, whether*

14j What is an interjection?

An **interjection** is a word or expression that conveys surprise or a strong emotion. Alone, an interjection is usually punctuated with an exclamation mark (!). As part of a sentence, an interjection is usually set off by one or more commas.

Hooray! I won the race.

Oh, my friends missed seeing the finish.

EXERCISE 14-4 Identify the part of speech of each numbered and underlined word. Choose from noun, pronoun, verb, adjective, adverb, preposition, coordinating conjunction, correlative conjunction, and subordinating conjunction. For help, consult 14b through 14i.

                                                            1

The geneticist Barbara McClintock was a nonconformist. She

   2   3   4

preferred the company of the corn plants that she eagerly studied to

          5

the companionship of many of the people she knew. When she won

                                                 6

the Nobel Prize in 1983, she learned of it over the radio because she

had no telephone.

7

McClintock worked <u>alone</u> throughout her fifty-year career at the

8   9

Cold Spring Harbor Laboratory <u>in</u> New York. In the 1940s <u>and</u> 1950s,

10

McClintock <u>discovered</u> that parts of chromosomes break off and

11   12   13

<u>recombine</u> with <u>neighbouring</u> chromosomes to create <u>unique</u> genetic

14

combinations. This process, known <u>as</u> crossing over, amazed

scientists and demonstrated that chromosomes formed the basis

of genetics. Still, scientists resisted McClintock's findings and did not

15   16   17

recognize the importance <u>of</u> her research for many <u>years</u>. Only <u>after</u>

18   19

geneticists <u>found</u> crossing-over genes in <u>both</u> plants <u>and</u> animals was

the great value of McClintock's discovery acknowledged. Years later, she

20

<u>won</u> the Nobel Prize for her groundbreaking achievement.

21   22

Overall, McClintock's life was <u>lonely</u>, but her career was very

productive. By the time of her death in 1992, her colleagues had

23   24   25

<u>finally</u> <u>come</u> to realize that Barbara McClintock was <u>one</u> of the

towering giants of genetics.

SENTENCE STRUCTURES

14k How is a sentence defined?

A **sentence** is defined in several ways: On a strictly mechanical level, a sentence starts with a capital letter and finishes with a period, question mark, or exclamation mark. Grammatically, a sentence consists of an INDEPENDENT CLAUSE: *skydiving is dangerous*. You might hear a sentence described as a "complete thought," but that definition is too vague to help much. Quick Reference 14.8 defines types of sentences by their purposes.

QUICK REFERENCE   **14.8**

Sentences and their purposes

- A **declarative sentence** makes a statement: *Skydiving is dangerous.*
- An **interrogative sentence** asks a question: *Is skydiving dangerous?*
- An **imperative sentence** gives a command: *Be careful when you skydive.*
- An **exclamatory sentence** express strong feeling: *How I love skydiving!*

14I   **What are a subject and a predicate in a sentence?**

The **subject** and **predicate** of a sentence are its two essential parts. Without both, a group of words isn't a sentence. Quick Reference 14.9 shows the sentence pattern with both.

QUICK REFERENCE   **14.9**

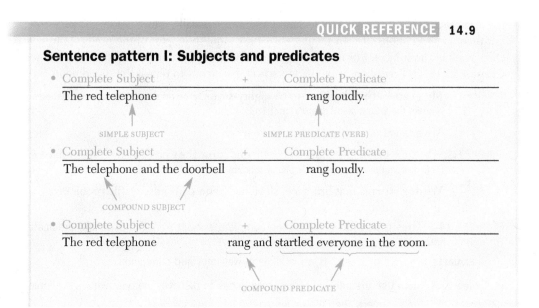

Sentence pattern I: Subjects and predicates

- Complete Subject   +   Complete Predicate

  The red telephone   rang loudly.

  SIMPLE SUBJECT   SIMPLE PREDICATE (VERB)

- Complete Subject   +   Complete Predicate

  The telephone and the doorbell   rang loudly.

  COMPOUND SUBJECT

- Complete Subject   +   Complete Predicate

  The red telephone   rang and startled everyone in the room.

  COMPOUND PREDICATE

The **simple subject** is the word or group of words that acts, is described, or is acted upon.

The **telephone** rang. [Simple subject, *telephone*, acts.]

The **telephone** is red. [Simple subject, *telephone*, is described.]

The **telephone** was being connected. [Simple subject, *telephone*, is acted upon.]

The **complete subject** is the simple subject and its MODIFIERS.

The red telephone rang.

A **compound subject** consists of two or more NOUNS or PRONOUNS.

The telephone and the doorbell rang.

The **predicate** contains the VERB in the sentence. The predicate tells what the subject is doing or experiencing or what is being done to the subject.

The telephone **rang**. [*Rang* tells what the subject, *telephone*, did.]

The telephone **is** red. [*Is* tells what the subject, *telephone*, experiences.]

The telephone **was being connected.** [*Was being connected* tells what was being done to the subject, *telephone*.]

A **simple predicate** contains only the verb.

The lawyer **listened.**

A **complete predicate** contains the verb and its modifiers.

The lawyer **listened carefully**.

A **compound predicate** contains two or more verbs.

The lawyer **listened and waited**.

ESL TIPS: (1) The subject of a declarative sentence usually comes before the predicate, but there are exceptions (9r). In sentences that ask a question, part of the predicate usually comes before the subject. For more information about word order in English sentences, see Chapter 52. (2) In English, don't add a PERSONAL PRONOUN to repeat the stated noun.

NO   My **grandfather** he lived to be eighty-seven. [The personal pronoun, *he,* mistakenly repeats the stated noun, *grandfather.*]

YES   My **grandfather** lived to be eighty-seven.

NO   **Winter storms** that bring ice, sleet, and snow **they** can cause traffic problems. [The personal pronoun, *they,* mistakenly repeats the stated noun, *winter storms.*]

YES   **Winter storms** that bring ice, sleet, and snow can cause traffic problems. ●

EXERCISE 14-5   Use a slash to separate the complete subject from the complete predicate. For help, consult 14l.

EXAMPLE A smart shopper / is an intelligent, well-informed consumer.

1. Wise consumers use the Internet to compare prices to discover the best values available.
2. Smart clothing shoppers keep their eyes on the sale racks.
3. They buy summer clothes in the winter and winter clothes in the summer.
4. The financial savings make them content to wait a few months to wear their new clothes.
5. Another good way to earn money for clothing is for people to sell their good used clothing to a resale store.

((•● **14m**   What are direct and indirect objects?

Subject-
Object
Agreement
and
Subject-
Complement
Agreement

A **direct object** is a noun, pronoun, or group of words acting as a noun that receives the action of a TRANSITIVE VERB. To check for a direct object, make up a *whom?* or *what?* question about the verb.

An **indirect object** is a noun, pronoun, or group of words acting as a noun that tells *to whom* or *for whom* the action expressed by a transitive verb was done. To check for an indirect object, make up a *to whom? for whom? to what?* or *for what?* question about the verb.

Direct and indirect objects always fall in the PREDICATE of a sentence. Quick Reference 14.10 shows how direct and indirect objects function in sentences.

ESL TIPS: (1) Verbs that normally do not take an indirect object can instead be followed by a PREPOSITIONAL PHRASE consisting of *to* or *for* with a noun or a pronoun that corresponds to an indirect object.

NO   Please do **Femi** the exercise.

YES   Please do the exercise **for Femi**.

Sentence pattern II: Direct and indirect objects

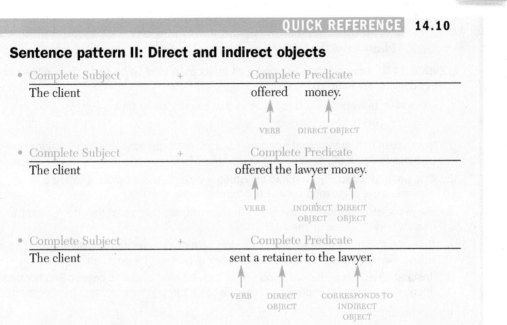

• Complete Subject	+	Complete Predicate
The client		offered money.
		↑ ↑
		VERB DIRECT OBJECT

• Complete Subject	+	Complete Predicate
The client		offered the lawyer money.
		↑ ↑ ↑
		VERB INDIRECT DIRECT
		OBJECT OBJECT

• Complete Subject	+	Complete Predicate
The client		sent a retainer to the lawyer.
		↑ ↑ ↑
		VERB DIRECT CORRESPONDS TO
		OBJECT INDIRECT
		OBJECT

| NO | Explain **me** the rule. |
| YES | Explain the rule **to me**. |

(2) Always put the direct object before a phrase made up of *to* or *for* and words that correspond to an indirect object.

NO	Will you please give **to John** this letter?
YES	Will you please give this letter **to John?**
NO	Explain **to me** the rule.
YES	Explain the rule **to me**.

(3) When the direct object is a pronoun, put it first and replace the indirect object with a phrase beginning with *to*.

NO	He gave **me it**.
YES	He gave it **to me**.
NO	She gave **Avi it.**
YES	She gave **it to Avi.**

(4) Any indirect object can be replaced by a phrase beginning with *to*. Make sure you put the direct object before this phrase (Rule 2).

| YES | Please give **Ivana** the CD. |
| YES | Please give the CD **to Ivana.** |

| YES | Please hand **me** the letter.

| YES | Please hand the letter **to me.** ●

EXERCISE 14-6   Draw a single line under all direct objects of verbs and a double line under all indirect objects. For help, consult 14m.

> **EXAMPLE**   Universities and colleges in this country serve their <u>students</u> countless <u>meals</u> every year.

1. Who doesn't know that students bring their parents and school administrations endless complaints about the food served on campus?

2. One western university even had to defuse a violent incident after it invited a representative of its food service to attend a public meeting.

3. For years, students have been telling anyone who will listen that they have a right to healthy meals served in interesting ways.

4. One bright spot is the University of Guelph, with its famous agricultural program, which hasn't awarded a major outside firm a catering contract for decades.

5. Instead, Guelph runs its own food operations, offering students organic and fair trade menus and giving its captive customers a voice through their student food ombudsman.

((•   **14n**   What are complements, modifiers, and appositives?

Copular Verbs (Linking Verbs)

COMPLEMENTS

((•

Subject-Object Agreement and Subject-Complement Agreement

A **complement** renames or describes a SUBJECT or an OBJECT. It appears in the PREDICATE of a sentence.

A **subject complement** is a NOUN, PRONOUN, or ADJECTIVE that follows a LINKING VERB. **Predicate nominative** is another term for a noun used as a subject complement, and **predicate adjective** is another term for an adjective used as a subject complement.

An **object complement** follows a DIRECT OBJECT and either describes or renames the direct object. Quick Reference 14.11 shows how subject and object complements function in a sentence.

QUICK REFERENCE **14.11**

Sentence pattern III: Complements

● Complete Subject   +   Complete Predicate

| The caller | | was a student. |

LINKING   SUBJECT
VERB   COMPLEMENT

● Complete Subject   +   Complete Predicate

| The student | | called himself a victim. |

VERB   DIRECT   OBJECT
OBJECT   COMPLEMENT

EXERCISE 14-7 Underline all complements and identify each as a subject complement (SUB) or an object complement (OB).

SUB

   EXAMPLE Architect Frank Gehry's buildings have been called <u>bizarre</u>.

1. Frank Gehry's colleagues consider him brilliant for his work in designing remarkable structures.
2. In 1989, he was awarded the Pritzker Architecture Prize, which is said to be equivalent to winning a Nobel.
3. From a distance, his Guggenheim Museum in Bilbao, Spain, seems poised over the city like a huge, splashing silver whale.
4. Gehry was born Canadian, but he made his career in California.
5. For years he wondered why no Canadian individuals or institutions ever found him appropriate to design their projects.

MODIFIERS

A **modifier** is a word or group of words that describes or limits other words. Modifiers appear in the SUBJECT or the PREDICATE of a sentence.

   The **large red** telephone rang. [The adjectives *large* and *red* modify the noun *telephone*.]

   The lawyer answered **quickly**. [The adverb *quickly* modifies the verb *answered*.]

   The person **on the telephone** was **extremely** upset. [The prepositional phrase *on the telephone* modifies the noun *person*; the adverb *extremely* modifies the adjective *upset*.]

   Therefore, the lawyer spoke **gently**. [The adverb *therefore* modifies the independent clause *the lawyer spoke gently*; the adverb *gently* modifies the verb *spoke*.]

   Because the lawyer's voice was calm, the caller felt reassured. [The adverb clause *because the lawyer's voice was calm* modifies the independent clause *the caller felt reassured.*]

APPOSITIVES

An **appositive** is a word or group of words that renames the NOUN or PRONOUN preceding it.

   The student's story, **a tale of broken promises**, was complicated. [The appositive *a tale of broken promises* renames the noun *story*.]

   The lawyer consulted an expert, **her law professor**. [The appositive *her law professor* renames the noun *expert*.]

   The student, **Jamil Amin,** asked to speak to his lawyer. [The appositive *Jamil Amin* renames the noun *student*.]

    ALERT: When an appositive is not essential for identifying what it renames (that is, when it is NONRESTRICTIVE), use a comma or commas to set off the appositive from the rest of the sentence; see 24f. ●

140 **What is a phrase?**

A **phrase** is a group of words that does not contain both a SUBJECT and a PREDICATE and therefore cannot stand alone as an independent unit.

NOUN PHRASE

A **noun phrase** functions as a NOUN in a sentence.

   The **modern census** dates back to the seventeenth century.

VERB PHRASE

A **verb phrase** functions as a VERB in a sentence.

> Two military censuses **are mentioned** in the Bible.

PREPOSITIONAL PHRASE

A **prepositional phrase** always starts with a PREPOSITION and functions as a MODIFIER.

> William the Conqueror conducted a census **of landowners in newly conquered England in 1086.** [three prepositional phrases in a row, beginning with *of, in, in*]

ABSOLUTE PHRASE

An **absolute phrase** usually contains a noun or PRONOUN and a PRESENT or PAST PARTICIPLE. An absolute phrase modifies its entire sentence.

> **Censuses being the fashion,** Quebec and Nova Scotia took sixteen counts between 1665 and 1754.

> Eighteenth-century Sweden and Denmark had complete records of their populations, **each adult and child having been counted.**

VERBAL PHRASE

A **verbal phrase** contains a verbal—a verb part that functions not as a verb, but as a noun, an ADVERB, or an ADJECTIVE. Verbals are INFINITIVES, GERUNDS, present participles, and past participles.

> In 1624, Virginia began **to count its citizens** in a census. [*To count its citizens* is an infinitive phrase.]

> **Going from door to door,** census takers used to interview millions of people. [*Going from door to door* is a present participial phrase.]

> **Amazed by some people's answers,** census takers always listened carefully. [*Amazed by some people's answers* is a past participial phrase.]

A **gerund phrase** functions as a noun. Telling the difference between a gerund phrase and a present participial phrase can be tricky because both use the *-ing* verb form (14e). The key is to determine how the phrase functions in the sentence: A gerund phrase functions only as a noun, and a participial phrase functions only as a modifier.

> **Including each person in the census** was important. [This is a gerund phrase because it functions as a noun and is the subject of the sentence.]

> **Including each person in the census,** Abby spent many hours on the crowded city block. [This is a present participial phrase because it functions as a modifier, namely, an adjective describing Abby.]

EXERCISE 14-8   Combine each set of sentences into a single sentence by converting one sentence into a phrase—a noun phrase, verb phrase, prepositional phrase, absolute phrase, verbal phrase, or gerund phrase. You can omit, add, or change words. Identify which type of phrase you created.

You can combine most sets in several correct ways, but make sure the meaning of your finished sentence is clear. For help, consult 14o.

> **EXAMPLE**   Large chain stores often pose threats to local independent retailers. Smaller store owners must find innovative ways to stay in business.

With large chains posing threats to local independent retailers, smaller store owners must find innovative ways to stay in business. (prepositional phrase)

1. Independent stores develop creative marketing strategies to compete with chain stores. Independent stores figure out ways to offer special features.

2. One independent children's bookstore attracted new customers. It did that by bringing live animals into the store.

3. Animals are popular with children. The store purchased two pet chickens, plus tarantulas, rats, cats, and fish.

4. This children's bookstore did not need to lower prices to draw customers. The store could survive by owning animals that appeal to youngsters.

5. Other sorts of independent stores sometimes take a slightly different approach. They compete by offering better service than the large chain stores can.

6. For example, independent hardware and housewares stores can be service-oriented and customer friendly. They sometimes can thrive financially doing this.

7. Many independent hardware and housewares store owners have begun to offer home-repair and decorating advice as well as to recommend house calls from staff members. They do this to attract and hold customers.

8. These store owners also feature high-end items that chains do not carry. They feature in-store displays and advertise their high-end items.

9. Independent hardware and housewares stores often stock fine items such as expensive lawn ornaments, costly brand-name paints, and rare Italian tiles. These stores tend to attract wealthier customers.

14p What is a clause?

A **clause** is a group of words with both a SUBJECT and a PREDICATE. Clauses can be either *independent clauses,* also called *main clauses,* or *dependent clauses,* also called *subordinate clauses.*

INDEPENDENT CLAUSES

An **independent clause** contains a subject and a predicate and can stand alone as a sentence. Quick Reference 14.12 shows the basic pattern.

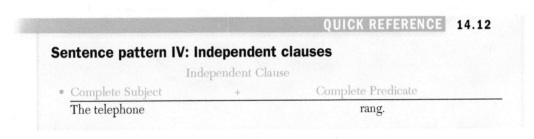

QUICK REFERENCE **14.12**

Sentence pattern IV: Independent clauses

Independent Clause

- Complete Subject   +   Complete Predicate
  The telephone   rang.

DEPENDENT CLAUSES

A **dependent clause** contains a subject and a predicate but can't stand alone as a sentence. To be part of a complete sentence, a dependent clause must be joined to an independent clause. Dependent clauses may be *adverb clauses, adjective clauses,* or certain *noun clauses.*

ADVERB CLAUSES

An **adverb clause** starts with a SUBORDINATING CONJUNCTION, such as *although, because, when,* or *until.* A subordinating conjunction expresses a relationship between a dependent clause and an independent clause; see Quick Reference 14.7. Adverb clauses usually answer some question about the independent clause: *How? Why? When? Under what circumstances?*

> **If the vote passes,** the city will install new sewers. [The adverb clause modifies the verb phrase *will install*; it explains under what circumstances.]

> They are drawing up plans **as quickly as they can**. [The adverb clause modifies the verb phrase *drawing up*; it explains how.]

> The homeowners feel happier **because they know the flooding will soon be better controlled**. [The adverb clause modifies the entire independent clause; it explains why.]

❶ ALERT: When you write an adverb clause before an independent clause, separate the clauses with a comma; see 24c. ●

ADJECTIVE CLAUSES

An **adjective clause**, also called a *relative clause,* starts with a RELATIVE PRONOUN, such as *who, which,* or *that,* or with a RELATIVE ADVERB, such as *when* or *where.* An adjective clause modifies the NOUN or PRONOUN that it follows. Quick Reference 14.13 shows how adverb and adjective clauses function in sentences.

> The car **that Jack bought** is practical. [The adjective clause describes the noun *car*; *that* is a relative pronoun referring to *car*.]

> The day **when I can buy my own car** is getting closer. [The adjective clause modifies the noun *day*; *when* is a relative adverb referring to *day*.]

Sentence pattern V: Dependent clauses

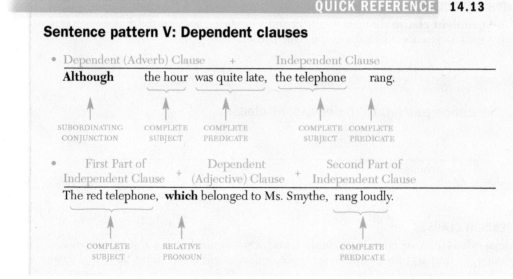

- Dependent (Adverb) Clause   +   Independent Clause

Although   the hour was quite late, the telephone   rang.

SUBORDINATING   COMPLETE   COMPLETE   COMPLETE COMPLETE
CONJUNCTION   SUBJECT   PREDICATE   SUBJECT   PREDICATE

- First Part of   Dependent   Second Part of
  Independent Clause + (Adjective) Clause + Independent Clause

The red telephone, **which** belonged to Ms. Smythe, rang loudly.

COMPLETE   RELATIVE   COMPLETE
SUBJECT   PRONOUN   PREDICATE

Use *who, whom, whoever, whomever,* and *whose* when an adjective clause refers to a person or to an animal with a name.

The di Pietros, **who collect cars,** are wealthy.

Their dog Bowser, **who is large and loud,** has been spoiled.

Use *which* or *that* when an adjective clause refers to a thing or to an animal that isn't a pet. Sometimes, writers omit *that* from an adjective clause. For grammatical analysis, however, consider the omitted *that* to be implied and, therefore, present.

For help in deciding whether to use *that* or *which,* see Quick Reference 16.4 in section 16s.

ALERT: When an adjective clause is NONRESTRICTIVE, use *which* and set it off from the independent clause with commas. Don't use commas with *that* in a RESTRICTIVE CLAUSE.

My car, **which** I bought used, needs major repairs. [The adjective clause is nonrestrictive, so it begins with *which* and is set off with commas.]

The car **that** I want to buy has a GPS. [The adjective clause uses *that* and is restrictive, so it is not set off with commas.] ●

EXERCISE 14-9   Underline the dependent clause in each sentence, and label it an ADJ or an ADV clause. For help, consult 14p.

ADV
EXAMPLE <u>When city dwellers want a quick lunch,</u> they often line up at a food cart.

1. Although lunchtime may be peak hour for food carts, street food is also popular at other times.
2. Club districts that attract late-night partiers have crowds lining up for hot dogs until dawn.
3. Because Vancouver is such a culturally diverse city, it provides a wide choice of street foods for its population and its many visitors.
4. Some other places make do with hot dog carts and trucks selling french fries or poutine, which is increasingly popular.
5. That approach has been abandoned in Vancouver, where people can also sample Mexican and Vietnamese specialties from the street vendors.

NOUN CLAUSES

Noun clauses function as nouns. Depending on their function in a sentence, they may be either independent or dependent clauses (9j). Dependent noun clauses can begin with many of the same words that begin adjective clauses: *that, who, which,* and their derivatives; both dependent and independent noun clauses can begin with *when, where, whether, why,* and *how.*

Promises are not always dependable. [noun]

What politicians promise is not always dependable. [independent noun clause]

The electorate often cannot figure out the **truth**. [noun]

The electorate often cannot know **that the truth is being manipulated**. [dependent noun clause]

Because they start with similar words, noun clauses and adjective clauses are sometimes confused with each other. One way to tell them apart is that the word starting an adjective clause has an ANTECEDENT, while the word starting a noun clause doesn't.

Good politicians **who make promises** know to keep the important ones. [Adjective clause modifies *politicians*, which is the antecedent of *who*.]

Good politicians understand **whom they must please**. [Noun clause; *whom* does not have an antecedent.]

Another way to distinguish noun clauses from other clauses is that any noun clause can be replaced by a pronoun: *It is not always dependable. Good politicians understand **it***. A pronoun renames a noun.

ESL TIP: Noun clauses in INDIRECT QUESTIONS are phrased as statements, not questions: *Kara asked why we needed the purple dye.* Don't phrase a noun clause this way: *Kara asked why **did** [or **do**] we need the purple dye?* If you prefer to change to a direct question, usually VERB TENSE, PRONOUN, and other changes are necessary; see 22e. ●

ELLIPTICAL CLAUSES

In an **elliptical clause**, one or more words are deliberately left out for CONCISENESS. For an elliptical clause to be correct, the one or more words you leave out need to be identical to those already appearing in the clause.

Engineering is one of the majors **[that] she considered.** [*that*, functioning as a relative pronoun, omitted from adjective clause]

She decided **[that] she would rather major in management**. [*that*, functioning as a conjunction, omitted from noun clause]

After [he takes] a refresher course, he will be eligible for a raise. [subject and verb omitted from adverb clause]

Broiled fish tastes better **than boiled fish [tastes]**. [second half of the comparison omitted]

Lucie attended graduate school **with the aid of a big scholarship** and **[with the aid of] a huge student loan.** [part of the parallel structure omitted]

EXERCISE 14-10 Use subordinate conjunctions and relative pronouns from the list below to combine each pair of sentences. You may use words more than once, but try to use as many different ones as possible. Some sentence pairs may be combined in several ways. Create at least one elliptical construction.

since   which   if   after   when   as   that   although   so that   unless   because

EXAMPLE Reports of flying snakes have been around for hundreds of years. Scientists have never believed them.

Even though reports of flying snakes have been around for hundreds of years, scientists have never believed them.

1. The idea that snakes can fly or even glide from treetops seems impossible. They lack wings, feathers, or any other kind of flying or gliding apparatus.

2. Yet, what seems impossible is not so for the paradise tree snake. This snake possesses many adaptations to allow it to soar long distances through the air.

3. The paradise tree snake has evolved into an animal of amazing agility. This allows it both to escape from predators and to catch its prey.

4. The paradise tree snake can land as far as 21 metres from its launch point. People who visit the jungles of Southeast Asia can see this.

5. The snake dangles like the letter *J* from a tree branch. It throws itself upward and away from the branch, giving the impression of leaping in midair.

6. Immediately, it begins to fall at a steep angle. It then takes on an *S*-shape, ripples through the air, and appears to be crawling.

7. The snake changes to an *S*-shape. Its fall becomes much less steep, enabling the snake to soar outward from its launch point.

8. A special characteristic permits the snake to change its shape and begin to glide. This characteristic permits the snake to flatten its body.

9. Most snakes cannot glide through the air. The paradise tree snake most certainly can.

10. The paradise tree snake must maintain its ability to glide effortlessly through the treetops. Otherwise, birds and mammals may eat it into extinction.

14q What are the four sentence types?

English uses four **sentence types**: simple, compound, complex, and compound-complex. A **simple sentence** is composed of a single INDEPENDENT CLAUSE and no DEPENDENT CLAUSES.

> Douglas Coupland was born in Germany in 1961.
>
> As a child, he moved to West Vancouver.

A **compound sentence** is composed of two or more independent clauses. These clauses may be connected by a COORDINATING CONJUNCTION (*and, but, for, or, nor, yet, so*), a semicolon alone, or a semicolon and a CONJUNCTIVE ADVERB.

> Coupland's father was a medical officer in the Canadian military, **and** Coupland inherited his father's interest in the sciences.
>
> The novel *Generation X* made Coupland a celebrity; it also gave us a new phrase.
>
> Some people know only his books; **however,** others have seen his sculptures, too.

A **complex sentence** is composed of one independent clause and one or more dependent clauses.

> Although some people think that Coupland invented the expression *Generation X*, he took it from the name of a punk band, which had borrowed it from a sociology book. [This sentence contains a dependent clause starting with *Although*, a dependent clause starting with *that*, an independent clause starting with *he*, and a dependent clause starting with *which*.]

A **compound-complex sentence** joins a compound sentence and a complex sentence. It contains two or more independent clauses and one or more dependent clauses.

> When journalists began calling him the spokesperson for his generation, Coupland denied it, **but** his continuing success as a writer cemented the unwanted reputation. [This sentence contains a dependent clause starting with *When*, an independent clause starting with *Coupland*, and an independent clause starting with *his*.]

237

🛈 **ALERTS:** (1) Use a comma before a coordinating conjunction connecting two independent clauses; see 24b. (2) When independent clauses are long or contain commas, use a subordinating conjunction—or use a semicolon to connect the sentences; see 25d. ●

EXERCISE 14-11   Decide whether each of the following sentences is simple, compound, complex, or compound-complex. For help, consult 14q.

> **EXAMPLE** Many people would love to eat a healthy meal at a fast-food restaurant or a food concession at the movies. *(simple)*

1. Fast-food restaurants and healthy meals rarely go together.

2. A fried-chicken sandwich packs an enormous number of calories and fat, and a fried-fish sandwich is no better.

3. A double cheeseburger with bacon at a fast-food restaurant can contain over 1000 calories and 80 grams of fat, but a plain burger reduces the unhealthy overload considerably.

4. You can purchase other relatively healthy meals at a fast-food restaurant, if you first do some research.

5. Even though governments and medical associations release vast amounts of reliable advice, consumers often ignore the information, and they choose main meals and side dishes with the most flavour, calories, and fat.

6. A healthy meal available at many fast-food restaurants is a salad with low-fat dressing, along with bottled water.

7. The temptations of high fat and calories also entice people at the food concessions in movie theatres.

8. Because calories from sugar have zero nutritional value, health experts use the expression "empty calories" for all sugar products, yet sales of colossal sugar-laden soft drinks at the movies continue to increase yearly.

9. The silent ingredient in a serving of chips with melted cheese, or nachos, is artery-clogging fat, and the culprits in extra-large candy bars are not only fat but also "empty calories."

10. In truth, many people need to stay away from fast-food restaurants and food concessions at the movies and thereby avoid the tasty temptations of high-calorie foods.

Chapter 15

VERBS

((• AUDIO LESSON Section 1: Big Ideas—Verbs

((• AUDIO LESSON Section 2: Practice Questions—Verbs

((• AUDIO LESSON Section 3: Rapid Review—Verbs

15a What do verbs do?

A **verb** expresses an action, an occurrence, or a state of being.

> Many people **overeat** on Thanksgiving. [action]
>
> Mother's Day **fell** early this year. [occurrence]
>
> New Years Day **is** tomorrow. [state of being]

Verbs also reveal when something occurs—in the present, the past, or the future. Verbs convey other information as well; see Quick Reference 15.1. For types of verbs, see Quick Reference 15.2 on the next page.

QUICK REFERENCE **15.1**

Information that verbs convey

PERSON	First person (the speaker: *I dance*), second person (the one spoken to: *you dance*), or third person (the one spoken about: *the man dances*).
NUMBER	Singular (one) or plural (more than one).
TENSE	Past (*we danced*), present (*we dance*), or future (*we will dance*); see 15g through 15k.
MOOD	Indicative (*we dance*), imperative (commands and polite requests: *Dance*), or subjunctive (speculation, wishes: *if we were dancing* . . .); see 15l and 15m.
VOICE	Active voice or passive voice; see 15n through 15p.

LINKING VERBS

Linking verbs are main verbs that indicate a state of being or a condition. They link a SUBJECT with one or more words that rename or describe the subject, called a SUBJECT COMPLEMENT. A linking verb is like an equal sign between a subject and its complement. Quick Reference 15.3 (p. 240) shows how linking verbs function in sentences.

Types of verbs

MAIN VERB The word in a PREDICATE that says something about the SUBJECT: *She **danced** for the group.*

AUXILIARY VERB A verb that combines with a main verb to convey information about TENSE, MOOD, or VOICE (15e). The verbs *be, do,* and *have* can be auxiliary verbs or main verbs. The verbs *can, could, may, might, should, would, must,* and others are MODAL AUXILIARY VERBS. They add shades of meaning such as ability or possibility to verbs: *She **might** dance* again.

LINKING VERB The verb that links a subject to a COMPLEMENT, a word or words that rename or describe the subject: *She **was** happy dancing. Be* is the most common linking verb; sometimes sense verbs (*smell, taste*) or verbs of perception (*seem, feel*) function as linking verbs. See also Quick Reference 15.3.

TRANSITIVE VERB The verb followed by a DIRECT OBJECT that completes the verb's message: *They **sent** her a fan letter.*

INTRANSITIVE VERB A verb that does not require a direct object: *Yesterday she **danced**.*

Linking verbs

- Linking verbs may be forms of the verb *be* (*am, is, was, were;* see 15e for a complete list).

Pierre Trudeau	**was**	prime minister.
SUBJECT	LINKING VERB	COMPLEMENT (PREDICATE NOMINATIVE: RENAMES SUBJECT)

- Linking verbs may deal with the senses (*look, smell, taste, sound, feel*).

Brian Mulroney	**sounded**	confident.
SUBJECT	LINKING VERB	COMPLEMENT (PREDICATE ADJECTIVE DESCRIBES SUBJECT)

- Linking verbs can be verbs that convey a sense of existing or becoming—*appear, seem, become, get, grow, turn, remain, stay,* and *prove,* for example.

Lester Pearson	**grew**	old.
SUBJECT	LINKING VERB	COMPLEMENT (PREDICATE ADJECTIVE DESCRIBES SUBJECT)

- To test whether a verb other than a form of *be* is functioning as a linking verb, substitute *was* (for a singular subject) or *were* (for a plural subject) for the original verb. If the sentence makes sense, the original verb is functioning as a linking verb.

  NO   Pierre Trudeau **grew** a beard ⟶ Pierre Trudeau **was** a beard. [*Grew* is not functioning as a linking verb.]

  YES   Lester Pearson **grew** old ⟶ Lester Pearson **was** old. [*Grew* is functioning as a linking verb.]

VERB FORMS

15b   What are the forms of main verbs?

Common Grammar Errors: 11. Wrong Verb Tense or Verb Form

A **main verb** names an action (*People **dance***), an occurrence (*Christmas **comes** once a year*), or a state of being (*It **will be** warm tomorrow*). Every main verb has five forms.

- The **simple form** conveys an action, occurrence, or state of being taking place in the present (*I **laugh***) or, with an AUXILIARY VERB, in the future (*I **will laugh***).
- The **past-tense form** conveys an action, occurrence, or state completed in the past (*I **laughed***). REGULAR VERBS add *-ed* or *-d* to the simple form. IRREGULAR VERBS vary (see Quick Reference 15.4 (p. 243) for a list of common irregular verbs).
- The **past participle** in regular verbs uses the same form as the past tense. Irregular verbs vary; see Quick Reference 15.4 (p. 243). To function as a verb, a past participle must combine with a SUBJECT and one or more auxiliary verbs (*I **have laughed***). Otherwise, past participles function as ADJECTIVES (***crumbled*** *cookies*).
- The **present participle** adds *-ing* to the simple form (***laughing***). To function as a verb, a present participle combines with a subject and one or more auxiliary verbs (*I **was laughing***). Otherwise, present participles function as adjectives (*my **laughing** friends*) or as NOUNS (***Laughing*** *is healthy*).
- The **infinitive** usually consists of *to* followed by the simple form (*I started **to laugh** at his joke*); see 16i. The infinitive functions as a noun or an adjective, not a verb.

ESL TIP: When verbs function as other parts of speech, they're called VERBALS. Verbals are INFINITIVES, PRESENT PARTICIPLES, PAST PARTICIPLES, and GERUNDS. For information about using gerunds and infinitives as OBJECTS after certain verbs, see Chapter 54.

15c   What is the -s form of a verb?

The **-s form of a verb** is the third-person singular in the PRESENT TENSE. The ending *-s* (or *-es*) is added to the verb's SIMPLE FORM (*smell* becomes *smells,* as in *The bread **smells** delicious*).

Be and *have* are irregular verbs. For the third-person singular, present tense, *be* uses *is* and *have* uses *has*.

The cheesecake **is** popular.

The éclair **has** chocolate icing.

Even if you tend to drop the *-s* or *-es* ending when you speak, always use it when you write. Proofread carefully to make sure you haven't omitted any *-s* forms.

EXERCISE 15-1   Rewrite each sentence, changing the subjects to the word or words given in parentheses. Change the form of the verbs shown in italics to match the new subject. Keep all sentences in the present tense. For help, consult 15c.

> **EXAMPLE**   The song of a bird *represents* different things to different listeners. (the songs of birds)
>
> *The songs of birds represent different things to different listeners.*

1. The poet Keats *imagines* a songbird as a fellow poet creating beautiful art. (The poets Keats and Shelley)

2. To a biologist, however, singing birds *communicate* practical information. (a singing bird)

3. A male sparrow that *whistles* one melody to attract a mate *sings* a different tune to warn off other male sparrows. (Male sparrows)

4. Female redwing blackbirds usually *distinguish* a male redwing's song from a mockingbird's imitation, but a male redwing almost never *hears* the difference. (A female redwing blackbird) (male redwings)

5. Nevertheless, in experiments, female birds *are* sometimes fooled by a carved wooden male and a recorded mating song. (the female bird)

Writing in
Action: Using
Irregular
Verbs

15d What is the difference between regular and irregular verbs?

A **regular verb** forms its PAST TENSE and PAST PARTICIPLE by adding *-ed* or *-d* to the SIMPLE FORM: *type, typed; cook, cooked; work, worked.* Most verbs in English are regular.

In informal speech, some people skip over the *-ed* sound, pronouncing it softly or not at all. In ACADEMIC WRITING, however, you're required to use it. If you're not used to hearing or pronouncing this sound, proofread carefully to see that you have all the needed *-ed* endings in your writing.

> NO   The cake was **suppose** to be tasty.
>
> YES   The cake was **supposed** to be tasty.

Irregular verbs, in contrast, don't consistently add *-ed* or *-d* to form the past tense and past participle. Some irregular verbs change an internal vowel to make the past tense and past participle: *sing, sang, sung.* Some change an internal vowel and add an ending other than *-ed* or *-d: grow, grew, grown.* Some use the simple form throughout: *cost, cost, cost.* Unfortunately, a verb's simple form doesn't provide a clue about whether the verb is irregular or regular.

Although you can always look up the principal parts of any verb, memorizing any you don't know is much more efficient in the long run. About two hundred verbs in English are irregular. Quick Reference 15.4 lists the most frequently used irregular verbs.

ALERT: For information about changing *y* to *i*, or doubling a final consonant before adding the *-ed* ending, see 31d. ●

EXERCISE 15-2 · Write the correct past-tense form of the regular verbs given in parentheses. For help, consult 15d.

> **EXAMPLE** Research in Motion (launches) *launched* its BlackBerry handheld device upon an eager world just in time for the new millennium.

(1) The BlackBerry was the first device that (allows) _____ busy people to get instant e-mail anywhere. (2) It soon (adds) _____ new features that (include) _____ text messaging, advanced Web browsing, Internet faxing, and the whole range of cell phone capabilities. (3) Technophiles who (love) _____ gadgets (admire) _____ the BlackBerry for uniting a host of wireless functions to a handheld keyboard. (4) Meanwhile, as high-powered executives (boast) _____ that the

BlackBerry (liberates) _____ them from their offices, bemused onlookers (watch) _____ them typing furiously with their thumbs on the tiny keyboard at restaurant tables and even at the gym. (5) The remarkable phenomenon (helps) _____ push Internet addiction to a whole new level.

QUICK REFERENCE 15.4

Common irregular verbs

SIMPLE FORM	PAST TENSE	PAST PARTICIPLE
arise	arose	arisen
awake	awoke *or* awaked	awaked *or* awoken
be (am, is, are)	was, were	been
bear	bore	borne *or* born
beat	beat	beaten
become	became	become
begin	began	begun
bend	bent	bent
bet	bet	bet
bid ("to offer")	bid	bid
bid ("to command")	bade	bidden
bind	bound	bound
bite	bit	bitten *or* bit
blow	blew	blown
break	broke	broken
bring	brought	brought
build	built	built
burst	burst	burst
buy	bought	bought
cast	cast	cast
catch	caught	caught
choose	chose	chosen
cling	clung	clung
come	came	come
cost	cost	cost
creep	crept	crept
cut	cut	cut
deal	dealt	dealt
dig	dug	dug
dive	dived *or* dove	dived
do	did	done
draw	drew	drawn
dream	dreamt *or* dreamed	dreamt *or* dreamed
drink	drank	drunk
drive	drove	driven
eat	ate	eaten
fall	fell	fallen
feed	fed	fed

continued ➤

Common irregular verbs

SIMPLE FORM	PAST TENSE	PAST PARTICIPLE
feel	felt	felt
fight	fought	fought
find	found	found
flee	fled	fled
fling	flung	flung
fly	flew	flown
forbid	forbade *or* forbad	forbidden
forget	forgot	forgotten *or* forgot
forgive	forgave	forgiven
forsake	forsook	forsaken
freeze	froze	frozen
get	got	got *or* gotten
give	gave	given
go	went	gone
grow	grew	grown
hang ("to suspend")*	hung	hung
have	had	had
hear	heard	heard
hide	hid	hidden
hit	hit	hit
hurt	hurt	hurt
keep	kept	kept
know	knew	known
lay	laid	laid
lead	led	led
leap	leaped *or* lept	leaped *or* leapt
leave	left	left
lend	lent	lent
let	let	let
lie	lay	lain
light	lighted *or* lit	lighted *or* lit
lose	lost	lost
make	made	made
mean	meant	meant
pay	paid	paid
prove	proved	proved *or* proven
quit	quit	quit
read	read	read
rid	rid	rid
ride	rode	ridden
ring	rang	rung
rise	rose	risen
run	ran	run

*When it means "to execute by hanging," *hang* is a regular verb: *In wartime, some armies routinely **hanged** deserters.*

continued ➤

Common irregular verbs

SIMPLE FORM	PAST TENSE	PAST PARTICIPLE
say	said	said
see	saw	seen
seek	sought	sought
send	sent	sent
set	set	set
shake	shook	shaken
shine ("to glow")*	shone	shone
shoot	shot	shot
show	showed	shown *or* showed
shrink	shrank	shrunk
sing	sang	sung
sink	sank *or* sunk	sunk
sit	sat	sat
slay	slew	slain
sleep	slept	slept
sling	slung	slung
sneak	snuck *or* sneaked	snuck *or* sneaked
speak	spoke	spoken
spend	spent	spent
spin	spun	spun
spring	sprang *or* sprung	sprung
stand	stood	stood
steal	stole	stolen
sting	stung	stung
stink	stank *or* stunk	stunk
stride	strode	stridden
strike	struck	struck
strive	strove	striven
swear	swore	sworn
sweep	swept	swept
swim	swam	swum
swing	swung	swung
take	took	taken
teach	taught	taught
tear	tore	torn
tell	told	told
think	thought	thought
throw	threw	thrown
understand	understood	understood
wake	woke *or* waked	waked *or* woken
wear	wore	worn
wring	wrung	wrung
write	wrote	written

*When it means "to polish," *shine* is a regular verb: We **shined** our shoes.

EXERCISE 15-3   Write the correct past-tense form of the irregular verbs given in parentheses. For help, consult Quick Reference 15.4 (pp. 243–245) in 15d.

> **EXAMPLE**   In August 1969, the Woodstock music festival (begin) <u>began</u> as thousands of fans (drive) <u>drove</u> to upstate New York for three days of music.

(1) The official name of the Woodstock festival (is) _____ the Woodstock Music and Art Fair. (2) It (draw) _____ nearly half a million people to Max Yasgur's farm, which (stand) _____ in the small town of Bethel, New York. (3) The concert (have) _____ to move to Bethel at the last minute after residents of the town of Woodstock (forbid) _____ organizers to hold the festive in their town. (4) Those who (come) _____ to hear music were not disappointed, since several well-known artists (sing) _____ to the large crowd. (5) Performers such as Jimi Hendrix, Santana, and Janis Joplin (lend) _____ their talents to the festival. (6) Even though rain clouds occasionally (cast) _____ a shadow on the events, most people (stick) _____ it out the entire three days. (7) According to some reports, two women (give) _____ birth during the festival. (8) Because of the relatively peaceful atmosphere, many people (see) _____ the events as a symbol of countercultural ideals. (9) Filmmaker Michael Wadleigh (strive) _____ to capture that atmosphere in the film *Woodstock,* which he (shoot) _____ and edited with the help of a young Martin Scorsese. (10) The festival also (lead) _____ Joni Mitchell to write a song she called "Woodstock." (11) That song (become) _____ a hit for Crosby, Stills, Nash, and Young, which (make) _____ its debut as a group at Woodstock. (12) Although organizers (try) _____ to turn a profit with the events, they (lose) _____ money because many attendees did not purchase tickets but instead crashed the gates.

15e   What are auxiliary verbs?

Auxiliary verbs, also called *helping verbs*, combine with MAIN VERBS to make VERB PHRASES. Quick Reference 15.5 shows how auxiliary verbs work.

USING *BE, DO, HAVE*

The three most common auxiliary verbs are *be, do,* and *have.* These three verbs can also be main verbs. Their forms vary more than most irregular verbs, as Quick References 15.6 and 15.7 (p. 248) show.

ESL TIP: When *be, do,* and *have* function as auxiliary verbs, change their form to agree with a third-person singular subject—and don't add *-s* to the main verb.

> NO   **Does** the library **closes** at 6:00?
> YES   **Does** the library **close** at 6:00? •

MODAL AUXILIARY VERBS

Can, could, shall, should, will, would, may, might, and *must* are modal auxiliary verbs. Modal **auxiliary verbs** communicate ability, permission, obligation, advisability, necessity, or possibility. They never change form.

> Exercise **can lengthen** lives. [possibility]
> She **can jog** for ten kilometres. [ability]

The exercise **must occur** regularly. [necessity, obligation]

People **should protect** their bodies. [advisability]

May I **exercise**? [permission]

Auxiliary verbs

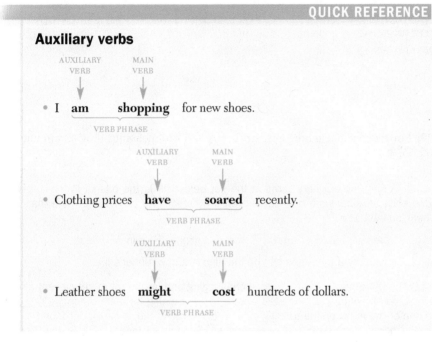

- I **am** **shopping** for new shoes.

- Clothing prices **have** **soared** recently.

- Leather shoes **might** **cost** hundreds of dollars.

Forms of the verb *be*

SIMPLE FORM	be
-S FORM	is
PAST TENSE	was, were
PRESENT PARTICIPLE	being
PAST PARTICIPLE	been

PERSON	PRESENT TENSE	PAST TENSE
I	am	was
you (singular)	are	were
he, she, it	is	was
we	are	were
you (plural)	are	were
they	are	were

Forms of the verbs *do* and *have*

SIMPLE FORM	do	have
-S FORM	does	has
PAST TENSE	did	had
PRESENT PARTICIPLE	doing	having
PAST PARTICIPLE	done	had

ESL TIP: For more about modal auxiliary verbs and the meanings they communicate, see Chapter 55. ●

EXERCISE 15-4   Using the auxiliary verbs in the list below, fill in the blanks in the following passage. Use each auxiliary word only once, even if a listed word can fit into more than one blank. For help, consult 15e.

| are | have | may | will | might | can | has |

EXAMPLE Completing a marathon <u>can</u> be the highlight of a runner's life.

(1) The marathon _____ been a challenging and important athletic event since the nineteenth century. (2) Athletes who _____ training for a marathon _____ use one of the many online training guides. (3) Running with a partner of friend _____ boost confidence and motivation. (4) Beginning runners _____ find the first few weeks difficult but _____ soon see dramatic improvement in their performance. (5) Those who _____ successfully finished the race often want to repeat the experience.

((•●   **15f**   **What are intransitive and transitive verbs?**

Lay Versus Lie   A verb is **intransitive** when an OBJECT isn't required to complete the verb's meaning: *I sing*. A verb is **transitive** when an object is necessary to complete the verb's meaning: *I need a guitar.* Many verbs have both transitive and intransitive meanings. Some verbs are only transitive: *need, have, like, owe.* Only transitive verbs function in the PASSIVE VOICE. Dictionaries label verbs as transitive (*vt*) or intransitive (*vi*).

The verbs *lie* and *lay* are particularly confusing. *Lie* means "to recline, to place oneself down, or to remain." *Lie* is intransitive (it cannot be followed by an object). *Lay* means "to put something down." *Lay* is transitive (it must be followed by an object). As you can see in Quick Reference 15.8, the word *lay* is both the past tense of *lie* and the present-tense simple form of *lay.* That makes things difficult. Our best advice is memorize these two verbs.

Using *lie* and *lay*

	lie	lay
SIMPLE FORM	lie	lay
-S FORM	lies	lays
PAST TENSE	lay	laid
PRESENT PARTICIPLE	lying	laying
PAST PARTICIPLE	lain	laid

Intransitive Forms

PRESENT TENSE	The hikers **lie** down to rest.
PAST TENSE	The hikers **lay** down to rest.

Transitive Forms

PRESENT TENSE	The hikers **lay** their backpacks on a rock. [*Backpacks* is a direct object.]
PAST TENSE	The hikers **laid** their backpacks on a rock. [*Backpacks* is a direct object.]

Two other verb pairs tend to confuse people because of their intransitive and transitive forms: *raise* and *rise* and *set* and *sit*.

Raise and *set* are transitive (they must be followed by an object). *Rise* and *sit* (in its usual meaning) are intransitive (they cannot be followed by an object). Fortunately, although each word has a meaning different from the other words, they don't share forms: *raise, raised, raised; rise, rose, risen;* and *set, set, set; sit, sat, sat.*

EXERCISE 15-5   Underline the correct word of each pair in parentheses. For help, consult 15f.

EXAMPLE During the summer, Caroline enjoys (<u>lying</u>/laying) on the beach.

(1) One day, after (setting/sitting) her chair on the sand, Caroline (lay/laid) her blanket near her umbrella. (2) Worried about getting a sunburn, she (raised/rose) her umbrella and (lay/laid) under it. (3) After a brief nap, Caroline began (rising/raising) to her feet when she realized she had forgotten where she had (lain/laid) her cooler. (4) She soon found it (lying/laying) near her car, just where she had (sat/set) it earlier. (5) She decided to pick it up and (lie/lay) it down near where her blanket (laid/lay).

VERB TENSE

15g What is verb tense?

Verb tense conveys time. Verbs show tense (time) by changing form. English has six verb tenses, divided into simple and perfect groups. The three **simple tenses** divide time into present, past, and future. The simple **present tense** describes what happens regularly,

Common Grammar Errors: 11. Wrong Verb Tense or Verb Form

249

what takes place in the present, and what is consistently or generally true. The simple **past tense** tells of an action completed or a condition ended. The simple **future tense** indicates action yet to be taken or a condition not yet experienced.

Rick **wants** to speak Spanish fluently. [simple present tense]

Rick **wanted** to improve rapidly. [simple past tense]

Rick **will want** to progress even further next year. [simple future tense]

The three **perfect tenses** also divide time into present, past, and future. They show more complex time relationships than the simple tenses. For information on using the perfect tenses, see section 15i.

The three simple tenses and the three perfect tenses also have **progressive forms**. These forms indicate that the verb describes what is ongoing or continuing. For information on using progressive forms, see section 15j. Quick Reference 15.9 summarizes verb tenses and progressive forms.

ESL TIP: Quick Reference 15.9 shows that most verb tenses are formed by combining one or more AUXILIARY VERBS with the SIMPLE FORM, the PRESENT PARTICIPLE, or the PAST PARTICIPLE of a MAIN VERB. Auxiliary verbs are necessary in the formation of most tenses, so never omit them.

    NO   I **talking** to you.

    YES   I **am talking** to you. ●

QUICK REFERENCE   **15.9**

Simple, perfect, and progressive tenses

Simple Tenses

	REGULAR VERB	IRREGULAR VERB	PROGRESSIVE FORM
PRESENT	I talk	I eat	I am talking; I am eating
PAST	I talked	I ate	I was talking; I was eating
FUTURE	I will talk	I will eat	I will be talking; I will be eating

Perfect Tenses

	REGULAR VERB	IRREGULAR VERB	PROGRESSIVE FORM
PRESENT PERFECT	I have talked	I have eaten	I have been talking; I have been eating
PAST PERFECT	I had talked	I had eaten	I had been talking; I had been eating
FUTURE PERFECT	I will have talked	I will have eaten	I will have been talking; I will have been eating

15h How do I use the simple present tense?

The **simple present tense** uses the SIMPLE FORM of the verb (15b). It describes what happens regularly, what takes place in the present, and what is generally or consistently true. Also, it can convey a future occurrence with verbs like *start, stop, begin, end, arrive,* and *depart.*

> Calculus class **meets** every morning. [regularly occurring action]
>
> Mastering calculus **takes** time. [general truth]
>
> The course **ends** in eight weeks. [specific future event]

ALERT: For a work of literature, always describe or discuss the action in the present tense. This holds true no matter how old the work.

> In Shakespeare's *Romeo and Juliet,* Juliet's father **wants** her to marry Paris, but Juliet **loves** Romeo. ●

15i How do I form and use the perfect tenses?

The **perfect tenses** generally describe actions or occurrences that are still having an effect at the present time or are having an effect until a specified time. The perfect tenses are composed of an AUXILIARY VERB and a main verb's PAST PARTICIPLE (15b).

For the **present perfect tense** (see Quick Reference 15.9), use *has* only for the third-person singular subjects and *have* for all other subjects. For the **past perfect**, use *had* with the past participle. For the **future perfect**, use *will have* with the past participle.

PRESENT PERFECT	Our government **has offered** to help. [having effect now]
PRESENT PERFECT	The drought **has created** terrible hardship. [having effect until a specified time—when the rains come]
PAST PERFECT	As soon as the tornado **had passed**, the heavy rain started. [Both events occurred in the past; the tornado occurred before the rain, so the earlier event uses *had.*]
FUTURE PERFECT	Our chickens' egg production **will have reached** five hundred per day by next year. [The event will occur before a specified time.]

15j How do I form and use progressive forms?

Progressive forms describe an ongoing event, action, or condition. They also express habitual or recurring actions or conditions. The **present progressive** uses the present-tense form of *be* that agrees with the subject in PERSON and NUMBER, plus the PRESENT PARTICIPLE (the *-ing* form) of the main verb. The **past progressive** uses *was* or *were* to agree with the subject in person and number, and it uses the present participle of the main verb. The **future progressive** uses *will be* and the present participle. The **present perfect progressive** uses *have been* or *has been* to agree with the subject, plus the present participle. The **past perfect progressive** uses *had been* and the present participle. The **future perfect progressive** uses *will have been* plus the present participle.

PRESENT PROGRESSIVE	The smog **is stinging** everyone's eyes. [event taking place now]
PAST PROGRESSIVE	Eye drops **were selling** well last week. [event ongoing in the past within stated limits]
FUTURE PROGRESSIVE	We **will be ordering** more eye drops than usual this month. [recurring event that will take place in the future]
PRESENT PERFECT PROGRESSIVE	Scientists **have been warning** us about air pollution for years. [recurring event that took place in the past and may still take place]
PAST PERFECT PROGRESSIVE	We **had been ordering** three cases of eye drops a month until the smog worsened. [recurring past event that has now ended]
FUTURE PERFECT PROGRESSIVE	By May, we **will have been selling** eye drops for eight months. [ongoing condition to be completed at a specific time in the future]

EXERCISE 15-6   Underline the correct verb in each pair of parentheses. If more than one answer is possible, be prepared to explain the differences in meaning between the two choices. For help, consult 15g through 15j.

> **EXAMPLE**   Before 1999, no head of state still holding office (has been charged, <u>had been charged</u>) with war crimes by an international court.

1. In May 1999, Judge Louise Arbour (accused, was accusing) the then president of Yugoslavia of committing crimes against humanity.

2. The crimes with which he was charged (have occurred, occurred) during the conflicts following the breakup of Yugoslavia in the early 1990s.

3. Arbour (was acting, has been acting) in her role as chief prosecutor of the United Nations International Criminal Tribunal for the former Yugoslavia.

4. This court (is known, is being known) also as the Hague Tribunal, after the Dutch city where it (has been, is) based since its establishment.

5. Its mission (is, has been) to prosecute crimes committed by all sides in the former Yugoslavia.

6. The last time such a court (existed, was existing) was after World War II, when the Nuremberg and Tokyo war crimes tribunals (have judged, judged) the defeated side.

7. Until her appointment to the Hague Tribunal in 1996, Arbour (was serving, has been serving) on the Ontario Court of Appeal. Before that, she (has been, had been) a leader of the Canadian Civil Liberties Association and a law professor at York University.

8. Arbour (is, was) a native of Quebec, however, and (is speaking, has spoken) English only since her early twenties.

9. In late 1999, Louise Arbour (has been appointed, was appointed) to the Supreme Court of Canada.

10. Arbour regularly (is taking on, takes on) new challenges; history (will judge, will be judging) how well she handled her term as UN High Commissioner for Human Rights, the position she held from 2004 to 2008.

15k   How do I use tense sequences accurately?

Common Grammar Errors: 4. Faulty Shift in Tense

Verb **tense sequences** communicate time relationships. They help deliver messages about actions, occurrences, or states that take place at different times. Quick Reference 15.10 shows how tenses in the same sentence can vary depending on the timing of actions (or occurrences or states).

Tense sequences

If your independent clause contains a simple-present-tense verb, then in your dependent clause you can

- use PRESENT TENSE to show same-time action:

  I **avoid** shellfish because I **am** allergic to it.

- use PAST TENSE to show earlier action:

  I **am** sure that I **deposited** the cheque.

- use the PRESENT PERFECT TENSE to show (1) a period of time extending from some point in the past to the present or (2) an indefinite past time:

  They **claim** that they **have visited** the planet Venus.

  I **believe** that I **have seen** that movie before.

- use the FUTURE TENSE for action to come:

  The book **is** open because I **will be reading** it later.

If your independent clause contains a past-tense verb, then in your dependent clause you can

- use the past tense to show another completed past action:

  I **closed** the door because you **told** me to.

- use the PAST PERFECT TENSE to show earlier action:

  The sprinter **knew** that she **had broken** the record.

- use the present tense to state a general truth:

  Christopher Columbus **determined** that the world **is** round.

If your independent clause contains a present-perfect-tense or past-perfect-tense verb, then in your dependent clause you can

- use the past tense:

  The bread **has become** mouldy since I **purchased** it.

  Sugar prices **had** already **declined** when artificial sweeteners first **appeared**.

If your independent clause contains a future-tense verb, then in your dependent clause you can

- use the present tense to show action happening at the same time:

  You **will be** rich if you **win** the prize.

- use the past tense to show earlier action:

  You **will** surely **win** the prize if you **remembered** to mail the entry form.

- use the present perfect tense to show future action earlier than the action of the independent-clause verb:

  The river **will flood** again next year unless we **have built** a better dam by then.

If your independent clause contains a future-perfect-tense verb, then in your dependent clause you can

- use either the present tense or the present perfect tense:

  Dr. Chang **will have delivered** five thousand babies by the time she **retires**.

  Dr. Chang **will have delivered** five thousand babies by the time she **has retired**.

253

ALERT: Never use a future-tense verb in a dependent clause when the verb in the independent clause is in the future tense. Instead, use a present-tense verb or present-perfect-tense verb in the dependent clause.

> NO   The river **will flood** us unless we **will prepare** our defence.
>
> YES   The river **will flood** us unless we **prepare** our defence. [*Prepare* is a present-tense verb.]
>
> YES   The river **will flood** us unless we **have prepared** our defence. [*Have prepared* is a present perfect verb.] ●

Tense sequences may include INFINITIVES and PARTICIPLES. To name or describe an activity or occurrence coming either at the same time as the time expressed in the MAIN VERB or after, use the **present infinitive**.

> I **hope to buy** a used car. [*To buy* comes at a future time. *Hope* is the main verb, and its action is now.]
>
> I **hoped to buy** a used car. [*Hoped* is the main verb, and its action is over.]
>
> I **had hoped to buy** a used car. [*Had hoped* is the main verb, and its action is over.]

The PRESENT PARTICIPLE (a verb's *-ing* form) can describe action happening at the same time as another action.

> **Driving** his new car, the man **smiled**. [the driving and the smiling happened at the same time.]

To describe an action that occurs before the action in the main verb, use the perfect **infinitive** (*to have gone, to have smiled*), the PAST PARTICIPLE, or the **present perfect participle** (*having gone, having smiled*).

> Candida **claimed to have written** fifty short stories in college. [*Claimed* is the main verb, and *to have written* happened first.]
>
> **Pleased** with the short story, Candida **mailed** it to several magazines. [*Mailed* is the main verb, and *pleased* happened first.]
>
> **Having sold** one short story, Candida **invested** in a laptop. [*Invested* is the main verb, and *having sold* happened first.]

EXERCISE 15-7   Underline the correct verb in each pair of parentheses that best suits the sequence of tenses. Be ready to explain your choices. For help, consult 15k.

> **EXAMPLE** When he (is, <u>was</u>) seven years old, Yo-Yo Ma, possibly the world's greatest living cellist, (moves, <u>moved</u>) to the United States with his family.

1. Yo-Yo Ma, who (had been born, was born) in France to Chinese parents, (lived, lives) in Boston, Massachusetts, today and (toured, tours) as one of the world's greatest cellists.

2. Years from now, after Mr. Ma has given his last concert, music lovers still (treasure, will treasure) his many fine recordings.

3. Mr. Ma's older sister, Dr. Yeou-Cheng Ma, was nearly the person with the concert career. She had been training to become a concert violinist when her brother's musical genius (began, had begun) to be noticed.

4. Even though Dr. Ma eventually (becomes, became) a physician, she still (had been playing, plays) the violin.
5. The family interest in music (continues, was continuing), for Mr. Ma's children (take, had taken) piano lessons.
6. Although most people today (knew, know) Mr. Ma as a brilliant cellist, he (was making, has made) films as well.
7. One year, while he (had been travelling, was travelling) in the Kalahari Desert, he (films, filmed) dances of southern Africa's Bush people.
8. Mr. Ma first (becomes, became) interested in the Kalahari people when he (had studied, studied) anthropology as an undergraduate at Harvard University.
9. When he shows visitors around Boston now, Mr. Ma has been known to point out the Harvard University library where, he claims, he (fell asleep, was falling asleep) in the stacks when he (had been, was) a student.
10. Indicating another building, Mr. Ma admits that in one of its classrooms he almost (failed, had failed) German.

MOOD

151 What is "mood" in verbs?

Mood in verbs conveys an attitude toward the action in a sentence. English has the *indicative, imperative,* and *subjunctive* moods. Use the **indicative mood** to make statements about real things, about highly likely things, and for questions of fact.

INDICATIVE   The door to the tutoring centre opened. [real]

She seemed to be looking for someone. [highly likely]

Do you want to see a tutor? [question about a fact]

The **imperative mood** expresses commands and direct requests. Often, the subject is omitted in an imperative sentence, but nevertheless the subject is implied to be either *you* or one of the indefinite pronouns such as *anybody, somebody,* or *everybody.*

ALERT: Use an exclamation mark after a strong command; use a period after a mild command or a request (23e, 23a).

IMPERATIVE   Please shut the door.

Watch out! That screw is loose.

The **subjunctive mood** expresses speculation, other unreal conditions, conjectures, wishes, recommendations, indirect requests, and demands. Often, the words that signal the subjunctive mood are *if, as if, as though,* and *unless.* Subjunctive verb forms were once used frequently in spoken English, but they're heard far less today. Nevertheless, in ACADEMIC WRITING, you need to use the subjunctive mood.

SUBJUNCTIVE   If I **were** you, I would ask for a tutor.

What are subjunctive forms?

For the **present subjunctive**, always use the SIMPLE FORM of the verb for all PERSONS and NUMBERS.

> The Crown attorney asks that she **testify** [not ~~testifies~~] again.

> It is important that they **be** [not ~~are~~] allowed to testify.

For the **past subjunctive**, use the simple past tense: *I wish that I **had** a car.* The one exception is for the past subjunctive of *be:* Use *were* for all forms.

> I wish that I **were** [not ~~was~~] leaving on vacation today.

> They asked if she **were** [not ~~was~~] leaving on vacation today.

USING THE SUBJUNCTIVE IN *IF, AS IF, AS THOUGH,* AND *UNLESS* CLAUSES

In dependent clauses introduced by *if, as if, as though,* and sometimes *unless,* the subjunctive describes speculations or conditions contrary to fact.

> If it **were** [not ~~was~~] to rain, attendance at the race would be disappointing. [speculation]

> The runner looked as if he **were** [not ~~was~~] winded, but he said he wasn't. [a condition contrary to fact]

In an *unless* clause, the subjunctive signals that what the clause says is highly unlikely.

> Unless rain **were** [not ~~was~~] to create floods, the race will be held this Sunday. [Floods are highly unlikely.]

Not every clause introduced by *if, unless, as if,* or *as though* requires the subjunctive. Use the subjunctive only when the dependent clause describes speculation or a condition contrary to fact.

> INDICATIVE   If she **is** going to leave late, I will drive her to the race. [Her leaving late is highly likely.]

> SUBJUNCTIVE   If she **were** going to leave late, I would drive her to the race. [Her leaving late is a speculation.]

USING THE SUBJUNCTIVE IN *THAT* CLAUSES

When *that* clauses describe wishes, requests, demands, or recommendations, the subjunctive can convey the message.

> I wish that this race **were** [not ~~was~~] over. [a wish about something happening now]

> He wishes that he **had seen** [not ~~saw~~] the race. [a wish about something that is past]

> The judges are demanding that the doctor **examine** [not ~~examines~~] the runners. [a demand for something to happen in the future]

Also, MODAL AUXILIARY VERBS *would, could, might,* and *should* can convey speculations and conditions contrary to fact. This is the *conditional* form of the verb.

> If the runner **were** [not ~~was~~] faster, we **would** see a better race. [*Would* is a modal auxiliary verb.]

Here, the DEPENDENT CLAUSE (beginning with *If*) takes the subjunctive verb, and the INDEPENDENT CLAUSE takes the conditional form of the verb, which uses the modal auxiliary. Don't use another modal auxiliary in the dependent clause.

NO   If I **would have trained** for the race, I **might have** won.

YES   If I **had trained** for the race, I **might have** won.

EXERCISE 15-8 Fill in each blank with the correct form of the verb given in parentheses. For help, consult 15l and 15m.

> **EXAMPLE** Imagining the possibility of brain transplants requires that we (to be) <u>be</u>
> open-minded.
>
> (1) If almost any organ other than the brain (to be) _____ the candidate for a swap, we would probably give our consent. (2) If the brain (to be) _____ to hold whatever impulses form our personalities, few people would want to risk a transplant. (3) Many popular movies have asked that we (to suspend) _____ disbelief and imagine the consequences should a personality actually (to be) _____ transferred to another body. (4) In real life, however, the complexities of a successful brain transplant require that not-yet-developed surgical techniques (to be) _____ used. (5) For example, it would be essential that during the actual transplant each one of the 500 trillion nerve connections within the brain (to continue) _____ to function as though the brain (to be) _____ lying undisturbed in a living human body.

VOICE

15n What is "voice" in verbs?

((◉
Passive Versus Active Voice

Voice in a verb tells whether a SUBJECT acts or is acted upon. English has two voices, *active* and *passive*. A subject in the **active voice** performs the action.

> Most clams **live** in salt water. [The subject *clams* does the acting: Clams *live*.]
>
> They **burrow** into the sandy bottoms of shallow waters. [The subject *they* does the acting: They *burrow*.]

A subject in the **passive voice** is acted upon. The person or thing doing the acting often appears in a PHRASE that starts with *by*. Verbs in the passive voice use forms of *be, have,* and *will* as AUXILIARY VERBS with the PAST PARTICIPLE of the MAIN VERB.

> Clams **are considered** a delicacy by many people. [The subject *clams* is acted upon *by many* people.]
>
> Some types of clams **are** highly **valued** by seashell collectors. [The subject *types* is acted upon *by seashell collectors*.]

15o How do I write in the active, not passive, voice?

((◉
Subjects and Verbs

Because the ACTIVE VOICE emphasizes the doer of an action, active constructions are more direct and dramatic. Active constructions usually require fewer words than passive constructions, which makes for greater conciseness (11c). Most sentences in the PASSIVE VOICE can be converted to active voice.

> PASSIVE   African tribal masks **are** often **imitated** by Western sculptors.
>
> ACTIVE   Western sculptors often **imitate** African tribal masks.

15p What are proper uses of the passive voice?

Although the active voice is usually best, in special circumstances you need to use the passive voice.

When no one knows who or what did something or when the doer of an action isn't important, writers use the passive voice.

The lock **was broken** sometime after four o'clock. [Who broke the lock is unknown.]

In 1899, the year I was born, a peace conference **was held** at The Hague. [The doers of the action—holders of the conference—aren't important.]

—E. B. White, "Unity"

Sometimes the action in the sentence is more important than the doer of the action. For example, if you want to focus on historical discoveries in a narrative, use the passive voice. Conversely, if you want to emphasize the people making the discoveries, use the active voice.

ACTIVE   Joseph Priestley **discovered** oxygen in 1774. [*Joseph Priestley* is the subject.]

PASSIVE   Oxygen **was discovered** in 1774 by Joseph Priestley. [*Oxygen* is the subject.]

ACTIVE   My e-mail program **delivered** the message before I **could delete** the embarrassing parts. [The emphasis is on the doer of the action, *my e-mail program,* and *I,* rather than on the events, *delivered* and *could delete.*]

PASSIVE   The e-mail **was delivered** before the embarrassing parts of the message **could be deleted.** [The emphasis is on the events, *was delivered* and *could be deleted,* not on the doers of the action.]

In former years, the social sciences and natural sciences preferred the passive voice. Recently, style manuals for these disciplines have been advising writers to use the active voice whenever possible. "Verbs are vigorous, direct communicators," point out the editors of the *Publication Manual of the American Psychological Association.* "Use the active rather than the passive voice."*

EXERCISE 15-9   First, determine which sentences are in the active voice and which the passive voice. Second, rewrite each sentence in the other voice, and then decide which voice better suits the meaning. Be ready to explain your choice. For help, consult 15n through 15p.

EXAMPLE   In the West African country of Ghana, a few woodcarvers are creating coffins that reflect their occupants' special interests. *(active; change to passive)*

In the West African country of Ghana, *coffins that reflect their occupants' special interests are being created by a few woodcarvers.*

1. A coffin in the shape of a green onion was chosen by a farmer.
2. A hunter's family buried him in a wooden coffin shaped like a leopard.
3. A dead chief was carried through his fishing village by friends and relatives bearing his body in a large pink wooden replica of a fish.
4. The family of a wealthy man who greatly admired cars buried him in a coffin shaped like a Mercedes car.
5. Although a few of these fantasy coffins have been displayed in museums, most of them end up buried in the ground.

---

*American Psychological Association, *Publication Manual of the American Psychological Association,* 6th ed. (Washington: APA, 2001), 77.

Chapter 16

PRONOUNS: CASE AND REFERENCE

PRONOUN CASE

16a What does "case" mean?

Case applies in different ways to PRONOUNS and to NOUNS. For pronouns, case refers to three pronoun forms: the **subjective** (pronoun as a SUBJECT), the **objective** (pronoun as an OBJECT), and the possessive (pronouns used in possessive constructions). For nouns, case refers to only one form: the possessive. (For help in using apostrophes in the possessive case, see Chapter 27.)

16b What are personal pronouns?

Writing in Action: Learning What Pronouns to Use

Personal pronouns refer to persons or things. Quick Reference 16.1 shows the case forms of personal pronouns (subjective, objective, and possessive), in both the singular and the plural.

QUICK REFERENCE **16.1**

Case forms of personal pronouns

	SUBJECTIVE	OBJECTIVE	POSSESSIVE
SINGULAR	I, you, he, she, it	me, you, him, her, it	my, mine, your, yours, his, her, hers, its
PLURAL	we, you, they	us, you, them, their, theirs	our, ours, your, yours,

The possessive words *my, your, her, his, its, our,* and *their* (*my book, her laptop*) are defined in some textbooks as pronouns and in others as adjectives. They share characteristics of both parts of speech.

Many of the most difficult questions about pronoun case concern *who/whom* and *whoever/whomever.* For a full discussion of how to choose between them, see 16g.

16c How do pronouns work in case?

Common Grammar Errors: 6. Pronoun Case Problems

In the subjective case, pronouns function as SUBJECTS.

We were going to get married. [*We* is the subject.]

John and **I** wanted an inexpensive band for our wedding. [*I* is part of the compound subject *John and I.*]

He and I found an affordable one-person band. [*He and I* is the compound subject.]

259

In the objective case, pronouns function as OBJECTS.

> We saw **him** perform in a public park. [*Him* is the direct object.]
>
> We showed **him** our budget. [*Him* is the indirect object.]
>
> He wrote down what we wanted and shook hands with **us**. [*Us* is the object of the preposition *with*.]

In the possessive case, nouns and pronouns usually indicate ownership or imply a relationship.

> The **musician's contract** was very fair. [The possessive noun *musician's* implies a type of ownership.]
>
> **His contract** was very fair. [The possessive pronoun *his* implies a type of ownership.]
>
> The **musicians' problems** stem from playing cheap instruments. [The possessive noun *musicians'* implies a type of relationship.]
>
> **Their problems** stem from playing cheap instruments. [The possessive pronoun *their* implies a type of relationship.]

Sometimes, however, the notion of ownership or relationship calls for a major stretch of the imagination in possessive constructions. In such cases, the possessive indicates an abstract relationship.

> The **musician's arrival** was eagerly anticipated. [The musician neither owns the arrival nor has a direct relationship with the arrival.]

ALERT: Never use an apostrophe in personal pronouns: *ours, yours, its, his, hers, theirs* (27c). ●

16d   Which case is correct when *and* connects pronouns?

When *and* connects pronouns, or nouns and pronouns, the result is a **compound construction**. Compounding has no effect on case. Always use pronouns in the subjective case when they serve as the subjects of a sentence, and use pronouns in the objective case when they serve as objects in a sentence. Never mix cases.

COMPOUND PRONOUN SUBJECT	**He and I** saw the solar eclipse. [*He and I* is a compound subject.]
COMPOUND PRONOUN OBJECT	That eclipse astonished **him and me**. [*Him and me* is a compound object.]

When you're unsure of the case of a pronoun, use the "Troyka test for case" in Quick Reference 16.2. In this four-step test, you drop some of the words from your sentence so that you can tell which case sounds correct.

When pronouns are in a PREPOSITIONAL PHRASE, they are always in the objective case. (That is, a pronoun is always the OBJECT of the preposition.) This rule holds whether the pronouns are singular or plural.

NO	Ms. Lester gave an assignment *to **Sam and I***. [The prepositional phrase, which starts with the preposition *to*, cannot use the subjective-case pronoun *I*.]
YES	Ms. Lester gave an assignment *to **Sam and me***.

Troyka test for case

SUBJECTIVE CASE

STEP 1: Write the sentence twice, once using the subjective case, and once using the objective case.

STEP 2: Cross out enough words to isolate the element you are questioning.

~~Janet and~~ **me**

> learned about the moon.

~~Janet and~~ **I**

STEP 3: Omit the crossed-out words and read each sentence aloud to determine which one sounds right.

> **NO** **Me** learned about the moon. [This doesn't sound right.]
>
> **YES** **I** learned about the moon. [This sounds right, so the subjective case is correct.]

STEP 4: Select the correct version and restore the words you crossed out.

Janet and I learned about the moon.

OBJECTIVE CASE

STEP 1: Write the sentence twice, once using the subjective case, and once using the objective case.

STEP 2: Cross out enough words to isolate the element you are questioning.

The astronomer taught ~~Janet and~~ **I**

> about the moon.

The astronomer taught ~~Janet and~~ **me**

STEP 3: Omit the crossed-out words and read each sentence aloud to determine which one sounds right.

> **NO** The astronomer taught **I** about the moon. [This doesn't sound right.]
>
> **YES** The astronomer taught **me** about the moon. [This sounds right, so the objective case is correct.]

STEP 4: Select the correct version and restore the words you crossed out.

The astronomer taught **Janet and me** about the moon.

Be especially careful when one or more pronouns follow the preposition *between*.

> **NO** The dispute is ***between Thomas and I***. [The prepositional phrase, which starts with the preposition *between*, cannot use the subjective-case pronoun I.]
>
> **YES** The dispute is ***between* Thomas and me**.

EXERCISE 16-1   Underline the correct pronoun of each pair in parentheses. For help, consult 16c and 16d.

> **EXAMPLE**   Mario and (<u>I</u>, me) noticed two young swimmers being pulled out to sea.

(1) The two teenagers caught in the rip current waved and hollered at Mario and (I, me). (2) The harder (they, them) both swam toward shore, the further away the undercurrent pulled them from the beach. (3) The yellow banners had warned Mario and (I, me) that a dangerous rip current ran beneath the water. (4) I yelled at Mario, "Between you and (I, me), (we, us) have to save them!" (5) (He and I, Him and me) both ran and leapt into the crashing waves. (6) As former lifeguards, Mario and (I, me) knew what to do. (7) (We, Us) two remembered that the rule for surviving a rip current is to swim across the current. (8) Only when swimmers are safely away from the current should (they, them) swim toward shore. (9) I reached the teenage girl, who cried, "My boyfriend and (I, me) are drowning." (10) Mario rescued the frightened teenage boy, and when they were safely on shore, the boy looked at (he and I, him and me) and gasped, "Thanks. The two of (we, us) know you saved our lives."

16e   How do I match cases with appositives?

You can match cases with APPOSITIVES by putting pronouns and nouns in the same case as the word or words the appositive is renaming. Whenever you're unsure about whether to use the subjective or objective case, use the "Troyka test for case" in Quick Reference 16.2 to get the answer.

> **We** [not *Us*] tennis players practise hard. [Here, the subjective-case pronoun *we* renames the noun phrase *tennis players*, which is the subject of this sentence.]

> The winners, **she and I** [not *her and me*], advanced to the finals. [The subjective-case pronouns in the phrase *she and I* rename the noun *winners*, which is the subject of this sentence.]

> The coach tells **us** [not *we*] tennis players to practise hard. [The objective-case pronoun *us* renames the noun phrase *tennis players*, which is the object in this sentence.]

> The crowd cheered the winners, **her and me** [not *she and I*]. [The objective-case pronouns in the phrase *her and me* rename the noun *winners*, which is the object in this sentence.]

16f   How does case work after linking verbs?

Copular Verbs (Linking Verbs)

A pronoun that comes after a LINKING VERB either renames the SUBJECT or shows possession. In both constructions, always use a pronoun in the subjective case. If you're unsure about how to identify a pronoun's case, use the "Troyka test for case" in Quick Reference 16.2.

> The contest winner was **I** [not *me*]. [*Was* is a linking verb. *I* renames the subject, the noun phrase *contest winner*, so the subjective-case pronoun *I* is correct.]

> The prize is **mine**. [*Is* is a linking verb. *Mine* shows possession, so the possessive-case pronoun *mine* is correct.]

EXERCISE 16-2   Underline the correct pronoun of each pair in parentheses. For help, consult 16c through 16f.

> **EXAMPLE**   My roommate and (<u>I</u>, me) have been interested in the entertainment scene in Quebec since (<u>we</u>, us) both visited Montreal last summer.

(1) Jen and (I, me) discovered that (we, us) knew nothing about popular culture in Quebec. (2) The two of (we, us) began by surfing the Web and watching the CBC in French. (3) Then, (we, us) two divided our responsibilities into two areas. (4) But between (she and I, her and me), her explorations in music and my forays into film were harder than expected. (5) (She and I, Her and me) still have trouble following fast-paced movie dialogue and colloquial, heavily accented song lyrics. (6) We had more luck with a variety show on TV hosted by Julie Snyder, whose delivery was easier for (we, us) beginners to understand. (7) Eventually, it was (I, me) who discovered a radio show in English, hosted by a French singer named Jim Corcoran, all about popular music in Quebec. (8) (He, him) and his guests translate the songs' lyrics and discuss the cultural scene that inspires (they, them) and their fellow composers. (9) If anyone can interpret Quebec music to people like (we, us), it's (he, him). (10) *Salut,* Jim Corcoran, and thanks—whether (he, him) is primarily a French-speaker or an English-speaker is unknown to Jen and (I, me).

16g   When should I use *who, whoever, whom,* and *whomever*?

The pronouns *who* and *whoever* are in the SUBJECTIVE CASE. The pronouns *whom* and *whomever* are in the OBJECTIVE CASE.

Informal spoken English tends to blur distinctions between *who* and *whom,* so with these words some people can't rely entirely on what "sounds right." Whenever you're unsure of whether to use *who* or *whoever* or to use *whom* or *whomever,* apply the "Troyka test for case" in Quick Reference 16.2 (p. 261). If you see *who* or *whoever,* test by temporarily substituting *he, she,* or *they.* If you see *whom* or *whomever,* test by temporarily substituting *him, her,* or *them.*

My father tells the same story to **whoever/whomever** he meets.

My father tells the story to ~~he~~/**him**. [Check to see if the pronoun you are testing is the subject of the verb that follows it. *If not,* end the sentence with the pronoun. Then, by substituting the subjective-case *he* and the objective-case *him* for *whoever/whomever,* you see that *him* is correct. Therefore, the objective-case *whomever* is correct.]

My father tells the same story to **whoever/whomever** is willing to listen.

She/~~Her~~ is willing to listen. [If the pronoun you are testing is the subject of the verb that follows it, drop from the sentence everything that precedes the pronoun. Then, by substituting the subjective-case *she* and the objective-case *her* for *whoever/whomever,* you see that *she* is correct. Therefore, the subjective-case *whoever* is correct.]

My father tells the same story to **whoever** is willing to listen.

Sometimes you will need to add a word before the substituted word set. In this example, you add the word *if.*

I wondered **who/whom** would vote for Ms. Wallace.

I wondered **if he**/~~if him~~ would vote for Ms. Wallace. [The subjective case *who* is correct because the sentence works when you substitute *if he* for *who/whom.* In contrast, the objective case *whom* is wrong because the sentence doesn't work when you substitute *if him* for *who/whom.*]

I wondered **who** would vote for Ms. Wallace.

Another variation of the test for *who, whom, whoever, whomever* calls for you to invert the word order in the test sentence.

Babies **who/whom** mothers cuddle grow faster and feel happier.

Mothers cuddle ~~they~~/**them**. [By inverting the word order of the phrase *who/whom* mothers cuddle (mothers cuddle *who/whom*) and substituting *they/them* for *who/whom*, you see that *them* is correct. Therefore, the objective case *whom* is correct.]

Babies **whom** mothers cuddle grow faster and feel happier.

At the beginning or end of a question, use *who* if the question is about the subject and *whom* if the question is about the object. To determine which case to use, recast the question into a statement, substituting *he* or *him* (or *she* or *her*).

Who watched the East Coast Music Awards? [*He* (not *Him*) *watched the East Coast Music Awards* uses the subjective case *who*.]

Ted admires **whom**? [*Ted admires him* (not *he*) uses the objective case *whom*.]

Whom does Ted admire? [*Ted admires him* (not *he*) uses the objective case *whom*.]

To **whom** does Ted speak about learning to play the fiddle? [*Ted speaks to them* (not *they*) uses the objective case *whom*.]

EXERCISE 16-3 Underline the correct pronoun of each pair in parentheses. For help, consult 16g.

> **EXAMPLE** Women (<u>who</u>, whom) both hold jobs outside the home and are mothers work a "double shift."

(1) Women (who, whom) raise families do as much work at home as at their jobs. (2) In North American society, it is still mainly women (who, whom) cook dinner, clean the house, check the children's homework, read to them, and put them to bed. (3) Nevertheless, self-esteem runs high, some researchers have found, in many women on (who, whom) families depend for both wage earning and child rearing. (4) Compared with women (who, whom) pursue careers but have no children, those (who, whom) handle a double shift experience less anxiety and depression, according to the research. (5) Perhaps the reason for this finding is that those for (who, whom) the extra paycheque helps pay the bills feel pride and accomplishment when they rise to the challenge. (6) However, other studies note that women (who, whom) have both jobs and children experience tremendous stress. (7) Those (who, whom) feel unable both to support and to nurture their children despite their maximum efforts are the women for (who, whom) the dual responsibility is an almost unbearable burden.

16h What pronoun case comes after *than* or *as*?

When *than* or *as* is part of a sentence of comparison, the sentence sometimes omits the words that complete the comparison. For example, *My two-month-old Saint Bernard is larger **than** most full-grown dogs [are]* doesn't need the final word *are*.

When a pronoun follows *than* or *as*, the meaning of the sentence depends entirely on whether the pronoun is in the subjective case or the objective case. Here are two sentences that convey two very different messages, depending on whether the subjective case (*I*) or the objective case (*me*) is used.

1. My sister loved that dog more **than** **I**.
2. My sister loved that dog more **than** **me**.

Sentence 1, because *I* is in the subjective case, means *My sister loved that dog more than* **I** *[loved it]*. Sentence 2, because *me* is in the objective case, means *My sister loved that dog more than [she loved]* me. In both situations, you can check whether you're using the correct case by supplying the implied words to see if they make sense.

16i How do pronouns work before infinitives?

Most INFINITIVES consist of the SIMPLE FORMS of verbs that follow *to:* for example, *to laugh, to sing, to jump, to dance.* (A few exceptions occur when the *to* is optional: *My aunt helped the elderly man [to] cross the street;* and when the *to* is awkward: *My aunt watched the elderly man [to] get on the bus.*) For both the SUBJECTS of infinitives and the OBJECTS of infinitives, use the objective case.

> Our tennis coach expects **me *to serve***. [Because the word *me* is the subject of the infinitive *to serve*, the objective-case pronoun is correct.]

> Our tennis coach expects **him *to beat*** me. [Because the word *him* is the subject of the infinitive *to beat*, and *me* is the object of the infinitive, the objective-case pronoun is correct for both.]

16j How do pronouns work with gerunds?

A GERUND is a verb's *-ing* form functioning as a NOUN: *Brisk **walking** is excellent exercise.* When a noun or PRONOUN comes before a gerund, the POSSESSIVE CASE is required: ***His** brisk **walking** built up his stamina.* In contrast, a PRESENT PARTICIPLE, which is a verb's *-ing* form functioning as a MODIFIER, requires the subjective case for the pronoun: ***He, walking** briskly, caught up to me.*

Here are two sentences that convey different messages, depending entirely on whether a possessive comes before the *-ing* word.

1. The detective noticed the **man *staggering***.
2. The detective noticed the **man's *staggering***.

Sentence 1 means that the detective noticed the *man;* sentence 2 means that the detective noticed the *staggering.* The same distinction applies to pronouns: When *the man* is replaced by *him* or *the man's* by *his*, the meaning is the same as in sentences 1 and 2.

1. The detective noticed **him *staggering***.
2. The detective noticed **his *staggering***.

In conversation, such distinctions are often ignored, but use them in ACADEMIC WRITING.

EXERCISE 16-4   Underline the correct pronoun of each pair in parentheses. For help, consult 16h through 16j.

> **EXAMPLE** The two inventors of the Quebec dish known as poutine say that no one is more surprised than (they, them) at its huge popularity.

> (1) Poutine was invented in 1957 when a truck driver named Eddy Lainesse pulled into Fernand Lachance's roadside diner and asked Lachance to serve (he, him) an order of french fries with melted cheese curds. (2) The diner was located in Quebec's dairy country, which accounts for (its, it) having fresh cheese curds for sale.

(3) Although Lachance found (them, their) appearing on a plate with french fries a strange idea, Lainesse was able to persuade (him, he) to give it a try. The new dish was a triumph. (4) Popular demand at Lachance's diner for an even more filling snack soon had (his, him) adding gravy, the way it is served today throughout Quebec. (5) Poutine's success—it is now on the menu of a nationwide hamburger chain and has been seen as far away as Florida—can be traced to (it, its) being a classic fast food: heavy, high in cholesterol, and gooey. (6) As far as Lainesse and Lachance are concerned, no one could be happier than (them, they) that Quebec is now known for this humble dish, even if Quebeckers who value their province's reputation for fine dining are annoyed at (it, its) winning such fame. (7) What explains (their, them) calling their invention "poutine," a slang word meaning a "mess"? (8) When Lainesse first asked for the dish, Lachance was not nearly as sure as (him, he) that it would work, and predicted, "If you do that, you'll get a real *poutine*."

16k What case should I use for -*self* pronouns?

Two types of pronouns end in -*self*: reflexive pronouns and intensive pronouns.

A **reflexive pronoun** reflects back on the subject. Without a subject, the reflexive pronoun cannot operate correctly.

> The **detective** disguised *himself*. [The reflexive pronoun *himself* reflects back on the subject *detective*.]

Never use a reflexive pronoun to replace a personal pronoun in the subjective case.

> NO My teammates and **myself** will vote for a team captain.
>
> YES My teammates and **I** will vote for a team captain.

Also, never use a reflexive pronoun to replace a personal pronoun in the objective case. The only exception is when the object restates the subject.

> NO That decision is up to my teammates and **myself**.
>
> YES That decision is up to my teammates and **me**.

Intensive pronouns, which reflect back in the same way as reflexive pronouns, provide emphasis by making the message of the sentence more intense in meaning.

> The detective felt that **his career** *itself* was at risk. [*Itself* intensifies the idea that the detective's career was at risk.]

PRONOUN REFERENCE

16l What is pronoun reference?

Writing in
Action:
Recognizing
Antecedents

The word or group of words that a pronoun replaces is called its **antecedent**. In order for your writing to communicate its message clearly, each pronoun must relate precisely to an antecedent.

> I knew a **woman**, lovely in **her** bones / When small **birds** sighed, **she** would sigh back at **them**.
>
> —Theodore Roethke, "I Knew a Woman"

16m What makes pronoun reference clear?

Pronoun reference is clear when your readers know immediately to whom or what each pronoun refers. Quick Reference 16.3 lists guidelines for using pronouns clearly, and the section in parentheses is where each is explained.

QUICK REFERENCE   16.3

Guidelines for clear pronoun reference

- Place pronouns close to their ANTECEDENTS (16n).
- Make a pronoun refer to a specific antecedent (16n).
- Do not overuse *it* (16q).
- Reserve *you* only for DIRECT ADDRESS (16r).
- Use *that, which,* and *who* correctly (16s).

16n How can I avoid unclear pronoun reference?

Every pronoun needs to refer to a specific, nearby ANTECEDENT. If the same pronoun in your writing has to refer to more than one antecedent, replace some pronouns with nouns.

> **NO** Fiona left for her summer job in Ft. McMurray two weeks before her friend Zahra took off for Banff. **She** [*Fiona or Zahra?*] had told all their friends that **she** [*Fiona or Zahra?*] just wanted to enjoy her summer, whether the pay was good or not. **She** [*Fiona or Zahra?*] had different ideas. As it turned out, **she** [*Fiona or Zahra?*] spent only a week at the site and returned home to Vancouver with a severe allergic attack.

> **YES** Fiona left for her summer job in Ft. McMurray two weeks before her friend Zahra took off for Banff. Fiona had told all their friends that Zahra just wanted to enjoy her summer, whether the pay was good or not. Fiona had different ideas. As it turned out, Zahra spent only a week at the site and returned home to Vancouver with a severe allergic attack.

ALERT: Be careful with the VERBS *said* and *told* in sentences that contain pronoun reference. To maintain clarity, use quotation marks and slightly reword each sentence to make the meaning clear.

> **NO** **Her** mother told **her she** was going to visit **her** grandmother.

> **YES** **Her** mother told **her,** "**You** are going to visit your grandmother."

> **YES** **Her** mother told **her,** "**I** am going to visit your grandmother." •

In addition, if too much material comes between a pronoun and its antecedent, readers can lose track of the meaning.

Alfred Wegener, a German meteorologist and professor of geophysics at the

University of Graz in Austria, was the first to suggest that all the continents on earth were originally part of one large landmass. According to this theory, the supercontinent

broke up long ago and the fragments drifted apart. ~~He~~ named this supercontinent
Wegener

Pangaea.

> [*He* can refer only to *Wegener*, but material about Wegener's theory intervenes, so using *Wegener* again instead of *he* jogs the reader's memory and makes reading easier.]

When you start a new paragraph, be cautious about beginning it with a pronoun whose antecedent is in a prior paragraph. You're better off repeating the word.

ESL TIP: Many languages omit a pronoun as a subject because the verb delivers the needed information. English requires the use of the pronoun as a subject. For example, never omit *it* in the following: *Political science is an important academic subject.* ***It** is studied all over the world.*

EXERCISE 16-5   Revise so that each pronoun refers clearly to its antecedent. Either replace pronouns with nouns or restructure the material to clarify pronoun reference. For help, consult 16n.

> **EXAMPLE** Pierre Trudeau became prime minister of Canada the year after Expo 67, the world's fair that presented it as youthful, exciting, and self-confident. These were the qualities that he embodied, too.
>
> Here is one acceptable revision: *Pierre Trudeau became prime minister of Canada the year after Expo 67, the world's fair that presented Canada as youthful, exciting, and self-confident. These were the qualities that Trudeau embodied, too.*

Trudeau exploded onto the scene as a sportscar-driving intellectual who—Canadians instantly recognized—was not like other politicians. He fascinated them, so they tolerated things from him that they would never accept from them: his dismissive shrugs, his arrogance, his insults. They were merely politicians; Trudeau was a star. Moreover, he combined them with an engaging playfulness. Most of them were delighted when he did an exaggerated pirouette behind the Queen's back at a royal reception.

Once, Trudeau had said "Just watch me." Journalists knew that Canada's "philosopher-king" was both spectacle and symbol to Canadians. They saw in him an idealized mirror of themselves. Significantly, when he retired, the critic Larry Zolf called the aging leader "our permanent Expo"—as though he were pure image.

Trudeau emerged again in the 1990s to launch his thunderbolts at Canada's new leaders, calling them "weaklings." When his son Michel died in 1998, he appeared frail and aged at his funeral. Then, when he died in late September 2000, Canadians acted much as Americans and British had at the deaths of Kennedy family members and of Princess Diana. They felt Trudeau's death as personally as they had felt their deaths. Mourning became a public spectacle.

Now they must ask themselves if this reaction represents their coming of age or is rather a sign of political immaturity. Perhaps when they say that he somehow touched them personally they are substituting emotions and wishes for political realism. Or perhaps Canadians have finally accepted their own identity and given it a necessary symbolic expression.

16o   How do I use *it, that, this,* and *which* precisely?

When you use *it, that, this,* and *which,* be sure that your readers can easily understand what each word refers to.

> NO   Comets usually fly by the earth at 160 000 km/ h, whereas asteroids sometimes collide with the earth. **This** interests scientists. [Does *this* refer to the speed of the comets, to comets flying by the earth, or to asteroids colliding with the earth?]

> YES   Comets usually fly by the earth at 160 000 km/h, whereas asteroids sometimes collide with the earth. **This difference** interests scientists. [Adding a noun after *this* or *that* clarifies the meaning.]

> NO   I told my friends that I was going to major in geology, **which** made my parents happy. [Does *which* refer to telling your friends or to majoring in geology?]

> YES   My parents were happy **because I discussed my major with my friends.**

> YES   My parents were happy **because I chose to major in geology.**

Also, the title of any piece of writing stands on its own. Therefore, in your introductory paragraph, never refer to your title with *this* or *that.* For example, if an essay's title is "Geophysics as a Major," the following holds for the first sentence:

> NO   **This subject** unites the sciences of physics, biology, and paleontology.

> YES   **Geophysics** unites the sciences of physics, biology, and paleontology.

16p   How do I use *they* and *it* precisely?

The expression *they say* can't take the place of stating precisely who is doing the saying. Your credibility as a writer depends on your mentioning a source precisely.

> NO   In Alberta **they say** that Eastern politicians have never understood the West. [*They* doesn't identify who has made the statement.]

> YES   **Many Albertans say** that Eastern politicians have never understood the West.

The expressions *it said* and *it is said that* reflect imprecise thinking. Also, they're wordy. Revising such expressions improves your writing.

> NO   **It said** in the newspaper that ranchers have demanded assistance in exporting their cattle. [*It said in the newspaper that* is awkward and wordy.]

> YES   **The newspaper reported** that ranchers have demanded assistance in exporting their cattle.

16q   How do I use *it* to suit the situation?

The word *it* has three different uses in English. Here are examples of correct uses of *it.*

1. PERSONAL PRONOUN: Kumar wants to visit the Canadian observatory where a supernova was discovered, but **it** is located in Chile.

2. EXPLETIVE (sometimes called a *subject filler,* it delays the subject): **It** is interesting to observe the stars.

3. IDIOMATIC EXPRESSION (words that depart from normal use, such as using *it* as the sentence subject when writing about weather, time, distance, and environmental conditions): **It** is sunny. **It** is midnight. **It** is not far to the hotel. **It** is very hilly.

All three uses listed above are correct, but avoid combining them in the same sentence. The result can be an unclear and confusing sentence.

> NO   Because our car was overheating, **it** came as no surprise that **it** broke down just as **it** began to rain. [*It* is overused here, even though all three uses—2, 1, and 3 on the above list, respectively—are acceptable.]

> YES   **It** came as no surprise that our overheating car broke down just as the rain began. [The word order is revised so that *it* is used once.]

ESL TIP: In some languages, *it* is not used as an expletive. In English, it is.

> NO   Is a lovely day.
> YES   **It** is a lovely day. ●

16r   Should I use *you* other than for direct address?

Reserve *you* for **direct address**, writing that addresses the reader directly. For example, we use *you* in this handbook to address you, the student. *You* is not a suitable substitute for specific words that refer to people, situations, or occurrences.

> NO   Prison uprisings often happen **when you allow** overcrowding. [The reader, *you*, did not allow the overcrowding.]

> YES   Prison uprisings often happen **when prisons are** overcrowded.

> NO   When **you** are crowned Queen of England, **you** automatically become Head of the Commonwealth. [Are *you*, the reader, planning to become Queen of England?]

> YES   **Queen Elizabeth, when she was crowned** Queen of England, automatically became Head of the Commonwealth.

EXERCISE 16-6   Revise these sentences so that all pronoun references are clear. If a sentence is correct, circle its number. For help, consult 16o through 16r.

> **EXAMPLE** They say that reaching the summit of Mount Everest is easiest in the month of May.
>
> *Experienced climbers say that reaching the summit of Mount Everest is easiest in the month of May.* [Revision eliminates imprecise use of *they*; see section 16p.]

1. Climbing Mount Everest is more expensive than you realize.
2. In addition to training, they need to raise as much as $60,000 for the expedition.
3. By contacting the Nepalese embassy, you can secure the help of Sherpa guides.
4. The government of Nepal requires permits, copies of passports, and letters of recommendation for each climbing team.
5. Climbers will need to pack oxygen bottles, a first aid kit, medications, a satellite phone, walkie-talkies, and a laptop computer. This will ensure a climber's safety.

6. Climbers often use yaks because they are stronger than you and can carry more equipment.

7. They do not offer direct flights, so climbers from Canada usually need a couple of days to get to Katmandu, Nepal.

8. Once atop the mountain, you should prepare for the descent, which is just as dangerous as the ascent.

16s When should I use *that, which,* and *who*?

To use the pronouns *that* and *which* correctly, you want to check the context of the sentence you're writing. *Which* and *that* refer to animals and things. Only sometimes do they refer to anonymous or collective groups of people. Quick Reference 16.4 shows how to choose between *that* and *which*. For information about the role of commas with *that* and *which*, see 24f.

Who refers to people and to animals mentioned by name.

John Polanyi, who was awarded the Nobel Prize in Chemistry, speaks passionately in favour of nuclear disarmament. [*John Polanyi* is a person.]

Lassie, who was known for her intelligence and courage, was actually played by a series of male collies. [*Lassie* is the name of an animal.]

Many professional writers reserve *which* for nonrestrictive clauses and *that* for restrictive clauses. Other writers use *that* and *which* interchangeably for restrictive clauses. Current practice allows the use of either as long as you're consistent in each piece of writing. However, for ACADEMIC WRITING, your instructor might expect you to maintain the distinction.

QUICK REFERENCE 16.4

Choosing between *that* and *which*

Choice: Some instructors and style guides use either *that* or *which* to introduce a RESTRICTIVE CLAUSE (a DEPENDENT CLAUSE that is essential to the meaning of the sentence or part of the sentence). Others may advise you to use only *that* so that your writing distinguishes clearly between restrictive and NONRESTRICTIVE CLAUSES. Whichever style you use, be consistent in each piece of writing.

- The zoos ***that*** (or which) **most children like** display newborn and baby animals. [The point in this sentence concerns children's preferences. Therefore, the words *most children like* are essential for delivering the meaning and make up a restrictive clause.]

No choice: You are required to use *which* to introduce a nonrestrictive clause (a dependent clause that isn't essential to the meaning of the sentence or part of the sentence).

- Zoos, **which most children like,** attract more visitors if they display newborn and baby animals. [The point in this sentence concerns attracting more visitors to zoos. Therefore, the words *most children like* are not essential to the meaning of the sentence and make up a nonrestrictive clause.]

🛈 **ALERT:** Use commas before and after a nonrestrictive clause. Don't use commas before and after a restrictive clause; see 24k.4. ●

EXERCISE 16-7 Fill in the blanks with *that, which,* or *who.* For help, consult 16s.

> **EXAMPLE** Antigua, <u>which</u> is an island in the West Indies, is a popular destination for European and North American tourists.

1. Those _____ like to travel to Antigua may enjoy online gambling, _____ is legal on the island.

2. The sport _____ is most popular in Antigua is cricket.

3. Celebrities _____ own homes on the island include Oprah Winfrey, Eric Clapton, and Jamaica Kincaid.

4. The main airport, _____ is named after Prime Minister V. C. Bird, is located in the capital, St. John's.

5. The cruise ships _____ travel to Antigua often stop at St. John's, _____ became the seat of government in 1981.

Chapter 17

AGREEMENT

17a What is agreement?

In everyday speech, agreement indicates that people hold the same ideas. Grammatical **agreement** is also based on sameness. Specifically, you need to match SUBJECTS and VERBS; see 17b through 17n. You also need to match PRONOUNS and ANTECEDENTS; see 17o through 17t.

SUBJECT-VERB AGREEMENT

17b What is subject-verb agreement?

Subject-verb agreement means that a SUBJECT and its VERB match in NUMBER (singular or plural) and PERSON (first, second, or third person). Quick Reference 17.1 presents these major concepts in grammatical agreement.

The **firefly glows**. [*Firefly* is a singular subject in the third person; *glows* is a singular verb in the third person.]

Fireflies glow. [*Fireflies* is a plural subject in the third person; *glow* is a plural verb in the third person.]

● Common Grammar Errors: 3. Lack of Subject-Verb Agreement

● Writing in Action: How to Recognize Subject-Verb Problems

QUICK REFERENCE 17.1

Grammatical agreement: first, second, and third person

- **Number**, as a concept in grammar, refers to *singular* (one) and *plural* (more than one).
- The **first person** is the speaker or writer. *I* (singular) and *we* (plural) are the only subjects that occur in the first person.

  SINGULAR **I see** a field of fireflies.

  PLURAL **We see** a field of fireflies.

- The **second person** is the person spoken or written to. *You* (for both singular and plural) is the only subject that occurs in the second person.

  SINGULAR **You see** a shower of sparks.

  PLURAL **You see** a shower of sparks.

- The **third person** is the person or thing being spoken or written about. *He, she, it* (singular) and *they* (plural) are the third-person subject forms. Most rules for subject-verb agreement involve the third person.

  SINGULAR The **scientist sees** a cloud of cosmic dust.

  PLURAL The **scientists see** a cloud of cosmic dust.

((•
AUDIO
LESSON
Section 1: Big
Ideas—
Correcting
Common
Errors:
Subject-Verb
Agreement
and Parallel
Structure

17c   Why is a final -s or -es in a subject or verb so important?

SUBJECT-VERB AGREEMENT often involves one letter: *s* (or *es* for words that end in -*s*). For verbs in the present tense, you form the SIMPLE FORM of third-person singular by adding -*s* or -*es: laugh, laughs; kiss, kisses*. Major exceptions are the verbs *be (is), have (has),* and *do (does)*; see 15c.

> That **student agrees** that **young teenagers spend** too much time online.

((•
AUDIO
LESSON
Section 2:
Practice
Questions—
Correcting
Common
Errors: Subject-
Verb Agreement
and Parallel
Structure

> Those **young teenagers are** taking valuable time away from studying.
>
> That **student has** a part-time job for ten hours a week.
>
> Still, that **student does** well in college.

For a subject to become plural, you add -*s* or -*es* to its end: *lip, lips; princess, princesses.* Major exceptions include most pronouns (*they, it*) and a few nouns that for singular and plural either don't change (*deer, deer*) or change internally (*mouse, mice*). Quick Reference 17.2 shows you how to visualize the basic pattern for agreement using -*s* or –*es*.

QUICK REFERENCE   **17.2**

Basic subject-verb agreement

The **student works** long hours.   The **students work** long hours.

SINGULAR   SINGULAR   PLURAL   PLURAL
SUBJECT   VERB   SUBJECT   VERB

((•
AUDIO LESSON
Section 3: Key
Terms—
Correcting
Common Errors:
Subject-Verb
Agreement and
Parallel
Structure

Here's a device for remembering how most subject-verb agreement works. Note that the final -*s* or -*es* can take only one path at a time—to the end of the verb or to the end of the subject.

((•
AUDIO
LESSON
Section 4:
Rapid
Review—
Correcting
Common
Errors:
Subject-Verb
Agreement
and Parallel
Structure

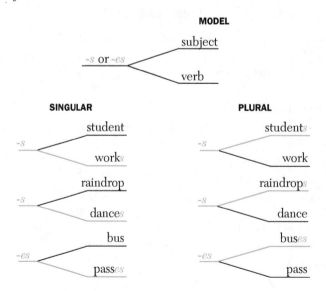

MODEL

subject
-*s* or -*es*
verb

SINGULAR   PLURAL

student   students
-*s*   -*s*
works   work

raindrop   raindrops
-*s*   -*s*
dances   dance

bus   buses
-*es*   -*es*
passes   pass

ESL TIP: When you use an AUXILIARY VERB with a main verb, never add -s or -es to the main verb: *The coach **can walk*** [not *can walks*] *to campus. The coach **does like*** [not *does likes*] *his job.* ●

EXERCISE 17-1 Use the subject and verb in each set to write two complete sentences—one with a singular subject and one with a plural subject. Keep all verbs in the present tense. For help, consult 17c.

> **EXAMPLE** climber, increase
>
> > **Singular subject:** Without proper equipment, a mountain *climber increases* the risk of falling.
> >
> > **Plural subject:** Without proper equipment, mountain *climbers increase* the risk of falling.

1. dog, bark
2. flower, bloom
3. girl, laugh
4. planet, rotate

5. author, write
6. singer, sing
7. hand, grab
8. professor, might quiz

17d Can I ignore words between a subject and its verb?

For purposes of subject-verb agreement, ignore all words between a subject and its verb. Focus strictly on the subject and its verb. Quick Reference 17.3 shows you this pattern.

> NO **Winners** of the regional contest **goes** to the national finals. [*Winners* is the subject; the verb must agree with it. Ignore the words *of the regional contest.*]
>
> YES **Winners** of the regional contest **go** to the national finals.

The words *one of the* . . . often require a second look. Use a singular verb to agree with the word *one.* Don't be distracted by the plural noun that comes after *of the.* (For information on the phrase *one of the* . . . *who,* see 17l.)

> NO **One** of the problems **are** the funds needed for travelling to the national finals.
>
> YES **One** of the problems **is** the funds needed for travelling to the national finals.

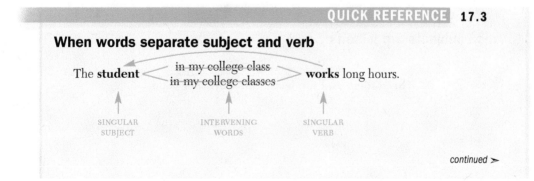

QUICK REFERENCE **17.3**

When words separate subject and verb

The **student** ⟨ in my college class / in my college classes ⟩ **works** long hours.

SINGULAR SUBJECT   INTERVENING WORDS   SINGULAR VERB

continued ➤

QUICK REFERENCE **17.3** *continued*

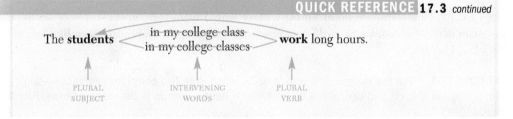

Similarly, eliminate all word groups between the subject and the verb, starting with *including, together with, along with, accompanied by, in addition to, except,* and *as well as.*

> NO   The **moon**, *as well as* the planet Venus, **are** visible in the night sky. [*Moon* is the subject. The verb must agree with it. Ignore the words *as well as the planet Venus*.]

> YES   The **moon**, as well as the planet Venus, **is** visible in the night sky.

17e   How do verbs work when subjects are connected by *and*?

When two SUBJECTS are connected by *and*, they create a single COMPOUND SUBJECT. A compound subject calls for a plural verb. Quick Reference 17.4 shows you this pattern. (For related material on PRONOUNS and ANTECEDENTS, see 17p.)

> **The Cascade Diner *and* the Wayside Diner *have*** [not *has*] fried halibut today. [These are two different diners.]

One exception occurs when *and* joins subjects that refer to a single thing or person.

> **My friend *and* neighbour *makes*** [not *make*] excellent chili. [In this sentence, the friend is the same person as the neighbour. If they were two different people, *makes* would become *make*.]

> **Macaroni *and* cheese *contains*** [not *contain*] carbohydrates, protein, and many calories. [*Macaroni and cheese* is one dish, not two separate dishes, so it requires a singular verb.]

QUICK REFERENCE **17.4**

When subjects are joined by *and*

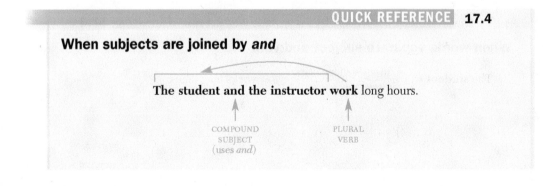

17f How do verbs work with *each* and *every*?

The words *each* and *every* are singular even if they refer to a compound subject. Therefore, they take a singular verb.

> **Each** human hand and foot *makes* [not *make*] a distinctive print.
>
> To identify lawbreakers, **every police chief, detective, and RCMP investigator** *depends* [not *depend*] on such prints.

ALERT: Use one word, either *each* or *every*, not both at the same time: **Each** [not *Each and every*] *robber has been caught.* (For more information about pronoun agreement for *each* and *every*, see 17i, 17p, and 17r.) ●

17g How do verbs work when subjects are connected by *or*?

As Quick Reference 17.5 shows, when SUBJECTS are joined by *or*, or by the sets *either . . . or, neither . . . nor, not only . . . but (also)*, the verb agrees with the subject closest to it. Ignore everything before the last-mentioned noun or pronoun. The box shows this pattern with *either . . . or.* (For related material on pronouns and antecedents, see 17q.)

> ~~Neither~~ this spider ~~nor those~~ **flies upset** me.
>
> ~~Not only~~ this spider ~~but also~~ all other **arachnids have** four pairs of legs.
>
> ~~Six clam fritters, four blue crabs, or one steamed~~ **lobster sounds** good to me.

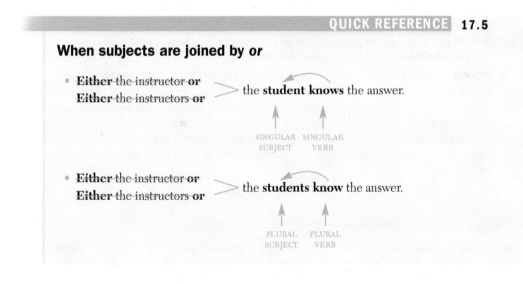

QUICK REFERENCE   17.5

When subjects are joined by *or*

- ~~Either~~ the instructor ~~or~~
  ~~Either~~ the instructors ~~or~~
  the **student knows** the answer.

  SINGULAR   SINGULAR
  SUBJECT   VERB

- ~~Either~~ the instructor ~~or~~
  ~~Either~~ the instructors ~~or~~
  the **students know** the answer.

  PLURAL   PLURAL
  SUBJECT VERB

17h How do verbs work with inverted word order?

In English sentences, the SUBJECT normally comes before its VERB: ***Astronomy*** is *interesting.* **Inverted word order** reverses the typical subject-verb pattern by putting the verb first. Most questions use inverted word order: *Is astronomy interesting?* In inverted word order, find the subject first and then check whether the verb agrees with it.

> Into deep space **shoot** probing **satellites**. [The plural verb *shoot* agrees with the plural subject *satellites*.]
>
> On the television screen **appears** an **image** of Saturn. [The singular verb *appears* agrees with the singular subject *image*.]

🛑 **ALERT:** When you start a sentence with *there*, check whether the subject is singular or plural, and then choose the right form of *be* to agree with the subject. If your sentence begins with *it*, always use the singular form of *be* (*is, was*) no matter whether the subject is singular or plural.

> There *are eight planets* in our solar system. [The verb *are* agrees with the subject *planets*.]
>
> There *is* probably no **life** on seven of them. [The verb *is* agrees with the subject *life*.]
>
> *It was* astronomers who demoted Pluto from planet status. [The verb *was* agrees with *it*, not with *astronomers*.] ●

EXERCISE 17-2 Supply the correct present-tense form of the verb in parentheses. For help, consult 17c through 17h.

> **EXAMPLE** Detectives and teachers (to know) <u>know</u> experienced liars can fool almost anybody, but a new computer can tell who is telling the truth.

1. Police officers and teachers often (to wish) _____ they could "read" people's facial expressions.
2. Trained police officers or a smart teacher (to know) _____ facial tics and nervous mannerisms (to show) _____ someone is lying.
3. However, a truly gifted liar, along with well-coached eyewitnesses, (to reveal) _____ very little through expressions or behaviour.
4. There (to be) _____ forty-six muscle movements that create all facial expressions in the human face.
5. Neuroscientist Terrence Seinowski, accompanied by a team of researchers, (to be) _____ developing a computer program to recognize even slight facial movements made by the most expert liars.

17i How do verbs work with indefinite pronouns?

Indefinite pronouns usually refer to nonspecific persons, things, quantities, or ideas. The nonspecific aspect is the reason these pronouns are labelled "indefinite." As part of a sentence, however, the indefinite pronoun usually takes on a clear meaning.

Most indefinite pronouns are singular and require a singular verb for agreement. Others are always plural, and a few can be singular *or* plural. Quick Reference 17.6 lists indefinite pronouns according to the verb form they require. (For related material on pronouns and antecedents, see 17r.)

Common indefinite pronouns

ALWAYS PLURAL

both   many

ALWAYS SINGULAR

another	every	no one
anybody	everybody	nothing
anyone	everyone	one
anything	everything	somebody
each	neither	someone
either	nobody	something

SINGULAR OR PLURAL, DEPENDING ON CONTEXT

all	more	none
any	most	some

Here are sample sentences:

SINGULAR INDEFINITE PRONOUNS

Everything about that intersection **is** dangerous.

But whenever **anyone says** anything, **nothing is** done.

Each of us **has** [not *have*] to shovel snow; **each is** [not *are*] expected to help.

Every snowstorm of the past two years **has** [not *have*] been severe.

Every one of them **has** [not *have*] caused massive traffic jams.

SINGULAR OR PLURAL INDEFINITE PRONOUNS (DEPENDING ON MEANING)

Some of our streams **are** polluted. [*Some* refers to the plural noun *streams*, so the plural verb *are* is correct.]

Some pollution **is** reversible, but **all** pollution **threatens** the balance of nature. [*Some* and *all* refer to the singular noun *pollution*, so the singular verbs *is* and *threatens* are correct.]

All that environmentalists ask **is** to give nature a chance. [*All* has the meaning here of "everything" or "the only thing," so the singular verb *is* is correct.]

Winter has driven the birds south; **all have** left. [*All* refers to the plural noun *birds*, so the plural verb *have* is correct.]

ALERTS: (1) Don't mix singular and plural with *this, that, these,* and *those* used with *kind* and *type. This* and *that* are singular, as are *kind* and *type; these* and *those* are plural, as are *kinds* and *types:* **This** [not *These*] **kind** of rainwear is waterproof. **These** [not *This*] **kinds** of sweaters keep me warm. (2) The rules for indefinite pronouns collide with one strategy for avoiding SEXIST LANGUAGE. For suggestions, see 17s and 12f. ●

17j   How do verbs work with collective nouns?

A **collective noun** names a group of people or things: *family, audience, class, number, committee, team, group,* and the like. When the group of people or things is acting as one unit, use a singular verb. When members of the group are acting individually, use a plural verb. As you're writing, be careful not to shift back and forth between a singular and a plural verb for the same noun.

> The graduating **class** nervously *awaits* final exams. [The *class* is acting as a single unit, so the verb is singular.]

> The graduating **class** *were fitted* for their graduation robes today. [The members (of the class) were fitted as individuals, so the verb is plural.]

ALERT: Although British usage allows plural verbs and pronouns with collective nouns and with proper names that act as collective nouns (*the government are considering their options; Sainsbury's are proud to present this award*), this practice is rare in North America and is usually considered wrong (see also 17n). ●

17k   Why does the linking verb agree with the subject, not the subject complement?

Even though a LINKING VERB connects a sentence's SUBJECT to its SUBJECT COMPLEMENT, the linking verb agrees with the subject. It does not agree with the subject complement.

> NO   The worst **part** of owning a car *are* the bills. [The subject is the singular *part*, so the plural verb *are* is wrong. The subject complement is the plural *bills* and doesn't affect agreement.]

> YES   The worst **part** of owning a car *is* the bills. [The singular subject *part* agrees with the singular verb *is*. The subject complement doesn't affect agreement.]

17l   What verbs agree with *who, which,* and *that?*

If the ANTECEDENT of *who, which,* or *that* is singular, use a singular verb. If the antecedent is plural, use a plural verb.

> The scientist will share the prize with the **researchers *who* work** with her. [*Who* refers to *researchers*, so the plural verb *work* is used.]

> David Pappas is the **student *who* works** in the science lab. [*Who* refers to student, so the singular verb *works* is used.]

If you use phrases including *one of the* or *the only one of the* immediately before *who, which,* or *that* in a sentence, be careful about the verb you use. *Who, which,* or *that* always refers to the plural word immediately following *one of the,* so the verb must be plural. Although *the only one of* is also always followed by a plural word, *who, which,* or *that* must be singular to agree with the singular *one.*

> Tracy is *one of the* students *who* **talk** in class. [*Who* refers to *students*, so the verb *talk* is plural. *Tracy* is pointed out, but the talking is still done by all of the students.]

Jim is **the only one of the** students **who talks** in class. [*Who* refers to *one*, so the verb *talks* is singular. *Jim* is the single person who is talking.]

EXERCISE 17-3   Supply the correct present-tense form of the verb in parentheses. For help, consult 17i through 17l.

> **EXAMPLE** Everybody on a class trip to the coastal waters of the Pacific Ocean (to enjoy) <u>enjoys</u> an opportunity to study dolphins in their natural habitat.

1. A class of students in marine biology (to take) _____ notes individually while watching dolphins feed off the British Columbia coast.
2. Everyone in the class (to listen) _____ as a team of dolphin experts (to explain) _____ some of the mammals' characteristics.
3. A group of dolphins, called a pod, usually (to consist) _____ of 24 000 to 30 000 members.
4. One unique characteristic of dolphins' brains (to be) _____ the sleep patterns that (to keep) _____ one-half of the brain awake at all times.
5. All (to need) _____ to stay awake to breathe, or else they would drown.

17m **How do verbs work with amounts, fields of study, and other special nouns?**

AMOUNTS

SUBJECTS that refer to time, sums of money, distance, or measurement are singular. They take singular verbs.

> **Two hours *is*** not enough time to finish. [time]
> **Three hundred dollars *is*** what we must pay. [sum of money]
> **Five kilometres *is*** a short sprint for some serious joggers. [distance]
> **Three-quarters of an inch *is*** needed for a perfect fit. [measurement]

FIELDS OF STUDY

The name for a field of study is singular even if it appears to be plural: *economics, mathematics, physics,* and *statistics.*

> ***Statistics is*** required of science majors. [*Statistics* is a course of study, so the singular verb *is* is correct.]
> ***Statistics* show** that a teacher shortage is coming. [*Statistics* isn't used here as a field of study, so the plural verb *show* is correct.]

SPECIAL NOUNS

Athletics, news, ethics, and *measles* are singular despite their plural appearance. Also, names such as *United States of America* and *United Nations* are singular: However, *politics* and *sports* take singular or plural verbs depending on the meaning of the sentence.

The **news gets** better each day. [*News* is a singular noun, so the singular verb *gets* is correct.]

Sports is a good way to build physical stamina. [*Sports* is one general activity, so the singular verb *is* is correct.]

Three **sports are** offered at the recreation centre. [*Sports* are separate activities, so the plural verb *are* is correct.]

Jeans, pants, scissors, clippers, tweezers, eyeglasses, thanks, and *riches* are some of the words that require a plural verb, even though they refer to one thing. However, if you use *pair* with *jeans, pants, scissors, clippers, tweezers,* or *eyeglasses,* use a singular verb for agreement.

Those **pants need** pressing. [plural]

That **pair** of pants **needs** pressing. [singular]

Series and *means* can be singular or plural, according to the meaning you intend.

Two new TV **series are** big hits. [*Series* refers to individual items (two different series), so the plural verb *are* is correct.]

A **series** of disasters **is** plaguing our production. [*Series* refers to a whole group (the whole series of disasters), so the singular verb *is* is correct.]

 How do verbs work with titles, company names, and words as themselves?

TITLES

A title itself refers to one work or entity (even when plural and compound NOUNS are in the title), so a singular verb is correct.

Fugitive Pieces by Anne Michaels **is** a prize-winning novel.

COMPANY NAMES

Many companies have plural words in their names. However, a company should always be treated as a singular unit, requiring a singular verb.

Cohn Brothers boxes and **delivers** fine art.

WORDS AS THEMSELVES

Whenever you write about words as themselves to call attention to those words, use a singular verb, even if more than one word is involved.

We implies that everyone is included.

Protective reaction strikes is a euphemism for *bombing*.

EXERCISE 17-4 Supply the correct present-tense form of the verb in parentheses. For help, consult 17i through 17n.

> **EXAMPLE** The movie *Wordplay* is about those who (to enjoy) <u>enjoy</u> solving crossword puzzles.

1. When the movie plays at theatres, the audience often (to consist) _____ of different ages and types of people.

2. For fans of crossword puzzles, the major attraction (to be) _____ the challenges they present.

3. Every creator of puzzles (to know) _____ that in the most successful puzzles all of the clues (to be) _____ interesting.

4. *Setters* (to be) _____ a term used by crossword puzzle fans to describe people who create puzzles.

5. Do crossword fans, who (to include) ——— people who love language, also spend time on the Sudoku puzzle that (to appear) _____ on the same page in many newspapers?

EXERCISE 17-5   This exercise covers all of subject-verb agreement (17b through 17n). Supply the correct form of the verb in parentheses.

> **EXAMPLE** Of the thirty thousand plant species on earth, the rose (to be) <u>is</u> the most universally known.

1. Each plant species (to invite) _____ much discussion about origins and meanings, and when talk turns to flowers, the rose is usually the first mentioned.

2. More fragrant and colourful (to be) _____ other types of flowers, yet roses (to remain) _____ the most popular worldwide.

3. Each of the types of roses (to symbolize) _____ beauty, love, romance, and secrecy.

4. There (to be) _____ more than two hundred pure species of roses and thousands of mixed species, thirty-five of which (to flourish) _____ in the soil of North America.

5. It's impossible to determine exactly where or when the first rose (to be) _____ domesticated, because roses have existed for so many centuries; one of the earliest references dates back to 3000 BCE.

6. One myth from Greek mythology (to suggest) _____ that the rose first appeared with the birth of the goddess Aphrodite.

7. Another myth, which focuses on the rose's thorns, (to say) _____ that an angry god shot arrows into the stem to curse the rose forever with arrow-shaped thorns.

8. While theories of this kind (to explain) _____ the significance and evolution of the rose, few people can explain the flower's enduring popularity.

9. Even today, a couple (to demonstrate) _____ love by purchasing red roses.

10. Of all flowers, the best seller (to remain) _____ the rose.

PRONOUN-ANTECEDENT AGREEMENT

170   What is pronoun-antecedent agreement?

Pronoun-antecedent agreement means that a PRONOUN matches its ANTECEDENT in NUMBER (singular or plural) and PERSON (first, second, or third person). Quick Reference 17.7 shows you how to visualize this pattern of grammatical agreement. You might also want to consult Quick Reference 17.1 (p. 273) in 17b for explanations and examples of the concepts *number* and *person.*

Writing in Action: Recognizing Antecedents

Writing in Action: Learning What Pronouns to Use

Pronoun-antecedent agreement

- Loud **music** has **its** harmful side effects.

  THIRD-PERSON THIRD-PERSON
  SINGULAR SINGULAR
  ANTECEDENT PRONOUN

- The **musicians** damaged **their** hearing.

  THIRD-PERSON THIRD-PERSON
  PLURAL PLURAL
  ANTECEDENT PRONOUN

The **firefly** glows when **it** emerges from **its** nest at night. [The singular pronouns *it* and *its* match their singular antecedent, *firefly*.]

Fireflies glow when **they** emerge from **their** nests at night. [The plural pronouns *they* and *their* match their plural antecedent, *fireflies*.]

17p How do pronouns work when *and* connects antecedents?

When *and* connects two or more ANTECEDENTS, they require a plural pronoun. This rule applies even if each separate antecedent is singular. (For related material on subjects and verbs, see 17e.)

> **The Cascade Diner *and* the Wayside Diner** closed for New Year's Eve to give **their** [not *its*] employees the night off. [Two separate diners require a plural pronoun.]

When *and* joins singular nouns that nevertheless refer to a single person or thing, use a singular pronoun.

> **My friend *and* neighbour** makes **his** [not *their*] excellent chili every Saturday. [The friend is the same person as the neighbour, so the singular *his* (or *her*) is correct. If two different people were involved, the correct pronoun would be *their*, and *make* would be the correct verb.]

EACH, EVERY

The words *each* and *every* are singular, even when they refer to two or more antecedents joined by *and*. The same rule applies when *each* or *every* is used alone (17i). (For related material on subjects and verbs, see 17f.)

> ***Each* human hand *and* foot** leaves **its** [not *their*] distinctive print.

The rule still applies when the construction *one of the* follows *each* or *every*.

> ***Each one of the* robbers** left **his** [not *their*] fingerprints at the scene.

17q   How do pronouns work when *or* connects antecedents?

When ANTECEDENTS are joined by *or*—or by CORRELATIVE CONJUNCTONS such as *either . . . or, neither . . . nor,* or *not only . . . but (also)*—the antecedents might mix singulars and plurals. For the purposes of agreement, ignore everything before the final antecedent. Quick Reference 17.8 shows you how to visualize this pattern. (For related material on subjects and verbs, see 17g.)

> ~~After the restaurant closes, *either* the resident mice *or*~~ **the owner's cat** gets **itself** a meal.
>
> ~~After the restaurant closes, *either* the owner's cat *or* the~~ **resident mice** get **themselves** a meal.

QUICK REFERENCE   17.8

When antecedents are joined by *or*

- ~~**Either** the loudspeakers **or**~~ **the microphone** needs **its** electric cord repaired.

  SINGULAR   SINGULAR
  ANTECEDENT   PRONOUN

- ~~**Either** the microphone **or**~~ **the loudspeakers** need **their** electric cords repaired.

  PLURAL   PLURAL
  ANTECEDENT   PRONOUN

17r   How do pronouns work when antecedents are indefinite pronouns?

(((•

None Is
Versus
None Are

INDEFINITE PRONOUNS usually refer to unknown persons, things, quantities, or ideas. The unknown aspect is the reason these pronouns are labelled "indefinite." But in a sentence, context gives an indefinite pronoun a clear meaning, even if the pronoun doesn't have a specific antecedent. Most indefinite pronouns are singular. Two indefinite pronouns, *both* and *many,* are plural. A few indefinite pronouns can be singular or plural, depending on the meaning of the sentence.

For a list of indefinite pronouns, grouped as singular or plural, see Quick Reference 17.6 (p. 279) in 17i. For more information about avoiding sexist language, especially when using indefinite pronouns, see 17s and 12f. (For related material on subjects and verbs, see 17i.)

SINGULAR INDEFINITE PRONOUNS

Everyone taking this course hopes to get **his or her** [not *their*] degree within a year.

Anybody wanting to wear a cap and gown at graduation must have **his or her** [not *their*] measurements taken.

Each of the students handed in **his or her** [not *their*] final term paper.

SINGULAR *OR* PLURAL INDEFINITE PRONOUNS

When winter break arrives for students, **most** leave **their** dormitories for home. [*Most* refers to *students*, so the plural pronoun *their* is correct.]

As for the luggage, **most** is already on **its** way to the airport. [*Most* refers to *luggage*, so the singular pronoun *its* is correct.]

None thinks that **he or she** will miss graduation. [*None* is singular as used in this sentence, so the singular pronoun phrase *he or she* is correct.]

None of the students has paid **his or her** [not *their*] graduation fee yet. [*None* is singular as used in this sentence, so the singular pronoun phrase *his or her* is correct.]

None are so proud as **they** who graduate. [*None* is plural as used in this sentence, so the plural pronoun *they* is correct.]

((• **17s** How do I use nonsexist pronouns?

Biased
and Sexist
Language

A word is **nonsexist** when it carries neither male or female gender. Each PRONOUN in English carries one of three genders: male (*he, him, his*); female (*she, her, hers*); or neutral (*you, your, yours, we, our, ours, them, they, their, theirs, it, its*). Usage today favours nonsexist terms in all word choices. Use gender-free pronouns whenever possible. In the past, it was conventional to use only masculine pronouns to refer to INDEFINITE PRONOUNS: "*Everyone* open **his** book." Today, however, people know that the pronouns *he, his, him,* and *himself* exclude women, who make up over half the population. Quick Reference 17.9 shows three ways to avoid using masculine pronouns when referring to males and females together. For more information on gender-neutral language, see 12f.

Questions often arise concerning the use of *he or she* and *his or her.* In general, writers find these gender-free pronoun constructions awkward. To avoid them, many writers make the antecedents plural. Doing this becomes problematic when the subject is a SINGULAR INDEFINITE PRONOUN (Quick Reference 17.6, p. 279, in section 17i). In the popular press (such as newspapers and magazines), the use of the plural pronoun *they, them, their,* or *theirs* with a singular antecedent has been gaining favour: "*Everyone* open **their** book." Indeed, some experts find that the history of English supports this use. In ACADEMIC WRITING, it is better for you not to follow the practice of the popular press. Language practice changes, however, so what we say here is our best advice as we write this book.

QUICK REFERENCE 17.9

Avoiding the masculine pronoun when referring to males and females together

- **Solution 1:** Use a pair of pronouns—as in the phrase *he or she.* However, avoid using a pair more than once in a sentence or in many sentences in a row. A *he or she* construction acts as a singular pronoun.

    Everyone hopes that **he or she** will win a scholarship.

    A **doctor** usually has time to keep up to date only in **his or her** specialty.

continued ➤

- **Solution 2:** Revise into the plural.

    Many students hope that **they** will win a scholarship.

    Most doctors have time to keep up to date only in **their** specialties.
- **Solution 3:** Recast the sentence.

    Everyone hopes to win a scholarship.

    Few specialists have time for general reading.

17t ## How do pronouns work when antecedents are collective nouns?

(((•●

Couple Is
Versus
Couple Are—
Collective
Nouns

A COLLECTIVE NOUN names a group of people or things, such as *family, group, audience, class, number, committee,* and *team.* When the group acts as one unit, use a singular pronoun to refer to it. When the members of the group act individually, use a plural pronoun. In the latter case, if the sentence is awkward, substitute a plural noun for the collective noun. (For related material on subjects and verbs, see 17j.)

The **audience** was cheering as **it** stood to applaud the performers. [The *audience* was acting as one unit, so the singular pronoun *it* is correct.]

The **audience** put on **their** coats and walked out. [The members of the audience were acting as individuals, so all actions become plural; therefore, the plural pronoun *their* is correct.]

The **family** is spending **its** vacation in the Laurentians. [All the family members went to one place together.]

The parallel sentence to the last example above would be *The **family** are spending **their** vacations in the Laurentians, the Rockies, and Rome,* which might mean that each family member is going to a different place. But such a sentence is awkward. Therefore, revise the sentence.

The **family members** are spending **their** vacations in the Laurentians, the Rockies, and Rome. [Substituting a plural noun phrase *family members* for the collective noun *family* sounds more natural.]

EXERCISE 17-6   Underline the correct pronoun in parentheses. For help, consult 17o through 17t.

> **EXAMPLE** Many people wonder what gives certain leaders (his or her, <u>their</u>) spark and magnetic personal appeal.

1. The cluster of personal traits that produces star quality is called *charisma*, a state that bestows special power on (its, their) bearers.

2. Charisma is the quality that allows an individual to empower (himself, herself, himself or herself, themselves) and others.

3. Power and authority alone don't guarantee charisma; (it, they) must be combined with passion and strong purpose.

4. A charismatic leader has the ability to draw other people into (his, her, his or her, their) dream or vision.

5. (He, She, He or she, They) can inspire followers to believe that the leader's goals are the same as (his, her, his or her, their) own.

6. Not all leaders who possess charisma enjoy having this ability to attract and influence (his, his or her, their) followers.

7. Charismatic leaders are often creative, especially in (his, her, his or her, their) capacity for solving problems in original ways.

8. A major corporation offering (its, their) employees charisma-training courses is no longer a rarity.

9. Usually, it's not the quiet, low-profile manager but rather the charismatic manager with strong leadership qualities who convinces others that (his, her, his or her, their) best interests are served by the course of action (he, she, he or she, they) is/are proposing.

10. Charisma trainers advise would-be leaders to start by bringing order to (his, her, his or her, their) activities; in stressful times, anyone who appears to have some part of (his, her, his or her, their) life under control makes others relax and perform (his, her, his or her, their) responsibilities better.

Chapter 18

ADJECTIVES AND ADVERBS

18a What are the differences between adjectives and adverbs?

Common
Grammar
Errors:
12. Adjective-
Adverb
Confusion

Both adjectives and adverbs are MODIFIERS—that is, words or groups of words that describe other words. **Adjectives** modify NOUNS and PRONOUNS. **Adverbs** modify VERBS, adjectives, and other adverbs.

ADJECTIVE   The **brisk** *wind* blew. [Adjective *brisk* modifies noun *wind*.]

ADVERB   The wind *blew* **briskly**. [Adverb *briskly* modifies verb *blew*.]

Not all adverbs end in *-ly*. While many adverbs do end in *-ly* (eat *swiftly*, eat *frequently*, eat *hungrily*), some do not (eat *fast*, eat *often*, eat *seldom*). To complicate matters further, some adjectives end in *-ly* (*lovely* flower, *friendly* dog). Use meaning, not an *-ly* ending, to identify adverbs.

ESL TIPS: (1) In English, the adjective is always singular, even if its noun is plural: *The hot* [not *hots*] *drinks warmed us up.* (2) Word order in English calls for special attention to the placement of adjectives and adverbs. Here is an example using the adverb *carefully: Thomas closed* [don't place *carefully* here] *the window* **carefully** (see 52b and 52c). ●

EXERCISE 18-1   Underline and label all adjectives (ADJ) and adverbs (ADV). Then, draw an arrow from each adjective and adverb to the word or words it modifies. Ignore *a, an,* and *the* as adjectives. For help, consult 18a.

ADJ   ADV   ADJ

EXAMPLE Leaky faucets are unexpectedly leading to genuine romance

ADJ   ADJ

in super-sized hardware stores.

1. Today's singles carefully look for possible mates at discount home improvement stores across the country.

2. Understandably, many people find these stores a healthy alternative to dark bars and blind dates.

3. Recently, an employee in the flooring department quietly confided that the best nights for singles are Wednesdays and Thursdays, while weekends generally attract families.

4. A young single mom returns home excitedly because a quick trip to the lumber department for a new door resulted in a date for Saturday night.

5. A lonely widower in his fifties jokingly says he wishes he had developed an interest in wallpapering and gardening earlier.

((•● **18b** **When should I use adverbs—not adjectives—as modifiers?**

Lesser-
Known
Adverbs

Adverbs MODIFY verbs, adjectives, and other adverbs. Don't use adjectives as adverbs.

> NO The candidate inspired us **great**. [Adjective *great* cannot modify verb *inspired*.]
>
> YES The candidate inspired us **greatly**. [Adverb *greatly* modifies verb *inspired*.]
>
> NO The candidate felt **unusual** energetic. [Adjective *unusual* cannot modify adjective *energetic*.]
>
> YES The candidate felt **unusually** energetic. [Adverb *unusually* modifies adjective *energetic*.]
>
> NO The candidate spoke **exceptional** forcefully. [Adjective *exceptional* cannot modify adverb *forcefully*.]
>
> YES The candidate spoke **exceptionally** forcefully. [Adverb *exceptionally* modifies adverb *forcefully*.]

18c **What is wrong with double negatives?**

A **double negative** is a nonstandard form. It is a statement with two negative MODIFIERS, the second of which repeats the message of the first. Negative modifiers include *no, never, not, none, nothing, hardly, scarcely,* and *barely.*

> NO The factory workers will **never** vote for **no** strike.
> YES The factory workers will **never** vote for **a** strike.
>
> NO The union members did **not** have **no** money in reserve.
> YES The union members did **not** have **any** money in reserve.
> YES The union members had **no** money in reserve.

Take special care to avoid double negatives with contractions of *not: isn't, don't, didn't, haven't,* and the like (27d). The contraction containing *not* serves as the negative. Don't add a second negative.

> NO He **didn't** hear **nothing**.
> YES He **didn't** hear **anything**.
>
> NO They **haven't** had **no** meetings.
> YES They **haven't** had **any** meetings.

Similarly, be careful to avoid double negatives when you use *nor.* The word *nor* is correct only after *neither* (14i). Use the word *or* after any other negative.

> NO Stewart **didn't** eat dinner **nor** watch television last night.
> YES Stewart **didn't** eat dinner **or** watch television last night.
> YES Stewart **neither** ate dinner **nor** watched television last night.

((•● **18d** **Do adjectives or adverbs come after linking verbs?**

Copular
Verbs
(Linking
Verbs)

LINKING VERBS connect a SUBJECT to a COMPLEMENT. Always use an adjective, not an adverb, as the complement.

> The *guests looked* **happy**. [Verb *looked* links subject *guests* to adjective *happy*.]

The words *look, feel, smell, taste, sound,* and *grow* are usually linking verbs, but sometimes they're simply verbs. Check how any of these verbs is functioning in a sentence.

Zora *looks* **happy**. [*Looks* functions as a linking verb, so the adjective *happy* is correct.]

Zora *looks* **happily** at the sunset. [*Looks* doesn't function as a linking verb, so the adverb *happily* is correct.]

BAD, BADLY

The words *bad* (adjective) and *badly* (adverb) are particularly prone to misuse with linking verbs.

((•
I Feel Bad
Versus I Feel
Badly

> NO   The students felt **badly**. [This means the students used their sense of touch badly.]
> YES   The student felt **bad**. [This means the student had a bad feeling about something.]
> NO   The food smelled **badly**. [This means the food had a bad ability to smell.]
> YES   The food smelled **bad**. [This means the food had a bad smell to it.]

GOOD, WELL

When the word *well* refers to health, it is an adjective; at all other times, *well* is an adverb. The word *good* is always an adjective.

Evander looks **well**. [This means that Evander seems to be in good health, so the adjective *well* is correct.]

Evander writes **well**. [This means that Evander writes skilfully, so the adverb *well* is correct.]

Avoid using *good* as the adjective referring to health following a linking verb. Do not use *good* as an adverb.

> NO   She is feeling **good**. [*Is feeling* is a linking verb, so *well* is the correct adjective, not *good*.]
> NO   She sings **good**. [*Sings* isn't a linking verb, so it calls for an adverb, not the adjective *good*.]
> YES   She sings **well**. [*Sings* isn't a linking verb, so the adverb *well* is correct.]

EXERCISE 18-2   Underline the correct uses of negatives, adjectives, and adverbs by selecting between the choices in parentheses. For help, consult 18a through 18d.

EXAMPLE   Sixty years ago, when (commercially, <u>commercial</u>) flight across the Atlantic was still (<u>new</u>, newly), most flights from Europe touched down at Gander International Airport.

(1) Gander, on the east coast of Newfoundland, is almost (exactly, exact) halfway between London and New York by air. (2) Until the 1960s, no (large, largely) passenger planes (couldn't, could) carry enough fuel to make the (complete, completely) crossing, so planes would (typically, typical) stop to refuel at Gander. (3) As a result, hundreds of thousands of Europeans caught their first glimpse of North America in Gander, which (modest, modestly) called itself "the crossroads of the world." (4) Visitors like Albert Einstein and the Beatles, Winston Churchill and Fidel Castro, and (countlessly, countless) others made this boast ring (truly, true).

(5) By the mid-1950s, travellers were demanding airport terminals that both looked (well, good) and functioned (well, good). (6) The Department of Transportation made plans to redesign (dreary, drearily) airports across the country. (7) Gander was (first, firstly). (8) The redesign transformed it into a futuristic environment of (cleanly, clean) lines and gleaming surfaces, the (characteristic, characteristically) features of twentieth-century modernist design. (9) With a gradual decline in activity at the airport and no need to expand, the terminal's dated interior has remained (nearly, near) (intact, intactly). (10) Now, (strange, strangely) enough, Gander's aging terminal has a reputation as the most (importantly, important) modernist room in Canada.

18e   What are comparative and superlative forms?

Comparatives and Superlatives

Faulty Comparison

When you write about comparisons, ADJECTIVES and ADVERBS often carry the message. The adjectives and adverbs also communicate degrees of intensity. When a comparison is made between two things, a **comparative** form is used. When a comparison is made about three or more things, a **superlative** form is used.

REGULAR FORMS OF COMPARISON

Most adjectives and adverbs are regular. They communicate degrees of intensity in one of two ways: either by adding -er and -est endings or by adding the words *more, most, less,* and *least* (see Quick Reference 18.1).

The number of syllables in the adjective or adverb usually determines whether to use -er, -est or *more, most* and *less, least.*

- **One-syllable words** usually take -er and -est endings: *large, larger, largest* (adjectives); *far, farther, farthest* (adverbs).

QUICK REFERENCE 18.1

Regular forms of comparison for adjectives and adverbs

POSITIVE	Use when nothing is being compared.
COMPARATIVE	Use when two things are being compared. Add the ending -er or the word *more* or *less.*
SUPERLATIVE	Use to compare three or more things. Add the ending -est or the word *most* or *least.*

POSITIVE [1]	COMPARATIVE [2]	SUPERLATIVE [3+]
green	greener	greenest
happy	happier	happiest
selfish	less selfish	least selfish
beautiful	more beautiful	most beautiful

That tree is **green**.

That tree is **greener** than this tree.

That tree is the **greenest** tree on the block.

- **Adjectives of two syllables** vary. If the word ends in *-y*, change the *y* to *i* and add *-er, -est* endings: *pretty, prettier, prettiest*. Otherwise, some two-syllable adjectives take *-er, -est* endings: *yellow, yellower, yellowest*. Others take *more, most* and *less, least: tangled, more tangled, most tangled; less tangled, least tangled*.
- **Adverbs of two syllables** take *more, most* and *less, least: quickly, more quickly, most quickly; less quickly, least quickly*.
- **Three-syllable words** take *more, most* and *less, least: dignified, more/most dignified, less/least dignified* (adjective); *carefully, more/most carefully, less/least carefully* (adverb).

ALERT: Be careful not to use a double comparative or double superlative. Use either the *-er* and *-est* endings or *more, most* or *less, least*.

He was **younger** [not *more younger*] than his brother.

Her music was the **loudest** [not *most loudest*] on the track. ●

IRREGULAR FORMS OF COMPARISON

A few comparative and superlative forms are irregular. Quick Reference 18.2 gives you the list. We suggest that you memorize them so they come to mind easily.

Irregular forms of comparison for adjectives and adverbs

POSITIVE [1]	COMPARATIVE [2]	SUPERLATIVE [3+]
good (*adjective*)	better	best
well (*adjective and adverb*)	better	best
bad (*adjective*)	worse	worst
badly (*adverb*)	worse	worst
many	more	most
much	more	most
some	more	most
little*	less	least

* When you're using *little* for items that can be counted (e.g., pickles), use the regular forms *little, littler, littlest*.

ALERTS: (1) Be aware of the difference between *less* and *fewer*. They aren't interchangeable. Use *less* with NONCOUNT NOUNS, either items or values: *The sugar substitute has less **aftertaste***. Use *fewer* with numbers or COUNT NOUNS: *The sugar substitute has fewer **calories***. (2) Don't use *more, most* or *less, least* with **absolute adjectives**, that is, adjectives that communicate a noncomparable quality or state, such as *unique* or *perfect*. Something either *is*, or *is not*, one of a kind. No degrees of intensity are involved: *This teapot is **unique*** [not *the most unique*]; *The artisanship is **perfect*** [not *the most perfect*]. ●

EXERCISE 18-3   Complete the chart that follows. Then, write a sentence for each word in the completed chart. For help, consult 18e.

> **EXAMPLE**   *funny, funnier, funniest:* My brother has a *funny* laugh; he thinks Mom has a *funnier* laugh; the person who has the *funniest* laugh in our family is Uncle Dominic.

POSITIVE	COMPARATIVE	SUPERLATIVE
small	_____	_____
_____	greedier	_____
_____	_____	most complete
gladly	_____	_____
_____	_____	fewest
_____	thicker	_____
some	_____	_____

18f   Why avoid a long string of nouns as modifiers?

NOUNS sometimes MODIFY other nouns: *truck driver, train track, security system.* Usually, these terms create no problems. However, avoid using several nouns in a row as modifiers. A string of too many nouns makes it difficult for your reader to figure out which nouns are being modified and which nouns are doing the modifying. You can revise such sentences in several ways.

REWRITE THE SENTENCE

> NO   I asked my adviser to write **two college recommendation letters** for me.
>
> YES   I asked my adviser to write *letters of recommendation to two colleges* for me.

CHANGE ONE NOUN TO A POSSESSIVE AND ANOTHER TO AN ADJECTIVE

> NO   Advanced students may use the **university psychology lab facilities** for **cognition research projects.**
>
> YES   Advanced students may use the *university's psychology lab facilities for cognitive research projects.*

CHANGE ONE NOUN TO A PREPOSITIONAL PHRASE

> NO   Our **student adviser training program** has won many awards.
>
> YES   Our *training program for student advisers* has won many awards. [This change requires a change from the singular *adviser* to the plural *advisers*.]

EXERCISE 18-4   Underline the better choice in parentheses. For help, consult this entire chapter.

> **EXAMPLE** A modern sculpture by Haida artist Bill Reid, done in a style that seems (traditionally, <u>traditional</u>), depicts his people's legend of the creation of mankind.

1. According to the Haida people of the Queen Charlotte Islands, before the (most early, earliest) humans appeared the world was the home of powerful beings.

2. One of these beings was the Raven, a playful bird who created the moon and the stars and did many other important deeds—but seldom out of the desire to do (good, well) at his tasks.

3. (Fewer, Less) of the Raven's creations were the product of his (well, good) intentions than of his sense of mischief.

4. While flying over a (more remote, remote) part of the islands, the Raven saw a clam shell lying on the beach and heard tiny creatures scrambling around inside it.

5. Although none of us (cannot, can) hear it today, the Raven had a beautiful voice, which he could use for magical purposes, in addition to his hoarse cawing sound.

6. The (curious, curiously) Raven used this beautiful voice to coax the creatures out of the shell, and so brought the first naked, helpless humans crawling (fearful, fearfully) into the world.

Chapter 19

SENTENCE FRAGMENTS

19a   What is a sentence fragment?

A **sentence fragment** looks like a sentence, but it's actually only part of a sentence. That is, even though a sentence fragment begins with a capital letter and ends with a period (or question mark or exclamation mark), it doesn't contain an INDEPENDENT CLAUSE. Fragments are merely unattached PHRASES or DEPENDENT CLAUSES.

FRAGMENT	The telephone with redial capacity. [no verb]
CORRECT	The telephone has redial capacity.
FRAGMENT	Rang loudly for ten minutes. [no subject]
CORRECT	The telephone rang loudly for ten minutes.
FRAGMENT	At midnight. [a phrase without a verb or subject]
CORRECT	The telephone rang at midnight.
FRAGMENT	Because the telephone rang loudly. [dependent clause starting with subordinating conjunction *because*]
CORRECT	Because the telephone rang loudly, the family was awakened in the middle of the night.
FRAGMENT	Which really annoyed me. [dependent clause starting with relative pronoun *which*]
CORRECT	The telephone call was a wrong number, which really annoyed me.

Sentence fragments can ruin the clarity of your writing. Moreover, in ACADEMIC WRITING and BUSINESS WRITING, sentence fragments imply that you don't know basic sentence structure or that you're a careless proofreader.

NO	The lawyer was angry. When she returned from court. She found the key witness waiting in her office. [Was the lawyer angry when she returned from court, or when she found the witness in her office?]
YES	The lawyer was angry when she returned from court. She found the key witness waiting in her office.
YES	The lawyer was angry. When she returned from court, she found the key witness waiting in her office.

Let's go beyond the grammatical terms to a more practical approach to recognizing sentence fragments, so that you can avoid them in your writing. To learn to recognize sentence fragments, see 19b; to learn several ways to correct sentence fragments, see 19c and 19d.

Many writers wait until the REVISING and EDITING stages of the WRITING PROCESS to check for sentence fragments. During DRAFTING, the goal is to get ideas down on paper or disk. As you draft, if you suspect that you've written a sentence fragment, simply underline or highlight it in boldface or italics and move on. Later, you can easily find it to check and correct.

If you tend to write SENTENCE FRAGMENTS, you want a system for recognizing them. Quick Reference 19.1 shows you a Sentence Test for checking that you haven't written a sentence fragment. We discuss each question in more detail in 19b.1 through 19b.3.

QUICK REFERENCE **19.1**

Sentence test to identify sentence fragments

QUESTION 1: IS THE WORD GROUP A DEPENDENT CLAUSE?

A DEPENDENT CLAUSE is a word group that has a subject and a verb but starts with a subordinating word—either a SUBORDINATING CONJUNCTION or a RELATIVE PRONOUN.

FRAGMENT   **When** winter comes early. [starts with *when,* a subordinating conjunction]

CORRECT   **When** winter comes early, **ships often rescue the stranded whales**. [adds an independent clause to create a sentence]

FRAGMENT   **Which** can happen quickly. [starts with *which,* a relative pronoun]

CORRECT   **Whales cannot breathe through the ice and will drown, which** can happen quickly. [adds an independent clause to create a sentence]

QUESTION 2: IS THERE A VERB?

FRAGMENT   Thousands of whales in the Arctic Ocean. [Because a verb is missing, this is a phrase, not a sentence.]

CORRECT   Thousands of whales **live** in the Arctic Ocean. [adds a verb to create a sentence]

QUESTION 3: IS THERE A SUBJECT?

FRAGMENT   Stranded in the Arctic Ocean. [Because a subject is missing, this is a phrase, not a sentence.]

CORRECT   **Many whales *were*** stranded in the Arctic Ocean. [adds a subject (and the verb *were* to *stranded*) to create a sentence]

19b.1   Question 1: Is the word group a dependent clause?

Writing in
Action:
Recognizing
Sentence
Fragments

If you answer yes to question 1, you're looking at a sentence fragment. A DEPENDENT CLAUSE is a word group that has a subject and a verb but starts with a subordinating word—either a SUBORDINATING CONJUNCTION or a RELATIVE PRONOUN. Such a word before an INDEPENDENT CLAUSE creates a dependent clause, which can't stand alone as a sentence and is therefore a sentence fragment. To become a complete sentence, the fragment needs either to be joined to an independent clause or to be rewritten.

FRAGMENTS WITH SUBORDINATING CONJUNCTIONS

A complete list of subordinating conjunctions appears in Quick Reference 14.7 in 14i. Some frequently used ones are *after, although, because, before, if, unless,* and *when.*

FRAGMENT   **Because** she returned my books. [*Because,* a subordinating conjunction, creates a dependent clause.]

CORRECT   **Because** she returned my books, *I can study*. [A comma and the independent clause *I can study* are added, and the sentence becomes complete.]

FRAGMENT	**Unless** I study. [*Unless*, a subordinating conjunction, creates a dependent clause.]
CORRECT	***I won't pass the test*** **unless** I study. [The independent clause *I won't pass the test* is added, and the sentence becomes complete.]

🛈 **ALERT:** When a dependent clause starts with a subordinating conjunction and comes before its independent clause, use a comma to separate the clauses (24c). ●

FRAGMENTS WITH RELATIVE PRONOUNS

Relative pronouns (see 14c), are *that, which, who, whom,* and *whose.*

FRAGMENT	**That** we had studied for all week. [*That*, a relative pronoun, creates a dependent clause here.]
CORRECT	***We passed the exam*** **that** we had studied for all week. [The independent clause *We passed the exam* is added, and the sentence becomes complete.]

When *which, who,* and *whose* begin questions, they function as INTERROGATIVE PRO-NOUNS, not relative pronouns. Questions are complete sentences, not fragments: *Which class are you taking? Who is your professor? Whose book is that?*

19b.2 Question 2: Is there a verb?

If you answer no to question 2, you're looking at a sentence fragment. When a VERB is missing from a word group, the result is a PHRASE, not a sentence. You can figure out if a word is a verb by seeing if it can change in TENSE.

Now the telephone **rings**. [present tense]

Yesterday, the telephone **rang**. [past tense]

When you check for verbs, remember that VERBALS (14e) are not verbs. Verbals might look like verbs, but they don't function as verbs.

FRAGMENT	Yesterday, the students **registering** for classes. [*Registering* is a verbal called a present participle, not a verb.]
CORRECT	Yesterday, the students **were registering** for classes. [Adding the auxiliary verb *were* to the present participle *registering* creates a verb.]
FRAGMENT	Now the students **to register** for classes. [*To register* is a verbal called an infinitive, not a verb.]
CORRECT	Now the students **want to register** for classes. [The verb *want* is added to the infinitive *to register*.]

19b.3 Question 3: Is there a subject?

If you answer no to question 3, you're looking at a sentence fragment. When a SUBJECT is missing from a word group, the result is a PHRASE, not a sentence. To see if a word is a subject, ask, "Who (*or* What) performs the action?"

FRAGMENT	Studied hard for class. [*Who* studied hard for class? unknown]
CORRECT	The students studied hard for class. [*Who* studied hard for class? *The students* is the answer, so a subject makes the sentence complete.]

FRAGMENT   Contained some difficult questions. [*What* contained some difficult questions? unknown]

CORRECT   The test contained some difficult questions. [*What* contained some difficult questions? *The test* is the answer, so a subject makes the sentence complete.]

Be especially careful with COMPOUND PREDICATES—for example, We **took** *the bus to the movie **and walked** home.* If you were to place a period after *movie*, the second part of the compound predicate would be a sentence fragment. Every sentence needs its own subject. To check for this kind of sentence fragment, ask the question "Who?" or "What?" of each verb.

NO   A few students organized a study group to prepare for midterm exams. **Decided to study together for the rest of the course.** [*Who* decided to study together? The answer is *The students* (who formed the group), but this subject is missing.]

YES   A few students organized a study group to prepare for midterm exams. ***The students* decided to study together for the rest of the course**.

IMPERATIVE SENTENCES—commands and some requests—may appear at first glance to be fragments caused by missing subjects. They're not fragments, however. Imperative sentences are complete sentences because their subjects are implied. An implied subject can be *you, anybody, somebody, everybody,* or another INDEFINITE PRONOUN.

Run! [This sentence implies the pronoun *you*.]

Return all library books to the front desk. [This sentence implies the indefinite pronoun *everyone*.]

EXERCISE 19-1   Identify each word group as either a complete sentence or a fragment. If the word group is a sentence, circle its number. If it's a fragment, tell why it's incomplete. For help, see Quick Reference 19.1 in 19b and sections 19b.1 through 19b.3.

EXAMPLE   Although antibacterial soaps have become popular. [Starts with a subordinating conjunction *(although)*, which creates a dependent clause, and lacks an independent clause to complete the thought; see Quick Reference 19.1 and section 19c.1]

1. Because antibacterial soaps do not provide protection against viruses.
2. Viruses responsible for a variety of common health problems.
3. Regular soap often successfully eliminates bacteria, viruses, and dirt.
4. Indicate that antibacterial soaps may wash away useful bacteria.
5. Eliminates most of the harmful bacteria as effectively as regular soap.
6. Careful hand washing cannot be stressed enough.
7. To work efficiently, antibacterial soaps, even those purchased in health food stores.
8. Most studies show that antibacterial soaps do not lead to resistant bacteria.
9. Although many people still believe they should not use antibacterial soaps.
10. Bacteria from overuse of antibiotics.

AUDIO
LESSON
Section 1:
Big Ideas—
Correcting
Common
Errors:
Fragments
and Run-On
Sentences

AUDIO
LESSON
Section 2:
Practice
Questions—
Correcting
Common
Errors:
Fragments
and Run-On
Sentences

Writing in
Action:
Combining
Sentences

19c What are major ways of correcting fragments?

Once you've identified a SENTENCE FRAGMENT (19b), you're ready to correct it. You can do this in one of two ways: by joining it to an independent clause (19c.1) or by rewriting it (19c.2).

19c.1 Correcting a sentence fragment by joining it to an independent clause

One way you can correct a sentence fragment is by joining it to an INDEPENDENT CLAUSE—that is, to a complete sentence. The first two examples below deal with dependent-clause fragments; the examples following the Alert examine fragments with missing subjects and/or verbs.

FRAGMENT **Because** the ice was thick. [Although this word group has a subject (*ice*) and verb (*was*), it starts with the subordinating conjunction *because*.]

CORRECT **Because** the ice was thick, *icebreakers were required to serve as rescue ships.* [Adding a comma and joining the fragment to the independent clause *icebreakers were required to serve as rescue ships* creates a complete sentence.]

CORRECT *Icebreakers were required to serve as rescue ships* **because** the ice was thick. [Joining the fragment to the independent clause *Icebreakers were required to serve as rescue ships* creates a complete sentence.]

FRAGMENT **Who** feared the whales would panic. [This fragment starts with the relative pronoun *who*.]

CORRECT *The noisy motors of the ships worried the crews,* **who** feared the whales would panic. [Joining the fragment to the independent clause *The noisy motors of the ships worried the crews* creates a complete sentence.]

! ALERT: Be careful with all words that indicate time, such as *after, before, since,* and *until.* They aren't always subordinating conjunctions. Sometimes they function as ADVERBS—especially if they begin a complete sentence. At other times, they function as PREPOSITIONS. When you see one of these words that indicate time, realize that you aren't necessarily looking at a dependent-clause fragment.

Before, the whales responded to classical music. [This is a complete sentence in which *Before* is an adverb that modifies the independent clause *the whales responded to classical music.*]

Before the whales responded to classical music, some crew members had tried rock and roll music. [If the word group before the comma stood on its own, it would be a sentence fragment because it starts with *Before* functioning as a subordinating conjunction.] ●

FRAGMENT **To announce new programs for crime prevention.** [*To announce* starts an infinitive phrase, not a sentence.]

CORRECT *The mayor called a news conference last week* **to announce** new programs for crime prevention. [The infinitive phrase starting with *to announce* is joined to an independent clause.]

FRAGMENT	**Hoping for strong public support.** [*Hoping* starts a present-participial phrase, not a sentence.]
CORRECT	**Hoping** for strong public support, *she gave examples of problems throughout the city*. [The present-participial phrase starting with *Hoping* is joined to an independent clause.]
FRAGMENT	**Introduced by her assistant.** [*Introduced* starts a past-participial phrase, not a sentence.]
CORRECT	**Introduced** by her assistant, *the mayor began with an opening statement*. [The past-participial phrase starting with *Introduced* is joined to an independent clause.]
FRAGMENT	**During the long news conference.** [*During* functions as a preposition—starting a prepositional phrase, not a sentence.]
CORRECT	*Cigarette smoke made the conference room seem airless* **during** the long news conference. [The prepositional phrase starting with *during* is joined with an independent clause.]
FRAGMENT	**A politician with fresh ideas.** [*A politician* starts an appositive phrase, not a sentence.]
CORRECT	*Most people respected the mayor,* **a politician** with fresh ideas. [The appositive phrase starting with *a politician* is joined with an independent clause.] ●

19c.2 Correcting a sentence fragment by rewriting it

A second way you can correct a sentence fragment is by rewriting it as an INDEPENDENT CLAUSE—that is, as a complete sentence. The first two examples below deal with dependent-clause fragments; the others examine fragments with missing subjects and/or verbs.

FRAGMENT	**Because** the ice was thick. [Although this word group has a subject (*ice*) and verb (*was*), it starts with the subordinating conjunction *because*.]
CORRECT	The ice was thick. [The fragment starting with *Because* is rewritten to become a complete sentence.]
FRAGMENT	**Who** feared the whales would panic. [This fragment starts with the relative pronoun *who*.]
CORRECT	*The crew* feared the whales would panic. [The fragment starting with *Who* is rewritten to become a complete sentence.]
FRAGMENT	**To announce** new programs for crime prevention. [*To announce* starts an infinitive phrase, not a sentence.]
CORRECT	*Last week, the mayor announced* new programs for crime prevention. [The infinitive phrase starting with *To announce* is rewritten to become a complete sentence.]
FRAGMENT	**Hoping for strong public support.** [*Hoping* starts a present-participle phrase, not a sentence.]
CORRECT	*She was* **hoping** for strong public support. [The present-participle phrase starting with *Hoping* is rewritten to become a complete sentence.]
FRAGMENT	**Introduced** by her assistant. [*Introduced* starts a past-participle phrase, not a sentence.]

301

> CORRECT   *Before she made her opening statement, the mayor was* **introduced** by her assistant. [The past-participle phrase starting with *Introduced* is rewritten to become a complete sentence.]

> FRAGMENT   **During** the long news conference. [*During* functions as a preposition that starts a prepositional phrase, not a sentence.]

> CORRECT   **During** the long news conference, **many proposals** *were announced*. [The prepositional phrase starting with *During* is rewritten to become a complete sentence.]

> FRAGMENT   **A politician** with fresh ideas. [*A politician* starts an appositive phrase, not a sentence.]

> CORRECT   *She seemed to be* **a politician** with fresh ideas. [The appositive phrase is rewritten to become a complete sentence.]

EXERCISE 19-2   Find and correct any sentence fragments. If a sentence is correct, circle its number. For help, consult 19a through 19c.

> **EXAMPLE**   Even though lice are a common problem for young children.
>
> Lice are a common problem for young children.

1. Even though lice are not dangerous and do not spread disease, parents tend to worry about their children. Who have been infected with this parasite.
2. Although good hygiene is important, it does not prevent lice infestation. Which can occur on clean, healthy scalps.
3. Spread only through direct contact. Lice are unable to fly or jump.
4. Evidence of lice has been found on ancient Egyptian mummies, which suggests that lice have been annoying humans for a long time.
5. While lice can spread among humans who share combs or pillows or hats. Lice cannot spread from pets to humans.
6. Doctors may prescribe special shampoos and soaps. To help get rid of the lice on a child's head.
7. Because lice do not like heat, experts recommend putting infected sheets and stuffed animals and pillows in a dryer for thirty minutes.
8. Just one is called a *louse,* and a louse egg is called a *nit.* Which is where we get the words *lousy* and *nitpick.*
9. Using a hair dryer after applying a scalp treatment can be dangerous. Because some treatments contain flammable ingredients.
10. Although lice cannot live for more than twenty-four hours without human contact.

19d   How can I fix a fragment that is part of a compound predicate?

A COMPOUND PREDICATE contains two or more VERBS. When the second part of a compound predicate is punctuated as a separate sentence, it becomes a sentence fragment.

> FRAGMENT   The reporters asked the mayor many questions about the new program. **And then discussed her answers among themselves.** [*And then discussed* starts a compound predicate fragment, not a sentence.]

CORRECT The reporters asked the mayor many questions about the new program and then discussed her answers among themselves. [The compound predicate fragment starting with *And then discussed* is joined to the independent clause.]

CORRECT The reporters asked the mayor many questions about the new program. ***Then the reporters*** discussed her answers among themselves. [The compound predicate fragment starting with *And then discussed* is rewritten as a complete sentence.]

EXERCISE 19-3 Go back to Exercise 19-1 and revise the sentence fragments into complete sentences. In some cases, you may be able to combine two fragments into one complete sentence.

19e What are the two special fragment problems?

Composing lists and examples sometimes leads writers into fragment problems. Lists and examples must be part of a complete sentence, unless they are formatted as a column.

You can connect a list fragment by attaching it to the preceding independent clause using a colon or a dash. You can correct an example fragment by attaching it to an independent clause (with or without punctuation, depending on the meaning) or by rewriting it as a complete sentence.

FRAGMENT You have a choice of desserts. **Carrot cake, butter tarts, apple pie, or peppermint ice cream.** [The list cannot stand on its own as a sentence.]

CORRECT You have a choice of desserts: carrot cake, butter tarts, apple pie, or peppermint ice cream. [A colon joins the sentence and the list.]

CORRECT You have a choice of desserts—carrot cake, butter tarts, apple pie, or peppermint ice cream. [A dash joins the sentence and the list.]

FRAGMENT Several good places offer brunch. **For example, the Bluenose Inn and Peggy's Retreat.** [Examples can't stand on their own as a sentence.]

CORRECT Several good places offer brunch—**for example**, the Bluenose Inn and Peggy's Retreat.

CORRECT Several good places offer brunch. **For example, *you could try* the** Bluenose Inn and Peggy's Retreat.

19f How can I recognize intentional fragments?

Professional writers sometimes intentionally use fragments for emphasis and effect.

> This is what mastery is like, he thought. **Being superb in one's chosen field, not merely in one's mother tongue. A respected performer in the lecture halls of the major universities, equipped by twenty years' research in the remotest libraries, and slowly giving it back to those who must have it. Dishing it out suavely, even wittily. Being a legend. Being loved and a little feared.**
>
> —Clark Blaise, "A Class of New Canadians"

Being able to judge the difference between an acceptable and unacceptable sentence fragment comes from years of reading the work of skilled writers. Most instructors don't accept sentence fragments in student writing until a student demonstrates a consistent ability to write well-constructed, complete sentences. As a rule, avoid sentence fragments in ACADEMIC WRITING.

EXERCISE 19-4   Revise this paragraph to eliminate all sentence fragments. In some cases, you can combine word groups to create complete sentences; in other cases, you must supply missing elements to rewrite. Some sentences may not require revision. In your final version, check not only the individual sentences but also the clarity of the whole paragraph. For help, consult 19a through 19f.

> **EXAMPLE**   Mordecai Richler was a novelist and essayist. Who was born in Montreal in 1931.
>
> Mordecai Richler was a novelist and essayist who was born in Montreal in 1931.

(1) Richler made his reputation with the satirical novel *The Apprenticeship of Duddy Kravitz*. A hard-edged portrait of a young entrepreneur and hustler from Montreal's Jewish quarter. (2) Still, Richler must have had warm feelings for his old St. Urbain neighbourhood and the remarkable characters who inhabited it. Because mingled with the satire are sympathy and even nostalgia. (3) Unless people can be convinced otherwise. They will continue to believe that there is much of Richler himself in his funny, pathetic, yet engaging anti-heroes. Who try to make their way in an unsympathetic world. (4) The writer was sensitive to this inference. And attached a preface to his second novel expressly to deny it. (5) Even though much of Richler's wit is aimed at people striving to escape their modest backgrounds. Satires like *Solomon Gursky Was Here* have not spared the Canadian elite, whom Richler shows with feet of clay and closets full of embarrassing secrets. (6) These satires may support Richler's contention that as a serious writer, he was obliged to serve a moral purpose. As well as act as the "loser's advocate." (7) In a series of essays, Richler turned his pen against nationalist intellectuals in Quebec. If Richler insisted. That his essay *Oh Canada! Oh Quebec!* with its sad subtitle *Requiem for a Divided Country* was serious political analysis. Why did his publisher catalogue it as "humour"?

EXERCISE 19-5   Revise this paragraph to eliminate all sentence fragments. In some cases, you can combine word groups to create complete sentences; in other cases, you must supply missing elements to revise word groups. Some sentences may not require revision. In your final version, check not only the individual sentences but also the clarity of the whole paragraph. Refer to 19a through 19f for help.

(1) Throughout his career as a philosopher and Cynic, Diogenes cultivated a following. That included the likes of Aristotle and Alexander the Great. (2) Diogenes was an important member of the Cynics, a group of people who rejected conventional life. The word *Cynic* comes from the Greek word for dog. (3) Diogenes lived like a beggar and slept in a tub. Which he carried around with him wherever he went. (4) He rejected the pursuit of wealth and once destroyed his wooden bowl. Because he saw a peasant boy drinking water with his hands. (5) Although none of his writings have survived, Diogenes produced dialogues and a play. That allegedly describes a social utopia in which people live unconventional lives. (6) Since he often walked around Athens in broad daylight with a lamp looking for an honest man. (7) When Plato defined *man* as a featherless biped, Diogenes plucked a chicken and said, "Here is Plato's man." (8) According to legend, Diogenes was once sunbathing when he was approached by Alexander the Great. Who was a fan of the eccentric Cynic. (9) Alexander asked if he could do anything for Diogenes. Which the philosopher answered by saying, "Don't block my sunlight." (10) Because Diogenes is a strange and interesting character. He has inspired works by such writers and artists as William Blake, Anton Chekhov, and François Rabelais.

Chapter 20

COMMA SPLICES AND FUSED SENTENCES

20a What are comma splices and fused sentences?

Comma splices and fused sentences are somewhat similar errors: One has a comma by itself between two complete sentences, and one has no punctuation at all between two complete sentences.

A **comma splice**, also called a *comma fault,* occurs when a comma, rather than a period, is used incorrectly between complete sentences. The word *splice* means "to fasten ends together," which is a handy procedure, except when splicing has anything to do with sentences.

A **fused sentence**, also called a *run-on sentence* and a *run-together sentence,* occurs when two complete sentences run into each other without any punctuation. Comma splices and fused sentences create confusion because readers can't tell where one thought ends and another begins.

COMMA SPLICE	The icebergs broke off from the **glacier, they** drifted into the sea.
RUN-ON SENTENCE	The icebergs broke off from the **glacier they** drifted into the sea.
CORRECT	The icebergs broke off from the **glacier. They** drifted into the sea.

There is one exception. You can use a comma between two independent clauses, but only if the comma is followed by one of the seven coordinating conjunctions: *and, but, for, or, nor, yet, so.* A comma in such a construction is correct; see Chapter 24.

CORRECT	The icebergs broke off from the **glacier, and** they drifted into the sea.

ALERT: Occasionally, when your meaning allows it, you can use a colon or a dash to join two independent clauses. ●

Many writers wait until the REVISING and EDITING stages of the WRITING PROCESS to check for comma splices and fused sentences. During DRAFTING, the goal is to put ideas down on paper or disk. As you draft, if you suspect that you've written a comma splice or a fused sentence, simply underline or highlight it in boldface or italics, and move on. Later, you can easily find it to check and correct.

20b How can I recognize comma splices and fused sentences?

When you know how to recognize an INDEPENDENT CLAUSE, you'll know how to recognize COMMA SPLICES and FUSED SENTENCES. An independent clause can stand alone as a complete sentence. An independent clause contains a SUBJECT and a PREDICATE. Also, an independent clause doesn't begin with a subordinating word—a SUBORDINATING CONJUNCTION or a RELATIVE PRONOUN.

Interestingly, almost all comma splices and fused sentences are caused by only four patterns. If you become familiar with these four patterns, listed in Quick Reference 20.1, you'll more easily locate them in your writing.

ALERT: To proofread for comma splices, cover all words on one side of the comma and see if the words remaining form an independent clause. If they do, next cover all the words on the other side of the comma. If that side is also an independent clause, you're looking at a comma splice. (This technique doesn't work for fused sentences because a comma isn't present.) •

QUICK REFERENCE **20.1**

Detecting comma splices and fused sentences

• Watch out for a PRONOUN starting the second independent clause.

> NO Grey Owl was an author and **conservationist, he** lived in northern Ontario and the Prairies.

> YES Grey Owl was an author and **conservationist. He** lived in northern Ontario and the Prairies.

• Watch out for a CONJUNCTIVE ADVERB (such as *furthermore, however, similarly, therefore,* and *then*) starting the second independent clause; see Quick Reference 14.5, section 14g, for a complete list.

> NO He passed himself off as a North American **Indian, however,** he was born Archibald Belaney in England.

> YES He passed himself off as a North American **Indian. However,** he was born Archibald Belaney in England.

• Watch out for a TRANSITIONAL EXPRESSION (such as *in addition, for example, in contrast, of course,* and *meanwhile*) starting the second independent clause; see Quick Reference 3.5, section 3g.1, for a reference list.

> NO Grey Owl served as a conservation **officer, in addition,** he lectured and wrote bestselling books.

> YES Grey Owl served as a conservation **officer; in addition,** he lectured and wrote bestselling books.

• Watch out for a second independent clause that explains, says more about, contrasts with, or gives an example of what's said in the first independent clause.

> NO Belaney appeared to be expert in First Nations **traditional lore, most of the traditions** he knew he learned from his Iroquois wife and his Ojibway friends.

> YES Belaney appeared to be expert in First Nations **traditional lore. Most of the traditions** he knew he learned from his Iroquois wife and his Ojibway friends.

Experienced writers sometimes use a comma to join very short independent clauses, especially if one independent clause is negative and the other is positive: *Mosquitoes don't* **bite, they** *stab.* In ACADEMIC WRITING, however, many instructors consider this an error, so you'll be safe if you use a period. (Another option is a semicolon, if the two independent clauses are closely related in meaning: *Mosquitoes don't* **bite; they** *stab.*)

20c How can I correct comma splices and fused sentences?

Once you have identified a COMMA SPLICE or a FUSED SENTENCE, you're ready to correct it. You can do this in one of four ways, as shown in Quick Reference 20.2 and discussed further in sections 20c.1 through 20c.4.

⊙ Common Grammar Errors: 1. Five Ways to Fix a Comma Splice Error

---

QUICK REFERENCE 20.2

Ways to correct comma splices and fused sentences

- Use a period between the INDEPENDENT CLAUSES (20c.1).
- Use a semicolon between the independent clauses (20c.2).
- Use a comma together with a COORDINATING CONJUNCTION (20c.3).
- Revise one independent clause into a DEPENDENT CLAUSE (20c.4).

20c.1 Using a period to correct comma splices and fused sentences

You can use a period to correct comma splices and fused sentences by placing the period between the two sentences. For the sake of sentence variety and emphasis (Chapter 9), however, you want to choose other options as well, such as those shown in 20c.3 and 20c.4. Strings of short sentences rarely establish relationships and levels of importance among ideas.

((•● AUDIO LESSON Section 1: Big Ideas— Correcting Common Errors: Fragments and Run-On Sentences

COMMA SPLICE	A shark is all **cartilage, it** doesn't have a bone in its body.
FUSED SENTENCE	A shark is all **cartilage it** doesn't have a bone in its body.
CORRECT	A shark is all **cartilage. It** doesn't have a bone in its body. [A period separates the independent clauses.]
COMMA SPLICE	Sharks can smell blood from 400 metres **away, they** then swim toward the source like a guided missile.
FUSED SENTENCE	Sharks can smell blood from 400 metres **away they** then swim toward the source like a guided missile.
CORRECT	Sharks can smell blood from 400 metres **away. They** then swim toward the source like a guided missile. [A period separates the independent clauses.]

((•● AUDIO LESSON Section 2: Practice Questions— Correcting Common Errors: Fragments and Run-On Sentences

20c.2 Using a semicolon to correct comma splices and fused sentences

You can use a semicolon to separate the independent clauses in comma splices and fused sentences. Use a semicolon only when the separate sentences are closely related in meaning. For the sake of sentence variety and emphasis, however, you'll want to choose other

((•● AUDIO LESSON Section 3: Rapid Review— Correcting Common Errors: Fragments and Run-On Sentences

307

Writing in
Action:
Combining
Sentences

options, such as those shown in 20c.1, 20c.3, and 20c.4; for correct semicolon use, see Chapter 25.

COMMA SPLICE   The great white shark supposedly eats **humans, research** shows that most white sharks spit them out after the first bite.

FUSED SENTENCE   The great white shark supposedly eats **humans research** shows that most white sharks spit them out after the first bite.

CORRECT   The great white shark supposedly eats **humans; research** shows that most white sharks spit them out after the first bite. [A semicolon separates two independent clauses that are close in meaning.]

20c.3 Using a comma together with a coordinating conjunction to correct comma splices and fused sentences

You can connect independent clauses by inserting a coordinating conjunction (*and, but, for, or, nor, yet, so*) following a comma to correct a comma splice or a fused sentence.

ALERT: Use a comma before a coordinating conjunction that links independent clauses (24b). ●

When you use a coordinating conjunction, be sure that your choice fits the meaning of the material. *And* signals addition; *but* and *yet* signal contrast; *for* and *so* signal cause; and *or* and *nor* signal alternatives.

COMMA SPLICE   All living creatures give off weak electrical charges in the **water, special** pores on a shark's skin can detect these signals.

FUSED SENTENCE   All living creatures give off weak electrical charges in the **water special** pores on a shark's skin can detect these signals.

CORRECT   All living creatures give off weak electrical charges in the **water, *and* special** pores on a shark's skin can detect these signals.

EXERCISE 20-1   Revise the comma splices and fused sentences by using a period, a semicolon, or a comma and coordinating conjunction. For help, consult sections 20c.1 through 20c.3.

EXAMPLE   Emily Carr was born in Victoria, British Columbia, in 1871, she died there in 1945.

Emily Carr was born in Victoria, British Columbia, *in 1871; she* died there in 1945.

1. Carr grew up in a disciplined, conventional household in a small and conservative city, however she went off to study art in San Francisco in 1891, after the death of her parents.

2. When she came home two years later, Carr set up a studio of her own, she roamed the beaches and forests of British Columbia sketching Indian totem poles and longhouses in their natural setting.

3. In 1910, Carr began her most important voyage she travelled to France where she developed the vivid postimpressionist style of painting for which she became known.

4. After Carr's return to Canada, her work showed new vigour clearly, her French experience had taught her how to interpret the powerful rhythms of Northwest Coast Indian art and the majesty of the region's mountains and forests.

5. Carr worked in obscurity until she was fifty-seven, she displayed her work that year in a national exhibition and, with the help of Lawren Harris and other members of the Group of Seven, she began to win wider recognition.

20c.4 Revising one independent clause into a dependent clause to correct comma splices and fused sentences

You can correct a comma splice or fused sentence by revising one of the two independent clauses into a dependent clause. This method is suitable only when one idea can logically be subordinated (9l) to the other. Also, be careful never to end the dependent clause with a period or semicolon. If you do, you've created the error of a SENTENCE FRAGMENT.

CREATE DEPENDENT CLAUSES WITH SUBORDINATING CONJUNCTIONS

One way to create a dependent clause is to insert a SUBORDINATING CONJUNCTION (such as *because, although, when,* and *if*—see Quick Reference 14.7, section 14i, for a complete list). Always choose a subordinating conjunction that fits the meaning of each particular sentence: *because* and *since* signal cause; *although* signals contrast; *when* signals time; and *if* signals condition. Dependent clauses that begin with a subordinating conjunction are called ADVERB CLAUSES.

COMMA SPLICE   Homer and Langley Collyer had packed their house from top to bottom with **junk, police** could not open the front door to investigate a reported smell.

FUSED SENTENCE   Homer and Langley Collyer had packed their house from top to bottom with **junk police** could not open the front door to investigate a reported smell.

CORRECT   **Because** Homer and Langley Collyer had packed their house from top to bottom with **junk, police** could not open the front door to investigate a reported smell. [*Because* starts a dependent clause that is joined by a comma with the independent clause starting with *police.*]

COMMA SPLICE   Old newspapers and car parts filled every room to the **ceiling, enough** space remained for fourteen pianos.

FUSED SENTENCE   Old newspapers and car parts filled every room to the **ceiling enough** space remained for fourteen pianos.

CORRECT   **Although** old newspapers and car parts filled every room to the **ceiling, enough** space remained for fourteen pianos. [The subordinating conjunction *although* starts a dependent clause that is joined by a comma with the independent clause starting with *enough.*]

ALERT: Place a comma between an introductory dependent clause and the independent clause that follows (24c). ●

309

CREATE DEPENDENT CLAUSES WITH RELATIVE PRONOUNS

You can create a dependent ADJECTIVE CLAUSE with a RELATIVE PRONOUN (*who, whom, whose, which, that*).

COMMA SPLICE	The Collyers had been crushed under a pile of **newspapers, the newspapers** had toppled onto the brothers.
FUSED SENTENCE	The Collyers had been crushed under a pile of **newspapers the newspapers** had toppled onto the brothers.
CORRECT	The Collyers had been crushed under a pile of **newspapers *that had toppled*** onto the brothers. [The relative pronoun *that* starts a dependent clause and is joined with the independent clause starting with *The Collyers*, after deletion of *the newspapers*.]

ALERT: Sometimes you need commas to set off an adjective clause from the rest of the sentence. This happens only when the adjective is NONRESTRICTIVE (nonessential), so check carefully (24f). ●

EXERCISE 20-2 Working individually or with your peer-response group, identify and then revise the comma splices and fused sentences. Circle the numbers of correct sentences. For help, consult 20b through 20c.4.

(1) Grey Owl's true identity was revealed after his death in 1938, the scandal that arose when his admirers discovered him to be an English writer stemmed from their anger at having been deceived. (2) At that time, few people asked Canadian Indians whether they were scandalized at having their identity taken by a stranger, few people probably cared. (3) Today, however, the concept of "cultural appropriation" provides a way to examine issues like this. (4) Actions like Grey Owl's, even when undertaken with respectful intent, lead to accusations that the minority group is being misrepresented perhaps its identity and culture are being appropriated—that is, taken over—unjustly. (5) Modern literary criticism is interested in this question it relates to the authenticity and "ownership" of stories and traditions. (6) Many writers commented on the accusation of cultural appropriation, this was brought against Robert Bringhurst in 1999, after he published his poetic retelling of Haida myths in *A Story as Sharp as a Knife*. (7) Questions like this can have one meaning for some minority groups at the same time they can have a very different meaning for members of the comfortable majority.

20d How can I correctly use a conjunctive adverb or other transitional expression between independent clauses?

CONJUNCTIVE ADVERBS and other TRANSITIONAL EXPRESSIONS link ideas between clauses or sentences. When these words begin an independent clause in mid-sentence, a semicolon must immediately precede them; a comma usually immediately follows them at the start of a sentence or a clause.

Conjunctive adverbs include such words as *however, therefore, also, next, then, thus, furthermore,* and *nevertheless* (see Quick Reference 14.5, section 14g, for a complete list). Be careful to remember that conjunctive adverbs are not COORDINATING CONJUNCTIONS (*and, but,* and so on; see 20c.3).

COMMA SPLICE   Buying or leasing a car is a matter of individual preference, **however,** it's wise to consider several points before making a decision.

FUSED SENTENCE   Buying or leasing a car is a matter of individual preference **however** it's wise to consider several points before making a decision.

CORRECT   Buying or leasing a car is a matter of individual preference. **However,** it's wise to consider several points before making a decision.

CORRECT   Buying or leasing a car is a matter of individual preference; **however,** it's wise to consider several points before making a decision.

Transitional expressions include *for example, for instance, in addition, in fact, of course,* and *on the one hand/on the other hand* (see Quick Reference 3.5, section 3g.1, for a complete list).

COMMA SPLICE   Car leasing requires a smaller down payment, **for example,** in many cases, you need only $1000 or $2000 and the first monthly payment.

FUSED SENTENCE   Car leasing requires a smaller down payment **for example** in many cases, you need only $1000 or $2000 and the first monthly payment.

CORRECT   Car leasing requires a smaller down payment. **For example,** in many cases, you need only $1000 or $2000 and the first monthly payment.

CORRECT   Car leasing requires a smaller down payment; **for example,** in many cases, you need only $1000 or $2000 and the first monthly payment.

ALERT: A conjunctive adverb or a transitional expression is usually followed by a comma when it starts a sentence (24c). ●

EXERCISE 20-3   Revise comma splices or fused sentences caused by incorrectly punctuated conjunctive adverbs or other transitional expressions. If a sentence is correct, circle its number. For help, consult 20d.

EXAMPLE   People used to say that East is East and West is West, however, the two cultures have met in a new clinical practice called energy psychology, which combines Eastern and Western therapies.

People used to say that East is East and West is *West. However,* the two cultures have met in a new clinical practice called energy psychology, which combines Eastern and Western therapies. [comma splice; corrected by inserting a period before a conjunctive adverb]

1. Leonard Holmes, PhD, has examined claims regarding the effectiveness of energy psychology; significantly, its proponents contend that stimulating acupuncture points while recalling an anxiety-causing incident can alleviate anxiety and phobias.

2. Holmes inquires whether this idea is true, in fact he goes on to question the connection that acupuncture points have to anxiety.

3. In the early 1980s, Roger Callahan, PhD, popularized a set of "thought field therapy" procedures therefore, these came to be called "the Callahan Technique."

4. Clinical psychologists such as Dr. David Feinstein have joined the ranks promoting energy psychology, furthermore Feinstein sells an interactive CD-ROM that presents guidance in therapy based on this theory.

5. Holmes thinks that energy psychotherapy is still too early in its development to be widely applied, indeed, he cautions the public to avoid trying it on their own.

EXERCISE 20-4   Revise all comma splices and fused sentences, using as many different methods of correction as you can. If a sentence is correct, circle its number.

(1) Shortly after midnight on August 21, 1853, the bow of the HMS *Breadalbane* was pierced by a huge shard of ice. (2) The wooden hull's copper sheathing was no protection against a summer storm in Canada's Arctic thus, within fifteen minutes the crew was standing on the pack ice, watching the last of their ship's three masts slip below the surface. (3) The *Breadalbane* was a sturdy Scottish-built merchant ship it had been pressed into service by the Royal Navy to help in the search for the missing Franklin Expedition. (4) Sir John Franklin's two ships and their crews had not returned from their attempt eight years earlier to navigate the Northwest Passage, they were never again seen alive by Europeans.

(5) The twenty-one sailors and officers of the *Breadalbane* were more fortunate they were plucked off the ice by their sister ship, the *Phoenix*. (6) They returned safely to England, however, their ship remained on the ocean floor, almost miraculously preserved by the freezing temperature. (7) Only in 1980 was the wreck located by Dr. Joseph MacInnis he had spent three years searching the southern coast of Beechey Island. (8) The following summer saw MacInnis return to continue studying the most northerly shipwreck ever discovered, it was also the best preserved wooden wreck. (9) MacInnis's team were forced to develop new diving and photographic techniques to use beneath the ice then in 1983 they employed an advanced arctic diving suit and miniature submersible vehicle to complete their exploration. (10) The underwater searchers found a ship that looks almost ready to set sail it still contains the crew's tools and personal effects, and above the deck hangs the signal lamp, forever dark.

Chapter 21

MISPLACED AND DANGLING MODIFIERS

21a What is a misplaced modifier?

A **modifier** is a word or group of words that describes or limits another word or group of words. A *misplaced modifier* is positioned incorrectly in a sentence, which means, therefore, that it describes the wrong word and changes the writer's meaning. Always place a modifier as close as possible to what it describes.

Common Grammar Errors: 10. Dangling or Misplaced Modifiers

AVOIDING SQUINTING MODIFIERS

A **squinting modifier** appears to modify both what comes before it and what follows it. Check that your modifiers are placed so that they communicate the meaning you intend.

> NO   Canadians watched the rower **anxiously** training for the Olympics as she recovered from a painful leg wound. [Was the training being done anxiously? Or was it being watched anxiously?]

> YES   Canadians watched the rower training **anxiously** for the Olympics as she recovered from a painful leg wound.

> YES   Canadians **anxiously** watched the rower training for the Olympics as she recovered from a painful leg wound.

PLACING LIMITING WORDS CAREFULLY

Words such as *only, not only, just, not just, almost, hardly, nearly, even, exactly, merely, scarcely,* and *simply* serve to limit the meaning of a word according to where they are placed. When you use such words, position them precisely. Consider how moving the placement of the word *only* changes the meaning of this sentence: *Professional coaches say that high salaries motivate players.*

Only professional coaches say that high salaries motivate players. [No one else says this.]

Professional coaches **only** say that high salaries motivate players. [The coaches probably do not mean what they say.]

Professional coaches say **only** that high salaries motivate players. [The coaches say nothing else.]

Professional coaches say that **only** high salaries motivate players. [Nothing except high salaries motivates players.]

Professional coaches say that high salaries **only** motivate players. [High salaries do nothing other than motivate players.]

Professional coaches say that high salaries motivate **only** players. [High salaries do motivate the players but not the coaches and managers.]

21b   How can I avoid split infinitives?

An INFINITIVE is a VERB form that starts with *to: to motivate, to convince, to create* are examples (14e). A **split infinitive** occurs when words are placed between the word *to* and its verb. The effect is awkward.

> NO   Overcoming the odds, Silken Laumann was able ***to, at the 1992 Barcelona Olympics, win*** a bronze medal in singles rowing.

> YES   Overcoming the odds, Silken Laumann was able ***to win*** a bronze medal in singles rowing at the 1992 Barcelona Olympics.

Often, the word that splits an infinitive is an ADVERB ending in *-ly.* In general, place adverbs either before or after the infinitive.

> NO   Originally favoured **to *easily* win** in her event, Olympic rower Laumann kept practising after her serious training accident.

> YES   Originally favoured **to win *easily*** in her event, Olympic rower Laumann kept practising after her serious training accident.

The rule about split infinitives has changed recently. Current usage says that when the best placement for a single adverb is actually between *to* and the verb, you may use that structure freely.

Who would have been able **to *accurately* foresee** her amazing comeback a few months later?

If you want to avoid splitting infinitives in your ACADEMIC WRITING, revise to avoid the split:

Who would have been able **to foresee *with any accuracy*** her amazing comeback a few months later?

21c   How can I avoid other splits in my sentences?

When too many words split a SUBJECT and its VERB or a verb and its OBJECT, the result is a sentence that lurches rather than flows.

> NO   **Silken Laumann,** like many other Olympic athletes, although her accomplishment in overcoming a serious training injury and her beaming smile put her in a class of her own, **has become** a popular motivational speaker. [The subject *Silken Laumann* is placed too far from the verb *has become*.]

> YES   Like many other Olympic athletes, **Silken Laumann has become** a popular motivational speaker, although her accomplishment in overcoming a serious training injury and her beaming smile put her in a class of her own.

> NO   Canadians **watched** with concern that quickly changed to enthusiasm **the brave athlete** as she recovered from her wound. [The verb *watched* is placed too far from its object *the brave athlete*.]

> YES   With concern that quickly changed to enthusiasm, Canadians **watched the brave athlete** as she recovered from her wound.

EXERCISE 21-1 Revise these sentences to correct misplaced modifiers, split infinitives, and other splits. If a sentence is correct, circle its number. For help, consult 21a through 21c.

> **EXAMPLE** When futurologists make predictions, probably, if their guesses turn out to be correct, they are relying on the science of demographics.
>
> When futurologists make predictions, if their guesses turn out to be correct, *they are probably relying* on the science of demographics.

1. Demographics, according to one researcher, David K. Foot, in this field, is capable of explaining "two-thirds of everything."

2. What Foot means is that most of the trends observed, from mortgage rate fluctuations to fast-food sales, in our society, can be traced to the study of human populations, and particularly their age structures.

3. When some futurologists speak of foreseeing changes in the "spirit of the times," these people only are obscuring the science that lies behind thoughtful trend-spotting.

4. Foot writes with amusement of popular authors who claim to with scientific accuracy predict "value shifts."

5. Demographers, because they can demonstrate that social values are linked to people's social and economic situations, insist that social values do not "shift" on their own.

6. Young adults tend to move into downtown neighbourhoods or onto university campuses for the first time where they are free from parental control.

7. When this age group explores its new freedom and consumes, limited by the relatively low income at its disposal, the "alternative" products aimed at the youth market, its behaviour *appears* to express the values of the youth culture.

8. Briefly, this is a description of the ten-million-strong Canadian Baby Boom generation, who were believed to have at one time permanently introduced a shift in values.

9. As young parents in the 1980s and 90s, these same "boomers" invested in suburban houses and minivans, took on mortgages, complained about dirty downtowns and unruly youth, and, while "cocooning" at home, set the tone for the so-called family values movement.

10. Foot observes that in countries that have had no comparable Baby Boom along with its related economic movements, such as Italy, there has been no parallel cycle of cultural trends and "value shifts."

EXERCISE 21-2 Using each list of words and phrases, create all the possible logical sentences. Insert commas as needed. Explain differences in meaning among the alternatives you create. For help, consult 21a through 21c.

> **EXAMPLE** exchange students
> learned to speak French
> while in Paris
> last summer

A. Last summer, / exchange students / learned to speak French / while in Paris.

B. While in Paris, / exchange students / learned to speak French / last summer.

C. Exchange students / learned to speak French / while in Paris / last summer.

D. Exchange students / learned to speak French / last summer / while in Paris.

1. chicken soup
   according to folklore
   helps
   cure colds
2. tadpoles
   instinctively
   swim
   toward
   their genetic relatives
3. the young driver
   while driving
   in the snow
   skidded
4. climbed
   the limber teenager
   a tall palm tree
   to pick a ripe coconut
   quickly
5. and cause mini-avalanches
   ski patrollers
   set explosives
   often
   to prevent big avalanches

DANGLING MODIFIERS

((•● **21d** **How can I avoid dangling modifiers?**

Dangling and
Misplaced
Modifiers

A **dangling modifier** describes or limits a word or words that never actually appear in the sentence. Aware of the intended meaning, the writer unconsciously supplies the missing words, but the reader gets confused. To correct a dangling modifier, clearly state your intended SUBJECT in the sentence.

> NO   While participating in a revolution in the Caribbean, terrible events overtook the novel's heroine. [The *terrible events* did not participate in the revolution.]

> YES   **While the novel's heroine was participating** in a revolution in the Caribbean, terrible events overtook her.

> YES   While **she** was participating in a revolution in the Caribbean, **the novel's heroine was overtaken** by terrible events.

> NO   Reading Margaret Atwood's novel *Bodily Harm,* the ending was shocking. [The *ending* did not read the novel.]

> YES   Reading Margaret Atwood's novel *Bodily Harm,* **I was shocked** by the ending.

> YES   **I read** Margaret Atwood's novel *Bodily Harm* and was shocked by the ending.

A major cause of dangling modifiers is the unnecessary use of the PASSIVE VOICE. Whenever possible, use the ACTIVE VOICE.

> NO   **Writing with a grim moral vision, the trap that fate prepares for foolish innocence** is explored by Atwood. [The *trap that fate prepares for foolish innocence* cannot write with a grim moral vision.]

> YES   **Writing with a grim moral vision, Atwood explores** the trap that fate prepares for foolish innocence.

EXERCISE 21-3   Identify and correct any dangling modifiers in these sentences. For help, consult 21d.

> **EXAMPLE**   Showing initiative and originality, the Nobel Peace Prize that was won by Lester Pearson in 1956 rewarded him for creating the first United Nations peacekeeping force.
>
> Showing initiative and originality, *Lester Pearson won the Nobel Peace Prize in 1956 for creating* the first United Nations peacekeeping force.

1. Stationed in the Sinai Desert, the task given to the first UN peacekeeping force was to observe the ceasefire between the armies of Egypt and Israel.
2. Emissaries of hope, the list of peacekeeping operations where UN troops have since served is a long one, including missions to the Congo, Cyprus, and Bosnia.
3. To accomplish the latest task demanded of them, the intervention in vicious wars against civilians, both physical danger and psychological trauma are risked by peacekeepers.
4. Therefore, having increased greatly in danger and complexity, the soldiers wearing the UN forces' blue beret are sometimes overwhelmed by their job.
5. Unable to stop the killing with the tiny UN force he was given, the world will not be allowed by General Roméo Dallaire to forget its indifference to the Rwandan genocide of 1994.

21e   **How can I proofread successfully for misplaced and dangling modifiers?**

Sentence errors like MISPLACED MODIFIERS and DANGLING MODIFIERS are hard to spot because of the way the human brain works. Writers know what they mean to say when they write. When they PROOFREAD, however, they often misread what they've written for what they intended to write. The mind unconsciously adjusts for the error. In contrast, readers see only what's on the paper or screen. We suggest that you read your writing aloud, or have someone else read it to you, to proofread it for these kinds of problems.

Chapter 22

SHIFTING AND MIXED SENTENCES

SHIFTING SENTENCES

22a What is a shifting sentence?

A **shift** within a sentence is an unnecessary, abrupt change in PERSON, NUMBER, SUBJECT, VOICE, TENSE, MOOD, or DIRECT or INDIRECT DISCOURSE. These shifts blur meaning. Sometimes a shift occurs between two or more sentences in a paragraph. If you set out on one track (writing in FIRST PERSON, for example), your readers expect you to stay on that same track (and not shift unnecessarily to THIRD PERSON, for example). When you go off track, you have written a shifting sentence or paragraph.

((•
AUDIO
LESSON
Section 1:
Big Ideas—
Correcting
Common
Errors:
Subject-Verb
Agreement
and Parallel
Structure

22b How can I avoid shifts in person and number?

Who or what performs or receives an action is defined by the term *person*. FIRST PERSON (*I, we*) is the speaker or writer; SECOND PERSON (*you*) is the one being spoken or written *to;* and THIRD PERSON (*he, she, it, they*) is the person or thing being spoken or written *about.*

The essential point is that shifts are incorrect unless the meaning in a particular context makes them necessary.

((•
AUDIO
LESSON
Section 2:
Practice
Questions—
Correcting
Common
Errors:
Subject-Verb
Agreement
and Parallel
Structure

> NO **I** enjoy reading financial forecasts of the future, but **you** wonder which will turn out to be correct. [The first person/shifts to the second person *you*.]

> YES **I** enjoy reading financial forecasts of the future, but **I** wonder which will turn out to be correct.

NUMBER refers to whether words are *singular* (one) or *plural* (more than one) in meaning. Do not start to write in one number and then shift for no reason to the other number.

> NO Because **people** are living longer, **an employee** now retires later. [The plural *people* shifts to the singular *employee*.]

> YES Because **people** are living longer, **employees** now retire later.

In ACADEMIC WRITING, reserve *you* for addressing the reader directly. Use the third person for general statements.

> NO *I* like my job in customer service because **you** get to solve people's problems. [I is in the first person, so a shift to the second person *you* is incorrect.]

> YES *I* like my job in customer service because **I** get to solve people's problems.

((•
AUDIO
LESSON
Section 3:
Key Terms—
Correcting
Common
Errors:
Subject-Verb
Agreement
and Parallel
Structure

NO **People** enjoy feeling productive, so when a job is unsatisfying, **you** usually become depressed. [*People* is in the third person, so a shift to the second person *you* is incorrect.]

YES **People** enjoy feeling productive, so when a job is unsatisfying, **they** usually become depressed.

Be careful with words in the singular (usually NOUNS) used in a general sense, such as *employee, student, consumer, neighbour,* and *someone.* These words are always third-person singular. The only pronouns for these ANTECEDENTS in the third-person singular are *he, she,* and *it.* Remember that *they* is plural, so the word *they* can't be used with singular nouns.

NO When **an employee** is treated with respect, **they** are more motivated to do a good job. [*Employee* is third-person singular, so the shift to the third-person plural *they* is incorrect.]

YES When **an employee** is treated with respect, **he or she** is more motivated to do a good job.

YES When **employees** are treated with respect, **they** are more motivated to do a good job.

YES **An employee** who is treated with respect is more motivated to do a good job.

YES **Employees** who are treated with respect are more motivated to do a good job.

🛈 **ALERT:** When you use INDEFINITE PRONOUNS (such as *someone, everyone,* or *anyone*), use GENDER-NEUTRAL LANGUAGE. For advice, see 17s and 12f. •

EXERCISE 22-1 Eliminate shifts in person and number between, as well as within, sentences. Some sentences may not need revision. For help, consult 22b.

(1) Fans of the fictional wizard Harry Potter have read about Quidditch and seen it on film, but at the University of Toronto you can find real-life teams competing in the sport. (2) A Quidditch player is supposed to be a wizard, because they can fly on the broomsticks that are part of every player's regulation equipment. (3) Unfortunately, at the university's Trinity College, where the league practises, sports fans can find only "Muggles" running up and down the playing field. (4) He or she won't see a single flying broomstick. (5) Muggles, in Harry Potter language, are people like most of us; they have no wizard powers. (6) Nonetheless, every member of a Quidditch team must keep a broom between their legs at all times as he or she scrambles after the ball, trying to score goals against their opponents. (7) Meanwhile, special team personnel called a "seeker" tries to capture another small, light ball, the "snitch," which is carried by a speedy player who may be wearing golden wings. (8) The University of Toronto isn't the only Canadian school whose students play competitive Quidditch. (9) McGill has had more success than Toronto in international tournaments, raising the possibility in some people's minds that they have been using players who aren't strictly Muggles.

Passive Versus Active Voice

22c   How can I avoid shifts in subject and voice?

A SHIFT in SUBJECT is rarely justified when it is accompanied by a shift in VOICE. The voice of a sentence is either *active (People expect changes)* or *passive (Changes are expected)*. Some subject shifts, however, are justified by the meaning of a passage: for example, *People look forward to the future, but the future holds many secrets.*

> NO   Most **people expect** major improvements in the future, but some **hardships are** also **anticipated**. [The subject shifts from *people* to *hardships,* and the voice shifts from active to passive.]

> YES   Most **people expect** major improvements in the future, but **they** also **anticipate** some hardships.

> YES   Most **people expect** major improvements in the future but also **anticipate** some hardships.

Common Grammar Errors: 4. Faulty Shift in Tense

22d   How can I avoid shifts in tense and mood?

TENSE refers to the time in which the action of a VERB takes place—past, present, or future: *We **will go** to the movies after we **finish** dinner.* An unnecessary tense SHIFT within or between sentences can make the statement confusing or illogical.

> NO   Canada **gave** its music industry a boost in the 1970s when government regulations **require** AM radio stations to play a minimum of 30 percent Canadian content. [The tense shifts from past to present, even though the action of both verbs occurred in the past.]

> YES   Canada **gave** its music industry a boost in the 1970s when government regulations **required** AM radio stations to play a minimum of 30 percent Canadian content.

> NO   Pop music **was** the greatest beneficiary of the new Canadian content regulations. However, the artists rushing into production with their recordings in the 1970s **include** a large number of failures as well as many well-known stars. [The illogical tense shift here occurs between sentences.]

> YES   Pop music **was** the greatest beneficiary of the new Canadian content regulations. However, the artists rushing into production with their recordings in the 1970s **included** a large number of failures as well as many well-known stars.

MOOD indicates whether a sentence is a statement or a question (INDICATIVE MOOD), a command or request (IMPERATIVE MOOD), or a wish or other-than-real statement (SUBJUNCTIVE MOOD). A shift in mood creates an awkward construction and can cause confusion.

> NO   The government issued a set of rules defining Canadian content: **Include** songs with music or lyrics composed or performed by a Canadian, and production details **are also to be taken** into account. [The verbs shift from the imperative mood to the indicative mood.]

> YES   The government issued a set of rules defining Canadian content: **Include** songs with music or lyrics composed or performed by a Canadian, and also **take** production details into account.

> YES   The government issued a set of rules defining Canadian content: Songs with music or lyrics composed or performed by a Canadian **are included,** and production details **are also to be taken** into account.

22e How can I avoid shifts between indirect and direct discourse?

Indirect discourse is not enclosed in quotation marks because it reports, rather than quotes, something that someone said. In contrast, **direct discourse** is enclosed in quotation marks because it quotes exactly the words that someone said. It's incorrect to write direct discourse and omit the quotation marks. Also, it's incorrect to write sentences that mix indirect and direct discourse. Such SHIFT errors confuse readers, who can't tell what was said and what is being merely reported.

> NO   Some record companies said that the Canadian content rules were too complicated and **these rules are excluding genuine Canadian music.**
> [*Said that* sets up indirect discourse, but *these rules are excluding genuine Canadian music* is direct discourse, although lacking quotation marks.]

> YES   Some record companies said that the Canadian content rules were too complicated and **that the rules were excluding genuine Canadian music.** [This revision uses indirect discourse consistently.]

> YES   Some record companies said that the Canadian content rules were too complicated and claimed, **"These rules are excluding genuine Canadian music."** [This revision distinguishes between indirect and direct discourse.]

Whenever you change your writing from direct discourse to indirect discourse (when you decide to paraphrase rather than quote someone directly, for example), you need to make changes in VERB TENSE and other grammatical features for your writing to make sense. Simply removing the quotation marks is not enough.

> NO   He asked **did we buy that CD?** [This version has the verb form needed for direct discourse, but the pronoun *we* is wrong and quotation punctuation is missing.]

> YES   He asked **whether we bought that CD.** [This version is entirely indirect discourse, and the verb has changed from *buy* to *bought*.]

> YES   He asked, **"Did you buy that CD?"** [This version is direct discourse. It repeats the original speech exactly, with correct quotation punctuation.]

EXERCISE 22-2   Revise these sentences to eliminate incorrect shifts within sentences. Some sentences can be revised in several ways. For help, consult 22b through 22e.

> **EXAMPLE**   Novelists such as Timothy Findley and Rohinton Mistry have won the Governor General's Literary Award, and more recently, translators such as Patricia Claxton and Linda Gaboriau won as well.
>
> Novelists such as Timothy Findley and Rohinton Mistry have won the Governor General's Literary Award, and more recently, translators such as Patricia Claxton and Linda Gaboriau *have won* as well.

1. Although some winners of the Governor General's Award have sunk into obscurity, fame has been won beyond Canada's borders by many others.

2. Examine the list of winners for proof of the award's prestige, and one can take a look at the stories surrounding the award for a glimpse at Canada's literary scene.

3. Leonard Cohen sparked a controversial episode when he announced that he was refusing the award for his *Selected Poems, 1956–1968,* explaining that much in me strives for this honour, but the poems themselves forbid it absolutely.

4. About the same time, a less enigmatic explanation for refusing the award was given by several nationalistic Quebec writers who announced they were rejecting them for political reasons.

5. However, in 1992 Cohen said that he will accept the newly instituted Governor General's Performing Arts Award, so apparently his songs, unlike his poems, did permit that honour.

EXERCISE 22-3   Revise this paragraph to eliminate incorrect shifts between sentences and within sentences. For help, consult 22b through 22e.

(1) According to sociologists, people experience role conflict when we find ourselves trying to juggle too many different social roles. (2) When people reach overload, he or she decided, "to cut back somewhere." (3) For example, a well-known politician might decide not to run for re-election because family life would be interfered with by the demands of the campaign. (4) In other cases, you may delay having children so they can achieve early career success. (5) A person might say to themselves that I can't do this right now and focus instead on career goals. (6) In yet another example, a plant manager might enjoy social interaction with employees but consequently find themselves unable to evaluate him or her objectively. (7) In short, sociologists find that although not all role conflicts cause problems, great hardships are suffered by some individuals faced with handling difficult balancing acts. (8) People can minimize role conflicts, however, if we learn to compartmentalize our lives. (9) A good example of this is people saying that I'm going to stop thinking about my job before I head home to my family.

MIXED SENTENCES

22f   What is a mixed sentence?

A mixed sentence has two or more parts, with the first part starting in one direction and the rest of the parts going off in another. This mixing of sentence parts leads to unclear meaning. To avoid this error, as you write each sentence, remember how you started it and make sure that whatever comes next in the sentence relates grammatically and logically to that beginning.

NO   Because our side lost the contest eventually motivated us to do better. [*Because our side lost the contest* starts the sentence in one direction, but *eventually motivated us to do better* goes off in another direction.]

YES   Because our side lost the contest, **we** eventually became motivated to do better.

YES   Our side lost the contest, **which** eventually motivated us to do better.

NO   Because television's first large-scale transmissions included news programs became popular with the public. [The opening dependent clause starts off on one track (and is not correctly punctuated), but the independent clause goes off in another direction. What does the writer want to emphasize, the first transmissions or the popularity of news programs?]

YES   Because television's first large-scale transmissions included news, programs became popular with the public. [The revision helps but is partial: The dependent clause talks about the news, but the independent clause goes off in another direction by talking about the popularity of the programs in general.]

YES   Television's first large-scale transmissions included news programs, **which were** popular with the public. [Dropping *because* and adding *which were* solves the problem by keeping the focus on news programs throughout.]

NO   By increasing the time for network news to thirty minutes increased the prestige of network news programs. [A prepositional phrase, such as *by increasing*, can't be the subject of a sentence.]

YES   Increasing the time for network news to thirty minutes increased the prestige of network news programs. [Dropping the preposition *by* clears up the problem.]

YES   By increasing the time for network news to thirty minutes, **the network executives** increased the prestige of network news programs. [Inserting a logical subject, *the network executives*, clears up the problem.]

The phrase *the fact that* lacks CONCISENESS, and it also tends to cause a mixed sentence.

NO   The fact that quiz show scandals in the 1950s prompted the networks to produce even more news shows.

YES   The fact **is** that quiz show scandals in the 1950s prompted the networks to produce even more news shows. [Adding *is* clarifies the meaning.]

YES   Quiz show scandals in the 1950s prompted the networks to produce even more news shows. [Dropping *the fact that* clarifies the meaning.]

22g How can I correct a mixed sentence resulting from faulty predication?

Faulty predication, sometimes called *illogical predication*, occurs when a SUBJECT and its PREDICATE don't make sense together.

NO   The purpose of television was invented to entertain people. [A *purpose* cannot be *invented*.]

YES   The purpose of television was to entertain people.

YES   Television was invented to entertain people.

Faulty predication often results from a lost connection between a subject and its SUBJECT COMPLEMENT.

NO   Peter Mansbridge's outstanding **characteristic** as a newscaster **is credible**. [The subject complement *credible* could logically describe *Peter Mansbridge*, but *Peter Mansbridge* is not the sentence's subject. Rather, the sentence's subject is his *characteristic*. Therefore, the sentence lacks a subject complement that would name a *characteristic* of Peter Mansbridge as a newscaster.]

YES   Peter Mansbridge's outstanding **characteristic** as a newscaster **is credibility**. [When *credibility* is substituted for *credible*, the sentence is correct.]

YES   Peter Mansbridge is credible as a newscaster. [When Peter Mansbridge becomes the sentence's subject, *credible* is correct.]

In ACADEMIC WRITING, avoid nonstandard constructions such as *is when* and *is where*. They should be avoided not only because they are nonstandard, but also because they usually lead to faulty predication.

> NO   A disaster **is when** TV news shows get some of their highest ratings.

> YES   TV news shows get some of their highest ratings during a disaster.

In academic writing, avoid constructions such as *the reason . . . is because*. Using both *reason* and *because* makes the construction redundant (it says the same thing twice). Instead, use either *the reason . . . is that* or *because* alone.

> NO   One **reason** that TV news captured widespread attention in the 1960s **is because** it covered the Vietnam War thoroughly.

> YES   One **reason** TV news captured widespread attention in the 1960s **is that** it covered the Vietnam War thoroughly.

> YES   TV news captured widespread attention in the 1960s **because** it covered the Vietnam War thoroughly.

EXERCISE 22-4   Revise the mixed sentences so that the beginning of each sentence fits logically with its end. If a sentence is correct, circle its number. For help, consult 22f and 22g.

> **EXAMPLE** The reason a newborn baby may stare at her hands or feet is because she can only focus on nearby objects.
>
> *A newborn baby may stare at her hands or feet* because she can only focus on nearby objects.

1. By showing babies plain, black-and-white images will help them learn to recognize shapes and focus their vision.
2. Even though babies can see their parents' faces will not respond with a smile until they are a few weeks old.
3. Babies may gaze intently into a small, unbreakable mirror attached to the inside of their cribs.
4. While following an object with her eyes is when eye coordination develops.
5. Because of a newborn's limited ability to see colour forces him to focus only on bright colours.
6. The reason babies occasionally cross their eyes is because they are perfecting their tracking skills.
7. Whether a light sleeper or a heavy sleeper, a typical baby does not need complete silence in order to rest well.
8. The fact that newborns can vary dramatically in their sensitivity to sounds and ability to sleep in noisy environments.
9. The reason that a two-month-old baby turns her head toward her parents' voice is because she is beginning to recognize familiar sounds.
10. Through changing his facial expression indicates he may find a particular sound soothing or comforting.

How can I proofread successfully for little words I forget to use?

22j

22h What are correct elliptical constructions?

An **elliptical construction** deliberately leaves out one or more words in a sentence for CONCISENESS.

Victor has his book and Joan's. [This means *Victor has his book* and *Joan's book*. The second *book* is left out deliberately.]

For an elliptical construction to be correct, the one or more words you leave out need to be identical to those already appearing in the sentence. For instance, the sample sentence above about Victor and Joan would have an incorrect elliptical construction if the writer's intended meaning were *Victor has his book, and Joan has her own book.*

> NO   In the 1980s, software expertise and communications equipment **were becoming** two major Canadian exports, and comedy talent a third. [The plural verb *were becoming* cannot take the place of *was becoming*, which the singular subject *comedy talent* requires.]

> YES   In the 1980s, software expertise and communications equipment **were becoming** two major Canadian exports, and comedy talent **was becoming** a third.

> YES   In the 1980s, software expertise and communications equipment **became** two major Canadian exports, and comedy talent a third. [*Became* works because it goes with both singular and plural subjects.]

22i What are correct comparisons?

((•
Faulty
Comparison

When you write comparisons, make sure that no important words are omitted.

> NO   Individuals driven to achieve make **better** business executives. [*Better* is a word of comparison (18e), but no comparison is stated.]

> YES   Individuals driven to achieve make **better** business executives **than do people not interested in personal accomplishments**.

> NO   Most personnel officers value high achievers **more than risk takers**. [*More* is a word of comparison, but it's unclear whether the sentence says *personnel officers value high achievers over risk takers* or *personnel officers value high achievers more than risk takers value them.*]

> YES   Most personnel officers value high achievers **more than they value** risk takers.

> YES   Most personnel officers value high achievers **more than** risk takers **do**.

22j How can I proofread successfully for little words I forget to use?

If you're rushing or distracted as you write, you might unintentionally omit little words, such as ARTICLES, PRONOUNS, CONJUNCTIONS, and PREPOSITIONS. Lynn does, unfortunately. She solves this by reading her writing aloud, word by word; or, better still, she asks someone else to read it aloud because she tends to fill in mentally any missing words in her own work.

> NO On May 2, 1808, citizens Madrid rioted against French soldiers and were shot.

> YES On May 2, 1808, citizens **of** Madrid rioted against French soldiers and were shot.

> NO The Spanish painter Francisco Goya recorded both the riot the execution in a pair of pictures painted 1814.

> YES The Spanish painter Francisco Goya recorded both the riot **and** the execution in a pair of pictures painted **in** 1814.

EXERCISE 22-5   Revise this paragraph to create correct elliptical constructions, to complete comparisons, and to insert any missing words. For help, see 22h through 22j.

(1) In late 2005, the scientific journal *Nature* gave some added credibility Wikipedia's experiment in creating an open, collaborative encyclopedia. (2) The respected British journal found that Wikipedia "comes close to" the Internet version of the *Encyclopaedia Britannica* in the accuracy its scientific entries. (3) Even though *Nature* was careful not to claim that the collaborative online encyclopedia was equal or better than the prestigious *Britannica*, the article raised a storm.

(4) The radical philosophy behind Wikipedia is that anyone—or nearly—is free to contribute, or to edit existing articles in, its database. (5) Wikipedia's founders hope that this buzz of voluntary, undirected activity will lead constant improvement. (6) To keep Wikipedia from filling up with junk, though, in recent years they have had to start imposing more editorial control over its contributions than its earliest years.

Using Punctuation and Mechanics

MyCanadianCompLab

Visit MyCanadianCompLab at **mycanadiancomplab.ca** for

- Diagnostic tests
- Punctuation and mechanics exercises
- Other resources, including an eText version of this book

Chapter 23

PERIODS, QUESTION MARKS, AND EXCLAMATION MARKS

Periods, question marks, and **exclamation marks** are collectively called *end punctuation* because they occur at the ends of sentences.

I love you. Do you love me? I love you!

PERIODS

((•
AUDIO
LESSON
Section 1:
Big Ideas—
Punctuation
and Mechanics

23a When does a period end a sentence?

A **period** ends a statement, a mild command, or an INDIRECT QUESTION.* Never use a period to end a DIRECT QUESTION, a strong command, or an emphatic declaration.

((•
AUDIO
LESSON
Section 2:
Practice
Questions—
Punctuation
and
Mechanics

END OF A STATEMENT

A journey of a thousand leagues begins with a single step.

—Lao-tsu, *The Way of Lao-tsu*

MILD COMMAND

Put a gram of boldness into everything you do.

—Baltasar Gracian

((•
AUDIO
LESSON
Section 3:
Rapid
Review—
Punctuation
and
Mechanics

INDIRECT QUESTION

I asked if they wanted to climb Mt. Everest. [As an indirect question, this sentence reports that a question was asked. If it were a direct question, it would end with a question mark: I asked, "Do you want to climb Mt. Everest?"]

23b How do I use periods with abbreviations?

Most **abbreviations**, though not all, call for periods. Typical abbreviations with periods include *Mt., St., Dr., Mr., Ms., Mrs., Jr., Fri., Feb., a.m.,* and *p.m.* (For more about *a.m.* and *p.m.*, see Chapter 13, "Usage Glossary," and section 30j; for more about abbreviations in general, see 30i through 30l.)

ALERT: Spell out the word *professor* in ACADEMIC WRITING; never abbreviate it. •

---

*Words printed in SMALL CAPITAL LETTERS are discussed elsewhere in the text and are defined in the Terms Glossary at the back of the book.

Abbreviations without periods include the two-letter postal code abbreviations for the names of provinces and US states and some organizations and government agencies (for example, CBC and NFB).

Ms. Yuan, who works at **the NFB,** lectured to **Dr.** Benet's film class at 9:30 **a.m.**

● **ALERT:** When the period of an abbreviation falls at the end of a sentence that calls for a period, the period of the abbreviation serves also to end the sentence. If, however, your sentence ends in a question mark or an exclamation mark, put it after the period of the abbreviation.

The phone rang at 4:00 **a.m.**

It's upsetting to answer a wrong-number call at 4:00 **a.m.!**

Who would call at 4:00 **a.m.?** ●

QUESTION MARKS

23c   When do I use a question mark?

A **question mark** ends a **direct question**, one that quotes the exact words the speaker used. (In contrast, an **indirect question** reports a question and ends with a period.)

How many attempts have been made to climb Mt. Everest? [An indirect question would end with a period: *She wants to know how many attempts have been made to climb Mt. Everest.*]

● **ALERT:** Never use a question mark with a period, comma, semicolon, or colon.

NO   She asked, "How are you**?.**"

YES   She asked, "How are you**?**" ●

Each question in a series is followed by a question mark, whether or not each question is a complete sentence.

After the fierce storm, the mountain climbers debated what to do next. Turn back**?** Move on**?** Rest for a while**?**

● **ALERT:** When questions in a series are not complete sentences (as in the preceding example), you can choose whether to capitalize the first letter, but be consistent within each piece of writing. ●

Sometimes a statement or mild command is phrased as a question to be polite. In such cases, a question mark is optional, but be consistent in each piece of writing.

Would you please send me a copy**.**

23d   When can I use a question mark in parentheses?

The only time to use a question mark in parentheses (?) is if a date or other number is unknown or doubtful. Never use (?) to communicate that you're unsure of information.

Mary Astell, a British writer of pamphlets on women's rights, was born in 1666 (**?**) and died in 1731.

The word *about* is often a more graceful substitute for (?): *Mary Astell was born* **about** *1666.*

Also, never use (?) to communicate IRONY or sarcasm. Choose words to deliver your message.

> NO   Having altitude sickness is a pleasant (**?**) experience.
>
> YES   Having altitude sickness is **as** pleasant **as having a bad case of the flu.**

EXCLAMATION MARKS

23e   When do I use an exclamation mark?

An **exclamation mark** ends a strong command or an emphatic declaration. A strong command is a firm and direct order: *Look out behind you!* An emphatic declaration is a shocking or surprising statement: *There's been an accident!*

ⓘ ALERT: Never combine an exclamation mark with a period, comma, semicolon, or colon.

> NO   "There's been an accident**!**," she shouted.
>
> YES   "There's been an accident**!**" she shouted.
>
> YES   "There's been an accident," she shouted. [Use this form if you prefer not to use an exclamation mark.] ●

23f   What is considered overuse of exclamation marks?

In ACADEMIC WRITING, words, not exclamation marks, need to communicate the intensity of your message. Reserve exclamation marks for an emphatic declaration within a longer passage.

> When we were in Nepal, we tried each day to see Mt. Everest. But each day we failed. **Clouds defeated us!** The summit never emerged from a heavy overcast.

Also, using exclamation marks too frequently suggests an exaggerated sense of urgency.

> NO   Mountain climbing can be dangerous. You must know correct procedures**!** You must have the proper equipment**!** Otherwise, you could die**!**
>
> YES   Mountain climbing can be dangerous. You must know correct procedures**.** You must have the proper equipment**.** Otherwise, you could die**!**

Never use (!) to communicate amazement or sarcasm. Choose words to deliver your message.

> NO   At 8882 metres (**!**), Mt. Everest is the world's highest mountain. Yet, Chris (**!**) wants to climb it.
>
> YES   At **a majestic** 8882 metres, Mt. Everest is the world's highest mountain. Yet, Chris, **amazingly**, wants to climb it.

EXERCISE 23-1   Insert any needed periods, question marks, and exclamation marks and delete any unneeded ones. For help, consult all sections of this chapter.

> **EXAMPLE** Dr Madan Kataria, who calls himself the Giggling Guru (!), established the world's first laughter club in 1995.
>
> Dr. Madan Kataria, who calls himself the Giggling Guru, established the world's first laughter club in 1995.

1. More than 1000 (?) laughter clubs exist throughout the world, each seeking to promote health by reducing stress and strengthening the immune system!

2. Dr Madan Kataria, a physician in Bombay, India, developed a yoga-like (!) strategy based on group (!) laughter and then set up laughter clubs.

3. Laughter clubs say, "Yes!" when asked, "Is laughter the best medicine."

4. The clubs' activities include breathing and stretching exercises and playful (?) behaviours, such as performing the opera laugh (!), the chicken laugh (!), and the "Ho-Ho, Ha-Ha" (?) exercise.

5. According to the German psychologist Dr Michael Titze, "In the 1950s people used to laugh eighteen minutes a day (!), but today we laugh not more than six (?) minutes per day, despite huge rises in the standard of living."

EXERCISE 23-2   Insert needed periods, question marks, and exclamation marks. For help, consult all sections of this chapter.

New York's Ellis Island immigration facility is famous as the place where millions of newcomers arrived in the United States How many people have heard of its Canadian counterpart It may be better to speak of its Canadian counterparts, rather Before the age of airplane travel, there were two important entry points for immigrants taking the Atlantic route to Canada Pier 21 in Halifax, which opened in 1928, was the arrival point for more than one million new Canadians Grosse Île, a small island near Quebec City on the St Lawrence River, was still receiving immigrants when Pier 21 opened, although the island facility closed a few years later What a contrast these two locations make Grosse Île was a quarantine station for severely ill arrivals When it opened in 1832, cholera was raging in the slums of Europe English and Irish immigrants brought this feared disease to Canada Thousands died of cholera in Quebec City and Montreal, despite the quarantine Then, in 1847, more than ninety thousand Irish immigrants arrived, fleeing the potato famine in their homeland Thousands were infected with typhus; the medical staff led by Dr Douglas worked heroically but were unable to save many of the ill This unhappy history may have led Canadians to ignore Grosse Île's heritage until recently In contrast, Pier 21 is celebrated as the place where refugees fleeing Nazism and war reached a safe shore

Chapter 24

COMMAS

Common
Grammar
Errors: 13.
Missing or
Unnecessary
Commas

((•
AUDIO
LESSON
Section 1:
Big Ideas—
Punctuation
and Mechanics

((•
AUDIO LESSON
Section 2:
Practice
Questions—
Punctuation
and Mechanics

24a What is the role of the comma?

Commas are the most frequently used marks of punctuation, occurring twice as often as all other punctuation marks combined. A comma must be used in certain places, it must not be used in other places, and it's optional in still other places. This chapter helps you sort through the various rules.

For quick access to most answers when you have a comma question, consult Quick Reference 24.1. The sections in parentheses indicate where you can find fuller explanations.

QUICK REFERENCE 24.1

Key uses of commas

COMMAS WITH COORDINATING CONJUNCTIONS LINKING INDEPENDENT CLAUSES (24B)

Postcards are ideal for brief greetings, **and** they can also be miniature works of art. [*and* is a coordinating conjunction]

COMMAS AFTER INTRODUCTORY ELEMENTS (24C)

Although most postcards cost less than a dollar, one recently sold for thousands of dollars. [clause]

On postcard racks, several designs are usually available. [phrase]

For example, animals are timeless favourites. [transitional expression]

However, most cards show local landmarks. [word]

COMMAS WITH ITEMS IN A SERIES (24D)

Places, paintings, and people appear on postcards. [*and* between last two items]

Places, paintings, people, animals occupy dozens of display racks. [no *and* between last two items]

COMMAS WITH COORDINATE ADJECTIVES (24E)

Some postcards feature **appealing, dramatic** scenes.

NO COMMAS WITH CUMULATIVE ADJECTIVES (24E)

Other postcards feature **famous historical** scenes.

continued ➤

COMMAS WITH NONRESTRICTIVE ELEMENTS (24F)

Four years after the first postcard appeared, some governments began to issue pre-stamped postcards. [nonrestrictive element introduces independent clause]

The Golden Age of postcards, **which lasted from about 1900 to 1929,** yielded many especially valuable cards. [nonrestrictive element interrupts independent clause]

Collectors attend postcard shows, **which are similar to baseball-card shows.** [nonrestrictive element ends independent clause]

NO COMMAS WITH RESTRICTIVE ELEMENTS (24F)

Collectors **who attend these shows** may specialize in a particular kind of postcard. [restrictive clause]

COMMAS WITH QUOTED WORDS (24H)

One collector told me, "Attending a show is like digging for buried treasure." [quoted words at end of sentence]

"I always expect to find a priceless postcard," he said. [quoted words at start of sentence]

"Everyone there," he joked, "believes a million-dollar card is hidden in the next stack." [quoted words interrupted mid-sentence]

24b How do commas work with coordinating conjunctions?

Never use a comma when a coordinating conjunction links only two words, two PHRASES, or two DEPENDENT CLAUSES.

> NO   Habitat for Humanity depends on volunteers for **labour, and donations** to help with its construction projects. [*Labour* and *donations* are two words; the conjunction explains their relationship. No comma is needed.]

> YES   Habitat for Humanity depends on volunteers for **labour and donations** to help with its construction projects.

> NO   Each language has **a beauty of its own, and forms of expression** that are duplicated nowhere else. [*A beauty of its own* and *forms of expression* are only two phrases.]

> YES   Each language has **a beauty of its own and forms of expression** that are duplicated nowhere else.
> —Margaret Mead, "Unispeak"

When a coordinating conjunction links two or more INDEPENDENT CLAUSES, place a comma before the coordinating conjunction.

The sky turned dark grey, **and** the wind died suddenly.

The November morning had just begun, **but** it looked like dusk.

Shopkeepers closed their stores early, **for** they wanted to get home.

Soon high winds would start, **or** thick snow would begin silently.

Farmers could not continue harvesting, **nor** could they round up their animals in distant fields.

People on the road tried to reach safety, **yet** a few unlucky ones were stranded.

The firehouse whistle blew four times, **so** everyone knew a blizzard was closing in.

EXCEPTIONS

- When two independent clauses are very short and they contrast with each other, you can link them with a comma without using a coordinating conjunction: *Mosquitoes don't bite, they stab.* Some instructors consider this an error, so in ACADEMIC WRITING, you'll never be wrong if you use a period or semicolon (Chapter 25) instead of a comma.
- When one or both independent clauses linked by a coordinating conjunction happen to contain other commas, dropping the coordinating conjunction and using a semicolon instead of the comma can help clarify meaning.

> With temperatures below freezing, the snow did not melt; and **people** wondered, gazing at the white landscape, when they would see grass again.

ALERTS: (1) Never put a comma *after* a coordinating conjunction that joins independent clauses.

> NO   A house is renovated in two weeks **but,** an apartment takes a week.
>
> YES   A house is renovated in two weeks, **but** an apartment takes a week.

(2) Never use a comma alone between independent clauses, or you'll create the error known as a COMMA SPLICE (see Chapter 20).

> NO   Twenty centimetres of snow fell in two hours, driving was hazardous.
>
> YES   Twenty centimetres of snow fell in two hours, **and** driving was hazardous.

EXERCISE 24-1   Working individually or in a group, combine each pair of sentences using the coordinating conjunction shown in parentheses. Rearrange words when necessary. For help, consult 24b.

> **EXAMPLE** Children spend less time playing outdoors than ever before. That has been found to be a significant problem. (and)
>
> Children spend less time playing outdoors than ever before, **and** that has been found to be a significant problem.

1. If your parents ever said to you, "Go outside and burn off some energy," you should thank them. They did you a big favour. (for)

2. Spending time outside as children is good for people. Now there is scientific proof. (and)

3. As children play outside, their senses are stimulated. That helps them learn in numerous ways. (and)

4. For example, children's vision is fully stimulated by being outside. They should spend more time playing outdoors than reading or watching TV, which stimulates only a narrow part of their vision. (so)

5. When children spend time playing outside, they may engage in intense physical activity. They may be less active but still discover the magic of the natural world. (or)

6. The outdoors can be a child's greatest source of stimulation. Many parents don't realize this. (yet)

7. Sadly enough, recess at many schools has been reduced. Children miss out on an opportunity for what scientists now know is another form of education. (so)

8. But as people learn more about the many benefits of outdoor play for children, parents will not allow children to spend so much time on indoor activities. Schools will not continue to reduce recess time. (nor)

9. Instead, school leaders may heed renowned educators such as Maria Montessori, Rudolf Steiner, and Howard Gardner, who understood the close connection between movement and learning. Children will once again enjoy the benefits of a longer recess. (and)

10. Enjoying the natural world may be part of our genetic makeup. It only makes sense that children should be encouraged to get their vitamin D from sunlight and to use up some energy. (so)

How do commas work with introductory clauses, phrases, and words?

A comma follows any introductory element that comes before an INDEPENDENT CLAUSE. An introductory element can be a CLAUSE, PHRASE, or words—that is, an element that is not a sentence by itself.

When the topic is dieting, many people say sugar craving is their worst problem. [introductory dependent clause]

Between 1544 and 1818, sugar refineries appeared in London, New York, and Halifax. [introductory prepositional phrase]

Beginning in infancy, we develop lifelong tastes for sweet foods. [introductory participial phrase]

Sweets being a temptation for many adults, most parents avoid commercial baby foods that contain sugar. [introductory absolute phrase]

For example, fructose comes from fruit, but it's still sugar. [introductory transitional expression]

Nevertheless, many people think fructose isn't harmful. [introductory conjunctive adverb]

To satisfy a craving for ice cream, even timid people sometimes brave midnight streets. [introductory infinitive phrase]

EXCEPTION

When an introductory element is short, and the sentence can be understood easily, some writers omit the comma. However, in ACADEMIC WRITING, you'll never be wrong if you use the comma.

> In 1921, William Lyon Mackenzie King became prime minister for the first time. [preferred]

> In 1921 William Lyon Mackenzie King became prime minister for the first time.

An **interjection** is an introductory word that conveys surprise or other emotions. Use a comma after an interjection at the beginning of a sentence: ***Oh,*** *we didn't realize that you're allergic to cats.* To express strong emotion, use an exclamation mark (23e).

ALERT: Use a comma before and after a transitional expression that falls in the middle of a sentence. When the transitional expression starts a sentence, follow it with a comma. When the transitional expression ends a sentence, put a comma before it.

> **By the way,** the parade begins at noon. [introductory transitional expression with comma after it]
>
> The parade, **by the way,** begins at noon. [transitional expression with comma before and after it, in middle of sentence]
>
> The parade begins at noon, **by the way.** [transitional expression with comma before it, at end of sentence]
>
> **However,** our float isn't finished. [introductory conjunctive adverb with comma after it]
>
> Our float, **however,** isn't finished. [conjunctive adverb with comma before and after it, in middle of sentence]
>
> Our float isn't finished, **however.** [conjunctive adverb with comma before it, at end of sentence]? ●

EXERCISE 24-2 Working individually or with a group, combine each set of sentences into one sentence according to the direction in parentheses. Use a comma after the introductory element. You can add, delete, and rearrange words as needed. For help, consult 24c.

> **EXAMPLE** People have known that humour is good for them. They have known this for a long time. (Begin with *for a long time*.)
>
> **For a long time,** people have known that humour is good for them.

1. People laugh. Scientists study them to find out what actually happens. (Begin with *when*.)
2. Scientists track our physiological reactions. They discover the chemicals we produce while we are laughing. (Begin with *in fact*.)
3. Our brains use dopamine when we laugh. Dopamine is a chemical we produce that makes us feel good. (Begin with *produced*.)
4. We sometimes activate our tear ducts by laughing. That reduces stress. (Begin with *interestingly*.)
5. Scientists tested people's saliva immediately after they laughed. Scientists concluded that immune systems may benefit from laughter. (Begin with *immediately*.)
6. Blood pressure and heart rates tend to go below baseline after we laugh. People should be happy about this effect because that's what happens after we exercise well. (Begin with *although*.)
7. Laughter causes the inner lining of our blood vessels to expand. This expansion produces beneficial chemicals in our bodies. (Begin with *in addition*.)
8. One of these chemicals is nitric oxide. It reduces inflammation and clotting. (Begin with *in the human body*.)
9. Laughter may even help with pain management. Laughter seems to have an analgesic effect. (Begin with *seeming*.)
10. Humour has so many physical benefits, and it makes us feel better. Try to enjoy a few laughs every day. (Begin with *because*.)

Serial
Commas

A **series** is a group of three or more elements—words, PHRASES, or CLAUSES—that match in grammatical form and are of equal importance in a sentence.

Marriage requires **sexual, financial, and emotional** discipline.
> —Anne Roiphe, "Why Marriages Fail"

Culture is a way of **thinking, feeling, believing**.
> —Clyde Kluckhohn, *Mirror for Man*

My love of flying goes back to those early days **of roller skates, of swings, and of bicycles**.
> —Tresa Wiggins, student

We have been taught **that children develop by ages and stages, that the steps are pretty much the same for everybody, and that to grow out of the limited behavior of childhood, we must climb them all**.

> —Gail Sheehy, *Passages*

Many authorities omit the comma between the next to last item of a series and the coordinating conjunction. This handbook uses the comma here (a style known as the serial comma) for clarity. Check with your instructor for his or her preference.

> NO   Ivan wears only **natural fibres, nylon and Thinsulate.** [This appears to say that nylon and Thinsulate are natural fibres.]

> YES   Ivan wears only **natural fibres, nylon, and Thinsulate.** [This makes it clear that Ivan wears clothes made from three types of fabric.]

At all times, however, follow the "toast, juice, and ham and eggs rule." That is, when one of the items in a series contains *and,* don't use a comma in that item.

When items in a series contain commas or other punctuation, separate them with semicolons instead of commas (25e).

> If it's a bakery, they have to sell cake; if it's a photography shop, they have to develop film; and if it's a dry-goods store, they have to sell warm underwear.
> —Art Buchwald, "Birth Control for Banks"

Numbered or lettered lists within a sentence are considered items in a series. With three or more items, use commas (or semicolons if the items themselves contain commas) to separate them.

> To file your insurance claim, please enclose (1) a letter requesting payment, (2) a police report about the robbery, **and** (3) proof of purchase of the items you say are missing.

ALERT: In a series, never use a comma before the first item or after the last item, unless a different rule makes it necessary.

> NO   Many **artists, writers, and composers, have indulged** in daydreaming.

> YES   Many artists, writers, and composers have indulged in daydreaming.

|NO| Such dreamers include, Miró, Debussy, Dostoevsky, and Dickinson.|
|YES| Such dreamers include Miró, Debussy, Dostoevsky, and Dickinson.|
|YES| Such dreamers include, **of course,** Miró, Debussy, Dostoevsky, and Dickinson. [As a transitional expression, *of course* is set off from the rest of the sentence by commas before and after it (24c).] ●|

EXERCISE 24-3   Insert commas to separate the items in a series. If a sentence needs no commas, explain why. For help, consult 24d.

> **EXAMPLE** Our longest serving prime minister, William Lyon Mackenzie King, left us the unemployment insurance program, the first Citizenship Act and a legacy of puzzling ambiguity.
>
> Our longest serving prime minister, William Lyon Mackenzie King, left us the unemployment insurance program, the first Citizenship Act, and a legacy of puzzling ambiguity.

1. During World War II, pulled by English-Canadian loyalty to the Allies pushed by French-Canadian protests against conscription and hounded by generals who needed more soldiers, King announced, "Conscription if necessary, but not necessarily conscription."

2. When he heard how severely London was being bombed in the Blitz, King asked Lester Pearson to send him pieces of damaged buildings to decorate his garden: souvenirs of a city that was being pounded burned shattered terrorized.

3. Although he was often accompanied by women on public occasions, King never married or lived with a woman friend, nor did he have children.

4. In public, King was a colourless, pragmatic politician, yet his diaries reveal a man obsessed by strange fads fears and enthusiasms.

5. Since his death in 1950, King's reputation has suffered, for his interest in attending seances communing with his dead mother and asking political advice from his dog has drawn embarrassing attention to his private life.

((⦿   **24e** **How do commas work with coordinate adjectives?**

Commas between Coordinate Adjectives

Coordinate adjectives are two or more ADJECTIVES of equal weight that modify a NOUN. In contrast, **cumulative adjectives** build meaning from word to word, as they move toward the noun. The key to applying this rule is recognizing when adjectives are coordinate and when they aren't. Quick Reference 24.2 tells you how.

The audience cheered when the **pulsating, rhythmic** music filled the stadium. [*Pulsating* and *rhythmic* are coordinate adjectives.]

Each band had a **distinctive musical** style. [*Distinctive* and *musical* aren't coordinate adjectives.]

❶ **ALERT:** Don't put a comma between a final coordinate adjective and the noun it modifies.

|NO| Hundreds of **roaring, cheering, yelling, fans** filled the stadium.|
|YES| Hundreds of **roaring, cheering, yelling fans** filled the stadium. ●|

Tests for coordinate and cumulative adjectives

If either one of these tests works, the adjectives are coordinate and require a comma between them.

- Can the order of the adjectives be reversed without changing the meaning or creating nonsense? If yes, use a comma.

  NO   The concert featured **new several** bands. [*New several* makes nonsense.]

  YES   The **huge, restless** crowd waited for the concert to begin. [*Restless, huge* still carries the same meaning, so these coordinate adjectives.]

- Can *and* be sensibly inserted between the adjectives? If yes, use a comma.

  NO   The concert featured **several and new** bands. [*Several and new* makes no sense.]

  YES   The **huge and restless** crowd waited. [Modifier *huge and restless* makes sense, so these are coordinate adjectives.]

EXERCISE 24-4   Insert commas to separate coordinate adjectives. If a sentence needs no commas, explain why. For help, consult 24e.

EXAMPLE   Only corn grown for popcorn pops consistently because all other kinds of corn lack tough enamel-like shells.

Only corn grown for popcorn pops consistently because all other kinds of corn lack *tough, enamel-like* shells.

1. The outside of an unpopped popcorn kernel is a hard plastic-like coating.
2. Inside an unpopped kernel is a soft starchy substance combined with water.
3. Applying heat causes the water molecules to expand until the pressure pops the dark yellow kernel.
4. The popped kernel turns itself inside out and absorbs air into its white pulpy matter.
5. The thinner softer shells of non-popping corn don't allow water to heat to the high popping temperature.

24f   How do commas work with nonrestrictive elements?

A **restrictive element** contains information (a descriptive word, clause, or phrase) that's essential for a sentence to deliver its message; thus, it is often called an *essential element*. A **nonrestrictive element** contains information that's not essential for a sentence to deliver its meaning, and therefore, it is often called a *nonessential element*. The key is in recognizing what's essential (restrictive) and what's nonessential (nonrestrictive) in a sentence. Quick Reference 24.3 defines and explains the differences in the meanings of these terms.

Restrictive and nonrestrictive defined

RESTRICTIVE

A restrictive element contains information essential for the sentence to deliver its message. By being essential, the words in the element limit—that is, "restrict"—the meaning in some way. Don't use commas with restrictive elements.

> Some provinces retest drivers **who are over sixty-five** to check their driving competency.

The information *who are over sixty-five* is essential to understanding the sentence because it limits or restricts the meaning of *drivers* to only those over the age of sixty-five. Drivers *under* sixty-five are not included. To check whether an element is essential, drop it and read the sentence. If the meaning of the sentence changes, then the information element is essential in delivering the message intended in the sentence. This means the element is restrictive (essential), and commas are not used.

NONRESTRICTIVE

A nonrestrictive element contains information that's *not* essential for the sentence to deliver its message. By being nonessential, the words in the element don't limit—or "restrict"—the meaning. Use commas with nonrestrictive (nonessential) elements.

> My parents, **who are both over sixty-five,** took a defensive-driving course.

The information *who are both over sixty-five* is not essential because the words *my parents* carry the sentence's message so that we know who took a defensive-driving course. (Information about their age is "extra" to this message, so commas are required.)

Quick Reference 24.4 shows the pattern for comma use with nonrestrictive elements. The pattern for restrictive elements calls for no commas.

Commas with nonrestrictive elements

> **Nonrestrictive element,** independent clause.
> Beginning of independent clause, **nonrestrictive element,** end of independent clause.
> Independent clause, **nonrestrictive element**.

Restrictive and nonrestrictive elements can fall at the beginning, in the middle, or at the end of a sentence. To test whether an element is nonrestrictive, read the sentence without the element. If the meaning of the sentence does not change, the element is nonrestrictive.

MORE EXAMPLES OF RESTRICTIVE ELEMENTS

Some people **in my neighbourhood** enjoy jogging. [The reader needs the information *in my neighbourhood* to know which people enjoy jogging. The information is essential, so no commas are used.]

Some people **who are in excellent physical condition** enjoy jogging. [The reader needs the information *who are in excellent physical condition* to know which people enjoy jogging. The information is essential, so no commas are used.]

The agricultural scientist **Wendy Singh** has developed a new fertilization technique. [*Wendy Singh* is essential to identify exactly which agricultural scientist developed the new technique, so no commas are used.]

MORE EXAMPLES OF NONRESTRICTIVE ELEMENTS

An energetic person, Anna Hom enjoys jogging. [Without knowing that Anna Hom is *an energetic person,* the reader can understand that she enjoys jogging. The information is nonessential, so a comma is used.]

Anna Hom**, who is in excellent physical condition,** enjoys jogging. [Without knowing Anna Hom's *physical condition,* the reader can understand that Anna Hom enjoys jogging. The information is nonessential, so commas are used.]

Anna Hom enjoys jogging**, which is also Adam's favourite pastime**. [Without knowing about *Adam's favourite pastime,* the reader can understand that Anna Hom enjoys jogging. The information is nonessential, so commas are used.]

The agricultural scientist**, a new breed of farmer,** explains how to control a farming environment. [Without knowing that the scientist is *a new breed of farmer,* the reader can understand that the agricultural scientist explains how to control a farming environment. The information is nonessential, so commas are used.]

EXERCISE 24-5   Using your knowledge of restrictive and nonrestrictive elements, insert commas as needed. If a sentence is correct, explain why. For help, consult 24f.

> **EXAMPLE** During the summer when butterflies are most active gardeners can attract them by planting the right flowers.
>
> During the summer, when butterflies are most active, gardeners can attract them by planting the right flowers.

1. In spring as birds and bees look for water and food certain plants and trees provide those needs and thus attract the greatest number of airborne visitors.
2. Gardeners who learn to attract birds may find they have fewer problems with insects and other unwelcome pests.
3. During periods of suburban sprawl when cities eat up more and more land birds adapt by putting their nests in buildings.
4. Birds are attracted to pines and evergreens where they can find food and shelter.
5. Hungry birds who are not picky will enjoy a feeder stocked with sunflower seeds.
6. Birds also need to eat insects which provide a higher protein content than seeds.
7. Some plants such as milkweed and lantana are ideal for attracting butterflies.
8. Because they have the nectar that butterflies want these plants enhance any butterfly garden.
9. As butterflies pass by a garden looking for bright colours and strong fragrances they will notice flowers planted in large clumps.
10. Gardens that are favourable to birds and butterflies will also invite honeybees and other pollinators.

24g How do commas set off parenthetical expressions, contrasts, words of direct address, and tag sentences?

Parenthetical expressions are "asides." They add information but aren't necessary for understanding the message of a sentence. Set them off with parentheses or commas.

Sales of Canadian tobacco (**according to recent statistics**) have been steadily decreasing.

Tobacco farmers, **it is clear,** must find other means of support.

Expressions of **contrast** state what is *not* the case. Set them off with commas.

Feeding the world's population is a serious, **though not impossible,** problem.

We must work against world hunger continuously, **not only when famines strike**.

Words of **direct address** name the person or group being spoken to (addressed). Set them off with commas.

Join me, **brothers and sisters,** to end hunger.

Your contribution to the Relief Fund, **Steve,** will help us greatly.

A **tag sentence** is a normal sentence that ends with a "tag," an attached phrase or question. Set off a tag with a comma. When the tag is a question, the sentence ends with a question mark. This holds whether or not the **tag question** is formed with a CONTRACTION.

Canadians' response to the Manitoba flood was impressive, **wasn't it?**

The response to future crises will be as generous, **I hope.**

EXERCISE 24-6 Add commas to set off any parenthetical or contrasting elements, words of direct address, and tag sentences. Adjust end punctuation as necessary. For help, consult 24g.

EXAMPLE Writer's block it seems to me is a misunderstood phenomenon.

Writer's block, it seems to me, is a misunderstood phenomenon.

1. An inability to write some say stems from lack of discipline and a tendency to procrastinate.
2. In other words the only way to overcome writer's block is to exert more willpower.
3. But writer's block is a complex psychological event that happens to conscientious people not just procrastinators.
4. Such people strangely enough are often unconsciously rebelling against their own self-tyranny and rigid standards of perfection.
5. If I told you my fellow writer that all it takes to start writing again is to quit punishing yourself, you would think I was crazy wouldn't you?

24h How do commas work with quoted words?

Explanatory words are words such as *said, stated, declared,* and others that introduce DIRECT DISCOURSE. When they fall in the same sentence, quoted words are set off from explanatory words.

Speaking of ideal love, the poet William Blake wrote, "Love seeketh not itself to please."

"My love is a fever," said William Shakespeare about love's passion.

"I love no love," proclaimed the poet Mary Coleridge, "but thee."

EXCEPTION

When the quoted words are blended into the grammatical structure of your sentence, don't use commas to set them off. These are instances of INDIRECT DISCOURSE, usually occurring with *as* and *that*.

> The duke describes the duchess **as** "too soon made glad."
>
> The duchess insists **that** "appearing glad often is but a deception."

🛈 **ALERT:** When the quoted words end with an exclamation mark or a question mark, retain that original punctuation, even if explanatory words follow.

QUOTED WORDS	"*O Romeo! Romeo!*"
NO	"O Romeo! Romeo**!,**" whispered Juliet from her window.
NO	"O Romeo! Romeo**,**" whispered Juliet from her window.
YES	"O Romeo! Romeo**!**" whispered Juliet from her window.
QUOTED WORDS	"*Wherefore art thou Romeo?*"
NO	"Wherefore art thou Romeo**?,**" continued Juliet as she thought of fate's cruel tricks.
NO	"Wherefore art thou Romeo**,**" continued Juliet as she thought of fate's cruel tricks.
YES	"Wherefore art thou Romeo**?**" continued Juliet as she thought of fate's cruel tricks. ●

EXERCISE 24-7   Punctuate the following dialogue correctly. If a sentence is correct, explain why. For help, consult 24h.

> **EXAMPLE**   "Can you tell me just one thing?," asked the tourist.
>   "Can you tell me just one thing?" asked the tourist.

1. "I'm happy to answer any questions you have" said the rancher to the tourist.
2. "Well, then" said the tourist "I'd like to know how you make ends meet on such a tiny ranch."
3. "Do you see that man leaning against the shed over there?" asked the rancher, pointing with a twig.
4. The rancher continued "He works for me, but I don't pay him any money. Instead, I promised him that after two years of work, he will own the ranch."
5. "Then, I'll work for him, and in two more years, the ranch will be mine again!," said the rancher with a smile.

<h2>24i   How do commas work in dates, names, addresses, correspondence, and numbers?</h2>

When you write dates, names, addresses, correspondence, and numbers, use commas according to accepted practice. Quick Reference 24.5 through 24.8 provide some guidelines.

Commas with dates

- Use a comma between the date and the year: **April 11, 2000.**
- Use a comma between the day and the date: **Tuesday, April 11, 2000.**
- Within a sentence, use a comma on both sides of the year in a full date: The morning of **April 11, 2000,** saw RIM introduce the first palm-sized BlackBerry.
- Never use a comma when only the month and year, or the month and day, are given. Also, never use a comma between the season and year.

    YES   A larger BlackBerry had come out in **January 1999** in North America.

    YES   Its shareholders remember the date **April 11** fondly.

    YES   The **spring 2000** launch of its slim new device gave a big boost to RIM.

- Never use a comma in an inverted date (day-month-year).

    YES   RIM's quarterly report of **16 September 2011** painted a darker picture for the company.

Commas with names, places, and addresses

- When an abbreviated academic degree *(MD, PhD)*comes after a person's name, use a comma between the name and the title *(Angie Eng, MD)*, and also after the title if other words follow in the sentence: *The jury listened closely to the expert testimony of **Angie Eng, MD, last week.***
- When an indicator of birth order or succession *(Jr., Sr., III, IV)* follows a name, never use a comma: *Martin Luther **King Jr.*** or *Henry **Ford II***
- When you invert a person's name, use a comma to separate the last name from the first: ***Troyka, David***
- When city and province or territory names are written together, use a comma to separate them: ***Estevan, Saskatchewan**. If the city and province fall within a sentence, use a comma after the province as well: The town of **Estevan, Saskatchewan,** recorded the highest number of hours of sunshine in Canada in 1993.*
- When a complete address is part of a sentence, use a comma to separate all the items, except the postal code and the standard abbreviation for the province. The postal code follows the province after a space and is not followed by a comma: *I wrote to **Shelly Kupperman, 1001 Rule Road, Mississauga ON L5A 2Z2** for more information about the comma.*

Commas in correspondence

- For the opening of an informal letter, use a comma: **Dear Betty,**
- For the opening of a business or formal letter, use a colon:

  Dear Ms. Kiviat:
- For the close of a letter, use a comma:

  Sincerely yours,   Best regards,   Love,

Commas with numbers

SI—the international system of metric measurements used in Canada—does not use commas in numbers; it uses spaces to separate sets of three digits. Nevertheless, many people still use commas. This section explains both number systems.

RULES FOR NUMBERS IN SI

- Counting from the right, put a space after every three digits in numbers with more than four digits.

  72 867   150 567 066
- In four-digit numbers, a space is optional for money, distance, amounts, and most other measurements. Be consistent within each piece of writing.

  $1867 $1 867

  1867 km   1 867 km

  1867 potatoes   1 867 potatoes

  Never use a space in a four-digit year: **1990.** (*Note:* If the year has five digits or more, do insert a space: **25 000** BCE. Always use a space in four-digit numbers when they are aligned in columns in a table or a chart.

RULES FOR NUMBERS IN SYSTEMS USING COMMAS

- Counting from the right, put a comma after every three digits in numbers with more than four digits.

  72,867   150,567,066
- A comma is optional in four-digit numbers. Be consistent within each piece of writing.

  $1867 $1,867

  1867 km   1,867 km

  1867 potatoes   1,867 potatoes

continued ➤

- Never use a comma in a four-digit year: **1990** (*Note:* If the year has five digits or more, do use a comma: **25,000** BCE.)
- Never use a comma in an address of four digits or more: ***12161 Dean Drive***
- Never use a comma in a page number of four digits or more: ***see page 1338***
- Use a comma to separate related imperial measurements written as words: ***five feet, four inches***
- Use a comma to separate a scene from an act in a play: ***act II, scene iv*** (or ***act 2, scene 4***)
- Use a comma to separate references to a page and a line: ***page 10, line 6***

EXERCISE 24-8   Insert commas where they are needed. For help, consult 24i.

> **EXAMPLE** The heaviest hailstone recorded in Canada fell on Cedoux Saskatchewan.
>
> The heaviest hailstone recorded in Canada fell on Cedoux, Saskatchewan.

1. With a rainfall of 6655 mm, Henderson Lake British Columbia has the most annual precipitation in the country.
2. Burgeo Newfoundland has the second highest average annual precipitation with 1699.7 mm.
3. The warmest temperature in Canada—45 degrees Celsius—was recorded on July 5 1937 at Midale Saskatchewan.
4. Windsor Ontario with more than 200000 population holds the record for the highest average number of days per year with thunderstorms: 34 days.
5. Snag Yukon Territory has the record for the coldest temperature ever recorded in Canada; it was minus 63 degrees Celsius on February 3 1947.

24j How do commas clarify meaning?

A comma is sometimes needed to clarify the meaning of a sentence, even though no rule calls for one. A better solution is to revise the sentence.

NO   Of the gymnastic team's twenty five were injured.

YES   Of the gymnastic team's **twenty, five** were injured.

YES   Of **twenty on** the gymnastic team, five were injured. [preferred]

NO   Those who can practise many hours a day.

YES   **Those who can,** practise many hours a day.

YES   **They** practise many hours a day **when they can**. [preferred]

NO   George dressed and performed for the sellout crowd.

YES   **George dressed,** and performed for the sellout crowd.

YES   **After** George dressed, **he** performed for the sellout crowd. [preferred]

EXERCISE 24-9 Working individually or with a group, insert commas to prevent misreading. For help, consult 24j.

> **EXAMPLE** Tracking and measuring hurricanes say scientists are still inexact sciences.
>
> Tracking and measuring hurricanes, say scientists, are still inexact sciences.

1. Lasting for thirteen days in August 1992 Hurricane Andrew after 2005's Katrina was the second most expensive hurricane.

2. Andrew was rated a category four smaller than 2005's Katrina when it made landfall in south Florida.

3. The highest gust officially recorded 262 kilometres per hour at 40 metres above the ground occurred before Andrew shut down the measuring devices that were tracking its intensity.

4. The thousands of vortexes within Andrew as with many high-intensity storms are what caused the worst damage.

5. Andrew difficult to measure accurately was upgraded from a category four to a category five hurricane ten years after it occurred.

24k How can I avoid misusing commas?

Most comma misuses are overuses—inserting a comma where one is unnecessary. This section summarizes this chapter's Alert notes and lists other frequent misuses of the comma.

When advice against overusing a comma clashes with a rule requiring one, follow the rule that requires the comma.

> Banff, Alberta, attracts thousands of tourists each year. [Although the comma after *Alberta* separates the subject and verb, the comma is correct because it is required to set off a city–province combination within a sentence (24i).]

AUDIO LESSON Section 3: Rapid Review—Punctuation and Mechanics

Writing in Action: Comma Problems and Word Processing

24k.1 Commas with coordinating conjunctions

Never use a comma after a COORDINATING CONJUNCTION that joins two INDEPENDENT CLAUSES, unless another rule makes it necessary (24b). Also, don't use a comma to separate two items joined with a coordinating conjunction—there must be at least three (24d).

> NO The sky was dark grey **and,** it looked like dusk.
>
> YES The sky was dark grey**, and** it looked like dusk.

> NO **The moon, and the stars** were shining last night.
>
> YES **The moon and the stars** were shining last night.

24k.2 Commas with subordinating conjunctions and prepositions

Never put a comma after a SUBORDINATING CONJUNCTION or a PREPOSITION, unless another rule makes it necessary.

> NO **Although,** the storm brought high winds, it did no damage.
>
> YES **Although the storm brought high winds,** it did no damage. [comma follows full subordinated dependent clause, not the subordinate conjunction that begins it]

NO	The storm did no damage **although,** it brought high winds.
YES	The storm did no damage **although it brought high winds.** [no comma after a subordinating conjunction]
NO	People expected worse **between,** the high winds and the heavy downpour.
YES	People expected worse **between the high winds and the heavy downpour.** [preposition begins sentence element that needs no comma before or after]

24k.3   Commas in a series

Never use a comma before the first, or after the last, item in a series, unless another rule makes it necessary (24d).

NO	This October Ivan wore**, galoshes, sneakers,** and **sandals** to school.
NO	This October Ivan wore **galoshes, sneakers,** and **sandals,** to school.
YES	This October Ivan wore **galoshes, sneakers,** and **sandals** to school.

Never put a comma between a final COORDINATE ADJECTIVE and the NOUN that the adjectives modify. Also, don't use a comma between adjectives that are not coordinate (24e).

NO	He wore an **old, baggy, sweater.**
YES	He wore an **old, baggy sweater.** [coordinate adjectives]
NO	He has **several, new sweaters.**
YES	He has **several new sweaters.** [noncoordinate, or cumulative, adjectives]

24k.4   Commas with restrictive elements

Never use a comma to set off a RESTRICTIVE (essential) element from the rest of a sentence (24f).

NO	**Vegetables, stir-fried in a wok,** are crisp and flavourful. [The words *stir-fried in a wok* are essential, so they are not set off with commas.]
YES	**Vegetables stir-fried in a wok** are crisp and flavourful.

24k.5   Commas with quotations

Never use a comma to set off INDIRECT DISCOURSE; use a comma only with DIRECT DISCOURSE (24h).

NO	Jon said **that, he likes** stir-fried vegetables.
YES	Jon said **that he likes** stir-fried vegetables.
YES	**Jon said,** "**I like** stir-fried vegetables."

24k.6   Commas that separate a subject from its verb, a verb from its object, or a preposition from its object

A comma does not make sense between a subject and its verb, a verb and its object, or a preposition and its object, though in some cases another comma rule might supersede this guideline (as in the first example in section 24k).

NO   **The National Aircraft Museum, attracts** enthusiasts from all over Canada. [As a rule, a comma doesn't separate a subject from its verb.]

YES   **The National Aircraft Museum attracts** enthusiasts from all over Canada.

NO   The many small airplanes developed in Canada **include, the de Havilland Otter and Dash 7.** [As a rule, a comma doesn't separate a verb from its object.]

YES   The many small airplanes developed in Canada **include the de Havilland Otter and Dash 7.**

NO   The Twin Otter did much to open up the Arctic **in, the mid-twentieth century.** [As a rule, a comma doesn't separate a preposition from its object.]

YES   The Twin Otter did much to open up the Arctic **in the mid-twentieth century.**

EXERCISE 24-10   Some commas have been deliberately misused in these sentences. Consulting 24k and the other sections in this chapter that are referred to in 24k, delete unneeded commas. If a sentence is correct, circle its number.

EXAMPLE   The "Persons Case" is the name of the court case, that finally gave women in Canada the right to serve in the Senate.

The "Persons Case" is the name of the court case that finally gave women in Canada the right to serve in the Senate.

1. In 1919, Judge Emily Murphy asked the prime minister to appoint a woman to the Senate but, she received a disappointing reply.

2. Prime Minister Borden informed her that only "persons" could sit in the Senate, and, the 1867 British North America Act did not recognize women as persons.

3. Murphy, and four other women petitioned the Supreme Court of Canada to decide if the word *persons* in the BNA Act, which served as Canada's constitution, included female persons.

4. After many, long weeks of deliberation, the Court said that, the BNA Act did not count women as persons.

5. The basis of the Court's decision was, the argument that the authors of the 1867 Act, who had not given women the vote, never intended them to become senators.

6. In response, one petitioner tartly expressed the disappointment, shock, and surprise of all the women "who had not known they were not persons" until the Court told them so.

7. The five, anxious petitioners could still appeal the decision of Canada's Supreme Court to, the Privy Council in London.

8. The Privy Council ruled in 1929 that the term *persons*, must be understood in the BNA Act to include women; further, it called, the exclusion of women from politics "a relic of days more barbarous than ours."

9. Ironically, women, had already won the right to be elected to Parliament and to every provincial legislature except Quebec's.

10. To commemorate this court case, someone, who has worked to achieve justice and equality, each year is presented with the cleverly named Persons Award.

241 How can I avoid comma errors?

You can avoid most comma errors with these two bits of advice:

- As you write or reread what you've written, never insert a comma simply because you happen to pause to think or take a breath before moving on. Pausing isn't a reliable guide for writers, although that myth continues to thrive. People's breathing rhythms, accents, and thinking patterns vary greatly.

- As you're writing, if you're unsure about a comma, insert it and circle the spot. Later, when you're EDITING, check this handbook for the rule that applies.

Chapter 25

SEMICOLONS

25a What are the uses of a semicolon?

While a period signals the complete separation of INDEPENDENT CLAUSES, a semicolon indicates only a partial ("semi") separation. Use a semicolon in only two situations. A semicolon can replace a period between sentences that are closely related in meaning (25b and 25c). Also, a semicolon belongs between sentence structures that already contain one or more commas (25d) and with certain lists (25e). Quick Reference 25.1 shows differents patterns for using semicolons.

((•
Colons and
Semicolons

QUICK REFERENCE 25.1

Semicolon patterns

- Independent clause; independent clause. [25b]
- Independent clause; conjuctive adverb, independent clause. [25c]
- Independent clause; transitional expression, independent clause. [25c]
- Independent clause, one that contains a comma; coordinating conjunction followed by independent clause. [25d]
- Independent clause; coordinating conjunction followed by independent clause, one that contains a comma. [25d]
- Independent clause, one that contains a comma; coordinating conjunction followed by independent clause, one that contains a comma [25d]
- Independent clause containing a series of items, any of which contains a comma; another item in the series; and another item in the series. [25e]

25b When can I use a semicolon, instead of a period, between independent clauses?

The choice between a period and a semicolon for separating independent clauses depends on whether your meaning is better communicated by a complete separation (period) or a partial separation (semicolon).

British Columbia has some of the wettest territory in Canada; it also has some of the driest.

ALERT: Never use a comma alone between independent clauses—this rule will prevent you from creating the error known as a COMMA SPLICE (Chapter 20). ●

25c When else can I use a semicolon between independent clauses?

When the second of a set of independent clauses closely related in meaning starts with a CONJUNCTIVE ADVERB or a TRANSITIONAL EXPRESSION, you can choose to separate the clauses with a semicolon instead of a period. Also, insert a comma following a conjunctive adverb or transitional expression that starts an independent clause. Although some writers today omit the comma after short words (*then, next, soon*), the rule remains for most ACADEMIC WRITING.

> The average annual rainfall in the Okanagan Valley is less than 40 cm**; nevertheless,** it lies in the shadow of the rainy Cascade Mountains. [conjunctive adverb]

> Irrigation came to the semidesert valley in the 1930s**; as a result,** it now produces much of Canada's fruit and wine. [transitional expression]

ALERT: Never use only a comma between independent clauses that are connected by a conjunctive adverb or word of transition—this rule will prevent you from creating the error known as a COMMA SPLICE. ●

25d How do semicolons work with coordinating conjunctions?

As a general rule, when INDEPENDENT CLAUSES are linked by a COORDINATING CONJUNCTION, good practice calls for a comma, not a period or semicolon, before the coordinating conjunction (24b). However, when one or more of the independent clauses already contain a comma, link the independent clauses by substituting a semicolon for the period. This can help your reader see the relationship between the ideas more clearly.

> Summers are long, hot, and dry in the Okanagan Valley**; yet** visitors can ski down the surrounding mountains all summer long.

> The Okanagan was once famous for its ranches**; and** ranches, including some of Canada's oldest, still stretch out over its broad, dry plain.

> A tour operator in the British Columbia interior offers a package that includes skiing, either downhill or cross-country, in the morning**; but** the afternoon activities it offers are soccer, tennis, and other warm-weather sports.

25e When should I use semicolons between items in a series?

Serial Commas

When a sentence contains a series of items that are long or that already contain one or more commas, separate the items with semicolons. Punctuating this way groups the elements so that your reader can see where one item ends and the next begins.

> Alexander Mackenzie's overland voyage to the Pacific took him through grassy uplands, steep canyons, and tangled swamp**;** into the habitats of the grizzly bear, bald eagle, and sea otter**; and** down rivers that required running rapids, portaging, and even towing his canoe.

NOT USING A SEMICOLON AFTER AN INTRODUCTORY PHRASE

If you use a semicolon after an introductory PHRASE, you create the error known as a SENTENCE FRAGMENT (Chapter 19).

> NO **Sent by the North West Company in 1793;** Mackenzie hoped to locate the great river whose mouth Captain Cook thought he had seen fifteen years earlier.

> YES **Sent by the North West Company in 1793,** Mackenzie hoped to locate the great river whose mouth Captain Cook thought he had seen fifteen years earlier.

NOT USING A SEMICOLON AFTER A DEPENDENT CLAUSE

If you use a semicolon after a DEPENDENT CLAUSE, you create the error known as a sentence fragment.

> NO **Although the expedition was trespassing on valuable Indian trade routes;** Mackenzie used negotiation, not firearms, to penetrate this well-defended territory.

> YES **Although the expedition was trespassing on valuable Indian trade routes,** Mackenzie used negotiation, not firearms, to penetrate this well-defended territory.

NOT USING A SEMICOLON TO INTRODUCE A LIST

When the words that introduce a list form an independent clause, use a colon, never a semicolon (26b).

> NO **The Mackenzie expedition hunted and traded for fresh food;** venison, trout, and especially salmon.

> YES **The Mackenzie expedition hunted and traded for fresh food:** venison, trout, and especially salmon.

EXERCISE 25-1 Insert semicolons as needed in these items. Also, fix any incorrectly used semicolons. If a sentence is correct, explain why. For help, consult all sections of this chapter.

> **EXAMPLE** Bicycle racing is as popular in Europe as hockey or baseball is here, it is even more heavily commercialized.
>
> Bicycle racing is as popular in Europe as hockey or baseball is here; it is even more heavily commercialized.

1. The Tour de France is the world's best-known bicycle race, the century-old Giro d'Italia runs a close second.
2. Both are gruelling, three-week-long events that require cyclists to cover 4000 km of difficult, mountainous terrain, and both are eagerly anticipated, draw enormous crowds along their routes, and receive extensive media coverage.
3. That media attention leads to marketing opportunities for the events' sponsors; which place ads along each race's route, in the nearby towns, and on the cyclists themselves.

4. Martin Hvastija, a participant in the 2003 Giro d'Italia, had no chance of winning the race, nevertheless, he drew extensive media attention for his sponsors.

5. His method was simple; he managed to ride out in front of the field for a few kilometers.

6. Although he had no chance of winning the race; newscasters beamed his image around the world while at the same time; showing the world the brightly coloured advertising logos on his jersey.

7. In addition to sponsoring individual athletes, corporations plaster ads all over the towns that the race goes through, they toss samples, coupons, and gadgets to spectators from promotional vehicles that ride ahead of the cyclists, and they run TV and radio ads.

8. In 2003, the organizers of the Giro took in over $10 million in fees from advertisers and $16 million in broadcast rights from the Italian state-owned TV network, RAI, however, these figures were down a bit from the previous year.

9. An additional source of revenues for race organizers is fees from the towns where the race starts and ends each day, as a result, organizers determine the actual course according to which cities are willing to pay the $160 000 charge.

10. Media watchers think the Giro d'Italia could become even more profitable and popular, especially among young adults, but only if it took a cue from the Tour de France by encouraging; more international press coverage, more star riders, and even heavier corporate sponsorship.

EXERCISE 25-2   Combine each set of sentences into one sentence so that it contains two independent clauses. Use a semicolon between the two clauses. You may add, omit, revise, and rearrange words. Try to use all the patterns in this chapter, and explain the reasoning behind your decisions. More than one revision may be correct. For help, consult all sections of this chapter.

> **EXAMPLE** A Canadian-led team of archaeologists has been excavating a site. The site is on the south shore of Crete. Scholars from Greece, the United Kingdom, the United States, and other countries as well have taken part.
>
> A Canadian-led team of archaeologists has been excavating a site on the south shore of *Crete; scholars* from Greece, the United Kingdom, the United States, and other countries as well have taken part.

1. Archaeologists have been excavating the site of Kommos in southern Crete for more than twenty-five years. The site has not yet yielded up all its secrets.

2. Ancient Crete was the home of the legendary King Minos. In Crete, according to Greek myth, lived the Minotaur. This was a man with the head of a terrible bull.

3. Kommos was a small seaport. Kommos was far from Knossos. Knossos was the great city at the centre of the Minoan civilization that preceded the Greeks.

4. Only a temple remained at Kommos after Crete passed to Greek rule. Phoenician merchants seem to have been the worshippers at this temple during the early Greek period.

5. The Phoenicians were a seafaring people from the Lebanese coast. They taught the Greeks to use the alphabet. Archaeologists have found few places where Phoenicians and Greeks could have lived side by side. Kommos may be one, though.

Chapter 26

COLONS

26a What are the uses of a colon?

Colons and
Semicolons

A **colon** is a full stop that draws attention to the words that follow. It can be placed only at the end of an INDEPENDENT CLAUSE. A colon introduces a list, an APPOSITIVE, or a QUOTATION. Quick Reference 26.1 shows different patterns for using a colon.

QUICK REFERENCE 26.1

Colon patterns

Independent clause: list. [26b]

Independent clause: appositive. [26b]

Independent clause: "Quoted words." [26b]

Independent clause: Independent clause that explains or summarizes the prior independent clause. [26c]

26b When can a colon introduce a list, an appositive, or a quotation?

When a complete sentence—that is, an INDEPENDENT CLAUSE—introduces a list, an APPOSITIVE, or a QUOTATION, place a colon before the words being introduced. These words don't have to form an independent clause themselves, but a complete sentence before the colon is essential.

INTRODUCING LISTED ITEMS

When a complete sentence introduces a list, a colon is required, as demonstrated in the following example.

If you really want to lose weight, you must do three things: eat smaller portions, exercise, and drink lots of water. [The required independent clause comes before the listed items, so a colon is correct.]

When the lead-in words at the end of an independent clause are *such as, including, like,* or *consists of,* never use a colon. In contrast, if the lead-in words at the end of an independent clause are *the following* or *as follows,* do use a colon.

The students demanded improvements *such as* an expanded menu in the cafeteria, improved janitorial services, and more up-to-date textbooks.

355

The students demanded *the following*: an expanded menu in the cafeteria, improved janitorial services, and more up-to-date textbooks.

INTRODUCING APPOSITIVES

An APPOSITIVE is a word or words that rename a NOUN or PRONOUN. When an appositive is introduced by an independent clause, use a colon.

The UBC Museum of Anthropology has one outstanding exhibit: its collection of Northwest Coast Indian artifacts. [The independent clause containing *outstanding exhibit* precedes the appositive *its collection of . . . artifacts.*]

INTRODUCING QUOTATIONS

When an independent clause introduces a quotation, use a colon after it. (If the words introducing a quotation don't form an independent clause, use a comma.)

The little boy in *E.T.* did say something neat: "How do you explain school to a higher intelligence?" [The required independent clause comes before the quotation.]

—George F. Will, "Well, I Don't Love You, E.T."

26c   When can I use a colon between two independent clauses?

When a second INDEPENDENT CLAUSE explains or summarizes a first independent clause, you can use a colon to separate them.

ALERT: You can choose to use a capital letter or a lowercase letter for the first word of an independent clause that follows a colon. Whichever you choose, be consistent within a piece of writing. We use a capital letter in this handbook.

We will never forget the first time we made dinner together**: He** got stomach poisoning and was too sick to go to work for four days.

—Lisa Baladendrum, student ●

26d   What standard formats require a colon?

A variety of standard formats require a colon. Also, colons are used in many DOCUMENTATION STYLES, as shown in Chapters 36, 37, and 38.

TITLE AND SUBTITLE
*A Brief History of Time***:** *From the Big Bang to Black Holes*

HOURS, MINUTES, AND SECONDS
The plane took off at 7:15 p.m.

The runner passed the halfway point at 1:23:02.

ALERT: In the military, hours and minutes are written without colons and with four digits on a 24-hour clock: *The staff meeting originally scheduled for Tuesday at **0930** will be held Tuesday at **1430** instead.* ●

REFERENCES TO BIBLE CHAPTERS AND VERSES
Psalms 23:1–3

ALERT: MLA style (Chapter 36) recommends use of a period in place of the colon in biblical references, but notes that the colon is customary. ●

MEMOS

Date: January 9, 2006

To: Dean Kristen Olivero

From: Professor Daniel Black

Re: Student Work-Study Program

SALUTATION IN A BUSINESS LETTER

Dear Dr. Jewell:

26e When is a colon wrong?

INDEPENDENT CLAUSES

A colon can introduce a list, an APPOSITIVE, or a QUOTATION, but only when an INDEPENDENT CLAUSE does the introducing. Similarly, a colon can be used between two independent clauses when the second summarizes or explains the first. In following these rules, be sure that you're dealing with independent clauses, not other word groups.

> NO   The cook bought: eggs, milk, cheese, and bread. [*The cook bought* isn't an independent clause.]

> YES   The cook bought eggs, milk, cheese, and bread.

Never use a colon to separate a PHRASE or DEPENDENT CLAUSE from an independent clause. Otherwise, you'll create the error known as a SENTENCE FRAGMENT.

> NO   Day after day: the drought dragged on. [*Day after day* is a phrase, not an independent clause.]

> YES   Day after day, the drought dragged on.

> NO   After the drought ended: the farmers celebrated. [*After the drought ended* is a dependent clause, not an independent clause.]

> YES   After the drought ended, the farmers celebrated.

LEAD-IN WORDS

Never use a colon after the lead-in words *such as, including, like, consists of,* and *re* (when you use *re* in a sentence).

> NO   The health board discussed many problems **such as:** poor water quality, aging sewage treatment systems, and the lack of alternative water supplies.

> YES   The health board discussed poor water quality, aging sewage treatment systems, and the lack of alternative water supplies. [*Such as* is dropped and the sentence slightly revised so that the colon is not needed.]

> YES   The health board discussed many problems, **such as** poor water quality, an aging sewage treatment system, and the lack of alternative water supplies. [Comma before *such as* tells the reader that the list coming up is nonrestrictive (nonessential)—it illustrates *problems*.]

357

YES   The health board discussed many problems: poor water quality, aging sewage treatment systems, and the lack of alternative water supplies. [If *such as* is dropped, a colon after the independent clause is correct.]

EXERCISE 26-1   Insert colons where needed and delete any not needed. If a sentence is correct, explain why. For help, consult all sections of this chapter.

> **EXAMPLE**   The twentieth century saw a flowering of Irish literature, W. B. Yeats, G. B. Shaw, Samuel Beckett, and Seamus Heaney all won the Nobel Prize for Literature.
>
> The twentieth century saw a flowering of Irish literature: W. B. Yeats, G. B. Shaw, Samuel Beckett, and Seamus Heaney all won the Nobel Prize for Literature.

1. People who work the night shift are typically deprived of essential sleep, an average of nine hours a week.
2. The Iroquois of the Great Lakes region lived in fortified villages and cultivated: corn, beans, and squash.
3. Five nations originally formed the Iroquois Confederacy: the Mohawk, the Oneida, the Onondaga, the Cayuga, and the Seneca.
4. Later, these five Iroquois nations were joined by: the Tuscarora.
5. Shouting: "Come back!" Adam watched the vehicle speed down the highway.
6. When a runner breaks through that unavoidable wall of exhaustion, a very different feeling sets in; an intense sense of well-being known as the "runner's high."
7. However: the "runner's high" soon disappears.
8. Two new nations were born on the same day in 1947, India and Pakistan achieved their independence from Britain at midnight on August 15.
9. Date   December 8, 2013
   To   English 101 Instructors
   From   Dean of Instruction
   Re   Classroom Assignments
10. Only a hurricane could have kept Lisa from meeting Nathaniel at 800 p.m.; unfortunately, that night a hurricane hit.
11. When he was sixteen, George's interests were the usual ones, cars, music videos, and dating.
12. Like many people who have never learned to read or write, the woman who told her life story in *Aman; The Story of a Somali Girl* was able to remember an astonishing number of events in precise detail.
13. The Greek philosopher Socrates took these words as his motto, "The unexamined life is not worth living."
14. Socrates was executed: after being found guilty of teaching young people new ideas.
15. The voice coming from the radio could belong to only one person; the great jazz singer Ella Fitzgerald.

Chapter 27

APOSTROPHES

Writing in Action: How to Recognize Apostrophe Problems

27a   What is the role of the apostrophe?

The **apostrophe** plays four roles in writing: It creates the POSSESSIVE of NOUNS, forms the possessive case of INDEFINITE PRONOUNS, stands for one or more omitted letters in a word (a CONTRACTION), and can help form plurals of letters and numerals.

In contrast, here are two roles the apostrophe doesn't play: It doesn't belong with plurals of nouns, and it doesn't form the plural of PERSONAL PRONOUNS in the possessive case.

27b   How do I use an apostrophe to show a possessive noun?

Singular Possessives Ending in "s"

An apostrophe works with a NOUN to form the POSSESSIVE CASE, which shows ownership or a close relationship.

Happy Holidays from the Thomases— Plurals and Possessives of Proper Names

OWNERSHIP	The **writer's** pen ran out of ink.
CLOSE RELATIONSHIP	The **novel's** plot is complicated.

Possession in nouns can be communicated in two ways: by a PHRASE starting with *of* (*comments **of** the instructor; comments **of** Professor Furman*) or by an apostrophe and the letter *s* (*the instructor**'s** comments; Professor Furman**'s** comments*). Here's a list of specific rules governing the usage of *'s*.

- **Add 's to nouns not ending in -*s*:**

  She felt a **parent's** joy. [*Parent* is a singular noun not ending in -s.]

  They care about their **children's** education. [*Children* is a plural noun not ending in -s.]

- **Add 's to singular nouns ending in -*s*:**

  You can add *'s* or the apostrophe alone to show possession when a singular noun ends in -*s*. In this handbook, we use *'s* to clearly mark singular-noun possessives, no matter what letter ends the noun. Whichever rule variation you choose, be consistent within each piece of writing.

  The **bus's** (or **bus'**) air conditioning is out of order.

  Chris's (or **Chris'**) ordeal ended.

  If you encounter a tongue-twisting pronunciation (*Charles **Dickens's** novel*), you may decide not to add the additional -*s* (*Charles **Dickens'** novel*). You must, however, be consistent in each piece of writing.

- **Add only an apostrophe to a plural noun ending in -*s*:**

  The **boys'** statements were taken seriously.

  Three **months'** parental leave is in the **workers'** contract.

- **Add 's to the last word in compound words and phrases:**

  His **mother-in-law's** corporation has bought out a competitor.

  The **tennis player's** strategy was brilliant.

  We want to hear the **caseworker's** recommendation.

- **Add 's to each noun in individual possession:**

  Shirley's and **Kayla's** houses are next to each other. [Shirley and Kayla each own a house; they don't own the houses jointly.]

- **Add 's to only the last noun in joint or group possession:**

  Kareem and Brina's house has a screened porch. [Kareem and Brina own one house.]

  Avram and Justin's houses always have nice lawns. [Avram and Justin jointly own more than one house.]

27c   How do I use an apostrophe with possessive pronouns?

When a PRONOUN expressing possession (16b) ends with the letter *-s* (*hers, his, its, ours, yours,* and *theirs*), never add an apostrophe. Following is a list of PERSONAL PRONOUNS and their possessive forms.

PERSONAL PRONOUNS	POSSESSIVE FORMS
I	my, mine
you	your, yours
he	his
she	her, hers
it	its
we	our, ours
they	their, theirs
who	whose

27d   How do I use an apostrophe with contractions?

Apostrophes in Its, Lets, Who's, They're

In a **contraction**, an apostrophe takes the place of one or more omitted letters. Be careful not to confuse a contraction with a possessive PRONOUN. Doing so is a common spelling error, one that many people—including employers—consider evidence of a poor education.

it's (contraction for *it is, it has*)	**its** (possessive pronoun)
they're (contraction for *they are*)	**their** (possessive pronoun)
who's (contraction for *who is, who has*)	**whose** (possessive form of *who*)
you're (contraction for *you are*)	**your** (possessive pronoun)

NO   The government promises to balance **it's** budget.

YES   The government promises to balance **its** budget.

NO   The professor **who's** class was cancelled is ill.

YES   The professor **whose** class was cancelled is ill.

In choosing whether or not to use a contraction, consider that many instructors think contractions aren't appropriate in ACADEMIC WRITING. Nevertheless, the *MLA Handbook* accepts contractions, including '90s for *the 1990s*. In this handbook, we use contractions because we're addressing you, the student. We suggest, however, that before you use contractions in your academic writing, you check with your instructor. Here's a list of common contractions.

COMMON CONTRACTIONS

aren't = *are not*	she's = *she is, she has*
can't = *cannot*	there's = *there is, there has*
didn't = *did not*	they're = *they are*
don't = *do not*	wasn't = *was not*
he's = *he is, he has*	we're = *we are*
I'd = *I would, I had*	weren't = *were not*
I'm = *I am*	we've = *we have*
isn't = *is not*	who's = *who is, who has*
it's = *it is, it has*	won't = *will not*
let's = *let us*	you're = *you are*

ALERT: One contraction required in all writing is *o'clock* (which stands for *of the clock,* an expression used long ago). ●

27e **How do I use an apostrophe with possessive indefinite pronouns?**

An apostrophe works with an INDEFINITE PRONOUN (see list in Quick Reference 17.6 in 17i) to form the POSSESSIVE CASE, which shows ownership or a close relationship.

OWNERSHIP **Everyone's** dinner is ready.

CLOSE RELATIONSHIP **Something's** aroma is appealing.

Possession in indefinite pronouns can be communicated in two ways: by a PHRASE starting with *of* (*comments of everyone*) or by an apostrophe and the letter *s* (*everyone's comments*).

27f **How do I form the plural of miscellaneous elements?**

Some writers form the plural of elements such as letters meant as letters, words meant as words, numerals, and symbols by adding *'s*. Others add *s*. The most current MLA guidelines endorse the use of *s* only, with the exception of adding *'s* to letters meant as letters. MLA recommends italics for letters meant as letters and words meant as words. The examples below reflect MLA practices.

PLURAL OF LETTERS MEANT AS LETTERS Printing ***M*'s** and ***N*'s** confuses young children.

Printing ***m*'s** and ***n*'s** confuses young children.

PLURAL OF LETTERS MEANT AS WORDS	He was surprised to get all **Bs** in his courses.
PLURAL OF WORDS MEANT AS WORDS	Too many *ifs* in a contract make me suspicious.
PLURAL OF NUMBERS	Her e-mail address contains many **7s**.
PLURAL OF YEARS	I remember the **1990s** well.
PLURAL OF SYMBOLS	What do those **&s** mean?

27g When is an apostrophe wrong?

If you're a writer who makes the same apostrophe errors repeatedly, memorize the rules you need (you may know some almost without thought). Then, you won't be annoyed by "that crooked little mark," a nickname popular with students who wish the apostrophe would go away. Quick Reference 27.1 lists the major apostrophe errors.

QUICK REFERENCE 27.1

Leading apostrophe errors

- Never use an apostrophe with a PRESENT-TENSE VERB.

  Cholesterol **plays** [not **play's**] an important role in how long we live.
- Always use an apostrophe after the -s in a POSSESSIVE plural of a noun.

  Patients' [not **Patients**] questions seek detailed answers.
- Never add an apostrophe at the end of a nonpossessive noun ending in -s.

  Medical **studies** [not **studies'** or **study's**] show this to be true.
- Never use an apostrophe to form a nonpossessive plural.

  Teams [not **Team's**] of doctors have studied the effects of cholesterol.

EXERCISE 27-1 Rewrite these sentences to insert 's or an apostrophe alone to make the words in parentheses show possession. (Delete the parentheses.) For help, consult 27b and 27e.

> **EXAMPLE** Every box, can, and bottle on a (supermarket) shelves is designed to appeal to (people) emotions.
>
> Every box, can, and bottle on a *supermarket*'s shelves is designed to appeal to *people*'s emotions.

1. A (product) manufacturer designs packaging to appeal to (consumers) emotions through colour and design.
2. Marketing specialists know that (people) beliefs about a (product) quality are influenced by their emotional response to the design of its package.
3. Circles and ovals appearing on a (box) design supposedly increase a (product user) feelings of comfort, while bold patterns and colours attract a (shopper) attention.
4. Using both circles and bold designs in (Arm & Hammer) and (Tide) packaging produces both effects in consumers.

5. (Heinz) ketchup bottle and (Coca-Cola) famous logo achieve the same effects by combining a bright colour with an old-fashioned, "comfortable" design.

6. Often, a (company) marketing consultants will custom-design products to appeal to the supposedly "typical" (adult female) emotions or to (adult males), (children), or (teenagers) feelings.

7. One of the (marketing business) leading consultants, Stan Gross, tests (consumers) emotional reactions to (companies) products and their packages by asking consumers to associate products with well-known personalities.

8. Thus, (test takers) responses to (Gross) questions might reveal that a particular brand of laundry detergent has (Mark Messier) toughness, (Oprah Winfrey) determination, or (someone else) sparkling personality.

9. Manufacturing (companies) products are not the only ones relying on (Gross) and other corporate (image makers) advice.

10. (Sports teams) owners also use marketing specialists to design their (teams) images, as anyone who has seen the unforgettable angry bull logo of the Chicago Bulls basketball team will agree.

EXERCISE 27-2   Rewrite these sentences so that each contains a possessive noun. For help, consult 27b and 27e.

    EXAMPLE The light of a firely gives off no heat.

        A *firefly's* light gives off no heat.

1. The scientific name of a firefly is *lampyridae,* but the nicknames of the bug include *glowworm* and *lightning bug.*

2. More than two thousand species of fireflies can be found throughout the temperate climates of the world.

3. The light of a firefly is caused by a chemical reaction in the organs of the abdomen.

4. Fireflies played a role in the mythology of ancient Mayans and were often compared to the light of a star.

5. Although it may be in the interest of nobody to know, fireflies are not flies at all; they are, according to the classification of scientists, beetles.

Chapter 28

QUOTATION MARKS

28a What is the role of quotation marks?

Quotation marks are used most often to enclose **direct quotations**—the exact spoken or written words of a speaker or writer. Quotation marks also set off some titles, and they can call attention to words used in a special sense.

Double quotation marks (" ") are standard. In most computer fonts, the opening marks differ slightly in appearance from the closing marks. The opening marks look like tiny 6s, the closing marks like tiny 9s. In some computer fonts, the opening and closing marks look the same (" "). Single quotation marks (' or ' ') are used for quotations within quotations: *Gregory said, "I heard the man shout 'Help me' but I could not reach him in time."* Quotation marks operate only in pairs: to open and to close. When you proofread your writing, check carefully that you've inserted the closing mark.

Please note that we use MLA STYLE to format the examples here and in other chapters. This affects the documentation features and the lengths of "short" and "long" quotations, which vary with different documentation styles. For MLA style, used in most English courses, see Chapter 36. For APA STYLE, see Chapter 37.

28b How do I use quotation marks with short direct quotations?

DIRECT QUOTATIONS are exact words from print or nonprint sources. In MLA STYLE, a quotation is considered *short* if it occupies no more than four typed lines. Use double quotation marks at the start and finish of a short quotation. Give DOCUMENTATION information after a short quotation, before the sentence's ending period.

> **SHORT QUOTATIONS**
>
> Gardner has suggested the possibility of a ninth intelligence: existential, "the proclivity to pose (and ponder) questions about life, death, and ultimate realities" (72).
>
> Susana Urbina, who surveyed many studies about intelligence, found that intelligence "is such a multifaceted concept that no single quality can define it . . ." (1130).

28c Are quotation marks used with long quotations?

Don't use quotation marks with a long DIRECT QUOTATION. In MLA STYLE, a quotation is *long* if it occupies more than four typed lines. Instead of using quotation marks with a long quotation, indent all its lines as a block (that is, the quotation is "set off" or "displayed"). This format makes quotation marks unnecessary. Give DOCUMENTATION information after the period that ends the quotation.

LONG QUOTATIONS

Gardner uses criteria by which to judge whether an ability deserves to be categorized as an "intelligence." Each must confer

> a set of skills of problem solving—enabling the individual *to resolve genuine problems or difficulties* [author's emphasis] that he or she encounters and, when appropriate, to create an effective product—and must also entail the potential for *finding or creating problems*—thereby laying the groundwork for the acquisition of new knowledge. These prerequisites represent [Gardner's] effort to focus on those intellectual strengths that prove of some importance within a cultural context. (*Frames* 60–61)

In the Gardner example above, note that a capital letter is *not* used to start the quotation. The lead-in words (*Each must confer*) are an incomplete sentence, so they need the quotation to complete the sentence.

> Goleman also emphasizes a close interaction of the emotional and rational states with the other intelligences that Gardner has identified:

> These two minds, the emotional and the rational, operate in tight harmony for the most part, intertwining their very different ways of knowing to guide us through the world. Ordinarily there is a balance between emotional and rational minds, with emotion feeding into and informing the operations of the rational mind, and the rational mind refining and sometimes vetoing the inputs of the emotions. (9)

In the Goleman example above, note that a capital letter starts the quotation because the lead-in words are a complete sentence. (A colon can—but isn't required to—end the lead-in sentence because it's an independent clause; see 26b.)

ALERT: Even if a quotation is a single word, document its SOURCE. Record the words just as they appear in the original. ●

28d How do I use quotation marks for quotations within quotations?

In short quotations of prose, which are themselves enclosed in double quotation marks, use single quotation marks for any internal quotation marks. In MLA STYLE, give DOCUMENTATION information after the entire quotation, before the sentence's ending period. For other documentation styles, check each style's manual.

In long quotations of prose—those that are displayed (set off in a block) and not enclosed in quotation marks—keep the double quotation marks as they appear in the original. In MLA style, give DOCUMENTATION information after the long quotation following any closing punctuation, and before the period that ends a short quotation.

SHORT QUOTATIONS: USE SINGLE WITHIN DOUBLE QUOTATION MARKS (MLA STYLE)

With short quotations, the double quotation marks show the beginning and end of words taken from the source; the single quotation marks replace double marks used in the source.

ORIGINAL SOURCE

Most scientists concede that they don't really know what "intelligence" is. Whatever it might be, paper and pencil tests aren't the tenth of it.

—Brent Staples, "The IQ Cult," p. 293

STUDENT'S USE OF THE SOURCE

Brent Staples argues in his essay about IQ as object of reverence, "Most scientists concede that they don't really know what 'intelligence' is. Whatever it might be, paper and pencil tests aren't the tenth of it" (293).

LONG QUOTATIONS: USE QUOTATION MARKS AS IN SOURCE

All long quotations must be set off (displayed) without being enclosed in quotation marks. Therefore, show any double and single quotation marks exactly as the source does.

28e How do I use quotation marks for quotations of poetry and dialogue?

POETRY (MLA STYLE)

A quotation of poetry is *short* if it includes three lines or fewer of the poem. As with prose quotations (28d), use double quotation marks to enclose the material. If the poetry lines have internal double quotation marks, change them to single quotation marks. To show when a line of poetry breaks to the next line, use a slash (/) with one space on each side. Give DOCUMENTATION information after a short poetry quotation, before the period that ends the sentence (see also 29e).

> As Auden wittily defined personal space, "some thirty inches from my nose / The frontier of my person goes" (*Complete* 205).

A quotation of poetry is *long* if it includes more than three lines of the poem. As with prose quotations (28d), indent all lines as a block, without quotation marks to enclose the material. Start new lines exactly as they appear in your source. Give documentation information after the long quotation and after the period that ends the quotation.

 ALERT: When you quote lines of poetry, follow the capitalization of your source. ●

DIALOGUE (MLA AND APA STYLES)

Dialogue, also called DIRECT DISCOURSE, presents a speaker's exact words. Enclose direct discourse in quotation marks. In contrast, INDIRECT DISCOURSE reports what a speaker said. Don't enclose indirect discourse in quotation marks. In addition to these differences in punctuation, PRONOUN use and VERB TENSES also differ for these two types of discourse.

DIRECT DISCOURSE   The mayor said, **"I** intend to oppose that bylaw.**"**

INDIRECT DISCOURSE   The mayor said **that he intended** to oppose that bylaw.

When you're reporting the words of a speaker, whether real or fictional, use double quotation marks at the beginning and end of the speaker's words. This tells your reader which words are the speaker's. Also, start a new paragraph each time the speaker changes.

> Becky Tyde climbed up on Flo's counter, made room for herself beside an open tin of crumbly jam-filled cookies.
> "Are these any good?" she said to Flo, and boldly began to eat one. "When are you going to give us a job, Flo?"
> "You could go and work in the butcher shop," said Flo innocently. "You could go and work for your brother."
>
> —Alice Munro, "Royal Beatings"

If two or more paragraphs present a single speaker's words, use double opening quotation marks at the start of each paragraph, but save the closing double quotation marks until the end of the last quoted paragraph.

EXERCISE 28-1 Decide whether each sentence below is direct or indirect discourse and then rewrite each sentence in the other form. Make any changes needed for grammatical correctness. With direct discourse, put the speaker's words wherever you think they belong in the sentence. For help, consult 28b through 28e.

> **EXAMPLE** A school counsellor told Betty, a fourth-year student, that she needed to take one more three-unit elective to graduate in May.
>
> A school counsellor told Betty, a fourth-year student, "You need to take one more three-unit elective to graduate in May."

1. "Betty, would you be interested in taking an introductory electronics course?" asked the counsellor.
2. Betty asked why she would take such a course when she was a nursing major.
3. The counsellor looked Betty straight in the eye and said, "Some knowledge of electronics may not be part of your major, but it's a very important modern subject, nevertheless."
4. Betty wondered whether it might give her a greater understanding of all the electronics used in medical diagnosis and treatment today. But she also asked if there wasn't another elective that might do more to enhance her nursing career.
5. The counsellor was quiet for a moment and then declared, "And don't forget, electronics is something you can always fall back on, Betty. And the more you have to fall back on, the softer the landing."

28f How do I use quotation marks with titles of short works?

When you refer to certain short works by their titles, enclose the titles in quotation marks (other works, usually longer, need to be in italics; see 30g). Short works include short stories, essays, poems, articles from periodicals, pamphlets, brochures, songs, and individual episodes of a series on television or radio.

> What is the rhyme scheme of Andrew Marvell's "Delight in Disorder"? [poem]
>
> Have you read "Insecurity" by Neil Bissoondath? [short story]
>
> The best source I found is "The Myth of Political Consultants." [magazine article]
>
> "Shooting an Elephant" describes George Orwell's experiences in Burma. [essay]

Titles of some other works are neither enclosed in quotation marks nor written in italics or underlined. For guidelines, see Quick Reference 30.1 in 30e and Quick Reference 30.2 in 30g.

ALERT: When placing the title of your own piece of writing on a title page or at the top of a page, never use quotation marks. ●

EXERCISE 28-2 Insert any needed quotation marks. For help, consult 28f.

1. Northrop Frye's essay The Bush Garden, which discusses the presence of nature as a theme in Canadian literature, was published in a volume that is also called *The Bush Garden*.

2. The same theme was taken up by Margaret Atwood in her book *Survival* and in poems such as Paths and Thingscape, expressing an early pioneer's awkward attempt to come to terms with the wild landscape.

3. Season one of *Heartland,* a CBC television series based on the works of Lauren Brooke, began with the episode Coming Home.

4. Lennie Gallant's song Pieces of You and Natalie MacMaster's Get Me Through December were nominated for the East Coast Music Awards.

5. In her short story The Lady from Lucknow, Bharati Mukherjee describes a visitor from India who resents being treated as an exotic object.

28g How do I use quotation marks for words used as words?

When you refer to a word as a word, you can choose to either enclose it in quotation marks or put it in italics (or use underlining). Whichever you choose, be consistent throughout each piece of writing.

> NO   Many people confuse affect and effect.
>
> YES   Many people confuse "affect" and "effect."
>
> YES   Many people confuse *affect* and *effect*.

Always put quotation marks around the English translation of a word or PHRASE. Also, use italics (or underlining) for the word or phrase in the other language.

> My grandfather usually ended arguments with *de gustibus non disputandum est* ("there is no disputing about tastes").

Many writers use quotation marks around words or phrases meant ironically or in other nonliteral ways.

> The proposed tax "reform" is actually a tax increase.

Some writers put technical terms in quotation marks and define them—but only the first time they appear. Never repeat quotation marks after a term has been introduced and defined.

> A "chinook" is a warm wind that blows eastward across the Rockies. Chinooks can transform an Alberta winter day into a brief anticipation of spring.

Some student writers put quotation marks around words that they sense might be inappropriate for ACADEMIC WRITING, such as a slang term or a CLICHÉ used intentionally to make a point. However, when possible, use different language—not quotation marks. Take time to think of accurate, appropriate, and fresh words instead. If you prefer to stick with the slang or cliché, use quotation marks.

> They "eat like birds" in public, but they "stuff their faces" in private.
>
> They **eat almost nothing** in public, but they **gorge themselves** in private.

A nickname doesn't call for quotation marks, unless you use the nickname along with the full name. When a person's nickname is widely known, you don't have to give both the nickname and the full name. For example, use *Joe Clark* or *Charles Joseph Clark*, whichever is appropriate in context. Because he's well known as a former prime minister, don't use *Charles Joseph "Joe" Clark*.

EXERCISE 28-3 Correct any quotation mark errors. If you think a sentence is correct, explain why. For help, consult 28g.

> **EXAMPLE** The word asyndeton simply means that a conjunction has been omitted, as when Shakespeare writes, A woman mov'd is like a fountain troubled, / Muddy, ill seeming, thick, bereft of beauty.
>
> The word "asyndeton" simply means that a conjunction has been omitted, as when Shakespeare writes, "A woman mov'd is like a fountain troubled, / Muddy, ill seeming, thick, bereft of beauty."

1. Shakespeare's phrases such as the sound and the fury from *Macbeth* and pale fire from *The Tempest* have been used by authors such as William Faulkner and Vladimir Nabokov as titles for their books.

2. Shakespeare's understanding of human nature was "profound" and helped him become a "prolific" writer.

3. Many words used commonly today, such as "addiction" and "alligator," were first used in print by Shakespeare.

4. To understand the difference between the words sanguinary and *sanguine* is important for a reader of Shakespeare because the former means bloody and the latter means optimistic.

5. In the play *Romeo and Juliet*, one of Shakespeare's most famous quotations is What's in a name? That which we call a rose / By any other name would smell as sweet.

28h How do I use quotation marks with other punctuation?

Quotation Marks with Other Punctuation

COMMAS AND PERIODS WITH QUOTATION MARKS

A comma or period that is grammatically necessary is always placed inside the closing quotation mark.

> Because the class enjoyed Michel Tremblay's "The Thimble," they were looking forward to his longer works. [comma before closing quotation mark]
>
> Max said, "Don't stand so far away from me." [comma before opening quotation mark (24k.5); period before closing quotation mark]
>
> Edward T. Hall coined the word "proxemia." [period before closing quotation mark]

SEMICOLONS AND COLONS WITH QUOTATION MARKS

A semicolon or colon is placed outside the closing quotation mark, unless it is part of the quotation.

> Computers offer businesses "opportunities that never existed before"; some workers disagree. [semicolon after closing quotation mark]
>
> We have to know each culture's standard for "how close is close": No one wants to offend. [colon after closing quotation mark]

QUESTION MARKS, EXCLAMATION MARKS, AND DASHES WITH QUOTATION MARKS

If the punctuation marks belong to the words enclosed in quotation marks, put them inside the quotation marks.

"Did I Hear You Call My Name?" was the winning song.

"I've won the lottery!" Arielle shouted.

"Who's there? Why don't you ans—"

If a question mark, an exclamation mark, or a dash doesn't belong to the material being quoted, put the punctuation outside the quotation marks.

Have you read Al Purdy's poem "The Country North of Belleville"?

If only I could write a story like Roch Carrier's "The Hockey Sweater"!

Weak excuses—a classic is "I have to visit my grandparents"—change little.

If you want to know how quotation marks work with capital letters, see 30d; with brackets, 29c; with ellipsis points, 29d; and with the slash, 29e.

28i   When are quotation marks wrong?

Never enclose a word in quotation marks to call attention to it, to intensify it, or to be sarcastic.

> NO   The collapse of an overpass near Montreal was a "wakeup call" to our cities.
>
> YES   The collapse of an overpass near Montreal was a wakeup call to our cities.

Never enclose the title of your paper in quotation marks (or italicize it). However, if the title of your paper contains another title that requires quotation marks, use those marks only for the included title.

> NO   "The Elderly in Nursing Homes: A Case Study"
>
> YES   The Elderly in Nursing Homes: A Case Study
>
> NO   Character Development in Shirley Jackson's Story The Lottery
>
> YES   Character Development in Shirley Jackson's Story "The Lottery"

EXERCISE 28-4   Correct any errors in the use of quotation marks and other punctuation with quotation marks. If you think a sentence is correct, explain why. For help, consult 28e through 28i.

1. For reasons unknown to me, the meteorologist said, *The Canadian Encyclopedia* contains a statistical analysis of groundhog weather predictions.

2. "No", Michael Ondaatje said, describing how he invented the intricate plot of his novel *The English Patient*," the plot wasn't there until I finished the book, probably.

3. Pierre Trudeau's claim that he used the expression fuddle-duddle, instead of a taboo four-letter word, led a member of Parliament to quip, "Mr. Trudeau wants to be obscene but not heard".

4. In his poem A Supermarket in California, Allen Ginsberg addresses the dead poet Walt Whitman, asking, Where are we going, Walt Whitman? The doors close / in an hour. Which way does your beard point tonight?

5. Gordie Howe was once asked how hockey players were coping with Canada's "language problem;" he replied, All pro athletes are bilingual. They speak English and profanity.

Chapter 29

OTHER PUNCTUATION MARKS

This chapter explains the uses of **dashes, parentheses, brackets, ellipsis points, slashes,** and **hyphens**. Some of these punctuation marks aren't used often, but each serves a purpose and gives you options with your writing style.

DASH

29a **When can I use a dash in my writing?**

The **dash,** or a pair of dashes, lets you interrupt a sentence to add information. Such interruptions can fall in the middle or at the end of a sentence. To make a dash, hit the hyphen key twice (--). Do not put a space before, between, or after the hyphens. Some word-processing programs automatically convert two hyphens into a dash; either form is correct. In print, the dash appears as an unbroken line approximately the length of two or three hyphens joined together (—). If you handwrite, make the dash at least twice as long as a hyphen.

USING DASHES FOR SPECIAL EMPHASIS

If you want to emphasize an example, a definition, an APPOSITIVE, or a contrast, you can use a dash or dashes. Some call a dash "a pregnant pause"—that is, take note, something special is coming. Use dashes sparingly so that you don't dilute their impact.

EXAMPLE

Urban centres in Canada—Montreal, Toronto, Winnipeg, Vancouver—share problems of crime and prostitution in core areas.

—Lovus Devine, student

DEFINITION

Our aboriginal peoples—Inuit, Indian, and Métis—challenge the model of two founding peoples that excludes them.

—William Thorsell, "Let Us Compare Mythologies"

APPOSITIVE

When we use that strange expression—reasonable accommodation—to refer to how we respond to other people's customs, it simply makes people on all sides feel uncomfortable.

CONTRAST

What could be less appropriate—or more offensive—than making a pun on your own friend's name?

Place what you emphasize with dashes next to or nearby the material it refers to so that what you want to accomplish with your emphasis is not lost.

NO	The current **argument is**—one that faculty, students, and coaches debate fiercely—whether to hold athletes to the same academic standards as others face.
YES	The current **argument**—one that faculty, students, and coaches debate fiercely—is whether to hold athletes to the same academic standards as others face.

USING DASHES TO EMPHASIZE AN ASIDE

An **aside** is a writer's comment, often the writer's personal views, on what's been written. Generally, this technique isn't appropriate for ACADEMIC WRITING, so before you insert an aside, carefully consider your writing PURPOSE and your AUDIENCE.

> As I observed all this and felt its effects on my daily life—and received wounds from my struggle to be part of it—another part of me itched to make a record of what I was seeing.
> —Sharon Butala, *Rural Saskatchewan: Creating the Garden*

ALERTS: (1) If the words within a pair of dashes require a question mark or an exclamation mark, place it before the second dash.

> A first date—do you remember?—stays in the memory forever.

(2) Never use commas, semicolons, or periods next to dashes. If such a need arises, revise your writing.

(3) Never enclose quotation marks in dashes except when the meaning requires them. These two examples show that, when required, the dash stops before or after the quotation marks; the two punctuation marks do not overlap.

> Many of George Orwell's essays—"A Hanging," for example—draw on his experiences as a civil servant.

> "Shooting an Elephant"—another Orwell essay—appears in many anthologies. ●

EXERCISE 29-1   Write a sentence about each topic, shown in italics. Use dashes to set off what is asked for, shown in roman, in each sentence. For help, consult 29a.

> **EXAMPLE**   *science*, a definition
>
> *Ecology*—the study of the interactions among animals, plants, and the physical environment—is closely related to both biology and geology.

1. *occupation*, a contrast
2. *sport*, an appositive
3. *public transportation*, an example
4. *ice cream flavour*, an aside
5. *a shape*, a definition

6. *animal*, a contrast
7. *Canadian region*, an example
8. *country*, an appositive
9. *musical instrument*, a definition
10. *technology*, an aside

PARENTHESES

29b   When can I use parentheses in my writing?

Parentheses let you interrupt a sentence to add various kinds of information. Parentheses are like dashes (29a) in that they set off extra or interrupting words—but unlike dashes, which emphasize material, parentheses de-emphasize what they enclose. Use parentheses sparingly because overusing them can make your writing lurch, not flow.

USING PARENTHESES TO ENCLOSE INTERRUPTING WORDS

EXPLANATION

After they've finished with the pantry, the medicine cabinet, and the attic, they will throw out the red geranium **(**too many leaves**)**, sell the dog **(**too many fleas**)**, and send the children off to boarding school (too many scuffmarks on the hardwood floors)**.**

—Suzanne Britt, "Neat People vs. Sloppy People"

EXAMPLE

Though other cities **(**Dresden, for instance**)** had been utterly destroyed in World War II, never before had a single weapon been responsible for such destruction.

—Laurence Behrens and Leonard J. Rosen
Writing and Reading Across the Curriculum

ASIDE

The older girls **(**non-graduates, of course**)** were assigned the task of making refreshments for the night's festivities.

—Maya Angelou, *I Know Why the Caged Bird Sings*

When it tastes pungent and hot **(**remember that the pungency will be cut by the beans**)** stir in a large quantity of molasses. Most people don't put in enough molasses, and yet this is the essence of all good baked bean dishes.

—Pierre Berton, "Baked Beans"

USING PARENTHESES FOR LISTED ITEMS AND ALTERNATIVE NUMBERS

When you number listed items within a sentence, enclose the numbers (or letters) in parentheses. Never use closing parentheses to set off numbers in a displayed list; use periods.

Four items are on the agenda for tonight's meeting: **(1)** current treasury figures, **(2)** current membership figures, **(3)** the budget for renovations, and **(4)** the campaign for soliciting additional public contributions.

ALERTS: For listed items that fall within a sentence, (1) use a colon before a list only if an INDEPENDENT CLAUSE comes before the list, and (2) use commas or semicolons to separate three or more items, but be consistent within a piece of writing. If, however, any item contains internal punctuation, use a semicolon to separate the items. ●

In legal writing and in some BUSINESS WRITING, you can use parentheses to enclose a numeral that repeats a spelled-out number.

The monthly rent is three hundred fifty dollars ($350).

Your order of fifteen (15) gross was shipped today.

In ACADEMIC WRITING, especially in subjects in which the use of figures or measurements is frequent, enclose alternative or comparative forms of the same number in parentheses: *3.2 km (2 mi.)*.

USING OTHER PUNCTUATION WITH PARENTHESES

When a complete sentence enclosed in parentheses stands alone, start it with a capital letter and end it with a period. When a sentence in parentheses falls within another sentence, never start with a capital or end with a period.

NO	Looking for his car keys (He had left them at my sister's house.) wasted an entire hour.
YES	Looking for his car keys (he had left them at my sister's house) wasted an entire hour.
YES	Looking for his car keys wasted an entire hour. (He had left them at my sister's house.)

If the material before the parenthetical material requires a comma, place that comma after the closing parenthesis unless you're using commas to set off numbers in a list.

NO	Although clearly different from my favourite film, (*The Wizard of Oz*) *Barney's Version* is also outstanding.
YES	Although clearly different from my favourite film (*The Wizard of Oz*), *Barney's Version* is also outstanding.
YES	Dorothy wore (1) a white blouse, (2) a blue pinafore, and (3) ruby slippers.

You can use a question mark or an exclamation point within parentheses that occur in a sentence.

Looking for clues (what did we expect to find?) wasted four days.

Place parentheses around quotation marks that come before or after any quoted words.

NO	Alberta Hunter "(Down Hearted Blues)" revived her singing career when she was in her seventies.
YES	Alberta Hunter ("Down Hearted Blues") revived her singing career when she was in her seventies.

BRACKETS

29c When do I need to use brackets in my writing?

Brackets (also called square brackets) allow you to enclose words that you want to insert into quotations, but only in the specific cases discussed below.

ADJUSTING A QUOTATION WITH BRACKETS

When you use a quotation, you might need to change the form of a word (a verb's tense, for example), add a brief definition, or fit the quotation into the grammatical structure of your sentence. In such cases, enclose the material you have inserted into the quotation in brackets. (These examples use MLA STYLE for PARENTHETICAL REFERENCES; see 36b.)

ORIGINAL SOURCE

Current research shows that successful learning takes place in an active environment.
—Deborah Moore, "Facilities and Learning Styles," p. 22

QUOTATION WITH BRACKETS

Deborah Moore supports a student-centred curriculum and agrees with "current re-search [which] shows that successful learning takes place in an active environment" (22).

ORIGINAL SOURCE

The logic of the mind is *associative;* it takes elements that symbolize a reality, or trigger a memory of it, to be the same as that reality.
—Daniel Goleman, *Emotional Intelligence,* p. 294

QUOTATION WITH BRACKETS

The kinds of intelligence are based in the way the mind functions: "The logic of the mind is *associative* [one idea connects with another]; it takes elements that symbolize a reality, or trigger a memory of it, to be the same as that reality" (Goleman 294).

USING BRACKETS TO POINT OUT AN ERROR IN A SOURCE OR TO ADD INFORMATION WITHIN PARENTHESES

Sometimes you find a mistake in the original version of words you want to quote—a wrong date, a misspelled word, or an error of fact. You fix that mistake by putting your correction in brackets, without changing the words you want to quote. This tells your readers that the error was in the original work and not made by you.

USING [SIC] TO SHOW A SOURCE'S ERROR

Insert *sic* (without italics), enclosed in brackets, in your MLA-style essays and research papers to show your readers that you've quoted an error accurately. *Sic* is a Latin word that means "so" or "thus" and expresses the thought "It is thus in the original."

USE FOR ERROR

A journalist wrote, "The judge accepted an [sic] plea of not guilty.

USE FOR MISSPELLING

The building inspector wrote about the consequence of doubling the apartment's floor space: "With that much extra room per person, the tennants [sic] would sublet."

USING BRACKETS WITHIN PARENTHESES

Use brackets to insert information within parentheses.

That expression (**first used in** *A Fable for Critics* **[1848] by James R. Lowell**) was popularized in the early twentieth century by Ella Wheeler Wilcox.

ELLIPSIS POINTS

29d How do I use ellipsis points in my writing?

The word *ellipsis* means "omission." **Ellipsis points** in writing are a series of three spaced dots (use the period key on the keyboard). You're required to use ellipsis points to indicate you've intentionally omitted words—perhaps even a sentence or more—from within the source you're quoting. These rules apply to both prose and poetry.

29d.1 Using ellipsis points with prose

ORIGINAL SOURCE

These two minds, the emotional and the rational, operate in tight harmony for the most part, intertwining their very different ways of knowing to guide us through the world. Ordinarily, there is a balance between emotional and rational minds, with emotion feeding into and informing the operations of the rational mind, and the rational mind refining and sometimes vetoing the inputs of the emotions. Still, the emotional and rational minds are semi-independent faculties, each, as we shall see, reflecting the operation of distinct, but interconnected, circuitry in the brain.

—Daniel Goleman, *Emotional Intelligence*, p. 9

QUOTATION OF SELECTED WORDS, NO ELLIPSIS NEEDED

Goleman explains that the "two minds, the emotional and the rational" usually provide "a balance" in our daily observations and decision making (9).

QUOTATION WITH ELLIPSIS MID-SENTENCE

Goleman emphasizes the connections between parts of the mind: "Still, the emotional and rational minds are semi-independent faculties, each . . . reflecting the operation of distinct, but interconnected, circuitry in the brain" (9).

QUOTATION WITH ELLIPSIS AND PARENTHETICAL REFERENCE

Goleman emphasizes that the "two minds, the emotional and the rational, operate in tight harmony for the most part . . ." (9). [*Note:* In MLA style, place a sentence-ending period after the parenthetical reference.]

QUOTATION WITH ELLIPSIS ENDING THE SENTENCE

On page 9, Goleman states, "These two minds, the emotional and the rational, operate in tight harmony for the most part. . . ." [*Note:* In MLA style, when all needed documentation information is written into a sentence—that is, not placed in parentheses at the end of the sentence—there's no space between the sentence-ending period and an ellipsis.]

QUOTATION WITH SENTENCE OMITTED

Goleman explains: "These two minds, the emotional and the rational, operate in tight harmony for the most part, intertwining their very different ways of knowing to guide us through the world. . . . Still, the emotional and rational minds are semi-independent faculties" (9).

QUOTATION WITH WORDS OMITTED FROM THE MIDDLE OF ONE SENTENCE TO THE MIDDLE OF ANOTHER

Goleman states, "Ordinarily, there is a balance between emotional and rational minds . . . reflecting the operation of distinct, but interconnected, circuitry in the brain" (9).

QUOTATION WITH WORDS OMITTED FROM THE MIDDLE OF ONE SENTENCE TO THE BEGINNING OF ANOTHER

Goleman explains, "there is a balance between emotional and rational minds. . . . Still, the emotional and rational minds are semi-independent faculties, each, as we shall see, reflecting the operation of distinct, but interconnected, circuitry in the brain" (9).

When you omit words from a quotation, you also omit punctuation related to those words, unless it's needed for the sentence to be correct.

Goleman explains, "These two minds . . . operate in tight harmony" (9). [comma in original source omitted after *minds*]

Goleman explains that the emotional and rational minds work together while, "still, . . . each, as we shall see, [reflects] the operation of distinct, but interconnected, circuitry in the brain" (9). [comma kept after *still* because it's an introductory word; *still* changed to begin with lowercase letter because now middle of sentence; form of *reflecting* changed for sense of sentence]

29d.2   Using ellipsis points with poetry

When you omit one or more words from a line of poetry, follow the rules stated above for prose. However, when you omit a full line or more from poetry, use a full line of spaced dots.

ORIGINAL SOURCE

Little Boy Blue

Little boy blue, come blow your horn,
The sheep's in the meadow, the cow's in the corn
Where is the little boy who looks after the sheep?
He's under the haystack, fast asleep.

QUOTATION WITH LINES OMITTED

Little Boy Blue

Little boy blue, come blow your horn,

. . . .

Where is the little boy who looks after the sheep?
He's under the haystack, fast asleep.

SLASH

29e   When can I use a slash in my writing?

The **slash** (/), also called a *virgule* or *solidus*, is a diagonal line that separates or joins words in special circumstances.

USING A SLASH TO SEPARATE QUOTED LINES OF POETRY

When you quote more than three lines of a poem, no slash is used; you merely follow the rules in 28e. When you quote three lines or fewer, enclose them in quotation marks and run them into your sentence—and use a slash to divide one line from the next. Leave a space on each side of the slash.

One of my mottoes comes from the beginning of Anne Sexton's poem "Words": "Be careful of words, / even the miraculous ones."

Capitalize and punctuate each line of poetry as in the original—but even if the quoted line of poetry doesn't have a period, use one to end your sentence. If your quotation ends before the line of poetry ends, use ellipsis points (29d).

USING A SLASH FOR NUMERICAL FRACTIONS IN MANUSCRIPTS

To type numerical fractions, use a slash (with no space before or after the slash) to separate the numerator and denominator. In mixed numbers—that is, whole numbers with fractions—leave a space between the whole number and its fraction: 1 2/3, 3 7/8. Do not use a hyphen. (For information about using spelled-out and numerical forms of numbers, see 30m through 30o.)

USING A SLASH FOR *AND/OR*

When writing in the humanities, try not to use word combinations connected with a slash, such as *and/or*. In academic disciplines in which such combinations are acceptable, separate the words with a slash. Leave no space before or after the slash. In the humanities, listing both alternatives in normal sentence structure is usually better than separating choices with a slash.

> **NO** The best quality of reproduction comes from 35 mm slides/direct-positive films.

> **YES** The best quality of reproduction comes from 35 mm slides **or** direct-positive films.

EXERCISE 29-2 Supply needed dashes, parentheses, brackets, ellipsis points, and slashes. If a sentence is correct as written, circle its number. In some sentences, when you can use either dashes or parentheses, explain your choice. For help, consult all sections of this chapter.

> **EXAMPLE** In Canada, there are almost four times as many managerial and administrative nonclerical workers as there are farmers.
>
> In Canada, there are almost four times as many managerial and administrative (nonclerical) workers as there are farmers.

1. In *The Color Purple* a successful movie as well as a novel, Alice Walker explores the relationships between women and men in traditional African American culture.

2. The three longest rivers in Canada are 1 the Mackenzie 4241 km, 2 the Yukon 3185 km, and 3 the St. Lawrence 3058 km.

3. Calgary's Saddledome, the broad roof of the arena dips like a saddle, was used in the 1988 Winter Olympic Games, several years after it first opened.

4. All the really interesting desserts ice cream, chocolate fudge cake, pumpkin pie with whipped cream are fattening, unfortunately.

5. Thunder is caused when the flash of lightning heats the air around it to temperatures up to 30 000°C (55 000°F).

6. Christina Rossetti wonders if the end of a life also means the end of love in a poem that opens with these two lines: "When I am dead, my dearest, Sing no sad songs for me."

7. The federal election held in May 2011 began as a quiet, low-key event, but by voting day Canadians were holding their breath in suspense.

8. Oscar Peterson has written, "To my way of thinking it the recording his friend Clifford Brown made in 1955 with Max Roach epitomizes the highest achievement in the world of Jazz—spontaneity."

9. Of his decision to resign as prime minister in 1984, Pierre Trudeau said, "I listened to my heart and saw if there were any signs of my destiny in the sky, and there were none there were just snowflakes."

10. Anyone in Canada who performs in public for private profit, of course a play, opera, or musical composition subject to copyright is liable to a fine of two hundred and fifty dollars $250.

11. Kim Campbell does anyone here remember Kim Campbell? used to fascinate us.

12. Patients who pretend to have ailments are known to doctors as "Munchausens" after Baron Karl Friedrich Hieronymus von Münchhausen he was a German army officer who had a reputation for wild and unbelievable tales.

EXERCISE 29-3   Follow the directions for each item. For help, consult all sections of this chapter.

> **EXAMPLE** Write a sentence about getting something right using a dash.
>
>   *I tried and failed, I tried and failed again—and then I did it.*

1. Write a sentence that quotes only three lines of the following sonnet by William Shakespeare:

   Let me not to the marriage of true minds
   Admit impediments. Love is not love
   Which alters when it alteration finds,
   Or bends with the remover to remove.
   O, no! it is an ever-fixèd mark
   That looks on tempests and is never shaken;
   It is the star to every wand'ring bark,
   Whose worth's unknown, although his height be taken.
   Love's not Time's fool, though rosy lips and cheeks
   Within his bending sickle's compass come;
   Love alters not with his brief hours and weeks,
   But bears it out even to the edge of doom.
       If this be error, and upon me proved,
       I never writ, nor no man ever loved.

2. Write a sentence using parentheses to enclose a brief example.

3. Write a sentence using dashes to set off a definition.

4. Write a sentence that includes four numbered items in a list.

5. Quote a few sentences from any source you choose. Omit words without losing meaning or use brackets to insert words to maintain meaning or grammatical structure. Use ellipsis points to indicate the omission, and place the parenthetical reference where it belongs.

HYPHEN

29f **When do I need a hyphen in my writing?**

((i•
Hyphenation

A **hyphen** divides words at the end of a line and combines words into compounds, and is used in spelling out certain numbers.

29g **When do I use a hyphen at the end of a line?**

Generally, try not to divide a word with a hyphen at the end of a line. (In printed books, hyphens are acceptable because of the limits on line length.) If you must divide a word, try hard not to divide the last word on the first line of a paper, the last word in a paragraph, or the last word on a page.

When you can't avoid using a hyphen at the end of a line, break the word only between syllables. If you aren't sure about the syllables in a word, consult a dictionary. Never divide words that are short, or that contain only one syllable or are pronounced as one syllable.

wealth   envy   screamed

Divide words between two consonants according to pronunciation.

full-ness   omit-ting   punc-ture

Never divide a word when only one or two letters would be left or carried over to another line.

alive   touchy   helicop-ter

29h How do I use a hyphen with prefixes and suffixes?

Prefixes are syllables in front of a **root**—a word's core, which carries the origin or meaning—and **suffixes** follow a root. Both modify the root's meaning. Some prefixes and suffixes are attached to root words with hyphens, but others are not. Quick Reference 29.1 shows you how to decide.

QUICK REFERENCE 29.1

Hyphens with prefixes and suffixes

* Use hyphens after the prefixes *all-*, *ex-*, *quasi-*, and *self-*,

    YES   all-inclusive   self-reliant

* Never use a hyphen when *self* is a root word, not a prefix.

    NO   self-ishness   self-less
    YES   selfishness   selfless

* Use a hyphen to avoid a distracting string of letters.

    NO   antiintellectual   belllike   prooutsourcing
    YES   anti-intellectual   bell-like   pro-outsourcing

* Use a hyphen to add a prefix or suffix to a numeral or a word that starts with a capital letter.

    NO   post1950   proAmerican   Rembrandtlike
    YES   post-1950   pro-American   Rembrandt-like

* Use a hyphen before the suffix *-elect*.

    NO   presidentelect
    YES   president-elect

* Use a hyphen to prevent confusion in meaning or pronunciation.

    YES   re-dress (means *dress again*)   redress (means *set right*)
    YES   un-ionize (means *remove the ions*)   unionize (means *form a union*)

* Use a hyphen when two or more prefixes apply to one root word.

    YES   pre- and post-Renaissance

29i How do I use hyphens with compound words?

A **compound word** combines two or more words to express one concept. Compound words come in three forms: open compounds as in *night shift;* hyphenated words, as in *tractor-trailer;* and closed compounds, as in *handbook.* Quick Reference 29.2 lists basic guidelines for positioning hyphens in compound words.

QUICK REFERENCE **29.2**

Hyphens with compound words

- At the end of a line, divide a compound word already containing a hyphen only after that hyphen, if possible. Also, divide a closed-compound word only between the two complete words, if possible.

NO	self-con-scious	sis-ter-in-law	mas-terpiece
YES	self-conscious	sister-in-law	master-piece

- Use a hyphen between a prefix and an open-compound word.

NO	antigun control [*gun control* is an open-compound word]
YES	anti-gun control

- Use a hyphen for most ADJECTIVE compounds that you create out of two or more words when the compound precedes the noun it modifies, but not when the words follow the noun (31g).

YES	well-researched report	report is well researched
YES	problem-solving skills	skills in problem solving

- Use hyphens when a compound modifier includes a series.

YES	two-, three-, or four-year program

- Never use a hyphen when a compound modifier starts with an *–ly* adverb.

NO	happily-married couple	loosely-tied package
YES	happily married couple	loosely tied package

- Avoid using a hyphen in compounds made with the COMPARATIVE and SUPERLATIVE forms *more, less* and *most, least.* (Compounds made with other comparatives and superlatives are sometimes hyphenated for clarity or by convention.)

NO	more-appropriate idea
YES	more appropriate idea
NO	least-significant factors
YES	least significant factors

- Never use a hyphen when a compound modifier is a foreign phrase.

YES	*post hoc* fallacies

- Never use a hyphen with a possessive compound.

NO	a full-week's work	eight-hours' pay
YES	a full week's work	eight hours' pay

EXERCISE 29-4   Provide the correct form of the words in parentheses, according to the rules in 29f through 29i. Explain your reasoning for each.

1. The tiger is (all powerful) _____ in the cat family.

2. (Comparison and contrast) _____ studies of tigers and lions show that the tiger is the (more agile) _____ and powerful.

3. Male tigers and lions look similar except for their hair length: Tigers have (ultra short) _____ hair and male lions have (extra long) _____ hair in their manes.

4. The tiger's body is a (boldly striped) _____ yellow, with a white (under body) _____.

5. The Bengal tiger, the largest of the family, is aggressive and (self confident) _____.

6. In India, where the Bengal tiger is called a (village destroyer) _____, it goes (in to) _____ villages to hunt for food.

7. Entire villages have been temporarily abandoned by (terror stricken) _____ people who have seen a Bengal tiger nearby.

8. Villagers seek to protect their homes by destroying tigers with traps, (spring loaded) _____ guns, and (poisoned arrows) _____.

9. Bengal tigers are also called (cattle killers) _____, although they attack domestic animals only when they cannot find wild ones.

10. Many people who do not live near a zoo get to see tigers only in (animal shows) _____, although (pro animal) _____ activists try to prevent tigers from being used this way.

Chapter 30

CAPITALS, ITALICS, ABBREVIATIONS, AND NUMBERS

CAPITALS

30a When do I capitalize a "first" word?

Common
Grammar
Errors: 18.
Capitalization
Errors

FIRST WORD IN A SENTENCE

Always capitalize the first letter of the first word in a sentence.

> **N**early two metres of snow fell last winter.

A SERIES OF QUESTIONS

If questions in a series are complete sentences, start each with a capital letter. If, however, the questions aren't complete sentences, you can choose to capitalize or not. Whatever your choice, be consistent in each piece of writing. In this handbook, we use capitals for a series of questions.

> What facial feature would most people like to change? **E**yes? **E**ars? **N**ose?
> What facial feature would most people like to change? **e**yes? **e**ars? **n**ose?

SMALL WORDS IN TITLES OR HEADINGS

Capitalize small words (*the, a, an,* and short PREPOSITIONS such as *of, to*) in a title or heading only when they begin or end the title or when the source capitalizes these small words.

Always capitalize *I*, no matter where it falls in a sentence or group of words: ***I** love you now, although **I** didn't use to.* The same holds for *O*, the INTERJECTION: *You are, **O** my fair love, a burning fever; **O** my gentle love, embrace me.* In contrast, never capitalize the interjection *oh*, unless it starts a sentence or is capitalized in words you're quoting.

AFTER A COLON

When a complete sentence follows a colon, you can choose to start that sentence with either a capital or a lowercase letter, but be consistent in each piece of writing. When the words after a colon are not a complete sentence, do not capitalize.

> She reacted instantly: **S**he picked up the ice cream and pushed it back into her cone.
> She reacted instantly: **s**he picked up the ice cream and pushed it back into her cone.
> She bought four pints of ice cream: **v**anilla, chocolate, strawberry, and butter pecan.

> ⚠ **ALERT:** A colon can follow only a complete sentence (an INDEPENDENT CLAUSE; see 26a). ●

FORMAL OUTLINE

In a formal outline (2f), start each item with a capital letter. Use a period only when the item is a complete sentence.

30b When do I use capitals with listed items?

A LIST RUN INTO A SENTENCE

If run-in listed items are complete sentences, start each with a capital and end each with a period (or question mark or exclamation point). If the run-in listed items are incomplete sentences, start each with a lowercase letter and end each with a comma—unless the items already contain commas, in which case use semicolons. If you list three or more items that are incomplete sentences, use *and* before the last item.

> **YES** We found three reasons for the delay: (1) **B**ad weather held up delivery of materials. (2) **P**oor scheduling created confusion. (3) **I**mproper machine maintenance caused an equipment failure.

> **YES** The reasons for the delay were (1) **b**ad weather, (2) **p**oor scheduling, **and** (3) **e**quipment failure.

> **YES** The reasons for the delay were (1) **b**ad weather, which had been predicted; (2) **p**oor scheduling, which is the airline's responsibility; **and** (3) **e**quipment failure, which no one can predict.

A DISPLAYED LIST

In a displayed list, each item starts on a new line. If the items are sentences, capitalize the first letter and end with a period (or question mark or exclamation point). If the items are not sentences, you can use a capital letter or not. Whichever you choose, be consistent in each piece of writing. Punctuate a displayed list as you would a run-in list.

> **YES** We found three reasons for the delay:
> 1. **B**ad weather held up delivery of materials.
> 2. **P**oor scheduling created confusion.
> 3. **I**mproper machine maintenance caused an equipment failure.

> **YES** The reasons for the delay were
> 1. **b**ad weather,
> 2. **p**oor scheduling, **and**
> 3. **e**quipment failure.

ALERTS: (1) If a complete sentence leads into a displayed list, you can end the sentence with a colon. However, if an incomplete sentence leads into a displayed list, use no punctuation.

(2) Use PARALLELISM for items in a list. For example, if one item is a sentence, use sentences for all the items (10e); or if one item starts with a VERB, start all items with a verb in the same TENSE; and so on. ●

30c When do I use capitals with sentences in parentheses?

When you write a complete sentence within parentheses that falls within another sentence, don't start with a capital or end with a period—but do use a question mark or exclamation mark, if needed. When you write a sentence within parentheses that doesn't fall within another sentence, capitalize the first word and end with a period (or question mark or exclamation mark).

> You may have to line the section of river between the Mazinaw Lake Dam and Marble Lake when water levels are low. (**L**ining is guiding the canoe along from shore with ropes tied to bow and stern.) To the right, a 150-metre portage works around the worst of this shallow stretch.

After turning off Highway 38 onto Perth Road, north of Kingston, and picking up our vehicle permit at the park office trail centre (**b**ooking a reservation for this route is strongly recommended), we drove down bumpy Salmon Road to the designated launch site.

—Kevin Callan, *Up the Creek*

30d When do I use capitals with quotations?

If a quotation within your sentence is itself less than a complete sentence, never capitalize the first quoted word. If the quotation you have used in your sentence is itself a complete sentence, capitalize the first word.

Mme Paquette says that students who are learning a new language should visit that country and "**a**bsorb a good accent with the food."

Mme Paquette likes to point out that when students live in a new country, "**T**hey'll absorb a good accent with the food."

When you write DIRECT DISCOURSE—which you introduce with verbs such as *said, stated, reported,* and others (see 35k) followed by a comma, capitalize the first letter of the quoted words. However, never capitalize a partial quotation, and never capitalize the continuation of a one-sentence quotation within your sentence.

Mme Paquette said, "**S**tudents who are learning a new language should visit that country. They'll absorb a good accent with the food." [complete sentence]

Mme Paquette told me that the best way to "**a**bsorb a good accent" in a language is to visit the country and eat its food. [part of a quotation integrated in a sentence]

"Of course," she continued with a smile, "**t**he accent lasts longer than the food." [continuation of a one-sentence quotation]

30e When do I capitalize nouns and adjectives?

Capitalize PROPER NOUNS (nouns that name specific people, places, and things): *Michael J. Fox, Mexico, World Wide Web*. Also, capitalize **proper adjectives** (adjectives formed from proper nouns): *a Mexican entrepreneur, a Web address*. Don't capitalize ARTICLES (*the, a, an*) that accompany proper nouns and proper adjectives, unless they start a sentence.

When a proper noun or adjective loses its very specific "proper" association, it also loses its capital letter: *french fries, pasteurized*. When you turn a common noun (*lake*) into a proper noun (*Lake Erie*), capitalize all words.

Expect sometimes that you'll see capitalized words that this handbook says not to capitalize. For example, a corporation's written communications usually capitalize its own entities (*our Board of Directors* or *this Company*), even though the rule calls for lowercase (*the board of directors, the company*). Similarly, the administrators of your school might write *the Faculty* and *the College* (or *the University*), even though the rule calls for a lower-case *f, c,* and *u*. How writers capitalize can depend on AUDIENCE and PURPOSE in each specific context.

Quick Reference 30.1 (p. 386) is a capitalization guide. If you don't find what you need, locate an item in it (or in Quick Reference 30.2 on p. 389) that's close to what you want, and use it as a model.

Capitalization

	CAPITALS	LOWERCASE LETTERS
NAMES	Mother Teresa (*also, used as names;* Mother, Dad, Mom, Pa)	my mother [relationship]
	Doctor Ruth	the doctor [role]
TITLES	Prime Minister Campbell	a prime minister
	Liberal [party member]	liberal [a believer in liberal ideals]
	Member of Parliament Peggy Nash	a member of Parliament
	the Honourable Mr. Justice John Sopinka	the judge
	Queen Elizabeth II	the queen [*also* the Queen, referring to Canada's queen]
GROUPS OF PEOPLE	Caucasian [race]	white, black [*also* White, Black]
	Native Canadian, First Nations, South Asian [ethnic group]	
	Irish, Korean [nationality]	
	Jewish, Catholic, Protestant, Buddhist [religious affiliation]	
ORGANIZATIONS	Parliament	parliamentary
	the Supreme Court of Canada	the court [*also* the Court]
	the Conservative Party	the party
	the Canadian Broadcasting Corporation	the corporation
	Calgary Flames	hockey team
	Canadian Medical Association	professional group
	Alcoholics Anonymous	self-help group
PLACES	Whitehorse	the city
	the West [region]	turn west [direction]
	the West Coast	the western coast of Canada
	King Street	the street
	Atlantic Ocean	the ocean
	the Rocky Mountains	the mountains
BUILDINGS	the House of Commons	the legislature [*but* the House, the Commons]
	Pauline Johnson High School	a high school
	Front Road Café	a restaurant
	Highland Hospital	a hospital
SCIENTIFIC TERMS	Earth [as one of nine planets]	the earth [otherwise]
	The Milky Way, the Galaxy [as name]	our galaxy, the moon, the sun
	Streptococcus aureus	a streptococcal infection
	Gresham's law	the theory of relativity
LANGUAGES	Spanish, Chinese	
SCHOOL COURSES	Chemistry 342	a chemistry course
	English 111	my English class
	Introduction to Photography	a photography course

continued ➤

Capitalization

	CAPITALS	LOWERCASE LETTERS
NAMES OF SPECIFIC THINGS	Black Parrot tulip Lakehead University Heinz ketchup a Toyota Camry Twelfth Dynasty the *Calgary Herald*	climbing rose the university ketchup, sauce a car the dynasty a newspaper

TIMES, SEASONS, HOLIDAYS	Monday, Fri.
	September, February
	the Roaring Twenties
	the Christmas season
	
	New Year's Day
	Passover, Ramadan,
	    Kwanzaa
		today
		a month
		the decade
		spring, summer, autumn, winter,
		    the fall semester
		feast day, the holiday
		religious holiday or observance

HISTORICAL PERIODS, EVENTS, AND DOCUMENTS	World War I
	Battle of Vimy Ridge
	the Great Depression
	    (of the 1930s)
	the Reformation
	Paleozoic
	the Quiet Revolution
	the Charter of Rights
		the war
		the battle
		the depression [any serious
		    economic downturn]
		the sixteenth century
		era or age, prehistory
		a sociopolitical movement
		twentieth-century documents

RELIGIOUS TERMS	Athena, God Islam the Torah, the Koran the Bible, Scripture	a goddess, a god a religion a holy book biblical, scriptural
LETTER PARTS	Dear Ms. Schultz: Sincerely, Yours truly,	

PUBLISHED AND RELEASED MATERIAL	"The Hockey Sweater"
	*The Canadian
	    Encyclopedia*
	Jazz on Ice
	the Meech Lake Accord
	Mass in B Minor
		[Capitalize first letter of first
		    and last word and all other
		    major words]
		the show, a performance
		a federal-provincial agreement
		the B minor mass

ACRONYMS AND INITIALISMS	NASA, NATO, NFB, UBC, NAFTA, DNA	
COMPUTER TERMS	Microsoft Word, WordPerfect, Linux Firefox the Internet World Wide Web, the Web	computer software a browser a computer network www (in URLs)
PROPER ADJECTIVES AND THEIR COMPOUNDS	Victorian post-Victorian Indo-European pre-Confederation	

EXERCISE 30-1   Add capital letters as needed. See 30a through 30e for help.

1. When Antonine Maillet was awarded france's prix goncourt in 1979, she said of the acadian people who are the subject of her prizewinning novel, "we don't have much to say. Just that we're alive."

2. Wai-Yee turned to face west and looked out over the pacific, imagining her grandfather's journey across that wide ocean.

3. The fine art course taught by professor Sanzio accepts only students who already have credits in fine art 101 and Renaissance studies 211.

4. For years, a european travel guide written by Arthur Frommer (it advised tourists how to live on five dollars a day) could be found in the backpacks and suitcases of thousands of north American travellers.

5. The north pole is surrounded by an icy sea; the south pole lies in the middle of a frozen land mass, the continent known as antarctica.

6. As a packed mass of men brushed by the reporters, a single voice arose: "may I ask you a question, prime minister Tupper?"

7. How should we think of the start of the french revolution? Was it the best of times? the worst of times? a time of indecision, perhaps?

8. According to the chapter "the making of a new world," among those credited with the discovery of the Americas before Columbus are (1) the vikings, (2) various groups of european fishers and whalers, and (3) the peoples who crossed the Bering strait to Alaska in prehistoric times.

9. People who are accustomed to one of the lovely and powerful English translations of the bible sometimes forget that the bible was not originally written in English.

10. The African union (AU), which came into existence in 2002, has many of the same structures and institutions as the older european union (EU).

ITALICS

((•
AUDIO LESSON
Section 1: Big
Ideas—
Punctuation
and Mechanics

30f   What are italics?

Italic typeface slants to the right (*like this*); **roman typeface** does not (like this). MLA STYLE requires italics, not underlining, in all documents.

     ROMAN   your writing

     ITALICS   *your writing*

((•
AUDIO LESSON
Section 2:
Practice
Questions—
Punctuation
and Mechanics

30g   How do I choose between using italics and quotation marks?

As a rule, use italics for titles of long works (*The Matrix*, a movie) or for works that contain subsections (*Masterpiece Theater*, a television show). Generally, use quotation marks for titles of shorter works ("I Wanna Hold Your Hand," a song) and for titles of subsections within longer works such as books (Chapter 1, "Loomings").

((•
AUDIO LESSON
Section 3:
Rapid
Review—
Punctuation
and Mechanics

     Quick Reference 30.2 is a guide for using italics, quotation marks, or nothing. If you don't find what you need, locate an item that is as much like what you want as possible and use it as a model.

Italics, quotation marks, or nothing

ITALICS

TITLES AND NAMES

The Englishman's Boy [a novel]
Farther West [a play]
Exotica [a film]
Who Do You Think You Are?
  [a book]
*Simon & Schuster Handbook
  for Writers* [a textbook]
The Prose Reader [a collection
  of essays]
Iliad [a book-length poem]
Equinox [a magazine]
Symphonie Fantastique [a long
  musical work]

Thank Me Later [a CD]
Degrassi [a television series] .
Kids Count [a website title]
the *Brandon Sun* [a newspaper]*

OTHER WORDS

a mari usque ad mare [words in
  a language other than English]
What does *our* imply? [a word
  meant as a word]
the *abc*'s; the letter *x* [letters
  meant as letters]

QUOTATION MARKS OR NOTHING

Title of Student Essay
act 2 [part of a play]
the epilogue [a part of a film or book]
"Royal Beatings" [a story in a book]

"Agreement" [a chapter in a book]

"Putting in a Good Word for Guilt"
  [an essay in a book]
"Whatever You Do" [a short poem]
"Nanook Passage" [an article in a magazine]
Violin Concerto No. 2 in B-flat Minor [a musical
  work identified by form, number, and key—
  neither quotation marks nor underlining]
"Up All Night" [a song]
"Breakaway" [an episode of a television series]
Excel [a software program]

burrito, chutzpah [widely understood
  non-English words]

6s and 7s; & [numerals and symbols]

*In MLA style and CM style, if *The* is part of a newspaper's title, don't capitalize or italicize it in the body of
your paper. In MLA style and CM-style documentation, omit the word *The* entirely. In APA-style and CSE-style
documentation, capitalize and italicize *The*.

30h   Can I use italics for special emphasis?

In ACADEMIC WRITING, you're expected to convey special emphasis through your choice
of words and sentence structure, not with italics. If your message absolutely calls for it, use
italics sparingly—and only after you're sure nothing else will do.

Many people we *think* are powerful turn out on closer examination to be merely frightened
and anxious.

—Michael Korda, *Power!*

EXERCISE 30-2   Edit these sentences for correct use of italics, quotation marks, and capitals. For help, consult 30a through 30h.

1. The article on "The Canoe" in The Canadian Encyclopedia says that birchbark canoes were "perfectly adapted to summer travel" along the shallow streams and swift rivers of early Canada.

2. According to one source, Canada's name is derived from the *Huron-Iroquois* word kanata, meaning a village or settlement.

3. The writer of a humour column in The Globe and Mail described an imaginary paper called The Mop and Pail, where things were just slightly more ridiculous than in real life.

4. Atom Egoyan's adaptation of the Strauss opera "Salome" had a stage full of TV monitors and other modern paraphernalia.

5. When a small business chooses a name beginning with the letter a repeated four times, as in AAAAbco Auto Body, we can be sure its marketing plan includes being noticed at the start of *The Telephone Directory*.

ABBREVIATIONS

30i   What are standard practices for using abbreviations?

Some abbreviations are standard in all writing circumstances (*Mr.,* not *Mister,* in a name; *St.* Catharines, the city, not *Saint* Catharines). In some situations, you may have a choice whether to abbreviate or spell out a word. Choose what seems suited to your PURPOSE for writing and your AUDIENCE, and be consistent within each piece of writing.

> NO   The great painter Vincent Van Gogh was **b.** in Holland in 1853, but he lived most of his life and died in **Fr.**

> YES   The great painter Vincent Van Gogh was **born** in Holland in 1853, but he lived most of his life and died in **France.**

> NO   Our hockey team left after Casey's **psych** class on **Tues., Oct.** 10, but the flight had to make an unexpected stop (in **N.B.**) before reaching **St. FXU.**

> YES   Our hockey team left after Casey's **psychology** class on **Tuesday, October** 10, but the flight had to make an unexpected stop (in **New Brunswick**) before reaching **St. Francis Xavier University.**

> NO   Please confirm in writing your order for one **doz.** helmets in **lg** and x-**lg.**

> YES   Please confirm in writing your order for one **dozen** helmets in **large** and **extra large.**

ALERTS: (1) Many abbreviations call for periods (*Mrs., Ms., Dr.*), but the practice is changing. The trend today is to drop the periods (*PS,* not *P.S.; MD,* not *M.D.; US* and *UK,* not *U.S.* and *U.K.*), yet firm rules are still evolving.

(2) **Acronyms** (pronounceable words formed from the initials of a name) generally have no periods: *NAFTA* (*N*orth *A*merican *F*ree *T*rade *A*greement) and *AIDS* (*a*cquired *immune deficiency syndrome*).

(3) **Initialisms** (names spoken as separate letters) usually have no periods (*IBM, CBC, UN*).

(4) Postal abbreviations for provinces and US states have no periods (30k).

(5) When the final period of an abbreviation falls at the end of a sentence, that period serves also to end the sentence. ●

30j How do I use abbreviations with months, time, eras, and symbols?

MONTHS

According to MLA STYLE, abbreviations for months belong only in Works Cited lists, tables, charts, and the like. Write out the full spelling in your ACADEMIC WRITING.

TIMES

Use the abbreviations *a.m.* and *p.m.* only with exact times: *7:15 a.m.; 3:47 p.m.* Although some publication styles use the capitalized versions, *A.M.* and *P.M.*, MLA style calls for the use of lowercase letters.

 ALERTS: (1) Never use *a.m.* and *p.m.* in place of the words *morning, evening,* and *night.*

> NO My hardest final exam is in the **a.m.** tomorrow, but by early **p.m.**, I'll be ready to study for the rest of my finals.

> YES My hardest final exam is in the **morning** tomorrow, but by early **evening**, I'll be ready to study for the rest of my finals.

(2) Specify *12:00 noon* and *12:00 midnight*, not *12:00 a.m.* and *12:00 p.m.* (because *a.m.* and *p.m.* mean, respectively, *before* noon and *after* noon). *Noon* and *midnight* are also acceptable on their own. ●

ERAS

In MLA style, use capital letters, without periods, in abbreviations for eras. Some writers prefer using *CE* ("common era") in place of *AD* (from the Latin *anno Domini,* "in the year of our Lord") as the more inclusive term. The equivalent to *CE* is *BCE* ("before the common era") in place of *BC* ("before Christ").

When writing the abbreviations for eras, place *AD* before the year (*AD 476*) and all the others after the year (*29 BC; 165 BCE; 1100 CE*).

SYMBOLS

In MLA style, decide whether to use symbols or spelled-out words according to your topic and the focus of your document (see also 30m). However, never use a freestanding symbol, such as $, %, or ¢ in your sentences; always use it with a numeral. Many writers abbreviate SI units (24i) in almost any context, but if you spell out a number, you should write out any unit that accompanies it (*6 km* but *six kilometres*).

Conversely, always use a numeral with the abbreviations of units of measure (both SI and imperial) and scientific or other symbols: *6 kg; 9 lbs.; 15 cm; 6"; $18; 24 KB; 6:34 a.m.; 32°;* and numbers in addresses, dates, page references, and decimal fractions (*8.3*). In writing about money, the form *$25 million* is an acceptable combination of symbol, numeral, and spelled-out word.

In confined spaces, such as charts and tables, use symbols with numerals (*20¢*). In documents that focus on technical matters, use numerals but spell out the imperial unit of measurement (*2500 pounds*)—in MLA style. In other documentation styles, such as APA, CM, CSE, and IEEE, the guidelines differ somewhat, so you need to check each style's manual.

30k How do I use abbreviations for other elements?

TITLES

Use either a title of address before a name (**Dr.** *Daniel Klausner*) or an academic degree after a name (*Daniel Klausner,* **PhD**), not both. However, because *Jr., Sr., II, III,* and so forth (rare in Canada but rather common in the United States) are part of a given name, you can use both titles of address and academic degree abbreviations: **Dr**. *Martin Luther King* **Jr.**; *Gavin Alexander* **II, MD**.

ALERTS: (1) Insert a comma both before and after an academic degree that follows a person's name, unless it falls at the end of a sentence: *Daljit Singh,* **LLD**, *is our guest speaker,* or *Our guest speaker is Daljit Singh,* **LLD**.

(2) Never put a comma before an abbreviation that is part of a given name: *Steven Elliott* **Sr.**, *Douglas Young* **III**. ●

NAMES AND TERMS

If you use a term frequently in a piece of writing, follow these guidelines: The first time you use the term, spell it out completely and put its abbreviation in parentheses immediately after. In later references, use the abbreviation alone.

Some new democracies in Eastern Europe quickly joined the **North Atlantic Treaty Organization (NATO)**, but full **NATO** membership came slowly for others.

When referring to the *United States* or *United Kingdom,* you can use the abbreviation *US (U.S.)* or *UK (U.K.)* as a modifier before a noun (*the* **US** *ski team; the* **UK** *skating team*). You must spell out the name when you use it as a noun.

ADDRESSES

If you include a full address—street, city, province, and postal code—in the body of your writing, you can abbreviate the province name. Both two-letter postal abbreviations (*AB*) and traditional abbreviations (*Alta.*) are used in writing in Canada. Spell out any other combination of a city and a province, and spell out the name of a province by itself.

ALERT: When you write the names of a city and province or territory within a sentence, use a comma before and after the province or territory. Don't insert a comma before a postal code.

NO   St. John, New Brunswick is too often confused with St. John's, Newfoundland.

YES   St. John, New Brunswick, is too often confused with St. John's, Newfoundland. ●

SCHOLARLY WRITING (MLA STYLE)

MLA style permits abbreviations for a selection of scholarly terms. These are listed in Quick Reference 30.3. Never use them in the body of your ACADEMIC WRITING. Reserve them for your Works Cited lists and for any notes you might write in a separate list at the end of your research paper.

30l When can I use *etc.?*

The abbreviation *etc.* comes from the Latin *et cetera,* meaning "and the rest." In ACADEMIC WRITING, don't use *etc.* Accepted substitutes include *and the like, and so on, and so forth,* among others. Even better is a more concrete description. An acceptable use of *etc.* is in tables and charts.

QUICK REFERENCE 30.3

Major scholarly abbreviations—MLA style

anon.	anonymous	**i.e.**	that is
b.	born	**ms., mss.**	manuscript,
c. *or* ©	copyright		manuscripts
c. *or* **ca.**	circa (about)	**NB**	note well (*nota bene*)
	[with dates]	**n.d.**	no date (of
cf.	compare		publication)
col., cols.	column, columns	**p., pp.**	page, pages
d.	died	**par.**	paragraph
ed., eds.	edition, edited by,	**pref.**	preface, preface by
	editor(s)	**rept.**	report, reported by
e.g.	for example	**rev.**	review, reviewed by;
esp.	especially		revised, revised by
et al.	and others	**sec., secs.**	section, sections
ff.	following pages,	**v.** *or* **vs.**	versus [*v.* in legal
	following lines,		cases]
	folios	**vol., vols.**	volume, volumes

NO   The names Baldwin and LaFontaine, Macdonald and Cartier, **etc.,** are linked in historical memory.

YES   The names Baldwin and LaFontaine, Macdonald and Cartier, **and other political allies** are linked in historical memory.

ALERT: If you do write *etc.,* always put a comma after the period if the abbreviation falls in the middle of a sentence. ●

EXERCISE 30-3 Revise these sentences for correct use of abbreviations. For help, consult 30i through 30l.

1. Although she took her degree in a tech. field, Charlene made a point of getting as many lib. arts credits as she could.

2. The U of M in Winnipeg, Man., was the first institution of higher ed. to be established in W Canada.

3. Graham knew instantly from Lucinda's accent that she came from NS and could not possibly be a native of Alta. as she claimed.

4. Lamont gave generously to all the charities, political orgs., etc., that asked him, until the day in Nov. 2011 when he was approached by a rep of the Flat Earth Society.

5. Dozens of hrs. and thousands of $$ later, the contractors finally extended the driveway to the main rd., a mere four m away.

NUMBERS

30m When do I use spelled-out numbers?

Your decision to write a number as a word or as a figure depends on what you're referring to and how often numbers occur in your piece of writing. The guidelines we give in this handbook are for MLA STYLE, which focuses on writing in the humanities. For other disciplines, follow the guidelines in their style manuals.

Reserve figures for some categories of numbers and spelled-out words for other categories. Never mix spelled-out numbers and figures for a particular category.

> NO   In **four** days, our volunteers increased from **five** to **eight** to **17** to **233**.
>
> YES   In **four** days, our volunteers increased from **5** to **8** to **17** to **233**.
> [Numbers referring to volunteers are in numerals, while *four* is spelled out because it refers to a different category: days.]

ALERT: When you write a two-word number, use a hyphen between the spelled-out words, starting with *twenty-one* and continuing through *ninety-nine*. ●

If you use numbers infrequently in a document, spell out all numbers that call for no more than two words: *fifty-two cards, twelve hundred students*. If you use specific numbers often in a document (temperatures when writing about climate, percentages in an economics essay, or other specific measurements of time, distance, and other quantities), use figures: *11 nanoseconds*. If you give only an approximation, and you are not writing scientific or technical prose, spell out the numbers: *About fifteen centimetres of snow fell*.

In the humanities, the names of centuries are always spelled out: *the eighteenth century*.

When you write for courses in the humanities, never start a sentence with a figure. Spell out the number—or better still, revise the sentence so that the number doesn't need to fall at the beginning. For practices in other disciplines, consult their manuals.

> NO   **$375 dollars** for each credit is the tuition rate for non-residents.
>
> YES   **Three hundred seventy-five dollars** for each credit is the tuition rate for non-residents.
>
> YES   The tuition rate for non-residents is **$375** for each credit.

30n What are standard practices for writing numbers?

Quick Reference 30.4 shows standard practices for writing numbers. Consider it a basic guide, and rely on the manual of each documentation style for answers to other questions you may have.

QUICK REFERENCE 30.4

Specific numbers in writing

DATES	August 6, 1941
	1732–1845
	from 34 BC to AD 244 (*or* 34 BCE to 230 CE)

continued ➤

Specific numbers in writing

ADDRESSES	10 Downing Street
	237 North 8th Street
	London ON N6A 3K7
TIMES	8:09 a.m., 6:00 p.m.
	six o'clock (*not* 6 o'clock)
	four in the afternoon *or* 4 p.m. (*not* four p.m.)
DECIMALS	0.01
AND FRACTIONS	98.6
	3.1416
	7/8
	12 1/4
	a sixth
	three-quarters (*not* 3-quarters)
	one-half
CHAPTERS	Chapter 27, page 2
AND PAGES	p. 1023
	pp. 660–62 (MLA style)
SCORES	a 6–0 score
AND STATISTICS	29% (*or* twenty-nine percent)
	a 5 to 1 ratio (*and* a ratio of 5:1)
	a one percent change (*and* at the 1 percent level)
IDENTIFICATION	94.4 FM (radio frequency)
NUMBERS	please call (012) 345–6789 (*or* 012-345-6789)
MEASUREMENTS	90 kilometres per hour (*or* 100 km/h)
	a 700-word essay
	8 1/2-by-11-inch paper (MLA style)
	2 metres (*or* 2 m)
	1.5 litres (*or* 1.5 L)
	350 millilitres (*or* 350 mL)
ACT, SCENE,	act 2, scene 2 (*or* act II, scene ii)
AND LINE	lines 75–79
TEMPERATURES	20°C; 7.5°C; –20°C
	40° F *or* 25°F
MONEY	$1.2 billion
	$3.41
	25¢ (*or* twenty-five cents)
	$10 000 (*or* $10,000)

EXERCISE 30-4 Revise these sentences so that the numbers are in correct form, either spelled out or as figures. For help, consult 30m and 30n.

1. At five fifteen p.m., the nearly empty city streets filled with 1000's of commuters.

2. A tarantula spider can survive without food for about two years and 3 months.

3. By the end of act one, scene five, Romeo and Juliet are in love and at the mercy of their unhappy fate.

4. Sound travels through air at a speed of 331 metres per second, but in water it travels four hundred and fifty percent faster, at 1481 metres per second.

5. 21 years old and unhappily married, Cleopatra met middle-aged Julius Caesar in forty-eight BCE.

6. A blue whale, which can weigh one hundred tonnes—the combined weight of 44 elephants—gains over three-point-four kilograms an hour until it reaches adolescence.

7. On the morning of August thirteen, nineteen hundred thirty, 3 huge meteorites smashed into the Amazon jungle.

8. 2 out of every 5 people who have ever lived on earth are alive today, according to 1 estimate.

9. The house at six hundred and fifty-three Oak Street—the 1 that children think is haunted—has been empty for 8 years, waiting for a buyer willing to pay its price of $ six million, forty-nine thousand dollars.

10. The 1912 sinking of the *Titanic*, in which one thousand five hundred and three people drowned, is widely known, but few people remember that more than three thousand people lost their lives aboard the ferryboat *Doña Paz* when it hit an oil tanker in the Philippines in nineteen eighty-seven.

30o How do I use hyphens with spelled-out numbers?

A spelled-out number uses words, not figures. Quick Reference 30.5 gives you guidelines.

! **ALERT:** Use figures rather than words for a fraction written in more than two words. If your context calls for figures, use hyphens only between the words of the numerator and only between the words of the denominator—but never between the numerator and the denominator: two one-hundredths (*2/100*), thirty-three ten-thousandths (*33/10 000*). ●

QUICK REFERENCE **30.5**

Hyphens with spelled-out numbers

- Use a hyphen between two-word numbers from *twenty-one* through *ninety-nine*, whether they stand alone or are part of a larger number.

  YES thirty-five two hundred thirty-five

continued ➤

- Use a hyphen in a COMPOUND-WORD modifier formed from a number and a word, whether the number is in words or figures.

  YES   fifty-minute class [*also* 50-minute class]

  YES   three-to-one odds [*also* 3-to-1 odds]

- Use a hyphen between the numerator and the denominator of two-word fractions.

  YES   one-half   two-fifths   seven-tenths

- Use a hyphen between compound nouns joining two units of measure.

  YES   light-years   kilowatt-hours

Chapter 31

SPELLING

31a What makes a good speller?

You might be surprised to hear that good spellers don't know how to spell and hyphenate every word they write. What they do know, however, is to check if they're not sure of a word's spelling. If your inner voice questions a spelling, do what good spellers do—consult a dictionary.

What do you do if even the first few letters of a word seem mysterious? This is a common problem among writers. Our best advice is that you think of an easy-to-spell SYNONYM for the word you need; look up that synonym in a thesaurus; and among the synonyms, find the word you need to spell.

Many people incorrectly believe that only naturally skilled spellers can write well. The truth is that correct spelling matters a great deal in final drafts, but not in earlier drafts. The best time to check spellings you doubt is when you're EDITING.

The various origins of words and ways that English-speaking people around the world pronounce words make it almost impossible to rely solely on pronunciation to spell a word. What you can rely on, however, are the proofreading hints and spelling rules explained in this chapter.

ALERT: Word-processing software usually includes a spell-check program that searches for words that don't match the spellings in the software's dictionary. Such programs have one major drawback. The programs can't detect that you've spelled a word incorrectly if what you've typed is a legitimate spelling of a legitimate word. For example, if you mean *top* but type *too,* or if you mean *from* and type *form,* no spell-check program "sees" a mistake. In these and similar cases, only the human eye can discover the errors. ●

Canadian spelling, because it has been influenced by both British and American spelling conventions, contains elements of both. Some people claim to notice a drift toward American conventions because of the influence of the media and new information technologies. Others, however, point to the popularity of new Canadian reference works, notably the *Canadian Oxford Dictionary.* Both British and American spellings may appear in any given piece of writing. Here are some examples:

labour	*or*	labor	encyclopaedia	*or*	encyclopedia
theatre	*or*	theater	catalogue	*or*	catalog
cheque	*or*	check	realise	*or*	realize
defence	*or*	defense	programme	*or*	program

In both academic and business writing, your purpose for writing and the expectations of your audience often determine your choice of spelling conventions. Readers in the scientific and medical fields, and especially in information technologies, often expect

American spellings to be used. Writing in other fields, including (but certainly not limited to) Canadian history and literature, typically uses a more British-oriented style to produce the hybrid that has become the *Canadian* spelling style.

Whichever spellings you choose, aim for a logical and consistent style. If you use the spelling *labour* in a document, use *colour* as well; and if you spell *theatre,* use the spelling *centre*. Each of the Canadian dictionaries listed in section 12d has its own version of Canadian spelling that can guide you in finding a consistent spelling style.

31b **How can I proofread for errors in spelling and hyphen use?**

Many spelling errors are the result of illegible handwriting, slips of the pen, or typographical mistakes. Catching these "typos" requires especially careful proofreading, using the techniques in Quick Reference 31.1.

QUICK REFERENCE   **31.1**

Proofreading for errors in spelling

- Slow down your reading speed to allow yourself to concentrate on the individual letters of words rather than on the meaning of the words.
- Stay within your "visual span," the number of letters you can identify with a single glance (for most people, about six letters).
- Put a ruler or large index card under each line as you proofread, to focus your vision and concentration.
- Read each paragraph in reverse, from the last sentence to the first. This method can keep you from being distracted by the meaning of the material.

31c **How are plurals spelled?**

The most common way to form a plural is to add *-s* or *-es* at the end of the word. The following list covers all variations of creating plurals.

- **Adding -s or -es:** Plurals of most words are formed by adding *-s,* including words that end in "hard"-*ch* (sounding like *k*): *leg, leg**s***; *shoe, shoe**s***; *stomach, stomach**s***. Words ending in *-s, -sh, -x, -z,* or "soft"-*ch* (as in *beach*) are formed by adding *-es* to the singular: *lens, lens**es***; *tax, tax**es***; *beach, beach**es***.
- **Words ending in -o:** Add *-s* if the *-o* is preceded by a vowel: *radio, radio**s***; *cameo, cameo**s***. Add *-es* if the *-o* is preceded by a consonant: *potato, potato**es***. With a few words, you can choose the *-s* or *-es* plural form, but current practice generally supports adding *-es*: *cargo, cargo**es***; *tornado, tornado**es***; *zero, zero**s*** or *zero**es***.
- **Words ending in -f or -fe:** Some words ending in *-f* and *-fe* are made plural by adding *-s*: *belief, belief**s***. Others require changing *-f* or *-fe* to *-ves*: *life, live**s***; *leaf, leave**s***. Words ending in *-ff* or *-ffe* simply add *-s*: *staff, staff**s***; *giraffe, giraffe**s***.
- **Compound words:** For most compound words, add *-s* or *-es* at the end of the last word: *chequebooks, player-coach**es***. In a few cases, the first word is made plural: *sister-in-law, sister**s**-in-law*; *kilometre**s** per hour.* (For information about hyphens in compound words, see 31g.)
- **Internal changes and endings other than -s:** A few words change internally or add endings other than *-s* to become plural: *foot, fe**et***; *man, m**en***; *crisis, cris**es***; *child, child**ren***.

- **Foreign words:** The best advice is to check your dictionary. In general, many Latin words ending in *-um* form the plural by changing *-um* to *-a*: *curriculum, curricula*; *datum, data*; *medium, media*. Also, Latin words that end in *-us* usually form the plural by changing *-us* to *-i*: *alumnus, alumni*; *syllabus, syllabi*. Additionally, Greek words that end in *-on* usually form the plural by changing *-on* to *-a*: *criterion, criteria*; *phenomenon, phenomena*.

- **One-form words:** Some words have the same form in both the singular and the plural: *deer, elk, fish*. You need to use modifiers, as necessary, to indicate which form you mean: **one** *deer,* **nine** *deer.*

EXERCISE 31-1   Write the correct plural form of these words. For help, consult 31c.

1. yourself
2. sheep
3. photo
4. woman
5. appendix
6. millennium
7. lamp
8. runner-up
9. criterion
10. lunch
11. echo
12. syllabus
13. wife
14. get-together
15. crisis

31d   How are suffixes spelled?

A **suffix** is an ending added to a word that changes the word's meaning or its grammatical function. For example, adding the suffix *-able* to the VERB *depend* creates the ADJECTIVE *dependable*.

- ***-y* words:** If the letter before a final *-y* is a consonant, change the *-y* to *-i* and add the suffix: *try, tries, tried*. In the case of *trying* and similar words, the following rule applies: Keep the *-y* when the suffix begins with *-i* (*apply, applying*). If the letter before the final *-y* is a vowel, keep the final *-y*: *employ, employed, employing*. These rules don't apply to IRREGULAR VERBS (see Quick Reference 15.4 in section 15d).

- ***-e* words:** Drop a final *-e* when the suffix begins with a vowel, unless doing this would cause confusion: for example, *be* + *ing* can't be written *bing*, but *require* does become *requiring*; *like* does become *liking*. Keep the final *-e* when the suffix begins with a consonant: *require, requirement*; *like, likely*. Exceptions include *argue, argument*; *true, truly*.

- **Words that double a final letter:** If the final letter is a consonant, double it *only* if it passes these tests: (1) Its last two letters are a vowel followed by a consonant; and (2) the suffix begins with a vowel: *drop, dropped*; *begin, beginning*; *forget, forgettable*. (American spelling adds a third test. The word must have one syllable or be accented on the last syllable: *begin* [accent on last syllable], *beginning*; but *travel* [accent on first syllable], *traveling*. British and Canadian spelling doubles the final consonant in many words even when the accent is not on the last syllable: *travel, travelling*; *worship, worshipper*. A notable exception is *novelist*, which has the same form in British, Canadian, and American spelling.)

- ***-cede, -ceed, -sede* words:** Only one word in the English language ends in *-sede*: *supersede*. Only three words end in *-ceed*: *exceed, proceed, succeed*. All other words with endings that sound like "seed" end in *-cede*: *concede, intercede, precede*.

- ***-ally* and *-ly* words:** The suffixes *-ally* and *-ly* turn words into adverbs. For most words ending in *-ic*, add *-ally*: *logically, statistically*. Otherwise, add *-ly*: *quickly, sharply, publicly*.

- ***-ance, -ence,* and *-ible, -able:*** No consistent rules govern words with these suffixes. When in doubt, look up the word.

31e · What is the *ie, ei* rule?

The famous rhymed rule for using *ie* and *ei* is usually true:

> *I* before *e* [believe, field, grief],
>
> Except after *c* [ceiling, conceit],
>
> Or when sounded like "ay"—
>
> As in n*ei*ghbour and w*ei*gh [eight, vein].

There are major exceptions (sorry!) to the *ie, ei* rule, listed here. Our best advice is that you memorize them.

- *ie:* consc*ie*nce, financ*ie*r, sc*ie*nce, spec*ie*s
- *ei:* *ei*ther, n*ei*ther, l*ei*sure, s*ei*ze, counterf*ei*t, for*ei*gn, forf*ei*t, sl*ei*ght (as in *sleight of hand*), w*ei*rd

EXERCISE 31-2   Follow the directions for each group of words. For help, consult 31d and 31e.

1. Add *-able* or *-ible:* (a) profit; (b) reproduce; (c) control; (d) coerce; (e) recognize.
2. Add *-ance* or *-ence:* (a) luxuri_____; (b) prud_____; (c) devi_____; (d) resist_____; (e) independ_____.
3. Drop the final *-e* as needed: (a) true + ly; (b) joke + ing; (c) fortunate + ly; (d) appease + ing; (e) appease + ment.
4. Change the final *-y* to *-i* as needed: (a) happy + ness; (b) pry + ed; (c) pry + ing; (d) dry + ly; (e) beautify + ing.
5. Double the final consonant as needed: (a) commit + ed; (b) commit + ment; (c) drop + ed; (d) occur + ed; (e) regret + ful.
6. Insert *ie* or *ei* correctly: (a) rel_____f; (b) ach_____ve; (c) w_____rd; (d) n_____ce; (e) dec_____ve.

31f   How are homonyms and other frequently confused words spelled?

Common Grammar Errors: 16. Spelling Errors

Homonyms are words that sound exactly like other words: *to, too, two; no, know.* The different spellings of homonyms tend to confuse many writers. The same holds for words that sound almost alike (*accept, except; conscience, conscious*).

Another reason for spelling problems is so-called swallowed pronunciation, which means one or more letters at the end of a word aren't pronounced clearly. For example, the *-d* ending in *used to* or *prejudiced* or the *-ten* ending in *written* are often swallowed rather than pronounced. When writers spell as they mispronounce, spelling errors result.

For more information about word usage that affects spelling, see Chapter 13, "Usage Glossary." Quick Reference 31.2 (p. 402) lists homonyms and other words that can be confused and lead to misspellings.

Homonyms and other frequently confused words

•	ACCEPT	to receive
	EXCEPT	with the exclusion of
•	ADVICE	recommendation
	ADVISE	to recommend
•	AFFECT	to influence [verb]; emotion [noun]
	EFFECT	result [noun]; to bring about or cause [verb]
•	AISLE	space between rows
	ISLE	island
•	ALLUDE	to make indirect reference to
	ELUDE	to avoid
•	ALLUSION	indirect reference
	ILLUSION	false idea, misleading appearance
•	ALREADY	by this time
	ALL READY	fully prepared
•	ALTAR	sacred platform or place
	ALTER	to change
•	ALTOGETHER	thoroughly
	ALL TOGETHER	everyone or everything in one place
•	ARE	PLURAL form of *to be*
	HOUR	sixty minutes
	OUR	plural form of *my*
•	ASCENT	the act of rising or climbing
	ASSENT	consent [noun]; to consent [verb]
•	ASSISTANCE	help
	ASSISTANTS	helpers
•	BARE	nude, unadorned
	BEAR	to carry; an animal
•	BOARD	piece of wood
	BORED	uninterested
•	BRAKE	device for stopping
	BREAK	to destroy, make into pieces
•	BREATH	air taken in
	BREATHE	to take in air
•	BUY	to purchase
	BY	next to, through the agency of
•	CAPITAL	major city; money [noun]; main [adjective]
	CAPITOL	government building (US)
•	CHOOSE	to pick
	CHOSE	PAST TENSE of *choose*

continued ➤

CITE	to point out
SIGHT	vision
SITE	a place
CLOTHES	garments [noun]; third-person singular PRESENT TENSE form of *to clothe*
CLOTHS	pieces of fabric
COARSE	rough
COURSE	path; series of lectures
COMPLEMENT	something that completes
COMPLIMENT	praise, flattery
CONSCIENCE	sense of morality
CONSCIOUS	awake, aware
COUNCIL	advisory or governing body
COUNSEL	advice [noun]; to advise [verb]
DAIRY	place associated with milk production
DIARY	personal journal
DESCENT	downward movement
DISSENT	disagreement
DESERT	to abandon [verb]; abandoned area, often dry or sandy [noun]
DESSERT	final, sweet course in a meal
DEVICE	a plan; an implement
DEVISE	to create
DIE	to lose life (dying) [verb]; one of a pair of dice [noun]
DYE	to change the colour of something (dyeing)
DOMINANT	commanding, controlling
DOMINATE	to control
ELICIT	to draw out
ILLICIT	illegal
EMINENT	prominent
IMMANENT	living within; inherent
IMMINENT	about to happen
ENVELOP	to surround
ENVELOPE	container for a letter or other papers
FAIR	light-skinned; just, honest
FARE	money for transportation; food
FORMALLY	conventionally, with ceremony
FORMERLY	previously
FORTH	forward
FOURTH	number four in a series
GORILLA	animal in ape family
GUERRILLA	fighter conducting surprise attacks

continued ➢

HEAR	to sense sound by ear
HERE	in this place
HOLE	opening [noun]
WHOLE	complete [noun or **adjective**]; an entire thing
HUMAN	relating to the species *Homo sapiens*
HUMANE	compassionate
INSURE	to buy or give insurance
ENSURE	to guarantee, protect
ITS	POSSESSIVE form of *it*
IT'S	CONTRACTION for *it is* or *it has*
KNOW	to comprehend
NO	negative
LATER	after a time
LATTER	second one of two things
LEAD	heavy metal substance [noun]; to guide [verb]
LED	past tense of *lead*
LIGHTNING	storm-related electricity
LIGHTENING	making lighter
LOOSE	unbound, not tightly fastened
LOSE	to misplace
MAYBE	perhaps [adverb]
MAY BE	might be [verb]
MEAT	animal flesh
MEET	to encounter
MINER	a person who works in a mine
MINOR	underage; less important
MORAL	distinguishing right from wrong; the lesson of a fable, story, or event
MORALE	attitude or outlook, usually of a group
OF	PREPOSITION indicating origin
OFF	away from; not on
PASSED	past tense of *pass*
PAST	at a previous time
PATIENCE	forbearance
PATIENTS	people under medical care
PEACE	absence of fighting
PIECE	part of a whole; musical arrangement
PERSONAL	intimate
PERSONNEL	employees
PLAIN	simple, unadorned
PLANE	to shave wood; aircraft; carpentry tool

continued ➤

• PRECEDE	to come before
PROCEED	to continue
• PRESENCE	being at hand; attendance at a place or in something
PRESENTS	gifts
• PRINCIPAL	foremost [adjective]; school head [noun]
PRINCIPLE	moral conviction, basic truth
• QUIET	silent, calm
QUITE	very
• RAIN	water that falls to earth [noun]; to fall like rain [verb]
REIGN	to rule
REIN	strap to guide or control an animal [noun]; to guide or control [verb]
• RAISE	to lift up
RAZE	to tear down
• RESPECTFULLY	with respect
RESPECTIVELY	in that order
• RIGHT	correct; opposite of *left*
RITE	ritual
WRITE	to put words on paper
• ROAD	path
RODE	past tense of *ride*
• SCENE	place of an action; segment of a play
SEEN	viewed
• SENSE	perception, understanding
SINCE	measurement of past time; because
• STATIONARY	standing still
STATIONERY	writing paper
• THAN	in comparison with; besides
THEN	at that time; next; therefore
• THEIR	possessive form of *they*
THERE	in that place
THEY'RE	contraction of *they are*
• THROUGH	finished; into and out of
THREW	past tense of *throw*
THOROUGH	complete
• TO	toward
TOO	also; indicates degree (*too much*)
TWO	number following *one*
• WAIST	midsection of the body
WASTE	discarded material [noun]; to squander, to fail to use up [verb]

continued ➤

• WEAK	not strong
WEEK	seven days
• WEATHER	climatic conditions
WHETHER	if, when alternatives are expressed or implied
• WHERE	in which place
WERE	past tense of *be*
• WHICH	one of a group
WITCH	female sorcerer
• WHOSE	possessive form of *who*
WHO'S	contraction for *who is* or *who has*
• YOUR	possessive form of *you*
YOU'RE	contraction for *you are*
YORE	long past

EXERCISE 31-3   Circle the correct homonym or commonly confused word of each group in parentheses.

Imagine that you (are, our) standing in the middle of a busy sidewalk, with a worried look on (your, you're, yore) face. In your hand (your, you're, yore) holding a map, (which, witch) you are puzzling over. If that happened in (real, reel) life, (its, it's) almost certain that within (to, too, two) or three minutes a passerby would ask if you (where, were) lost and would offer you (assistance, assistants). That helpful passerby, (buy, by) taking a (personal, personnel) interest in your problem, is displaying a quality known as empathy— the ability (to, too, two) put oneself in another person's place. Some researchers claim that empathy is an instinct that (human, humane) beings share with many other animals. Other scientists wonder (weather, whether) empathy is instead a (conscience, conscious) (moral, morale) choice that people make. Whatever explanation for the origin (of, off) empathy is (right, rite, write), such empathy generally has a positive (affect, effect)— especially if (your, you're, yore) a person who (maybe, may be) (to, too, two) lost to (know, no) (where, were) (to, too, two) turn.

31g   What are compound words?

A **compound word** puts together two or more words to express one concept.

Open compound words remain as separate words, such as *decision making, problem solving,* and *editor in chief.* Those compounds that can be used as ADJECTIVES are often hyphenated when they precede a NOUN. For advice about hyphens, see 29i.

Hyphenated compound words use a hyphen between the words, such as *trade-in, fuel-efficient,* and *tax-sheltered.* See 29i.

Closed compound words appear as one word, such as *proofread, website,* and *workweek.*

Single-word compounds usually started as open (two-word) compounds and then became hyphenated compounds before ending up as closed compounds. To check whether a compound term consists of closed, hyphenated, or open words, consult an up-to-date dictionary.

Research and Writing

MyCanadianCompLab

Visit MyCanadianCompLab at
mycanadiancomplab.ca for

- Access to EBSCO's ContentSelect database of source material
- Citation exercises
- Model documents
- Other resources, including an eText version of this book

Chapter 32

TYPES AND USES OF RESEARCH IN WRITING

((•
AUDIO
LESSON
Section 1:
Big Ideas—
Finding a
Research
Topic

((•
AUDIO
LESSON
Section 2:
Practice
Questions—
Finding a
Research
Topic

((•
AUDIO
LESSON
Section 3:
Rapid
Review—
Finding a
Research
Topic

32a What is the role of research in writing?

Research is a systematic process of gathering information to answer a question. You're doing research when you're trying to decide which college or university to attend, which MP3 player to buy, or which summer job to accept. Perhaps you find information in print or online. You analyze and evaluate what you learn and then make a decision.

Other kinds of research are more formal, and we don't mean just the type conducted by scientists in white lab coats. People wanting to start small businesses usually have to research the local business climate and present their findings to lenders to get a loan. Citizens wanting to oppose a new construction project have to research its impact and present their findings.

The amount of research in a piece of writing can vary, depending on your audience, purpose, and type of writing (1b; 7a). You might be familiar with RESEARCH* papers or term papers, which are dense with sources, synthesizing information to support a thesis. Chapter 33 will help you with extended formal research projects.

However, any essay might potentially benefit from even a little research. Finding a crucial fact might improve an argument. Consider the following paragraph:

> The homeless situation is even more serious when we understand the variety of people who lack a place to sleep every night. It's not just a problem that afflicts single men or individuals with physical or mental problems. Many families are homeless.

An improved paragraph might specifically answer the research question, "How many families are homeless?" Whenever writing has a vague term like "many" or "some," research can improve it with more precise information. Specific totals and percentages can lay the basis for informed analysis and discussion.

EXERCISE 32-1 The following paragraph has a number of general statements. Generate a list of all the possible research questions you might pursue to strengthen the paragraph.

> **EXAMPLE** "If we fail to act on global warming, our coastal cities will be damaged by rising ocean levels."

> **POSSIBLE** How will global warming affect oceans? How much will oceans rise? Which **QUESTIONS** cities will be affected?

In a troubling reversal of roles, boys are now considerably more at risk in school than are girls. Girls used to be denied many opportunities in schools, as boys enjoyed several unfair advantages. Now, however, girls are graduating from high schools at much higher rates. They

---

*Words printed in SMALL CAPITAL LETTERS are discussed elsewhere in the text and are defined in the Terms Glossary at the back of this book.

are performing better on standardized tests and entering colleges and universities at much higher levels. Women substantially outnumber men in admission to medical and law schools. Several factors are responsible, but unless we take action to ensure academic success for both boys and girls, we will need to create affirmative action programs for men.

32b What are the reasons for doing research?

Writers do research for several reasons and at different points in the writing process, from generating and planning to revising.

1. **To find a fact or piece of information.** Sometimes you simply need to answer a direct question of "how much?" or "when?" or "where?" or "who?" In each case, you need to find a credible source and extract only the specific information necessary to answer the question. Example: How does the cost of university today compare to the cost twenty years ago?

2. **To understand an issue or situation more fully.** Sometimes you need to learn basic information about a topic, even before writing. You're trying to learn not only information new to you but also the range of viewpoints or opinions on a particular topic. Rather than identifying a single fact from a source, you're reading many sources, sometimes with the goal of synthesizing them, sometimes with the goal of generating more specific research questions. Example: What are the effects of globalization?

3. **To synthesize current information.** Even if you know a good deal about a topic, you many need to bring together the most current information. A **review of the literature** is a synthesis of the latest knowledge on a particular topic. It may be part of a longer project, as in the case of **science reports** (41i.1), or it may be the project itself as in the case of **science reviews** (41i.2). Example: What treatments are now possible for Alzheimer's disease?

4. **To identify a specific opinion or point of view.** A good strategy in argumentative writing is to state and refute counter arguments. You might research in order to find out what people who disagree with you believe and, more important, why they hold their beliefs. You can then explain the shortcomings of their views or explain why your position is better. You might also look for expert viewpoints that support your own. Example: What are the main arguments in favour of censoring cable television programs? For more information on writing arguments, see Chapter 5.

5. **To create new knowledge.** Writers often research in order to create new knowledge. This is the kind of research that chemists and biologists do, but so do psychologists, sociologists, journalists, and so on. This research includes experiments, surveys, interviews, ethnographies, and observations. For example, if you were writing a guide to coffee houses in a certain area, you'd need to visit all of them, take notes, and present your findings to readers. Field research (32e) is a general name for this kind of research.

Report 4: Research Report

32c What is the process of doing research?

Although the research process varies according to the specific reason you're doing research (32b) and to your writing situation (1a), a few general steps are common to most projects involving research.

Writing in Action: Narrowing a Subject Online

1. **Develop a research question.** What is the question that you need to answer? Some question might be very specific, such as when you're looking for a piece of data; consider, for example, "What was the population of Canada in 1880?" With substantial projects, however,

Writing in Action: Comparing Online Sources

your research question involves more than looking for a single fact. Consider, for example, "What is the most practical way to reduce automobile emissions?" Section 33e has more advice about developing effective research questions.

2. **Decide what kinds of sources will best answer your question.** Some research questions are best answered by finding appropriate published sources, generally through the library (Chapter 34). Others might require **field research**, gathering data firsthand through surveying, interviewing, or observing (32e). We talk about kinds of sources in 32d.

3. **Develop a search strategy.** Once you determine the sources you need, develop a plan for finding them. How will you search the library, for example (34b)? Whom will you contact to interview? When will you visit a location for direct observations, and how will you take notes? Be purposeful in designing your strategy so your research will be effective and efficient.

4. **Gather your sources.** This is the stage where you not only find appropriate books and articles, for example, but also take notes (33k). Your goal is to accumulate more than enough materials so that you feel confident you can answer your research question.

5. **Interpret your source materials.** Having a bunch of reading notes, a lot of survey answers, a transcript of an interview, or a list of direct observations is only part of the process. Organizing and interpreting them to understand how they answer your research question is just as vital. This stage can also tell you whether your search strategy has been successful or whether you need to gather even more sources. Look for themes or patterns. Look not only for information and ideas that seem to fit together but also conflicts or tensions.

6. **Draft, revise, edit, and proofread your paper.** The general writing processes that we explained in Chapter 2 apply. In sections 33n and 33o, we explain how to apply those processes to research papers.

32d What kinds of sources do writers use?

Office Hours:
Evaluating
Sources

AUDIO
LESSON
Section 1:
Big Ideas—
Researching
Your Topic

A **source** is any form of information that provides ideas, examples, information, or evidence. Different kinds of writing require different kinds of sources (7b). You're probably most familiar with published sources: books, magazine or journal articles, sources from organizational websites, and so on. However, writers use others source, too. These include interviews; surveys; direct observations of situations, places, or people; performances or lectures; museums; and so on.

AUDIO
LESSON
Section 2:
Practice
Questions—
Researching
Your Topic

ESL TIP: In Canada, PLAGIARISM is a major offence in academic writing. In some cultures, it's customary to take material from scholarly authorities on your topic. However, this practice is forbidden in Canada unless you use quotation marks around the exact words and then state the source of those words. For detailed information about how to avoid plagiarism, see Chapter 35. ●

AUDIO
LESSON
Section 3:
Rapid
Review—
Researching
Your Topic

A source is either primary or secondary. **Primary sources** are firsthand evidence based on your own or someone else's original work or direct observation. Primary sources can take the form of experiments, surveys, interviews, memoirs, FIELD RESEARCH (32e), or original creative works (for example, poems, novels, paintings and other art, plays, films, or musical compositions). **Secondary sources** report, describe, comment on, or analyze the experiences or work of others. Quick Reference 4.4 illustrates the difference.

Suppose you're researching student attitudes toward marriage. Surveying several students would be primary research. Consulting scholars' books and articles about students and marriage would be secondary research. Your decision to use primary or secondary sources depends on your RESEARCH QUESTION or the nature of your assignment.

32e What is field research?

Field research involves going into real-life situations to observe, survey, interview, or be part of some activity firsthand. A field researcher might, for example, go to a factory, a lecture, a daycare centre, or a mall—anywhere that people engage in everyday activities. A field researcher might also conduct interviews of experts and other identified individuals. Because field research yields original data, it's a PRIMARY SOURCE.

Conducting field research takes careful planning. Be sure to allow time to gather the data you want, ANALYZE it, and then SYNTHESIZE it with other sources and with your own knowledge and experience. Field research often involves events that can't be revisited. Therefore, record as much information as possible during your research and decide later what information you can use. Afterwards, while your memory is fresh, go over your notes and highlight major categories of information. Also, fill in any details you might not have written down.

32e.1 Surveying

Surveys use several questions to gather information from a number of people, asking about experiences, situations, opinions, or attitudes. Responses to multiple-choice or true/false questions are easy for people to complete and for researchers to summarize and report, as totals or averages. Open-ended questions, in which people are asked to respond in writing to a question, require more effort on the part of researchers and people completing the survey. However, they sometimes have the advantage of providing more complete or accurate information.

If you want to survey a group of people, allow time to write, reflect on, and revise a questionnaire. Test the questionnaire on a few people. Revise any questions that don't work well. For advice, see Quick Reference 32.1.

QUICK REFERENCE **32.1**

Guidelines for developing a questionnaire

1. Define what you want to learn.
2. Identify the appropriate type and number of people to answer your survey so that you get the information you need.
3. Write questions to elicit the information.
4. Phrase the questions so that they are easy to understand.
5. Make sure that your wording does not imply what you want to hear.
6. Decide whether to include open-ended questions that allow people to write their own answers.
7. Test a draft of the questionnaire on a small group of people. If any question is misinterpreted or difficult to understand, revise and retest it.

When you report findings from a survey, keep within your limitations. For example, if the only people who answer your survey are students at a particular school or people at a particular shopping mall, you can't claim your results represent "all students" or "all North Americans." For further advice on writing about quantitative information, see section 7e.

32e.2 Observing people and situations

Case studies (7d.4) and ETHNOGRAPHIES (7d.5) are examples of researching people in specific situations. For observations of behaviour (for example, the audience at a sporting event or elementary school children at play during recess), you can take notes during the activity. Permission to videotape is hard to get because of privacy concerns. Try to remain objective so that you can see things clearly. One strategy is to take notes in a two-column format. On the left, record only objective observations; on the right, record comments or possible interpretations. Figure 32.1 is an example of a double-column note strategy.

32e.3 Interviewing

An expert can offer valuable information, a new point of view, and firsthand facts, statistics, and examples. Probably the best place to start is with the faculty at your college or university. Your instructors are also scholars and researchers with expertise in many areas. They may suggest good additional sources, as well as other experts to contact. Indeed, your family and friends might qualify as experts, if they've been involved with an issue you're researching. Corporations, institutions, and professional organizations often have public relations offices that can answer questions or put you in contact with experts.

Make every attempt to conduct interviews in person so that you can observe body language and facial expressions as you talk. However, if distance is a problem, you can conduct interviews over the phone or online. Quick Reference 32.2 provides specific suggestions for conducting interviews.

Notes	Comment/Analyses
Small conference room; round table covered with papers	
JP suggests fundraising plan	JP seems nervous. Her normal behaviour, or is it this situation?
AR and CT lean forward; SM leans back	
SM interrupts JP's plan, asks for more; CT silent	The fact that JP and AR are women might explain SM's response. Or is it that he's more senior?
JP continues proposal	
SM looks out window, taps pencil	Seems to have made up his mind. A power move?

Figure 32.1 A double-column field research note

Conducting research interviews

- Arrange the interview well in advance, conduct background research, prepare specific questions, and show up on time.
- Rehearse how to ask your questions without reading them (perhaps highlight the key word in coloured ink). Looking your interviewee in the eye as you ask questions establishes ease and trust. If you're interviewing on the telephone, be organized and precise.
- Create a shortcut symbol or letter for key terms you expect to hear during the interview. This cuts down on your time needed to look away from your interviewee.
- Take careful notes, listening especially for key names, books, or other print or online sources.
- Use standard 8 1/2-by-11-inch paper so that you have room to write.
- Bring extra pens or pencils.
- Never depend on recording an interview. People have become very reluctant to permit anyone to record them, and many will cancel appointments on the spot if recording is even mentioned.

32e.4 Gathering data about things or practices

Some kinds of primary research involve looking at objects, artifacts, or practices, describing or counting what you observe, and reporting what you find. Consider three research questions:

1. How are women portrayed on the covers of national magazines?
2. What are the most popular colours used to paint houses in middle-class neighbourhoods and in wealthy neighbourhoods?
3. Are characters with foreign-sounding names or accents in current movies more likely to be heroes or villains?

Although you might be able to answer these questions by finding published sources or interviewing experts, it is likely that you'd need to collect this information yourself, by directly and systematically looking at examples. Quick Reference 32.3 summarizes steps for this kind of research.

Research using direct observation

1. Identify your research question.
2. Identify the sample (the group of individual examples) that you're going to examine, count, describe, or analyze.
3. Develop a system for recording your observations.
4. After recording all observations, look for patterns, make conclusions, or draw inferences.
5. If appropriate to your purpose, explore questions such as "Why are things as I found them?" or "What might be the implications of my findings?"

EXERCISE 32-2   For each of these research questions, what kinds of research would be appropriate? Discuss all the kinds of research that might apply to each question.

1. What types of television programs most appeal to students?

2. Do men and women behave differently in fast-food restaurants?

3. What factors led to the genocide in Rwanda in the 1990s?

4. What are the working conditions in a job that interests me?

5. How do clothing displays in upscale stores differ from clothing displays in discount stores?

Chapter 33

WRITING RESEARCH PAPERS

33a What is a research paper?

A **research paper** (sometimes called a *term paper*) is a specific kind of researched writing common in many university and college courses. In Chapter 32, we explained the role of research in many writing situations and examined different kinds of sources. Research papers usually require the use of several published sources (Chapter 34) throughout. Your mission is to synthesize those sources into a project of fairly significant length.

Every research activity, formal or informal, involves two processes:

1. Gathering information
2. Analyzing, synthesizing, and evaluating what you've gathered

Academic research writing (and many business and public reports), involves a third process:

3. Writing an accurately documented paper based on your ANALYSIS, SYNTHESIS, and EVALUATION of what you've gathered

Some research papers use information from PRIMARY SOURCES and FIELD RESEARCH. However, most use information from published sources such as SECONDARY SOURCES.

Research is an absorbing, creative activity. It lets you come to know a subject deeply and leads to fresh insights. The entire process, especially when repeated in a number of courses and settings, helps to shape you into a self-reliant learner. Nevertheless, many researchers—inexperienced and experienced—feel intimidated at the beginning of a research project. We find that research writing goes most easily when you deliberately break it down into organized steps using a manageable research plan.

33b How do I plan a research project?

Research takes time, so plan ahead and budget your efforts intelligently. As soon as you get an assignment for a research paper, plan your schedule, using Quick Reference 33.1 as a model. Because no two research paper projects are alike, adapt this schedule to your needs. You might, for example, need only one day for some steps but two weeks for others. So, while you stay flexible, keep your eye on the calendar.

Report 4:
Research
Report

Office Hours:
Prewriting

About the
Audio
Lessons for
Before You
Write,
Organize

AUDIO
LESSON
Section 1:
Big Ideas—
Before You
Write,
Organize

Sample schedule for a research project

Assignment received _____

Assignment due date _____

PLANNING	FINISH BY (DATE)
1. Start my research log (33c).	_____
2. Choose a topic suitable for research (33d).	_____
3. Draft my research question (33e).	_____
4. Understand my writing situation (33f).	_____
5. Take practical steps (33g):	
a. Gather materials and supplies.	_____
b. Learn how to use my school's library.	_____
6. Decide what documentation style I'll use (33h).	_____

RESEARCHING

7. Plan my search strategy, but modify as necessary (34b).	_____
8. Decide the kinds of research I need to do:	
a. Field research (32e). If yes, schedule tasks.	_____
b. Published sources (Chapter 34).	_____
9. Locate and evaluate sources (34d, 34j).	_____
10. Compile a working bibliography (33i) or annotated bibliography (33j).	_____
11. Take content notes from sources I find useful (33k).	_____

WRITING

12. Draft my thesis statement (33l).	_____
13. Outline, as required (33m).	_____
14. Draft my paper (33n).	_____
15. Use correct parenthetical citations (35b–c, 36b–c, 37b–c, 38c.2).	_____
16. Revise my paper (33o).	_____
17. Compile my final bibliography (works cited or references), using the documentation style required (Chapters 36–38).	_____

((•
AUDIO
LESSON
Section 2:
Practice
Questions—
Before You
Write,
Organize

((•
AUDIO
LESSON
Section 3:
Rapid
Review—
Before You
Write,
Organize

33c What is a research log?

A research log is your diary of your research process. Use a separate notebook for the log, or create a new folder or file on the computer. Whichever format you rely on, make your research schedule one of the first entries.

Although much of your research log will never find its way into your research paper itself, what you write in it greatly increases your efficiency. A well-kept log traces your line of reasoning as your project evolves, tells where you've ended each work session, and suggests what your next steps might be. Keeping a research log can also help you avoid plagiarizing any of the sources you locate. In your log, always record the date as well as the following elements:

- Your current step in your search for information; the search strategy you used to find that information; the name, location, and other details of exactly where you found the information; the main point of the information you found; and the exact file or folder name in which you've stored your detailed content notes.
- Your suggested next step for when you return to your research.
- Your evolving overall thoughts and insights as you move through the research and writing processes.
- Your awareness that you're becoming ready to move away from gathering material to organizing it; from organizing it to writing about it; and from drafting to revising.

Figure 33.1 shows a selection from the research log of Andrei Gurov, who wrote the MLA-style research paper shown in section 36e.

33d How do I choose and narrow a research topic?

Sometimes, of course, you don't choose a research topic. Research in the workplace and many public arenas often emerges from specific situations. A doctor needs to decide the best way to treat a patient. An office manager needs to make a decision about purchasing new computers. An actor needs to research a time period to better portray a character.

In college or university, some instructors assign a specific topic for research (for example, "Are there scientific theories to explain false memory?"). Others leave more choice to you, assigning a general subject (for example, "memory") and expecting you to narrow it to a manageable topic. Still other instructors expect you to choose a topic on your own (for example, "Write a research paper on a topic of current interest or importance").

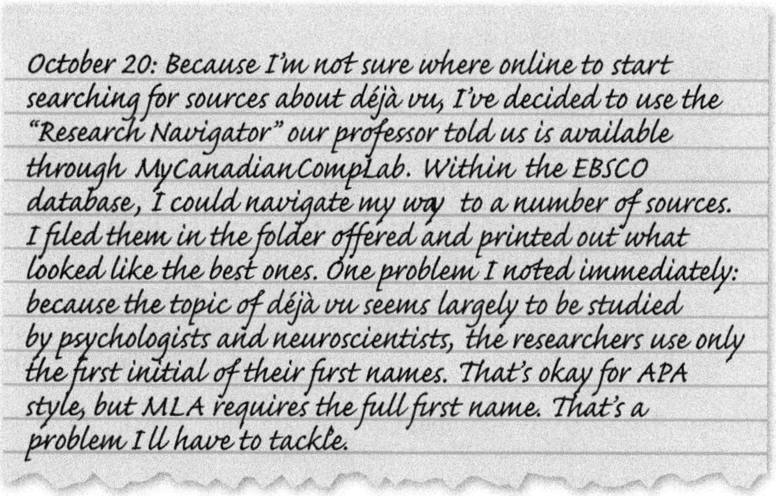

((•
AUDIO LESSON
Section 1:
Big Ideas—
Finding a
Research
Topic

((•
AUDIO LESSON
Section 2:
Practice
Questions—
Finding a
Research
Topic

((•
AUDIO LESSON
Section 3:
Rapid
Review—
Finding a
Research
Topic

> *October 20: Because I'm not sure where online to start searching for sources about déjà vu, I've decided to use the "Research Navigator" our professor told us is available through MyCanadianCompLab. Within the EBSCO database, I could navigate my way to a number of sources. I filed them in the folder offered and printed out what looked like the best ones. One problem I noted immediately: because the topic of déjà vu seems largely to be studied by psychologists and neuroscientists, the researchers use only the first initial of their first names. That's okay for APA style, but MLA requires the full first name. That's a problem I'll have to tackle.*

Figure 33.1 A selection from the research log of Andrei Gurov, who wrote the MLA-style research paper shown in section 36e

33d.1 Choosing a topic on your own

The freedom to choose any topic you want can sometimes lead to what is called "research topic block." Don't panic. Instead, use some of the strategies for generating ideas in Quick Reference 33.2

Finding general ideas for research

- **Talk with others.** Ask instructors or other experts in your area of interest what issues currently seem "hot" to them. Ask them to recommend readings or the names of authorities on those issues.

- **Browse some textbooks.** Read the table of contents and major headings of textbooks for subjects that interest you. As you narrow your focus, note the names of important books and experts, often mentioned in reference lists at the end of chapters or in the final pages of the book.

- **Browse the library or a well-stocked bookstore.** Stroll through the **stacks** (the rows of shelves) to find subjects that interest you. Look at books as well as periodicals. Thumb through popular magazines, and browse academic journals in fields that interest you.

- **Browse the Internet.** Many search engines provide topic directories. Click on some general categories and review subcategories until you locate specific topics that interest you. Then try further subject searches or KEYWORD searches (34d) to see where they lead.

- **Read encyclopedia articles about your interests.** General encyclopedias survey a wide range of topics, while specialized encyclopedias concentrate on a specific area. Never, however, stop with encyclopedias—they are too basic for college- and university-level research.

- **Get ready.** Carry a small notebook and a pen, a laptop, or a PDA. Ideas have a way of popping into your mind when you least expect them. Jot down your thoughts on the spot so that they don't slip away.

33d.2 Narrowing a general topic into a workable one

Whether you're working with a topic of your choice or an assigned one, check that it's sufficiently narrow for the time frame and other requirements of your research paper. Also, be sure that the narrowed topic is worthy of an academic research project.

- **Expect to consider various topics before making your final choice.** Give yourself time to think. Keep your mind open to flashes of insight and to alternative ideas. At the same time, be careful not to let indecision paralyze you.

- **Select a topic that interests you.** Your topic will be a companion for a while, sometimes for most of a semester. Select a topic that arouses your interest and allows you the pleasure of satisfying your intellectual curiosity.

- **Choose a sufficiently narrow topic.** You want to be successful within the time and length given by the assignment. Avoid topics that are too broad, such as "emotions." A better choice would be "how people perceive and respond to anger in others."

- **Choose a topic worth researching.** Avoid trivial topics that prevent you from doing what instructors and others expect of a student researcher: investigating ideas, analyzing them critically, and creating a synthesis of complex concepts.
- **Choose a topic that has a sufficient number of appropriate sources available.** If you can't find useful sources—ones that relate directly to your topic and that are credible, not simply plentiful—drop the topic.
- **Talk with a professor in your field of interest, if possible.** Before the meeting, read a little about your topic so that you can ask informed questions. Ask whether you've narrowed your topic sufficiently and productively. Also, ask for the titles of major books and names of major authorities on your topic.

A good academic topic allows you to demonstrate your critical thinking abilities. There are two broad ways of doing so. First, you might choose a topic on which intelligent people have formed different opinions. Then, you might analyze your sources and draw on your own experiences to decide which position appears best. The purpose of such a paper would be to attempt to PERSUADE readers that you've considered the various positions and reached a reasonable conclusion.

Alternatively, you might choose to INFORM readers in a paper that synthesizes several sources related to a complex subject. Writing a SYNTHESIS means pulling together extensive information from varied sources to examine essential points that relate to a topic. For example, imagine you've been assigned to write the sample research paper about déjà vu in 36e. After you've read a dozen articles on the topic of déjà vu, you might try to identify three or four key points and then organize information from your reading around those points. Your goal is to clarify complicated or scattered information for your readers.

For a more detailed narrative of Andrei Gurov's research process and the final draft of his research paper, see 36e.1 and 36e.2.

33e What is a research question?

(((•
AUDIO LESSON
Section 1: Big Ideas—Constructing an Argument

(((•
AUDIO LESSON
Section 2: Practice Questions—Constructing an Argument

(((•
AUDIO LESSON
Section 3: Rapid Review—Constructing an Argument

A **research question** is the controlling question that drives your research. Few research paper assignments are phrased as questions. Therefore, most research writing calls on you to ask a thought-provoking, underlying question and then to search for answers to it. Regarding research as a quest for an answer gives your work a specific focus: You can't know whether you've found useful source material unless you know what you're looking for.

Research questions, whether stated or implied, and the strategies needed to answer them vary widely. Your purpose might be to present and explain information: "How does penicillin destroy bacteria?" Or your purpose might be to argue one side of an issue: "Is Parliament still more important than the Supreme Court in setting social policy?" You can then consult various sources in an attempt to work toward an answer.

Attempt is an important word in relation to research. Some research questions lead to a final, definitive answer, but some do not. The previous question about penicillin leads to a reasonably definitive answer (you describe how the antibiotic penicillin destroys the cell walls of some bacteria); this means your writing has an informative purpose. The other question about social policy has no definitive answer, so you're asked to offer an informed opinion based on facts and authoritative viewpoints gathered from your research; this means your writing has a persuasive purpose.

To formulate a research question, begin by BRAINSTORMING a list of questions that come to mind about your topic. Write your list of ideas in your research log (33c).

AUDIO
LESSON
Section 1:
Big Ideas—
Writing Well
in College

AUDIO
LESSON
Section 1:
Big Ideas—
Using
Language
Well and
Addressing
Your
Audience

AUDIO
LESSON
Section 2:
Practice
Questions—
Using
Language
Well and
Addressing
Your
Audience

AUDIO
LESSON
Section 3:
Rapid
Review—
Using
Language
Well and
Addressing
Your
Audience

AUDIO
LESSON
Section 1:
Big Ideas—
Researching
Your Topic

AUDIO
LESSON
Section 2:
Practice
Questions—
Researching
Your Topic

AUDIO
LESSON
Section 3:
Rapid
Review—
Researching
Your Topic

Suppose, for example, the topic you want to write about is "homelessness." Here are some typical questions you might ask.

- Why can't a rich country like Canada eliminate homelessness?
- Who is homeless?
- How do people become homeless?
- Is it true that many families—not just adults—are homeless?
- Is the homelessness problem getting better or worse?
- What are we doing to solve the problem of homelessness?
- What is it like to be homeless?

Some questions will interest you more than others, so begin with one of those. If a question leads to a dead end, pursue another. Only when you find yourself accumulating answers— or in the case of questions without definitive answers, accumulating viewpoints—is it likely you're dealing with a usable research question. Once you have an explicitly stated research question, you can streamline your research by taking notes only from those sources that help you answer your research question. If your paper requires you to support an opinion, keep in mind that dealing with opposing positions is crucial to writing an effective argument (5l).

Stay flexible as you work. The results of your research may lead you to modify the research question slightly. Actually, such modifying is part of the "moving ahead and circling back" that characterizes research writing. When you've finished researching and note-taking in response to your final research question, you have a starting place for formulating the preliminary THESIS STATEMENT (see 2d).

33f How does the writing situation shape my research paper?

Your TOPIC, PURPOSE, AUDIENCE, ROLE, and any **special requirements** (1b) all influence your research paper. Even if you are given an open assignment, you'll find it useful to create a writing situation, especially purpose and audience. Doing so will give you a guidepost to see if you're on the right track. To decide whether your paper will have an informative purpose or a persuasive purpose, see what your research question asks. If the answer to it involves giving facts, information, and explanation, your purpose is to inform. For example, "How have computers changed over time?" calls for INFORMATIVE WRITING. Conversely, if the answer involves offering an educated opinion based on contrasting views and supporting evidence, your purpose is to persuade. For example, "Why should people be aware of current developments in computers?" calls for PERSUASIVE WRITING. You may find that your purpose shifts during your research process.

AUDIENCES for research papers vary. In some situations, only your instructor will read your paper. Sometimes your audience starts with your peers, the other students in your class. Next, it moves on to a general public audience or to specialists on your topic, with your instructor as one among many readers. Your sense of these other readers' expertise in your topic can guide your decisions about content, level of detail, and DICTION. Section 1d provides advice for analyzing audience.

33g What practical steps can help me work efficiently?

To conduct your research with greatest efficiency, you need to do some footwork before you start researching. First, gather the materials listed in Quick Reference 33.3 so that they're organized and ready for use at a moment's notice. Second, become familiar with your school's library (34c–h). Third, be sure to become skilled in finding and evaluating online resources (34k–m).

Materials you might need for research

1. A copy of your assignment.
2. This handbook, especially Part Five, or access to the Internet so that you can read the book online and use its guidelines.
3. Your research log (33c).
4. Index cards for taking notes (unless you use a laptop). If you use different colours of index cards, you might colour-code the different categories of information you find. Also, you might use one size for bibliography cards and the other for content note cards. Another coding strategy is to use pens of different ink colours or self-sticking dots of various colours.
5. Cash or a debit card for copy machines or printers.
6. A flash drive or other means for storing downloaded source materials, if you're using the library's computer.
7. If you use index cards and other paper, a small stapler, paper clips, and elastic bands.
8. A separate bag or backpack with wheels to carry research-project materials and books you check out from the library. (Librarians joke about researchers with wheelbarrows.)

33g.1   Learning how to use library resources

When you learn how your college or university library functions, your research efficiency increases. Though almost all libraries in Canada and the United States are organized around the same principles for organizing information, physical layouts and procedures differ considerably. If you visit your library for the sole purpose of figuring out what's located where, you'll feel comfortable and confident when you work there.

Some academic libraries provide orientations through English courses; some offer individual training sessions; and most offer informative websites or handouts describing their resources. Quick Reference 33.4 provides a checklist for familiarizing yourself with your library.

Learning your library's resources

- How do you get access to the library's catalogue and databases, both from inside the library and, if possible, through the Internet? What are the log-in procedures?
- How does the library's catalogue work?
- What periodical indexes or databases does your library have, online or in print? (*Indexes* and *databases* are lists of articles in journals and magazines, grouped by subject areas.)

continued ➤

- Where is the general reference collection? (You can't check out reference books, so when you need to use them, build extra time into your schedule to spend at the library.)
- Where is the special reference collection? (Same rules apply as for general reference books.)
- Are the book and journal stacks open (fully accessible shelves) or closed (request each item by filling out a form to hand to library personnel)? If the latter, become familiar with the required procedures not only for asking for a book or journal but also for picking it up when it's ready.
- Where are the library's physical collections of journals and magazines stored? Libraries are increasingly moving to digital storage, but some publications may exist only in print. Most libraries place periodicals published in the past year in open areas and older periodicals in bound volumes, on microfiche, or online. Learn to use whatever system is in place at your library.
- What periodicals exist online in full-text formats (copies you can read online rather than only from a print copy)?
- What, if anything, is stored on microfilm or microfiche? If you think you'll use that material, take the time to learn how to use the machines. (We find that each library's machines work differently—and many of them have stumped us on occasion.)
- Does the library have special collections, such as local historical works or the writings of notable persons?

Office Hours:
Citing
Sources

((•
AUDIO
LESSON
Section 1:
Big Ideas—
Working with
Sources and
Avoiding
Plagiarism

33g.2   Deciding how you'll use the computer

Office Hours:
Avoiding
Plagiarism

How you use the computer in the research process is largely a matter of personal preference. Some students use a computer only for finding sources and for DRAFTING and REVISING the paper itself. These students do the rest of their research steps by hand on index cards and sheets of paper: keeping their research log (33c), compiling their WORKING BIBLIOGRAPHY (33i), taking content notes (33k), and so forth.

((•
AUDIO
LESSON
Section 2:
Practice
Questions—
Working with
Sources and
Avoiding
Plagiarism

Other students carry out their entire research process on computer. They set up folders for every phase of their project. To accumulate print sources for their working bibliography, these students download them onto a computer hard drive or a flash drive—always carefully recording the origin of the source in the documentation style they've selected (33h). They type their research log, working bibliography, and content notes directly into computer files.

33h   What documentation style should I use?

A **documentation style** is a system for providing information about each source you've used in your research paper. Documentation styles vary from one academic discipline to another. The humanities often use MLA (Modern Language Association) style (Chapter 36). The social sciences frequently use APA (American Psychological Association) style (Chapter 37). Biology and other natural sciences often use CSE (Council of Science Editors) style (Chapter 38). CM (*Chicago Manual*) style is used in various disciplines, generally in the humanities (Chapter 38). Engineers often use IEEE style (Chapter 38). If you don't know which style to use, ask your instructor. Never mix documentation styles; use only one style in each piece of writing.

Determining the documentation style you need to follow at the start of the process helps to guarantee that you'll write down the exact details you need to document your sources. You'll need to document all secondary sources. If you're doing primary research, decide what you must document before you begin. Your instructor may have special requirements, such as asking you to submit your research notes or results from observations, questionnaires, surveys, interviews, or anything else that produces primary data.

33i What is a working bibliography?

A **working bibliography** is a preliminary list of the PRIMARY and SECONDARY SOURCES you gather in your research. It contains information about the source and where others might find it. Following is a list of basic elements to include (see more detailed information about documenting specific types of sources in Chapters 36–38).

BOOKS	PERIODICAL ARTICLES	ONLINE SOURCES
Author(s)	Author(s)	Author (if available); editor or sponsor of site, translator, director, performer
Title	Title	Title of document and title of site; if you are citing a book or journal, bibliographic information for that source
Publisher and place of publication	Name of periodical, volume number, issue number	Name of database or sponsor of online source
Year of publication	Date of issue	Date of electronic publication
Call number	Page numbers of article	Date you accessed the source

Begin your working bibliography as soon as you start identifying sources. Compiling a working bibliography will help you find out what is available on a particular subject before you do extensive reading and notetaking. If your search turns up very few sources, you may want to change your topic. If it reveals a vast number of sources, you definitely want to narrow your topic or even choose a different one. At the outset, don't leave anything out; even an unpromising source may later prove useful. Expect to add and drop sources throughout the research writing process. As a rough estimate, your working bibliography needs to be about twice as long as the list of sources you end up using. You can record your working bibliography on note cards or on a computer.

On the one hand, note cards have the advantage of being easy to sift through and rearrange. You can also carry them with you when you do library research. At the end of your writing process, you can easily sort and alphabetize them to prepare your final bibliography. Write only one source on each card. Figure 33.2 (p. 424) displays a handwritten bibliography note card by Andrei Gurov for his MLA-style research paper in section 36e.

On the other hand, putting your working bibliography on a computer saves you from having to type your list of sources later. If you use a computer for this purpose, clearly separate one entry from another. You can organize the list alphabetically, by author, or according to your subtopics.

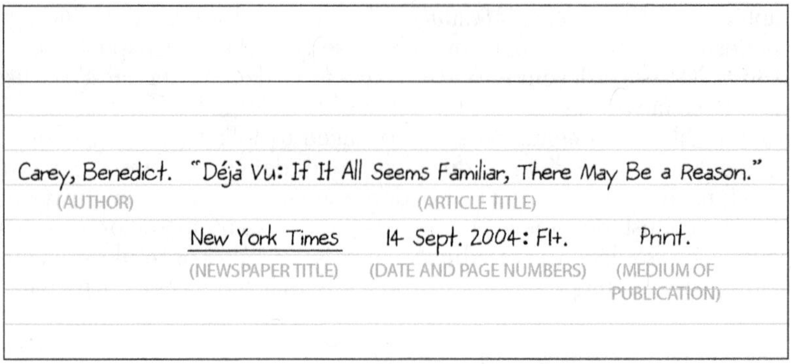

Carey, Benedict. "Déjà Vu: If It All Seems Familiar, There May Be a Reason."
   (AUTHOR)   (ARTICLE TITLE)

New York Times   14 Sept. 2004: F1+.   Print.
(NEWSPAPER TITLE) (DATE AND PAGE NUMBERS) (MEDIUM OF
                                           PUBLICATION)

Figure 33.2 Sample bibliography note card in MLA style

Whichever method you use, when you come across a potential source, immediately record the information exactly as you need it to fulfill the requirements of the DOCUMENTATION STYLE you need to use for your assignment (33h). Spending a few extra moments at this stage can save you hours of work and frustration later on.

33j What is an annotated bibliography?

An **annotated bibliography** includes not only publishing information about your sources but also your brief summary of each one, and perhaps a commentary. Figure 33.3 shows part of an annotated bibliography for sources used in the APA-style student paper in Chapter 37.

McKenna, K. Y., Green, A. S., & Gleason, M. E. (2003). Relationship formation on the Internet: What's the big attraction? *Journal of Social Issues, 58,* 9–31.

Two studies show that people who share "true selves" over the Internet often form closer relationships than when they meet face to face. One study surveyed Internet users. A second study found that students who meet first on the Internet tend to like each other better than students who meet first in person.

Miyake, K., & Zuckerman, M. (1993). Beyond personality impressions. *Journal of Personality, 61*(3), 411–436.

This research study examines how both physical and vocal attractiveness affect judges' responses to individuals. The researchers found that, for five different personality measures, judges rate more attractive people more highly.

Figure 33.3 Section from an annotated bibliography in APA style

33k How do I take content notes?

Content notes record information from your sources. As with your working bibliography, you can make content notes either in a computer file or on index cards.

- If you're using index cards, put a heading on each card that gives a precise link to one of your bibliography items. Include the source's title and the numbers of the pages from which you're taking notes.

- On the computer, keep careful track of what ideas came from each source. One strategy is to open a new file for each. Later, after you've taken notes on many of your sources, you can determine what subtopics are important for your paper. You can then open a new file for each topic and use the "Cut" and "Paste" functions to gather notes from all of your sources under each topic.

- On every note card or every note in your computer, do one of three things: (1) Copy exact words from a source, enclosing the quotation in quotation marks; (2) write a paraphrase of the source; or (3) write a summary of the source. Keeping track of the kind of note you're taking will help you avoid PLAGIARISM. You might use the codes Q for QUOTATION, P for PARAPHRASE, and S for SUMMARY. Or you might use a different typeface or ink colour.

- As you're taking notes, separately record your own reactions and ideas, but take care to differentiate your ideas from those found in your sources. You might write your own thoughts in a different coloured ink (note card) or font (computer); you might use the back of your note cards or a computer's "Comment" feature. You can also record your thinking in your **research log**.

Figure 33.4 shows one of Andrei Gurov's note cards for his paper in 36e.2.

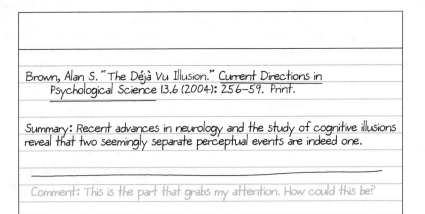

Brown, Alan S. "The Déjà Vu Illusion." *Current Directions in Psychological Science* 13.6 (2004): 256–59. Print.

Summary: Recent advances in neurology and the study of cognitive illusions reveal that two seemingly separate perceptual events are indeed one.

Comment: This is the part that grabs my attention. How could this be?

Figure 33.4 A handwritten content note card

33l How do I draft a thesis statement for a research paper?

Finding a Topic for Argument

Drafting a THESIS STATEMENT for a research paper marks the transition from the research process to the writing process. A thesis statement in a research paper sets out the central theme, which you need to sustain throughout the paper (see 2d, especially Quick Reference 2.3, and see 5d). As with any piece of writing, your research paper must fulfill the promise of its thesis statement.

You might begin thinking of a preliminary thesis statement at some middle point in the research process, although it's perfectly acceptable to wait until you've completely finished researching. You might try to convert your RESEARCH QUESTION into a preliminary thesis statement, stating it, of course, as a DECLARATIVE SENTENCE, not as a question. Remember that a good thesis statement makes an assertion that conveys your point of view about your topic and foreshadows the content of your paper (see Quick Reference 2.3 in 2d). It introduces the position you intend to argue. And not least, remember that your research needs to support your thesis statement. Ask yourself whether the material you've gathered from sources can effectively give support. If not, revise your thesis statement, conduct further research, or do both.

Here are examples of subjects narrowed to topics, focused into research questions, and then cast as thesis statements.

SUBJECT	*computers*
TOPIC	Artificial intelligence
RESEARCH QUESTION	How close are researchers to developing artificial intelligence in computers?
INFORMATIVE THESIS STATEMENT	Scientists disagree about whether computers need emotions to have artificial intelligence.
PERSUASIVE THESIS STATEMENT	Because emotions play a strong role in human intelligence, computers must have emotions before they can truly have artificial intelligence.
SUBJECT	*nonverbal communication*
TOPIC	Personal space
RESEARCH QUESTION	How do standards for personal space differ among cultures?
INFORMATIVE THESIS STATEMENT	Everyone has expectations concerning the use of personal space, but accepted distances for that space are determined by each person's culture.
PERSUASIVE THESIS STATEMENT	To prevent intercultural misunderstandings, people must be aware of cultural differences in standards for personal space.
SUBJECT	*literature*
TOPIC	The historical novel
RESEARCH QUESTION	How does Timothy Findley's *The Wars* represent the historical novel?
INFORMATIVE THESIS STATEMENT	In Findley's *The Wars*, the protagonist, Robert Ross, undergoes a moral journey as he experiences the futile 1916 Flanders offensive in World War I.
PERSUASIVE THESIS STATEMENT	In the art of the historical novel as represented by Findley's *The Wars*, historical events are merely the backdrop to the novelist's main purpose of developing the protagonist's moral journey.

Andrei Gurov (whose research paper appears in 36e) revised his preliminary thesis statement twice before he felt that it expressed the point he wanted to make. Andrei also took the key step of checking that he would be able to support it sufficiently with sources throughout the paper.

FIRST PRELIMINARY THESIS STATEMENT

Déjà vu can be explained by a variety of scientific theories. [Andrei realized that this draft thesis would lead to a paper that would merely list, paragraph by paragraph, each theory, and that the paper would lack synthesis.]

SECOND PRELIMINARY THESIS STATEMENT

Many people believe feelings of déjà vu have mysterious origins, but science has shown this is not true. [Andrei liked this statement better because it began to get at the complexity of the topic, but he wanted to work on it more because he felt the second part was too general.]

FINAL THESIS STATEMENT

Although a few people still believe that feelings of déjà vu have mysterious or supernatural origins, research in cognitive psychology and the neurosciences has produced laboratory experments that could explain the phenomenon rationally.

33m How do I outline a research paper?

Some instructors require an OUTLINE of your research paper, either before you hand in the paper or along with the paper. In such cases, your instructor probably expects you to be working from an outline as you write your drafts. Your research log often comes in handy when you group ideas, especially for a first draft of your paper—and as you make an *informal outline* for it. An outline can serve as a guide as you plan and write your paper. For directions on composing a *formal outline*, see section 2f. To see a topic outline of Andrei Gurov's research paper, turn to section 36e.

33n How do I draft a research paper?

Office Hours: Drafting

DRAFTING and REVISING a research paper is like drafting and revising any other piece of writing (Chapter 2). Yet to write a research paper, you need extra time for planning, drafting, thinking, redrafting, rethinking, and creating a final draft because you need to demonstrate all of the following:

- You've followed the steps of the research process presented in Chapters 32–35.
- You understand the information that you've located during your research.
- You've evaluated the SOURCES you've used in your research.
- You haven't PLAGIARIZED your material from someone else (35b).
- You've used sources well in your writing, correctly employing QUOTATIONS, PARAPHRASES, and SUMMARIES (35f–k).
- You've moved beyond SUMMARY to SYNTHESIS so that your sources are interwoven with each other and with your own thinking, not merely listed one by one (4f).
- You've used DOCUMENTATION accurately. (For MLA STYLE, see Chapter 36; for APA STYLE, see Chapter 37; for other documentation styles, see Chapter 38.)

Expect to write a number of drafts of your research paper. The first draft is your chance to discover new insights and connections. Successive drafts help you master the information you've learned and add it authoritatively to the knowledge you already had about the topic. In the first draft, organize the broad categories of your paper. Quick Reference 33.5 suggests some ways to write your first draft.

Suggestions for drafting a research paper

- Some researchers categorize notes and write a section at a time. They organize the notes into broad categories by making a separate group for each topic. As patterns begin to emerge, these writers might move material from one category to another. Each category becomes a section of the first draft. This method not only assures researchers that their first draft will include all of the material from their research, but reveals any gaps in information that call for additional research. Of course, you may discover that some of your research doesn't fit your topic and thesis. Put it aside; it might be useful in a later draft.

- Some writers generate a list of questions that their paper needs to address and then answer each question, one at a time, looking for the content notes that will help them. Generating and answering questions can be a way of turning a mass of information into manageable groupings.

- Some researchers finish their research and then slowly review half of the information they've gathered. Next, setting aside that information, they write a partial first draft by drawing on the information they remember from their reading. Then, they use the same process with the second half of the information that they've gathered. Finally, with their two partial drafts and all of their research notes in front of them, they write a complete first draft. Researchers who use this method say it gives them a broad overview of their material quickly and identifies any gaps in information that they need to fill in with further research.

- Some researchers stop at various points during their research and use FREEWRITING to get their ideas into words. Researchers who use this method say that it helps them recognize when they need to adjust their RESEARCH QUESTION or change the emphasis of their search. After a number of rounds of researching and freewriting, these researchers find that they can write their complete first draft relatively easily.

- Some writers review their sources and create an OUTLINE before drafting (2f). Some find a formal outline helpful, while others use a less formal approach.

Office Hours:
Revising

AUDIO
LESSON
Section 1:
Big Ideas—
Revising,
Editing, and
Proofreading

AUDIO
LESSON
Section 2:
Practice
Questions—
Revising,
Editing, and
Proofreading

330 How do I revise a research paper?

Before you write each new draft, read your previous draft with a sharp eye. For best results, take a break of a few days (or at least a few hours) before beginning this process. This gives you distance from your material and a clearer vision of what you need to revise. For a more objective point of view, consider asking a few people you respect to read and react to your first, or perhaps your second, draft.

AUDIO
LESSON
Section 3:
Rapid
Review—
Revising,
Editing, and
Proofreading

One key to REVISING any research paper is to examine carefully the evidence you have included. **Evidence** consists of facts, statistics, expert studies and opinions, examples, and stories. As a reader, you expect writers to provide solid evidence to back up their claims and conclusions. Similarly, when you write, readers expect you to provide evidence that clearly supports your claims and conclusions. Use RENNS (3f) to see if you can develop paragraphs more fully. Identify each of the points you have made in your paper, including your thesis and all your subpoints. Then ask the questions in Quick Reference 33.6

Questions for evaluating your evidence

- **Is the evidence sufficient?** To be sufficient, evidence can't be thin or trivial. As a rule, the more evidence you present, the more convincing your thesis will be to readers.

- **Is the evidence representative?** Representative evidence is customary and normal, not based on exceptions. When evidence is representative, it provides a view of the issue that reflects the usual circumstances rather than rare ones.

- **Is the evidence relevant?** Relevant evidence relates directly to your thesis or topic sentence. It illustrates your reasons straightforwardly and never introduces unrelated material.

- **Is the evidence accurate?** Accurate evidence is correct, complete, and up to date. It comes from a reliable SOURCE. Equally important, you present it honestly, without distorting or misrepresenting it.

- **Is the evidence reasonable?** Reasonable evidence is not phrased in extreme language, such as *all*, *never*, or *certainly*. It is well thought out and free of logical fallacies (4i).

Experienced writers know that writing is really *rewriting*. Research papers are among the most demanding composition assignments, and most writers revise several times. Once you've produced a *final draft*, you're ready to edit (2j), proofread (2k), and format (Chapter 45) your work. Check for correct grammar, punctuation, capitalization, and spelling. (No amount of careful research and good writing can make up for an incorrectly presented, sloppy, error-laden document.)

Consult Quick References 2.8 and 2.9 to remind yourself of the general principles of revising, and consult the research paper revision checklist in Quick Reference 33.7. Apply the strategies of critical thinking (Chapter 4) to your own writing. Read your paper as if you were an outside critical reader. Additionally, have a classmate or trusted friend provide a peer response (6c).

Revising a research paper

If the answer to any of the following questions is no, you need to revise. The section numbers in parentheses tell you where to find useful information.

WRITING

- Does your introductory paragraph lead effectively into the material? (3b)

- Have you met the basic requirements for a written thesis statement? (2d and 33l)

- Do your thesis statement and the content of your paper address your research question(s)? (33e)

continued ➤

- Have you developed effective body paragraphs? (3d, 3f, Quick Reference 3.3)
- Does the concluding paragraph end your paper effectively? (3k)
- Does your paper satisfy a critical thinker? (Chapter 4)

RESEARCH

- Have you included appropriate and effective evidence? (4d and Quick Reference 33.6)
- Have you deleted irrelevant or insignificant information? (3g)
- Have you used quotations, paraphrases, and summaries well? (35f–k)
- Have you integrated your source material well without plagiarizing? (35c)

FORMAT AND DOCUMENTATION

- Have you used the correct format for your parenthetical citations or other documentation style? (Chapters 36–38)
- Does each citation tie into an item in your WORKS CITED (MLA style) or REFERENCES (APA style) list of sources at the end of your paper? (36d and 37f)
- Does the paper exactly match the format you've been assigned to follow? Check margins, spacing, title, headings, page number, font, and so on (Chapter 45).

To see one example of the research writing process in action, turn to section 36e. There you'll see the final draft of an MLA-style research paper; a narrative of decisions that the student made during his research process; and commentary (on the text page facing each page of the student's paper) that gives you insight into specific aspects of his paper.

For an APA-style research paper, turn to section 37h. There you'll see the final draft of a student's paper and a narrative of the decisions that the student made during his research process.

Chapter 34

FINDING AND EVALUATING PUBLISHED SOURCES

34a What is a published source?

A published source is a book, article, webpage, or other type of writing that appears in print or in electronic format. While the kinds of field research we discuss in section 32e require you to gather information and turn it into words, in published sources other writers have already done that work. However, it's up to you to decide whether they have done it accurately, fairly, and well. Your goal is to find sources needed to answer your research question, evaluate their quality, and SYNTHESIZE them into your own writing, using QUOTATION, SUMMARY, or PARAPHRASE. Published sources are PRIMARY if they are first-hand reports of experiments, observations, and so on, or if they are creative works like poems, letters, or stories. A SECONDARY published source is one that reports, describes, or comments on someone else's work. Section 4d explains the differences.

34b What is a search strategy?

A search strategy is an organized procedure for locating and gathering information to answer your specific RESEARCH QUESTION. Assignments that involve fully understanding an issue or synthesizing current knowledge require care and planning. Using a search strategy guarantees that you'll work systematically rather than haphazardly.

Following are three frequently used search strategies. If no single one meets your requirements, create your own.

The **expert method** is useful when you know your specific topic. Begin by reading articles or books by an expert in the field. Of course, this means that you have to know who the experts are, and sometimes that's difficult. Talk with people who are generally knowledgeable about your topic, learn what you can from them, and ask them to refer you to work by experts on the topic. (For example, if you're interested in researching Internet dating, a psychology instructor may be able to tell you who the leading experts are on that topic.) Alternatively, or in addition, interview an expert in person, on the phone, or through e-mail. Turn to 32e.3 for detailed advice about conducting effective interviews.

The **chaining method** is useful when your topic is a general one. Start with reference books and bibliographies in current articles or on websites; use them to link to additional sources. Keep following the links until you reach increasingly expert sources. Alternatively, talk with people who have some general knowledge of your topic and ask them to refer you to experts they might know.

The **question method** means breaking your overall research question into several smaller questions and finding sources to answer each of them. This method has the advantage of allowing you to see if your sources cover all the areas important to your research question. Suppose your research question is, "How successful are relationships that begin

((•
AUDIO LESSON Section 1: Big Ideas— Working with Sources and Avoiding Plagiarism

((•
AUDIO LESSON Section 2: Practice Questions— Working with Sources and Avoiding Plagiarism

((•
AUDIO LESSON Section 3: Rapid Review— Working with Sources and Avoiding Plagiarism

((•
AUDIO LESSON Section 1: Big Ideas— Researching Your Topic

((•
AUDIO LESSON Section 2: Practice Questions— Researching Your Topic

((•
AUDIO LESSON Section 3: Rapid Review— Researching Your Topic

on the Internet?" The list of questions you brainstorm might include, "Who participates in Internet dating? Are there typical ways Internet relationships develop? How may Internet contacts result in actual meetings?" Generating a list of questions like this can give your search a direction and purpose.

You may find yourself switching or combining methods. That's fine. "Flexibility with focus" is the guiding principle for experienced researchers. Discovering early in the process what sources are available allows you time to find those that are harder to locate; to use interlibrary loan if an item isn't available in your library or online; to wait for someone to return checked-out books you need; or to schedule interviews, arrange visits, or conduct surveys.

As you locate, assemble, and evaluate sources, expect to accumulate much more information than you'll actually use. The quality of a research paper depends partly on your ability to eliminate inadequate or repetitive sources and to recognize what is valuable. Turn to section 34j for detailed guidelines for evaluating sources.

One more piece of advice: Avoid getting too far along in your search until you're reasonably certain you're going in a useful direction. Rather than spending endless hours simply gathering sources, read and analyze some of your materials to make sure your topic is a good one. Your **research log** can be useful for this purpose.

34c What are library-based sources?

((•
AUDIO
LESSON
Section 1:
Big Ideas—
Researching
Your Topic

((•
AUDIO
LESSON
Section 2:
Practice
Questions—
Researching
Your Topic

((•
AUDIO
LESSON
Section 3:
Rapid
Review—
Researching
Your Topic

In an age when the Web contains billions of pages of information, it might seem almost prehistoric to talk about libraries. After all, the library is where generations of students have traditionally gone to find sources: books and periodicals organized by catalogues and indexes. However, notice that we've referred to "library-based" sources and not necessarily to the library itself. In many respects, the function that a library performs is even more important than its physical building. Librarians and scholars have systematically gathered and organized sources so that students and researchers can find the best ones efficiently and reliably. Many libraries give you remote access to their holdings and to the advice and expertise of their personnel via the Internet, so you might use library-based sources without ever setting foot in the building.

Still, the building itself continues to be a vital place for all research. One key advantage of going to the library is your chance to consult face-to-face with librarians. They train for their profession by learning how to advise students and other researchers about using library resources to greatest advantage. Never hesitate to ask questions about how to proceed or where to find a resource.

Catalogues list sources—usually books, but also films, recordings, and documents—that the library owns (34d). **Databases** contain extensive lists of articles, reports, and books, organized and searchable in many ways. You can access and search catalogues and databases from computers in the library or by connecting to the library online. Both academic and public libraries subscribe to databases. Many businesses and corporations also subscribe to databases. A law firm, for example, may subscribe to LexisNexis, which provides searchable access to legal cases and decisions.

If you're accessing a database by connecting to the library online, you need to use a **browser** (such as Firefox or Internet Explorer), a software program that gives you access to the Web.

34d How do I use catalogues and databases?

Sources that you identify through catalogues and scholarly databases are almost always more reliable and appropriate than sources you find by simply browsing the Web. The reliability of scholarly databases stems from their origins: Only experts and professionals who recognize works of merit compile them.

The best way to access a database at your school's library is to go to the library's website.

The home page of a library shows the resources available through that website, although more might be available in the library itself. Most academic libraries subscribe to one or more database services, such as EBSCO, FirstSearch, and ProQuest. Because the institution pays for these services, you don't have to, but you'll need an ID or password to use them.

Each entry in a database contains bibliographic information, including a title, author, date of publication, and publisher (in the case of books or reports) or periodical (in the case of articles). The entry might also provide an abstract, or summary, of the material. Once you locate an entry that seems promising, you need to find the book or the complete article itself. We explain how to do that in 34e (for books) and 34f (for periodicals).

EXERCISE 34-1 Working either individually or as part of a group, access your library's website. List all of the types of information available. In particular, list the catalogues and databases you can search and the subject areas each one covers. Note whether any of the databases have full-text versions of articles.

USING KEYWORDS

When you search library databases, **keywords,** also called *descriptors* or *identifiers,* are your lifeline to success. Keywords are the main words in a source's title or the words that the author or editor has identified as central. Without keywords, you'd have great difficulty accessing sources listed in electronic databases.

When you search using keywords, chances are you'll come up with a large or even overwhelming number of sources. Much of what turns up won't be relevant to your topic. The two main ways to make keyword searches more efficient are using guided searches (answers to prompts) and using Boolean expressions (keyword combinations).

USING GUIDED SEARCHES

Guided searches, also called *advanced searches,* allow you to look through a database or search engine by answering prompts provided in an onscreen form. A typical search involves selecting a range of dates of publication (for example, after 2008 or between 1990 and 1995) and specifying only a certain language (such as English) or a certain format (such as books). Figure 34.1 is an example of a search for sources that have the words *déjà vu* in their titles and sources that use *false memory* as another keyword but are not about *crime.*

USING BOOLEAN EXPRESSIONS

Using **Boolean expressions** means that you search a database or search engine by typing keyword combinations that narrow and refine your search. To combine keywords, use the words *AND, OR,* and *NOT,* or the symbols that represent those words. Boolean expressions, generally placed between keywords, instruct the search engine to list only those websites in which your keywords appear in certain combinations and to ignore others. Quick Reference 34.1 explains a few ways to search with keywords more effectively, using the subject "relationships" as an example.

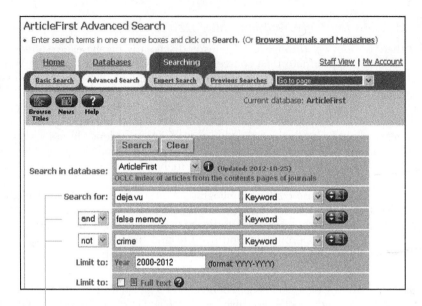

Users can list the keywords
they want to search for or
not to search for.

Figure 34.1 A guided or advanced search

Refining keyword searches with Boolean expressions

AND or the + ("plus") symbol: Narrows the focus of your search because both keywords must be found. For example, if you were researching the topic of the APA paper in section 37h (the role of physical attractiveness in new relationships over the Internet) you would try the expression *relationships AND attractiveness AND Internet.* Many search engines, such as Google, don't require the word *AND* between terms. Figure 34.2 illustrates the results.

NOT or the – ("minus") symbol: Narrows a search by excluding texts containing the specified word or phrase. If you want to eliminate instant messaging from your search, type *relationships AND attractiveness AND Internet NOT instant messaging.*

OR: Expands a search's boundaries by including more than one keyword. If you want to expand your search to include sources about relationships begun through either instant messaging or chat rooms, try the expression *relationships AND attractiveness AND Internet AND instant messaging OR chat rooms.* You'll get pages mentioning relationships and attractiveness only if they also mention instant messaging or chat rooms.

" ": Quotation marks direct a search engine to match your exact word order on a webpage. For example, a search for "online relationships" will find pages that contain the exact phrase *online relationships.* However, it won't return pages with the the phrase *relationships online.* If you search for *James Joyce* without using quotation marks, most engines will return all pages containing the words *James* and *Joyce* anywhere in the document; however, a search using "James Joyce" brings you closer to finding websites about the Irish writer.

continued ➤

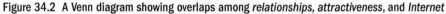

Relationships

Internet AND Relationships

Internet AND Relationships AND Attractiveness

Internet

Internet AND Attractiveness

Relationships AND Attractiveness

Attractiveness

Figure 34.2 A Venn diagram showing overlaps among *relationships*, *attractiveness*, and *Internet*

34e How do I find books?

A library's **book catalogue,** which lists its holdings (its entire collection), exists as a computer database in almost every modern library. You can find a book by searching by **author**, by **title**, by **subject**, and by KEYWORD. When you search the book catalogue, some computer programs ask which of these four categories you would like to search.

Try searching your school's library online. You might also try searching in the online library catalogue of any large university that gives you access, or of a major municipal reference library.

Suppose you want to find a book by Naomi Klein, but you don't know its title. You can search the online catalogue for books by this author. Click on "Author" in the drop-down menu next to the catalogue search window on the computer screen. In the catalogue search window, you type in "klein, naomi." (Usually you enter the last name first, but check to see how your library's system works.) If the library owns any books by Naomi Klein, the catalogue will show you their titles and other information. Among the books you might find is *No Logo: Taking Aim at the Brand Bullies* (Toronto: Knopf Canada, 2000). Or suppose you know this title, and want to see if the library owns the book. Click on "Title" next to the catalogue search window and type in "no logo." Usually you do not need to include the full title or words like *the* or *a*.

Often you don't know either an author's name or a book's title. Instead, you have a research topic and need to find sources. In this case you need to search by subject, using the terms listed in the *Library of Congress Subject Headings (LCSH)* or another subject directory. The *LCSH* is a multivolume catalogue available in the reference section of your library. It lists only subject headings, organized from most general to most narrow. If you are researching a Canadian topic, consult the National Library of Canada's *Canadian Subject Headings (CSH)* at <http://www.collectionscanada.gc.ca/csh/index-e.html>. Suppose you are researching the topic "brand name products—public opinion." If you enter that term in the space for subject searches, *No Logo: Taking Aim at the Brand Bullies* by Naomi Klein will be listed—if your library owns that book. Finally, you may wish to search by keyword. You could find Klein's book using the keywords "brand name," "logo," and so on.

An entry in the library's book catalogue contains a great deal of useful information: a book's title, author, publisher, date and place of publication, and length, along with its location in the library. A full-record catalogue entry (a complete set of information about the source rather than a brief listing that may have only author, title, and call number) lists additional subjects covered in that book. The list of additional subjects can provide valuable clues for further searching.

Many libraries allow you to print out this information, send it to your e-mail account, or download and save it. Whether you choose one of these options or copy the information yourself directly into your WORKING BIBLIOGRAPHY, it's crucial to record the **call number** exactly as it appears, with all numbers, letters, and decimal points. The call number tells where the book is located in the library's stacks (storage shelves). If you're researching in a library with *open stacks* (that is, you're permitted to go where books are shelved), the call number leads you to the area in the library where you can find all books on the same subject. Simply looking at what's on the shelves may yield useful sources. Keep in mind that in physically browsing the stacks, however, you're missing sources that other students have checked out or that are "on hold" at the library's reserve desk. The book catalogue generally will contain information about whether a book is checked out or on reserve.

A call number is especially crucial in a library or special collection with *closed stacks* (that is, a library where you fill in a call slip, hand it in at the call desk, and wait for the book to arrive). Such libraries don't permit you to browse the stacks, so you have to rely entirely on the book catalogue. If you fill in the wrong number or an incomplete number, your wait will be in vain.

34f How do I find periodicals?

Periodicals are newspapers, magazines, and journals published at set intervals. Different kinds of periodicals meet different research purposes. Quick Reference 34.2 describes several types. To use periodicals efficiently, consult databases or indexes to periodicals, which allow you to search by subject, title, keyword, or author. Most exist as online databases that are updated frequently. Your library very likely subscribes to several of the ones that you'll need, and you can access them through the library's website.

QUICK REFERENCE 34.2

Types of periodicals

TYPE	CHARACTERISTICS	USEFUL FOR
JOURNALS	Scholarly articles written by experts for other experts; usually focus on one academic discipline or field; published relatively infrequently (often 3–6 times per year, generally not more than once per month); examples are *Canadian Journal of Public Health* and *The Canadian Journal of Sociology*	The most reliable expert research on a particular subject; detailed articles and extensive bibliographies that can point to other sources or experts; may also have book reviews

continued ➤

TYPE	CHARACTERISTICS	USEFUL FOR
NEWS MAGAZINES	Short to mid-length articles on current events or topics of interest to a broad readership; lots of photographs and graphics; may have opinions or editorials, as well as reviews; generally are published weekly; examples are *Maclean's* and *Time*	Easily understandable and timely introductions to current topics; often point to more expert sources, topics, and keywords
SPECIAL INTEREST OR "LIFESTYLE" MAGAZINES	Written for audiences (including fans and hobbyists) interested in a particular topic; include news and features on that topic; generally published monthly, with entertainment as an important goal; examples include *wired* and *Zoomer*	Providing "how to" information on their topics of focus, as well as technical information or in-depth profiles of individuals, products, or events; many include reviews; the more serious examples are well written and reliable
"INTELLECTUAL" OR LITERARY MAGAZINES	Publish relatively longer articles that provide in-depth analysis of issues, events, or people; may include creative work as well as nonfiction; aimed at a general well-educated audience; usually published monthly; examples include *The Walrus* and *Literary Review of Canada*	Learning about a topic in depth but in a way that's more accessible than scholarly journals; becoming aware of major controversies and positions; learning who experts are and what books or other sources have been published; reading arguments on topics
TRADE MAGAZINES	Focus on particular businesses, industries and trade groups; discuss new products, legislation, or events that will influence individuals or businesses in that area; examples include *Canadian Poultry* and *Broadcaster*	Specialized information focusing on applying information or research in particular settings; seeing how specific audiences or interest groups may respond to a particular position
NEWSPAPERS	Publish articles about news, sports, and cultural events soon after they happen; contain several sections, including opinions and editorials, lifestyle (home, food, movies, etc.), sports and so on; most appear daily, though some smaller ones are weekly or twice-weekly	Very current information on things as they happen; national newspapers cover world events and frequently have analysis and commentary; local newspapers cover small happenings you likely won't find elsewhere; opinion sections and reviews are stimulating sources of ideas and positions

ALERT: The terms **database** and **index** are often used interchangeably, but there are differences between the two. Before electronic means of storing information in databases became common, periodical information was organized in lists of references called indexes, which existed only in print. An index only had bibliographic information. A database often includes not only that information but also connections to the articles themselves. A database is more comprehensive than an index. Generally, if you're referring to online lists of sources, you can't go wrong simply using the broader term *database*. ●

34f.1   Using databases to find periodicals

Your library's home page generally provides different ways to access various databases. For instance, users who select "Articles" on the home page of the University of Alberta Libraries are given the option "Add More Databases." Clicking on that link opens up at a page that lists article databases that include *Academic Search Complete, Medline, PsycINFO,* and others. Users who select "Browse by Subject" on the library system's home page can click on a subject area to open a list of relevant databases. It's important to choose the right database for your search because the wrong one may miss some of the best sources for your paper.

General databases index articles in journals, magazines, and newspapers. Large libraries have many general databases. Among them are the following:

- **Academic Search Premier** covers thousands of general and scholarly publications in the social sciences, humanities, education, computer sciences, engineering, language and linguistics, arts and literature, medical sciences, and ethnic studies. Most of the sources in this database are available in full text. This database is suitable for academic research projects, as long as you take care to focus on journal articles and well-regarded general publications.
- **General Reference Center Gold** covers current events, popular culture, business and industry, the arts and sciences, and sports published in newspapers, reference books, and periodicals; it focuses on general interest periodicals.
- **LexisNexis Academic** provides abstracts of news, business, and legal information. Sources include foreign news publications; regional US news services; radio and television transcripts; US federal and state case law; medical, legislative, and industry news; and so on.

For research in Canadian periodicals, see *A Bibliography of Canadian Bibliographies, A Guide to Basic Reference Materials for Canadian Libraries, Canadian Newspaper Index,* and *Canadian Periodical Index.* Major newspapers have online archives that include articles from recent years, and sometimes from decades long past.

Specialized databases are more appropriate than general ones for most post-secondary-level research. They list articles in journals published by and for expert, academic, or professional readers. Many specialized databases include the abstract, or summary, that is printed at the beginning of each scholarly article. Examples include *General Science Abstracts, Business Abstracts, Humanities Index, Social Sciences Abstracts, MLA International Biography,* and *PsycINFO.*

Keyword search

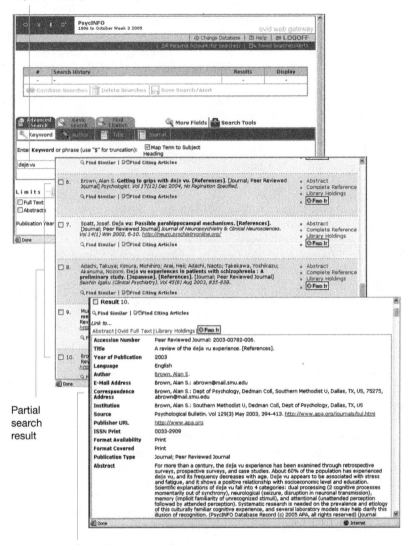

Partial
search
result

One article selected from database

Figure 34.3 Keyword search of *PsycINFO*

You search periodical indexes by using KEYWORDS. Shown in Figure 34.3 are three screens from a keyword search of *PsycINFO* for Andrei Gurov's research paper that appears in section 36e.2.

34f.2   Locating the articles themselves

Periodical indexes help you locate the titles of specific articles on your topic. Once you have the listing, through, how do you get your hands on the article itself? Often you can find a

Figure 34.4 Location information in a database

full-text online version of the article to read, download, or print. A full-text version may be either in HTML format or PDF. The listing will tell you which one; if you have a choice, we recommend using the PDF version, which is easier to cite because it has the layout of a common article. Figure 34.4 shows location information in a typical database entry.

Sometimes, however, you need to find a printed copy of the periodical. Often, the database listing will tell you if you library owns a print copy and what its call number is. Otherwise, you'll need to check if the periodical is listed in the library's catalogue. Search for the periodical name you want, not for the article's author or title. If your library subscribes to that periodical, you use its call number to find its location. You then need to find the specific article you want by looking for the issue in which the article you're looking for is printed.

Few libraries subscribe to all of the periodicals listed in specialized indexes. For advice on locating sources that your library doesn't own, see 34i.

EXERCISE 34-2   Use two databases that are available through your library to conduct two searches for one or more of the terms below. (Alternatively, your instructor may suggest a different term or have you pursue a topic of your own choosing.)

If possible, choose one general and one specialized database. Compile a brief report that compares the sources you generate. You might address questions like these: How many sources did each search turn up? Is there any overlap? What kinds of periodicals are represented in each database? What access does your library provide to the several sources you find most interesting in each search? Note: If you're generating lots of hits, restrict your search to the past year or two.

Suggested terms for searching (with type of specialized database to consult in parentheses): *memory* (psychology); *globalization* (business, economics, sociology); *cloning* (biology); *Troy* (classics, humanities, film, archaeology); *obesity* (medicine).

34g   How do I use reference works?

Reference works include encyclopedias, almanacs, yearbooks, fact books, atlases, dictionaries, biographical reference works, and bibliographies. Some references are *general,* providing information on a vast number of subjects, but without any depth. Others are *specialized,* providing information on selected topics, often for more expert or professional audiences.

34g.1 General reference works

Reference works are the starting point for many researchers—but they're no more than a starting point. **General reference works** by themselves are insufficient for academic research. Still, they help researchers identify useful KEYWORDS, find examples, and verify facts. Most widely used reference works are available in electronic versions, usually online. Check your library website to see if the reference work you want is available online through a subscription or licence the library has purchased. Alternatively, you can search the Web by entering the work's name to see if it's available there. (For example, *Encyclopaedia Britannica* is at <http://www.britannica.com>.) Be aware that often you have to pay a fee for works you don't access through the library.

GENERAL ENCYCLOPEDIAS

Articles in multivolume general encyclopedias, such as the *Encyclopaedia Britannica,* summarize information on a wide variety of subjects. The articles can give you helpful background information and the names of major figures and experts in the field. Best of all, many articles end with a brief bibliography of major works on the subject. General encyclopedias aren't the place to look for information on recent events or current research, although sometimes they cover a field's ongoing controversies up until the date that the reference was published.

The *Canadian Encyclopedia* and *Colombo's Canadian References,* an encyclopedic dictionary, are important sources of information on Canadian topics.

ALMANACS, YEARBOOKS, FACT BOOKS

Almanacs, yearbooks, and fact books are huge compilations of facts in many subject areas. They're often available both in print and online. They're excellent for verifying information from other sources and, in some cases, for finding supporting facts and figures. *The Canadian Global Almanac* and *The World Almanac* present capsule accounts of a year's events and data about government, politics, economics, science and technology, sports, and many other categories. *Facts on File,* which is indexed online by LexisNexis, covers world events in a weekly digest and in an annual one-volume yearbook.

Sources of Canadian information include *Canada Year Book, Canadian Almanac and Directory,* and *Canadian News Facts.* The annual *Statistical Abstract of the United States,* the international *Demographic Yearbook,* and the *United Nations Statistical Yearbook* carry a wealth of data.

ATLASES AND GAZETTEERS

Atlases contain maps of our planet's continents, seas, and skies. Gazetteers provide comprehensive geographical information on topography, climates, populations, migrations, natural resources, crops, and so on. Examples include *The Atlas of Canada, Canada Gazetteer Atlas,* the *Times Atlas of the World,* and *The Columbia Gazetteer of the World.*

DICTIONARIES

Dictionaries define words and terms. In addition to general dictionaries, specialized dictionaries exist in many academic disciplines to define words and phrases specific to a field.

BIOGRAPHICAL REFERENCE WORKS

Biographical reference books give brief factual information about famous people—their accomplishments along with pertinent events and dates in their lives. Biographical references include the *Who's Who* series (including *Canadian Who's Who*), *The Dictionary of*

Canadian Biography, and many others. Specialized biographical references in various fields are also available.

BIBLIOGRAPHIES

Bibliographies list books, articles, documents, films, and other resources and provide publication information so that you can find those sources. Some bibliographies are comprehensive and list sources on a wide range of topics. Others list only sources on a particular subject. Specialized bibliographies can be very helpful in your research process. Annotated or critical bibliographies describe and evaluate the works that they list. These resources are increasingly available online but require you either to access them through a library's paid subscription service or to pay a fee each time you use them.

34g.2 Specialized reference works

Specialized reference works provide more authoritative and specific information than do general reference works. Specialized reference works are usually appropriate for postsecondary-level research. They can be invaluable for introducing you to the controversies and KEYWORDS in a subject area. In particular, finding authors' names in such books can help you begin to accumulate a list of credible authors.

There are hundreds of specialized references. A few examples are the *Encyclopedia of Banking and Finance,* the *New Grove Dictionary of Music and Musicians,* the *Dictionary of Canadian Biography,* the *New Cambridge Modern History,* the *Oxford Companion to Canadian Literature, The Canadian Annual Review of Politics and Public Affairs,* and the *Encyclopedia of the Biological Sciences.*

Hundreds of highly specific one-volume works are not listed here. Check what specialized reference books your library has available that might help you in your search.

34h How do I find government publications?

Canadian government publications are available in astounding variety. You can find information on laws, regulations, populations, weather patterns, agriculture, national parks, education, and health, and many other topics.

A federal government website known as the Canada Site <http://www.canada.gc.ca/> is an excellent starting point for online research into current Canadian government publications. It provides direct access to federal departments, boards, and agencies and their publications, as well as to public records, including parliamentary debates and hearings, and to databases. You can also follow its links to provincial and territorial government sites. Statistics Canada <http://www.statcan.gc.ca/> collects and analyzes a wide range of data.

34i What if my library doesn't have a source I need?

No library owns every book or subscribes to every periodical. However, many libraries are connected electronically to other libraries' catalogues and can give you access to additional holdings. The Canadian Library Gateway, a project of Library and Archives Canada <http://www.collectionscanada.gc.ca/index-e.html>, coordinates an interlibrary loan system linking the catalogues of university and other large libraries throughout the country. The Internet gives you access to the catalogues of many large libraries worldwide. Librarians can request materials from other libraries through interlibrary loan, which is generally free of charge. Alternatively, your school may have a different document delivery system.

Evaluating Sources—Interactive Tutorial

Office Hours: Evaluating Sources

34j **How do I evaluate sources?**

Finding a source is only part of your effort. Your next step is to evaluate the quality of each source. Your critical thinking skills (Chapter 4) will be important in this effort. First, decide whether the information in the source relates to your topic in more than a vague, general sense. Ask how a source might help you answer your research question (33e). Finally, using the criteria in Quick Reference 34.3, evaluate each source with a cold, critical eye.

QUICK REFERENCE 34.3

Evaluating sources

1. **Is the source authoritative?** Generally, academic journals and books published by university presses and by publishers that specialize in scholarly books are authoritative. Encyclopedias and textbooks are usually trustworthy but are not adequate sources for advanced research. Material published in newspapers, in general-readership magazines, and by established commercial publishers is usually reliable, but you want to apply the other criteria in this list with special care, cross-checking names and facts whenever possible. Websites maintained by professional organizations are often authoritative.

2. **Is the author an expert?** Biographical material in the article or book may tell you if the author is an expert on the topic. Look up the author in a recent biographical dictionary. Alternatively, enter the author's name in an Internet search engine. Look to see if the author has a degree in this field and whether he or she is affiliated with a reliable institution. Also, if an author is often cited by professionals in the field and published in journals, he or she is probably considered an expert.

3. **Is the source current?** Check the publication date. Research is ongoing in most fields, and information is often modified or replaced by new findings. Check databases and online subject directories to see if newer sources are available.

4. **Does the source support its information sufficiently?** Are its assertions or claims supported with sufficient evidence? Separate facts from opinions (4d.1) and see if the writer relies too much on opinion. Look for evidence that backs up the writer's position (4d.2) and for reasonable claims of cause and effect (4d.3). Reject arguments that rely on logical fallacies (4i). If the author expresses a point of view but offers little evidence to back up that position, reject the source.

5. **Is the author's tone balanced?** If the TONE is unbiased and the reasoning is logical, the source is probably useful (4d.4, 4e.2). Some warning signs of biased tone are name calling, sarcasm, stereotyping, or absolute assertions about matters that are open to interpretation (using *always, everyone,* and similar words). Note, however, that a forcefully argued thesis that takes a definite point of view can still be a trustworthy source.

34k What should I know about searching the Web?

Sources from the library or from library databases have the advantage of being selected by experts. While you still have to evaluate them, they have passed a screening process. On the other hand, anyone can put anything on the Web. This makes the Web a rich source of information, but it also makes finding what you need difficult, and it opens the possibility of encountering inaccurate or biased materials. Therefore, searching library databases remains an indispensable method of finding many scholarly sources.

Writing in
Action:
Conducting
Online
Keyword
Searches

34l How do I search the Web?

Finding information on the Web has become so common that "google" has become a verb. The principles for searching the Web are much like those for searching databases (34d). Once you use a browser to get on the Web, you can search for sites by using a SEARCH ENGINE or by typing an address (called a **URL**, for "universal resource locator" or "uniform resource locator") into the search box. **Search engines** are programs designed to hunt the Internet for sources on specific topics that you identify by using keywords (34l.1) or through subject directories (34l.2).

Search engines are constantly acquiring new features. A special feature of the Google search engine, Google Scholar <http://scholar.google.ca> permits scholarly searches that have features in common with searches of library databases.

Quick Reference 34.4 lists some of the many types of sources found on the Web.

QUICK REFERENCE | **34.4**

Types of sources on the Internet

Periodicals and news sites. Many newspapers and magazines put content online, although some of them give access to all of their material only to subscribers. Some periodicals have extra content that appears only on the Web. Finally, there are periodicals that exist only online. Examples include *Salon.com* and *Kairos* <http://english.ttu.edu/Kairos>.

Mainstream news organizations frequently have sites, in which they publish video and sound clips as well as articles.

Organizational websites. Interest groups, clubs, businesses, museums, universities, and similar organizations usually have websites. They often provide basic facts and information about the organization, and may include articles, reports, research findings, position papers, policy statements, and so on. Some of them can be authoritative and useful; others require cautious evaluation, especially when the organization is promoting itself.

Government websites. Governments at all levels maintain websites to provide all sorts of information to their citizens. This frequently includes not only news about laws or events, but often research or articles. See 34h for information and leads.

Blogs. Much of what appears now on the Web is in the form of blogs, regular short articles published by people ranging from experts to amateurs. (Several well-regarded

continued ➤

scholars and other experts keep blogs.) Blogs tend to be highly opinionated, so evaluate them carefully.

Images, sounds, and videos. These appear on the Web as parts of other sites and in sites of their own. A podcast or a documentary may offer expert information. You can often find videos of press conferences or recordings of speeches.

ALERT: When you write a URL, such as <http://www.pearsoned.com>, the Modern Language Association (MLA) tells you to surround it with angle brackets so that readers can clearly distinguish the URL from the body text. However, don't use angle brackets when you type a URL in the locator box at the top of a webpage. ●

34l.1   Using keywords

In the same way you use KEYWORDS to find materials in library databases (34d), you use them to find information on the Internet. Type a word or group of words in the search box on the opening page of the search engine, and click on the "Search" or "Enter" button. The engine scans for your word(s) in webpages, and then lists sites that contain them.

34l.2   Using subject directories

Subject directories provide a good alternative to keyword searches. These directories are lists of topics (education, computing, entertainment, and so on) or resources and services (shopping, travel, and so on), with links to websites on those topics and resources. Many search engines' home pages have one or more subject directories. In addition, there are some independent subject directories. Some examples are Educator's Reference Desk <http://www.eduref.org/>, *Library of Congress* <http://www.loc.gov>, *Refdesk.com* <http://www.refdesk.com/>, *UBC Library Research Guides* <http://guides.library.ubc.ca/>, and *University of Toronto Libraries Portal* <http://discover.library.utoronto.ca/resources-research/>.

Clicking on a general category within a subject directory will take you to lists of increasingly specific categories. Eventually, you'll get a list of webpages on the most specific subtopic you select. These search engines also allow you to click on a category and enter keywords for a search.

Quick Reference 34.5 summarizes the information in this section by providing some general guidelines for using search engines and directories with keywords.

QUICK REFERENCE **34.5**

Tips on using search engines and directories

● Use keyword combinations or BOOLEAN EXPRESSIONS (Quick Reference 34.1) unless you have a very specific, narrow topic with unique keywords. A search for even a moderately common topic may produce thousands of hits, many of which won't be relevant to your topic. You might also switch to a subject directory.

continued ➤

- Most search engines attempt to search as much of the Web as possible. But because the Web is vast and unorganized, different search engines will give different results for the same search. Try using more than one search engine, or use a **metasearch engine** that searches several search engines at once.

- Use the "Advanced Search" page, if one is available. It allows you to search or sort by date, language, file format, and domain type, as well as by combining keywords.

- When you find a useful site, go to the toolbar at the top of the screen and click on "Bookmark" or "Favorites" and then click on "Add." This will make it easy for you to return to a good source.

- Use the "History" or "Go" function to track the sites you visit, in case you want to revisit one you previously thought was not helpful.

- Sources on the Web may come in various formats. Most common are webpages in HTML (Hypertext Markup Language) format. You may also encounter Word or Excel documents, PowerPoint slides, or PDF (portable document format) files, each of which requires specific software. PDF files, which require the free Adobe Acrobat Reader that you can download from <http://www.adobe.com>, allow people to preserve documents in their original formats.

EXERCISE 34-3   Use a search engine of your choice to search for sources on "déjà vu." (To make the search easier, you may omit the accents.) For each option below, record how many hits occur.

1. Enter the phrase *"deja vu"*
2. Enter the word *"memory"*
3. Enter the word *"memory"* AND the phrase *"deja vu"*
4. Enter the phrase *"deja vu"* AND the word *"consciousness"*
5. To any of the searches above, add the word *"research"*
6. Repeat this exercise by searching another topic that interests you.

34m   How do I evaluate Web sources?

Writing in
Action:
Comparing
Online
Sources

The same strategies for evaluating library sources, discussed in 34j, apply to evaluating Web sources. Ask if the Web source is well supported with evidence and free from fallacies or bias. Use strategies for critical thinking and analysis (Chapter 4).

Office Hours:
Evaluating
Sources

However, you need to evaluate Web sources with additional care for two reasons. First, because anyone can post anything on the Web, some sources may very well be plagiarized. Second, many sources on the Web have been written by individuals posing as experts and, as a result, may offer false or misleading information.

You're always accountable for the sources you choose. Most sites contain material that will help you assess their credibility, such as a bibliography, links to the author or editor, or a description of the sponsoring organization. Discard sites that do not contain such verifying information, however useful they may seem. Err on the side of caution.

An important question to ask about any website is why the information exists and why it was put on the Internet. What motives might the site's authors have? Are you asked to take action of any kind? If yes, take special care to judge the source's bias.

Quick Reference 34.6 summarizes the questions to ask about websites.

EXERCISE 34-4   Working as part of a group, assemble a maximum of three sources per person on a single topic, choosing from media such as newspapers, magazines, advertisements, and Internet sources. Select a topic of your choice, use one that your instructor assigns, or pick one from the list below. Look for materials that take no more than about five minutes each to read. Then give every member of the group the opportunity to read all the sources that the group has assembled.

Discuss the sources together as a group, evaluating and comparing them in terms of accuracy, bias, completeness, verifiability, purpose, or any other criteria that you think are relevant. (Refer to Quick References 34.3 and 34.6.) Have one member of the group take notes and then, as a group, compile a brief report summarizing your findings. Keep the discussion focused on the sources—avoid getting into a discussion of the topics themselves.

Suggested topics: a particular political party or its leader; fossil fuels; a healthy diet; a recent Canadian military intervention; globalization; genetically modified organisms; immigration; storage of nuclear waste.

QUICK REFERENCE **34.6**

Judging the reliability of Web sources

RELIABLE SOURCES ARE . . .

From educational, not-for-profit, or government organizations. One sign is an Internet address ending in *.edu, .org, .gc, .gov,* or a country abbreviation such as *.ca* or *.uk.* However, if any of these organizations fail to list their sources, don't use them. After all, many colleges and universities now host student websites, whose addresses also end identically to the school's address.

From expert authors. Experts have degrees or credentials in their fields that you can check. See if their names appear in other reliable sources, in bibliographies on your topic, or in reference books in an academic library; check whether the site's author gives an e-mail address for questions or comments.

QUESTIONABLE SOURCES ARE . . .

From commercial organizations advertising to sell a product (*.com*); websites that are advertisements or personal pages; junk mail. These sites may or may not list sources. If they fail to, don't use them. If they do, check that the sources are legitimate, not a front for some commercial enterprise.

From anonymous authors or authors without identifiable credentials. Chat rooms, discussion groups, bulletin boards, and similar networks are questionable because they don't give credentials or other qualifying information.

continued ➤

From reliable print sources. Online versions of major newspapers, magazines, and other publications that are produced by the publisher are just as reliable as the print versions.

Secondhand excerpts and quotations. Materials that appear on a site that is not the official site of the publisher may be edited in a biased or misleading manner. Such sources may be incomplete and inaccurate.

Well supported with evidence. The information is presented in a balanced, unbiased fashion.

Unsupported or biased. These sites carry declarations and assertions that have little or no supporting evidence.

Current. The site's information is regularly updated.

Outdated. The site's information hasn't been updated in a year or more.

Chapter 35

USING SOURCES AND AVOIDING PLAGIARISM

35a How do I use sources well?

Office Hours: Citing Sources

Using sources well means using QUOTATIONS (35h), PARAPHRASES (35i), and SUMMARIES (35j) to create a synthesis of those materials and your own thoughts. It also means documenting your sources and avoiding PLAGIARISM. Generally, you'll begin this process after you've located most of your sources and evaluated them (Chapter 34), written a WORKING BIBLIOGRAPHY (33i), and taken content notes (33k). Of course, during the process of DRAFTING, you might discover the need to do some additional research, and that's fine. Be careful, though, to avoid a trap into which we see some writers fall—endlessly researching to put off the challenging work of drafting.

Pulling together a SYNTHESIS of your sources and your own thinking about the topic means

- Mastering the information from each source
- Finding relationships among the pieces of information from various sources
- Adding your own thinking to the mix

To write effectively, organize your paper around a logical sequence based on the main points in your synthesis. Further, support each main point and important subpoint with specific evidence, ideas, or facts drawn from your sources. You'll also want to support your points with ideas generated through your own CRITICAL THINKING (Chapter 4). If your PURPOSE is persuasive rather than informative, remember to present opposing viewpoints evenhandedly and then refute them reasonably (5e, 5l).

All SOURCE-BASED WRITING needs to be

- Accurate
- Effective
- Honest (the only way to avoid plagiarism)

Honesty requires using correct documentation (Chapters 36–38). **Documentation** means making two types of entries in your research paper each time you use a source:

1. Writing a parenthetical citation for each quotation, paraphrase, and summary you take from sources (for examples in MLA STYLE, see 36c; for APA, see 37c).
2. Composing a BIBLIOGRAPHY for the end of your paper. MLA calls this list of sources WORKS CITED, while APA calls it REFERENCES. This list needs to include full bibliographic information on each source from which you have quoted, paraphrased, and summarized in your paper (for examples, see 36d for MLA style, and 37f for APA).

Today's bibliographies differ from those of the past. The root word *biblio-* means "book," so traditionally, the bibliographic information referred to a book's title, author, publisher, and place and year of publication. In the age of digital technology, researchers include in their bibliographies sources not only from printed books but also from electronic sources.

Documentation is vital for three reasons. It tells your readers where to find your sources in case they want to consult those sources in greater depth or to verify that you've used them properly. It lends credibility to your writing, strengthening your **ethos** as someone who does the careful work needed to develop well-supported papers. Documentation also gives credit to others for their work. A **documentation style** refers to a specific system for providing information on sources used in a research paper. Documentation styles vary among the disciplines. This handbook presents five documentation styles in Chapters 36–38.

Office Hours:
Avoiding
Plagiarism

35b What is plagiarism?

Plagiarism is presenting another person's words, ideas, or visual images as if they were your own. Plagiarizing is like stealing: It is a form of academic dishonesty or cheating. Plagiarism is a serious offence that can be grounds for a failing grade or expulsion from a college or university. Beyond that, you're hurting yourself. If you're plagiarizing, you're not learning.

Plagiarism isn't something that just professors and instructors get fussy about. In the workplace, it can get you fired and hinder your being hired elsewhere. Plagiarism at work also has legal implications; words, ideas, and images, especially those that describe or influence business practices and decisions, are *intellectual property*. Using someone else's intellectual property without permission or credit is a form of theft that may land you in court. Furthermore, plagiarism in any setting—academic, business, or civic—hurts your credibility and reputation. Quick Reference 35.1 lists the major types of plagiarism.

QUICK REFERENCE 35.1

Types of plagiarism

You're plagiarizing if you . . .

- Buy a paper from an Internet site, another student or writer, or any other source and pass it off as your own.
- Turn in any paper that someone else has written, whether the person has given it to you, you've downloaded it from the Internet, or you've copied it from any other source.
- Change selected parts of an existing paper and claim the paper as your own.
- Neglect to put quotation marks around words that you quote directly from a source, even if you document the source.
- Copy or paste into your paper any *key terms, phrases, sentences,* or *longer passages* from another source without using documentation to tell precisely where the material came from.
- Use *ideas* from another source without correctly citing and documenting that source, even if you put the ideas into your own words.
- Combine ideas from many sources and pass them off as your own without correctly citing and documenting the sources.
- Take language, ideas, or visual images from anyone (colleagues, companies, organizations, and so on) without obtaining permission or crediting them.

ESL TIP: Perhaps you come from a country or culture that has a different understanding of plagiarism than Canada. Here, and in most Western settings, using others' words without citing them is considered unacceptable. Use the strategies we discuss in this chapter to avoid suspicions of plagiarism. •

35c How do I avoid plagiarism?

((•
AUDIO
LESSON
Section 1:
Big Ideas—
Working with
Sources and
Avoiding
Plagiarism

You can avoid plagiarism two ways. First, be very systematic and careful when you take content notes and when you quote, paraphrase, or summarize materials. Second, become comfortable with the concept of **documentation**, which you need each time you use a source. Quick Reference 35.2 describes the main strategies you can use to avoid plagiarism.

QUICK REFERENCE 35.2

Strategies for avoiding plagiarism

- Use DOCUMENTATION to acknowledge your use of the ideas or phrasings of others, taken from the sources you've compiled on your topic.

- Become thoroughly familiar with the documentation style that your instructor tells you to use for your research paper (Chapters 36–38). To work efficiently, make a master list of the information required to document all sources that you quote, paraphrase, or summarize according to your required documentation style.

- Write down absolutely all the documentation facts that you'll need for your paper, keeping careful records as you search for sources. Otherwise, you'll waste much time trying to retrace your steps to get a documentation detail you missed.

- Use a consistent system for taking **content notes**, making sure to maintain the distinction between your own thinking and the ideas that come directly from a source. Perhaps use different colours of ink or another coding system to keep these three uses of sources separate:
  1. Quotations from a source (documentation required)
  2. Material paraphrased or summarized from a source (documentation required)
  3. Thoughts of your own triggered by what you've read or experienced in life (no documentation required)

- Write clear, perhaps oversized, quotation marks when you're directly quoting a passage. Make them so distinct that you can't miss seeing them later.

- Consult with your instructor if you're unsure about any phase of the documentation process.

((•
AUDIO
LESSON
Section 2:
Practice
Questions—
Working with
Sources and
Avoiding
Plagiarism

Another important way to avoid plagiarism is to dive willingly into any interim tasks your instructors build into research assignments. For example, many instructors set interim deadlines such as a date for handing in a WORKING BIBLIOGRAPHY (33i) or an **annotated bibliography** (33j). Further, some instructors want to read and coach you about how to improve one or more of your research paper drafts. In some cases, they might want to look over your research log (33c), content notes (33k), and/or photocopies of your sources.

((◦•
AUDIO
LESSON
Section 3:
Rapid
Review—
Working with
Sources and
Avoiding
Plagiarism

👁
Writing in
Action: How
to Avoid
Plagiarism

👁
Writing in
Action:
Understanding
Online
Citation

Never assume that your instructor can't detect plagiarism. Instructors have keen eyes for writing styles that are different from the ones students generally produce and from your own style in particular. They recognize professionally drawn visuals and charts. Instructors can access websites that electronically check your submitted work against all material available online. Further, sites such as <http://www.turnitin.com> allow instructors to check your writing against hundreds of thousands of papers for free or for sale on the Internet. (Also, that site adds your paper to its huge database of student papers so that no one can plagiarize your work.) Moreover, when instructors receive papers that they suspect contain plagiarized passages, they can check with other professors to see whether a student paper looks familiar.

35d How do I work with Internet sources to avoid plagiarism?

Online sources can both greatly help researchers and create new problems. Because it's so easy to download source materials, it's potentially easy to misrepresent someone else's work as your own, even if you don't intend to be dishonest.

You might be tempted to download a completed research paper from the Internet. *Don't.* That's intellectual dishonesty, which can get you into real trouble. Or you might be tempted to borrow wording from what you wrongly consider an "obscure" Internet source. *Don't.* Not only is this intellectual dishonesty, but instructors will easily detect it. Even if you have absolutely no intention of plagiarizing, being careless, especially with cutting and pasting, can easily lead to trouble. Quick Reference 35.3 suggests ways to avoid plagiarism when you're working with digital or online sources.

QUICK REFERENCE 35.3

Guidelines for avoiding plagiarizing online sources

- Never cut material from an online source and paste it directly into your paper. You can too easily lose track of which wording is your own and which comes from a source.

- Keep material that you downloaded or printed from the Internet separate from your own writing, whether you intend to QUOTE, SUMMARIZE, or PARAPHRASE the material. Be careful how you manage copied files. Use another colour or a distinct font as a visual reminder that this isn't your work. Just as important, make sure that you type in all of the information you need to identify each source, according to the documentation style you need to use.

- Copy or paste downloaded or printed material into your paper only when you intend to use it as a direct quotation or visual. Immediately place quotation marks around the material, or set off a long passage as a block quotation. Be sure to document the source at the same time as you copy or paste the quotation into your paper. (You can start by copying the URL or bookmarking the page.) Don't put off documenting the passage until later, because you may forget to do it or do it incorrectly.

- Summarize or paraphrase materials *before* you include them in your paper. If you have printed or downloaded Internet sources to separate files, don't copy directly

continued ➤

from those files into your paper. Summarize or paraphrase the sources in a different file, and then paste the summaries or paraphrases into your paper. Document the source of each passage at the same time as you insert it in your paper. If you put off this task until later, you may forget to do it or get it wrong.

- Use the Internet to check a passage you're not sure about. If you're concerned that you may have plagiarized material by mistake, try submitting one or two sentences that concern you to <http://www.google.ca>. To make this work, always place quotation marks around the sentences you want to check when you type them into the search window.

Many resources are available online to help students understand what plagiarism is and how they can avoid it. Some include interactive components. Here is a sample of Canadian resources that you can use.

http://www.library.ubc.ca/home/plagiarism/

http://www.academicintegrity.uoguelph.ca/plagiarism.cfm

http://www.writing.utoronto.ca/advice/using-sources/how-not-to-plagiarize

http://www.yorku.ca/tutorial/academic_integrity/

35e What don't I have to document?

You don't have to document common knowledge or your own thinking. **Common knowledge** is information that most educated people know, although they may need to remind themselves of certain facts by looking up information in a reference book. For example, here are a few facts of common knowledge that you don't need to document.

- Newfoundland entered Confederation in 1949.
- Mercury is the planet closest to the sun.
- Normal human body temperature is 37°C.
- All the oceans on our planet contain salt water.

Sometimes, of course, a research paper doesn't contain common knowledge. For example, Andrei Gurov, whose research paper appears in 36e.2, had only very general common knowledge about the topic of déjà vu. Most of his paper consists of ideas and information that he quotes, paraphrases, and summarizes from sources.

A very important component of a research paper that doesn't need documentation is **your own thinking**, which is based on what you've learned as you built on what you already knew about your topic. It consists of your ANALYSIS, SYNTHESIS, and interpretation of new material as you read or observe it. You don't have to document your own thinking. Your own thinking helps you formulate a THESIS STATEMENT and organize your research paper by composing TOPIC SENTENCES that carry along your presentation of information. For example, suppose that you're drawing on an article about the connections between emotions and logic in people. While reading the article, you come to a personal conclusion that computers can't have emotions. This idea is not stated anywhere in the article you are reading or in any other source you use. Certainly, you need to cite the ideas from the article that led to your conclusion, but you don't need to cite your own thinking. On the other hand, if you find a source that states this very idea, you must cite it. Doing so adds force to your paper and strengthens your credibility.

35f   What must I document?

You must document everything that you learn from a source. This includes ideas as well as specific language. Expressing the ideas of others in your own words doesn't release you from the obligation to tell exactly where you got those ideas—you need to use complete, correct documentation. Here's an example in action.

SOURCE

Park, Robert L. "Welcome to Planet Earth." *The Best American Science Writing 2001.* Ed. Jesse Cohen. New York: Ecco/Harper, 2001. 302-08. Print. [This source information is arranged in MLA documentation style.]

ORIGINAL (PARK'S EXACT WORDS)

The widespread belief in alien abductions is just one example of the growing influence of pseudoscience. Two hundred years ago, educated people imagined that the greatest contribution of science would be to free the world from superstition and humbug. It has not happened. (304)

PLAGIARISM EXAMPLE

Belief in alien kidnappings illustrates <u>the influence of pseudoscience</u>. In the nineteenth century, educated people imagined that science would <u>free the world from superstition</u>, but they were wrong.

Even though the student changed some wording in the example above, the ideas aren't original to her. To avoid plagiarism she's required to document the source. The underlined phrases are especially problematic examples of plagiarism because they're Park's exact wording.

CORRECT EXAMPLE (USING QUOTATION, PARAPHRASE, AND DOCUMENTATION)

Robert Park calls people's beliefs in alien kidnapping proof of "the growing influence of pseudoscience" (304). Centuries of expectation that science would conquer "superstition and humbug" are still unfulfilled (304). [This citation is arranged in MLA documentation style.]

The writer of the correct example above has used Park's ideas properly through a combination of **quotation** and **paraphrase**, and **attribution** and **documentation**. For example, she correctly quotes the phrase "the growing influence of pseudoscience," and she paraphrases the statement "Two hundred years ago, educated people imagined that the greatest contribution of science would be to free the world," rephrasing it as "Centuries of expectation that science would conquer." She also attributes the ideas to Park, giving the author's name in the sentence, and twice includes parenthetical citations, which would lead the reader to find the source on the WORKS CITED page. Sections 35g through 35j explain exactly how to use sources effectively and document correctly.

35g How can I effectively integrate sources into my writing?

Integrating sources means blending information and ideas from others with your own writing. Before trying to integrate sources into your writing, you need to ANALYZE and SYNTHESIZE your material. Analysis requires you to break ideas down into their component parts so that you can think them through separately. Do this while reading your sources and reviewing your notes. Synthesis requires you to make connections among different ideas, seeking relationships and links that tie them together.

35h How can I use quotations effectively?

A **quotation** is the exact words of a source enclosed in quotation marks. Well-chosen quotations can lend a note of authority and enliven a document with someone else's voice. Think, for example, of a good marketing campaign. A company can incorporate real-life quotes to help support its claim that a product or service works effectively. In academic writing, you achieve some of the same benefits by supporting your work with quotations.

You face conflicting demands when you use quotations in your writing. Although quotations provide support, you can lose coherence in your paper if you use too many of them. If more than a quarter of your paper consists of quotations, you've probably written what some people call a "cut and paste special"—merely stringing together someone else's words. Doing so gives your readers—including instructors—the impression that you've not bothered to develop your own thinking and you're letting other people do your talking.

In addition to avoiding too many quotations, you also want to avoid using quotations that are too long. Readers tend to skip over long quotations and lose the drift of the paper. Also, your instructor might assume that you just didn't take the time required to PARAPHRASE or SUMMARIZE the material. Generally, summaries and paraphrases are more effective for reconstructing someone else's argument. If you do need to quote a long passage, make sure every word in the quotation counts. Edit out irrelevant parts, using ellipsis points to indicate deleted material (29d and 35h.1). Quick Reference 35.4 provides guidelines for using quotations. Sections 35h.1 and 35h.2 give examples of acceptable and unacceptable quotations.

QUICK REFERENCE 35.4

Guidelines for using quotations

1. Use quotations from authorities on your subject to support or dispute what you write in your paper.
2. Never use a quotation to present your THESIS STATEMENT or a TOPIC SENTENCE.
3. Select quotations that fit your message. Choose a quotation for these reasons:
   - Its language is particularly appropriate or distinctive.
   - Its idea is particularly hard to paraphrase accurately.
   - The source's authority is especially important to support your thesis or main point.
   - The source's words are open to interpretation.

continued ➤

4. Never allow quotations to make up more than a quarter of your paper. Instead, rely on paraphrases (35i) and summaries (35j).

5. Quote accurately. Always check each quotation against the original source—and then recheck it.

6. Integrate quotations smoothly into your writing.

7. Avoid PLAGIARISM (35b–d).

8. Document quotations carefully.

35h.1   Making quotations fit smoothly with your sentences

When you use quotations, the greatest risk you take is that you'll end up with incoherent, choppy sentences. You can avoid this problem by making the words you quote fit smoothly with three aspects of your writing: grammar, style, and logic. Here are some examples of sentences that don't mesh well with quotations, followed by revised versions.

SOURCE

Goleman, Daniel. *Emotional Intelligence.* New York: Bantam, 1995. Print. [This source information is arranged in MLA documentation style.]

ORIGINAL (GOLEMAN'S EXACT WORDS)

These two minds, the emotional and the rational, operate in tight harmony for the most part, intertwining their very different ways of knowing to guide us through the world. [from p. 9]

INCOHERENT GRAMMAR PROBLEM

Goleman explains how the emotional and rational <u>minds "intertwining</u> their very different ways of knowing to guide us through the world" (9). [Corrected: Goleman explains how emotional and rational minds mix "their very different ways of knowing to guide us through the world" (9).]

INCOHERENT STYLE PROBLEM

Goleman explains how <u>the "tight harmony" of "the emotional and the rational"</u> minds work together while "intertwining their very different ways of knowing to guide us through the world" (9). [Corrected: Goleman explains how the "emotional and the rational" minds work together "in tight harmony" while "intertwining their very different ways of knowing to guide us through the world" (9).]

INCOHERENT LOGIC PROBLEM

Goleman explains how the emotional and rational minds <u>work together</u> by "their very different ways of knowing to guide us through the world" (9). [Corrected: Goleman explains how the emotional and rational minds work together by combining "their very different ways of knowing to guide us through the world" (9).]

CORRECT USE OF THE QUOTATION

Goleman explains how the emotional and rational minds work together by "intertwining their very different ways of knowing to guide us through the world" (9). [This citation is arranged in MLA documentation style.]

After writing sentences that contain quotations, read the material aloud and listen to whether the language flows smoothly and gracefully. Perhaps you need to add a word or two placed in brackets (29c) within the quotation so that the wording works grammatically and effortlessly with the rest of your sentence. Of course, make sure your bracketed additions don't distort the meaning of the quotation. For example, the following quotation comes from the same page of the source quoted above. The bracketed material explains what the phrase *these minds* refers to in the original quotation—this helps the reader understand what was clear in the context of the original source but isn't clear when quoted in isolation.

ORIGINAL (GOLEMAN'S EXACT WORDS)

In many or most moments, these minds are exquisitely coordinated; feelings are essential to thought, thought to feeling. [from p. 9]

QUOTATION WITH EXPLANATORY BRACKETS

"In many or most moments, these minds [emotional and rational] are exquisitely coordinated; feelings are essential to thought, thought to feeling" (Goleman 9). [This citation is arranged in MLA documentation style.]

Another way to integrate a quotation smoothly into your sentence is to delete some words, always using an ellipsis where the deletion occurs. You also might delete any part of the quotation that interferes with conciseness and the focus you intend in your sentence. When you use an ellipsis, make sure that the remaining words accurately reflect the source's meaning and that your sentence structure still flows smoothly.

ORIGINAL (GOLEMAN'S EXACT WORDS)

These two minds, the emotional and the rational, operate in tight harmony for the most part, intertwining their very different ways of knowing to guide us through the world. [from p. 9]

QUOTATION WITH ELLIPSIS

Goleman contends that, generally, "these two minds, the emotional and the rational, operate in tight harmony . . . to guide us through the world" (9). [This citation is arranged in MLA documentation style.]

In the preceding example, the words "for the most part, intertwining their very different ways of knowing" have been deleted from the original material so that the quotation is more concise and focused.

35h.2 Using quotations to enhance meaning

Perhaps the biggest complaint instructors have about student research papers is that sometimes quotations are simply stuck in, for no apparent reason. Whenever you place words between quotation marks, they take on special significance for your message as well as your language. Without context-setting information in the paper, the reader can't know exactly what logic leads the writer to use a particular quotation.

Furthermore, always make sure your readers know who said each group of quoted words. Otherwise, you've used a *disembodied quotation* (some instructors call them "ghost quotations"), which reflects poorly on your writing.

SOURCE

Wright, Karen. "Times of Our Lives." *Scientific American* Sept. 2002: 58–66. Print. [This source information is arranged in MLA documentation style.]

ORIGINAL (WRIGHT'S EXACT WORDS)

In human bodies, biological clocks keep track of seconds, minutes, days, months and years. [from p. 66]

INCORRECT (DISEMBODIED QUOTATION)

The human body has many subconscious processes. People don't have to make their hearts beat or remind themselves to breathe. "In human bodies, biological clocks keep track of seconds, minutes, days, months and years" (Wright 66).

CORRECT

The human body has many subconscious processes. People don't have to make their hearts beat or remind themselves to breathe. However, other processes are less obvious and perhaps more surprising. Karen Wright observes, for example, "In human bodies, biological clocks keep track of seconds, minutes, days, months and years" (66).

Rarely can a quotation begin a paragraph effectively. Start your paragraph by relying on your TOPIC SENTENCE, based on your own thinking. Then, you can fit in a relevant quotation somewhere in the paragraph, if it supports or extends what you have said.

Another strategy for working quotations smoothly into your paper is to integrate the name(s) of the author(s), the source title, or other information into your paper. You can prepare your reader for a quotation using one of these methods:

- Mention in your sentence directly before or after the quotation the name(s) of the author(s) you're quoting.
- Mention in your sentence the title of the work you're quoting from.
- Give additional authority to your material. If the author of a source is a noteworthy figure, you gain credibility when you refer to his or her credentials.
- Mention the name(s) of the author(s), with or without the name of the source and any author credentials, along with your personal introductory lead-in to the material.

Here are some examples, using the original source material from Karen Wright (above), of effective integration of an author's name, source title, and credentials, along with an introductory analysis.

AUTHOR'S NAME

Karen Wright explains that "in human bodies, biological clocks keep track of seconds, minutes, days, months and years" (66).

AUTHOR'S NAME AND SOURCE TITLE

Karen Wright explains in "Times of Our Lives" that "in human bodies, biological clocks keep track of seconds, minutes, days, months and years" (66).

AUTHOR'S NAME AND CREDENTIALS

Karen Wright, an award-winning science journalist, explains that "in human bodies, biological clocks keep track of seconds, minutes, days, months and years" (66).

AUTHOR'S NAME WITH STUDENT'S INTRODUCTORY ANALYSIS

Karen Wright reviews evidence of surprising subconscious natural processes, explaining that "in human bodies, biological clocks keep track of seconds, minutes, days, months and years" (66).

ALERT: After using an author's full name in the first reference, you can decide to use only the author's last name in subsequent references. This holds unless another source has that same last name. ●

EXERCISE 35-1 Read the original material, a passage taken from pages 16 and 17 of *Outliers: The Story of Success* by Malcolm Gladwell (New York: Little, 2008). Then, evaluate the passages that show unacceptable uses of quotations, either individually or with your peer-response group. Describe the problems, and then revise each passage. End four of the quotations with this MLA parenthetical reference: (Gladwell 16-17). Introduce one quotation with an attribution (see 35f) to Gladwell, and end it with this MLA parenthetical reference: (16-17).

ORIGINAL

Canadian hockey is a meritocracy. Thousands of Canadian boys begin to play the sport at the "novice" level, before they are even in kindergarten. From that point on, there are leagues for every age class, and at each of those levels, the players are sifted and sorted and evaluated, with the most talented separated out and groomed for the next level. By the time players reach their midteens, the very best of the best have been channeled into an elite league known as Major Junior A, which is the top of the pyramid. And if your Major Junior A team plays for the Memorial Cup, that means you are at the very top of the top of the pyramid.

This is the way most sports pick their future stars. It's the way soccer is organized in Europe and South America, and it's the way Olympic athletes are chosen. For that matter, it is not all that different from the way the world of classical music picks its future virtuosos, or the way the world of ballet picks its future ballerinas, or the way our elite educational system picks its future scientists and intellectuals.

UNACCEPTABLE USES OF QUOTATIONS

1. Only some Canadian hockey players are good enough to play in the Major Junior A league. "It's the way soccer is organized in Europe and South America, and it's the way Olympic athletes are chosen" (Gladwell 16-17).

2. The principle of meritocracy used in Canadian junior hockey "is not all that different from the way our elite educational system picks its future scientists and intellectuals" (Gladwell 16-17).

3. Players who begin to develop before they start kindergarten and pass through one level after another, "at each of those levels, the players are sifted and sorted and evaluated, with the most talented separated out and groomed for the next level. . . . This is the way most sports pick their future stars" (Gladwell 16-17).

4. The parents of a teenage boy sent to play competitive hockey even before he began kindergarten may want him to become one of "the very best of the best and be channeled into an elite league known as Major Junior A, which is the top of the pyramid" (Gladwell 16-17).

5. From childhood on, according to Gladwell, Canadian hockey players are sorted by ability, with the top teenage players going into the Major Junior A league. Therefore, as Gladwell writes, players on the two Major Junior A teams that complete for the Memorial Cup each year know that "you are at the very top of the top of the pyramid" (16-17).

EXERCISE 35-2   Working individually or with your peer-response group, do the following:

1. For a paper analyzing modern conceptions of place and identity, write a three- to four-sentence passage that includes your own words and a quotation from this paragraph, taken from pages 267–68 of Mark Kingwell's *Marginalia* (Toronto: Penguin, 1999). After the quoted words, use this parenthetical reference: (Kingwell 267-68).

ORIGINAL

I have been away from home a lot lately, travelling from city to city across this country and south of the border. Last Sunday I had breakfast with my wife in Boston, lunch with a friend in Toronto, and dinner with a colleague in Ottawa. I started writing this essay in Montreal, worked on it in Vancouver, Edmonton, and Calgary, fiddled with the first few paragraphs in Winnipeg, fleshed out some other parts in upstate New York, and then finished it in Toronto. Covering all those miles, trundling in and out of departure lounges, and putting in hours in rental cars, gives you an appreciation for the vastness and variety of Canada: The way cool kids are cool differently in Quebec than on the West Coast. The way provincial politics dominates Edmonton in a way it doesn't in Winnipeg. The way Vancouver has, like Paris, apparently cornered the regional market on beautiful people. The way the smog and driving habits get worse every year in Toronto.

2. For a paper arguing that writers of children's books should not impose their own views on their readers, quote from the Landsberg paragraph in Exercise 35-6 (section 35j). Be sure to include in your quotation some of the strengths that Landsberg sees in the novel she is discussing, in addition to one or more of its weaknesses. The paragraph appears on page 109 of Landsberg's book.

3. Write a two- to three-sentence passage that includes your own words and a quotation from a source you're currently using for a paper assigned in one of your courses. If you have no such assignment, choose any material suitable for a college-level or university-level research paper. Your instructor might request a photocopy of the material from which you're quoting, so make a copy to have on hand.

35i   How can I write good paraphrases?

A **paraphrase** precisely restates in your own words and your own writing style the written or spoken words of someone else. Select for paraphrase only the passages that carry ideas you need to reproduce in detail. Because paraphrasing calls for a very close approximation of a source, avoid trying to paraphrase more than a paragraph or two; for longer passages, use SUMMARY instead. Expect to write a number of drafts of your paraphrases, each time getting closer to effectively rewording and revising the writing style so that you avoid PLAGIARISM. Quick Reference 35.5 provides guidelines for writing paraphrases.

Guidelines for writing paraphrases

1. Paraphrase authorities on your subject to support or dispute what you write in your paper.
2. Never use a paraphrase to present your THESIS STATEMENT or a TOPIC SENTENCE.
3. Say what the source says, but no more.
4. Reproduce the source's sequence of ideas and emphases.
5. Use your own words and writing style to restate the material. If some technical words in the original have no or awkward synonyms, you may quote the original's words—but do so very sparingly. For example, you can use the term *literate civilization* if you're paraphrasing the original source by Robert Bringhurst in the example below.
6. Never distort the source's meaning as you reword and change the writing style.
7. Expect your material to be as long as, and often longer than, the original. (A paraphrase is sometimes used to clarify a difficult passage.)
8. Integrate your paraphrases smoothly into your writing.
9. Avoid plagiarism (35b–d).
10. Enter all DOCUMENTATION precisely and carefully.

Here's an example of an unacceptable paraphrase and an acceptable one.

SOURCE

Bringhurst, Robert. *The Solid Form of Language*. Kentville, NS: Gaspereau, 2004. Print. [This source information is arranged in MLA documentation style.]

ORIGINAL (BRINGHURST'S EXACT WORDS)

A script is not a language—and the classification of scripts is as different from the classification of languages as the classification of clothes is from the classification of people. Writing, nevertheless, is many things, used by different people in many different ways. In itself, it is both less and more than language. More because it can develop into rich and varied forms of graphic art. Less because, much as we love it, it is not an inescapable part of the human experience or the perennial human condition. If language is lost, humanity is lost. If writing is lost, certain kinds of civilization and society are lost, but many other kinds remain—and there is no reason to think that those alternatives are inferior. Humans lived on the earth successfully—and so far as we know, quite happily—for a hundred thousand years without the benefit of writing. They have never lived, nor ever yet been happy, so far as we know, in the absence of language. [from p. 69]

UNACCEPTABLE PARAPHRASE (UNDERLINED WORDS ARE PLAGIARIZED)

Script is not the same as language, <u>and the classification of scripts is different from the classification of languages.</u> A script is like the garment in which a language is clothed. <u>Writing, nevertheless,</u> has many uses and forms. In one sense, it is more than language because it can evolve into <u>rich and varied forms of graphic art.</u> In another sense, writing is less than language because, even if we are attached to it, human experience and the human condition do not depend on it. There is no humanity without language, but if writing is lost, not all civilization or society is lost. What remains may not even be inferior to literate civilization. For most of their time on earth, human beings lived successfully—and perhaps even happily—without the benefit of writing. However, we have never lived, much less been happy, in the absence of language (Bringhurst 69).

ACCEPTABLE PARAPHRASE

Script is not the same as language. Bringhurst points out that scripts are classified differently from the languages that use them just as clothes are classified differently from the people who wear them. In one sense, he explains, writing is more than language because it can evolve into a variety of artistic forms. In another sense, writing is less than language because, even if we are attached to it, writing can be separated from what it means to be human. There is no humanity without language, but civilization and human society can survive without writing. What remains may not even be inferior to literate civilization. For most of their time on earth, human beings had no writing and, Bringhurst claims, they still lived successfully and even happily. However, he concludes, we have never lived, much less been happy, without language (69). [This citation is arranged in MLA documentation style.]

The first attempt to paraphrase is not acceptable. The writer simply changed a few words. What remains is plagiarized because the passage keeps most of the original's language, has much of the same sentence structure as the original, and uses no quotation marks. The documentation is correct, but its accuracy doesn't make up for the unacceptable paraphrasing. The second paraphrase is acceptable. It captures the meaning of the original in the student's own words.

EXERCISE 35-3   Working individually or with your peer-response group, read the original material, a paragraph from page 49 of *Uniforms: Why We Are What We Wear* by Paul Fussell (Boston: Houghton, 2002). Then, read the unacceptable paraphrase, and point out each example of plagiarism. Finally, write your own paraphrase, starting it with a phrase naming Fussell and ending it with this parenthetical reference: (49).

ORIGINAL (FUSSELL'S EXACT WORDS)

Until around 1963, part of the routine for Levi's wearers was shrinking the trousers to fit, and the best way to do that was to put them on wet and let them dry on your body. This gave the wearer the impression that he or she was actually creating the garment, or at least emphasizing one's precious individuality, and that conviction did nothing to oppose the illusion of uniqueness precious to all American young people.

UNACCEPTABLE PARAPHRASE

Paul Fussell says that until around 1963 Levi's wearers used to shrink new trousers to fit. The best way to do that was to put them on wet and let them dry while wearing them. Doing this created the impression that wearers were actually creating the garment or emphasizing their precious individuality. It reinforced the illusion of uniqueness precious to all American teens (49).

EXERCISE 35-4   Working individually or with your peer-response group, do the following:

1. For a paper on the place of censorship in the coverage of military conflicts, paraphrase the following paragraph from page 65 of *Regarding the Pain of Others* by Susan Sontag (New York: Farrar, 2003). Start with words mentioning Sontag, and end with this parenthetical reference: (65).

   ORIGINAL (SONTAG'S EXACT WORDS)

   There had always been censorship, but for a long time it remained desultory, at the pleasure of generals and heads of state. The first organized ban on press photography at the front came during the First World War; both the German and French high commands allowed only a few selected military photographers near the fighting. (Censorship of the press by the British General Staff was less inflexible.) And it took another fifty years, and the relaxation of censorship with the first televised war coverage, to understand what impact shocking photographs could have on the domestic public. During the Vietnam era, war photography became, normatively, a criticism of war. This was bound to have consequences: Mainstream media are not in the business of making people feel queasy about the struggles for which they are being mobilized, much less of disseminating propaganda against waging war.

2. In one of your sources for a current research assignment, locate a paragraph that is at least 150 words in length and write a paraphrase of it. If you have no such assignment, choose any material suitable for a college-level or university-level paper. Your instructor may request that you submit a photocopy of the original material, so make a copy to have on hand.

35j   How can I write good summaries?

A **summary** differs from a PARAPHRASE (35i) in one important way: A paraphrase restates the original material completely, but a summary provides only the main point of the original source. A summary is much shorter than a paraphrase. Summarizing is the technique you'll probably use most frequently in writing your research paper, both for taking notes and for integrating what you have learned from sources into your own writing.

As you summarize, you trace a line of thought. This involves deleting less central ideas and sometimes transposing certain points into an order more suited to summary. In summarizing a longer original—say, ten pages or more—you may find it helpful first to divide the original into subsections and summarize each. Then, group your subsection summaries and use them as the basis for further condensing the material into a final summary. You'll probably have to revise a summary more than once. Always make sure that a summary accurately reflects the source and its emphases.

When you're summarizing a source in your **content notes**, resist the temptation to include your personal interpretation along with something the author says. Similarly, never include in your summary your own judgment about the point made in the source. Your own opinions and ideas, although they have value, don't belong in a summary. Instead, jot them down immediately when they come to mind, but separate them clearly from your summary. Write your notes so that when you go back to them you can be sure to distinguish your opinions or ideas from your summary. On a computer, highlight your personal writing with a screen of yellow or some other colour, or use an entirely different font for it. Quick Reference 35.6 provides guidelines for writing good summaries.

Guidelines for writing summaries

1. Use summaries from authorities on your subject to support or dispute what you write in your paper.
2. Identify the main points you want to summarize and condense them using your own words without losing the meaning of the original source.
3. Never use a summary to present your THESIS STATEMENT or a TOPIC SENTENCE.
4. Keep your summary short.
5. Integrate your summaries smoothly into your writing.
6. Avoid PLAGIARISM (35b–d).
7. Enter all DOCUMENTATION precisely and carefully.

Here's an example of an unacceptable summary and an acceptable one.

SOURCE

Frye, Northrop. *Anatomy of Criticism*. 1957. Princeton: Princeton UP, 1973. Print. [This source information is arranged in MLA documentation style.]

ORIGINAL (FRYE'S EXACT WORDS)

The repetition of certain common images of physical nature like the sea or the forest in a large number of poems cannot in itself be called even "coincidence," which is the name we give to a piece of design when we cannot find a use for it. But it does indicate a certain unity in the nature that poetry imitates, and in the communicating activity of which poetry forms part. Because of the larger communicative context of education, it is possible for a story about the sea to be archetypal, to make a profound imaginative impact, on a reader who has never been out of Saskatchewan. And when pastoral images are deliberately employed in *Lycidas,* for instance, merely because they are conventional, we can see that the convention of the pastoral makes us assimilate these images to other parts of literary experience. [from p. 99]

UNACCEPTABLE SUMMARY (UNDERLINED WORDS ARE PLAGIARIZED)

The fact that common images of physical nature like the sea or the forest are repeated in many poems is not in itself coincidence. It indicates the unity of the natural world, which poetry imitates, and unity in poetry's aspect as a communicating activity. For example, a story about the sea can be archetypal and therefore able to impact readers who have never been out of Saskatchewan. A pastoral work assimilates its images to other parts of the literary experience.

ACCEPTABLE SUMMARY

Frye simply sees the repetition of images from nature in poetry as a result of the unity of nature—but more important, he argues that this repetition reveals the unity of literature as a form of communication. Thus he sees particular natural images, such as the sea or the pastoral landscape, as archetypes that connect to other elements in the literary experience (99). [This citation is arranged in MLA documentation style.]

The unacceptable summary above has several major problems: It doesn't isolate the main point. It plagiarizes by taking much of its language directly from the source. Examples of plagiarized language include all the underlined phrases. The acceptable summary concisely isolates the main point, puts the source into the writer's own words, calls attention to the author by including his name in the summary, and remains objective throughout.

EXERCISE 35-5   Working individually or with your peer-response group, read the original material from *No Logo: Taking Aim at the Brand Bullies* by Naomi Klein (Toronto: Knopf, 2000): 195–96. Then, read the unacceptable summary. Point out each example of plagiarism. Finally, write your own summary, starting it with a phrase mentioning Klein and ending it with this parenthetical reference: (195-96).

ORIGINAL (KLEIN'S EXACT WORDS)

Many brand-name multinationals, as we have seen, are in the process of transcending the need to identify with their earthbound products. They dream instead about their brands' deep inner meanings—the way they capture the spirit of individuality, athleticism, wilderness or community. In this context of strut over stuff, marketing departments charged with the managing of brand identities have begun to see their work as something that occurs not in conjunction with factory production but in direct competition with it. "Products are made in the factory," says Walter Landor, president of the Landor branding agency, "but brands are made in the mind." Peter Schweitzer, president of the advertising giant J. Walter Thompson, reiterates the same thought: "The difference between products and brands is fundamental. A product is something that is made in a factory; a brand is something that is bought by a customer." Savvy ad agencies have all moved away from the idea that they are flogging a product made by someone else, and have come to think of themselves instead as brand factories, hammering out what is of true value: the idea, the lifestyle, the attitude. Brand builders are the new primary producers in our so-called knowledge economy.

UNACCEPTABLE, PLAGIARIZED SUMMARY

According to Naomi Klein, many multinational corporations are transcending the need to identify with their products. Instead, they think of the inner meanings of their brands and how they represent individuality, athleticism, and other attributes. Marketing departments today see branding as competing with factory production: The brand is an idea and what a customer buys, while the product is manufactured in a factory. Advertisers no longer think that they are selling products made by someone else. Instead, they consider themselves brand factories, creating the real value in the form of ideas, lifestyles, and attitudes (195-96).

EXERCISE 35-6   Working individually or with your peer-response group, do the following:

1. For a paper examining the author's point of view in Canadian children's literature, summarize this paragraph from *Michele Landsberg's Guide to Children's Books* (Toronto: Penguin, 1985): 109. Start your summary with a mention of the author, and end with this parenthetical reference: (109).

ORIGINAL (LANDSBERG'S EXACT WORDS)

One-sidedness is a sore (and fatal) temptation for a novelist, to which too many of Canada's accomplished storywriters have succumbed—particularly, alas, those of dissenting views. Perhaps they have been provoked by the national complacency that smothers critics of the status quo like a monstrous clammy blanc mange. Silver Donald Cameron's novel, *The Baitchopper*, about a Nova Scotia fishermen's strike, has a memorable title, an exciting climactic scene at sea in a storm, and some fine salty local language. Unfortunately, it is weakened by a black-and-white finality about heroic proletarian strikers versus the smug establishment. I would share Cameron's conclusions about the rights and wrongs of the strike and about the base self-interest of those who opposed it, but the writer's fixed viewpoint robs his young characters of the opportunity to come to these conclusions for themselves. Ironically, the drama of that inner struggle would have been far more effective in making the point.

2. Write a summary of your paraphrase of the Sontag material in Exercise 35-4. Use the parenthetical reference given there.

3. Write a summary of a passage from a source you're currently using for a paper assigned in one of your courses. If you have no such assignment, choose any material suitable for a college-level or university-level research paper. Your instructor might request a photocopy of the material you're summarizing, so make a copy to have on hand.

35k Which verbs can help me weave source material into my sentences?

The verbs listed in Quick Reference 35.7 can help you work quotations, paraphrases, and summaries smoothly into your writing. Some of these verbs imply your position toward the source material (for example, *argue, complain, concede, deny, grant, insist,* and *reveal*). Other verbs imply a more neutral stance (for example, *comment, describe, explain, note, say,* and *write*). For many examples of effective use of such verbs, see the student research papers presented in sections 36e.2 and 37h.2.

QUICK REFERENCE 35.7

Verbs useful for integrating quotations, paraphrases, and summaries

acknowledges	claims	contends
agrees	comments	contradicts
analyzes	compares	contrasts
argues	complains	declares
asks	concedes	demonstrates
asserts	concludes	denies
balances	confirms	describes
begins	connects	develops
believes	considers	discusses

continued ➤

distinguishes between/among	introduces	rejects
emphasizes	maintains	remarks
endeavours to	means	reports
establishes	negates	reveals
estimates	notes	says
explains	notices	sees
expresses	observes	shows
finds	offers	signals
focuses on	organizes	specifies
grants	points out	speculates
illuminates	prepares	states
illustrates	promises	suggests
implies	proves	supports
indicates	questions	supposes
informs	recognizes	thinks
insists	recommends	wishes
	refutes	writes

Chapter 36

MLA DOCUMENTATION WITH CASE STUDY

Here are two directories. The first lists examples of MLA in-text parenthetical citations. The second lists examples of MLA Works Cited entries.

continued ➤

continued ➢

36a What is MLA style?

A DOCUMENTATION STYLE* is a standard format that writers follow to tell readers what SOURCES they used in conducting their research and how to find those sources. Different disciplines follow different documentation styles. The one most frequently used in the humanities (Chapter 40) is that recommended by the Modern Language Association (MLA).

MLA style requires you to document your sources in two equally important ways.

1. Within the text of the paper, use parenthetical documentation, as described in section 36b. Section 36c shows twenty models of in-text parenthetical documentation, each for a different type of source.

2. At the end of the paper, provide a WORKS CITED list of the sources you used in your paper. Title this list "Works Cited." It should include only the sources you've actually used in your research paper, not any you've consulted but haven't used. Section 36d gives instructions for composing a Works Cited list, followed by ninety-six models, each based on different kinds of sources (book, article, website, and so on) that you might use.

For an example of a research paper that uses MLA-style parenthetical documentation and a Works Cited list, see section 36e.2. As you read the research paper, notice how the two requirements for crediting sources work together so that readers can learn the precise origin of QUOTATIONS, PARAPHRASES, and SUMMARIES. If you need more information than we cover in this chapter, consult the *MLA Handbook for Writers of Research Papers*, Seventh Edition (New York: Modern Language Association of America, 2009).

---

*Words printed in SMALL CAPITAL LETTERS are discussed elsewhere in the text and are defined in the Terms Glossary at the back of the book.

36b   What is MLA in-text parenthetical documentation?

MLA-style **parenthetical documentation** (also called **in-text citation**) places SOURCE information in parentheses within the sentences of your research papers. This information is given each time that you quote, summarize, or paraphrase source materials. It signals materials used from outside sources and enables readers to find the originals.

If you include an author's name (or, if none, a shortened title of the work) in the sentence to introduce the source material, you include in parentheses only the page number where you found the material:

> According to Brent Staples, IQ tests give scientists little insight into intelligence (293). [Author name cited in text; page number cited in parentheses.]

For readability and good writing technique, try to introduce names of authors (or titles of sources) in your own sentences. If you don't include this information in your sentence, you need to insert it before the page number, in parentheses. There is no punctuation between the author's name and the page number:

> IQ tests give scientists little insight into intelligence (Staples 293). [Author name and page number cited in parentheses.]

When possible, position a parenthetical reference at the end of the quotation, summary, or paraphrase it refers to—preferably at the end of a sentence, unless that would place it too far from the source's material. When you place the parenthetical reference at the end of a sentence, insert it before the sentence-ending period.

If you're citing a quotation enclosed in quotation marks, place the parenthetical information after the closing quotation mark but before sentence-ending punctuation.

> Coleman summarizes research that shows that "the number, rate, and direction of time-zone changes are the critical factors in determining the extent and degree of jet lag symptoms" (67). [Author name cited in text; page number cited in parentheses.]

The one exception to this rule concerns quotations that you set off in BLOCK STYLE, meaning one inch (about 2.5 cm) from the left margin. (MLA requires that quotations longer than four typed lines be handled this way.) For block quotations, put the parenthetical reference after the period.

> Bruce Sterling worries about what he calls "medical tourism":
>
> > Offshore docs offer medical services that are faster, cheaper, and safer than anything available at home. . . . Medical tourism is already in full swing. Thailand is the golden shore for wealthy, sickly Asians and Australians. Fashionable Europeans head to South Africa for embarrassing plastic surgery. Crowds of scrip-waving Americans buy prescription drugs in Canada and Mexico. (92)

If you quote more than one paragraph, indent the first line of each paragraph an additional quarter inch (0.5 cm; 1¼ inches or 3 cm in all).

36c   What are MLA guidelines for parenthetical documentation?

This section shows examples of how to handle parenthetical documentation in the text of your research papers. The directory at the beginning of this chapter corresponds to the numbered examples in the following pages. Most of these examples show the author's name or the title included in the parenthetical citation, but remember that it's usually more effective to integrate that information into your sentences.

1. Paraphrased or Summarized Source—MLA

According to Brent Staples, IQ tests give scientists little insight into intelligence (293). [Author name cited in text; page number cited in parentheses.]

In "The IQ Cult," the journalist Brent Staples states that IQ tests give scientists little insight into intelligence (293). [Title of source, author name, and author credentials cited in text; page number cited in parentheses.]

IQ tests give scientists little insight into intelligence (Staples 293). [Author name and page number cited in parentheses.]

2. Source of a Short Quotation—MLA

Given that "thoughts, emotions, imagination and predispositions occur concurrently . . . [and] interact with other brain processes" (Caine and Caine 66), it is easy to understand why "whatever [intelligence] might be, paper and pencil tests aren't the tenth of it" (Staples 293).

O'Connor asks, "What actually happened in Walkerton?" (2).

3. Source of a Long Quotation—MLA

A long quotation in MLA style consists of more than four typed lines. It's set off block style, indented one inch (about 2.5 cm) from the left margin. Never put quotation marks around a set-off quotation, because the indentation and block style communicate that the material is quoted. At the end of an indented quotation, place the parenthetical reference after the end punctuation mark.

Gray and Viens explain how, by tapping into a student's highly developed spatial-mechanical intelligence, one teacher can bolster a student's poor writing skills:

> The teacher asked that during "journal time" Jacob create a tool dictionary to be used as a resource in the mechanical learning center. After several entries in which he drew and described tools and other materials, Jacob confidently moved on to writing about other things of import to him, such as his brothers and a recent birthday party. Rather than shy away from all things linguistic—he previously had refused any task requiring a pencil—Jacob became invested in journal writing. (23-24)

4. One Author—MLA

Give an author's name as it appears on the source: for a book, on the title page; for an article, directly below the title or at the end of the article.

One test asks four-year-olds to choose between one marshmallow now or two marshmallows later (Gibbs 60).

Many nonprint sources also name an author; for CDs or DVDs, for example, check the printed sleeve or cover. For an online source, look at the beginning or end of the file for a link to the author, or at the site's home page. (For more information about citing electronic sources, see items 18 through 20.)

5. Two or Three Authors—MLA

Give the names in the same order as in the source. Spell out *and*. For three authors, use commas to separate the authors' names.

> As children get older, they begin to express several different kinds of intelligence (Todd and Taylor 23).

> Another measure of emotional intelligence is the success of inter- and intrapersonal relationships (Voigt, Dees, and Prigoff 14).

6. More Than Three Authors—MLA

If your source has more than three authors, you can name them all or use the first author's name only, followed by *et al.*, either in a parenthetical reference or in your sentence. In MLA citations, do not underline or italicize *et al.*

> Emotional security varies, depending on the circumstances of the social interaction (Carter et al. 158).

ALERTS: (1) *Et al.* is an abbreviation of the latin *et alii*, meaning "and others." No period follows *et*, but one follows *al.* (2) When an author's name followed by *et al.* is the subject of a verb, use a plural verb.

> Carter et al. have found that emotional security varies, depending on the circumstances of the social interaction (158). ●

7. More Than One Source by an Author—MLA

When you use two or more sources by an author, include the relevant title in each citation. In parenthetical citations, use a shortened version of the title. For example, in a paper using two of Howard Gardner's works, *Frames of Mind: The Theory of Multiple Intelligences* and "Reflections on Multiple Intelligences: Myths and Messages," use *Frames* and "Reflections." Shorten the titles as much as possible without making them ambiguous to readers, and start them with the word by which you alphabetize each work in your Works Cited list. Separate the author's name and the title with a comma, but do not use punctuation between the title and the page number. When you incorporate the title into your own sentences, you can omit a subtitle, but never shorten the main title.

> Although it seems straightforward to think of multiple intelligences as multiple approaches to learning (Gardner, *Frames* 60-61), an intelligence is not a learning style (Gardner, "Reflections" 202-03).

8. Two or More Authors with the Same Last Name—MLA

Use each author's first initial and full last name in each parenthetical citation. This is the only instance in MLA style where you use an initial in a parenthetical reference. If both authors have the same first initial, use the full name in all instances.

> According to Anne Cates, psychologists can predict how empathetic an adult will be from his or her behaviour at age two (41), but other researchers disagree (T. Cates 171).

9. Work with a Group or Corporate Author—MLA

When a corporation or other group is named as the author of a source you want to cite, use the corporate name just as you would an individual's name.

> In a five-year study, the Canadian Institute of Child Health reported that these tests are usually unreliable (11).

> A five-year study shows that these tests are usually unreliable (Canadian Institute of Child Health 11).

10. Work Listed by Title—MLA

If no author is named, use the title in citations. In your own sentences, use the full main title and omit a subtitle, if any. For parenthetical citations, shorten the title as much as possible (making sure that the shortened version refers unambiguously to the correct source), and always make the first word the one by which you alphabetize it in the Works Cited. "Are You a Day or Night Person?" is the full title of the article in the following citation.

> The "morning lark" and "night owl" connotations are typically used to categorize the human extremes ("Are You" 11).

11. Multivolume Work—MLA

When you cite more than one volume of a multivolume work, include the relevant volume number in each citation. Give the volume number first, followed by a colon and one space, and then the page number(s).

> By 1900, the Amazon forest dwellers had been exposed to these viruses (Rand 3: 202).

> Rand believes that forest dwellers in Borneo escaped illness from retroviruses until the 1960s (4: 518-19).

12. Material from a Novel, Play, Poem, or Short Story—MLA

Literary works frequently appear in different editions. When you cite material from literary works, providing the part, chapter, act, scene, canto, stanza, or line numbers usually helps readers locate what you are referring to more than page numbers alone. Unless your instructor tells you not to, use arabic numerals for these references, even if the literary work uses roman numerals.

For novels that use them, give part and/or chapter numbers after page numbers. Use a semicolon after the page number but a comma to separate a part from a chapter.

> Flannery O'Connor describes one character in *The Violent Bear It Away* as "divided in two—a violent and a rational self" (139; pt. 2, ch. 6).

For plays that use them, give act, scene, and line numbers. Use periods between these numbers. For short stories, use page numbers.

> Among the most quoted of Shakespeare's lines is Hamlet's soliloquy beginning "To be, or not to be: that is the question" (3.1.56).

> The old man in John Collier's short story "The Chaser" says about his potions, "I don't deal in laxatives and teething mixtures . . . " (79).

For poems and plays that use them, give canto, stanza, and line numbers. Use periods between these numbers.

In "To Autumn," Keats's most melancholy image occurs in the lines "Then in a wailful choir the small gnats mourn / Among the river swallows" (3.27-28).

13. Bible or Sacred Text—MLA

Give the title of the edition you're using, the book (in the case of the Bible), and the chapter and verse. Spell out the names of books in sentences, but use abbreviations in parenthetical references. (See also 36d, item 21.)

> He would certainly benefit from the advice in Ephesians to "get rid of all bitterness, rage, and anger" (*Holy Bible*, 4.31).

> He would certainly benefit from the advice to "get rid of all bitterness, rage, and anger" (*Holy Bible*, Eph. 4.31).

14. Work in an Anthology or Other Collection—MLA

You may want to cite a work you have read in a book that contains many works by various authors and that was compiled or edited by someone other than the person you're citing. Your in-text citation should include the author of the selection you're citing and the page number. For example, suppose you want to cite the poem "Several Things" by Martha Collins, in a literature text edited by Pamela Annas and Robert Rosen. Use Collins's name and the title of her work in the sentence, and give the line numbers (see item 12) in a parenthetical citation.

> In "Several Things," Martha Collins enumerates what could take place in the lines of her poem: "Plums could appear, on a pewter plate / A dead red hare, hung by one foot. / A vase of flowers. Three shallots" (2-4).

15. Indirect Source—MLA

When you want to quote words that you found quoted in someone else's work, put the name of the person whose words you're quoting into your own sentence. Cite the work where you found the quotation either in your sentence or in a parenthetical citation beginning with *qtd. in* (not in italics).

> Pierre Trudeau makes a notably populist statement: "The ordinary person can be appealed to through common sense. Beyond the effects of technology. My grandfather, for instance, was not especially literate but he was able to reason choices out" (qtd. in Powe 126).

> Powe quotes Pierre Trudeau as having made a notably populist statement: "The ordinary person can be appealed to through common sense. Beyond the effects of technology. My grandfather, for instance, was not especially literate but he was able to reason choices out" (126).

16. Two or More Sources in One Reference—MLA

If more than one source has contributed to an idea, opinion, or fact in your paper, cite them all. Suppose, as in the following example, that three sources all make the same point. An efficient way to credit all is to include them in a single parenthetical citation, with a semicolon separating each block of information.

> Once researchers agreed that multiple intelligences existed, their next step was to try to measure or define them (West 17; Arturi 477; Gibbs 68).

17. Entire Work—MLA

References to an entire work usually fit best into your own sentences.

> In *Convergence Culture*, Henry Jenkins explores how new digital media create a culture of active participation rather than passive reception.

18. Electronic Source with Page Numbers—MLA

The principles that govern in-text parenthetical citations of electronic sources are exactly the same as the ones that apply to books, articles, or other sources. When an electronically accessed source identifies its author, use the author's name for parenthetical references. If no author is named, use the title of the source. When an electronic source has page numbers, use them exactly as you would the page numbers of a print source.

> Learning happens best when teachers truly care about their students' complete well-being (Anderson 7).

19. Electronic Source with Paragraph or Screen Numbers—MLA

When an electronic source has numbered paragraphs or screens (instead of page numbers), use them for parenthetical references, with two differences: (1) Put a comma followed by one space after the name (or title); and (2) use the abbreviation *par.* for a reference to one paragraph or *pars.* for a reference to more than one paragraph, followed by the number(s) of the paragraph(s) you are citing. Note that the practice of numbering paragraphs or screens is rare.

> Artists seem to be haunted by the fear that psychoanalysis might destroy creativity while it reconstructs personality (Francis, pars. 22–25).

> The renovation cost $25 million, according to Conklin (screen 5).

20. Electronic Source Without Page or Paragraph Numbers—MLA

Many online sources don't number pages or paragraphs. Simply refer to those works in their entirety. Here are two examples referring to "What Is Artificial Intelligence?" by John McCarthy; this website does not use page numbers or paragraph numbers. Include the name of the author in your sentence; it is also helpful to include the title.

> According to McCarthy, the science of artificial intelligence includes efforts beyond trying to simulate human intelligence.

> In "What Is Artificial Intelligence?" John McCarthy notes that the science of artificial intelligence includes efforts beyond trying to simulate human intelligence.

36d What are MLA guidelines for a Works Cited list?

In MLA-STYLE DOCUMENTATION, the Works Cited list gives complete bibliographic information for each SOURCE used in your paper. Include only the sources from which you quote, paraphrase, or summarize. Never include sources that you consulted but don't refer to in the paper. Quick Reference 36.1 gives general information about the Works Cited list. The rest of this chapter gives models of many specific kinds of Works Cited entries.

Guidelines for an MLA-style Works Cited list

TITLE

Works Cited

PLACEMENT OF LIST

Start a new page numbered sequentially with the rest of the paper, following the Notes pages, if any.

CONTENT AND FORMAT

Include all sources quoted from, paraphrased, or summarized in your paper. Start each entry on a new line and at the regular left margin. If the entry uses more than one line, indent the second and all following lines one-half inch (about 1.25 cm) from the left margin. Double-space all lines.

SPACING AFTER PUNCTUATION

The *MLA Handbook* uses one space after punctuation at the end of a sentence. However, you should use two spaces if that's the style your instructor prefers. Always put only one space after a comma, a colon, or a semicolon.

ARRANGEMENT OF ENTRIES

Alphabetize by author's last name. If no author is named, alphabetize by the title's first significant word (ignore *A, An,* or *The*).

AUTHORS' NAMES

Use first names and middle names or middle initials, if any, as given in the source. Don't reduce to initials any name that is given in full. For one author or the first-named author in multiauthor works, give the last name first. Use the word *and* with two or more authors. List multiple authors in the order given in the source. Put a comma between the first author's last and first names and after each complete author name except the last, which ends with a period: Fein, Ethel Andrea, Bert Griggs, and Delaware Rogash.

Include *Jr., Sr., II,* or *III* but no other titles and degrees before or after a name. For example, an entry for a work by Edward Meep III, MD, and Sir Richard Bolton would start like this: Meep, Edward III, and Richard Bolton.

CAPITALIZATION OF TITLES

Capitalize all major words and the first and last words of all titles and subtitles. Don't capitalize ARTICLES (*a, an, the*), PREPOSITIONS, COORDINATING CONJUNCTIONS (*and, but, for, nor, or, so, yet*), or *to* in INFINITIVES in the middle of a title.

SPECIAL TREATMENT OF TITLES

Use quotation marks around titles of shorter works (poems, short stories, essays, articles). Italicize titles of longer works (books, periodicals, plays).

When a book title includes the title of another work that is usually italicized (as with a novel, play, or long poem), the preferred MLA style is not to italicize the incorporated title: *Decoding* Jane Eyre. For an alternative that MLA accepts, see item 20 in 36d.1.

continued ➤

If the incorporated title is usually enclosed in quotation marks (such as a short story or short poem), keep the quotation marks and italicize the complete title of the book: *Theme and Form in "I Shall Laugh Purely": A Brief Study*.

Drop *A, An,* or *The* as the first word of a periodical title.

PLACE OF PUBLICATION

If several cities are listed for the place of publication, give only the first. MLA doesn't ask for province, territory, state, or country names to accompany even confusing or obscure city names, but your instructor may ask you to include their abbreviations.

PUBLISHER

Use shortened names as long as they are clear: *Random* for *Random House.* For companies named for more than one person, name only the first: *Prentice* for *Prentice Hall.* For university presses, use the capital letters *U* and *P* (without periods): Oxford UP; U of Chicago P

PUBLICATION MONTH ABBREVIATIONS

Abbreviate all publication months except *May, June,* and *July.* Use the first three letters followed by a period (*Dec., Feb.*) except for September (*Sept.*).

PAGE, PARAGRAPH, AND SCREEN NUMBERS IN ELECTRONIC SOURCES

Some electronic sources number paragraphs or screens instead of pages. If paragraphs are numbered, some instructors ask to give the total number of paragraphs at the end of the publication information followed by the abbreviation *pars.*: 77 *pars.* If screens are numbered, you may give the number of screens. If you cite a source (like a journal) where pages are normally numbered but that does not number pages or anything else, use the abbreviation *n. pag.*

PAGE RANGES

Give the page range—the starting page number and the ending page number, connected by a hyphen—of any paginated electronic source and any paginated print source that is part of a longer work (for example, a chapter in a book, an article in a journal). A range indicates that the cited work is on those pages and all pages in between. If that isn't the case, use the style shown next for discontinuous pages. In either case, use numerals only, without the word *page* or *pages* or the abbreviation *p.* or *pp.*

Use the full second number through 99. Above that, use only the last two digits for the second number unless to do so would be unclear: 103-04 and 113-14 are clear, but 567-602 requires full numbers.

DISCONTINUOUS PAGES

A source has discontinuous pages when the source is interrupted by material that's not part of the source (for example, an article beginning on page 32, interrupted on page 40, and continued on page 54). Use the starting page number followed by a plus sign (+): 32+.

MEDIUM OF PUBLICATION

Include the medium of publication in each works cited entry: *Web, Print, E-mail, CD, DVD, Film, Television, Performance, Personal interview, Lecture, Photograph, CD-ROM, Microform,* and so forth.

continued ➤

QUICK REFERENCE **36.1** *continued*

VOLUME AND ISSUE NUMBERS FOR SCHOLARLY JOURNALS

Include both a volume and issue number for each Works Cited entry for scholarly journals. This applies both to journals that are continuously paginated through each annual volume and those that are not.

WORKS CITED INFORMATION REQUIRED FOR INTERNET SOURCES

For online sources, provide as much of the following information as you can.

1. The author's name if given, or the compiler, editor, director, performer, etc.
2. Title of the work (italicized if the work is independent; in quotation marks if the work is part of a larger work). If the work has no title, describe it: for example, *Home page, Introduction, Online posting* (not italicized and without quotation marks).
3. The italicized title of the website, if distinct from the title of the work.
4. The version or edition used, if relevant.
5. The publisher or sponsor of the site (if not available, use *N.p.*)
6. The date of electronic publication or the most recent update (if not given, use *n.d.*).
7. The medium of publication (*Web*).
8. The date you accessed the site.

If you are also citing publication information for a print version of the online source, begin the entry with that information but omit the original medium (*Print*). Then provide the following information.

9. The italicized title of the website or database.
10. The medium of publication you consulted (*Web*).
11. The date you accessed the site.

Give any supplementary information that normally follows the medium of publication in a print citation immediately before the title of the website or database.

URLS IN ELECTRONIC SOURCES

Entries for online citations should not include the URL, unless the reader probably could not locate the source without it. Enclose a URL in angle brackets and put it after the access date, followed by a period. If your computer automatically creates a hyperlink when you type a URL, format the URL to look the same as the rest of the entry using the command "remove hyperlink," which you can usually find on the "Insert" menu or by right-clicking on the hyperlink. If a URL is very long, shorten it by giving just the URL for the site's search page. To divide a URL between two lines, break it after a slash and do not insert a hyphen.

36d.1 Following MLA guidelines for specific sources in a Works Cited list

The Works Cited directory at the beginning of this chapter corresponds to the numbered entries in this section. Not every possible documentation model is shown in this chapter. You may find that you have to combine features of models to document a particular source. You'll also find more information in the *MLA Handbook for Writers of Research Papers*. Figure 36.1 provides another tool to help you find the Works Cited model you need: a decision-making flowchart.

MLA

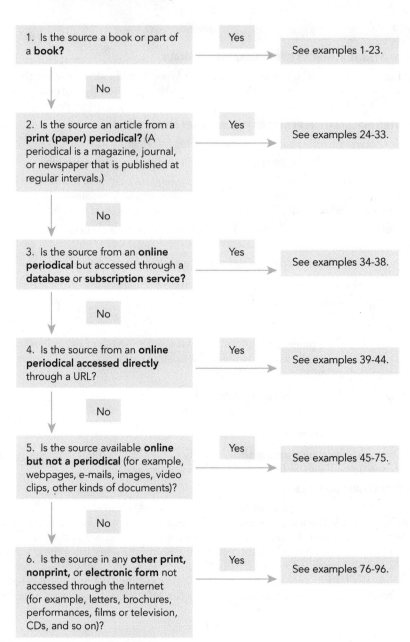

1. Is the source a book or part of a **book?** → Yes → See examples 1-23.

No ↓

2. Is the source an article from a **print (paper) periodical?** (A periodical is a magazine, journal, or newspaper that is published at regular intervals.) → Yes → See examples 24-33.

No ↓

3. Is the source from an **online periodical** but accessed through a **database** or **subscription service?** → Yes → See examples 34-38.

No ↓

4. Is the source from an **online periodical accessed directly** through a URL? → Yes → See examples 39-44.

No ↓

5. Is the source available **online but not a periodical** (for example, webpages, e-mails, images, video clips, other kinds of documents)? → Yes → See examples 45-75.

No ↓

6. Is the source in any **other print, nonprint,** or **electronic form** not accessed through the Internet (for example, letters, brochures, performances, films or television, CDs, and so on)? → Yes → See examples 76-96.

Figure 36.1 MLA Works Cited visual directory

BOOKS

Citations for books have three main parts: author, title, and publication information (place of publication, publisher, date of publication, and medium of publication). Figure 36.2 illustrates where to find this information and the proper citation format.

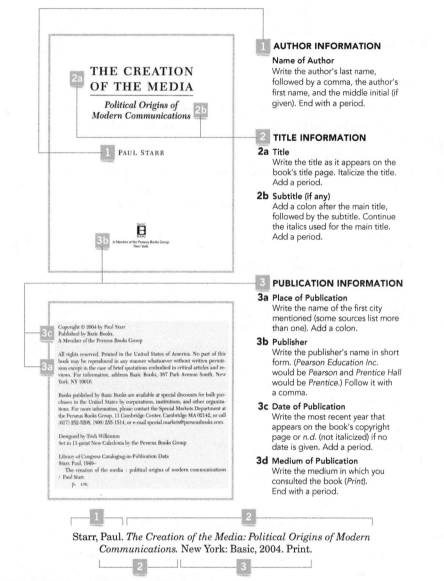

Figure 36.2 Locating and citing source information in a book

1. Book by One Author—MLA

Trudeau, Pierre E. *Federalism and the French Canadians.* Toronto: Macmillan, 1968. Print.

2. Book by Two or Three Authors—MLA

Doob, Anthony, and Carla Cesaroni. *Responding to Youth Crime in Canada.* Toronto: U of Toronto P, 2004. Print.

Scardamalia, Marlene, Carl Bereiter, and Bryant Fillion. *Writing for Results: A Sourcebook of Consequential Composing Activities.* Toronto: OISE, 1981. Print.

3. Book by More Than Three Authors—MLA

Give only the first author's name, followed by a comma and the phrase *et al.* ("and others"), or list all names in full and in the order in which they appear on the title page.

Saul, Wendy, et al. *Beyond the Science Fair: Creating a Kids' Inquiry Conference*. Portsmouth: Heinemann, 2005. Print.

4. Two or More Works by the Same Author(s)—MLA

Give author name(s) in the first entry only. In the second and subsequent entries, use three hyphens and a period to stand for exactly the same name(s). If the person served as editor or translator, put a comma and the appropriate abbreviation (*ed.* or *trans.*) after the three hyphens. Arrange the works in alphabetical (not chronological) order according to book title, ignoring labels such as *ed.* or *trans.*

Atwood, Margaret. *The Handmaid's Tale*. Toronto: McClelland, 1985. Print.

---. *Survival*. Toronto: Anansi, 1972. Print.

---. *Writing with Intent: Essays, Reviews, Personal Prose 1983–2005*. New York: Carroll, 2005. Print.

5. Book by Group or Corporate Author—MLA

Cite the full name of the corporate author first, omitting the first articles *A, An,* or *The*. When a corporate author is also the publisher, use a shortened form of the corporate name in the publication information. (The CBC Massey Lectures Series is considered the corporate author of the book in the second item.)

American Psychological Association. *Publication Manual of the American Psychological Association*. 6th ed. Washington: APA, 2009. Print.

CBC Massey Lectures Series. *The Lost Massey Lectures: Recovered Classics from Five Great Thinkers*. Toronto: Anansi, 2007.

6. Book with No Author Named—MLA

If there is no author's name on the title page, begin the citation with the title. Alphabetize the entry according to the first significant word of the title, ignoring *A, An* or *The*.

The Chicago Manual of Style. 16th ed. Chicago: U of Chicago P, 2010. Print.

7. Book with an Author and an Editor—MLA

If your paper refers to the work of the book's author, put the author's name first; if your paper refers to the work of the editor, put the editor's name first.

Trudeau, Pierre Elliott. *The Essential Trudeau*. Ed. Ron Graham. Toronto: McClelland, 1998. Print.

Graham, Ron, ed. *The Essential Trudeau*. By Pierre Elliott Trudeau. Toronto: McClelland, 1998. Print.

8. Translation—MLA

Tremblay, Michel. *A Thing of Beauty*. Trans. Sheila Fischman. Vancouver: Talon, 1998. Print.

9. Work in Several Volumes or Parts—MLA

If you're citing only one volume, put the volume number before the publication information. If you wish, you can give the total number of volumes at the end of the entry. MLA recommends using arabic numerals, even if the source uses roman numerals (*Vol. 6* rather than *Vol. VI*).

Chrisley, Ronald, ed. *Artificial Intelligence: Critical Concepts*. Vol. 1. London: Routledge, 2000. Print. 4 vols.

10. Anthology or Edited Book—MLA

Use this model if you are citing an entire anthology. In the following example, *ed.* stands for "editor," so use *eds.* when more than one editor is named; also see items 9, 11, and 12.

New, W. H., ed. *Canadian Short Fiction: From Myth to Modern.* Scarborough: Prentice, 1986.
Print.

11. One Selection from an Anthology or an Edited Book—MLA

Give the author and title of the selection first and then the full title of the anthology. Information about the editor starts with *Ed.* (for "Edited by"), so don't use *Eds.* when there is more than one editor. Give the name(s) of the editor(s) in normal order rather than reversing first and last names. Give the page range after the publication date.

Morrisseau, Norval. "The Indian That Became a Thunderbird." *Canadian Short Fiction: From Myth
to Modern.* Ed. W. H. New. Scarborough: Prentice, 1986. 26-29. Print.

12. More Than One Selection from the Same Anthology or Edited Book—MLA

If you cite more than one selection from the same anthology, you can list the anthology as a separate entry with all the publication information. Also, list each selection from the anthology by author and title of the selection, but give only the name(s) of the editor(s) of the anthology and the page number(s) for each selection. Here, *ed.* stands for "editor," so it is correct to use *eds.* when more than one editor is named. List selections separately in alphabetical order by author's last name.

Davis, Robertson, "The Charlottetown Banquet." Ioannou and Missen 40-52.

Ioannou, Greg, and Lyanne Missen, eds. *Shivers: An Anthology of Canadian Ghost Stories.*
Toronto. McClelland, 1989. Print.

Mistry, Rohinton. "The Ghost of Firozsha Baag." Ioannou and Missen 198-216.

13. Signed Article in a Reference Book—MLA

If the articles in the book are alphabetically arranged, you don't need to give volume and page numbers.

Shadbolt, Doris. "Carr, Emily." *The Canadian Encyclopedia.* 2nd ed. Edmonton: Hurtig, 1988.
Print.

14. Unsigned Article in a Reference Book—MLA

Begin with the title of the article. If you're citing a widely used reference work, give only the edition, year of publication, and medium of publication.

"Ireland." *The New Encyclopaedia Britannica: Macropaedia.* 15th ed. 2002. Print.

15. Second or Later Edition—MLA

If a book isn't a first edition, the edition number appears on the title page. Place the abbreviated information (*2nd ed., 3rd ed.,* etc.) between the title and the publication information. Give only the latest copyright date for the edition you're using.

Pratt, E. J. *The Collected Poems of E. J. Pratt.* Ed. Northrop Frye. 2nd ed. Toronto: Macmillan, 1958.
Print.

16. Introduction, Preface, Foreword, or Afterword—MLA

Give first the name of the writer of the part you're citing and then the name of the cited part, capitalized but not italicized or in quotation marks. After the book title, write *By* or *Ed.* and the full name(s) of the book's author(s) or editor(s), if different from the writer of the cited material. If the writer of the cited material is the same as the book author, include only the last name after *By*. If a single author has written the entire book including the introduction, preface, and so forth, and there is no editor listed, cite the entire book instead of creating a separate entry for this part. Following the publication information, give inclusive page numbers for the cited part, using roman or arabic numerals as the source does.

Hesse, Doug. Foreword. *The End of Composition Studies.* By David W. Smit. Carbondale: Southern
> Illinois UP, 2004. ix-xiii. Print.

When the introduction, preface, foreword, or afterword has a title (as in the next example), include it in the citation before the section name.

Fox-Genovese, Elizabeth. "Mothers and Daughters: The Ties That Bind." Foreword. *Southern Mothers.*
> Ed. Nagueyalti Warren and Sally Wolff. Baton Rouge: Louisiana State UP, 1999. iv-xviii. Print.

17. Unpublished Dissertation or Essay—MLA

State the author's name first, then the title in quotation marks (not italicized), then a descriptive label (such as *Diss.* or *Unpublished essay*), followed by the degree-granting institution (for dissertations), and, finally, the date. Treat published dissertations as books. In the following example, the title of the television series is italicized (see item 87).

Byers, Michele. *"Buffy the Vampire Slayer:* The Insurgence of Television as a Performance Text."
> Diss. U of Toronto, 2000. Print.

18. Reprint of an Older Book—MLA

Republishing information can be found on the copyright page. Give the date of the original version before the publication information for the version you're citing.

Lampman, Archibald. *Lyrics of Earth.* 1895. Ottawa: Tecumseh, 1978. Print.

19. Book in a Series—MLA

Give the series name and number, if any, as supplementary information at the end of the entry, after the publication medium.

Courchene, Thomas J. *In Praise of Renewed Federalism.* Toronto: C. D. Howe Institute, 1991. Print.
> The Canada Round.

Mukherjee, Meenakshi. *Jane Austen.* New York: St. Martin's, 1991. Print. Women Writers Ser.

20. Book with a Title Within a Title—MLA

The MLA recognizes two distinct styles for handling normally independent titles when they appear within an italicized title. (Use whichever style your instructor prefers.) When using the MLA's preferred style, do not italicize the embedded title or set it within quotation marks.

Lumiansky, Robert M., and Herschel Baker, eds. *Critical Approaches to Six Major English Works:*
> Beowulf *through* Paradise Lost. Philadelphia: U of Pennsylvania P, 1968. Print.

However, because MLA also accepts a second style for handling such embedded titles, you can set the normally independent titles within quotation marks and italicize them.

Lumiansky, Robert M., and Herschel Baker, eds. *Critical Approaches to Six Major English Works:*
> *"Beowulf" through "Paradise Lost."* Philadelphia: U of Pennsylvania P, 1968. Print.

21. Bible or Sacred Text—MLA

With a named version of a book such as the Bible, you may record the name of the version as supplementary information after the publication medium.

Bhagavad Gita. Trans. Juan Mascaro. Rev. ed. New York: Penguin, 2003. Print.

The Holy Bible. New York: Harper, 1983. Print. New International Version.

The Qur'an. Trans. Abdullah Yusuf Ali. 13th ed. Elmhurst: Tahrike Tarsile Qur'an, 1999. Print.

22. Government Publication—MLA

For government publications that name no author, start with the name of the government (such as Canada). Then name the branch of government or the government agency next (such as Department of Finance or Task Force on Program Review).

Canada. Indian and Northern Affairs Canada. *The Inuit.* Ottawa: Supply and Services Canada, 1986. Print.

Canada. Royal Commission on Bilingualism and Biculturalism. *Preliminary Report.* Ottawa: Queen's Printer, 1965. Print.

23. Published Proceedings of a Conference—MLA

Smith, Donald B., ed. *Forging a New Relationship: Proceedings of the Conference on the Report of the Royal Commission on Aboriginal Peoples.* 31 Jan.-2 Feb. 1997. Montreal: McGill Institute for the Study of Canada, 1997. Print.

PERIODICAL PUBLICATIONS—PRINT VERSIONS

Citations for periodical articles contain three major parts: author information, title information, and publication information. Figure 36.3 (p. 486) shows a citation for an article in a journal (see item 27).

24. Signed Article in a Weekly or Biweekly Periodical—MLA

Johnson, Brian D. "Why Six Dylans Are Better Than One." *Maclean's* 26 Nov. 2007: 43-46. Print.

25. Signed Article in a Monthly or Bimonthly Periodical—MLA

Fallows, James. "The 1.4 Trillion Question." *Atlantic* Jan.-Feb. 2008: 36-48.

26. Unsigned Article in a Periodical—MLA

"The Price Is Wrong." *Economist* 2 Aug. 2003: 58-59. Print.

27. Article in a Scholarly Journal—MLA

Provide both volume and issue number (if available).

Adler-Kassner, Linda, and Heidi Estrem. "Rethinking Research Writing: Public Literacy in the Composition Classroom." *WPA: Writing Program Administration* 26.3 (2003): 119-31. Print.

1 AUTHOR INFORMATION
Name of Author
Write the author's last name, followed by a comma, the author's first name, and the middle initial (if given). End with a period.

2 TITLE INFORMATION
2a Article Title
Write the title (with subtitle, if there is one), and include a period, inside the quotation marks. Capitalize all major words.
2b Journal Title and Volume
Italicize the title. Capitalize all major words. Include the volume and issue number, separated by a period.

3 PUBLICATION INFORMATION
3a Date of Publication
Journals: Include the year of publication in parentheses, followed by a colon. *Monthly periodicals*: Include the month and year, followed by a colon. *Weekly and biweekly periodicals*: List the day, month, and year, followed by a colon.
3b Page Numbers
Provide the page numbers on which the article begins and ends, separated by a hyphen. For numbers up to 99, include both digits. For higher numbers, include only the last two digits (145-57) unless doing so would be unclear (295-307). End with a period.
3c Medium of Publication
Write the medium in which you consulted the work (*Print*). End with a period.

Malinowitz, Harriet. "Business, Pleasure, and the Personal Essay." *College English* 65.3 (2003): 305-22. Print.

Figure 36.3 Locating and citing source information for a journal article

28. Article in a Collection of Reprinted Articles—MLA

First include the original publication information, then *Rpt.* and information about the place the article was republished. If you cite only one volume of a series, it is optional to give the volume number and series title (Vol. 14 of *The Gorbachev Era*).

Brumberg, Abraham. "Russia after Perestroika." *New York Review of Books* 27 June 1991: 53-62. Rpt. in *Russian and Soviet History*. Ed. Alexander Dallin. New York: Garland, 1992. 300-20. Print. Vol. 14 of *The Gorbachev Era*.

Textbooks used in writing courses often collect previously printed articles.

Rothstein, Richard. "When Mothers on Welfare Go to Work." *New York Times* 5 June 2002: A20. Rpt. in *Writing Arguments: A Rhetoric with Readings*. Ed. John D. Ramage, John C. Bean, and June Johnson. New York: Longman, 2004. 263. Print.

29. Signed Article in a Daily Newspaper—MLA

Omit *A, An,* or *The* as the first word in a newspaper title. Give the day, month, and year of the issue (and the edition, if applicable). If sections are designated, give the section letter as well as the page number. If an article runs on nonconsecutive pages, give the starting page number followed by a plus sign (for example, 23+ for an article that starts on page 23 and continues on page 42).

McCarthy, Shawn. "Sale Puts Ottawa out of Nuclear Business." *Globe and Mail* 28 June 2011: A1+ Print.

30. Unsigned Article in a Daily Newspaper—MLA

"Private Water May Violate Constitution." *Ottawa Citizen* 27 Nov. 2002: A1. Print.

If the city of publication is not part of the title, put it in square brackets after the title, not italicized.

"Judge Bars Public from CNR Building in Interim Order." *Beacon Herald* [Stratford] 24 July 2004: A1. Print.

31. Editorial, Letter to the Editor, or Review—MLA

After the author's name or title, provide information about the type of publication.

"London Doomed to Repeat Its History on Heritage." Editorial. *London Free Press* 20 July 2011: B8. Print.

Hurka, John. Letter. *Calgary Sun* 5 July 1994: A18. Print.

Toews, Wendy. "Politics of the Mind." Rev. of *They Say You're Crazy: How the World's Most Powerful Psychiatrists Decide Who's Normal*, by Paula J. Caplan. *Winnipeg Free Press* 26 Aug. 1995: C3. Print.

32. Article in a Looseleaf Collection of Reprinted Articles—MLA

Give the citation for the original publication first, followed by the citation for the collection.

Hayden, Thomas. "The Age of Robots." *US News and World Report* 23 Apr. 2001: 44+. Print. *Applied Science 2002*. Ed. Eleanor Goldstein. Boca Raton: SIRS, 2002. Art. 66.

33. Abstract in a Collection of Abstracts—MLA

To cite an abstract, first give information for the full work: the author's name, the title of the article, and publication information about the full article. If a reader could not know that the cited material is an abstract, write the word *Abstract*, not italicized, followed by a period. Give publication information about the collection of abstracts. For abstracts identified by item numbers rather than page numbers, use the word *item* before the item number.

Marcus, Hazel R., and Shinobu Kitayamo. "Culture and the Self: Implications for Cognition, Emotion, and Motivation." *Psychological Review* 88.2 (1991): 224-53. *Psychological Abstracts* 78.2 (1991): item 23878. Print.

MLA

PERIODICALS—ONLINE VERSIONS FROM SUBSCRIPTION SERVICES

A large (and increasing) number of periodicals are available online, as well as in print; some are available only online. Online periodicals fall into two categories: (1) periodicals you access through a **database** or **subscription service** paid for by your library or company, such as EBSCO or FirstSearch, or through an online service to which you personally subscribe (examples 34–38); and (2) periodicals you directly access by entering a specific URL (examples 39–44). Articles you access through a subscription service are the most important for academic research. Many other online sources are not from periodicals; we explain them in examples 45–75.

ALERT: Online periodical articles are frequently available in both HTML (hypertext mark-up language) and PDF (portable document format) versions. The PDF versions are almost always preferable for research and citation because they present an image of articles exactly as they appear in print, including page numbers, images and graphics, headings, and so on. The HTML version of an article includes all of the text; however, because it has been formatted to work efficiently in databases, it contains no page numbers or graphics. With academic journals, if page numbers are not included, use *n. pag.* ●

34. Subscription Service: Article with a Print Version—MLA

Jackson, Gabriel. "Multiple Historic Meanings of the Spanish Civil War." *Science and Society* 68.3
    (2004): 272-76. *Academic Search Elite*. Web. 7 Mar. 2013.

Figure 36.4 illustrates citing an article that has a print version but has been accessed through a subscription service.

35. Subscription Service: Material with No Print Version—MLA

Siemens, Raymond G. "A New Computer-Assisted Literary Criticism?" *Computers and the
    Humanities* 36.3 (2002): n. pag. *AOL Canada*. Web. 12 Nov. 2013.

36. Subscription Service: Abstract with a Print Version—MLA

Marcus, Hazel R., and Shinobu Kitayamo. "Culture and the Self: Implications for Cognition,
    Emotion, and Motivation." *Psychological Abstracts* 78.2 (1991): n. pag. *PsycINFO*.
    Web. 10 Apr. 2012.

This entry is for the same abstract shown on item 33, but here it is accessed from an online database (*PsycINFO*) by means of a library subscription service. The name of the subscription service (*Ovid*) could be included as optional supplementary information at the end of the entry.

37. Subscription Service Access with a Keyword: Article in a Periodical with a Print Version—MLA

Electronic versions of sources that also appear in print start with information about the print version. Here is an entry for a journal article accessed through a computer service; it also has a print version.

Wynne, Clive D. L. "'Willy' Didn't Yearn to Be Free." Editorial. *New York Times* 27 Dec. 2003.
    New York Times Online. AOL Canada. Web. 29 Dec. 2012. Keyword: nytimes.

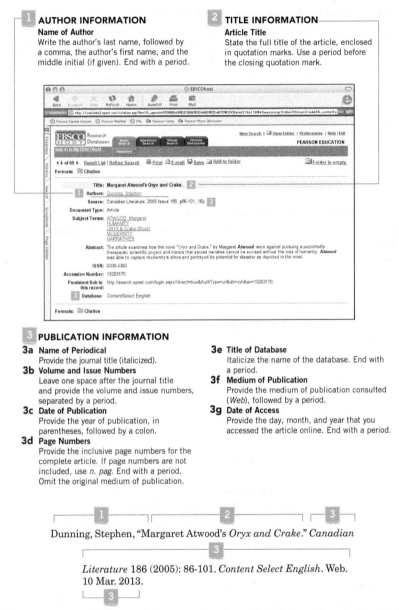

AUTHOR INFORMATION
Name of Author
Write the author's last name, followed by a comma, the author's first name, and the middle initial (if given). End with a period.

TITLE INFORMATION
Article Title
State the full title of the article, enclosed in quotation marks. Use a period before the closing quotation mark.

PUBLICATION INFORMATION

3a Name of Periodical
Provide the journal title (italicized).

3b Volume and Issue Numbers
Leave one space after the journal title and provide the volume and issue numbers, separated by a period.

3c Date of Publication
Provide the year of publication, in parentheses, followed by a colon.

3d Page Numbers
Provide the inclusive page numbers for the complete article. If page numbers are not included, use *n. pag.* End with a period. Omit the original medium of publication.

3e Title of Database
Italicize the name of the database. End with a period.

3f Medium of Publication
Provide the medium of publication consulted (*Web*), followed by a period.

3g Date of Access
Provide the day, month, and year that you accessed the article online. End with a period.

Dunning, Stephen, "Margaret Atwood's *Oryx and Crake*." *Canadian Literature* 186 (2005): 86-101. *Content Select English*. Web. 10 Mar. 2013.

Figure 36.4 Locating and citing source information for a journal article found in an online database

Information applying to the print version of this article in the *New York Times* ends with the publication date, and information about the online version starts with the title of the database, *New York Times Online. AOL Canada* is the service through which the database was accessed, and 29 Dec. 2012 is the access date. The keyword *nytimes* was used to access *New York Times Online.*

38. Subscription Service Access Showing a Path—MLA

When you access a source by choosing a series of keywords, menus, or topics, end the entry with the "path" of words you used. Use semicolons between items in the path, and put a period at the end.

Futrelle, David. "A Smashing Success." *Money.com* 23 Dec. 1999. AOL Canada. Web. 26 Dec. 1999.

   Path: Personal Finance; Business News; Business Publications; Money.com.

PERIODICALS—ONLINE VERSIONS ACCESSED DIRECTLY

You can access some online versions of periodicals directly, without going through a paid subscription service. Newspapers and magazines often publish some of their articles from each issue online this way. Often, however, you can't access every single article—or any older articles—without being a subscriber.

39. Online Version of a Print Magazine Article—MLA

The example is for the online version of the same article cited in 25, above. In addition to the print information (but omitting the original medium—*print*), include the italicized title of the website, the name of the site publisher (which may be the publication name), the publication date, the medium of publication you consulted (*Web*), and the date you accessed the online version. (If the page numbers from the print version are available, include them, too, after the publication date.)

Fallow, James. "The $1.4 Trillion Question." *The Atlantic.com.* Atlantic Monthly Group, Jan.-Feb. 2008.
   Web. 2 May 2013.

If the article is unsigned, begin with the title.

"Too Smart to Marry." *The Atlantic.com.* Atlantic Monthly Group, 14 Apr. 2005. Web. 7 Mar. 2012.

40. Online Version of a Print Journal Article—MLA

Archibald, W. Peter. "Small Expectations and Great Adjustments: How Hamilton Workers Most
   Often Experienced the Great Depression." *Canadian Journal of Sociology* 21.3 (1996): 359-402.
   Web. 22 Feb 2013.

41. Periodical Article Published Only Online—MLA

Many periodicals are published only online; other have "extra" online content that doesn't appear in print. Figure 36.5 illustrates how to cite an article that appears only online.

Shipka, Jody. "This Was (Not!!) an Easy Assignment." *Computers and Composition Online.*
   Computers and Composition Online, Fall 2007. Web. 2 May 2011.

42. Online Version of a Print Newspaper Article—MLA

If the article is signed, begin with the author's name, last name first.

El Akkad, Omar. "New Identification Rules Bar Some Canadians from Casting Ballots" *Globe and
   Mail.* Globe and Mail, 15 Oct. 2008. Web. 20 Nov. 2009.

If the article is unsigned, begin with the article title.

43. Online Editorial or Letter to the Editor—MLA

"Katrina, Climate Change and the Poor." Editorial. *CMAJ* 173.8 (2005): 837. Web. 22 Nov. 2012.

Sklar, Brian, Letter. "Pay-or-Die Medicine in the U.S." *Leader-Post* [Regina]. Canwest, 23 Nov. 2005.
   Web. 23 Nov. 2012.

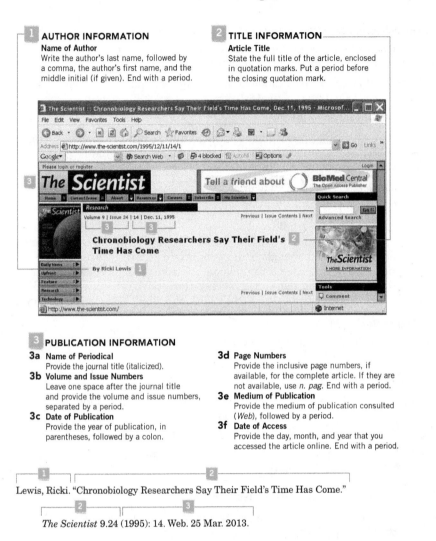

AUTHOR INFORMATION
Name of Author
Write the author's last name, followed by a comma, the author's first name, and the middle initial (if given). End with a period.

TITLE INFORMATION
Article Title
State the full title of the article, enclosed in quotation marks. Put a period before the closing quotation mark.

PUBLICATION INFORMATION

3a Name of Periodical
Provide the journal title (italicized).
3b Volume and Issue Numbers
Leave one space after the journal title and provide the volume and issue numbers, separated by a period.
3c Date of Publication
Provide the year of publication, in parentheses, followed by a colon.

3d Page Numbers
Provide the inclusive page numbers, if available, for the complete article. If they are not available, use *n. pag.* End with a period.
3e Medium of Publication
Provide the medium of publication consulted (*Web*), followed by a period.
3f Date of Access
Provide the day, month, and year that you accessed the article online. End with a period.

Lewis, Ricki. "Chronobiology Researchers Say Their Field's Time Has Come."

The Scientist 9.24 (1995): 14. Web. 25 Mar. 2013.

Figure 36.5 Locating and citing source information for a journal article published only online

44. Online Material from a Newspaper or News Site Published Only Online—MLA

Perkins, Tara. "Conrad Black's Chicago Court Date Set for Tuesday: U.S. Attorney's Office." *CP Online.* Canadian Press, 18 Nov. 2005. Web. 22 Nov. 2005.

OTHER INTERNET SOURCES

This section shows models for other online sources. For such sources, provide as much of the following information as you can.

1. The author's name, if given, or the compiler, editor, director, performer, etc.
2. Title of the work (italicized if the work is independent; in quotation marks if the work is part of a larger work). If the work has no title, describe it; for example, *Home page, Introduction, Online posting* (not italicized and without quotation marks).

3. The italicized title of the website, if distinct from the title of the work.

4. The version or edition used, if relevant.

5. The publisher or sponsor of the site (if not available, use *N.p.*)

6. The date of electronic publication or the most recent update (if not given, use *n.d.*).

7. The medium of publication (*Web*).

8. The date you accessed the site.

If you are also citing publication information for a print version of the online source, begin the entry with that information but omit the original medium (*Print*). Then provide the following information.

9. The italicized title of the website or database.

10. The medium of publication you consulted (*Web*).

11. The date you accessed the site.

Give any supplementary information that normally follows the medium of publication in a print citation immediately before the title of the website or database. Include the URL at the end of the entry only if you think that it is the only way to locate the source. Enclose it in angle brackets(< >), with a period after the closing bracket. If the URL is long, use the URL of the site's search page or a subscription service. Break a URL only after a slash and do not insert a hyphen.

45. Online Book—MLA

The first example shows the format for citing a book accessed from a database on the Web. With a book published before 1900, you may omit the publisher after the place of publication. The second example shows the format for citing a book that appears independently on the Web. In this example, only the Web edition is cited. Therefore, the publisher or sponsor of the website is listed with the date of online publication, but the publication information for the print version is omitted.

Eaton, Arthur W. *Acadian Legends and Lyrics.* London, 1889. *Early Canadiana Online.* Web. 25 May 2013.

Thomson, A. B. R., and E. A. Shaffer, eds. *First Principles of Gastroenterology.* 3rd ed.
    Gastroenterology Resource Centre, 2005. Web. 22 Mar. 2013.

46. Online Book in a Scholarly Project—MLA

Herodotus. *The History of Herodotus.* Trans. George Rawlinson. *Internet Classics Archive.* Ed.
    Daniel C. Stevenson. MIT, 11 Jan. 1998. Web. 15 May 2012.

47. Online Government-Published Book—MLA

Start with the name of the government or government body, and then name the government agency, and the title. Only the online version of the work is being cited in these entries. In the first entry, the title of the work (*Report*) is followed by the name of the website (italicized) and the sponsoring agency.

Canada. Royal Commission on Bilingualism and Biculturalism. *Report. Commissions of Inquiry.*
    Library and Archives of Canada, 12 Apr. 2005. Web. 12 Sept. 2011.

MLA also permits an alternative format, with the author's name first, then title, and then government body. In the second entry, the title of the website is *Reports*; it is followed by the name of the sponsoring agency.

Savoie, Donald J. *Horizontal Management of Official Languages. Reports.* Canada. Office of the
    Commissioner of Official Languages, 2008. Web. 14 Nov. 2013.

48. Professional Home Page—MLA

Treat home pages like other works you cite in only their online versions. Provide as much of the following information as you can find.

1. The name of the person who created or put up the home page, last name first.
2. The name of the sponsoring organization and the date the page was posted.
3. The date you accessed the material.

Mountain Culture. Banff Centre for Continuing Education, 2006. Web. 22 Nov. 2006.

This is the home page of an institute based at the Banff Centre.

49. Personal Home Page—MLA

Follow guidelines for professional home pages, but give the name of the person who created the page, last name first. Include the page's title, if there is one, italicized; if there is no title, add the description *Home page,* not italicized, followed by a period.

Hesse, Doug. Home page. 5 Mar. 2005. Web. 1 Nov. 2007.

50. Page from a Website—MLA

Provide as much information as you can (see Figure 36.6 on page 494).

"About the Manitoba Geocaching Association." *Manitoba Geocaching
     Association*. 2007. Web. 29 Nov. 2007.

Statistics Canada. "Hours Worked and Labour Productivity in the Provinces
     and Territories." *Daily* 27 Jan. 2010. Web. 14 July 2011.

51. Entire Internet Site—MLA

WebdelSol.Com. Ed. Michael Neff. Web del Sol, 2008. Web. 4 Aug. 2008.

52. Academic Department Home Page—MLA

Write the nature of the academic department, followed by the words *Home page.* (Do not put any words in quotations or in italics.) Also include the name of the institution (as sponsor of the site), the date and medium of publication, and the date you accessed the page.

English Department. Home page. Simon Fraser U, 2011. Web. 26 Feb. 2011.

53. Course Home Page—MLA

Cramer, Peter. "Controversy as Media Discourse." *Undergraduate Courses: Fall 2007.* Dept. of
     English, Simon Fraser U, 2007. Web. 15 June 2007.

54. Government or Institutional Website—MLA

The Banff Centre. Banff Centre for Continuing Education, 2006. Web. 22 Nov. 2006

The title of the home page of the Banff Centre for Continuing Education is *The Banff Centre.*

1 TITLE

Title of the Work
State the full title of the work cited, enclosed in quotation marks. Use a period before the closing quotation mark.

2 PUBLICATION INFORMATION

2a Title of the Overall Website
Provide the title of the website (italicized), followed by a period.

2b Publisher or Sponsor of the Website
Leave one space after the title of the overall website and provide the publisher or sponsor. If this information is not available, use *N.p.* End with a comma.

2c Date of Publication
Provide the available date (day, month, and year) of publication, followed by a period. If no date is available, use *n.d.*

2d Medium of Publication
Provide the medium of publication consulted (*Web*), followed by a period.

2e Date of Access
Provide the day, month, and year that you accessed the article online. End with a period.

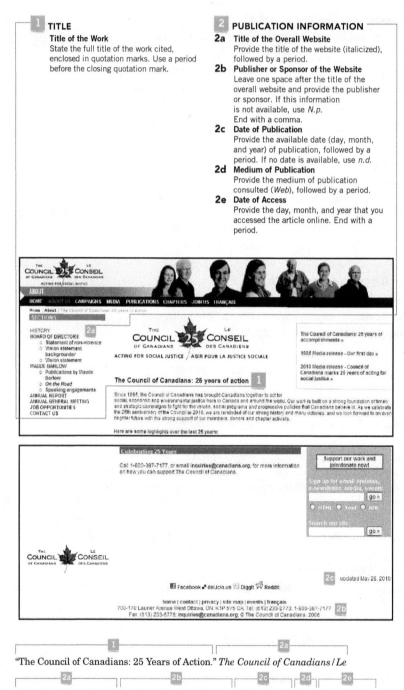

"The Council of Canadians: 25 Years of Action." *The Council of Canadians / Le Conseil des Canadiens.* The Council of Canadians, 28 May 2010. Web. 20 July 2010.

Figure 36.6 Locating and citing source information for a webpage

55. Online Poem—MLA

Nelligan, Émile. "Automne." *Émile Nelligan et son oeuvre*. E. Garand: Montreal, 1925. *Canadian Poetry Archive*. National Library of Canada, 2 Jan. 2002. Web. 22 Nov. 2012.

56. Online Work of Art—MLA

Provide artist, title of work, creation date, medium of composition, the museum or individual who owns it, and the name of the database or website (italicized) on which you accessed it. Then list the medium of publication (*Web*) and access date.

Anghik, Abraham. *Kittigazuti—1918*. 2000. Lithograph. Winnipeg Art Gallery. *The Inuit Shaman*. Web. 18 Nov. 2011.

57. Online Images or Photograph—MLA

As with images from print publications (see item 88), include information about the photographer and title, if known. Otherwise, describe the photograph briefly and give information about the website, the medium of publication, and the access date.

Stafford, Mark, *20 Victoria Bus to Downtown*. N.d. Photograph. *The Black & White Gallery*, 2005. Web. 15 Nov. 2005.

58. Online Interview—MLA

Pope, Carole. Interview by Amy Standen. *Salon.com*. Salon Media Group, 29 Apr. 2002. Web. 27 Jan. 2010.

59. Online Video or Film Clip—MLA

See Figure 36.7 on page 496.

Reeves, Matt, dir. *Cloverfield*. Trailer. Bad Robot, 2008. Web. 18 Jan. 2011.

60. Online Cartoon—MLA

Turner, Jason. "Jason and the Comics." Cartoon. *Broken Pencil*. Broken Pencil Magazine, Winter 2011. Web. 9 May 2011.

61. Online Television or Radio Program—MLA

Give the same information as in item 87, but omit the local station (unless it is important information) and the broadcast medium, and add the name of the website, the medium on which you accessed the program (*Web*), and the date of access.

Walsh, Mary. "*Regeneration* Triology by Pat Barker." *Mary Walsh: Open Book*. CBC, 29 Sept. 2002. *CBC.ca*. Web. 15 Nov. 2006.

62. Online Discussion Posting—MLA

Give the author's name (if any), the title of the message in quotation marks, and then the name of the discussion list and sponsor. Give the date of the posting and the medium of publication. Then give the access date.

Firrantello, Larry. "Van Gogh on Prozac." Salon *Table Talk*. Salon Media, 23 May 2005. Web. 7 June 2009.

Be cautious about using online postings as sources. Some postings contain cutting-edge information from experts, but some contain trash.

1 **TITLE**

Title of the Work
State the full title of the work cited, enclosed in quotation marks. Use a period before the closing quotation mark.

2 **PUBLICATION INFORMATION**

2a **Title of the Overall Website**
Provide the title of the website (italicized), followed by a period.

2b **Publisher or Sponsor of the Website**
Leave one space after the title of the overall website and provide the publisher or sponsor of the website. If this information is not available, use *N.p.* End with a comma.

2c **Date of Publication**
Provide the day, month, and year of publication, followed by a period. If no date is available, use *n.d.*

2d **Medium of Publication**
Provide the medium of publication consulted (*Web*), followed by a period.

2e **Date of Access**
Provide the day, month, and year that you accessed the article online. End with a period.

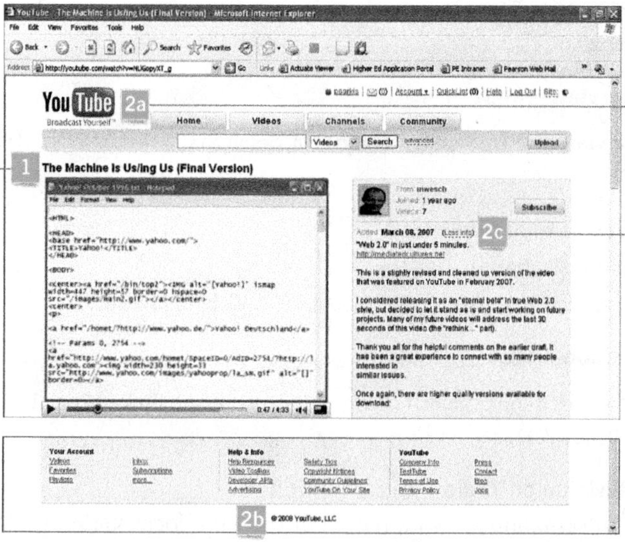

"The Machine Is Us/ing Us (Final Version)." *YouTube*. YouTube, 8 Mar. 2007. Web. 10 June 2012.

Figure 36.7 Locating and citing source information for an online video

63. Real-Time Communication—MLA

Give the name of the speaker or writer, a title for the event (if any), the forum, date, publication medium, access date, and URL if needed.

Berzsenyi, Christyne. Online discussion of "Writing to Meet Your Match: Rhetoric, Perceptions, and Self-Presentation for Four Online Daters." *Computers and Writing Online*. AcadianaMOO. 13 May 2007. Web. 13 May 2007.

64. E-mail Message—MLA

Start with the name of the person who wrote the e-mail message. Give the title or subject line in quotation marks. Then identify the recipient. Add the date and the medium (*E-mail*).

Parks, George. "Atwood's Library Tweets: What the Mayor Didn't Know." Message to Mike Liston.
26 July 2011. E-mail.

65. Part of an Online Book—MLA

Teasdale, Sara. "Driftwood." *Flame and Shadow*. Ed. A. Light. N.p., 1920. *Project Gutenberg*. 1 July
1996. Web. 18 Aug. 2008.

66. Online Review—MLA

Baird, Daniel. Rev. of Once, by Rebecca Rosenblum. *Walrusmagazine.com*. The Walrus
Foundation, Oct./Nov. 2008. Web. 20 July 2011.

67. Online Abstract—MLA

McIntyre, John W. R., and C. Stuart Houston. "Smallpox and Its Control in Canada." *CMAJ* 161.12
(1999): 1543-47. Abstract. Web. 14 Aug. 2010.

68. Posting on a Blog—MLA

McLemee, Scott. "To Whom It May Concern." *Quick Study*, 1 Jan. 2008. Web. 14 May 2011.

69. Online Sound Recording or Clip—MLA

Atwood, Margaret. "Writing Women's Fiction." *CBC Digital Archives*. CBC, 9 Apr. 1981. Web. 12 June
2011.

70. Online Advertisement—MLA

BlackBerry PlayBook. Advertisement. *Edmonton Journal*. Postmedia Network, 2 May 2011. Web. 24
July 2011.

71. Online Manuscript or Working Paper—MLA

Follow the basic model for a work you cite only in a Web version. If you include an explanation of the work (such as *Unpublished article*), put it after the title. *N.p.* indicates that there is no publisher or sponsor of the site. Include the URL at the end of the entry only if you think that it is the only way to locate the source.

deGrandpre, Andrew. *Baseball Destined to Die in Hockey Town*. N.p., 2002. Web. 7 Mar. 2009.

72. Podcast—MLA

A podcast is an audio recording that is posted online. Include as much of the following information as you can: author, title, sponsoring organization, and website, date posted, medium of publication, and date accessed.

Karchut, Paul. "Parkour Turns the Urban Jungle into a Jungle Gym." Podcast. *Extreme Canada*.
CBC Radio, 25 July 2011. Web. 26 July 2011.

73. Online Slide Show—MLA

Erickson, Britta, narr. *Visionaries from the New China*. Slide show. July 2007. Web. 11 Sept. 2012.

74. Online Photo Essay—MLA

"Gallery: G8 and G20 summits." *National Post. Photo essay*. 29 June 2010. Web. 5 July 2010.

75. Online Map, Chart, or Other Graphic—MLA

"+15 Walkway System." Graphic. *DowntownCalgary.com.* Calgary Downtown Assn., 2010. Web.
     21 May 2012.

OTHER PRINT, NONPRINT, AND ELECTRONIC SOURCES

76. Published or Unpublished Letter—MLA

Begin the entry with the author of the letter. Note the recipient, too. Unpublished letters include a description of the format, either *MS* (manuscript, meaning handwritten) or *TS* (typescript).

Irvin, William. Letter to Lesley Osburn. 7 Dec. 2007. TS.

Williams, William Carlos. Letter to his son. 13 Mar. 1935. *Letters of the Century: America 1900-1999.*
     Ed. Lisa Grunwald and Stephen J. Adler. New York: Dial, 1999: 225-26. Print.

77. Microfiche Collection of Articles—MLA

A microfiche is a transparent sheet of film (a *fiche*) that needs to be read through a special magnifier. Each fiche holds several pages, with each page designated by a grid position. A long document may appear on more than one fiche. The medium of publication (*Microfiche, Microform*) follows the original publication information and precedes the fiche information.

Smith, David. "Creators Ready to Unveil Super Tape." *Vancouver Sun* 6 Apr. 1988: C12. Microform,
     BCARS Newspaper Index 32 (1990): fiche 2, grid D12.

78. Map or Chart—MLA

Gibsons-Sechelt Sunshine Coast. Map. Coquitlam: Canadian Cartographics, 1996. Print.

79. Report or Pamphlet—MLA

Use the format for books, to the extent possible.

Assembly of First Nations. *Annual Report 2009–2010*. Ottawa: AFN, 2010. Print.

80. Legal Source—MLA

If you are writing for a general audience, use only familiar abbreviations in citing laws, bills, and cases. At a minimum, give the name of a law or case, or the number of a bill and the parliamentary session at which the bill was debated, and the date.

Bill C-50, An Act to Amend the Criminal Code in Respect of Cruelty to Animals. 1st Sess. 38th Parl.,
     2005. Print.

Legal writers follow the *Canadian Guide to Uniform Legal Citation* (7th edition, 2010) and include abbreviated publication information for laws and court cases.

Canada Labour Code. R.S.C. 1985, c. L-2, S. 12. Print.

Delgamuukw v. British Columbia, [1997] 3 S.C.R. 1010. Print.

81. Interview—MLA

Note the type of interview, for example "Telephone" or "Personal" (face-to-face). For a published interview, give the name of the interviewed person first, identify the source as an interview, and then give details as for any published source: title; author, preceded by the word *By*; and publication details.

Brooks, Max. Telephone interview. 30 Aug. 2012.

Kettlitz, Nicola. "C-Suite: Interviews with Canada's Top Decision Makers." By Mary Teresa Bitti.
    Financial Post 28 June 2011: FP14. Print.

82. Lecture, Speech, or Address—MLA

Barlow, Maude. League of Canadian Poets. Toronto. 25 May 1991. Address.

83. Film, Videotape, or DVD—MLA

Give the title first, and include the director, the distributor, and the year of release and medium consulted. If you use a DVD or videotape, give its year; as an option, you may also give the original year of release before the name of the distributor of the medium you have consulted. Other information (writer, producer, major actors) is optional but helpful; it follows the title and precedes the distributor. Put first names first.

Shakespeare in Love. Screenplay by Marc Norman and Tom Stoppard. Dir. John Maddon.
    Prod. David Parfitt, Donna Gigliotti, Harvey Weinstein, Edward Zwick, and Mark
    Norman. Perf. Gwyneth Paltrow, Joseph Fiennes, and Judi Dench. 1988. Miramax,
    2003. Film.

Calendar. Screenplay by Atom Egoyan. Dir. Atom Egogyan. Prod. Ego Film Arts/ZDF.
    Perf. Atom Egoyan and Arsinée Khanjian. 1993. Alliance Atlantis, 2001. DVD.

84. Musical Recording—MLA

Put first the name most relevant to what you discuss in your paper (performer, conductor, the work performed). Include the recording's title, the artist(s) (if distinct from the first item), the issuer, the year of issue, and the medium (*CD, LP, Audiocassette*).

Smetana, Bedrich. *My Country.* Czech Philharmonic Orch. Cond. Karel Ancerl. Vanguard, 1975. LP.

Cohen, Leonard. "Tower of Song." *I'm Your Man.* Sony, 1988. CD.

85. Live Performance (Play, Concert, etc.)—MLA

Twelfth Night. By William Shakespeare. Dir. Des McAnuff. Perf. Suzy Jane Hunt, Brian Dennehy,
    and Tom Rooney. Festival Theatre, Stratford. 3 July 2011. Performance.

86. Work of Art, Photograph, or Musical Compostion—MLA

Pratt, Christopher. *Shop on an Island.* 1969. Oil on Canvas. London Regional Art Gallery, London.

Don't italicize or put in quotation marks music identified only by form, number, and key.

Schubert, Franz. Symphony no. 8 in B minor.

Italicize any work that has a title, such as an opera or ballet or a named symphony.

Schubert, Franz. *Unfinished Symphony.*

Cite a musical performance as a live performance, and cite a published score as a book.

Schubert, Franz. *Symphony in B minor (Unfinished).* Ed. Martin Cusid. New York: Norton, 1971. Print.

87. Television or Radio Program—MLA

Include at least the title of the program (italicized), the network, the local station and its city, the date of the broadcast, and the medium of broadcast.

"Chasing Pavements: Part 2." *Degrassi: The Next Generation.* Perf. Charlotte Arnold, Luke Bilyk,

and Stefan Brogren. CTV. CFTO, Toronto. 8 Apr. 2011. Television.

For a series, supply the title of the specific episode (in quotation marks) before the title of the program or series (italicized).

88. Image or Photograph in a Print Publication—MLA

Give the photographer (if known) or artist, the title or caption of the image (italicized) and its date, the medium of composition, and complete publication information, as for an article. If the image has no title, provide a brief description.

Greene, Herb. *Grace Slick.* 2004. Photograph. *Rolling Stone* 30 Sept. 2004: 102. Print.

89. Advertisement—MLA

WestJet Airlines. Advertisement. CTV. 24 June 2011. Television.

McCord Museum. Advertisement. *Walrus* July/Aug. 2011: 24. Print.

90. Video Game or Software—MLA

Tom Clancy's Splinter Cell Trilogy. Montreal: Ubisoft, 2011. Game.

91. Nonperiodical Publications on CD, DVD, CD-ROM, or Other Recording Formats—MLA

Citations for publications on CD, DVD, CD-ROM, or other recording formats follow guidelines for print publications, with these additions: give the vendor's name and the publication date as shown in the source; the publication date or update, if available, if the source is a database; and the publication medium.

Perl, Sondra. *Felt Sense: Guidelines for Composing.* Portsmouth: Boyton, 2004. CD.

92. Materials on CD or DVD with a Print Version—MLA

"The Price Is Right." *Time* 20 Jan. 1992: 38. *Time Man of the Year.* New York: Compact, 1993. CD-ROM.

Information for the print version ends with the article's page number, 38. The title of the CD-ROM is *Time Man of the Year,* its producer is the publisher Compact, and its copyright year is 1993. Both the title of the print publication and the title of the CD-ROM are italicized.

93. Materials on CD or DVD with No Print Version—MLA

"Artificial Intelligence." *Encarta 2003.* Redmond: Microsoft, 2003. CD-ROM.

Encarta 2003 is a CD-ROM encyclopedia with no print version. "Artificial Intelligence" is the title of an article in *Encarta 2003.*

94. Book in Digital Format—MLA

Many books are available for downloading from the Internet in digital format; some are intended to be read on special players.

Heintzman, Andrew. *The New Entrepreneurs: Building a Green Economy for the Future.* Toronto:

Anansi, 2010. Kindle Edition.

95. PowerPoint or Similar Presentation—MLA

To cite a digital file in a version that has not been published on the Web or as a CD (such as a PDF file stored on a computer, a word-processed document, a PowerPoint presentation, an image received as an e-mail attachment, or a recording formatted for an MP3 player), follow the guidelines for the kind of work being cited. The medium of publication may be *PDF file,* Microsoft Word *file, JPEG file, MP3 file, XML file,* or something else, neither italicized (except for titles of software programs) nor inside quotation marks. For an unknown file type, use *Digital file.*

Cite more facts about the file (such as date of last modification), if needed, in the place reserved for version or edition.

Leung, Valerie. "The New Canadian Graphic Novel." File last modified on 24 Feb. 2008. *Microsoft Word* file.

Bayrakdarian, Isabel, perf. "Che Tango Che." *Tango Notturno.* CBC Records, 2006. MP3 file.

Laursen, Finn. "European Union Centre of Excellence (EUCE) Dalhousie University." EUCE Directors Meeting, Ottawa. 18 Jan. 2007. *PowerPoint* file.

96. Work in More Than One Publication Medium—MLA

Follow the format for the medium of the component or version that you primarily used. For medium of publication, list all the media you consulted in alphabetical order.

Thomson, A. B. R., and E. A. Shaffer, eds. *First Principles of Gastroenterology.* 3rd ed. Gastroenterology Resource Centre, 2005. Print, Web. 12 Feb. 2012.

This entry follows the format for citing a book that appears independently on the Web, as the online version was the one primarily consulted.

36d.2 Using content or bibliographic notes in MLA style

In MLA style, footnotes or endnotes serve two specific purposes: (1) You can use them for content (ideas and information) that does not fit into your paper but is still worth relating; and (2) you can use them for bibliographic information that would intrude if you were to include it in your text. Place a note number at the end of a sentence, if possible. It comes after any punctuation mark except the dash. Do not put any space before a note number; put one space after it. Raise the note number a little above the line of words (called a *superscript* number), as shown in the following examples.

TEXT OF PAPER

Ronald Wright's *Stolen Continents* surprises us by telling the story of the European conquest of North and South America "through Indian eyes."[1]

CONTENT NOTE—MLA

1. Wright, who was born and educated in England, brings an outsider's point of view to his adopted country, Canada. This may explain his willingness to examine the post-conquest history of the First Nations from a new and disturbing perspective.

TEXT OF PAPER

Barbara Randolph believes that enthusiasm is contagious (65).[1] Many psychologists have found that panic, fear, and rage spread more quickly in crowds than positive emotions do, however.

BIBLIOGRAPHIC NOTE—MLA

1. Others who agree with Randolph include Thurman 21, 84, 155; Kelley 421-25; and Brookes 65-76.

A student's MLA-style research paper

36e.1   Researching and writing the paper

The following is student writer Andrei Gurov's assignment for an MLA-style research paper.

> Write an MLA-style research paper on the general subject of memory. You are required to write 1800 to 2000 words, using a variety of sources. Your final paper is due in six weeks. Interim deadlines for parts of the work will be announced. To complete this assignment, you need to engage in three interrelated processes: conducting research, understanding the results of that research, and writing a paper based on the first two processes. Consult the *Simon & Schuster Handbook for Writers,* especially Chapter 33–35 for guidance on how to complete this assignment, and Chapter 36 for guidance on MLA-style parenthetical citations and Works Cited entries. You may also consult the MLA website at <http://www.mla.org>.

Andrei's instructor also assigned a bonus exercise asking students to chronicle their research processes in a brief informal narrative. This exercise could help students see what worked well for them and what didn't, and then they could apply that knowledge when researching future papers. The following is from Andrei's narrative about how he researched his topic and sources for his MLA-style paper about déjà vu.

I started by filling in a research schedule, then thought about how to find ideas for research. In the past, brainstorming has worked well for me, so I just started listing anything that came to mind about the assigned topic of "memory" (e.g., how much memory is on my iPod, past vacations, forgetfulness, flashbacks). I had a lot of personal memories to write about, but those wouldn't have worked for a formal research paper.

So, I turned to the Web and searched Google using the keyword "memory." The 326 million hits generally pointed to four large categories: brain memory, computer memory, entertainment venues, and music. I didn't expect so many directions. In an attempt to narrow this down, I tried some Boolean NOT instructions, but even eliminating "computer + music + entertainment + girls" made little difference. Then I tried Google Scholar, and although I reduced the number of hits, there were still millions.

To spark ideas, I decided to flip through some textbooks. My anthropology book came with a study skills guide that offered some tips about memory retention. That could've been a topic, but it really didn't interest me enough to want to learn more about it. My intro sociology textbook had some information about eyewitness testimony and false memory—both pretty interesting, so I kept those topics in reserve. Then, a chapter in my intro psychology textbook turned up a topic that I'd always been curious about: déjà vu. I'd experienced that weird feeling of being somewhere before—even though I'd never been there in my life—and was really curious to know what caused it. So, I decided to narrow my formal research question to "What is known today about the experience of déjà vu?"

A Google Scholar search using "déjà vu" still brought up 14 million hits, but at least the first few pages seemed relevant, and I chose eleven sources that looked interesting. To help me determine how scholarly the online resources were, I went to the library and skimmed a couple of scholarly psychology books. I found I'd been fooled three times out of eleven. When I read the printouts, I knew almost immediately that two of the sources were unreliable, but figuring out a third bad one took me a while longer.

continued ➤

I took notes, carefully recorded my sources, then organized the notes into folders. At that point, I felt ready to do some planning. I knew my audience was mainly my instructor, but because my first draft was going to be peer-edited, I wanted to make sure my paper also appealed to other students in my class. I wasn't too sure about which purpose I wanted to tackle. Originally, I had wanted to write with a persuasive purpose and argue against the concept of déjà vu having anything to do with witchcraft, reincarnation, and that stuff. But the more I read, the more I wanted to educate people about the scientific aspects of déjà vu experiences. So, I switched to an informative purpose.

I used the note documents that I had created, making sure that I kept track of when I was quoting, summarizing, and paraphrasing. I kept a separate document as my working bibliography, to make it easier to list each of my sources in my Works Cited list at the end of my paper.

At this stage, I felt ready to write my first draft. I sorted all my printed notes into categories and then wrote a very rough draft with numbers where I thought notes would fit. Next I went to the computer and strung my paper together. My first draft ran on for too many pages. It was time to cut. My major cuts had to do with (a) at least two pages about other terms related to déjà vu but not the same as déjà vu, and (b) a table reporting an unscientific survey I had taken of the déjà vu memories of each member in a family of fifteen.

I then worked through the paper and worked on conciseness and tried to draft my concluding paragraph. It was a struggle. I had to synthesize complicated material in a fairly limited space. I kept wanting to introduce new information, but I knew that would only set me off track and confuse readers. I rejected the first draft of my concluding paragraph because it had too much about the paranormal and déjà vu, which definitely didn't work for the paper I wrote.

Overall, my research and writing process went well. Learning how to brainstorm ideas and how to do keyword searches effectively definitely saved me some anxiety, time, and effort in getting the topic and the information I needed.

36e.2   Formatting the MLA-style research paper

TITLE PAGE

MLA style doesn't call for a title page for research papers or any other types of writing. Many instructors, however, do require one. If you're asked to use a title page, follow the format of the example on page 506. Never assign a page number to a title page.

Whether or not you use a title page, use the headings shown on the first page of the sample research paper on page 508. If you're required to hand in a formal outline with your paper, place the outline after the title page, unless told to do otherwise by your instructor.

PAGE 1 OF PAPER WITH OR WITHOUT A TITLE PAGE

On the first page of your paper, in the upper right corner, type your last name, followed by a space, and then followed by the numeral 1 placed one-half inch (about 1.25 cm) below the top edge of the page. Next, at the left margin, type the four lines with the information shown on the first page of the sample paper on page 508. Finally, type your paper's title centred one double space below the last of the four lines that you just finished typing flush left.

Double-space after the title, and start your paper, indenting the first line of the first—and all—paragraphs one-half inch (1.25 cm). This is equal to the first-line indent in Microsoft Word. Use one-inch (2.5 cm) margins on both sides of the sheet of paper and the bottom.

OUTLINES

Even though MLA doesn't officially endorse using outlines, some instructors, including Andrei Gurov's, require that students submit formal outlines with their research papers. In this handbook, you'll find examples of two formal outlines in section 2f. The traditional formal outline follows long-established conventions for using numbers and letters to show relationships among ideas. A less traditional formal outline includes these elements but also includes the planned content for a research paper's introductory and concluding paragraphs. Both the traditional and the less traditional outlines can be sentence outlines (composed entirely of complete sentences) or topic outlines (composed only of words and phrases). Never mix the two styles.

The outline that follows is for Andrei Gurov's research paper about déjà vu. To format the outline, he used the less traditional outline, which was what his instructor preferred and asked her class to use. In the name-page number line in the upper right corner of his outline, Andrei typed his last name, left one space, and then typed the lowercase roman numeral *i* for the page number, the conventional way of indicating any page that comes before the first page of the essay itself. He placed that information one-half inch (1.25 cm) from the top of the page and kept it within the one-inch (2.5-cm) margin at the right. He then left a half-inch space below the name-number heading and centred the word *Outline.* The thesis statement in the outline matches the last sentence of the first paragraph of his paper (see p. 508).

Even if your instructor doesn't require an outline, you'll probably find that developing one to go with a later draft will help you clarify the overall organization and logic of your research paper (or, indeed, any essay you write). Examining the paper's "skeleton" enables you to focus on the overall shape of the paper and may reveal gaps in your paper's development that you can fill in.

Title page of Andrei Gurov's MLA-style research paper

One-third
down from
top of page

Double-space title if
more than one line

Déjà Vu: At Last a Subject for Serious Study

Lowercase "by" and
double-space

by

Andrei Gurov

Instructor

Institution

Course and section

Date order:
day month year

Professor Ryan

Glengarry University

English 101, Section A4

12 December 2013

½" (1.25 cm)

1" (2.5 cm)

Gurov i

Outline

Double-space

I. Introduction

    A. The meaning of the term *déjà vu*

    B. <u>Thesis statement</u>: Although a few people still believe that feelings of déjà vu have mysterious or supernatural origins, research in cognitive psychology and the neurosciences has produced laboratory experiments that could explain the phenomenon rationally.

II. Percentage of people who report experiencing déjà vu

III. Misunderstandings of the phenomenon of déjà vu

1"
(2.5 cm)

    A. Precognition

    B. False memory

IV. New psychological and medical theories of déjà vu

    A. Human sight's two pathways

    B. Implanted memories

        1. Natural: from old memories long forgotten

        2. Manipulated: from subliminal stimulation

        3. Inattentional blindness

V. Conclusion

    A. Many years of paranormal explanations of déjà vu

    B. Scientific research after 1980

    C. Much promise for further research

Put identifying information in upper left corner.

Quotation marks around phrases show they appeared separately in the source.

The ellipsis indicates words omitted from a quotation.

World Wide Web source has no page numbers or paragraph numbers.

1" (2.5 cm)

Use ½-inch (1.25 cm) top margin, 1-inch (2.5 cm) bottom and side margins; double-space throughout.

½" (1.25 cm)

Gurov 1

Andrei Gurov

Professer Ryan

English 101, Section A4

12 December 2013

Déjà Vu: At Last a Subject for Serious Study

"Brain hiccup" might be another name for *déjà vu*, French for "already seen." During a moment of déjà vu, a person relives an event that in reality is happening for the first time. The hiccup metaphor seems apt because each modern scientific explanation of the déjà vu phenomenon involves a doubled event, as this paper will demonstrate. However, such modern scientific work was long in coming. In his article "The Déjà Vu Illusion," today's leading researcher in the field, Alan S. Brown at Southern Methodist University, states that "for over 170 years, this most puzzling of memory illusions has intrigued scholars" but research was hampered when "during the behaviorist era . . . the plethora of parapsychological and psychodynamic interpretations" multiplied rapidly (256). Thus, its identification with the supernatural halted the scientific study of déjà vu for decades in the twentieth century when it was considered an unscientific topic. Although a few people still believe that feelings of déjà vu have mysterious or supernatural origins, research in cognitive psychology and the neurosciences has produced laboratory experiments that could explain the phenomenon rationally.

Some people report never having experienced déjà vu, and the percentages vary for the number of people who report having lived through at least one episode of it. Brown reports that of the subjects he has interviewed, an average of 66 percent say that they have had one or more déjà vu experiences during their lives (*Experience* 33). However, in "Strangely Familiar," Uwe Wolfradt reports that "various studies indicate that from 50 to 90 percent of the people [studied] can recall having had at least one such déjà vu incident in their lives."

Perhaps part of the reason for this variation in the range of percentages stems from a general misunderstanding of the phrase *déjà vu*, even by some of the earlier scientific researchers twenty or more years ago. Indeed, in today's society, people throw around the term *Déjà vu* without much thought. For example, it is fairly common for someone to see or hear about an event and then say, "Wow. This is déjà vu. I had a dream that this exact same thing happened."

continued ➤

(Proportions shown in this paper are adjusted to fit space limitations of this book. Follow actual dimensions discussed in this book and your instructor's directions.)

PAGE NUMBERING AFTER THE FIRST PAGE OF THE PAPER

In the upper right corner, type your last name, followed by a space and by the arabic numeral of the page in sequence (2, 3, and so on). Place this name-number heading in the same location as on page 1. Number the pages consecutively, including the last page of your Works Cited. Many writers use the "header and footer" word-processing function that inserts last names and sequential page numbers, updating automatically. This feature is especially convenient during revision, as the pagination changes.

Commentary

1. **Computer tip.** Following MLA style, Andrei uses his last name and the page number as a header (that is, text in the top margin) throughout the paper. To do this, he accesses the "header and footer" option in the "View" choice on the toolbar in his Microsoft Word word-processing program and inserts the proper information so that it will appear automatically on each page.

2. **Introductory strategy.** Andrei hopes to attract his readers' interest by making up the unusual phrase "brain hiccups," which ties into the dual visual processing that he describes later in his paper. He also refers briefly to the paranormal and immediately discredits it by quoting the leading modern researcher into déjà vu, Alan S. Brown.

3. **PROCESS NOTE:** I use a quotation from Brown's journal article "The Déjà Vu Illusion," so I include the page number in parentheses.

4. **Thesis statement.** The last sentence of Andrei's introductory paragraph is his THESIS STATEMENT. He drafted two preliminary thesis statements, shown in section 33l. The thesis statement is a bridge from his introduction to the rest of his paper and helps his readers anticipate the main message of his paper. All of his topic sentences have to tie into his thesis statement.

5. **Summarizing and citing a source by an author of two different sources used in this paper.** Andrei summarizes the percentage information that Brown gives in his book *The Déjà Vu Experience* and cites his source with a shortened title and page number. He includes a title because he has been drawing on two of Brown's writings for this paper—one book and one journal article that he accesses online—and he knows that he needs to make a clear distinction between them whenever he cites them.

6. **The insertion of words to fit a quotation into the writer's sentence.** Nothing is wrong with Uwe Wolfradt's sentence, but Andrei needs to add the word *studied* to make the meaning clear within his research paper. To do this in proper MLA form, Andrei put his added word in brackets to indicate that he is adding the word—that is, the word is not in the original text by Uwe Wolfradt.

7. **Figuring out a page number from an online source.** Andrei found the article "Strangely Familiar" by Uwe Wolfradt online through his search using Google Scholar. Even though the citation for the article on the opening screen page says that the page range is pages 32–37, and Andrei might feel quite safe in assuming that his information is on the first page—namely, page 32—he can't be sure, so he can't include a page number.

8. **PROCESS NOTE:** I kept being distracted about using the word *déjà vu* as a term or as the name of an experience. As I was drafting, I purposely overlooked the problem, but I circled each use so that I could tackle the issue in my final draft.

9. **PROCESS NOTE:** I'm fairly certain that my instructor will know that this quotation is not from a source, but it's rather one I made up from everyday speech.

Header
has student's
last name and
page number.

Gurov 2

However, dreaming about an event ahead of time is a different phenomenon known as *precognition*, which relates to the paranormal experience of extrasensory perception. To date, precognition has never been scientifically demonstrated. As Johnson explains about dreams, however,

Use block
indent of 1 inch
(2.5 cm) for a
quotation
longer than four
typed lines.

> . . . there is usually very little "data," evidence, or documentation to confirm that a Precognition has taken place. If a person learns about some disaster and THEN [author's emphasis] tells people that he/she has foreseen it the day before, that may or may not be true, because there is usually not corroborative confirmation of what the person claims.

Thus, precognition, a phenomenon talked about frequently but one that has never held up under scientific scrutiny, is definitely not the same as déjà vu.

False memory is another phenomenon mislabelled *déjà vu*. It happens when people are convinced that certain events took place in their lives, even though the events never happened. This occurs when people have strong memories of many unrelated occurrences that suddenly come together into a whole that's very close to the current experience. It seems like a déjà vu experience.

Introductory
phrase
smoothly leads
into direct
quotation.

This occurs from the "converging elements of many different but related experiences. When this abstract representation, which has emerged strictly from the melding together of strongly associated elements, happens to correspond to the present experience, a déjà vu may be the outcome" (Brown, *Experience* 160). To illustrate lab-induced false memory, Brown in *Experience* cites investigations in which subjects are shown lists of words related to sleep; however, the word *sleep* itself is not on the list. In recalling the list of words, most subjects insist that the word *sleep* was indeed on the list, which means that the memory of a word that was never there is false memory. This is exactly what happens when well-intentioned eyewitnesses believe they recall certain criminal acts even though, in fact, they never saw or experienced the events at all (159).

Put only page
number in
parentheses
when author is
named in text.

In the last twenty years especially, new theories have come to the fore as a result of rigorous work from psychological and medical points of view. In *The Déjà Vu Experience*, Brown surveys the literature and concludes that this relatively young field of investigation is dividing itself into four categories: (1) dual processing, (2) memory, (3) neurological, and (4) attentional. This paper briefly discusses the first

10

11

12

13

14

15

16

continued ➤

Commentary

10. **No capital letter to start block-indented quotation.** Andrei took this quotation from the middle of a sentence in the source, so he can't start it with a capital letter. The ellipsis indicates he omitted words to make the quotation fit stylistically.

11. **How "[author's emphasis]" is used.** When a source uses a typographical technique of emphasis—such as italics or all capital letters—the writer who quotes that source sometimes indicates that the emphasis belongs to the source, not to the writer. Some instructors ask for the wording "author's emphasis" to be used.

12. **MLA style for a block-indent quotation.** MLA style requires, when a quotation takes up four or more lines in a research paper, that it be set off in a block. A block indent calls for all lines to be indented one inch (2.5 cm) from the left margin. It has to end with a period. Then the source information has to come after the period in parentheses. Because Andrei's online source did not provide page, paragraphs, or screen numbers, he could not include a parenthetical citation after the quotation.

13. **PROCESS NOTE:** I want to use Brown in two different ways in this paragraph because I've drawn on Brown as a major reference throughout my paper. I don't want to use only quotations or only summaries. Here I use a quotation but don't call attention to the source. I place all source information in parentheses after the end of the quotation. I include a shortened version of the title of the source because I've used two different sources by the same author to write this paper.

14. **PROCESS NOTE:** To follow up on Process Note 13, this time I summarize Brown's words and fit in his name and the shortened title of the source.

15. **PROCESS NOTE:** I now need to write a paragraph of transition from what is *not* déjà vu to what is. My plan is to write about two types of phenomena that aren't déjà vu, and then write about three types of phenomena that are. I checked my outline to make sure I was adhering to my plan.

16. **PROCESS NOTE:** Every time I type the word *attentional* (using Microsoft Word) into my paper, a red wavy line pops up under it, which means a misspelling. However, because the word is spelled that way consistently in all my sources, I've just ignored the red wavy line and added the word, with confidence, to my personal dictionary provided by the Microsoft Word program.

and second as each relates to the third. Next, this paper discusses the fourth as it relates to the second.

Brain-based studies of the human sense of sight are one heavily researched theory of déjà vu that has been partially explained in the last two decades. Such studies focus on the dual pathways by which the sight of an event reaches the brain (Glenn; Carey F1). For example, the left hemisphere processes information from the right eye and the right hemisphere processes information from the left eye. The brain is incapable of storing data with respect to time and is only able to "see" events in relation to others. Each eye interprets data separately, at the same precise time. According to research, the human brain can perceive two visual stimuli at one instant as long as they are "seen" less than 25 milliseconds apart. Since the human brain is capable of interpreting both signals within this time, when events are perceived normally, they are seen and recognized by the brain as one single event (Weiten 69, 97-99, 211).

Occasionally, however, the neurological impulses that carry data from each eye to the brain are delayed. As Johnson explains, the person might be fatigued or have had his or her attention seriously distracted (as when crossing the street at a dangerous intersection). As a result, one signal may reach the brain in under 25 milliseconds, while the other signal is slowed and reaches the brain slightly more than 25 milliseconds later. Even a few milliseconds' delay makes the second incoming signal arrive late—and, without fail, the brain interprets the stimuli as two separate events rather than one event. The person thus has the sensation of having seen the event before because the brain has recognized the milliseconds-later event as a memory.

Implanted memory is another well-researched explanation for the déjà vu phenomenon. Examples of this originate in both the natural and the lab-induced experiences of people. For instance, perhaps a person walks into the kitchen of a new friend for the first time and, although the person has never been there before, the person feels certain that he or she has. With hypnosis and other techniques, researchers could uncover that the cupboards are almost exactly like those that the person had forgotten were in the kitchen of the person's grandparents' house and that the scent of baking apple pie is identical to the smell the person loved when walking into the grandparents' home during holidays (Carey F1).

Put author and page number in parentheses when author is not named in the sentence.

Paragraph summarizes several pages of source material, as parenthetical citation shows.

17

18

19

20

continued ➤

Commentary

17. **Two sources for one piece of information.** When two sources contain the same information, MLA style permits the citing of both sources. Each source is given with its page number; don't provide a page number if you're using a one-page source or an online source with no page numbers. A semicolon divides the sources.

18. **Words used in a non-literal way.** The words *see* and *seen* here do not carry their literal meaning related to conscious sight. Rather, they refer to subconscious sight. Therefore, they belong in quotation marks.

19. **PROCESS NOTE:** Earlier in the paper, I devoted two paragraphs to each of two non-déjà vu topics. Now, I'm giving more attention to each of the three types of legitimate déjà vu phenomena that I've chosen to discuss (dual pathways of sight, implanted memories, and inattentional blindness). This paragraph is the second I'm writing about dual pathways of sight.

20. **PROCESS NOTE:** I'm now starting to write about the second of the three types of déjà vu that I'm covering in this paper. I'm intentionally using the word *another* in my topic sentence to bridge from dual pathways of sight to implanted memories. Because there are so many concepts and examples of them in this paper, I'm trying to be very clear in my transitions.

Gurov 4

Thomas McHugh, a researcher at MIT, believes he has even discovered the specific "memory circuit" in the brain that is the source of this kind of déjà vu (Lemonick). This circuit allows people to complete memories with just a single cue. For example, you can remember much about a football game you saw even if someone just mentions the two teams involved. Sometimes, however, the circuit "misfires," and it signals that a new memory is actually part of the pattern of an old one.

Wolfradt describes a lab-induced experiment in which psychologist Larry   21
L. Jacoby in 1989 manipulated a group of subjects so that he could implant a memory that would lead to a déjà vu experience for each of them. He arranged for his subjects to assemble in a room equipped with a screen in front. He flashed on the screen one word so quickly that no one was consciously aware they had seen the word. Jacoby was certain, however, that the visual centres of the brain of each subject had indeed "seen" the word. Later, when he flashed the word, leaving it on   22
the screen long enough for the subjects to consciously see it, everyone indicated they had seen the word somewhere before. All the subjects were firmly convinced that the first time they had seen the word, it absolutely was not on the screen at the front of the room they were in. Some became annoyed at being asked over and over. Since Jacoby's work, lab-induced memory research has become very popular in psychology. In fact, it has been given its own name: *priming*.

Inattention, or what some researchers call "inattentional blindness," is also an extensively researched explanation for the déjà vu experience. Sometimes people can see objects without any impediment right before them but still not process the objects because they're paying attention to something else (Brown, *Experience* 181). The distraction might be daydreaming, a sudden lowering of energy, or simply being drawn to another object in the environment. As David Glenn explains in "The Tease of Memory,"

> Imagine that you drive through an unfamiliar town but pay little
> attention because you're talking on a cellphone. If you then drive back
> down the same streets a few moments later, this time focusing on the
> landscape, you might be prone to experience déjà vu. During your
> second pass, the visual information is consciously processed in the
> hippocampus but feels falsely "old" because the images from your
> earlier drive still linger in your short term memory.   23

continued ➤

Commentary

21. **PROCESS NOTE:** Specific examples are very important to me as I write this paper. It's far too easy for me to write on and on about theory and concepts. As I'm writing this paper, I find myself often cutting generalizations to make room for details. When I've read friends' papers from when they were in first year, I'm surprised to see how few specifics and concrete details they put in their first year composition papers—and their grades and the comments they got reflect this.

22. **PROCESS NOTE:** When I wrote my first draft, I felt that my discussion of implanted memories was pretty weak. I did some further research and was happy to find enough information to write this additional paragraph in my second draft. It is, to me, a dramatic demonstration of laboratory-manipulated implanted memory.

23. **PROCESS NOTE:** Here's how I wasted a day of researching for this paper. I know it's not unusual for students to go off the topic and waste their time, so I am trying to stay very conscious of what I am doing so that I can learn what NOT to do in the future. What happened was that I was becoming aware that psychologists have named many phenomena that are closely related to déjà vu, each somewhat different from it and from each other. For example, Brown in *Experience* names over twenty relatives of déjà vu. This captured my interest, but once I got into writing up the information, I realized that I was going off topic. I'll list here some that had potential but that I never used in my paper:

- *Déjà éprouvé:* A sense that one has experienced or attempted something.
- *Déjà senti:* A mental feeling that one is *feeling* something again. It is limited to feeling, and does not include a sense of being in a place.
- *Déjà visité:* The knowledge of a large place, such as an entire village, but knowing that one has never been there.
- *Jamais vu:* This is the opposite of déjà vu. Even though one knows something has happened before, the experience feels completely unfamiliar.
- *Presque vu:* This is the sense of almost, but not quite, remembering something—as in "it's on the tip of my tongue."

Gurov 5

The busy lifestyle today would seem to lead to many distractions of perception and thus to frequent experiences of déjà vu; however, these are no more frequently reported than any other causes reported concerning déjà vu.

One compelling laboratory experiment studying inattention is described by   24
Carey in "Déjà Vu: If It All Seems Familiar, There May Be a Reason." He recounts a test with many students from Duke University in Durham, North Carolina. The students were asked to look at a group of photographs of the campus of Southern Methodist University in Dallas, Texas, that were flashed before them at a very quick speed. A small black or white cross was superimposed on each photograph, and the students were instructed to find the cross and focus on it (F6). Brown in *Experience* explains that the researchers assumed that the quick speed at which the photographs had been shown would result in no one's having noticed the background scenes. A week's time passed, and the same students were shown the pictures again, this time without the crosses. Almost all insisted that they had been to the campus shown in the photos, which was physically impossible for that many students since they lived in Durham, North Carolina, and the campus in the photographs was in Dallas, Texas (182-83). This means that the scenes in the photographs did indeed register in the visual memories of the students in spite of the quick speed and the distraction of looking only for the crosses.

Concluding paragraph summarizes paper.

The worlds of psychology and neurology have learned much since the age   25
of paranormal interpretations of déjà vu experiences, starting around 1935. That is when rational science energetically began its disciplined investigations of brain-based origins of the déjà vu phenomenon. Concepts such as dual processing of sight, implanted memories, and inattentional blindness, among other theories, have gone far in opening the door to the possibilities of many more inventive theories to explain incidents of déjà vu. The leading researcher in the field today, Alan S. Brown, is among the strongest voices urging a vast expansion of investigations into this still relatively unexplored phenomenon. He is optimistic this will happen, given his whimsical remark to Carlin Flora of *Psychology Today*: "We are always fascinated when the brain goes haywire."

continued ➤

Commentary

24. **PROCESS NOTE:** To stay on the topic, I needed a third type of déjà vu—for which I used inattentional blindness—to drive home my thesis statement.

25. **PROCESS NOTE:** In my second draft, I decided to check whether all my topic sentences tied together with each other. (They are listed below.) I remembered that neither the introductory nor the concluding paragraphs have topic sentences.

Thesis Statement: Although a few people still believe that feelings of déjà vu have mysterious or supernatural origins, research in cognitive psychology and the neurosciences has produced laboratory experiments that could explain the phenomenon rationally.

(1) Some people report never having experienced déjà vu, and the percentages vary for the number of people who report having lived through at least one episode of it.

(2) Perhaps part of the reason for this variation in the range of percentages stems from a general misunderstanding of the phrase *déjà vu*, even by some of the earlier scientific researchers twenty or more years ago.

(3) False memory is another phenomenon mislabelled *déjà vu*.

(4) In the last twenty years especially, new theories have come to the fore as a result of rigorous work from psychological and medical points of view.

(5) Brain-based studies of the human sense of sight are one heavily researched theory of déjà vu that has been partially explained in the last two decades.

(6) Occasionally, however, the neurological impulses that carry data from each eye to the brain are delayed.

(7) Implanted memory is another well-researched explanation for déjà vu.

(8) Wolfradt describes a lab-induced experiment in which psychologist Larry L. Jacoby in 1989 manipulated a group of subjects so that he could implant a memory that would lead to a déjà vu experience for each of them.

(9) Inattention, or what some researchers call "inattentional blindness," is also an extensively researched explanation for the déjà vu experience.

(10) One compelling laboratory experiment studying inattention is described by Carey in "Déjà Vu: If It All Seems Familiar, There May Be a Reason."

Works Cited

Brown, Alan S. *The Déjà Vu Experience: Essays in Cognitive Psychology*. New York: Psychology, 2004. Print.

---. "The Déjà Vu Illusion." *Current Directions in Psychological Science* 13.7 (2004): 256-59. Print.

Carey, Benedict. "Déjà Vu: If It All Seems Familiar, There May Be a Reason." *New York Times* 14 Sept. 2004: F1+. *LexisNexis*. Web. 11 Nov. 2013.

Flora, Carlin. "Giving Déjà Vu Its Due." *Psychology Today* Mar.-Apr. 2005: 27. *Academic Search Premier*. Web. 7 Nov. 2013.

Glenn, David. "The Tease of Memory." *Chronicle of Higher Education* 23 July 2004: A12. Print.

Johnson, C. *A Theory on the Déjà Vu Phenomenon*. 8 Dec. 2001. *Public Service Projects Index*. Web. 20 Nov. 2013.

Lemonick, Michael D. "Explaining Déjà Vu." *Time* 20 Aug. 2007. *Academic Search Premier*. Web. 5 Dec. 2013.

Weiten, Wayne. *Psychology Themes and Variations*. Belmont: Wadsworth, 2005. Print.

Wolfradt, Uwe. "Strangely Familiar." *Scientific American Mind* 16.1 (2005): 32-37. *Academic Search Elite*. Web. 7 Nov. 2013.

Works Cited begins on a new page. Double-space throughout.

List sources in alphabetical order.

26
27
28
29

Commentary

26. **Working versus final bibliography.** In keeping with MLA style, Andrei developed a working bibliography using those sources referred to in his research paper. His bibliography contained over twice the number of sources in his Works Cited. He dropped sources he considered less authoritative and ones that were not specifically targeted to the subjects that he chose to discuss related to déjà vu.

27. **Balance of source types.** Andrei's final list of Works Cited contains nine works, five from online databases and four from print sources—a proportion that is typical of today's undergraduate research papers.

28. **What is LexisNexis?** LexisNexis is an online database, available to students through their school's library, that contains a large number of research and other scholarly collections, including the LexisNexis Academic and Library Solutions. Originally a document service for law students and lawyers, it now includes areas of study such as government, business, and environmental issues.

29. **What is Academic Search Premier?** Academic Search Premier is a widely used online database in English studies and the humanities. It's available to students through their school's library and gives access to over one hundred reference databases, thousands of online journals, lists of book titles at some libraries, linking services, and much more.

Chapter 37

APA DOCUMENTATION WITH CASE STUDY

Following are two directories that point you to guidance you'll find in this chapter. The first lists examples of APA in-text citations. The second lists examples of APA References entries.

continued ➤

APA

What is APA documentation style?

The American Psychological Association (APA) sponsors a DOCUMENTATION system widely used in the social sciences. APA style involves two equally important features that need to appear in research papers.

1. Within the body of your paper, use **in-text citations**, in parentheses, to acknowledge your SOURCES. This chapter explains the proper way to provide APA in-text citations. Section 37b explains how they work, and section 37c shows sixteen models, each of which gives one or more examples of different types of sources.

2. At the end of the paper, provide a list of the sources you used—and only those sources. Title this list, which contains complete bibliographic information about each source, **References**. It needs to appear on a separate page at the end of your research paper. It includes only the sources you've actually used in your paper, not any you've consulted but haven't used. Section 37f gives instructions for composing your References pages, followed by seventy-five models, each based on a different kind of source (book, article, website, and so on) that you might use.

For an example of a research paper that uses APA-style in-text citations in parentheses and a References list, see section 37h. As you read the paper, notice how the two requirements for crediting sources work together so that readers can learn the precise origin of the material that is quoted, paraphrased, and summarized.

What are APA parenthetical in-text citations?

The APA-STYLE DOCUMENTATION guidelines here follow the recommendations of the *Publication Manual of the American Psychological Association*, Sixth Edition (Washington, DC: American Psychological Association, 2009), which is the most current edition. For possible updates or if you need more information than we provide in this handbook, you may wish to consult the APA's own manual or its website at <http://www.apastyle.org>.

APA style requires parenthetical IN-TEXT CITATIONS that identify a SOURCE by the author's name (or a shortened version of the title if there is no author) and the copyright year. For readability and a good writing style, you can often incorporate the name, and sometimes the year, into your sentence. Otherwise, place this information in parentheses, located as close as possible to the material you quote, paraphrase, or summarize. Your goal is to tell readers precisely where they can find the original material.

APA style requires page numbers for DIRECT QUOTATIONS and recommends them for PARAPHRASES and SUMMARIES. Some instructors expect you to give page references for paraphrases and summaries, and others don't; so find out your instructor's preference to avoid any problems in properly crediting your sources.

Put page numbers in parentheses, using the abbreviation *p.* before a single page number and *pp.* when the material you're citing falls on more than one page. For a direct quotation from an electronic source that numbers paragraphs, give the paragraph number (or numbers). Handle paragraph numbers as you do page numbers, but use *para* rather than *p.* or *pp.* If there are headings but no page or paragraph numbers, cite the heading of the section you are using, and count and then cite the number of the paragraph, starting from that heading (Moon, 2007, Discussion, para. 2). Shorten long headings and put them inside quotation marks: (Hickson, 2005, "Judging People," para. 3).

If you refer to a work more than once in a paragraph, give the author's name and the date at the first mention; then you may use only the name after that. When you're citing two or more works by the same author, however, each citation must include the date. When two or more of your sources have the same last name, use both first and last names in the text or first initial(s) and last names in parentheses.

37c What are APA guidelines for in-text citations?

The following numbered examples show how to cite various kinds of sources in the body of your research paper. Remember, though, that you often can introduce source names, including titles when necessary, and sometimes even years, in your own sentences rather than in the parenthetical IN-TEXT CITATIONS.

1. Paraphrased or Summarized Source—APA

People from the Mediterranean prefer an elbow-to-shoulder distance from each other (Morris, 1977). [Author name and date cited in parentheses; note comma.]

Desmond Morris (1977) notes that people from the Mediterranean prefer an elbow-to-shoulder distance from each other. [Author name cited in text; date cited in parentheses.]

2. Source of a Short Quotation—APA

A recent report of reductions in SAD-related "depression in 87 percent of patients" (Binkley, 1990, p. 203) reverses the findings of earlier studies. [Author name, date, and page reference in parentheses immediately following the quotation.]

Binkley (1990) reports reductions in SAD-related "depression in 87 percent of patients" (p. 203). [Author name followed by the date in parentheses incorporated into the words introducing the quotation; page number in parentheses immediately following the quotation.]

3. Source of a Long Quotation (and Format of Quotation)—APA

Incorporate a direct quotation of fewer than forty words into your own sentence and enclose it in quotation marks. Place the parenthetical in-text citation after the closing quotation mark and, if the quotation falls at the end of the sentence, before the sentence-ending punctuation. When you use a quotation longer than forty words, set it off in block style indented one-half inch (about 1.25 cm) from the left margin. Never enclose a set-off quotation in quotation marks. Place the parenthetical reference citation one space after the end punctuation of the last sentence.

DISPLAYED QUOTATION (FORTY OR MORE WORDS)

Jet lag, with its characteristic fatigue and irregular sleep patterns, is a common problem among those who travel great distances by jet airplane to different time zones:

> Jet lag syndrome is the inability of the internal body rhythm to rapidly resynchronize after sudden shifts in the timing. For a variety of reasons, the system attempts to maintain stability and resist temporal change. Consequently, complete adjustment can often be delayed for several days—sometimes for a week—after arrival at one's destination. (Bonner, 1991, p. 72)

4. One Author—APA

In a parenthetical reference in APA style, a comma and a space separate a name from a year, and a year from a page reference. (Note: Examples 1 through 3 are also citations of works by one author.)

One of his questions is, "What actually happened in Walkerton?" (O'Connor, 2002, p. 2).

5. Two Authors—APA

If a work has two authors, give both names in each citation.

> One report describes 2123 occurrences (Krait & Cooper, 1994).

> The results that Krait and Cooper (1994) report would not support the conclusions Davis and Sherman (1992) draw in their review of the literature.

When you write a parenthetical in-text citation naming two (or more) authors, use an ampersand (&) between the final two names, but write out the word *and* for any reference in your own sentence.

6. Three, Four, or Five Authors—APA

For three, four, or five authors, use the last names of all the authors in the first reference. In all subsequent references, use only the first author's last name followed by *et al.* (a Latin term meaning "and others"). Note that *et al.* is followed by a period and is not italicized.

FIRST REFERENCE

> In one study, only 30% of the survey population could name the most commonly spoken language in five Middle Eastern countries (Ludwig, Rodriquez, Novak, & Ehlers, 2008).

SUBSEQUENT REFERENCE

> Ludwig et al. (2008) found that most people surveyed could identify the language spoken in Saudi Arabia.

7. Six or More Authors—APA

For six or more authors, name the first author followed by *et al.* in all in-text references, including the first.

> These injuries can lead to an inability to perform athletically, in addition to initiating degenerative changes at the joint level (Mandelbaum et al., 2005).

8. Author(s) with Two or More Works in the Same Year—APA

If you use more than one source written in the same year by the same author(s), alphabetize the works by their titles for the References list and assign letters in alphabetical order to the years—(1996a), (1996b), (1996c). Use the year-letter combination in parenthetical references. Note that a citation of two or more such works lists the years in alphabetical order.

> Most recently, Torrevillas (2007c) draws new conclusions from the results of eight experiments conducted with experienced readers (Torrevillas, 2007a, 2007b).

9. Two or More Authors with the Same Last Name—APA

Include first initials for every in-text citation of authors who share a last name. Use the initials appearing in the References list. (In the second example, a parenthetical citation, the name order is alphabetical, as explained in item 12.)

> R. A. Smith (2008) and C. Smith (1999) both confirm these results.

> These results have been confirmed independently (C. Smith, 1999; R. A. Smith, 2008).

10. Work with a Group or Corporate Author—APA

If you use a source in which the "author" is a corporation, agency, or group, an in-text reference gives that name as author. Use the full name in each citation, unless an abbreviated version of the name is likely to be familiar to your audience. In that case, use the full name and give its abbreviation at the first citation; then, use the abbreviation for subsequent citations.

FIRST REFERENCE

After 1949 the federal government took over responsibility for most public housing projects (Canada Mortgage and Housing Corporation [CMHC], 1990).

SUBSEQUENT REFERENCE

The cost of retrofitting older designs was substantial (CMHC, 1990).

11. Work Listed by Title—APA

If no author is named, use a shortened form of the title for in-text citations. Ignoring *A*, *An*, or *The*, make the first word the one by which you alphabetize the title in your References. The following example refers to an article fully titled "Are You a Day or Night Person?"

Scientists group people as "larks" or "owls" on the basis of whether individuals are more efficient in the morning or at night ("Are You," 1989).

12. Reference to More Than One Source—APA

If more than one source has contributed to an idea or opinion in your paper, cite the sources alphabetically by author in one set of parentheses; separate each block of information with a semicolon.

Conceptions of personal space vary among cultures (Morris, 1977; Worchel & Cooper, 1983).

13. Personal Communication, Including E-Mail and Other Nonretrievable Sources—APA

Telephone calls, personal letters, interviews, and e-mail messages are "personal communications" that your readers can't access or retrieve. Acknowledge personal communications in parenthetical references, but never include them in your References list.

Recalling his first summer at camp, one person said, "The proximity of 12 other kids made me—an only child with older, quiet parents—frantic for eight weeks" (A. Weiss, personal communication, January 12, 2011).

14. References to Retrievable Online Sources—APA

When you quote, paraphrase, or summarize an online source that is available to others, cite the author (if any) or title and the date as you would for a print source, and include the work in your References list.

It's possible that similarity in personality is important in having a happy marriage (Luo & Clonen, 2005, p. 324).

15. Reference to an Online Source with No Page Numbers—APA

If an online source doesn't provide page numbers, use the paragraph number, if available, preceded by the abbreviation *para.* If you can't find a page or paragraph number, cite a heading and count the paragraph numbers after it, if possible.

(Anderson, 2003, para. 14)

(Migueis, 2002, Introduction, para. 1)

16. Source Lines for Graphics and Table Data—APA

If you use a graphic from another source or create a table using data from another source, provide a note at the bottom of the table or graphic, crediting the original author and the copyright holder. Here are examples of two source lines—one for a graphic from an article, the other for a graphic from a book.

TABLE USING DATA FROM AN ARTICLE—APA

Note. The data in columns 1 and 2 are from "Advance Organizers in Advisory Reports: Selective Reading, Recall, and Perception" by L. Lagerwerf et al., 2008, *Written Communication, 25*(1), p. 68. Copyright 2008 by Sage Publications. Adapted with permission of the author.

GRAPHIC FROM A BOOK—APA

Figure 2. Additive approval cycle. From *Additive Alert: A Guide to Food Additives for the Canadian Consumer* (p. 28), by Linda R. Pim, 1979, Toronto: Doubleday. Copyright 1979 by Pollution Probe Foundation. Reprinted with permission.

37d What are APA guidelines for writing an abstract?

An abstract is comprehensive summary of a longer piece of writing. The APA estimates that an abstract should be no longer than about 150 to 250 words. Your instructor may require that you include an abstract at the start of a paper; if you're not sure, ask. Make the abstract accurate, objective, and exact. You may be familiar with effective abstracts, because many disciplines have online abstracts of longer sources. See 37g for guidelines on formatting an abstract. The student paper in 37h.2 has an abstract you can study as an example.

37e What are APA guidelines for content notes?

Content notes in APA-style papers add relevant information that can't be worked effectively into a text discussion. Use consecutive arabic numerals for note numbers, both within your paper and on any notes page(s) following the References section of your paper. Try to arrange your sentence so that the note number falls at the end. Use a numeral raised slightly above the line of words and immediately after the final punctuation mark. See 37g for instructions on formatting the notes page.

37f What are APA guidelines for a References list?

The REFERENCES list at the end of your research paper provides complete bibliographic information for readers who may want to access the sources you draw on for your paper.

Include in a References list all the sources you QUOTE, PARAPHRASE, or SUMMARIZE in your paper so that readers can find the same sources with reasonable effort. Never include in your References list any source that's not generally available to others (see item 13 in 37c). Quick Reference 37.1 presents general format guidelines.

Guidelines for an APA-style References list

TITLE

The title is "References" (centred without quotation marks, italics, or underlining).

PLACEMENT OF LIST

Start a new page. Number it sequentially with the rest of the paper and place it immediately after the body of the paper.

CONTENTS AND FORMAT

Include all quoted, paraphrased, or summarized sources in your paper that are not personal communications, unless your instructor tells you to include all the references you have consulted, not just those you have to credit. Start each entry on a new line, and double-space all lines. APA recommends a *hanging indent style*: The first line of each entry begins flush left at the margin, and all other lines are indented. Type the first line of each entry full width, and indent subsequent lines one-half inch (about 1.25 cm). The easiest way to do this is to use the word processor's ruler bar.

Shuter, R. (1977). A field study of nonverbal communication in Germany, Italy, and the
United States. *Communication Monographs, 44,* 298–305. doi:10.1080/03637757709390141

SPACING AFTER PUNCTUATION

In papers submitted to journals for publication, APA recommends putting two spaces after periods and other punctuation that ends a sentence. In other cases, only one space is used. Most word-processing programs single-space between sentences, and your instructor may prefer single spacing, so ask for his or her preferred style.

ARRANGEMENT OF ENTRIES

Alphabetize by the author's last name. If no author is named, alphabetize by the first significant word (ignore *A, An,* or *The)* in the title of the work.

AUTHORS' NAMES

Use last names, first initials, and middle initials, if any. Reverse the order for all authors' names, and use an ampersand (&) before the last author's name: Mills, J. F., & Holahan, R. H.

Give names in the order in which they appear on the work (on the title page of a book or under the title of an article or other printed work). Put a comma between each author's last name and first initial and after each complete name except the last. Use a period after the last author's name. If there are eight or more authors, give the first six authors' names, insert a comma and an ellipsis, and end with the last author's name, but don't use an ampersand.

DATES

Date information follows the name information and is enclosed in parentheses. Place a period followed by one space after the closing parenthesis.

For books, articles in journals that have volume numbers, and many other print and nonprint sources, the year of publication or production is the date to use. For articles from most general-circulation magazines and newspapers, use the year followed by a comma and then the exact date that appears on the issue (month and day for daily and weekly publications, month alone for monthly and bimonthly publications, and season for

continued ➤

quarterly publications). Capitalize any words and use no abbreviations. Individual entries that follow show how much information to give for various sources.

CAPITALIZATION OF TITLES

For book, article, and chapter titles, capitalize the first word, the first word after a colon between a title and subtitle, and any proper nouns. For names of journals and proceedings of meetings, capitalize the first word, all nouns, verbs, adverbs, and adjectives, and any other words four or more letters long.

SPECIAL TREATMENT OF TITLES

Use no special treatment for titles of shorter works (poems, short stories, essays, articles, webpages). Italicize titles of longer works (books, newspapers, journals, or websites). A rarely used alternative to italic typeface is underlining with an unbroken line.

Do not drop any words (such as *A, An,* or *The*) from the titles of PERIODICALS such as newspapers, magazines, and journals.

Information that helps identify a work by its format is placed in square brackets immediately after the last word of the title. Examples are [Audio podcast]; [Data file]; [Editorial]; [Letter to . . .]; [Online forum comment]; [Review of DVD . . .]; [Special issue]; [Web log message].

PUBLISHERS

Use a shortened version of the publisher's name except for an association, corporation, or university press. Drop *Co., Inc., Publishers,* and the like, but retain *Books* or *Press.*

PLACE OF PUBLICATION

For US publishers, give the city and add the state (use the two-letter postal abbreviations listed in most dictionaries) for all US cities. For Canadian cities, Canadian writers normally add the two-letter postal abbreviation for the province or territory. For publishers in other countries, give city and country spelled out. However, if the state or country is part of the publisher's name, omit it after the name of the city.

ABBREVIATIONS OF MONTHS

Don't abbreviate the names of months.

PAGE NUMBERS

Use all digits, omitting none. For references to books or newspapers only, use *p.* and *pp.* before page numbers. List all discontinuous pages, with numbers separated by commas: pp. 32, 44–45, 47–49, 53.

REFERENCES ENTRIES: BOOKS

Citations for books have four main parts: author, date, title, and publication information (place of publication and publisher). Each part ends with a period.

AUTHOR   DATE   TITLE

Kingwell, M. (1999). *Marginalia: A cultural reader.*

PUBLICATION INFORMATION

Toronto: Penguin Books.

, *continued* ➢

REFERENCES ENTRIES: ARTICLES

Citations for periodical articles contain four major parts: author, date, title of article, and publication information (usually, the periodical title, volume number, and page numbers). Each part ends with a period.

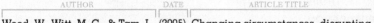

AUTHOR   DATE   ARTICLE TITLE

Wood, W., Witt, M. G., & Tam, L. (2005). Changing circumstances, disrupting

VOLUME PAGE
PERIODICAL TITLE   NUMBER RANGE

habits. *Journal of Personality and Social Psychology, 88,* 918–933.

REFERENCES ENTRIES: ELECTRONIC AND ONLINE SOURCES

The *Publication Manual of the American Psychological Association,* Sixth Edition (2009), updates both the previous (2001) edition of the manual and the *APA Style Guide to Electronic References* (Washington, DC: American Psychological Association, 2007). Its basic approach is still to include the familiar elements of a citation in the same order, before giving whatever retrieval information other readers need to locate the electronic source.

When citing electronic or online sources, include the name(s) of author(s) the same way as for books and journals. Always include the publication date in parentheses after the author(s)' name(s), followed by a period. Titles of books, periodicals, and whole websites should be italicized; titles of articles or pages in a website should not use italics. Journal articles retrieved online should always list the volume and issue number, if available. If the electronic source is based on a print source (including a PDF), give inclusive page numbers as you would for the same kind of print source.

You then include retrieval information for the electronic source. For articles with a DOI (Digital Object Identifier), this is simply the letters "doi" followed by a colon, then the numbers and letters of the identifier. Figure 37.1 (p. 530) shows how to find publication information in a journal article with a DOI. If an article has no DOI, give the URL of the journal's or publisher's home page. For an online book with no DOI, give the URL of its site, which may be the publisher's or the vendor's URL.

Figure 37.1A shows that the source is listed in a database. In general, you include the name of a database only when that information is essential for locating the source; usually, this means the source is a dissertation, an abstract, or an article found only on a specialized database. (Some databases specialize in archiving articles from journals that are no longer being published.)

Figure 37.1B illustrates the actual page of the article itself. We show an entry for it on the next page. Give retrieval information, beginning with the words "Retrieved from," only if you need to introduce a URL or database. If you know that the database is difficult to locate, give its URL as well. Do not give a retrieval date unless you cite a source that will change over time, such as a wiki.

Here are three examples of electronic source entries. The first is for an article that does not have a DOI.

AUTHOR   DATE   ARTICLE NAME

Ang, A. (2005, November 24). China reports second human death from bird flu.

ONLINE
NEWSPAPER TITLE   RETRIEVAL INFORMATION

The Globe and Mail. Retrieved from http://www.theglobeandmail.com

continued ➤

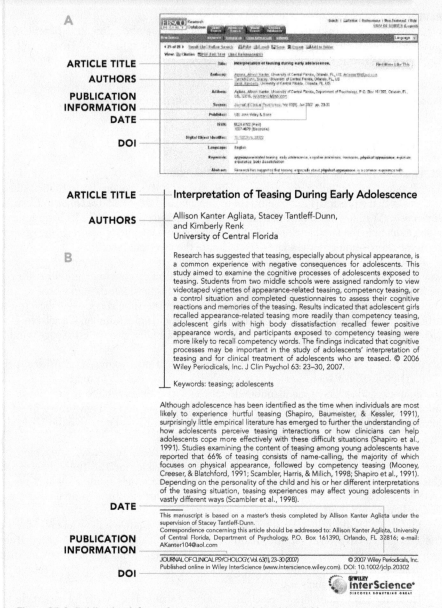

Figure 37.1 Publication information in a journal article with a DOI

If the newspaper's home page allows you to search for the article, give only its URL. Do not add a period after a URL.

The second example is for an electronic article that has a DOI. Note that this is for the article in Figure 37.1.

continued ➤

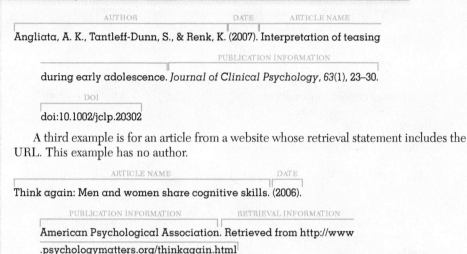

A third example is for an article from a website whose retrieval statement includes the URL. This example has no author.

ARTICLE NAME   DATE

Think again: Men and women share cognitive skills. (2006).

PUBLICATION INFORMATION   RETRIEVAL INFORMATION

American Psychological Association. Retrieved from http://www
.psychologymatters.org/thinkagain.html

The following samples of entries may appear in an APA References list. You can find others in the *Publication Manual of the American Psychological Association* or at <http://www.apastyle.org> for quick help in deciding which example to follow, see the decision flowchart in Figure 37.2 (p. 532).

PRINT REFERENCES—BOOKS

1. Book by One Author—APA

Note that all entries use the hanging indent style: The first line of an entry is flush to the left margin, and all other lines in the entry are indented five spaces or one-half inch (about 1.25 cm).

Trudeau, P. E. (1968). *Federalism and the French Canadians*. Toronto, ON: Macmillan Canada.

2. Book by Two Authors—APA

Doob, A., & Cesaroni, C. (2004). *Responding to youth crime in Canada*. Toronto, ON: University of Toronto Press.

3. Book by Three or More Authors—APA

For a work by three to seven authors, include all the author's names. For a work by eight authors or more, list the first six names followed by a comma, an ellipsis, and the name of the last author. See item 23.

Lynam, J. K., Ndiritu, C. G., & Mbabu, A. N. (2004). *Transformation of agricultural research systems in Africa: Lessons from Kenya*. East Lansing, MI: Michigan State University Press.

4. Two or More Books by the Same Author(s)—APA

Arrange references by the same author chronologically, with the earlier date of publication listed first.

Atwood, M. (1972). *Survival*. Toronto, ON: Anansi.

Atwood, M. (1981). *True stories*. Toronto, ON: Oxford University Press.

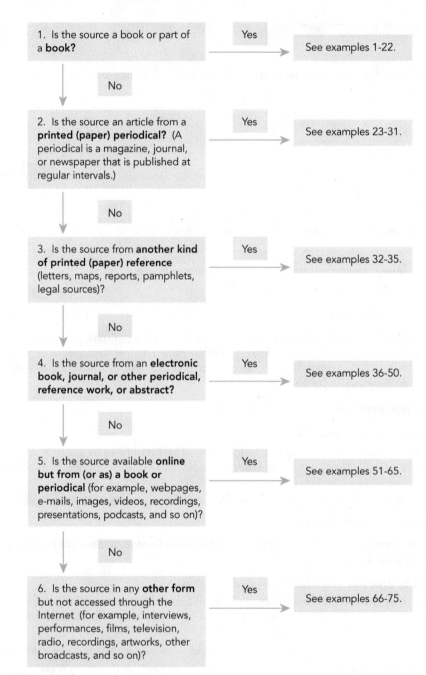

1. Is the source a book or part of a **book?** Yes → See examples 1-22.

No ↓

2. Is the source an article from a **printed (paper) periodical?** (A periodical is a magazine, journal, or newspaper that is published at regular intervals.) Yes → See examples 23-31.

No ↓

3. Is the source from **another kind of printed (paper) reference** (letters, maps, reports, pamphlets, legal sources)? Yes → See examples 32-35.

No ↓

4. Is the source from an **electronic book, journal, or other periodical, reference work, or abstract?** Yes → See examples 36-50.

No ↓

5. Is the source available **online but from (or as) a book or periodical** (for example, webpages, e-mails, images, videos, recordings, presentations, podcasts, and so on)? Yes → See examples 51-65.

No ↓

6. Is the source in any **other form** but not accessed through the Internet (for example, interviews, performances, films, television, radio, recordings, artworks, other broadcasts, and so on)? Yes → See examples 66-75.

Figure 37.2 APA References visual directory

5. Book by a Group or Corporate Author—APA

American Psychological Association. (2009). *Publication manual of the American Psychological Association* (6th ed.). Washington, DC: Author.

CBC Massey Lectures Series. (2007). *The Lost Massey Lectures: Recovered classics from five great thinkers.* Toronto, ON: Anansi.

Cite the full name of the corporate author first. If the author is also the publisher, use the word *Author* as the name of the publisher. (The CBC Massey Lectures Series is considered the corporate author of the book in the second item.)

6. Book with No Author Named—APA

The Chicago manual of style (16th ed.). (2010). Chicago, IL: University of Chicago Press.

Ignoring *The*, this would be alphabetized under *Chicago*, the first important word in the title.

7. Book with an Author and an Editor—APA

Trudeau, P. E. (1998). *The Essential Trudeau* (R. Graham, Ed.). Toronto, ON: McClelland & Stewart.

8. Translation—APA

Tremblay, M. (1998). *A thing of beauty* (S. Fischman, Trans.). Vancouver, BC: Talon.

9. Work in Several Volumes or Parts—APA

Chrisley, R. (Ed.). (2000). *Artificial intelligence: Critical concepts* (Vols. 1–4). London, UK: Routledge.

10. Anthology or Edited Book—APA

New, W. H. (Ed.). (1986). *Canadian short fiction: From myth to modern.* Scarborough, ON: Prentice Hall.

11. One Selection from an Anthology or an Edited Book—APA

Give the author of the selection first. The word *In* introduces the larger work from which the selection is taken. Note that names are inverted only in the author position; in all other circumstances, they are written in standard form.

Morrisseau, N. (1986). The Indian that became a thunderbird. In W. H. New (Ed.), *Canadian short fiction: From myth to modern* (pp. 26–29). Scarborough, ON: Prentice Hall.

12. Selection from a Work Already Listed in References—APA

Provide full information for the cited anthology (second example), along with information about the individual selection. Put entries in alphabetical order.

Bond, R. (2004). The night train at Deoli. In A. Chaudhuri (Ed). *The Vintage book of modern Indian literature* (pp. 415–418). New York, NY: Vintage Books.

Chaudhuri, A. (Ed.). (2004). *The Vintage book of modern Indian literature.* New York, NY: Vintage Books.

13. Signed Article in a Reference Book—APA

Use *In* to introduce the larger work from which the selection is taken.

Shadbolt, D. (1988). Emily Carr. In *The Canadian encyclopedia* (2nd ed., Vol. 1, p. 366). Edmonton, AB: Hurtig.

14. Unsigned Article in a Reference Book—APA

Ireland. (2002). In *The new encyclopaedia Britannica: Macropaedia* (15th ed., Vol. 21, pp. 997–1018). Chicago, IL: Encyclopaedia Britannica.

15. Second or Subsequent Edition—APA

A book usually doesn't announce that it's a first edition. However, after the first edition, the edition number appears on the title page. In your entry, place the abbreviated information (*2nd ed., 3rd ed.*, and so on) after the title and in parentheses.

Gibaldi, J. (2009). *MLA handbook for writers of research papers* (7th ed.). New York, NY: Modern Language Association.

16. Introduction, Preface, Foreword, or Afterword—APA

If you're citing an introduction, preface, foreword, or afterword, give its author's name first. After the year, give the name of the part cited. If the writer of the material you're citing isn't the author of the book, use the word *In* and the author's name before the title of the book.

Hasse, D. (2004). Foreword. In D. Smith, *The end of composition studies* (pp. ix–xiii). Carbondale, IL: Southern Illinois University Press.

17. Unpublished Dissertation or Essay—APA

Byers, M. (2000). Buffy the Vampire Slayer: *The insurgence of television as a performance text* (Unpublished doctoral dissertation), University of Toronto, Toronto, ON.

The title of the television series is taken out of italics when it is part of the italicized title of an independent work. See also item 20.

18. Reprint of an Older Book—APA

Lampman, A. (1978). *Lyrics of the earth.* Ottawa, ON: Tecumseh Press. (Original work published 1895)

You can find republishing information on the copyright page. The in-text citation for this book would be (Lampman, 1895/1978).

19. Book in a Series—APA

Give the title of the book but not of the whole series.

Courchene, T. J. (1991). *In praise of renewed federalism.* Toronto, ON: C. D. Howe Institute.

20. Book with a Title Within a Title—APA

Never italicize a title within a book title, even though it would appear in italic typeface if it were by itself. (See also item 17.)

Lumiansky, R. M., & Baker, H. (Eds.). (1968). *Critical approaches to six major English works:* Beowulf through Paradise Lost. Philadelphia, PA: University of Pennsylvania Press.

21. Government Publication—APA

Use the complete name of a government agency as author when no specific person is named.

Indian and Northern Affairs Canada. (1986). *The Inuit.* Ottawa, ON: Supply and Services Canada.

Royal Commission on Bilingualism and Biculturalism. (1965). *Preliminary report.* Ottawa, ON: Queen's Printer.

22. Published Proceedings of a Conference—APA

Smith, D. B. (Ed.). (1997). *Forging a new relationship: Proceedings of the conference on the Report of the Royal Commission on Aboriginal Peoples.* Montreal, QC: McGill Institute for the Study of Canada.

When citing a specific department or other university facility, put the name of the university first.

PRINT REFERENCES—PERIODICALS

23. Article in a Journal with Continuous Pagination—APA

Tyson, P. (1998). The psychology of women. *Journal of the American Psychoanalytic Association, 46,* 361–364.

Give the volume number, italicized, after the journal title; do not give the issue number, however, when the first page of each subsequent issue is one number higher than the last page of the previous issue.

Vaillancourt, T., Brittain, H., Bennett, L., Arnocky. S., McDougall, P., Hymel, S., . . . Cunningham, L. (2010). Places to avoid: Population-based study of student reports of unsafe and high bullying areas at school. *Canadian Journal of School Psychology, 25,* 40–54.

This article is by more than eight authors. The first six names are listed, followed by a comma, an ellipsis, and the name of the last author listed.

Use the following format to cite a special issue or section of a journal.

Poverty and human development [Special issue]. (2007). *Canadian Medical Association Journal, 177.*

Montazemi, A. R., & Irani, Z. (2009). Information technology in support of financial markets [Special section]. *Canadian Journal of Administrative Sciences, 26,* 122–124.

24. Article in a Journal That Pages Each Issue Separately—APA

Give the volume number, italicized with the journal title, followed by the issue number in parentheses (not italicized), and the page number(s).

Adler-Kassner, L., & Estrem, H. (2003). Rethinking research writing: Public literacy in the composition classroom. *WPA: Writing Program Administration, 26*(3), 119–131.

25. Signed Article in a Weekly or Biweekly Periodical—APA

Give year, month, and day for a periodical published every week or every two weeks. Don't use the abbreviation *p.* (or *pp.*) for magazines or journals.

Johnson, B. D. (2007, November 26). Why six Dylans are better than one. *Maclean's,* 43–46.

26. Signed Article in a Monthly or Bimonthly Periodical—APA

Give the year and month(s) for a periodical published every month or every other month. Insert the volume number, italicized with the periodical title. Put the issue number in parentheses; do not italicize it.

Fallows, J. (2008, January/February). The $1.4 trillion question. *The Atlantic, 301*(1), 36–48.

27. Unsigned Article in a Weekly or Monthly Periodical—APA

The price is wrong. (2003, August 2) *The Economist, 368,* 58–59.

28. Signed Article in a Daily Newspaper—APA

Use the abbreviation *p.* (or *pp.* for more than one page) for items from newspapers.

McCarthy, S. (2011, June 28). Sale puts Ottawa out of nuclear business. *The Globe and Mail*, pp. A1–A2.

29. Unsigned Article in a Daily Newspaper—APA

Private water may violate Constitution. (2002, November 27). *The Ottawa Citizen*, pp. A1, A7.

30. Editorial, Letter to the Editor, or Review—APA

London doomed to repeat its history on heritage. [Editorial]. (2011, July 20). *The London Free Press*, p. B8.

Hurka J. (1994, July 5). [Letter to the editor]. *The Calgary Sun*, p. A18.

Toews, W. (1995, August 26). Politics of the mind [Review of the book *They say you're crazy: How the world's most powerful psychiatrists decide who's normal*]. *Winnipeg Free Press*, p. C3.

Put information that helps identity the work, such as *Editorial* and *Review of . . .* , immediately after the title. Do not use the abbreviations *p.* or *pp.* for magazines or journals. Give year, month, and day for a periodical published every week or every two weeks.

31. Article in a Looseleaf Collection of Reprinted Articles—APA

Hayden, T. (2002). The age of robots. In E. Goldstein (Ed.), *Applied Science 2002. SIRS 2002*, Article 66. (Reprinted from *U.S. News & World Report*, pp. 44–50, 2001, April 23).

OTHER PRINT REFERENCES

32. Published and Unpublished Letters—APA

If they are not published, archived, or stored in a collection, letters are considered personal communications inaccessible to general readers, so they do not appear in the References list. They are cited only in the body of the paper (see item 66).

Williams, W. D. (1939, November 14). [Letter to David Williams]. Canada at War Archive (Series 2.1, Folder 20042), Ottawa, ON.

33. Map or Chart—APA

Gibsons-Sechelt Sunshine Coast [Map]. (1996). Coquitlam, BC: Canadian Cartographers.

34. Report or Pamphlet—APA

Assembly of First Nations. (2010). *Annual report 2009–2010* [Pamphlet]. Ottawa, ON: Author.

35. Legal Source—APA

Give the name of a law, the name and number of case, or the number of a bill and the parliamentary session at which the bill was debated, and the date. Also give the published source where the law is codified or the case is reported. See Appendix 7.1 of the APA *Publication Manual* for other types of legal citations.

Bill C-50. An Act to amend the Criminal Code in respect of cruelty to animals, 1st Sess., 38th Parl., 2005.

Legal writers follow the *Canadian Guide to Uniform Legal Citation* (7th edition, 2010), and include abbreviated publication information for laws and cases.

Canadian Labour Code, R.S.C. 1985, c.L.-2, s.12.

Delgamuukw v. British Columbia, [1997] 3 S.C.R. 1010.

ELECTRONIC AND ONLINE SOURCES

In general, for online sources APA recommends giving the same information, in the same order, as you would for a print source: author name(s), date of publication, title (italicized for books, periodicals, and whole websites), and publication information (title, volume, issue, pages). Online journal articles should always list the volume and issue number, if available. If the electronic source is based on a print source, give inclusive page numbers. Then add as much retrieval information as others will need to locate the source. This retrieval information may include a DOI or it may consist of a "Retrieved from" statement along with a URL or a database name. Only with wikis and some other sources that change over time do you need to include the date you retrieved the information.

- **DOI (Direct Object Identifier):** These codes are assigned to many journal articles and other publications, and are typically located on the first page of the online article or listed in the database. The DOI for a publication will be the same wherever the article appears. As a result, you don't use a URL or a "retrieved from" statement if an online source contains a DOI. Include the DOI after the publication information.
- **URL:** You should include the URL for most works accessed online, including databases, that don't have a DOI. If the source can be located from the site's home page, give only the URL of the home page. If a URL must be divided on two or more lines, only break the address before slashes or punctuation marks (except within "http://").
- **Databases:** In general, you include the name of a database only when it is essential for locating the source (such as a dissertation, an abstract, or an article found only on a specialized database). If you know that the database is difficult to locate, also give its URL.
- **Retrieval date:** Do not include the date you retrieved the information unless the item is likely to be changed in the future (such as a wiki).
- **Nonretrievable sources:** Don't include a personal communication such as an e-mail message in your References list; instead, cite it in the text with a parenthetical notation saying it's a personal communication. (Also see item 66.) If you have a scholarly reason to cite a message from a newsgroup, forum, or electronic mailing list that is available in an electronic archive, then see items 52 and 53.

ELECTRONIC BOOKS

36. Entire Electronic Book—APA

Provide information about the print version, if available. The retrieval statement gives the URL of the database containing the work. (See also item 37.)

Eaton, A. W. (1889). *Acadian legends and lyrics*. London, UK: White & Allen. Retrieved from http://
www.canadiana.org/

37. Chapter from Electronic Book—APA

Gembris, H. (2006). The development of musical abilities. In R. Colwell (Ed.). *MENC handbook of musical cognition and development* (pp. 124–164). New York, NY: Oxford University Press. Retrieved from http://site.ebrary.com

38. Thesis or Dissertation—APA

Stuart, G. A. (2006). *Exploring the Harry Potter book series: A study of adolescent reading motivation* [Doctoral dissertation]. Retrieved from ProQuest Digital Dissertations. (AAT 3246355)

The number in parentheses at the end is the accession number.

ELECTRONIC JOURNALS

39. Article with DOI Assigned—APA

Guring, R., & Vespia, K. (2007). Looking good, teaching well? Linking liking, looks, and learning. *Teaching of Psychology, 34*(1), 5–10. doi:10.1207/s15328023top3401_2

40. Article with No DOI Assigned—APA

Pollard, R. (2002). Evidence of a reduced home field advantage when a team moves to a new stadium. *Journal of Sports Sciences 20*, 969–974. Retrieved from http://0-find.galegroup.com

41. In-Press Article—APA

In-press means that an article has been accepted for publication but has not yet been published in its final form. Therefore, there is no publication date. If there is no DOI, give the full URL. Before you submit your paper, check again to see if the final version is available.

George, S. (in press). How accurately should we estimate the anatomical source of exhaled nitric oxide? *Journal of Applied Physiology.* doi:10.1152 /japplphysiol.00111.2008

OTHER ELECTRONIC PERIODICALS

42. Newspaper Article—APA

For articles accessed online, replace the page numbers with the news organization's URL.

Perkins, T. (2005, November 22). Conrad Black's Chicago court date set for Tuesday: U.S. Attorney's office. *CP Online.* Retrieved from http://www.thecanadianpress.com/

43. Online Magazine Content Not Found in Print Version—APA

MacQueen, K. (2011, June 8). The case for a national drug plan. *Macleans, ca.* Retrieved from http:// www2.macleans.ca/

44. Webpage or Article on Website—APA

The Banff Centre. (2010, July). *Parks Canada's youth videography project.* Retrieved from http://www.banffcentre.ca/

ELECTRONIC REFERENCE MATERIALS

45. Online Encyclopedia—APA

Turing test. (2008). In *Encyclopedia Britannica.* Retrieved from http://www.britannica.com/bps /topic/609757/Turing-test

46. Online Dictionary—APA

Asparagus, (n.d.). *Merriam-Webster's online dictionary.* Retrieved from http:// dictionary.reference.com/browse/asparagus

47. Online Handbook—APA

Gembris, H. (2006). The development of musical abilities. In R. Colwell (Ed.), *MENC handbook of musical cognition and development* (pp. 124–164). Retrieved from http://0-site.ebrary.com

48. Wiki—APA

Machine learning, (n.d.). Retrieved January 5, 2008, from Artificial Intelligence Wiki: http://www.ifi
.unizh.ch/ailab/aiwiki/aiw.cgi

Note that *n.d.* means "no date."

ELECTRONIC ABSTRACTS

49. Abstract from a Secondary Source—APA

Waulther, J. B., Van Der Heide, B., Kim, S., Westerman, D., & Tong, S. (2008). The role of friends'
appearance and behavior on evaluations of individuals on Facebook: Are we known by the
company we keep? *Human Communication Research 34*(1), 28–49. Abstract retrieved from
PsycINFO database. (Accession no. 200810185)

50. Abstract Submitted for Meeting or Poster Session—APA

Wang, H. (2007). Dust storms originating in the northern hemisphere of Mars. Paper presented at
the American Geophysical Union 2007 Fall Meeting, San Francisco, CA. Abstract retrieved
from http://www.agu.org /meetings/fm07/?content=program

OTHER ELECTRONIC REFERENCES

51. Personal or Professional Website—APA

Hesse, Doug. (2008, November). Home page. Retrieved from http://portfolio.du.edu/dhesse

The Banff Centre. (2010, July). Retrieved from http://www.banffcentre.ca/

52. Message on a Newsgroup, Online Forum, or Discussion Group—APA

Boyle, F. (2002, October 11). Psyche: Cemi field theory: The hard problem made easy [Online forum
comment]. Retrieved from news://sci.psychology.consciousness

53. Message on an Electronic Mailing List (LISTSERV)—APA

Haswell, R. (2005, October 17). Re: A new graphic/text interface [Electronic mailing list message].
Retrieved from http://lists.asu.edu/archives /wpa-l.html

APA advises using the term *electronic mailing list*, as LISTSERV is the name of specific
software.

54. Course Home Page—APA

Hart, A. (2011, Winter). Studies in contemporary literature [Course home page]. Retrieved from
http://www.english.ubc.ca/courses/winter20117474d-003.htm

55. Blog Post—APA

McLemee, S. (2008, January 1). To whom it may concern [Web log post]. Retrieved from http://
www.artsjournal.com/quickstudy/

56. Video Blog Post—APA

Wesch, M. (2007, January 31). Web *2.0 . . . the machine is us/ing us* [Video file]. Retrieved from
http://www.youtube.com/watch?v=6gmP4nkOEOE

57. Online Digital Recording—APA

Gould, G. (1981). *Tape 1087: Orillia Opera House test* [Audio file]. Retrieved from http://www
.collectionscanada.ca/glenngould/028010-700-e.html

58. Audio Podcast—APA

Suzuki, D. (2010, July 5). *The bottom line* [Audio podcast]. Retrieved from http://www.cbc.ca
/thebottomline/2010/07/

59. Online Television Program—APA

Mercer, R. (Writer/Actor). (2011, January 18). Season 8—episode 12 [Television series episode]. In
G. Lunz (Producer), *The Rick Mercer Report*. Retrieved from http://www.cbc.ca/video/#/Shows
/1221254309/ID=1750748073

If writers or directors can be identified, list them in the author position. Producers go in
the editor position. Include the episode title, if any, and the title of the series. If it is a
one-time program, list only the title.

60. Online Advertisement—APA

BlackBerry PlayBook. (2011, May 2). [Advertisement]. Retrieved from http://www.edmontonjournal.com

61. Computer Software or Video Game—APA

Tom Clancy's splinter cell trilogy [Video game]. (2011). Montreal, QC: Ubisoft.

Provide an author name, if available. Standard software (Microsoft Word) and program
languages (C++) don't need to be given in the References list. The name of a software
program is not italicized.

62. Brochure—APA

In Vancouver Web Services. (2010). *Website design and hosting in Vancouver* [Brochure]. Retrieved
from http://www.invancouver.com/

63. Policy Brief—APA

Sharpe, A., Arsenault, J.-F., Lapointe, S., & Cowan, F. (2009). *The effect of increasing Aboriginal
educational attainment on the labour force, output and the fiscal balance* (CSLS Research
Report 2009-3). Retrieved from Centre for the Study of Living Standards website: http://www
.csls.ca/reports/csls2009-3.pdf

With a brief, a report, or a corporate document that has an author, give the name of the
sponsoring organization.

64. Presentation Slides—APA

Laursen, F. (2007). *European Union Centre of Excellence (EUCE) Dalhousie University* [PowerPoint
slides]. Retrieved from http://euce.dal.ca/Files /EUCE-January2007.pdf

65. Graphs, Maps, Other Images—APA

Hurricane Rita [Interactive map]. (2005, September 24). Retrieved from http://www.nytimes.com
/packages/html/national/20050923_RITA_GRAPHIC/index.html

OTHER NONPRINT REFERENCES

66. Interview—APA

In APA style, a personal interview is not included in the References list. Cite the interview in the text as a personal communication.

Max Brooks (personal communication, August 30, 2012) endorses this view.

67. Lecture, Speech, or Address—APA

Hawking, S. (2010, June 20). Address given at the Perimeter Institute, Waterloo, ON. Retrieved from http://www.youtube.com/watch?v=IpT1ANHlXpk

68. Film, Videotape, or DVD—APA

Ego Filmarts/ZDF (Producer), & Egoyan, A. (Director). (1993). *Calendar* [Motion picture]. Canada/Armenia/Germany: Zeitgeist Films.

Madden, J. (Director), Parfitt, D., Gigliotti, D., Weinstein, H., Zwick, E., & Norman, M. (Producers). (2003). *Shakespeare in love* [DVD]. (Original motion picture released 1998).

69. Music Recording—APA

Cohen, L. (Performer). (1988). Tower of song. On *I'm your man* [CD]. Toronto, ON: Sony Music Canada.

Smetana, B. (1975). *My country* [Recorded by the Czech Philharmonic Orchestra with K. Ancerl conducting]. [Record]. London, UK: Vanguard Records.

70. Live Performance—APA

APA style does not require a live performance to be listed in the References list. You can follow this model, however, if it is essential to include the details of a performance.

Shakespeare, W. (Author), McAnuff, D. (Director), Hunt, S. J., Dennehy, B., & Rooney, T. (Performers). (2011, July 3). *Twelfth night* [Theatrical performance]. Stratford ON: Festival Theatre.

71. Work of Art, Photograph, or Musical Composition—APA

Pratt, C. (1968). Shop *on an island* [Artwork]. London, ON: London Regional Art Gallery.

McMillan, D. (2001). *Village grave. Commemoration Day, April, 1995* [Photograph]. Winnipeg, MB: Winnipeg Art Gallery.

Schubert, F. (1822). *Unfinished symphony* [Musical composition].

72. Radio or Television Broadcast—APA

Moore, Y., & Schuyler, L. (Writers), & Deacon, C. (Director). (2011, April 8). Chasing pavements: Part 2 [Television series episode]. In L. Schuyler & S. Stohn (Producers), *Degrassi: The Next Generation*. Toronto, ON: Epitome Pictures.

If you're citing a television series produced by and seen on only one station, cite its call letters.

73. Information Service—APA

Davies, S. (2002). *School choice by default? Understanding the growing demand for private tutoring in Canada* (Report No. NALL-WP-65). Toronto, ON: Research Network on New Approaches to Lifelong Learning, Ontario Institute for Studies in Education of the University of Toronto. (ERIC Documentation Reproduction Service No. ED479073)

74. Advertisement—APA

An appeal [Advertisement]. (2005). *Canadian Journal of Communication, 30*(3), 435.

75. Image—APA

If you're reproducing an image in your paper, follow the guidelines for graphics in item 16 in 37c. Include the citation in the body of your paper. If you're only referring to an image, cite the photographer or illustrator (if known), the title (or a brief description of the image), and source information.

Riel in court [Photograph]. (2005). *The Canadian Historical Review, 86*(3), 467.

37g What are APA format guidelines for research papers?

Ask whether your instructor has instructions for preparing a final draft. If not, you can use the APA guidelines here. For illustration of these guidelines, see the student paper in 37h.2.

GENERAL INSTRUCTIONS—APA

Use 8 1/2-by-11-inch (standard size) white paper. The APA *Publication Manual* recommends double-spacing for a final manuscript of a student research paper. Set at least a one-inch (about 2.5 cm) margin on the left (slightly more if you submit your paper in a binder) and leave no less than one inch on the right and at the bottom.

Leave one-half inch (about 1.25 cm) from the top edge of the paper to the title-and-page-number line (*header*). Leave another one-half inch (or one inch from the top edge of the paper) before the next line on the page, whether that's a heading (such as "Abstract" or "Footnotes") or a line of your paper.

ALERT: Most word-processing programs set the top and bottom margins at one inch (2.5 cm) as their default. Also, they generally set the "header" function at a default of one-half inch (1.25 cm). Therefore, formatting the margins for your paper is probably less troublesome than it might seem. You simply need to check the default settings. •

Use indents of one-half inch (1.25 cm) for the first line of all paragraphs, except in an abstract, the first line of which isn't indented. Don't justify the right margin. Indent footnotes one-half inch.

ORDER OF PARTS—APA

Number all pages consecutively. Use this order for the parts of your paper:

1. Title page
2. Abstract (if required)
3. Body of the paper
4. References
5. Footnotes, if any
6. Appendices and attachments, if any (questionnaires, data sheets, or other material your instructor asks you to include)

TITLE-AND-PAGE-NUMBER LINE FOR ALL PAGES—APA

Use a title-and-page-number line on all pages of your paper. Leaving a margin of one-half inch (about 1.25 cm) from the top edge of the paper, type the title (use a shortened version if necessary) at the left margin in capital letters, and then type the page number at the right margin. End the title-and-page-number line one inch (about 2.5 cm) from the right edge of the paper. Ask whether your instructor wants you to include your last name in this title-and-page-number line. The "header" feature on a word-processing program will help you create the title-and-page-number line.

TITLE PAGE—APA

Use a separate title page. On it, begin with the title-and-page-number line described above, using the numeral 1 for this first page. Then, centre the complete title horizontally and place it on the upper half of the page. Use two or more double-spaced lines if the title is long. Don't italicize (or underline) the title or enclose it in quotation marks. On the next line, centre your name, and below that centre the course title and section, your professor's name, and the date.

ALERTS: (1) Use the following guidelines for capitalizing the title of your own paper and for capitalizing titles you mention in the body of your paper. (For capitalization of titles in the References list, where different rules apply, see Quick Reference 37.1.)

(2) Use a capital letter for the first word of your title and for the first word of a subtitle, if any. Start every noun, pronoun, verb, adverb, and adjective with a capital letter. Capitalize each main word in a hyphenated compound word (two or more words used together to express one idea): *Father-in-Law, Self-Consciousness.* Capitalize the word after a colon or a dash.

(3) Don't capitalize articles (*a, an, the*) unless one of the other capitalization rules applies. Don't capitalize prepositions and conjunctions unless they are four or more letters long. Don't capitalize the word *to* used in an infinitive. ●

ABSTRACT—APA

See 37d for advice about what to include in an abstract of your paper. Type the abstract on a separate page, using the numeral 2 in the title-and-page-number line. Centre the word *Abstract* one inch (2.5 cm) from the top of the paper. Don't italicize or underline it or enclose it in quotation marks. Double-space below this title, and then start your abstract, double-spacing it. Don't indent the first line.

SET-OFF QUOTATIONS—APA

Set off (indent in block style) quotations of forty words or more. Double-space to start a new line for the quoted words, indenting each line of the (double-spaced) quotation one-half inch (about 1.25 cm) or five spaces from the left margin. Don't enclose the quoted words in quotation marks.

If you're quoting part of a paragraph or one complete paragraph, don't indent the first line more than one-half inch. But if you quote two or more paragraphs, indent the first line of the second and subsequent paragraphs one inch (about 2.5 cm).

At the end of the quotation, leave one space after the sentence-ending punctuation, and then give the parenthetical citation. Begin a new line to resume your own words.

REFERENCES LIST—APA

Start a new page for your References list immediately after the end of the body of your paper. Use a title-and-page-number line. Drop down one inch (about 2.5 cm) from the top of the paper and centre the word *References*. Don't italicize, underline, or put it in quotation marks. Double-space below it. Start the first line of each entry at the left margin, and indent any subsequent lines one-half inch (about 1.25 cm) from the left margin. Use this "hanging indent" style unless your instructor prefers a different one. Double-space within each entry and between entries.

NOTES—APA

Whenever you use a content note in your paper (37e), try to arrange your sentence so that the note number falls at the end. The best place for a note number is after the sentence-ending punctuation. Use a numeral raised slightly above the line of words and immediately after the final punctuation mark.

Put any notes on a separate page after the last page of your References list. Use a title-and-page-number line. Then, centre the word *Footnotes* one inch (about 2.5 cm) from the top of the paper. Don't italicize (or underline) it or put it in quotation marks. APA style uses the heading *Footnotes* even for one or more pages of endnotes; this reflects the needs of scholarly journals that format content notes as footnotes.

On the next line, indent one-half inch (about 1.25 cm) and begin the note. Raise the note number slightly (you can use the superscript feature in your word-processing program), and then start the words of your note, leaving no space after the number. If the note is more than one typed line, don't indent any line after the first. Double-space throughout.

37h A student's APA-style research paper

The final section of this chapter presents a student research paper prepared to conform to APA style. We discuss the research, planning, drafting, and revising processes of the student, Shawn Hickson, and show the final draft of the paper, including its abstract.

Case Study

Shawn Hickson was given this assignment for a research paper in a second-term writing class: Write a research paper of 1250 to 1700 words about an aspect of contemporary life that interests you. For guidance, refer to the *Simon & Schuster Handbook for Writers*, Chapters 32 through 34. Use the documentation style of the American Psychological Association (APA) explained in Chapter 37. Your topic and working bibliography are due in two weeks. An early draft of your paper is due two weeks later. (Try to get that early draft close to what you hope will be your last draft, so that comments from me and from your peers can concretely help you write an excellent final draft.) Your final draft is due one week after I've returned your early draft (with comments) to you.

37h.1 Researching and writing the paper

When Shawn Hickson read her assignment, she was both pleased and intimidated by the number of choices she had. She started PLANNING by listing several broad topics, finding that she was most interested in current technologies: cell phones, pagers, video games, computers, and MP3 players. She added to her list by thinking how each of these influenced several areas of life: school, work, entertainment, social life, communication. She recalled a lecture from a sociology course about how people today communicated more extensively than at any other point in history, yet they were spending less time together in person. This led to an early research question, "How do face-to-face interactions compare with cell-phone or online interactions?" While she personally thought online dating services were strange, she was intrigued that they seemed to be popular among many people. She wondered, then, what role physical appearance played.

Shawn checked to see whether she could find enough sources useful for research on this topic. From her home computer, she went to her university's library home page. She searched the catalogue with several keywords, including "physical appearance," "relationships," "dating," "physical attraction," and "Internet dating." She also used combinations of these terms in a Boolean search and generated a list of books, including several that hadn't been checked out. Next, she turned to online databases, which generated citations for dozens of journal, magazine, and newspaper articles. Some of them had full-text versions online, and she printed those that looked promising. Then, she went to the university library to check out several books and to review some other materials that were available only in the library.

Shawn also used the Google search engine to browse her keywords. However, she tended to turn up dating sites and bulletin boards. She thought some were entertaining and might be interesting as examples, but she ultimately decided they didn't have enough substance to use for this particular paper.

From all the sources she identified, Shawn compiled a WORKING BIBLIOGRAPHY, typing sources into a file on her computer. The working bibliography that she submitted consisted of twenty-nine SOURCES, though she had reviewed and rejected about ten others, including several eliminated because they were of poor quality or seemed too technical for her to grasp easily. Shawn didn't intend to use all twenty-nine sources, but she wasn't yet sure where her drafting would go. Not surprisingly, her instructor urged her to reduce the list once DRAFTING began; otherwise, Shawn would risk writing too little about too much. The instructor also recommended a colleague in the psychology department who had a scholarly interest in what attracted people to each other. Shawn arranged a brief interview with the psychology instructor, who directed her to some classic studies on the topic.

After spending several hours reading sources and taking content notes, Shawn began to weed out material. She narrowed her list to sixteen sources, took detailed notes on each, and began to group her material into emerging subtopics. Eventually, she dropped five of the sources.

Shawn realized that she'd still need to narrow the TOPIC sufficiently to shape a THESIS STATEMENT. The narrowing process worried her because she had been told in other courses that her topics for research papers were too broad. She was determined this time to avoid that same problem.

To start drafting her paper, Shawn spread her note cards around for easy reference, but she felt somewhat overwhelmed by the amount of information at hand, and she wrote only a few sentences. To break through, she decided to type a DISCOVERY DRAFT to see what she had absorbed from her reading and notetaking. That very rough draft became her vehicle for many things, including creating an effective thesis statement, inserting source information according to APA documentation style, and checking the logical arrangement of her material.

Revising for Shawn started with her thesis statement, a process that helped her further narrow her focus. She started with "Physical appearances affect people's responses to each other," which her research supported but which was extremely broad and bland. Her next version served her well: "When people meet face to face, they form opinions based on physical characteristics including age, attractiveness, ethnicity, and appearance of wealth, but when they meet online they have to form opinions using other criteria." This thesis proved very useful in revising the discovery draft into a true first draft, but the process made it clear to Shawn that she was covering too much for a 1250- to 1750-word research paper, and she dropped some material. She decided first to inform readers about the affect of appearances (or their absence) on first meetings and then to explore why people responded as they did. For her final draft, Shawn used this more focused thesis statement: "The presence or absence of physical characteristics during first meetings can influence how people respond to each other."

Shawn had to attend very closely to the details of correct parenthetical IN-TEXT CITATIONS (37b and 37c) within her paper and a correct REFERENCES list (37f and 37g) at the end. Because she'd used MLA DOCUMENTATION STYLE in other courses, she made sure not to confuse the two styles. For example, she saw that APA-style parenthetical citations include the year of publication (whereas MLA-style citations don't). For format and style details of the References list at the end of her paper, she found Quick Reference 37.1 especially helpful.

As Shawn checked the logical arrangement of her material, she dropped some aspects of physical appearance when she finally narrowed her topic sufficiently. A couple of hours at the computer led her to develop examples beyond attractions in dating, including how teachers and parents treat children whom they judge to be cute, and how gender and ethnicity influence people's expectations. Shawn learned from her research experiences the difference between researching a topic too broadly (and therefore gathering too many sources for the assignment) and researching a few aspects of a topic in depth by focusing on selected sources. Her final draft, which appears on the following pages, draws on eleven sources, a number that is down considerably from the twenty-nine with which she started.

37h.2 Analyzing the research paper

Shawn's paper, including her title page and abstract page, is shown here. For guidelines on writing an abstract, see 37d and 37g.

↑ ½ inch (1.25 cm)

EFFECT OF PHYSICAL CUES   1 ◄—►

Put shortened title at left margin and page number at right in the header.

1 inch (2.5 cm)

Use the first page for the title page.

Centre the title, student name, course, instructor, and date on the page. Use double spacing.

The Effect of Physical Cues on New Relationships

Shawn Hickson

General Psychology 131

Professor M. Staley

May 10, 2013

↑ ½ inch (1.25 cm)

EFFECT OF PHYSICAL CUES   2 ◄—►

1 inch (2.5 cm)

Abstract

Double-space

Place abstract if required, on the second page

Communication via the Internet has allowed people to form friendships and relationships in new ways. Research shows that individuals respond to new acquaintances at least partly according to how attractive they perceive the new friends to be. The absence of physical cues in Internet chat rooms or e-mail discussions means that people form impressions that are

◄—► less affected by superficial factors. As the Internet changes, however,

1 inch (2.5 cm) these differences may diminish.

continued ➤

The Effect of Physical Cues on New Relationships

Over the past 20 years, the Internet has enabled people to meet others from around the world with a few simple keystrokes. Occasionally, these interactions extend beyond the confines of chat rooms and e-mail discussions, so that individuals arrange to meet in person. Of course, people have learned to be cautious because others online can easily misrepresent themselves and their intentions. Nonetheless, lasting friendships, romances, and even marriages have resulted from first interactions that have happened online. Surprisingly, research shows that compared to people who meet face to face, those who meet on the Internet develop a greater liking for each other (McKenna, Green, & Gleason, 2003). This result is an example of a larger phenomenon: The presence or absence of physical characteristics during first meetings can influence how people respond to each other.

Judging People by Appearances

It can be troubling to know that something as shallow as someone's physical attractiveness can affect how people treat that person. However, the truth is that even if people do not mean to judge others based on their appearance, they tend to do so. Dion, Berscheid, and Walster (1972) showed research participants pictures of stereotypically attractive and unattractive individuals and then asked them to judge the people in the photographs according to several personality traits. The researchers found that the more attractive a person was judged to be, the more desirable traits that person was judged to have. For example, people might believe that beautiful women are smarter or that handsome men are more clever. Several studies found that individuals assume that attractive people will agree with them more often than those who are unattractive; they assume that the attractive person will be more like them (Miyake & Zuckerman, 1993).

APA STYLE: 1-inch (2.5-cm) margins; double-space throughout

INTRODUCTION

IN-TEXT CITATION: Page numbers not needed for paraphrase or summary; ask if your instructor wants them included

THESIS STATEMENT: Paper's focus

FIRST HEADING: Set headings in bold type

PARAGRAPH 2: Background information

APA-STYLE INTEGRATED CITATION: Author names cited in text; date cited in parentheses

(Proportions shown in this paper are adjusted to fit space limitations of this book. Follow actual dimensions discussed in this book and your instructor's directions.)

continued ➤

APA

PARA-
GRAPH 3:
Provides
further
examples of
thesis

Even when people are young, appearance colours how others perceive them. Studies of preschoolers show that both peers and teachers treat children differently on the basis of their physical appearances. Both expect attractive children to be more active socially, and teachers believe that attractive children have more academic potential (Kachel, 1996). More surprisingly, research from the University of Alberta (McLean, 2005) shows that children's physical appearances may affect how their very own parents treat them.

PARA-
GRAPH 4:
Provides
information
and bridges
to next
paragraph

Attractiveness has a different importance for men and women. While both sexes value physical attractiveness in brief relationships, men tend to view it as vital in long-term relationships. In contrast, women tend to regard other qualities more highly, especially financial stability and high social status (Singh, 2004).

PARA-
GRAPH 5:
Summarizes
research
findings

Replaces
names with
et al. because
this is second
reference to
same work
with multiple
authors

However, for men and women alike, physical cues at the first meeting can shape not only impressions but also behaviours. Snyder, Tanke, and Berscheid (1977) showed male participants a picture of either an attractive or an unattractive female and then asked the men to rate her personality traits. Results of this initial rating were very similar to those obtained by Dion et al. (1972). Snyder's group next took the study one step further. Each male participant then had a phone conversation with a female participant who he thought was the female from the picture. In these conversations, men treated their phone partners as if they possessed the characteristics they believed went along with the photograph. However, the men knew nothing about the women; they assigned the women traits simply on the basis of a photograph. Even more interesting, women responded in a manner that was consistent with the images that were being projected onto them. Attractive women who were treated as if they were unattractive actually behaved as if they were, and vice versa. What happened was a clear example of a self-fulfilling prophecy (Snyder et al., 1977). Judgments based on appearance clouded other realities.

continued ➤

Meeting on the Internet

Meeting people online, especially through e-mail or in a chat room, obviously differs from meeting them face to face because there are no physical cues, only other people's words. Do people meeting in that environment engage one another differently? A study conducted by McKenna et al. (2003) suggests that they do. McKenna and colleagues divided participants into two groups: an experimental group and a control group. All participants had two separate conversations, one in person and the other online. Both conversations took place with the same person. Those in the control group knew this, but those in the experimental group believed they were talking with two different people. Participants in both groups then rated the quality of the interactions on three factors: (a) the quality of the conversations, (b) the degree to which they felt they had gotten to know the other person, and (c) how well they liked the other person in general. For the control groups, the ratings were similar in all categories, for both in-person and online conversations. However, differences emerged with the participants who thought they had been interacting with two different people, not the same person: They consistently rated the Internet partner higher in all three categories.

One probable explanation for this occurrence is that Internet interactions do away with traditional physical judgments. Attractiveness, extreme shyness, speech impediments, and many other superficial factors can hinder people from expressing their true selves and accepting others who are deficient in one area or another (McKenna et al., 2003). Because early judgments determine how two people will interact, a physical meeting makes it harder for some individuals to become comfortable and disclose themselves at the same level as they would in a situation where physical cues don't matter.

By the time people engage in online romantic relationships, according to researcher Malin Sveningsson (2002), they have already established a written relationship based on common interests. They know each other on a basis other than physical characteristics. Most

SECOND HEADING

PARAGRAPH 6: Explains research on Internet meetings

Creates clarity by using letters in parentheses to identify factors

PARAGRAPH 7: Interprets findings summarized in previous paragraph

PARAGRAPH 8: Explains interests of people meeting online

continued ➤

APA-STYLE
IN-TEXT
CITATION:
Requires page
number for
direct quotation;
uses p. not
page

Shawn uses
brackets in
quotation to
show that she
(not the
speaker) has
altered wording
to improve
clarity

Uses statistics
to illustrate
example

people who enter chat rooms do so with the hope of making "contact with people, getting into a rewarding discussion, or just small-talking and having a good time in general" (p. 49). Those who meet on Internet chat sites or mailing lists nearly always come together over a shared interest. A chat room frequenter named Richard explained his reasons for taking part in online conversations: "When you enter a place like that, you just want somebody to talk to . . . so you actively [look] for people who [have] something to say. And all the time you [make] comments just to find someone who [has] something to tell" (p. 50). Women and men are nearly equal in their use of the Internet for purposes of community. The Cyber Dialogue group found that about 27% of women and 31% of men first went to the Internet to "join an online community" and that 85% of women and 82% of men came to believe that "the Internet community is an important part" of their lives (Hawfield & Lyons, 1998, p. 4). It appears, then, that the primary motivation for both is not physical but rather communicative.

PARA-
GRAPH 9:
Gives other
factors that
influence
relationships

Attractiveness is hardly the only physical quality by which men and women judge others. Broad features of identity such as race, gender, and ethnicity can also trigger uninformed responses. Researcher Lisa Nakamura (2002) found that when a person's race is revealed on the Internet, he or she can be just as subject to prejudicial assumptions as if the reality had been revealed face to face. Because of this, some people online deliberately try to mask their race or gender. They want others to judge them by what they say and think rather than by how they look, especially in a first encounter.

PARA-
GRAPH 10:
Explains how
increased use of
images and
sounds changes
nature of online
meetings

Whether Internet communication will continue to support first meetings that occur purely in writing is uncertain. With the increased use of digital images and audio, the Internet has begun to provide more and more physical cues. Participants in chat rooms tend to request images earlier as a sign of interest. People can post false photographs or videos, of course, but deception complicates any desired face-to-face meeting later on. Further, the sound of a person's voice shapes others' perceptions. When voice communication over the Internet becomes more prevalent, it is likely that our stereotypical notions

continued ➤

EFFECT OF PHYSICAL CUES   7

will return. Dr. Clifford Nass of Stanford University has predicted that

APA-STYLE
IN-TEXT
CITATION:

when voice becomes a part of online interaction, people will "apply

Includes
paragraph or

gender stereotypes" (as cited in Eisenberg, 2000, para. 6). Nass says that

screen number
for direct

people tend to interpret the female voice as being "less accurate," with

quotation from
online source

deeper male voices projecting authority. Some voices are perceived as

without
numbered pages

more attractive than others, too.

Conclusion

CONCLUSION:
Summarizes
main points
and looks to
the future

Research on Internet relationships suggests that communication
without visual cues can increase people's acceptance of one another. In
face-to-face meetings, people form impressions based solely on physical
appearance, impressions that influence both the way they treat others
and the way those people respond. People who are treated well, for example, tend to take on positive characteristics. Because Internet conversations rely more heavily on the quality of communication than on
superficial factors, meeting online allows people to suspend judgments
based on appearance. This advantage may disappear as images and
sounds increasingly accompany online meetings. Perhaps society
would be healthier if people judged others not by their looks but by their
character as expressed in words and ideas; however, the current tendency to treat stereotypically attractive and unattractive people differently shows the remoteness of that ideal.

continued ➢

APA

APA

References

Begins References on new page

Dion, K., Berscheid, E., & Walster, E. (1972). What is beautiful is good. *Journal of Personality and Social Psychology, 24*(3), 285–290. doi:10.1037/h0033731

Double-space throughout

Eisenberg, A. (2000, October 12). Mars and Venus on the Net: Gender stereotypes prevail. *New York Times on the Web*. Retrieved from http://www.nytimes.com

Lists References in alphabetical order by author

Hawfield, K., & Lyons, E. (1998). *Conventional wisdom about women and Internet use: Refuting traditional perceptions* [Unpublished research paper]. Retrieved from http://elab/vanderbilt./edu /research/papers/html/studentprojects/

Kachel, J. (1996, March). Good looks count during childhood. *Brown University Child and Adolescent Newsletter, 12*(3). Retrieved from http://www.childresearch.net

McKenna, K. Y., Green, A. S., & Gleason, M. E. (2003). Relationship formation on the Internet: What's the big attraction? *Journal of Social Issues, 58*(I), 9–31.

McLean, A. (2005, March 14). Ugly truth: Cute kids loved more. *The National Post*, p. A1.

Miyake, K., & Zuckerman, M. (1993). Beyond personality impressions. *Journal of Personality, 61*(3), 411–436.

Nakamura, L. (2002). *Cybertypes: Race, ethnicity, and identity on the Internet*. New York NY: Routledge.

Singh, D. (2004). Mating strategies of young women: Role of physical attractiveness. *Journal of Sex Research, 41*(1), 43–54. doi:10.1080/00224490409552212

Snyder, M., Tanke, E. D., & Berscheid, E. (1977). Social perception and interpersonal behavior: On the self-fulfilling nature of social stereotypes. *Journal of Personality and Social Psychology, 35*, 656–666.

Provides source information for chapter in a book

Sveningsson, M. (2002). Cyberlove: Creating romantic relationships on the Net. In J. Fornäs, K. Klein, M. Ladendorf, J. Sundén, & M. Sveningsson, (Eds.), *Digital borderlands: Cultural studies of identity and interactivity on the Internet* (pp. 48–78). New York, NY: Lang.

Chapter 38

CHICAGO MANUAL (CM), COUNCIL OF SCIENCE EDITORS (CSE), AND IEEE DOCUMENTATION

This chapter presents three more systems of documentation (in addition to MLA STYLE in Chapter 36 and APA STYLE in Chapter 37). They are the styles of the University of Chicago Press (CM), the Council of Science Editors (CSE), and the IEEE. The following directory provides a list of the CM-style entries you'll find in this chapter. For the CSE directory, turn to page 566, and for IEEE, turn to page 575.

CM-STYLE DOCUMENTATION

CM-STYLE DIRECTORY

CM

38a What is CM-style documentation?

The sixteenth edition of *The Chicago Manual of Style* (CM; Chicago: University of Chicago Press, 2010) presents the latest **CM style** recommendations on documentation, as outlined in this handbook. If you need more information than we provide here, consult *The Chicago Manual* itself or its website at <http://www.chicagomanualofstyle.org/>.

The CM endorses two styles of documentation. One CM style is an author-date style, similar to the APA style of IN-TEXT CITATIONS (Chapter 37), that includes a list of sources usually titled "Works Cited" or "References." The other CM style uses a **bibliographic note system**. This system gives information about each source in two places: (1) in a footnote (at the bottom of a page) or an endnote (on a separate page following your paper) and, (2) if required, in a BIBLIOGRAPHY that begins on a separate page. We present the bibliographic note system here because it's often used in such humanities subjects as art, music, history, philosophy, and sometimes English. Within the bibliographic note system, there are two sub-styles: "full" and "abbreviated."

THE FULL BIBLIOGRAPHIC NOTE SYSTEM IN CM STYLE

The CM full bibliographic note system requires you to give complete information, in a footnote or an endnote, the first time you cite a source. Because you're giving full information, you don't need to include a bibliography page. If you cite a source a second time, you provide shortened information that includes the last name(s) of the author(s) and the key words in the work's title. The following example uses the full bibliographic note system.

TEXT

Ignatieff opens his analysis of Quebec's place in the Canada of the 1990s with an anecdote from his childhood.[3]

FULL FOOTNOTE (SAME PAGE) OR ENDNOTE (SEPARATE PAGE FOLLOWING TEXT)

3. Michael Ignatieff, *Blood and Belonging: Journeys into the New Nationalism* (Toronto: Penguin, 1994), 148.

SECOND CITATION OF THIS SOURCE

6. Ignatieff, *Blood and Belonging*, 156.

THE ABBREVIATED BIBLIOGRAPHIC NOTE SYSTEM, PLUS BIBLIOGRAPHY, IN CM STYLE

In the abbreviated bibliographic note system, even your first endnote or footnote provides only brief information about the source. You provide complete information in a bibliography, which appears as a separate page at the end of the paper. Following is an example using the abbreviated bibliographic note system.

TEXT

Ignatieff opens his analysis of Quebec's place in the Canada of the 1990s with an anecdote from his childhood.[3]

ABBREVIATED FOOTNOTE (SAME PAGE) OR ENDNOTE (SEPARATE PAGE FOLLOWING TEXT)

3. Ignatieff, *Blood and Belonging*, 148.

BIBLIOGRAPHY (SEPARATE PAGE AT END OF THE PAPER)

Ignatieff, Michael. *Blood and Belonging: Journeys into the New Nationalism*. Toronto: Penguin, 1994.

ALERT: Ask your instructor which style he or she prefers. Remember that CM style requires a separate bibliography only if you use the abbreviated notes style. ●

Quick Reference 38.1 provides guidelines for compiling CM-style bibliographic notes.

QUICK REFERENCE 38.1

Guidelines for compiling CM-style bibliographic notes

TITLE AND PLACEMENT OF NOTES

If you're using endnotes, place them all on a separate page, before your bibliography. Centre the heading "Notes," without using italics, underlining, or quotation marks, an inch (about 2.5 cm) from the top of the page. If you're using footnotes, place them at the bottom of the page on which the source needs to be credited. Never place a title above a footnote. CM generally uses blank space to divide the footnote(s) from the body text but puts a line above the ending of a footnote that runs onto a second page.

TITLE AND PLACEMENT OF BIBLIOGRAPHY

The abbreviated notes style requires a bibliography, which begins on a separate page at the end of the paper, following the endnotes page. An inch (about 2.5 cm) from the top

continued ➤

of the page, centre the heading "Bibliography" or "Works Cited" (either is acceptable in CM style). Don't underline the heading or put it in quotation marks.

FORMAT FOR ENDNOTES AND FOOTNOTES

Include an endnote or a footnote every time you use a source. Number notes sequentially throughout your paper whether you're using endnotes or footnotes. Use superscript (raised) arabic numerals for the footnote or endnote numbers in your paper. Position note numbers after any punctuation mark except the dash and preferably at the end of a sentence, unless that is so far from the source material that the citation would be confusing. Ask your instructor if you may use raised numbers in the endnote or footnote itself, or if he or she prefers that you place the number, followed by a period, on the same line as the content of the note. Single-space both within each note and between notes. Indent each note's first line by a 0.3-inch tab (0.75 cm), which equals about three characters, but place subsequent lines flush left at the margin.

SPACING AFTER PUNCTUATION

A single space follows all punctuation, including the period.

AUTHORS' NAMES

In endnotes and footnotes, give the name in standard (first-name-first) order, with names and initials as given in the original source. Use the word *and* before the last author's name if your source has more than one author.

In the bibliography, invert the name: last name, first name. If a work has two or more authors, invert only the first author's name. If your source has up to ten authors, give all the authors' names. If your source has eleven or more authors, list only the first seven and use *et al.* for the rest.

CAPITALIZATION OF SOURCE TITLES

Capitalize the first and last words and all major words in titles.

SPECIAL TREATMENT OF TITLES

Use italics for titles of long works, and use quotation marks around the titles of shorter works. Omit *A, An,* and *The* from the titles of newspapers and periodicals. For an unfamiliar newspaper title, list the city (and province or state, in parentheses, where useful for clarity): *London (ON) Free Press,* for example. Use postal abbreviations for provinces and states.

PUBLICATION INFORMATION

Enclose publication information in parentheses. Use a colon and one space after the city of publication. Give complete publishers' names or abbreviate them according to standard abbreviations in *Books in Print.* Omit *Co., Inc.,* and so on. Spell out *University* or abbreviate to *Univ.* Never use *U* alone. Also spell out *Press;* never use *P* alone. Don't abbreviate publication months.

PAGE NUMBERS

For inclusive page numbers, give the full second number for 2 through 99. For 100 and beyond, give the full second number only if a shortened version would be ambiguous: 243–47, 202–6, 300–404. List all discontinuous page numbers. (See "First Endnote or

continued ➤

Footnote: Book" below in this box.) Use a comma to separate parenthetical publication information from the page numbers that follow it. Use the abbreviations *p.* and *pp.* with page numbers only for material from newspapers, for material from journals that do not use volume numbers, and to avoid ambiguity.

CONTENT NOTES

Try to avoid using content notes. If you must use them, use footnotes, not endnotes, with symbols rather than numbers: an asterisk (*) for the first note on a page and a dagger (†) for a second note on that page.

FIRST ENDNOTE OR FOOTNOTE: BOOK

For books, include the author, title, publication information, and page numbers when applicable.

    1. Eudora Welty, *One Writer's Beginnings* (Cambridge, MA: Harvard University Press, 1984), 25–26, 30, 43–51, 208.

FIRST ENDNOTE OR FOOTNOTE: ARTICLE

For articles, include the author, article title, journal title, volume number, year, and page numbers.

    1. D. D. Cochran, W. Daniel Hale, and Christine P. Hissam, "Personal Space Requirements in Indoor versus Outdoor Locations," *Journal of Psychology* 117 (1984): 132–33.

SECOND MENTION IN ENDNOTES OR FOOTNOTES

Second (or later) citations of the same source can be brief. See 38b, item 4 for an explanation.

ELECTRONIC SOURCES

Books and articles consulted online use the same citation formats as those consulted in print. However, in a footnote or endnote, you change the final period to a comma and follow that with the URL or, if possible, the DOI, and then end with a period. In a bibliographic citation, after the final period you include the item's URL or DOI, and follow it with a period. A DOI, or Digital Object Identifier, is a unique code assigned to many publications; it can usually be found on the first page of an online article or in the database. Because a given publication's DOI never changes, it is preferable to a URL for locating a source.

If you have to break a URL or DOI at the end of a line, break it after a colon or a double slash, but before other punctuation and symbols. (You may break it either before *or* after an equals sign or an ampersand.) Don't add a hyphen at the line break or set a hyphen that is part of a URL or DOI at the end of a line.

Some disciplines ask for an access date with all online sources; ask your instructor if you should include one. It goes immediately before the URL or DOI; see 38b, items 34 and 36. When doing your research, it is always a good idea to save a copy of any undated source or any source that seems likely to change without notice, along with the date you consulted it.

Citations of websites and parts of websites also include the date consulted and the URL, as well as the date of publication or last revision.

For electronic works not accessed online, include a description of the medium you consulted (e.g., DVD, CD-ROM); see 38b, item 44.

The CM directory that appears at the beginning of this chapter corresponds to the sample bibliographic note forms that follow. In a few cases, we give sample bibliography forms as well. If you need a model that isn't here, consult *The Chicago Manual of Style*, Sixteenth Edition (Chicago: University of Chicago Press, 2010), which gives footnote, endnote, and bibliography forms for a multitude of sources.

BOOKS AND PARTS OF BOOKS—PRINT

1. Book by One Author—CM

Footnote or Endnote

1. Pierre E. Trudeau, *Federalism and the French Canadians* (Toronto: Macmillan Canada, 1968), 25.

Bibliography

Trudeau, Pierre E. *Federalism and the French Canadians*. Toronto: Macmillan Canada, 1968.

In bibliographic form, the first line is placed flush left to the margin and the second and other lines are indented by a 0.3-inch tab, or 0.75 cm. Periods replace commas after the author's name and title, and parentheses are omitted.

Footnote or Endnote

2. John K. Lynam, Cyrus G. Ndiritu, and Adiel N. Mbabu, *Transformation of Agricultural Research Systems in Africa: Lessons from Kenya* (East Lansing: Michigan State University Press, 2004), 41.

Bibliography

Lynam, John K. Cyrus G. Ndiritu, and Adiel N. Mbabu. *Transformation of Agricultural Research Systems in Africa: Lessons from Kenya*. East Lansing: Michigan State University Press, 2004.

In a bibliography entry, invert only the name of the first author listed.

2. Book by Two or Three Authors—CM

Footnote or Endnote

1. Daniel Drache and Harry Glasbeek, *The Changing Workplace: Reshaping Canada's Industrial Relations System* (Toronto: Lorimer, 1992).

3. Book by More Than Three Authors—CM

For works by or edited by four to ten persons, in a footnote or endnote include only the name of the first author followed by *et al.*, but in the bibliography give all the names. For works with more than ten authors, list only the first seven in the bibliography, followed by *et al.*

1. Wendy Saul et al., *Beyond the Science Fair: Creating a Kids' Inquiry Conference* (Portsmouth, NH: Heinemann, 2005), 72.

4. Multiple Citations of a Single Source—CM

For subsequent references to a work you've already named, use a shortened citation. Give the last name of the author, the title of the work, and the page number, all separated by commas. Shorten the title if it's longer than four words. This example shows the form for a subsequent reference to the work fully described in item 1.

1. Trudeau, *Federalism*, 25.

If there are more than three authors for a source, use only the name of the first author followed by *et al.* The following example shows the shortened citation for the work in item 3.

> 2. Saul et al., *Beyond the Science Fair,* 72.

If you cite two or more authors with the same last name, include first names or initials in each note.

> 2. Pierre Trudeau, *Federalism,* 25.

> 3. G. B. Trudeau, *Revolt,* 128.

If you cite the same source as the source immediately preceding, you may use *Ibid.* (capitalized at the beginning of a note), followed by a comma and the page number, instead of repeating the author's name and the title. (If the page number is also identical to the preceding one, use *Ibid.* alone.)

> 5. Ibid., 152.

5. Book by a Group or Corporate Author—CM

> 1. American Psychological Association, *Publication Manual of the American Psychological Association,* 6th ed. (Washington, DC: American Psychological Association, 2009).

> 2. CBC Massey Lectures Series. *The Lost Massey Lectures: Recovered Classics from Five Great Thinkers* (Toronto: House of Anansi Press, 2007).

If a work issued by an organization has no author listed on the title page, give the name of the organization as the author of the work. The organization may also be the publisher of the work. (The CBC Massey Lectures Series is the corporate author of the book in the second item.)

6. Book with No Author Named—CM

> 1. *The Chicago Manual of Style,* 16th ed. (Chicago: University of Chicago Press, 2010).

Begin the citation with the name of the book.

7. Book with an Author and an Editor—CM

> 1. Pierre Elliott Trudeau, *The Essential Trudeau,* ed. Ron Graham (Toronto: McClelland & Stewart, 1998).

In this position, the abbreviation *ed.* stands for "edited by," not "editor." Therefore, *ed.* is correct whether a work has one or more than one editor. (Also see items 10 and 15.)

8. Translation—CM

> 1. Michel Tremblay, *A Thing of Beauty,* trans. Sheila Fischman (Vancouver: Talon Books, 1998), 44.

The abbreviation *trans.* stands for "translated by," not "translator."

9. Work in Several Volumes or Parts—CM

The following notes show ways to give bibliographic information for a specific place in one volume of a multivolume work. Use whichever you prefer, staying consistent throughout a paper.

> 1. Ernest Jones, *The Last Phase,* vol. 3 of *The Life and Work of Sigmund Freud* (New York: Basic Books, 1957), 97.

> 1. Ernest Jones, *The Life and Work of Sigmund Freud,* vol. 3, *The Last Phase* (New York: Basic Books, 1957), 97.

If you're citing an entire work in two or more volumes, use the form shown below.

> 2. Ronald Chrisley, ed., *Artificial Intelligence: Critical Concepts*, 4 vols. (London: Routledge, 2000).

10. One Selection from an Anthology or an Edited Book—CM

Footnote or Endnote

> 1. Norval Morrisseau, "The Indian That Became a Thunderbird." In *Canadian Short Fiction: From Myth to Modern*, ed. W. H. New, (Scarborough, ON: Prentice Hall, 1986), 27.

In a note, give the numbers of the pages cited; in a bibliography entry, give the page range of the full selection, and place it before the publication information.

Bibliography

> Morrisseau, Norval. "The Indian That Became a Thunderbird." In *Canadian Short Fiction: From Myth to Modern*, edited by W. H. New, 26–29. Scarborough, ON: Prentice Hall, 1986.

11. More Than One Selection from an Anthology or an Edited Book—CM

If you cite more than one selection from the same anthology or edited book, give complete bibliographical information in each citation.

12. Signed Article in a Reference Book—CM

> 1. Doris Shadbolt, "Emily Carr." In *The Canadian Encyclopedia*, 2nd ed. (Edmonton: Hurtig, 1988), 366.

13. Unsigned Article in a Reference Book—CM

> 1. *Encyclopaedia Britannica*, 15th ed., s. v. "Ireland."

The abbreviation *s .v.* stands for *sub verbo*, meaning "under the word." Capitalize the heading of the entry only if it's a proper noun. Omit publication information except for the edition number.

14. Second or Later Edition—CM

> 1. Anthony F. Janson, *History of Art*, 6th ed. (New York: Abrams, 2001).

Here the abbreviation *ed.* stands for "edition." Give the copyright date for the edition you're citing.

15. Anthology or Edited Book—CM

> 1. W. H. New, ed., *Canadian Short Fiction: From Myth to Modern* (Scarborough, ON: Prentice Hall, 1986), 124–26.

Here the abbreviation *ed.* stands for "editor." For a source with two or more editors, use the plural *eds.*

16. Introduction, Preface, Foreword, or Afterword—CM

> 1. Warren Allmand, foreword to *The Life and Death of Anna Mae Aquash*, by Johanna Brand (Toronto: Lorimer, 1993).

If the author of the book is different from the author of the cited part, give the name of the book's author or editor after the title of the book, preceded by the word *by* or *ed.* (for "edited by").

17. Unpublished Dissertation or Essay—CM

1. Michele Byers, "*Buffy the Vampire Slayer:* The Insurgence of Television as a Performance Text" (PhD diss., University of Toronto, 2000), 23–24.

List the author's name first, then the title in quotation marks (not italicized), a descriptive label (such as *PhD diss.* or *master's thesis*), the degree-granting institution, the date, and finally the page numbers you're citing.

1. Peter Leslie Mortensen, "Meet the Press: Reading News Coverage of Research on Writing" (paper presented at the annual meeting of the Modern Language Association, Washington, DC, December 29, 2005).

To cite a paper read at a meeting, give the name of the meeting in parentheses, along with the location and the date.

18. Reprint of an Older Book—CM

1. Archibald Lampman, *Lyrics of Earth* (1895; repr., Ottawa: Tecumseh Press, 1978).

Republishing information is located on the copyright page. List the original date of publication first, followed by the publication information for the reprint.

19. Book in a Series—CM

1. Thomas J. Courchene, *In Praise of Renewed Federalism*, The Canada Round (Toronto: C. D. Howe Institute, 1991), 54–66.

If the series numbers its volumes and the volume number isn't part of the title, you would include the volume number after the series title. Separate the volume number from the series title with a comma.

20. Book with a Title Within a Title—CM

1. Aljean Harmetz, *The Making of "The Wizard of Oz"* (New York: Hyperion, 1998).

Put the name of a work that appears in an italicized title inside quotation marks, whether it is usually shown in italics or in quotation marks.

21. Government Publication—CM

1. Indian and Northern Affairs Canada, *The Inuit* (Ottawa: Supply and Services Canada, 1986), 46.

If a government department, bureau, agency, or committee produces a document, cite that group as the author.

22. Published Proceedings of a Conference—CM

1. Ovide Mercredi, "The Future Is Our Collective Rights as Distinct Peoples," in *Forging a New Relationship: Proceedings of the Conference on the Report of the Royal Commission on Aboriginal Peoples*, ed. Donald B. Smith (Montreal: McGill Institute for the Study of Canada, 1997), 60.

Treat a selection from published conference proceedings as you would a chapter in a book.

23. Secondary Source from a Book—CM

When you quote on person's words, having found them in another person's work, give information as fully as you can about both sources. CM style recommends, however, that original sources be consulted and cited whenever practical.

1. Mary Wollstonecraft, *A Vindication of the Rights of Woman* (1792), 90, quoted in Caroline Shrodes, Harry Finestone, and Michael Shugrue, *The Conscious Reader*, 4th ed. (New York: Macmillan, 1988), 282.

561

2. Caroline Shrodes, Harry Finestone, and Michael Shugrue, *The Conscious Reader*, 4th ed. (New York: Macmillan, 1988), 282, quoting Mary Wollstonecraft, *A Vindication of the Rights of Woman* (1792), 90.

PERIODICALS—PRINT

24. Signed Article from a Daily Newspaper—CM

2. Shawn McCarthy, "Sale Puts Ottawa out of Nuclear Business," *Globe and Mail*, June 28, 2011, national edition, sec. A.

Many newspapers print more than one edition a day and reposition the same articles on different pages. CM style recommends that you omit page numbers from note entries. When applicable, identify the specific edition (such as *national edition* or *final edition*); put this information after the date, preceded by a comma. For a paper that specifies sections, put *sec.* before the section's letter or number or use *section* for a section's name (such as *Weekend section*). If a paper gives column titles, you may use the title (not italicized or in quotation marks) in addition to or in place of the article title. Separate all items with commas.

25. Editorial, Letter to the Editor, or Review—CM

1. "London Doomed to Repeat Its History on Heritage," editorial, *London Free Press*, July 20, 2011, sec. B.

2. John Hurka, letter to the editor, *Calgary Sun*, July 5, 1994, sec. A.

3. Wendy Toews, "Politics of the Mind," review of *They Say You're Crazy: How the World's Most Powerful Psychiatrists Decide Who's Normal*, by Paula J. Caplan, *Winnipeg Free Press*, August 26, 1995, sec. C.

Before page numbers, use a comma for popular magazines and a colon for journals.

26. Unsigned Article in a Daily Newspaper—CM

1. "Private Water May Violate Constitution," *Ottawa Citizen*, November 27, 2002, sec. A.

27 Signed Article in a Weekly or Biweekly Magazine or Newspaper—CM

1. Brian D. Johnson, "Why Six Dylans Are Better Than One," *Maclean's*, November 26, 2007, 43–46.

For general-readership weekly and biweekly magazines and newspapers, give the month, day, and year of publication. Separate page numbers from the year with a comma. In your footnotes or endnotes you give only the specific page(s) you are citing from a magazine or journal article; in the bibliography you give the first and last pages of the article.

28. Signed Article in a Monthly or Bimonthly Periodical—CM.

1. James Fallows, "The $1.4 Trillion Question," *The Atlantic*, January/February 2008, 36–48.

For general-readership monthly and bimonthly magazines, give the month and year of publication. Separate page numbers from the year with a comma.

29. Unsigned Article in a Weekly or Monthly Periodical—CM

1. "The Price Is Wrong," *Economist*, August 2, 2003, 58–59.

30. Article in a Collection of Reprinted Articles—CM

1. Thomas Hayden, "The Age of Robots," in *Applied Science*, Social Issues Resources Series (Boca Raton, FL: Social Issues Resources, 2002).

Cite only the publication actually consulted, not the original source. If you use a bibliography, cite its location in both the reprinted publication you consulted and the publication where the article first appeared.

31. Article in a Journal with Continuous Pagination—CM

1. Phyllis Tyson, "The Psychology of Women Continued," *Journal of the American Psychoanalytic Association* 46, (1998): 361–63.

You may omit the issue number if pagination is continuous throughout a volume or if a month or season precedes the year.

32. Article in a Journal That Pages Each Issue Separately—CM

1. Linda Adler-Kassner and Heidi Estrem, "Rethinking Research Writing: Public Literacy in the Composition Classroom," *WPA: Writing Program Administration* 26, no. 3 (2003): 119–31.

The issue number of a journal is required if each issue of the journal starts with page 1. In this example, the volume number is 26 and the issue number, abbreviated *no.*, is 3.

INTERNET SOURCES

If there is a print version of the source, use it as the basis for your entry and then add information about how to find the electronic version. Always cite the version you consulted, in case the print and electronic versions differ.

Electronic sources do not always include page numbers, and if they do, their page numbers may vary when pages are displayed. For such works, you may include a chapter or paragraph number (if available), a section heading, or a description of the part of the work you are using. Numbers or descriptions are usually unnecessary when you cite a short electronic work presented as a single, searchable document.

For an online work that gives no date of publication or revision, include the date you accessed the work. (Some disciplines expect the access date with any online source.) The final part of the entry is the URL or DOI.

33. Online Book—CM

1. Arthur W. Eaton, *Acadian Legends and Lyrics* (1889; Canadian Institute for Historical Microreproductions, 2002), http://www.canadiana.org/cgi-bin/ECO/mtq?doc=09066.

Include the author's name, the title, and access information—in this case, the name of the organization that sponsors the site—and the URL or DOI. For an older work whose place of publication may not be discoverable, the notation *n.p.* is not needed.

2. Joseph Pivato, ed., *The Anthology of Italian-Canadian Writing* (Toronto: Guernica Editions, 1998), section 2, accessed July 11, 2011, http://books.google.com/.

For an electronic edition of a printed book downloaded from a library or bookseller, omit the URL or DOI but include a notation such as *Kindle edition* or *PDF e-book*. The date is the year of electronic publication. Instead of page numbers, which may vary in online works, give the chapter or paragraph number, a section heading, or a descriptive phrase that readers can use to locate the citation.

3. Michael Ondaatje, *The English Patient* (Toronto: Vintage Canada, 2008), PDF e-book, chap. 3.

34. Article from a Periodical Available Only Online—CM

Cite an online periodical as you would a printed periodical, but add a URL or DOI. Your instructor may require you to include an access date as well; it precedes the URL or DOI. (For a newspaper citation, you can shorten a long URL to end after the forward slash that follows a domain extension such as *.com.*) If you need to cite a specific passage and there are no page numbers, you can use a section heading or other description of its location.

1. Jody Shipka, "This Was (NOT!!) an Easy Assignment," *Computers and Composition Online*, Fall 2007, accessed November 22, 2007, http://www.bgsu.edu/cconline/not_easy/.

Footnote or Endnote

2. Natalie Oake et al., "Effect of an Interactive Voice Response System on Oral Anticoagulant Management," *Canadian Medical Association Journal* 180 (April 20, 2009): 928, accessed July 5, 2012. doi:10.1503/cmaj.081659.

Bibliography

Oake, Natalie, Carl van Walraven, Marc A. Rodger, and Alan J. Forster. "Effect of an Interactive Voice Response System on Oral Anticoagulant Management." *Canadian Medical Association Journal* 180 (April 28, 2009): 927-33. doi:10.1503/cmaj.081659.

35. Article Accessed Through a Database—CM

For library and commercial databases, use the standard entry for the type of publication. Include the URL only if the database includes a stable URL with the document. Otherwise, give the name of the database and, in parentheses, the identification number given to the source. If the item doesn't include a publication or revision date, include an access date.

1. Gail Dutton, "Greener Pigs," *Popular Science* 255, no. 5 (November 1999): 38–39, ProQuest UMI (8320500510).

36. Source from a Website—CM

Provide the name of the website (if any), neither in italics nor in quotation marks, and the name of the sponsor or author. A site name like *www.google.com* is usually simply referred to as *Google*. If there is no title, use a descriptive phrase for the site. Treat a site name that resembles the title of a book, journal, or article as you would the title of that type of publication (italics or quotation marks). Place the titles of webpages or sections within a website in quotation marks.

Also include the date of publication or last revision (if available), an access date, and the URL.

1. The Banff Centre, accessed July 11, 2010, http://www.banffcentre.ca/.

2. "Computational Astrophysics," Canadian Institute for Theoretical Astrophysics, accessed January 22, 2008, http://www.cita.utoronto.ca/index.php/research_cita/computational_astrophysics.

3. "Privacy Policy," Research in Motion (RIM), last modified February 28, 2007, accessed August 12, 2011, http://na.blackberry.com/eng/legal/privacy_policy.jsp.

4. "Manual of Style," *Wikipedia*, last modified July 29, 2011, accessed August 3, 2011, http://en.wikipedia.org/wiki/wikipedia:Manual_of_Style.

37. Electronic Mailing List—CM

1. T. Caruso to Calls for Papers mailing list, June 30, 2002, no. 14, http://www.cfp.english.upenn.edu/archive/2002-09/0041.html.

38. E-Mail Message—CM

1. Eliana Pessin, e-mail message to Georgia Dobyns, November 11, 2012.

39. Blog Entry—CM

1. Scott McLemee, "To Whom It May Concern," *Quick Study* (blog), January 1, 2008, http://www.artsjournal.com/quickstudy/.

If the blog is part of a larger publication, put its name before the date. If you are citing a comment, start with the name of the commenter, include the date of the comment (if known) and the words "comment on," and give the citation information for the entry being commented on.

40. Online Video or Podcast—CM

1. Michael Wesch, *Web 2.0 . . . The Machine is Us/ing Us*, YouTube video, 4:32, accessed July 7, 2007, posted January 31, 2007, http://www.youtube.com/watch?v=6gmP4nkOEOE.

Wesch is the director and producer of this video, and *4:32* is its length. The medium is given as *video, YouTube video, podcast audio*, etc.

OTHER SOURCES

41. Speech or Conference Presentation—CM

1. Peter Leslie Mortensen, "Meet the Press: Reading News Coverage of Research on Writing" (paper presented at the annual meeting of the Modern Language Association, Washington, DC, December 29, 2005).

42. Personal Interview—CM

1. Max Brooks, interview by author, August 30, 2012, Victoria, BC.

For an unpublished interview, give the name of the interviewee and the interviewer, and the date and location of the interview. CM style recommends that you incorporate this information into the text, making a note unnecessary.

43. Published and Unpublished Letters—CM

1. William Carlos Williams to his son, 13 March 1935, in *Letters of the Century: America 1900–1999*, ed. Lisa Grunwald and Stephen J. Adler (New York: Dial, 1999), 225–26.

2. Theodore Brown, letter to author, December 7, 2005.

For an unpublished letter, give the name of the writer, the name of the recipient, and the date the letter was written.

44. Film, Videotape, CD-ROM, or DVD—CM

1. Marc Norman and Tom Stoppard, *Shakespeare in Love* (1998; New York: Miramax Films/Universal Pictures. 2003), DVD.

The note begins with the authors of the screenplay. If the point of the note was about the director or the producers, then the title would appear first and *directed by* and/or *produced by* would follow a comma after the title, along with the relevant names.

45. Sound Recording—CM

1. Bedrich Smetana, *My Country,* Czech Philharmonic, conducted by Karel Ancerl, Vanguard SV-9/10,1968, 33 ⅓ rpm.

Bedrich Smetana is the composer, and Karel Ancerl is the conductor. If your focus is on the conductor or performer, you may list that person's name first. If no date is given, use *n.d.*

2. Leonard Cohen, "Tower of Song," on *I'm Your Man,* Sony CK 44191, 1988, compact disc.

46. Computer Software—CM

1. Tom Clancy's Splinter Cell Trilogy, 2011, Unisoft, Montreal.

2. QNX Neutrino RTOS, Ver. 6.3, QNX Software Systems, Kanata, ON.

Place the version or release number, abbreviated *Ver.* or *Rel.,* directly after the name of the software. Then, list the company that owns the rights to the software, followed by that company's location.

CSE-STYLE DOCUMENTATION

CSE-STYLE DIRECTORY

38c What is CSE-style documentation?

The Council of Science Editors (CSE) produces a manual to guide publications in the mathematics, the life sciences, and the physical sciences. The information in 38c and 38d adheres to the style guidelines in the seventh edition of that manual, *Scientific Style and Format* (2006). For up-to-date information about any changes, go to the organization's website at <http://www.councilscienceeditors.org.>.

Scientific journals and publishers are notoriously independent in how they handle documentation, and scholars submitting work to specific journals always check which documentation rules apply. Similarly, students in science courses should ask their instructors about the specific guidelines they're to follow.

Like the MLA (Chapter 36) and APA (Chapter 37) styles, CSE has two components: (1) citations within the text (called "**in-text references**") tied to (2) a bibliography (called "**end references**") at the end of the text. However, CSE offers three different options for in-text references: the citation-sequence system, the name-year system, and the citation-name system. We explain each, below. CSE most strongly endorses the citation-name system. Therefore, if you have a choice, we advise to you follow the citation-name system. In any case, be consistent; don't mix systems.

38c.1 The CSE citation sequence system

The citation-sequence system uses numbers in the text to refer to a numerically arranged end reference list. Here's how it works.

1. The first time you cite each source in your paper, assign it an arabic number in sequence, starting with 1.
2. Mark each subsequent reference to that source with the assigned number.
3. Use superscript (raised) numbers for source citations in your sentences, although numbers in parentheses are also acceptable.
4. Don't use footnotes or endnotes to credit your sources. Use only a Cited References list, and number the entries in the order of their appearance in your paper. Start with the number 1, followed by a period, and then the content of the citation. Never list sources alphabetically. Never underline or use italics for titles of works.

Here's an example of a sentence that includes in-text citations and the corresponding cited references.

IN-TEXT CITATIONS

Sybesma[1] insists that this behaviour occurs periodically, but Crowder[2] claims never to have observed it.

END REFERENCES

1. Sybesma C. An introduction to biophysics. New York: Academic; 1977. 648 p.

2. Crowder W. Seashore life between the tides. New York: Dodd, Mead; 1931. New York: Dover Reprint; 1975. 372 p.

Thereafter, throughout your paper, follow each citation of Sybesma's *Introduction to Biophysics* by a superscript [1] and each citation of Crowder's *Seashore Life* by a superscript [2].

When you're citing more than one reference—for example, a new source and three previous sources as well as a source from your first page—list each source number, followed by a comma with no space. Use a hyphen to show the range of numbers in a continuous sequence, and put all in superscript:[2,5-7,9]

Quick Reference 38.2 gives guidelines for compiling a Cited References list for the citation-sequence system.

QUICK REFERENCE **38.2**

Guidelines for a References list (CSE-style)

TITLE

Use "Cited References" or "References" as the title (no underlining, no italics, no quotation marks). (CSE also permits "Bibliography" or "Literature Cited" as acceptable titles.)

PLACEMENT OF LIST

Begin the list on a separate page at the end of the research paper. Number the page sequentially with the rest of the paper.

CONTENT AND FORMAT OF CITED REFERENCES

Include all sources that you quote, paraphrase, or summarize in your paper. Centre the title one inch (2.5 cm) from the top of the page. Start each entry on a new line. If an entry takes more than one line, indent the second and all other lines under the first word, not the number. Single-space each entry and double-space between entries.

SPACING AFTER PUNCTUATION

CSE style specifies no space after date, issue number, or volume number of a periodical, as shown in the models in 38d.

ARRANGEMENT OF ENTRIES—CITATION-SEQUENCE SYSTEM

Sequence and number the entries in the precise order in which you first use them in the body of your paper. Put the number, followed by a period and a space, at the regular left margin.

ARRANGEMENT OF ENTRIES—NAME-YEAR SYSTEM

Sequence the entries in alphabetical order by author, then title, etc. Do not number the entries.

ARRANGEMENT OF ENTRIES—CITATION-NAME SYSTEM

Sequence the entries in alphabetical order by author, then title, etc. Number the entries. Put the number, followed by a period and a space, at the regular left margin.

AUTHORS' NAMES

Reverse the order of each author's name, giving the last name first. For book citations, you can give first names or use only the initials of first and (when available) middle names; CSE style recommends you use only initials. For journal citations, use only initials. Don't use a period or a space between first and middle initials. Use a comma to separate the names of multiple authors identified by initials; however, if you use full first names, use a

continued ➤

semicolon. Don't use *and* or *&* with authors' names. Place a period after the last author's name.

With journal citations, CSE style recommends listing the names of the first ten authors. For eleven or more authors, list the first ten followed by *et al.* (The CSE recognizes that not all publications accept this recommendation; follow your instructor's preference.)

TREATMENT OF TITLES

Never underline titles or enclose them in quotation marks. Capitalize a title's first word and any proper nouns. Don't capitalize the first word of a subtitle unless it's a proper noun. Capitalize the titles of academic journals. If the title of a periodical is one word, give it in full; otherwise, abbreviate the title according to recommendations established by the *American National Standard for Abbreviations of Titles of Periodicals.* Capitalize a newspaper title's major words, giving the full title but omitting *A, An,* or *The* at the beginning.

If a document has no title, create a title from the first few words of its text and place it within square brackets. If title is not in English, put the English translation, if you know it, in square brackets after the original title. When a bilingual text (such as some government publications) has a title in each language, give both titles and place an equals sign between them:

Health and welfare reports = Rapports sur la santé et le bien-être

PLACE OF PUBLICATION

Use a colon after the city of publication. If the city name could be unfamiliar to readers, add in parentheses the postal abbreviation for the province or US state. If the location of a city outside Canada or the United States will be unfamiliar to readers, add in parentheses the country name, abbreviating it according to International Organization for Standardization (ISO) standards. Find ISO abbreviations at <http://unstats.un.org/unsd/methods/m49/m49.htm>.

PUBLISHER

Give the name of the publisher, without periods after initials, and put a semicolon after the publisher's name. Omit *The* at the beginning and *Co., Inc., Ltd.,* or *Press* at the end. However, for a university press, abbreviate *University* and *Press* as *Univ* and *Pr,* respectively, without periods.

PUBLICATION DATE

If no year of publication can be determined, use the year of copyright preceded by *c:* ©2007. Abbreviate all month names longer than three letters to their first three letters, but do not add a period.

INCLUSIVE PAGE NUMBERS

In contrast to its earlier practice of shortening numbers as much as possible, CSE style now repeats all digits in inclusive page numbers: 44–45, 233–244, and 1233–1234.

DISCONTINUOUS PAGE NUMBERS

Give the numbers of all discontinuous pages, separating successive numbers or ranges with a comma: 54–57, 60–66.

continued ➤

TOTAL PAGE NUMBERS

In the citation for an entire book, the last information unit gives the total number of book pages, followed by the abbreviation *p* and a period.

FORMAT FOR REFERENCES ENTRIES: BOOKS

The basic format for the **citation-sequence** and **citation-name systems** is

> Author(s). Title. Edition [if other than first]. Place of publication: Publisher: Date. Pages.

As the last item, list total pages when citing an entire work or inclusive pages when citing part of a book. Note that the Author, Title, and Edition sections end with a period. Place of publication is followed by a colon, and Publisher by a semicolon. Date and Pages end with a period.

1. Primrose SB, Twyman RM, Old RW. Principles of gene manipulation. London: Blackwell; 2002. 390 p.

The basic format for the **name-date system** is

> Author(s). Date. Title. Edition [if other than first]. Place of publication: Publisher. Pages.
>
> Primrose SB, Twyman RM. Old RW. 2002. Principles of gene manipulation. London: Blackwell. 390 p.

FORMAT FOR CITED REFERENCES ENTRIES: ARTICLES

The basic format for the **citation-sequence** and **citation-name system** is

> Author(s). Article title. Journal title. Date;Volume(Issue):Pages.

Each section ends with a period. Notice there is no space after the semicolon, before the parentheses, or after the colon. Abbreviate a journal's name only if it's standard in your scientific discipline. For example, *Exp Neurol* is the abbreviated form for *Experimental Neurology*. In the following example, the volume number is 184, and the issue number, in parentheses, is 1.

1. Ginis I, Rao MS. Toward cell replacement therapy: promises and caveats. Exp Neurol. 2003;184(1):61–77.

The basic format for the **name-year system** is

> Author(s). Date. Article title. Journal title. Volume(Issue):Pages.
>
> Ginis I, Rao MS. 2003. Toward cell replacement therapy: promises and caveats. Exp Neurol. 184(1):61–77.

38c.2   The CSE name-year system

In the name-year system, in text references include the last name of the author or authors, along with the year of publication, placed in parentheses. The end references in this system are organized in alphabetical order by author and are not numbered. (This system resembles APA style.)

IN-TEXT REFERENCE

This behaviour occurs periodically (Sybesma 1977), although some claim never to have observed it (Crowder 1931).

or

Sysbesma (1977) insists that this behaviour occurs periodically, but Crowder (1931) claims never to have observed it.

END REFERENCE

Crowder W. Seashore life between the tides. New York: Dodd, Mead; 1931. New York: Dover Reprint; 1975. 372 p.

Sybesma C. An introduction to biophysics. New York: Academic; 1977. 648 p.

If there are two authors, give both names in the in-text reference, separated by *and*. If there are more than two authors, give only the first author's name, then include *et al.* and the publication year. If no author is given, include the first word or first few words of the title, followed by an ELLIPSIS and the date.

IN-TEXT-REFERENCE

Various therapies have proven effective (Treatment . . . 2007).

Quick Reference 38.2 gives guidelines for compiling a References list. Especially pay attention to the arrangement of entries in a name-year system.

38c.3   The CSE citation-name system

In the citation-name system, the in-text references use numbers to refer to end references that are arranged alphabetically. In other words, first complete the list of end references, arranging them alphabetically by author. Then, number each reference; for example, if you were documenting references by Schmidt, Gonzalez, Adams, and Zurowski, in your end references, they would be arranged like this:

1. Adams . . .
2. Gonzalez . . .
3. Schmidt . . .
4. Zurowski . . .

Finally, your in-text references should use a superscript number corresponding to the name in your end references. The system resembles the citation-sequence system, except that the alphabetical order of the end references determines the number rather than the order or appearance in the text.

IN-TEXT REFERENCES—CITATION-NAME

Sysbesma[2] insists that this behaviour occurs periodically, but Crowder[1] claims never to have observed it.

END REFERENCES—CITATION-NAME

1. Crowder W. Seashore life between the tides. New York: Dodd, Mead; 1931. New York: Dover Reprint; 1975. 372 p.

2. Sybesma C. An introduction to biophysics. New York: Academic; 1977. 648 p.

Quick Reference 38.2 gives guidelines for compiling a References list. Especially pay attention to the arrangement of entries in a citation-name system.

38d   What are CSE guidelines for sources in a list of references?

The directory that precedes section 38c corresponds to the sample references that follow. If you need a model not included in this book, consult the seventh edition of *Scientific Style and Format*. The examples that follow are for the citation-sequence and citation-name systems; the name-date system differs by the placement of the date and by not numbering the entries. See Quick Reference 38.2 for illustrations of the differences.

BOOK AND PARTS OF BOOKS

1. Book by One Author—CSE

1. Hawking SW. Black holes and baby universes and other essays. New York: Bantam Books; 1993. 320 p.

Use one space but no punctuation between an author's last name and the initial of the first name. Don't put punctuation or a space between first and middle initials (*Hawking SW*). Do, however, use the hyphen in a hyphenated first and middle name (for example, *Gille J-C* represents *Jean-Claude Gille* in the next item).

2. Book by More Than One Author—CSE

1. Wegzyn S, Gille J-C, Vidal P. Developmental systems: at the crossroads of system theory, computer science, and genetic engineering. New York: Springer; 1990. 595 p.

3. Book by a Group or Corporate Author—CSE

1. Canadian Institute of Child Health. Family-centred maternity and newborn care. 3rd ed. Ottawa: CICH; 1987. 121 p.

The group or organization that is the author may also be the publisher of a book. If a government agency is the publisher and its nationality is not included in its name, place the ISO two-letter country code (see Quick Reference 38.2) in parentheses following its name: National Academy of Sciences (US).

4. Anthology or Edited Book—CSE

1. Syzf M, editor. DNA methylation and center therapy. New York: Springer; 2005. 239 p.

5. One Selection or Chapter from an Anthology or Edited Book—CSE

1. Basov NG, Feoktistov LP, Senatsky YV. Laser driver for inertial confinement fusion. In: Bureckner KA, editor. Research trends in physics: inertial confinement fusion. New York: American Institute of Physics; 1992. p. 24–37.

6. Translation—CSE

1. Foucault M. Madness: the invention of an idea. Sheridan A, translator. New York: HarperCollins; 2011. 160 p. Translation of: Maladie mentale et psychologie.

7. Reprint of an Older Book—CSE

1. Carson R. The sea around us. New York: Oxford Univ Press; 1951. New York: Oxford Univ Press; 1991. 288 p.

8. Multivolume Work—CSE

1. Crane FL, Moore DJ, Low HE, editors. Oxidoreduction at the plasma membrane: relation to growth and transport. Boca Raton (FL): CRC; 1991. 2 vol.

The first item cites both volumes of the two-volume work.

1. Crane FL, Moore DJ, Low HE, editors. Oxidoreduction at the plasma membrane: relation to growth and transport. Vol. 2, Plants. Boca Raton (FL): CRC; 1991. 453 p.

The second item cites the work's second volume only.

9. Unpublished Dissertation or Thesis—CSE

1. McFayden RG. Sequential access in files used for partial match retrieval [dissertation]. [Waterloo (ON)]: University of Waterloo; 1990. 170 p. Available from: UMI; ADGNN-61072.

10. Published Article from Conference Proceedings—CSE

1. Tsang CP, Bellgard MI. Sequence generation using a network of Boltzmann machines. In: Tsang CP, editor. Proceedings of the 4th Australian Joint Conference on Artificial Intelligence; 1990 Nov 8–11; Perth, AU. Singapore: World Scientific; 1990. p 224–233.

PRINT ARTICLES FROM JOURNALS AND PERIODICALS

11. Article in a Journal—CSE

1. Lomas J, Woods J, Veenstra G. Devolving authority for health care in Canada's provinces: 1. an introduction to the issues. CMAJ. 1997;156(3):371–377.

2. Lowe M. Breeding a sustainable agriculture. World Watch. 2007 Nov-Dec:32–43.

Place a period after the journal title, unless the title is followed by a note specifying its medium. Include volume and issue numbers for any journal that gives them (in the first entry, *156* is the volume number and *3* is the issue number). If the journal uses no volume or issue number, put the month (and day, if available) or season after the year.

12. Journal Article on Discontinuous Pages—CSE

1. Richards FM. The protein folding problem. Sci Am. 1991;246(1):54–57, 60–66.

13. Article with No Identifiable Author—CSE

1. Cruelty to animals linked to murders of humans. AWIQ. 1993;42(3):16.

14. Article with Author Affilliation—CSE

1. DeMoll E, Auffenberg T (Department of Microbiology, University of Kentucky). Purine metabolism in *Methanococcus vannielii*. J Bacteriol. 1993;175:5754–5761.

15. Entire Issue of a Journal—CSE

1. Whales in a modern world: a symposium held in London, November 1988. Mamm Rev. 1990; 20(9).

The date of the symposium, November 1988, is part of the title of this issue.

16. Signed Newspaper Article—CSE

1. Weeks C. Social media could help detect pandemics. Globe and Mail. 2011 Jun 28:sect. L:5.

Sect. stands for *section.* Note that there is no space between the date and the section or between the section and the page number. Show just the first page of the article.

17. Unsigned Newspaper Article—CSE

1. Arctic drilling study. Globe and Mail. 1995 Sep 2:sect. D:8.

18. Editorial or Review—CSE

CSE allows "notes" after the page number(s) that will help readers understand the nature of the reference.

1. Leshner AI. "Glocal" science advocacy. Science 2008;319(5865):877. Editorial.

2. Myer A. Genomes evolve, but how? Nature 2008;451(7180):771. Review of Lynch M, The Origins of Genome Architecture.

ELECTRONIC SOURCES ON THE INTERNET

Cite electronic and online sources by including the author's name, if available; the work's title; the type of medium, in brackets, such as [*Internet*] or [*electronic mail on the Internet*]; the title of the publication if there's a print version or, if not, the place of publication and the publishing organization; the date the original was published or placed on the Internet; the date you accessed the publication, preceded by the word *cited* enclosed in brackets; and the address of the source, if from the Internet or a database. Omit end punctuation after an Internet address.

If the year of publication followed the year of copyright by three years or more, include both: 2006, c2002.

For non-Internet electronic sources, include a physical description and, if possible, notes to assist users of the source.

For online sources with no obvious title, use as a title the first series of significant words on the screen. With a home page, you can use the name of the person or organization responsible for the site as the title and also as the publisher.

19. Book on the Internet—CSE

1. Thomson ABR, Shaffer EA, editors. First principles of gastroenterology [Internet]. 3rd ed. Mississauga (ON): AstraZeneca Canada Inc., 1997 [updated 2005; cited 2011 Sep 14]. 849 p. Available from: http://www.gastroresource.com/.GITextbook/En/Default.htm

After the publication date comes the date of the latest update or revision; place that in brackets before the date you accessed (cited) the site. If there is no pagination, you may estimate the extent of an Internet source (other than a home page) or the location of the passage you are citing in screens, paragraphs, or bytes.

20. Article with Print Version on the Internet—CSE

1. Clark DR, McGrath PJ, MacDonald N. Members' of Parliament knowledge of and attitudes toward health research and funding. CMAJ [Internet]. 2007 [cited 2012 Nov 22]; 177(9):87–883. Available from: http://www.cmaj.ca/cgi/content/full/177/9/1045

21. Article Available Only on the Internet—CSE

1. Overbye D. Remembrance of things future: the mystery of time. The New York Times on the Web [Internet]. 2010 Jun 28 [cited 2010 Dec 11]. Available from: http://www.nytimes.com/2005/06/28/science/28time.html

22. Webpage—CSE

Begin with author, if available; otherwise, begin with title.

1. Think again: men and women share cognitive skills [Internet]. Washington DC:
   American Psychological Association; 2006 [cited 2012 Jan 17]. Available from:
   http://www.apa.org/research/action/share.aspx

2. Mountain culture [home page on the Internet]. Banff (AB): Banff Centre for Continuing
   Education; c2006 [cited 2006 Nov 22]. Available from: http://www.banffcentre.ca/mountainculture/

This home page has no author listed, so the item begins with the title of the home page.
For clarity, this item states the type of source before the medium: [*home page on the
Internet*]. The publisher here is the organization responsible for the site. This home page
gives no date of publication, so the copyright date is used instead *c2006*.

23. Video or Podcast—CSE

1. Wesch M. Web 2.0 . . . the machine is us/ing us [video on the Internet]. 2007 Jan 31 [cited 2012 Dec
   14]. Available from: http://www.youtube.com/watch?v=6gmP4nk0EOE

OTHER SOURCES

24. Map—CSE

1. Skoda L, cartographer. Kitimat-Stikine Regional District—regional resource inventory [resource
   map]. Coquitlam (BC): Canadian Cartographics; 1981. 2 sheets: colour, scale 1:500 00.

Begin the item with the name of the author, if available, followed by the word *cartographer*.
The physical description (such as number of sheets and scale) is optional.

25. Unpublished Letter—CSE

1. Darwin C. [Letter to Mr. Clerke, 1861]. Located at: University of Iowa Library, Iowa City (IA).

Place references to your own personal communications in the body of the paper, along with
appropriate identification, and not in the list of references.

26. Video Recording—CSE

1. Nova—the elegant universe [DVD]. Boston: WGBH; 2004. 2 DVDs: 180 min, sound, colour.

27. Slide Set—CSE

1. Human parasitology [slides]. Chicago; American Society of Clinical Pathologists; 1990. Colour.
   Accompanied by: 1 guide.

28. Presentation Slides—CSE

1. Beaulieu E. Fruit fly larvae [PowerPoint slides]. Halifax (NS): Dalhousie University; 2011 Oct 17.
   49 slides.

IEEE-STYLE DOCUMENTATION

38e What is IEEE-style documentation?

The IEEE, an international association for the advancement of engineering and technology, publishes the *IEEE Editorial Style Manual,* in which it presents a citation-sequence
system of documentation similar to one of the systems recommended by the CSE. In the
body of your text, place inside square brackets in-text reference numbers corresponding to
the numbered items in your References list.

1. The first time you cite each source in your paper, assign it an arabic number in sequence, starting with 1.
2. Mark each subsequent reference to that source with the same assigned number.
3. Create a References list whose entries follow the order in which you cite the corresponding sources in your paper. Number each entry in order.

Wherever possible, cite only the number, not the author's name and the number.

IN-TEXT CITATIONS

This phenomenon was thought to occur regularly [8], but [9]-[12] demonstrate frequent variations in the pattern. In fact, [9], [11], and [12] have performed studies calling the methods used by [8] into question. Other evidence [13, pp. 182-212] of similar phenomena has not yet been reproduced in controlled studies.

Items in the References list are listed and numbered according to their appearance in your text, not according to alphabetical order. You can find further information on IEEE style at <http://www.ieee.org/documents/stylemanual.pdf>.

REFERENCES LIST

Print Sources

1. Book—IEEE

[1] S. Wegzyn, J.-C. Gille, and P. Vidal, *Developmental Systems: At the Crossroads of System Theory, Computer Science, and Genetic Engineering*. New York: Springer, 1990.

2. Periodical—IEEE

[2] H. Eriksson and P. E. Danielsson, "Two problems on Boolean memories," *IEEE Trans. Electron. Devices*, vol. ED-11, pp. 32-33, Jan. 1959.

3. Published Article from Conference Proceedings—IEEE

[3] C. P. Tsang and M. I. Bellgard, "Sequence generation using a network of Boltzmann machines," in *Proc. 4th Australian Joint Conf. Artificial Intelligence*, C. P. Tsang, Ed., Perth, AU, 1990, pp. 224-233.

Electronic Sources

4. Book on the Web—IEEE

[4] A. B. R. Thomson and E. A. Shaffer, Eds. (2005). *First Principles of Gastroenterology* (3rd ed.) [Online]. Available: http://www.gastroresource.com/GITextbook/En/Default.htm

5. Periodical on the Web—IEEE

[5] D. R. Clark, P. J. McGrath, and N. MacDonald. (2007, Oct.). Members' of Parliament knowledge of and attitudes toward health research and funding. *CMAJ* [Online]. *177*(9), pp. 877-883. Available: http://www.cmaj.ca/cgi/content/full/177/9/1045

6. Home Page—IEEE

[6] C. Colligan. (2005, Sept. 15). *Theoretical Approaches To Print Culture* [Online]. Available: http://www.sfu.ca/english/gradwebpage/course053808.html

Writing Across the Curriculum— and Beyond

MyCanadianCompLab

Visit MyCanadianCompLab at
mycanadiancomplab.ca for

- More information on writing essays
- Chapter exercises
- Other resources including an eText version of this book

Chapter 39

COMPARING THE DISCIPLINES

((•●
AUDIO LESSON
Section 1: Big
Ideas—Writing
Successfully in
Other Courses

((•●
AUDIO LESSON
Section 2:
Practice
Questions—
Writing
Successfully in
Other Courses

((•●
AUDIO LESSON
Section 3:
Rapid Review—
Writing
Successfully in
Other Courses

39a   What is "writing across the curriculum"?

Writing across the curriculum refers to the writing you do in college and university courses beyond first-year composition. Good writing in various subject areas, such as history, biology, and psychology, has many common features, but also important differences. This section will help you adapt general principles of writing so you'll be successful in writing across the curriculum.

People commonly group academic disciplines into three broad categories: the humanities, the social sciences, and the natural sciences. Each has its own knowledge, vocabulary, and perspectives on the world; its own specialized assignments and purposes; its own common types of SOURCES;* and its own expected documentation styles (Chapters 36–38).

No matter what differences exist among the academic disciplines, writing processes and strategies interconnect and overlap across the curriculum. Chapters 1 and 2 discuss elements of the WRITING SITUATION and WRITING PROCESS that are common to various disciplines. Chapter 7 highlights specific types of papers common in many academic situations. Quick Reference 39.1 compares elements of the academic disciplines.

To understand some of the differences among the disciplines, consider these three quite different paragraphs about a mountain.

HUMANITIES

The mountain stands above all that surrounds it. Giant timber—part of a collage of evergreen and deciduous trees—conceals the expansive mountain's slope, where cattle once grazed. At the base of the mountain, a cool stream flows over rocks of all sizes, colours, and shapes. Next to the outer bank of the stream stands a shingled farmhouse, desolate, yet suggesting its active past. Unfortunately, the peaceful scene is interrupted by billboards and chairlifts, landmarks of a modern, fast-paced life.

SOCIAL SCIENCES

Among the favourite pastimes of Canadian city dwellers is the "return to nature." Many outdoor enthusiasts hope to enjoy a scenic trip to the mountains, only to be disappointed. They know they have arrived at the mountain that they have travelled hundreds of kilometres to see because huge billboards are directing them to its base. As they look up the mountain, dozens of people are riding over the treetops in a chairlift, littering the slope with paper cups and food wrappers. At the base of the mountain stands the inevitable refreshment stand, found at virtually all Canadian tourist attractions. Land developers consider such commercialization a way to preserve and utilize natural resources, but environmentalists are appalled.

---

*Words printed in SMALL CAPITAL LETTERS are discussed elsewhere in the text and are defined in the Terms Glossary at the back of this book.

Comparing the Disciplines

DISCIPLINE	TYPES OF ASSIGNMENTS	PRIMARY SOURCES	SECONDARY SOURCES	USUAL DOCUMENTATION STYLES
HUMANITIES				
e.g., history, languages, literature, philosophy, art, music, theatre	essays, response, statements, reviews, analyses, orginal works such as stories, poems, memoirs	literary works, manuscripts, paintings and sculptures, historical documents, films, plays, photographs, artifacts from popular culture, personal experiences	reviews, journal articles, research papers, books	MLA, CM
SOCIAL SCIENCES				
e.g., psychology, sociology, anthropology, education	research reports, case studies, reviews of the literature, analyses, ethnographies	surveys, interviews, observations, tests and measures	journal articles, scholarly books, literature reviews	APA
NATURAL SCIENCES				
e.g., biology, chemistry, physics, mathematics	research or lab reports, research proposals, science reviews	experiments, field notes and direct observations, measurements	journal reports, research papers, books	often CSE but varies by discipline

NATURAL SCIENCES

The mountain rises approximately 2100 metres above sea level. The underlying rock is igneous, of volcanic origin, composed primarily of granites and feldspars. Three distinct biological communities are present on the mountain. The community at the top of the mountain is alpine, dominated by very short grasses and forbs. At middle altitudes, the community is a typical northern boreal coniferous forest community, and at the base and lower altitudes, deciduous forest is the dominant community. This community has, however, been highly affected by agricultural development along the river at its base and by recreational development.

These examples illustrate that each discipline has its own perspective and emphasis. The paragraph written for the humanities describes the mountain from the writer's perspective—personal, yet representative of a wider human response. The paragraph written for the social sciences focuses on the behaviour of people as a group. The paragraph written for the natural sciences reports observations of natural phenomena.

((•
AUDIO LESSON
Section 1: Big
Ideas—
Researching
Your Topic

((•
AUDIO LESSON
Section 2:
Practice
Questions—
Researching
Your Topic

((•
AUDIO LESSON
Section 3:
Rapid Review—
Researching
Your Topic

39b What are primary research and secondary research in the disciplines?

Different source materials lead to different kinds of writing (Chapter 7). PRIMARY SOURCES offer you firsthand exposure to texts or information. In the humanities, primary sources are original creative works, including novels, stories, poems, autobiographies, plays, films, musical compositions, and works of art (Chapter 40). In the social and natural sciences, primary sources may include books and articles in which researchers report findings from their research studies for the first time. You might also complete your own primary research, conducting experiments, surveys, or careful observations (Chapter 41).

SECONDARY SOURCES are scholarly writings that SUMMARIZE, ANALYZE, or SYNTHESIZE primary sources. In the humanities, secondary sources offer analysis and interpretation of primary works. In the social and natural sciences, secondary sources summarize, then synthesize findings, and draw parallels that offer new insights. You might review Quick Reference 4.4 in section 4d to understand the difference between primary and secondary sources.

39c What can help me write assignments in various disciplines?

A useful strategy for writing assignments in different disciplines is to analyze successful writings that match the requirements of your assignment. Instructors sometimes provide models for such papers or point you to similar published works. Following are some types of questions that will help you analyze model writings.

1. Are papers divided by subheadings or not?
2. Are specific parts required? Is there a specified format?
3. Does the paper require sources? If so, do writers tend to cite most of their sources in one place (for example, near the beginning), or do they cite sources throughout?
4. What kinds of sources appear in the writing? Are they primary or secondary? Which kinds of books, periodicals, or other sources do the writers tend to use?
5. Is the tone informal or very formal? Do writers use first person or third person?
6. Is the writing characterized by explanations and discussions that are full and expansive or concise and terse?
7. To what extent are writers expected to include their opinions or personal experiences, and to what extent are they expected to rely on objective analyses or source materials?
8. What is the mix of summary and analysis or interpretation?
9. What are typical introduction and conclusion strategies in model sources?
10. What documentation style do the writers use?

39d How do I use documentation in the disciplines?

Writers use DOCUMENTATION to credit the sources they've used and to help their readers learn more. A writer who neglects to credit a source is guilty of PLAGIARISM (35b).

DOCUMENTATION STYLES differ among the disciplines. In the humanities, most fields use the documentation style of the Modern Language Association (MLA), as explained and illustrated in Chapter 36. Occasionally, the humanities use CM (Chicago Manual) style, as explained and illustrated in Chapter 38. In the social sciences, most fields use the documentation style of the American Psychological Association (APA), as explained and illustrated in Chapter 37. In the natural sciences, documentation styles vary, although the Council of Science Editors (CSE) style is frequently used, and some technical fields use the IEEE style (see Chapter 38). Ask each of your science and technology instructors about the particular documentation style required for his or her assignments.

Chapter 40

WRITING ABOUT THE HUMANITIES AND LITERATURE

AUDIO LESSON
Section 1: Big
Ideas—
Constructing an
Argument

AUDIO LESSON
Section 2:
Practice
Questions—
Constructing an
Argument

AUDIO LESSON
Section 3:
Rapid Review—
Constructing
an Argument

Into the Wind:
Understanding
the Rhetoric of
Arrangement

All in the
Family:
Understanding
the Rhetoric of
Subject

It's All About
the Food:
Understanding
the Rhetoric of
Argument

40a What are the humanities?

The humanities consist of a set of disciplines that seek to represent and understand human experience, creativity, thought, and values. These disciplines include literature, languages, philosophy, and sometimes history, which is often grouped with the social sciences, however. The fine arts (music, art, dance, theatre, and creative writing) may either be grouped with the humanities or given their own independent classification.

40b What types of sources do I use in the humanities?

In the humanities, existing documents or artifacts are PRIMARY SOURCES, and the writer's task generally is to analyze and interpret them. A humanities class assignment might invite you to create primary sources yourself.

Some humanities papers will require SECONDARY SOURCES. These are articles and books that someone has written to explain or interpret a primary source.

40c What types of papers do I write in the humanities?

Because the humanities cover an impressively broad range of knowledge, writing in the humanities covers many types and purposes.

SUMMARIES

Occasionally your instructor will request an objective summary of a text; you might need to tell the plot of a novel or present the main points of an article. Generally, however, summary is a means to a larger end. For example, writing an interpretation often requires you to summarize parts of the source. See 7f.1.

SYNTHESES

SYNTHESIS relates several texts, ideas, or pieces of information to one another (4f). For example, you might read several accounts of the origins of the Quebec independence movement and then write a synthesis that explains what caused the movement. See 7f.4.

RESPONSES

In a response, you give your personal reaction to a work, supported by explanations of your reasoning. Even though a response is a personal reaction, think of it as writing to inform or to argue; provide reasons for your response so your readers understand clearly why you believe as you do and see that your response is reasonable. Some instructors want you to justify your response with references to a text, while other instructors do not. Clarify what your instructor wants before you begin. See 7f.2.

NARRATIVES

When you write a NARRATIVE, you construct a coherent story out of separate facts or events. You might do the kind of work that a biographer does, gathering isolated events in people's lives and interviewing those people or others who knew them, or researching letters or other writings and related SOURCES.

INTERPRETATIONS

An interpretation explains the meaning or significance of a particular text, event, or work of art. You present your point of view and explain your reasoning. The quality of your reasoning determines how successfully you've conveyed your point. See 7f.3.

CRITIQUES

In a critique (also called a CRITICAL RESPONSE or a review), you present judgments about a particular work, supported by your underlying reasoning. Critical responses and reviews may focus on the literary form, or genre, of a work, or on a work's accuracy, logic, or conclusions. Finally, responses or reviews may analyze a work's relations to other works or a work's similarities to and differences from the "real" world.

ANALYSES

When you engage in analysis, you examine material by breaking it into its component parts and discovering how the parts interrelate. You explain texts, events, objects, or documents by identifying and discussing important elements in them. These elements can include matters of form (how the work is put together) or of ideas (what the work means). The humanities use a number of **analytic frameworks**, or systematic ways of investigating a work. Quick Reference 40.1 summarizes some common analytic frameworks used most notably in literary analysis.

QUICK REFERENCE **40.1**

Selected analytic frameworks used in the humanities

RHETORICAL

Examines how and why people use LOGIC, EMOTION, and ETHOS to create desired effects on specific audiences, in specific situations (see Chapter 4).

FEMINIST

Focuses on how women are presented and treated, concentrating especially on power relations between men and women.

CULTURAL/NEW HISTORICAL

Explores how social, economic, and other cultural forces influence the development of ideas, texts, art, laws, customs, and so on. Also explores how individual texts or events provide broader understanding of the past or present.

DECONSTRUCTIONIST

Assumes that the meaning of any given text is not stable or "in" the work. Rather, meaning always depends on contexts and the interests of those in power. The goal of deconstruction is to produce multiple possible meanings of a work, usually to undermine traditional interpretations.

continued ➤

FORMALIST

Centres on matters of structure, form, and traditional literary devices (plot, rhythm, images, symbolism, DICTION).

MARXIST

Assumes that the most important forces in human experience are economic and material ones. Focuses on power differences between economic classes and the effects of those differences.

READER-RESPONSE

Emphasizes how the individual reader determines meaning. The reader's personal history, values, experiences, relationships, and previous reading all contribute to how he or she interprets a particular work or event.

40d **Which documentation style do I use to write about the humanities?**

Most fields in the humanities use the documentation style of the Modern Language Association (MLA), as explained and illustrated in Chapter 36. Some disciplines in the humanities use Chicago Manual (CM) style, as explained in Chapter 38. Writers use documentation to give credit to the sources they've used. A writer who neglects to credit a source is guilty of PLAGIARISM.

EXERCISE 40-1 Consider how you could use some of the frameworks in Quick Reference 40.1 to analyze the photograph in Figure 40.1.

Figure 40.1 Use analytic frameworks to view this photograph.

Literature includes fiction (novels and short stories); drama (plays, scripts, and some films); poetry (poems and lyrics); as well as nonfiction with artistic qualities (memoirs, personal essays, and the like). Since ancient times, literature has represented human experiences, entertained readers, and enlarged people's perspectives.

AUDIO LESSON Section 1: Big Ideas— Becoming a Critical Reader and a Better Writer

Writing about literature generates insights about your reading. It helps you understand other people, ideas, times, and places. It shows you how authors use language to stir the imaginations, emotions, and intellects of their readers. Finally, writing is a way to share your own reading experiences and insights with other readers.

40f What general strategies can help me write about literature?

When you write about literature, you want to read the work closely as well as actively (Chapter 4). Such reading involves asking what the work means, why the author made a particular choice, what other works influenced the author, and why readers react to the work as they do. Quick References 40.2, 40.3, and 40.4 list several questions or elements that encourage active reading.

AUDIO LESSON Section 2: Practice Questions— Becoming a Critical Reader and a Better Writer

---

QUICK REFERENCE 40.2

Questions for an interpretation paper

1. What is a central theme of the work?
2. How do particular parts of the work relate to the theme?
3. If patterns exist in the work, what might they mean? Patterns include repeated images, situations, words, and so on.
4. What meaning does the author create through the elements listed in Quick Reference 40.3?
5. Why might the work end as it does?

QUICK REFERENCE 40.3

Major elements of formal analysis in literary works

PLOT	Events and their sequence
THEME	Central idea or message
STRUCTURE	Organization and relationship of parts to each other and to the whole
CHARACTERIZATION	Traits, thoughts, and actions of the characters
SETTING	Time and place of the action
POINT OF VIEW	Perspective or position from which the material is presented—by a narrator, a main character, another character, or an external observer

continued ➤

STYLE	How words and sentence structures present the material
IMAGERY	Descriptive or figurative language that creates mental pictures for the reader
TONE	Author's attitude toward the subject of the work—and sometimes toward the reader—expressed through choice of words, imagery, and point of view (Chapter 1)
FIGURE OF SPEECH	Unusual use or combination of words, as in metaphor and simile, for enhanced vividness or effect
SYMBOLISM	Meaning beneath the surface of the words and images
RHYTHM	Beat, metre
RHYME	Repetition of similar sounds for their auditory effect

QUICK REFERENCE **40.4**

Major topics for cultural analysis

GENDER	How does a work portray women or men and define—or challenge—their respective roles in society?
CLASS	How does a work portray relationships among the upper, middle, and lower economic classes? How do characters' actions or perspectives result from their wealth and power—or the lack of wealth and power?
RACE AND ETHNICITY	How does a work portray the influences of race and ethnicity on the characters' actions, status, and values?
HISTORY	How does a work reflect—or challenge—past events and values in a society?
AUTOBIOGRAPHY	How might the writer's experiences have influenced this particular work? Similarly, how might the times in which the writer lives or lived have affected his or her work?
GENRE	How is the work similar to or different from other works of its type (plays, sonnets, mysteries, comic novels, memoirs, and so on)?

Sometimes instructors ask students to answer questions that deal with material on a literal level. If a question asks what happens in the plot or what a passage is saying, you need to answer with a SUMMARY or PARAPHRASE of the work. If a question asks about the historical context of a work, or asks for biographical or situational information about the author, you probably need to do some research and then report exactly what you find.

More often, assignments call for making INFERENCES, reading "between the lines" to figure out what is implied but not stated. This reading skill is especially crucial for reading literature because literature tends to "show" rather than to "tell." Inferential thinking is necessary when your instructor asks you to discuss why a character does something for which the author provides no explicit reason. It's necessary when your instructor asks you to explain the effect of images in a poem, to discuss how a work implies the author's stance on a social issue, or to analyze how the author depicts the role of women, men, or specific ethnic groups.

Writing effective papers about literature involves more than summarizing the plot. It involves CRITICAL THINKING and SYNTHESIS. In such papers, you state a CLAIM (an observation or a position about the work of literature) and convince your readers that the thesis is reasonable. To be effective, your papers must be thorough and well supported. For support, you make direct references to the work, by SUMMARIZING, PARAPHRASING, and QUOTING specific passages (35h–j) and by explaining precisely *why* and *how* the selected passages support your interpretation.

40g How do I write different types of papers about literature?

When you read, look for details or passages that relate to your thesis. Mark up the text as you read by selectively underlining passages or by writing notes, comments, or questions in the margin. Alternatively, take notes separately.

WRITING A PERSONAL RESPONSE

In a personal response paper, you explain your reaction to a literary work or some aspect of it. You might write about why you did or did not enjoy reading a particular work; discuss whether situations in the work are similar to your personal experiences and why such observations deserve the reader's consideration; explain whether you agree or disagree with the author's point of view and why; or answer a question or explore a problem that the work raised for you.

WRITING AN INTERPRETATION

An interpretation explains the message or viewpoint that you think the work conveys. Most works of literature are open to more than one interpretation. Your task, then, is not to discover the single right answer. It is to determine a possible interpretation and provide an argument that supports it. The questions in Quick Reference 40.2 can help you write an effective interpretation paper.

WRITING A FORMAL ANALYSIS

A formal analysis explains how elements of a literary work function to create meaning or effect. Quick Reference 40.3 describes some of the major literary elements that you might expect to use in formal analyses.

To prepare to write a formal analysis, read the work thoroughly, looking for patterns and repetitions. Write notes as you read to help you form insights about these patterns and repetitions.

WRITING A CULTURAL ANALYSIS

A cultural analysis relates the literary work to broader historical, social, cultural, and political situations. Instructors might ask you to explain how events or prevailing attitudes influence the writing of a work or the way readers understand it. Quick Reference 40.4 lists some common focuses for cultural analysis.

40h What special rules apply to writing about literature?

When you write about literature, certain special elements come into play.

Into the Wind: Understanding the Rhetoric of Arrangement

All in the Family: Understanding the Rhetoric of Subject

Office Hours: Evaluating Sources

40h.1   Using present and past tense correctly

Always use the PRESENT TENSE when you describe or discuss a literary work or any of its elements: *Constance's adventures in Cyprus and Verona—the settings of the Shakespearean tragedies—are framed by two brief scenes set in her campus office.* The present tense is also correct for discussing what the author has done in a specific work: *By transforming Desdemona into a warrior, MacDonald is playing upon an imaginary implication of Desdemona's taste for Othello's gory tales.*

If you are discussing events that take place before the action of a literary work has begun, a PAST-TENSE VERB is correct: *But her own career has come* [before the action starts] *to a dead end.* Also use past tenses, as appropriate, to discuss historical events or biographical information: *MacDonald's play opens with an epigraph taken from the psychologist Carl Gustav Jung, who theorized that our unconscious combines archetypal characters found in myth and literature: the Fool, the Hero, and so on.*

40h.2   Using your own ideas and secondary sources

Office Hours:
Citing
Sources

Office Hours:
Avoiding
Plagiarism

Some assignments call for only your own ideas about the literary work that is the subject of your essay. Other assignments require you additionally to use SECONDARY SOURCES, books and articles in which experts discuss some aspect of the literary text or other material related to your topic.

You might use secondary sources to support your own ideas, perhaps by drawing on the ideas of a scholar who agrees with you or debating the ideas of a scholar who disagrees with you. Or, if you think that you have a new or different interpretation, you might summarize, analyze, or critique what others have written, to provide a framework for your own analysis. You can locate secondary sources by using the research process discussed in Chapter 34. A particularly important resource for research about literature is the *MLA International Bibliography,* which is the most comprehensive index to literary scholarship.

As with all source-based writing, you need to DOCUMENT primary and secondary sources to ensure that readers never mistake someone else's ideas for yours. Otherwise, you're PLAGIARIZING (see Chapter 35). Most literature instructors require students to use the DOCUMENTATION STYLE of the Modern Language Association (MLA) that we described in Chapter 36. Check with your instructor.

40i   Sample student essay

The student essay that follows uses one SECONDARY SOURCE in order to draw a parallel with that work. It uses MLA-STYLE DOCUMENTATION.

The essay examines a drama, *Goodnight Desdemona (Good Morning Juliet)* by Ann-Marie MacDonald, a playwright, novelist, and actor. MacDonald won the Governor General's Award for Drama for this comic play in 1990. Although the play's protagonist is apparently on a quest for the key to a strange manuscript that could unlock a literary mystery, her search takes her into the unexplored territory of her own personality. MacDonald shifts playfully among scenes, characters, and scripts, tantalizing us with clues to the play's deeper mystery. The student's paper examines how MacDonald uses the framework of the quest to "take apart" elements in two Shakespearean tragedies and in the process allow the main character to construct her own fully developed personality.

Simon Brook

Professor Boland

Drama 250

12 April 2013

The Construction of the Protagonist in

Goodnight Desdemona (Good Morning Juliet)

On the surface, Ann-Marie MacDonald's comedy *Goodnight Desdemona (Good Morning Juliet)* is the story of an imaginary literary puzzle. Constance, a talented but ineffectual academic, believes that the two Shakespearean tragedies *Othello* and *Romeo and Juliet* were originally written as comedies by an unknown author. By deciphering a mysterious manuscript, Constance hopes to find the original texts of the two plays and the identity of their author. MacDonald does not show us Constance's literary labours, however. Instead, most of the play is a dream sequence in which Constance becomes a character in the two Shakespearean tragedies. Only at the play's end do we learn that Constance's true search is not a literary quest at all: The dream sequence is a descent into Constance's unconscious, and her literary puzzle is a metaphor for her quest for herself.

Constance's adventures in Cyprus and Verona—the settings of the Shakespearean tragedies—are framed by two brief scenes set in her campus office. There we see her as a comical figure, timid and socially awkward; her nickname, we discover later on, is "Mouse." Constance's talents are exploited by the suave Professor Claude Night, with whom she is hopelessly in love, and who has built a successful career by plagiarizing Constance's work. But her own career has come to a dead end.

Her colleagues ridicule her bizarre theory about the two Shakespearean tragedies. From her observation that the tragic outcomes of the two plays turn on "flimsy mistakes—a lost hanky, a delayed wedding announcement" (21), Constance reasons that Shakespeare (as plagiarist) eliminated the role of a fool from each play. This "Wise Fool"

(Proportions shown in this paper are adjusted to fit space limitations of this book. Follow actual dimensions given in this book and in your instructor's directions.)

continued ➤   589

would have been the unknown author's agent in concocting and then correcting the "mistakes" in the original comic versions of *Othello* and *Romeo and Juliet*. By confronting the characters and situations in the plays, Constance believes, the Wise Fool would have engineered happy endings for them.

No sooner does Constance set this part of her thesis down on paper than Professor Night arrives to collect the latest scholarly pieces she has ghostwritten for him. He casually announces that he is eloping with one of his students and is taking the post at Oxford University that Constance has coveted. She takes it all quietly, as usual.

Betrayed in love and blocked in her career, Constance has reached the lowest point in her life. She imagines herself falling into a decline and dying pathetically. In her vision she is awarded a posthumous doctorate; a chastened Claude Night lays roses daily on her grave. Rousing herself from this hallucination, Constance immediately begins to discard the paraphernalia of her trivial and unsatisfying identity, tossing keepsakes into the wastebasket. When a few pages of the mysterious manuscript fall into the trash as well, the inscription on its cover catches her eye:

> You who possess the eyes to see
>
> this strange and wondrous alchemy,
>
> where words transform to vision'ry,
>
> where one plus two makes one, not three;
>
> open this book if you agree
>
> to be illusion's refugee,
>
> and of return no guarantee—
>
> unless you find your true identity.
>
> And discover who the Author be. (28-29)

Sent on her search with these words, Constance falls into her own wastebasket and directly into the action of *Othello*.

Constance enters Shakespeare's plots at two crucial moments: just as the jealous Othello is about to murder his innocent wife, Desdemona, in Cyprus, and at the moment when family hatreds in Verona lead Romeo to fight Juliet's cousin in the duel that sets in motion the lovers' downfall.

continued ➤

Brook 3

Constance struggles to set things right between the characters while she hunts unsuccessfully for the key to the original manuscript of the two plays. A comedy of errors and incongruities is the result.

As Constance stumbles through *Othello* and then *Romeo and Juliet*, we witness odds and ends of famous Shakespearean speeches and scenes. MacDonald's playing on stage reality and our reality is reminiscent of Tom Stoppard's absurdist version of *Hamlet* in *Rosencrantz and Guildenstern Are Dead*. When Constance hears gunfire at the siege of Cyprus, she wonders, "They can't use real blood, can they?" (37). She is an incongruous visitor, knowing more about the characters and their circumstances than they believe possible, intruding on their lives, demolishing Shakespeare's plots, answering Shakespearean speeches in colourless Canadian English. (At one point she remembers how she ought to be speaking as a character in an Elizabethan play and starts counting iambic pentameter on her fingers.)

By interfering in their plots, Constance inadvertently transforms the two plays into the comedies she believes they were intended to be. She saves Desdemona by revealing the trap that Iago had set to make Othello murderously jealous.

> CONSTANCE.   ...   I've preempted the Wise Fool! He must be here
>   somewhere—
>
> I'll track him down and reinstate him in the text . . . (38)

She cannot find her fool, however. Constance barely escapes with her life from *Othello*, falling suddenly into *Romeo and Juliet*, where she stops Romeo's fateful duel.

Revisiting these two plays with Constance forces us to reimagine their two heroines. As Constance suspected, in the "pre-Shakespearean" comic versions of their plays (that is, the plays as MacDonald shows them), Desdemona and Juliet are not innocent, helpless, doomed victims. Rather, Constance finds Desdemona to be a warlike woman who advises her:

> If thou wouldst know thyself an Amazon,
>
> acquire a taste for blood. (36-37)

In Shakespeare's *Othello*, the Venetian general has wooed Desdemona with stories of military victories in exotic lands. By transforming Desdemona into a warrior, MacDonald is playing

continued ➤

upon an imaginary implication of Desdemona's taste for Othello's gory tales and of her wish to accompany Othello to the battlefields in Cyprus.

The teenaged characters Constance meets in Verona really are teenagers—randy, brawling, and rather shallow. In MacDonald's version of her story, Juliet is independent and sexually adventurous. A piece of quasi-Shakespearean stage nonsense has Constance impersonating a man, and Romeo a woman; both Romeo and Juliet become infatuated with Constance/Constantine. A flustered Constance exclaims at the insistent Juliet:

> Heavenly days, what's come over you?!
>
> You're supposed to be all innocence. (69)

Desdemona and Juliet, as transformed by MacDonald, represent possible models for Constance as an autonomous twentieth-century woman.

Meanwhile, MacDonald has been dropping hints at the progress of Constance's quest.

> CONSTANCE.   . . . I have to find the Author first;
>
> or else the Fool to lead me to the bard.
>
> JULIET.   Author? Fool?
>
> CONSTANCE.   And Self. It is my quest, and means
>
> more to me than love or death. (71)

These hints are for the audience, but not for Constance. Bound up in the pursuit of her thesis, she follows false trails and misconstrues the message contained in the introduction to the manuscript: "where one plus two makes one, not three. . . ." She does not yet recognize that these words bid her to reconstruct her one-dimensional personality by reassembling the neglected parts of her "self," and that this is her true quest.

Earlier on, in her office, Constance had tossed the signs of her mouse-like identity into her wastebasket. Now she is inspired by the two not-quite-Shakespearean heroines. Desdemona, who knows the scholarly Constance as "the pedant," adds another dimension to Constance's personality by dubbing her an Amazon and inciting her to admit her hatred for her betrayer, Professor Night. Thinking of her own betrayer, Constance nearly kills the traitorous Iago in a swordfight.

continued ➤

I saw a flash of red before my eyes.

I felt a rush of power through my veins.

I tasted iron blood inside my mouth.

I loved it! (50)

Then, in Verona, Constance begins to reclaim her sexual and passionate side. Constance had earlier admitted to only a delayed adolescent crush on Claude Night—now Juliet coaxes her to proclaim that she once truly loved him. Juliet and Romeo nearly succeeded in drawing Constance into their romantic escapades. Finally, Desdemona and Juliet confront each other and stage a tug-of-war over Constance, who refuses to surrender completely to the obsessions of either one. In an instant, Constance realizes who the Wise Fool is. She is the Fool. And the Author.

In following her supposed scholarly quest, Constance has deconstructed Shakespeare's two plays, helped us to reimagine Desdemona and Juliet, and constructed her own identity. The Amazon in Desdemona and the sexual being in Juliet combine, in proper measure, with the pedant. The end of Constance's search is the integration of her personality followed by a symbolic rebirth—all three women have their birthday on the day the play ends. MacDonald's play opens with an epigraph taken from the psychologist Carl Gustav Jung, who theorized that our unconscious combines archetypal characters found in myth and literature: the Fool, the Hero, and so on. Hints scattered throughout the play seem to point to this idea of the self and its construction. Other hints, as we have seen, lead to the interpretation of Constance's quest as a quest for herself. Her dreamed adventures in Cyprus and Verona, therefore, may be seen as a healing journey into her unconscious. As Constance learns to act as an autonomous and complete personality, it becomes clear that she is the Author of the tale by the same token that she has become the author of her own life.

Works Cited

MacDonald, Ann-Marie. *Goodnight Desdemona (Good Morning Juliet).* Toronto: Playwrights Canada, 1997. Print.

Stoppard, Tom. *Rosencrantz and Guildenstern Are Dead.* New York: Grove, 1968. Print.

Chapter 41

WRITING IN THE SOCIAL SCIENCES AND NATURAL SCIENCES

SOCIAL SCIENCES

41a What are the social sciences?

The social sciences focus on the behaviour of people as individuals and in groups. The field includes disciplines such as economics, education, political science, psychology, sociology, and certain specializations in geography. At some colleges and universities, history is included in the social sciences; at others, it's part of the humanities.

41b What kinds of sources do I use in the social sciences?

((•
AUDIO
LESSON
Section 1:
Big Ideas—
Researching
Your Topic

Some methods used in the social sciences lead to **quantitative research**, which analyzes statistics and other numerical data. Other methods lead to **qualitative research**, which relies on careful descriptions and interpretations.

In the social sciences, PRIMARY SOURCES include surveys and questionnaires, observations, interviews, and experiments. When writing about information you gather, you analyze and explain what the sources mean or why they're significant.

((•
AUDIO
LESSON
Section 2:
Practice
Questions—
Researching
Your Topic

SURVEYS AND QUESTIONNAIRES

Surveys and questionnaires systematically gather information from a representative number of individuals. To prepare a questionnaire, use the guidelines in Quick Reference 32.1 on page 411.

((•
AUDIO
LESSON
Section 3:
Rapid Review—
Researching
Your Topic

OBSERVATIONS

Some writing in the social sciences requires direct observations of people's behaviours. In reporting your observations, tell what tools you used, because they might have influenced what you saw. For example, it is important to say if a photo was posed, because people behave differently when they know they are being photographed.

INTERVIEWS

You might interview people to gather opinions and impressions. Remember that interviews aren't always reliable because people's memories are imprecise, and their first impulse is to present themselves in the best light. Try to interview as many people as possible so that you can cross-check information.

EXPERIMENTS

The social sciences sometimes use data from experiments as a source. For example, if you want to learn how people react in a particular situation, you can set up that situation artificially and bring individuals (known as "subjects") into it to observe their behaviour.

With all methods of inquiry in the social sciences, you need to be ethical. Professional social scientists must seek explicit written permission from their subjects, and colleges and universities have official panels to review research proposals to make sure the studies are ethical. Check with your instructor to see whether you need to have your study approved.

41c What are writing purposes and practices in the social sciences?

The purpose of much writing in the social sciences is explanatory. Writers try to explain both what a behaviour is and why it happens. SUMMARY and SYNTHESIS (7f.1, 7f.4) are important fundamental strategies for explanatory writing in the social sciences. Interpretations and ANALYSES (7f.3) are common when social scientists write about problems and their solutions.

Other kinds of writing that are common in the social sciences include reports of observations (7d.1), case studies (7d.4), and ETHNOGRAPHIES (7d.5). Social scientists also write reports and analyses of data (7e.1–2), essays of application (7f.5), proposals (similar to business proposals, 43j), and, of course, research papers (Chapter 33).

Social scientists are careful to define their KEY TERMS when they write, especially when they discuss complex social issues. Without defining such terms, writers may confuse readers or lead them to wrong conclusions.

In courses in the social sciences, your goal is usually to be a neutral observer, so most of the time you need to use the THIRD PERSON (*he, she, it, one, they*) and comment impersonally on the data. Using the FIRST PERSON (*I, we, our*) is acceptable only when you write about your own reactions and experiences. Some writing in the social sciences overuses the PASSIVE VOICE (15o–p). Style manuals for the social sciences recommend using the ACTIVE VOICE whenever possible.

41d What are different types of papers in the social sciences?

Instructors in the social sciences will sometimes assign the same kinds of writing that are common in the humanities (40c). Three additional types of papers are case studies, research reports, and research papers (or reviews of the literature).

Report 4: Research Report

CASE STUDIES

A **case study** is an intensive study of one group or individual. We discussed these in 7d.4; here are some additional perspectives. If you write a case study, describe situations as a neutral observer. Refrain from interpreting them unless your assignment explicitly permits interpretation. Always differentiate between fact and opinion (4d.1).

A case study is usually presented in a relatively fixed format, but the specific parts and their order vary. Most case studies contain the following components: (1) basic identifying information about the individual or group; (2) a history of the individual or group; (3) observations of the individual's or group's behaviour; and (4) conclusions as well as possible recommendations that result from the observations.

RESEARCH REPORTS

Research reports explain your own original research based on PRIMARY SOURCES. These may result from interviews, questionnaires, observations, or experiments. Research reports in the social sciences often follow a prescribed format: (1) statement of the problem;

(2) background, sometimes including a review of the literature; (3) methodology; (4) results; and (5) discussion of findings.

RESEARCH PAPERS (OR REVIEWS OF THE LITERATURE)

More often, social science research requires undergraduate students to summarize, analyze, and synthesize SECONDARY SOURCES. To prepare a **review of the literature**, comprehensively gather and analyze the sources that have been published on a specific topic. "Literature" in this sense simply means "the body of work on a subject." Sometimes a review of the literature is a part of a longer paper, usually the "background" section of a research report. Other times the entire paper might be an extensive review of the literature.

ETHNOGRAPHIES

ETHNOGRAPHIES are comprehensive studies of a particular group of people interacting in a specific situation. Section 7d.5 provides advice on writing these.

41e What documentation style should I use in the social sciences?

If you use sources when writing about the social sciences, you must credit them using documentation. The American Psychological Association (APA) is the most commonly used documentation style in the social sciences. APA style uses PARENTHETICAL REFERENCES in the body of a paper and a list of REFERENCES at the end. We describe APA documentation style in detail in Chapter 37, providing a sample student research paper using APA style in section 37h.

Chicago Manual (CM) documentation style is sometimes used in the social sciences. The CM BIBLIOGRAPHIC NOTE style is described in detail in Chapter 38.

NATURAL SCIENCES

41f What are the natural sciences?

The natural sciences include disciplines such as astronomy, biology, chemistry, geology, and physics. Scientists form and test hypotheses, which are assumptions made to prove their logical soundness and consequences in the real world. They do this to explain CAUSE AND EFFECT (4d.3) as systematically and objectively as possible.

The scientific method, commonly used in the sciences to make discoveries, is a procedure for gathering information related to a specific hypothesis. The scientific method is the cornerstone of all inquiry in the sciences. Quick Reference 41.1 gives guidelines for using the scientific method.

41g What are writing purposes and practices in the natural sciences?

Plug It In:
Understanding
the Rhetoric of
Proof

Because scientists usually write to inform their AUDIENCE about factual information, SUMMARY and SYNTHESIS are important fundamental writing techniques.

Exactness is extremely important in scientific writing. Readers expect precise descriptions of procedures and findings, free of personal bias. Scientists expect to be able to *replicate*—repeat step by step—the experiment or process the researcher carried out and obtain the same outcome.

Guidelines for using the scientific method

1. Formulate a tentative explanation—known as a *hypothesis*—for a scientific phenomenon. Be as specific as possible.

2. Read and summarize previously published information related to your hypothesis.

3. Plan and outline a method of investigation to uncover the information needed to test your hypothesis.

4. Experiment, following exactly the investigative procedures you've outlined.

5. Observe closely the results of the experiment, and write notes carefully.

6. Analyze the results. If they prove the hypothesis to be false, rework the investigation and begin again. If the results confirm the hypothesis, say so.

7. Write a report of your research. At the end, you can suggest additional hypotheses that might be investigated.

Completeness is as important as exactness. Without complete information, a reader can misunderstand the writer's message and reach a wrong conclusion.

Because science writing depends largely on objective observation rather than subjective comments, scientists generally avoid using the FIRST PERSON (*I, we, our*) in their writing. The sciences generally focus on the experiment rather than on the person doing the experimenting.

When writing for the sciences, you're often expected to follow fixed formats, which are designed to summarize a project and present its results efficiently. In your report, organize the information to achieve clarity and precision. Writers in the sciences sometimes use charts, graphs, tables, diagrams, and other illustrations to present material. Illustrations may be more effective than words in explaining complex material, as in Figure 41.1.

COMMON DISEASES AND INFECTIONS WITH THEIR MICROBIAL CAUSES

	Bacteria	Fungus	Protozoa	Virus
Athlete's foot		▲		
Chickenpox				▲
Common cold				▲
Diarrheal disease	▲		▲	▲
Flu				▲
Genital herpes				▲
Malaria			▲	
Meningitis	▲			▲
Pneumonia	▲	▲		▲
Sinusitis	▲	▲		
Skin diseases	▲	▲	▲	▲
Strep throat	▲			
Tuberculosis	▲			
Urinary tract infection	▲			
Vaginal infections	▲	▲		
Viral hepatitis				▲

Figure 41.1 A table conveying data

41h What documentation style should I use in the natural sciences?

If you use secondary sources when you write about the sciences, you are required to credit your sources by using documentation. Documentation styles in the various sciences differ somewhat from discipline to discipline and, even, from publication to publication. Ask your instructor which style to use.

The Council of Science Editors (CSE) has compiled style and documentation guidelines for the life sciences, the physical sciences, and mathematics. CSE documentation guidelines are described in sections 38c and 38d.

41i How do I write different types of papers in the natural sciences?

Reports and analyses of data (7e.1–2), lab reports and empirical studies (7e.3), and research papers (Chapter 33) are common in the natural sciences. Two additional major types of papers in the sciences are reports and reviews.

41i.1 Science reports

Science reports tell about observations and experiments. When they describe laboratory experiments, they're usually called lab reports. Formal reports feature the eight elements identified in Quick Reference 41.2. Less formal reports, which are sometimes assigned in introductory courses, might not include an abstract or a review of the literature. Ask your instructor which sections to include in your report.

QUICK REFERENCE 41.2

Parts of a science report

1. **Title.** Precisely describes your report's topic. Your instructor may require a title page that lists the title, your name, the course name and section, your instructor's name, and the date. If so, there is no recommended format in CSE style; generally, students use APA format (37g) or their instructor's.

2. **Abstract.** Provides a short overview of the report to help readers decide whether your research interests them.

3. **Introduction.** States the purpose behind your research and presents the hypothesis. Any needed background information and a review of the literature appear here.

4. **Methods and Materials.** Describes the equipment, materials, and procedures used.

5. **Results.** Provides the information obtained from your efforts. Charts, graphs, and photographs help present the data in a way that is easy for readers to grasp.

6. **Discussion.** Presents your interpretation and evaluation of the results. Did your efforts support your hypothesis? If not, can you suggest why not? Use concrete evidence in discussing your results.

7. **Conclusion.** Lists conclusions about the hypothesis and the outcomes of your efforts, paying particular attention to any implications that can be drawn from your work. Be specific in suggesting further research.

8. **References.** Presents references cited in the review of the literature, if any. Its format conforms to the requirements of the documentation style preferred by your instructor.

SAMPLE STUDENT SCIENCE REPORT

The sample science report here was written by a student in an intermediate course in biology. Like this sample, your report would be likely to follow APA format for margins, page numbering, and title page. The text and references would follow CSE-style recommendations.

EFFECTIVENESS   1

Adam Furman

Biology 201, Lab

Professor Joshua Mann

November 13, 2013

Title of report →   The Effectiveness of Common Antibiotics

Title of subsection →   Introduction   ← *Abstract omitted in this sample*

The purpose of this experiment was to test the effectiveness of antibiotics against two common bacteria.

Antibiotics are substances that inhibit life processes of bacteria. There are two types of antibiotics. One interferes with cell wall synthesis, causing death. The other disrupts protein synthesis, thus preventing replication.

Escherichia coli is a gram-negative bacterium. It is found in the colon of many mammals, including humans. Commonly, it contaminates beef and chicken products. *Staphylococcus epidermidis* is a gram-positive bacterium found naturally on the skin. This bacterium is often the cause of infected burns and cuts. Both bacteria were used in this experiment.

It is hypothesized that five chemical antibiotics will be effective against both bacteria. Also hypothesized is that two natural antimicrobials, echinacea and garlic, would not work very well.

Methods and Materials

Using aseptic techniques, two petri dishes were inoculated. *Staphylococcus epidermidis* was used on one dish and *Escherichia coli* on the second dish. A sterile paper disc was saturated with streptomycin. The disc was placed on one of the dishes. The process was repeated for the other dish. Both dishes were marked with identification and location of the paper discs. Each of the following was also saturated on paper discs and placed into its own zone on both dishes: sterile water (control), ampicillin, erythromycin, chloramphenicol, tetracycline, gentamycin, echinacea, and garlic.

EFFECTIVENESS   2

The dishes were incubated overnight at room temperature. The zone of inhibition of growth in centimetres was measured and recorded.

Results

Streptomycin, a protein synthesis disrupter, worked effectively to prevent growth of the *S. epidermidis* and the *E. coli*. Tetracycline inhibited the reproduction of the *S. epidermidis* and the *E. coli*. Ampicillin, a common bactericide, worked better on the *S. epidermidis* than on the *E. coli*, because *S. epidermidis* is gram positive and *E. coli* is gram negative. Gentamycin effectively prevented the growth of *E. coli*. Erythromycin and chloramphenicol behaved similarly to the ampicillin.

The antibiotics behaved as expected in regard to effectiveness against gram-positive and gram-negative bacteria. As hypothesized, the echinacea inhibited growth only slightly, indicating that it probably would not function as an antibiotic. The garlic had a zone of inhibition greater than expected for a non-antibiotic. Zero centimetres of inhibition from the sterile water control demonstrates that there was no contamination of the experiment.

Conclusion ◄───────────────

Discussion section omitted in this sample

The results imply that the ampicillin would be an effective treatment against *S. epidermidis* infection and gentamycin would prove effective in treating an infection of *E. coli*.

As with any experiment, it would be wise to repeat the tests again to check for accuracy. Other antibiotics could be tested against a larger range of bacteria for broader results.

No Cited References needed in this type of science report ◄───────────────

41i.2 Science reviews

A science review is a paper discussing published information on a scientific topic. The purpose of the review is SUMMARY: to assemble for readers all the current knowledge about the topic or issue. Sometimes, the purpose of a science review is SYNTHESIS: to suggest a new interpretation of the old material. In such reviews, the writer must present evidence to persuade readers that the new interpretation is valid.

If you're required to write a science review, you want to (1) choose a very limited scientific issue currently being researched; (2) use information that is current—the more recently published the articles, books, and journals you consult, the better; (3) accurately PARAPHRASE (35i) and SUMMARIZE (35j) material; and (4) DOCUMENT your sources (Chapters 36–38). If your review runs longer than two or three pages, you might want to use headings to help your reader understand the organization and idea progression of your paper. See Chapters 32–34 for advice on finding and using sources.

Chapter 42

MAKING PRESENTATIONS AND USING MULTIMEDIA

42a What are presentations?

Presentations, which are speeches often supported with multimedia tools, are common not only in academic disciplines across the curriculum, but also in work and public settings. Preparing a presentation and drafting a paper involve similar processes, and a review of Chapters 1 and 2 will be helpful here. The rest of this chapter will provide additional information for preparing presentations and using multimedia tools.

42b How does my situation focus my presentation?

Just as you need to adjust your writing according to each WRITING SITUATION, so you need to adjust presentations to fit PURPOSES, AUDIENCES, **roles**, and any special considerations. Consider three different situations.

- You want to address a group of students to inform them about a film club you're starting.
- You need to persuade a management group at work to adopt a new set of procedures for making purchasing decisions.
- You plan to give a toast at a friend's wedding to express your feelings and to entertain the wedding guests.

Different approaches will be successful in each instance because your purpose and audience are different.

The three main purposes for presentations are to entertain, to INFORM, and to PERSUADE (1b). In academic and work situations, the last two are most important. For a presentation, determine your purpose, and keep it in mind as you draft and revise your speech. For an informative presentation, state your purpose in the form of an INFINITIVE PHRASE: *to explain why, to clarify, to show how, to report, to define, to describe, to classify.* For a persuasive presentation, state your purpose as one of the following: *to convince, to argue, to agree with, to disagree with, to win over, to defend, to influence.*

42c How do I adapt my message to my audience?

Adapting your presentation to your listening audience means grabbing and holding their interest and being responsive to their viewpoints. Especially consider your listeners' prior knowledge of your topic, their desire to learn more, and whether they agree with your point of view. You'll find that your audience falls into one of three categories: *uninformed, informed,* or *mixed.*

((•
AUDIO
LESSON
Section 1:
Big Ideas—
Using
Language
Well and
Addressing
Your
Audience

UNINFORMED AUDIENCE	Start with the basics, and then move to a few new ideas. Define new terms and concepts, and avoid unnecessary technical terms. Use visual aids and give examples. Repeat key ideas—but not too often.
INFORMED AUDIENCE	Don't waste your audience members' time with the basics. From the beginning, reassure them that you'll be covering new ground. Devote most of your time to new ideas and concepts.
MIXED AUDIENCE	In your introduction, acknowledge the more informed audience members who are present. Explain that you're going to review the basic concepts briefly so that everyone can build from the same knowledge base. Move as soon as possible toward more complex concepts.

Adapting your presentation to the general needs and expectations of your audience doesn't mean saying only what they might want to hear. It means rather that you need to consider their knowledge of your topic and their interest in it. You can then make your message understandable and relevant by using appropriate language and examples.

42d How do I organize my presentation?

As with essays, an oral presentation has three parts: **introduction**, **body**, and **conclusion**. Within the body, you present your major points, with two to three supports for each point. Drafting a SENTENCE OUTLINE gets you close to your final form and forces you to sharpen your thinking. Quick Reference 42.1 shows you a sample outline for an oral presentation.

QUICK REFERENCE 42.1

Organizational outline for an oral presentation

Title:

Topic: _____

Specific purpose: _____

Thesis statement: _____

   I. Introduction (followed by a clear transition to point 1 in the body)
  II. Body
     A. Major point 1 and specific supporting examples (followed by a clear transition from point 1 to point 2, perhaps with a brief reference to the introduction)
     B. Major point 2 and specific supporting examples (followed by a clear transition from point 2 to point 3, perhaps with a brief reference to point 1 and the introduction)
     C. Major point 3 and specific supporting examples (perhaps with a brief reference to points 1 and 2)
 III. Conclusion (Refer to your introduction but do not repeat it verbatim or your audience will lose interest.)

INTRODUCING YOURSELF AND YOUR TOPIC

Your *ethos* is perhaps even more important in speaking than in writing (5g). Your audience needs to trust you—even like you. All audience members want to know three things about a speaker: Who are you? What are you going to talk about? Why should I listen? To respond effectively to these unasked questions, try these suggestions.

- Grab your audience's attention with an interesting question, quotation, or statistic; a bit of background information; a compliment; or an anecdote. If it is necessary to establish your credibility—even if someone has introduced you—briefly and humbly mention your qualifications as a speaker about your topic.
- Give your audience a road map of your talk: Tell where you're starting, where you're going, and how you intend to get there. Your listeners need to know that you won't waste their time.

FOLLOWING YOUR ROAD MAP

Although much advice for writing applies to oral presentations, listening to a presentation is very different from reading an essay. When you're reading an article and lose sight of the main point, you can reread a few paragraphs. But when you're listening to a speech, you can't go back. As a result, audiences generally need help following the speaker's line of reasoning. Here are some strategies to keep your listeners' minds from wandering and to help them follow your points.

- Signal clearly where you are on your road map by using cue word transitions such as *first, second,* and *third;* or *subsequently, therefore,* and *furthermore;* or *before, then,* and *next.*
- Define unfamiliar terms and concepts, and follow up with strong, memorable examples.
- Occasionally tell the audience what you consider significant, memorable, or especially relevant, and why. Do so sparingly, at key points.
- Provide occasional summaries at points of transition. At each interval, recap what you've covered and say how it relates to what's coming next.

WRAPPING UP YOUR PRESENTATION

Demonstrate that you haven't let key points simply float away. Try ending with these suggestions.

- Never let your voice volume fall or your clarity of pronunciation falter because the end is in sight.
- Don't introduce new ideas at the last minute.
- Signal that you're wrapping up your presentation using verbal cues, such as "In conclusion" and "Finally." When you say "finally," mean it!
- Make a dramatic, decisive statement; cite a memorable quotation; or issue a challenge. Allow a few seconds of silence, and then say "thank you." Use body language, such as stepping slightly back from the podium, and then sit down.

42e How do I research and write a presentation?

Doing research for an oral presentation requires the same kind of planning as doing research for written documents. To keep yourself calm and focused, divide the preparation into manageable tasks according to a realistic time line. Set small goals and stick to them to give yourself enough time to research, organize, and practise your presentation. Review Chapters 33–35 for help on finding and evaluating sources, taking notes, planning a research strategy, and documenting sources. An oral presentation won't have a WORKS CITED or REFERENCES list to be read out, but your instructor might ask you to turn it in before or after you give your presentation.

Most of the preparation involved in an oral presentation is written work. Writing helps you take four important steps in your preparation: (1) organizing your thoughts; (2) distancing yourself from the ideas and remaining objective; (3) paying attention to words and language; and (4) polishing for clarity and impact.

When drafting your speech, it may help you to review Chapter 8 on style and TONE. In particular, see sections 8c and 8d for a discussion of a medium LEVEL OF FORMALITY in language, which is an appropriate level for most public speaking. Careful DICTION (12d) will make your speech both easy to listen to and memorable.

An oral presentation calls for the same careful language selection that you employ in your writing. Here are some tips on using language in oral presentations.

- Recognize the power of words. For example, read this statement by Winston Churchill, made during the Battle of Britain in World War II: "Never in the field of human conflict was so much owed by so many to so few." Now try substituting the word *history* for "the field of human conflict." Note that while the single word *history* is more direct, using it destroys the powerful impact of the original words. Note also the PARALLELISM in Churchill's sentence (Chapter 10).

- Never alienate your audience by using words, phrases, or examples that could offend your listeners or people connected with them.

- Use GENDER-NEUTRAL LANGUAGE by avoiding sexist terms and inappropriate words and expressions (12f).

- Present yourself with dignity in body language, tone of voice, and dress.

Informational Graphics

The Sleep of Reasoning (PowerPoint Presentation)

42f How do I incorporate multimedia into my oral presentation?

Multimedia elements such as visual aids, sound, and video can reinforce key ideas in your speech by providing illustrations or concrete images for the audience. If done well, they can make long explanations unnecessary and add to your credibility. Still, they can never take the place of a well-prepared presentation.

42f.1 Using traditional visual aids

Here are various types of visual aids and their uses. For each of them, always make text and graphics large enough for others to read and grasp at a distance.

- **Posters** can dramatize a point, often with colour or images. Because posters have to be large enough for everyone in your audience to see them, they tend to work best with audiences of thirty or fewer.

- **Dry-erase boards** are preferable to chalkboards because they let you use various colours that are visually appealing. Use them to roughly sketch an illustration or to emphasize a technical word; doing this adds a dynamic element to your presentation. Take care not to turn your back on the audience for more than a few seconds.

- **Handouts** are useful when the topic calls for a longer text or when you want to give your audience something to refer to later. Short, simple handouts work best during a presentation, but longer, more detailed ones are more effective at the end; remember that listeners can pay more attention to what's on the page than to you, and you don't want to compete with yourself! Always include DOCUMENTATION information for any SOURCES on the handout.

A strategic handout can be a useful backup just in case other technologies are missing or broken; remember to wait until everyone has one before you begin speaking about it.

- **Transparencies** require an overhead projector. You can prepare them in advance, either by hand or by using a computer and printer, which helps clarity and also allows you to incorporate visual materials. For emphasis during a presentation, you can write on transparencies with a marker.

42f.2 Using electronic media

Computers offer a range of possibilities for enhancing oral presentations. However, make sure that the electronic media you use add to your remarks rather than distract your audience. Above all, don't spend so much time developing multimedia materials that you neglect actually writing and practising your presentation.

POWERPOINT PRESENTATIONS

Microsoft PowerPoint is the most widely used presentation software for creating digital slides. A program called Impress is available for free from <www.openoffice.org>. These slides can contain words, images, or combinations of both; they can even include sound or video clips. To project your slides during a presentation, you need an LCD projector connected to your computer and a screen.

To design PowerPoint slides, follow the principles of unity, variety, balance, and emphasis discussed in Chapter 45. Never present so much information on each slide that your audience pays more attention to reading it than to listening to you. Also, never simply read large amounts of text from your slides; your audience will quickly—and rightfully—become bored. Remember the power of photographs, illustrations, or other visual materials for conveying information or making points (4j, 4k, 4m, and Chapter 45).

Figure 42.1 is an example of an effective PowerPoint slide prepared for a presentation about water-quality monitoring. The slide is clearly titled, is well balanced, and has images to capture attention. It presents the points concisely and clearly.

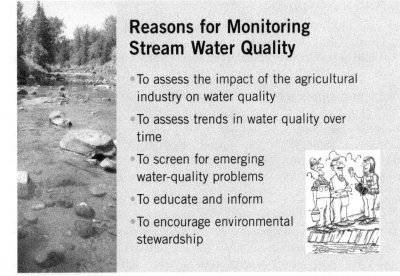

Figure 42.1 A PowerPoint slide from a presentation about monitoring water quality in Alberta

SOUND AND VIDEO CLIPS

A brief sound file (for example, a sentence or two from a speech) or a video clip (perhaps 20 to 30 seconds of footage from an event) can occasionally help you illustrate a point. These clips can be excerpts from a CD or DVD, or MP3, WAV, QuickTime, FLV, or other files on a computer. Always keep them brief and be absolutely sure that your audience will recognize immediately that they enhance your message and aren't just for show.

42g How do I plan for multimedia in my presentation?

Few things can frustrate you more than technology troubles. Always have a backup plan. Computers and projectors have a tendency to act up just at the times you're most nervous or the situation is most important, and few things annoy audience members more than watching people fiddle with technology. If you or a technician can't solve the problem in a minute or two, shift to your plan B, which might consist of selected transparencies, a strategic short handout, or even no multimedia at all. Plan and practise for all situations.

If you're making a PowerPoint presentation, you need to operate in advance the computer system you'll be using. If you intend to hook up your laptop computer to an LCD projector, make sure you bring with you—and practise installing—all of the connecting cables and cords. Arrive early to double-check that any technology you're planning to use is available and working, even if you've practised with it beforehand. Learn how to turn on computers, video players, and projectors. Learn how to raise or lower the screen, if you're using one, and how to dim the lights.

42h What presentation styles can I use?

Presentation style is the way you deliver what you have to say. You may memorize it, read it, map it, or speak without notes. In general, avoid the last style until you have considerable experience giving speeches, unless otherwise instructed by your professor or someone in your workplace.

MEMORIZING YOUR PRESENTATION

Memorized talks often sound unnatural. Unless you've mastered material well enough to recite it in a relaxed way, choose another presentation style. After all, no safety net exists if you forget a word or sentence. Fortunately, instructors rarely require you to memorize long presentations.

READING YOUR PRESENTATION

You can bore your audience when you read your entire presentation aloud. Burying your nose in sheets of paper creates an uncomfortable barrier between you and your audience because you appear painfully shy, unprepared, or insincere. If you have no choice but to read, avoid a monotone voice. Vary your pitch and style so that people can listen more easily. In addition, try these tips.

- Become familiar with your words as much as possible so that you can look up from the pages to make frequent eye contact with your audience.
- Place the sheets of paper on a podium instead of holding them.
- Keep your hands out of your pockets. Use them to gesture instead.
- Turn your body—not just your head—to your right, left, and straight ahead so that you can look at everyone in your audience.

MAPPING YOUR PRESENTATION

Mapping means creating a brief outline of the presentation's main points and examples and then using that outline to cue yourself as you talk. Quick Reference 42.2 contains additional suggestions for mapping your presentation.

QUICK REFERENCE 42.2

Preparing materials for delivering a mapped presentation

- Type your key words in a large font for easier reading.
- Highlight the most important point(s) you want to make.
- Use only one side of a page or card to avoid losing your place.
- Number your pages or cards in large type in case you drop them.
- Clearly distinguish the introduction, body, and conclusion so that your audience can follow along easily.
- Mark cues to yourself on your pages for pauses, emphasis, and use of visuals.
- Include information on your sources so that you can briefly mention them (and offer to give more details after your speech).

42i **How do I use my voice effectively?**

Your voice is the focus of any oral presentation. If you're unsure whether you can be heard in a particular setting, speak briefly and then ask your listeners whether they can hear you. When you use a microphone, speak into it without raising your voice. If the sound system "screeches" with feedback, step away from any speaker units on the stage or around the room.

Speak naturally but clearly. Articulate your words by pronouncing the end of each word. Swallowing word endings leads to poor speech delivery. Speak slowly and deliberately—but make sure that your words have rhythm and pace so that your listeners will stay engaged. Vary your tone of voice for emphasis and clarity. Pause every now and then to let your points sink in.

42j **How do I use nonverbal communication?**

Your body language can either add to or detract from your message. Eye contact is your most important nonverbal communication tool because it communicates confidence and shows respect for your listeners. If you have to walk up to the front of a room or a podium, don't begin speaking before you get there and are looking directly at the audience. Smile or nod at your listeners as you begin. To do this smoothly, you need to memorize your first few sentences.

Use appropriate facial expressions to mirror the emotions in your message. Gestures, if not overdone, contribute to your message by adding emphasis; they are best when they appear to be natural rather than forced or timed. If you use a podium, stand squarely behind it. When gestures aren't needed, rest your hands on the podium—don't scratch your head, dust your clothing, or fidget. You may step slightly forward or backward from a microphone to indicate transitions in your message, but never sway from side to side. And, of course, dress appropriately for your audience and the type of event.

42k **What can I do to practise for my oral presentation?**

Good delivery requires practice. In preparing to speak, figure in enough time for at least four complete run-throughs of your entire presentation, using visuals if you have them. When you practise, keep the following in mind:

- Practise conveying ideas rather than particular words so that your TONE doesn't become stilted.
- Time yourself and cut or expand material accordingly.
- Practise in front of a mirror or videotape yourself. As you watch yourself, notice your gestures. Do you look natural? Do you make nervous movements that you weren't aware of as you spoke?
- Practise in front of a friend. Ask for constructive feedback by posing these questions: What was my main point? Did the points flow? Did any information seem to come from out of nowhere or not fit in with the information around it? Did I sound natural? Did I look natural? How did the visuals add to my message?

42l **How can I overcome stage fright?**

If you suffer from stage fright, remember that the more prepared and rehearsed you are, the less frightened you'll be. Your aim is to communicate, not to perform. If you worry that your audience will see that you're nervous, refer to Quick Reference 42.3, which suggests ways to overcome physical signs of anxiety. The truth is that once you're under way, the momentum of your presentation will take over and you'll forget to be nervous. Try it.

QUICK REFERENCE **42.3**

Overcoming anxiety during an oral presentation

- **Pounding heart.** Don't worry: No one else can hear it!
- **Trembling hands.** Rest your hands on the podium, or put them behind your back or hold your outline or notes until the shaking stops. It will.
- **Shaky knees.** Stand behind the desk or podium. If neither is available, step forward to emphasize a point. Walking slowly from one place to another can also help you get rid of nervous energy.
- **Dry throat and mouth.** Place water at the podium. Never hesitate to take an occasional sip, especially at a transition point.
- **Quavering voice.** Speaking louder can help until this problem disappears on its own, which it always does. The sooner you ignore the quaver, the faster it will stop.
- **Flushed face.** Although you might feel as if you're burning up, audiences don't notice. The heat always fades as you continue speaking.

42m How do I make a collaborative presentation?

A common practice in many academic settings—and in business and public situations—is to present an oral report as part of a group. All members of the group are required to contribute in some way to the collaborative enterprise. The advice in section 6a will help you work together productively. Here are some additional guidelines:

- Make sure, when choosing a topic or a position on an issue, that most members of the group are familiar with the subject.

- Lay out clearly each member's responsibilities for preparing the presentation. Try to define roles that complement one another; otherwise, you may end up with overlap in one area and no coverage in another.

- Agree on firm time limits for each person, if all members of the group are expected to speak for an equal amount of time. If there is no such requirement, people who enjoy public speaking can take more responsibility for delivery, while others can do more of the preparatory work or contribute in other ways.

- Allow enough time for practice. Good delivery requires practice. Plan at least four complete run-throughs of your presentation, with any visuals you intend to use. Although each member can practise his or her own part alone, schedule practice sessions for the entire presentation as a group. This will help you (a) work on transitions, (b) make sure the order of presenters is effective, (c) clock the length of the presentation, and (d) cut or expand material accordingly.

- As you practise your presentation, have different group members watch in order to make suggestions or videotape. Notice your gestures. Do you look natural? Do you speak clearly and at an effective pace?

Chapter 43

BUSINESS AND PROFESSIONAL WRITING

(((• AUDIO
LESSON
Section 1:
Big Ideas—
Writing
Successfully
Beyond
College

43a Who writes in the workplace?

If you plan to have a job or already have one, chances are that writing is or will be a large part of your life. Writing infuses most job situations, from corporate offices, not-for-profit agencies, schools, and health care facilities to farms and factories. People write to co-workers inside organizations; they write to customers or service providers outside them. Even people who work independently (consultants, therapists, artists, craftspeople, and so on) keep records, apply for grants, correspond with customers, and advertise their services.

All workplace writing benefits from moving its way through the WRITING PROCESS as it seeks to INFORM or to PERSUADE. Never before in your writing have revising, editing, and proofreading carried as much weight as they do in business writing. The slightest error reflects negatively on the writer personally and on the company that employs the writer. Work-related correspondence needs to be professional in TONE, concise, and well informed. It can't contain slang, abbreviations, or informal words or expressions. Recipients expect it to use standard EDITED CANADIAN ENGLISH grammar, spelling, and punctuation.

ESL TIP: In some cultures, work-related correspondence is often sprinkled with elaborate language, many descriptive details, and even metaphors. Most North American businesses, however, expect correspondence that gets to the point quickly, is highly concise, and is written in clear language. •

43b What are typical policies concerning business writing?

Most workplaces have policies that strictly govern their employees' use of the organization's e-mail system and stationery. As soon as you start with a new employer, speak to your supervisor about policies. Also ask for the employee manual and take time to read it carefully. If no one seems to know the official policy, always assume that the policies are strict until you're told differently. See Quick Reference 43.1 for a list of typical business writing policies for employees.

QUICK REFERENCE **43.1**

Typical business writing policies for employees

- Companies reserve e-mail systems and any uses of company letterhead stationery for their operations only.
- Companies may insist that they own all correspondence written, sent, or received via e-mail or other means, including courier or regular mail. Furthermore, they may give administrators and supervisors complete access to view and save all of this correspondence.

continued ➤

- Companies prohibit employees from writing, sending, or receiving correspondence (by any means) with content that is potentially harmful to the company. This includes, among other things, content that makes libellous comments, enters into contracts, contains chain letters, degrades someone in the company, disseminates confidential or embarrassing information, or reveals other offensive material.

- Companies often ask their employees to sign a statement allowing the company to monitor employees' Internet use at work and reveal the results to others. Lawyers advise that these signed statements override the employees' right to privacy. Information collected this way has been used in internal disciplinary hearings and legal cases.

- Companies typically ask their employees to sign an agreement that assigns to the company ownership of the writing and other intellectual property that the employees produce in their employment.

43c What are legal considerations concerning business writing?

Legal considerations concerning business writing involve two entities at least: you as an employee and the company for which you work.

43c.1 Legal considerations involving you as an employee

In some cases, employers may attempt to use your business e-mail, business letters, and business memos as evidence of your job performance. (The Privacy Commissioner and the courts in Canada have not yet given consistent guidance in this area.) You might not be aware during the normal course of your workday that your supervisors have access to your written conduct of business. Judge your writing, therefore, as if it were being read in a formal assessment of your work.

43c.2 Legal considerations involving your company

For legal purposes, your business e-mail as well as your business letters and business memos witten on company letterhead stationery may be used as evidence in legal disputes, in court, and by the government, regarding you or the company you work for. In some situations, e-mails sent to customers or other parties within and outside the company may be construed as legally binding on the company.

43d What are special considerations concerning business e-mail?

E-mail is the primary form of written business communication today. Therefore, use it with special care, even though you might use it quite informally in your personal life. Here are some overriding guidelines for business use.

- Find out whether personal e-mail is tolerated. (You can usually find e-mail policies in an employee manual.) Even if personal e-mail is permitted, realize that workplace monitoring systems can quickly identify such e-mails. Therefore, you might want to avoid sending or receiving personal e-mails on your workplace computer.

E-mail 1:
Request or
Inquiry

E-mail 2:
Request or
Inquiry

E-mail 3:
Request or
Inquiry

611

- Scan for viruses to avoid the risk of infecting your organization's entire computer system. If you aren't sure how to do this skilfully, ask before trying to scan your first attachment.
- Ask your supervisor whether there are restrictions regarding the size of attachments that you can send or receive. (Large attachments can overload the computer system at work.) Use NETIQUETTE and alert your recipients to the size of any large attachments before you send them. In turn, ask senders to alert you before sending large ones to you.
- Protect the ID numbers and passwords you're assigned or have created to access your organization's electronic systems. As an employee, you may be held accountable for all activity conducted on password-protected accounts.

Some businesses automatically insert or require employees to insert a DISCLAIMER—a statement appended to the top or bottom of e-mails designed to protect the company from legal liability. The value of disclaimers is limited. Only a court of law can determine the effectiveness of such statements, but they might prove effective in limiting a company's liability in some cases.

✹ 43d.1 Following guidelines for content of work-related e-mail

E-mail 4: Announcement

The subject line in an e-mail tells your recipients how to sort, file, and prioritize a message. Be very specific in stating your subject so that you don't show disrespect for your recipient's time. You might have to write the same people more than one e-mail about different subjects in the same day, but at least your recipients will be able to keep their records straight.

NO (VAGUE)	**YES (SPECIFIC)**
Travel Approval	Approval Request for Winnipeg Trip
E-mail Policy	New E-mail Retention Policy
Meeting	Meeting on Annual Report Schedule
Schedule Change	Cancellation of Winnipeg Trip

In the "Cc" or "Copies" space, insert the e-mail addresses of people who need to see your message, even when they aren't expected to respond. Never send copies to people who don't really need the information; it can backfire and simply annoy someone who already has too many messages in his or her inbox. If you use the "Bcc" (blind copy) space, you're sending a copy to people without your primary recipients' knowledge. Generally, people consider blind copying rude because it's akin to talking behind someone's back. However, certain rare, delicate situations might call for it. For example, in a mass mail-out, it would be good netiquette to blind copy dozens of customers because you would be protecting their privacy by not disclosing their e-mail addresses to everyone else.

For the message of your e-mail, single-space the text, and double-space between paragraphs and before your complimentary closing. Start paragraphs flush left at the margin. When you need to include a separate document of more than a paragraph or two with your e-mail, such as a report, compose it as a separate document in your word-processing program, and attach it to your e-mail using the "Attachments" function of your e-mail service. Attached documents look better than copied and pasted documents because they maintain the original formatting (margins, spacing, italics). As you compose your message, follow the principles in Quick Reference 43.2.

Content of a business e-mail

- Keep the message brief and your paragraphs short. Reading a screen is harder on the eyes than reading a print document.
- Restrict each business e-mail to one topic, even if you have to write the recipients about more than one topic in the same day.
- Start your business e-mail with a sentence that tells what your message is about.
- Put the details of your business e-mail message in the second paragraph. Supply any background information that your recipients aren't already aware of or might have forgotten.
- Conclude your e-mail in a short, final paragraph by asking for explicit information or specific action, if needed, or by restating your reason for writing (for example, keeping someone apprised of a situation or reporting on a meeting).
- If your e-mail runs longer than three to four paragraphs, add topic headings (45d) to help your readers speed through the material.
- Never write in all capital letters or all lowercase letters. Not only are they annoying to read, but all capital letters are considered the written equivalent of rudely shouting. All lowercase letters suggest laziness and a lack of respect.
- At the end of your message, before your full name and position, use a commonly accepted complimentary closing, such as *Sincerely, Cordially,* or *Regards.*
- Be cautious about what you say in a business e-mail. After all, the recipient can forward any e-mail, including ones received as blind copies, to others without your permission, even though this practice is considered unethical and rude.
- Forward an e-mail message only if you've asked the original sender for permission.

43d.2 Using e-mail netiquette

E-mail 5: Workplace E-mail

Netiquette, a word coined from *net* and *etiquette,* refers to good e-mail manners. For example, unless your business recipients give you permission to loosen your level of formality, always address them by their full names and titles, especially when your recipients are people you've never met or corresponded with before. As important, always use GENDER-NEUTRAL LANGUAGE. Finally, try to reply to e-mail messages within one or two days after receiving them. When you can't respond quickly, always acknowledge that you've received a message. Say when you'll reply, and don't forget to follow up.

E-mail 6: Workplace E-mail

For an example of a business e-mail, see Figure 43.1 (p. 614).

43e How do I format and write memos?

Memo 1: Transmittal or Cover Memo

Memos are usually exchanged internally within an organization or business. Today e-mail takes the place of most memos, unless the correspondence requires a paper record or signature. The guidelines for writing e-mail (43d.1) also pertain to memos.

The standard format of a memo includes two major parts: the headings and the body.

To: [Name your audience—a specific person or group.]
From: [Give your name and your title, if any.]
Date: [Give the date on which you write the memo.]
Re: [State your subject as specifically as possible in the "Subject" or "Re" line.]

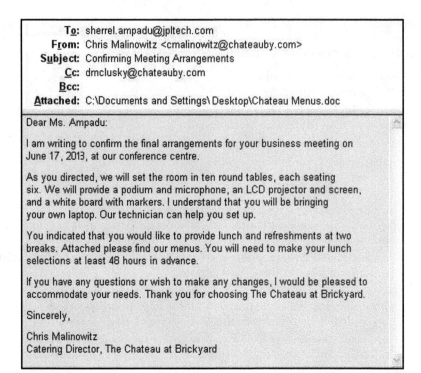

To: sherrel.ampadu@jpltech.com
From: Chris Malinowitz <cmalinowitz@chateauby.com>
Subject: Confirming Meeting Arrangements
Cc: dmclusky@chateauby.com
Bcc:
Attached: C:\Documents and Settings\Desktop\Chateau Menus.doc

Dear Ms. Ampadu:

I am writing to confirm the final arrangements for your business meeting on June 17, 2013, at our conference centre.

As you directed, we will set the room in ten round tables, each seating six. We will provide a podium and microphone, an LCD projector and screen, and a white board with markers. I understand that you will be bringing your own laptop. Our technician can help you set up.

You indicated that you would like to provide lunch and refreshments at two breaks. Attached please find our menus. You will need to make your lunch selections at least 48 hours in advance.

If you have any questions or wish to make any changes, I would be pleased to accommodate your needs. Thank you for choosing The Chateau at Brickyard.

Sincerely,

Chris Malinowitz
Catering Director, The Chateau at Brickyard

Figure 43.1 A professional e-mail

The content calls for a beginning, middle, and end, with all parts holding closely to your topic. Don't ramble. If you need more than one or, at most, two pages, change your format into that of a brief report. Here are some guidelines for preparing a memo.

- **Introduction:** Briefly state your purpose for writing and why your memo is worth your readers' attention. Mention whether the recipient needs to take action, making it clear either here or at the conclusion.
- **Body:** Present the essential information on your topic, including facts the recipient needs to know. If you write more than three or four paragraphs, use headings to divide the information into subtopics so that the memo can be scanned quickly.
- **Conclusion:** End with a one- to two-sentence summary, a specific recommendation, or what action is needed and by when. Finish with a thank-you sentence.

43f How do I write business letters?

Business letters are more formal and official than business e-mails or memos. Choose to write a business letter, rather than an e-mail, to add appropriate weight and respect to your message, for ceremonial occasions, and to ensure that your message is placed on the record and thereby becomes part of a "paper trail." Business letters generally fall into two official categories based on their purposes.

- **Regular business letters** are business-to-business communications. These letters make up the majority of business correspondence. Always use company letterhead stationery, and follow any special guidelines for style or format that your company uses.

- **Social business letters** are letters to business colleagues on matters that serve a business-related social function, such as congratulations on an achievement, condolences, thank-you letters, invitations to social events, and the like. Given that these letters are written in a business context, social business letters may be written on company letterhead stationery.

There are some general guidelines for addressing recipients in business letters. The old-fashioned "To Whom It May Concern" rarely reaches the right person in an organization. Use the full name of your recipient whenever possible. If you can't locate a name, either through a phone call to a central switchboard or on the Internet, use a specific category—for example, "Dear Billing Department," placing the key word "Billing" first (not "Department of Billing"). Always use gender-neutral language. Figure 43.2 is an example of a business letter from a not-for-profit group.

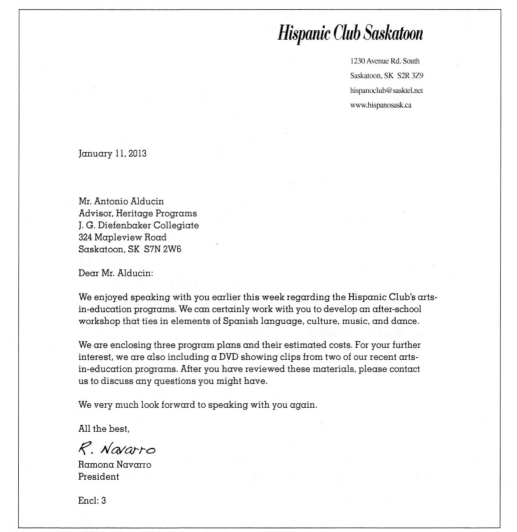

Figure 43.2 A sample business letter written in block style

Here are guidelines for the format and content of your business letters.

- **Paper:** Use 8½-by-11-inch paper. The most suitable colours are white, off-white, and light beige. Fold your business letters horizontally into thirds to fit into a standard number 10 business envelope. Never fold a business letterhead stationery page in half and then into thirds.
- **Letterhead stationery:** Use the official letterhead stationery (name, address, and logo, if any) of the business where you're employed. If no letterhead stationery exists, imitate the format that others have used. If no such tradition exists, centre the company's full name, address, and phone number at the top of the page, and use a larger and different font than for the content of your letter.
- **Format:** Without indents, use single spacing within paragraphs and double spacing between paragraphs. All lines start flush left, which means at the left margin. This is called **block style**. An equally acceptable alternative form is called **modified block style** in which the lines for the inside address and the body begin flush left but the heading, closing, and signature begin about halfway across the page. Quick Reference 43.3 lists the features of block-style and modified block-style letter formats.

QUICK REFERENCE **43.3**

Features of block and modified block styles

BLOCK-STYLE FORMAT

- Begin the dateline two inches (about 5 cm) below the top of the page or three lines below the last line of the letterhead, depending on the depth of the letterhead copy.
- Begin all elements at the left margin.
- Allow one inch (2.5 cm) for left, right, and bottom margins.
- Leave three blank lines between the dateline and the inside address.
- Leave one blank line between the inside address and the salutation.
- Leave one blank line between the salutation and the body.
- Type the body single-spaced and leave one blank line between paragraphs.
- Leave one blank line between the body and complimentary closing.
- Leave three blank lines between the complimentary closing and the signature block.

MODIFIED BLOCK-STYLE FORMAT

- Begin the dateline two inches (about 5 cm) below the top of the page or three lines below the last line of the letterhead, depending on the depth of the letterhead copy.
- Centre:
  - Dateline
  - Complimentary closing
  - Signature block
- Allow one inch (2.5 cm) for left, right, and bottom margins.
- Leave three blank lines between the dateline and the inside address.
- Leave one blank line between the inside address and the salutation.
- Leave one blank line between the salutation and the body.

continued ➤

- Type the body single-spaced and leave one blank line between paragraphs.
- Leave one blank line between the body and complimentary closing.
- Leave three blank lines between the complimentary closing and the signature block.

Use block or modified block formats for business correspondence of a personal nature, such as job application letters, letters of complaint concerning personal matters, or letters asking for information for you personally. Use plain white paper, and if you have personal stationery, use it.

43g How do I prepare a meeting agenda?

An agenda is a plan for a meeting. It lets everyone who is attending know the purpose of the meeting and the topics it will cover. The specific forms of an agenda can vary from company to company, so if you're asked to prepare one, the best way to begin is to study the agendas and minutes of prior meetings of the same group.

Sending out an agenda before a meeting can help participants prepare, especially if some are to give reports or review materials ahead of time. (In fact, preparing an agenda in advance might let you know a meeting is unnecessary, that information can be shared through an e-mail, or a decision can be made without getting everyone together; no one likes meetings that waste time.) Agendas generally provide the following information:

1. The time, date, and place of the meeting (and perhaps a list of who will attend).
2. The topics of the meeting, in the order in which the group will take them up (perhaps with the approximate amount of time to be devoted to each), with a note about who (if anyone) is in charge of the particular topics.
3. The purpose of each topic on the agenda. For example, is the purpose simply to share or discuss information? Is the purpose, rather, to make decisions or judgments? People attending the meeting need to know what they're expected to accomplish.
4. A list of what material needs to be reviewed ahead of time or what will be available at the meeting.

Figure 43.3 (p. 618) shows you the agenda for an informal meeting.

43h How do I write meeting minutes?

Minutes are the record of a meeting. Generally, minutes cover all important topics that were discussed, both those on the agenda and not. Exactly what is defined as "important" is hard to know when you're new to a company, so your best route is to write down just about everything that comes up. Pay special attention to any decisions the group made, any votes, and any assignments of tasks to individuals or groups. After the meeting you can ask at least two colleagues who were there to advise you about what to leave out when you write up the minutes.

On rare occasions, minutes are very detailed, recording all the points raised and their nuances. Most times, however, the minutes are much shorter, briefly summarizing the highlights and focusing on conclusions and decisions that were reached. Such minutes summarize outcomes, not entire discussions. Minutes generally have several elements:

1. Date, time, and place of the meeting, including when it began and ended.
2. Who was present (and perhaps who was absent).
3. Summaries of topics, decisions, and responsibilities.

Using headings or lists can help organize the minutes.

FORMAT OF HEADING
Name and title centred, single-spaced
Double-space to date and time on one line and location on one line
"Agenda" two lines below

Human Resources Department
Planning Meeting for Open Enrolment Communication

Wednesday, July 17, 2013, 3–4 p.m.
Third-Floor Conference Room

Agenda

Attendees
Margaret Alexander, HR
Joanna Bergstrom, HR Director-Organizer
Rebecca Greenfield, Freelance HR Writer/Editor
Larry Jun, HR Services
Bob LeGorce, Finance
Bhupal Mansingh, HR Services
Chris Papparello, Finance

Topics	**Discussion leader (time)**
• Introductions/roles and responsibilities	Joanna (5 minutes)
• Tentative enrolment dates	Joanna and Bob (5 minutes)
• Possible benefits plan changes	Bob (10 minutes)
• Goals/strategies for communication	Bob and Chris (10 minutes)
• Communication elements	Joanna and Beth (25 minutes)
• Next steps/assignments	Joanna (5 minutes)

REQUIRED IN INFORMAL AGENDA
Organization or department name
List of attendees
Topics to be discussed

OPTIONAL IN INFORMAL AGENDA
Statement of purpose after title of meeting
Bullets for names
Name of chair or organizer
Time allotments

Figure 43.3 An informal meeting agenda

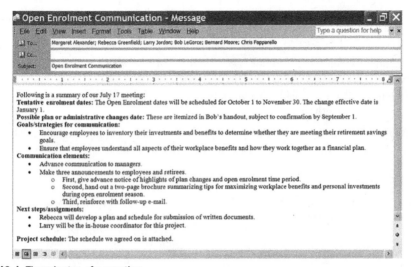

Figure 43.4 The minutes of a meeting

Sometimes taking minutes is assigned spontaneously at the beginning of a meeting. Therefore, always go to meetings prepared with a laptop or a notebook, pens or pencils—and a smile. Once they're written, minutes can be distributed in paper copies or, more frequently, as e-mail attachments, or on a protected company Intranet site or blog. You'll need to follow the method your company or supervisor prefers. It goes without saying that you edit and proofread the minutes very carefully.

The sample set of minutes shown in Figure 43.4 is being communicated by e-mail because the minutes-taker found out this is the traditional way the minutes of this particular group are circulated.

43i How do I write business reports and manuals?

Reports and manuals are documents that exist for the purpose of informing others inside or outside the workplace. Some manuals explain procedures or processes to help employees do their work consistently and effectively: how to handle specific situations (filing claims, dealing with customer concerns, processing orders, and so on). Customers often see "how-to" manuals when they buy a new product. Other manuals document policies. Among the most important of these are employee or personnel manuals, which explain things like workplace dress and behaviour, benefits, use of technology, and so on.

If you're in charge of writing a manual, clarity and completeness are your most important considerations. Readers need to be able to find information easily and use it accurately. As a writer, you need to anticipate the questions people will have and write the manual accordingly. Analyzing your audience is crucial. Document design is important as you lay out the information in the most effective way.

43i.1 Writing internal reports

Internal reports are designed to convey information to others in your workplace. They can be various lengths and serve various purposes. Consider four examples:

- You attend a professional meeting and provide a report on what you learned there for your supervisor and for colleagues who weren't there.

- You're working on a lengthy project. You report on your progress so that others can understand what you have completed, what remains, and what problems or delays you anticipate, if any.
- You conduct extensive consumer research through telephone interviews with potential customers, and you summarize and analyze your findings.
- You identify all the available solutions to a particular problem and write a report that discusses the strengths and weaknesses of each.

In each of these cases, follow the principles of reporting, analyzing, and interpreting information and data (7c–d). Being clear and concise is vital.

43i.2   Writing external reports

External reports inform audiences beyond the workplace. Generally, they have a secondary function of creating a good impression of the company or organization. Probably the most common examples are annual reports, in which companies summarize for investors their accomplishments during the previous years, especially their profits and losses. Other kinds of external reports include progress reports on student achievement written by school boards.

Because external reports are written for more general audiences, their writers must explain many terms and concepts that would be clear to co-workers. Document design is also important (Chapter 45). Many corporations put important resources into the design of their external reports.

43j   How do I write a business proposal?

Sales Proposal
(Interactive)

Abstract 2:
Proposal

Proposals persuade readers to follow a plan, choose a product or service, or implement an idea. A marketing specialist might propose a new product line. A teacher might propose a change in the curriculum. A leader in a not-for-profit organization might propose a way to raise funding. Proposals generally describe a project, the steps for starting and completing the project, and how much it will cost.

Readers evaluate proposals according to how well the writers have anticipated and answered their questions. If some readers have a high level of knowledge about the subject of the proposal, and others have little, then you need to explain the basic information and offer a glossary of terms. Here are some guidelines for preparing a proposal.

INTRODUCTION
Explain the purpose and scope of the project.
Describe the problem that the project seeks to solve.
Lay out the solution your project will provide.
Include dates for beginning and completing the work.
Forecast the outcomes and the costs.
Be accurate and precise.

BODY
Describe the product or service.
State what resources are needed.
Outline the phases of the project.
Present the detailed budget.
Describe precisely how each phase is to be completed.
Give the completion date for each phase.
State how the project will be evaluated.

CONCLUSION   Summarize briefly the benefits of this proposal.
              Thank readers for their time.
              Offer to provide further information.

Resumé 1:
Functional

Resumé 2:
Chronological

Resumé 3:
Archival
(Interactive)

43k How do I write a resume?

A **resume** details your accomplishments and employment history. Its purpose is to help a potential employer determine whether you'll be a suitable candidate for employment. To make a favourable impression, follow the guidelines for writing a resumé in Quick Reference 43.4.

QUICK REFERENCE 43.4

Guidelines for writing a resume

- Place your name, address, e-mail address, and telephone number at the top. Include the URL of your professional website or online portfolio, if you have one.
- Make sure to have a professional-sounding e-mail address.
- Make the resume easy to read. Label the sections clearly, and target it to the position you want. Help employers see your most significant attributes as quickly and as easily as possible.
- Adjust your resume to fit your PURPOSE. For example, if you're applying for a job as a computer programmer, you'll want to emphasize different facts than you would if you're applying for a job selling computers.
- Use headings to separate blocks of information. Include the following headings, as appropriate: Position Desired or Career Objective; Education; Experience; Licences and Certifications; Related Experience; Honours or Awards; Publications or Presentations; Activities and Interests; and Special Abilities, Skills, and Knowledge.
- When you list your work experience, place your most recent job first; when listing education, place your most recent degrees, certificates, or enrolments first.
- Write telegraphically. Start with verb phrases, not with the word *I*, and omit *a, an,* and *the*. For example, write "Created new computer program to organize company's spreadsheets" instead of "*I* created *a* new computer program to organize *the* company's spreadsheets."
- Include only relevant information.
- Tell the truth. Even if you get the job, an employer who discovers you lied will probably fire you.
- Include references, or state that you can provide them on request. (Be sure to have them at hand so that you can respond speedily to such a request.)
- Try to fit all of the information on one page. If you need a second page, make sure the most important information is on the first page.
- Use high-quality paper that is white or off-white.
- Prepare your resume in three formats: traditional print, digitally scannable, and plain text.
- Proofread carefully; even one spelling error or one formatting error can eliminate you from consideration.

Your resumé can take many formats, and an employer may specifically require one of them.

Traditional print resumés can take advantage of the full range of document design, including columns, different fonts, and graphics. Still, you want the overall effect to be clean and clear. Figure 43.5 shows an example of a traditional print resumé.

Scannable resumés are designed to be scanned by machines that digitize their content. Sophisticated software then searches the database to match key terms to position requirements. As a result, these resumés need to be simpler: don't use columns, different fonts, lines or other graphics, bold or italic fonts, and so on. Choose a clean sans serif font such as Arial or Geneva in a 10- to 12-point size. Include keywords that the computer can match to the job. Figure 43.6 (p. 624) shows a scannable version of the resumé in Figure 43.5.

Plain text resumés are simpler yet. They can be pasted directly into e-mails (for companies that won't open attachments for fear of viruses) or into application databases. If you have time to prepare only one type of resumé, we suggest you create one that's scannable.

Targeting Your Resumé

A resumé targeted to the specific company and the specific position you are applying for makes its reader think, "We should talk to this person. This candidate looks like someone who would be an asset to our business."

What is an "asset to the business"? Employers look for evidence of your attitude, work ethic, and "trainability"—your ability to help the company meet its goals and to fit into its corporate culture.

The first step in identifying what a particular company is looking for in an employee is to "decode" the job advertisement that led you to that company:

- Circle the terms (usually adjectives and adverbs) that describe the type of person the company is seeking.
- Underline terms that describe the specific skills required for the position.

Use the same or similar terms in your resumé and the job application letter that accompanies it to demonstrate your knowledge of the company and your "fit" with its corporate culture.

Supplement what you discover in the job advertisement by visiting the company's website to learn more about its products or services and to look at its mission statement and the terminology it uses. With the information you gather, you can "crack the code" and identify what that company considers essential in a successful applicant.

---

431 How do I write a job application letter?

Career Letter 1:
Application

Career Letter 2:
Application

Career Letter 3:
Application
(Interactive)

A **job application letter** always needs to accompany your resumé. Avoid repeating what's already on the resume. Instead, connect the company's expectations to your experience by emphasizing how your background has prepared you for the position. Your job application letter, more than your resumé, reflects your energy and personality. Here are guidelines for writing a job application letter.

- Use one page only.
- Overall, think of your letter as a polite sales pitch about yourself and what benefits you can bring to the company. Don't be shy, but don't exaggerate.

Margaret Lorentino
1338 Sunflower Lane
Halifax, NS B3J 3J6
(902) 555-3756
mlorentino3@gmail.com
Professional portfolio: www.lorentinopage.net

OBJECTIVE: Full/part-time position as a medical transcrip-
                 tionist to utilize my medical, computer, and office skills

EDUCATION: Certificate in Medical Transcription
                    Nova Scotia Community College,
                    Institute of Technology, Halifax, NS,
                    December 2012
                 Bachelor of Science
                    Dalhousie University, Halifax, NS, May 2011

EMPLOYMENT: Dalhousie University, January 2009–Present
                    Lab Assistant and Computer Skills Teacher
                 RTD Real Estate, Halifax, August 2004–August 2005
                    Receptionist, Accounting Assistant
                 Atlantic Mutual Life, Dartmouth, NS, May 2003–July 2004
                    Sales Assistant
                 Reliable Personnel, Summerside, PE, May 2002–May 2003
                    Temporary Employment Manager

SKILLS: Computer
                 • Expert in Microsoft Office Suite, Adobe Creative Suite
                 • Experienced in Internet research and Web design
                 • Have experience with Excel, PowerPoint, Access
                 • Teach basic computer skills in first-year
                   college English classes

                 Organizational
                 • Girl Scout leader, soccer coach, summer camp
                   counsellor
                 • Trained employees in data entry and accounting
                   principles
                 • Managed temporary workforce of 20–30 employees

REFERENCES: Available upon request

Figure 43.5 A traditional print resumé

Margaret Lorentino
1338 Sunflower Lane
Halifax, NS B3J 3J6
(902) 555-3756
mlorentino3@gmail.com
Professional portfolio: www.lorentinopage.net

KEYWORDS: Medical transcription, Bachelor of Science, lab assistant,
Web design, data entry, research, Microsoft Office Suite,
Adobe Creative Suite, Photoshop, Dreamweaver, Excel,
PowerPoint, Access, teaching, digital media, accounting,
manager, sales

OBJECTIVE: Full/part-time position as a medical transcriptionist

EDUCATION: Certificate in Medical Transcription,
Nova Scotia Community College,
Institute of Technology,
December 2012
Bachelor of Science
Dalhousie University, May 2011

EMPLOYMENT: Dalhousie University, Lab Assistant and Computer
Skills Teacher. January 2009 to present
RTD Real Estate, Halifax, NS, Receptionist,
Accounting Assistant. August 2004 to August 2005
Atlantic Mutual Life, Dartmouth, NS, Sales Assistant
May 2003 to July 2004
Reliable Personnel, Summerside, PE, Temporary
Employment Manager. May 2002 to May 2003

SKILLS: Computer
- Expert in Microsoft Office Suite, Adobe Creative Suite
- Experienced in Internet research and Web design
- Have experience with Excel, PowerPoint, Access
- Teach basic computer skills in first-year
college English classes

Organizational
- Girl Scout leader, soccer coach, summer camp
counsellor
- Trained employees in data entry and accounting
principles
- Managed temporary workforce of 20–30 employees

REFERENCES: Available upon request

Figure 43.6 A scannable resumé

624

- Use the same name, content, and format guidelines as for a business letter (43f).
- Address the letter to a specific person. If you can't discover a name, use a gender-neutral title such as *Dear Personnel Director.*
- Open your letter by identifying the position for which you're applying.
- Mention your qualifications, and explain how your background will meet the job requirements.

Margaret Lorentino
1338 Sunflower Lane
Halifax, NS B3J 3J6
(902) 555-3756
mlorentino3@gmail.com
www.lorentinopage.net

December 1, 2012

Ms. Arlene Chang
Employment Coordinator
Rockford Medical Centre
820 Cornwallis Rd.
Halifax, NS B5A 2C2

Dear Ms. Chang:

I had a chance to talk with you last spring about your company at the Medical Professions Job Fair. I am very interested in the medical transcription position that I noticed in the *Register Star* on November 29.

I will be completing my Certificate in Medical Transcription at the end of December. I have taken courses in medical transcription and medical office procedures, as well as numerous computer courses. In the course of obtaining a bachelor's degree in general science from Dalhousie University, I had extensive experience in Internet research and writing reports.

The enclosed resumé will give you the details of my experience and qualifications, which I think have prepared me for a position at Rockford Medical. I am available for an interview at your convenience.

Sincerely yours,

Margaret Lorentino

Margaret Lorentino

Figure 43.7 A job application letter

- Make clear that you're familiar with the company or organization; your research will impress the employer.
- End by being specific about what you can do for the company. If the job will be your first, give your key attributes—but make sure they're relevant. For instance, you might state that you're punctual, self-disciplined, eager to learn, and hard-working.
- State when you're available for an interview and how the potential employer can reach you.
- Edit and proofread the letter carefully. If you have to hand-correct even one error, print out the letter again.

For an example of a job application letter, see Figure 43.7.

ESL TIPS: In North America, job applications are not expected to include personal information such as an applicant's age, marital status, number of children, religion, or political beliefs. Such personal information does not help an employer determine how well you can perform a particular job, so avoid including it in your application. ●

Thinking, speaking, and writing using gender-neutral language (12f) is very important in the workplace, particularly when addressing recipients in memos, job application letters, and so on. Prepare yourself by following these guidelines.

1. Telephone or send an e-mail to the company to which you're sending the letter. State your reason for contacting them, and ask for the name of the person you want to receive your letter.
2. Address men as Mr., and address women as Ms., unless you're specifically told to use Miss or Mrs. If your recipient goes by another title such as Dr. or Professor, use it.
3. If you can't identify a proper name and must use a title alone, keep the title generic and gender-neutral.

> NO   Dear Sir: [sexist]
>
>   Dear Sir or Madam: [out of date, awkward]
>
> YES   Dear Human Resources Officer.
>
>   Dear Apple Sales Manager.

Chapter 44

WRITING FOR THE PUBLIC

44a What is public writing?

Public writing is intended for people who are reading for reasons other than work, school, or professional obligations. Instead, they read it out of interest or a desire to keep informed. Some public writing is also known as CIVIC WRITING because you're writing to affect the actions or beliefs of other citizens in a democratic society.

Examples of writing for the public include a letter or e-mail to refute a newspaper editorial, a program for a play or concert, a brochure to draw new members into a service organization, a proposal to build a park, a fundraising letter for a worthy cause, a script for a radio announcement, a website for a hobby or social cause that interests you, or an e-mail to your MPP or MLA inquiring about his or her position on health care funding.

44b How can I understand public writing situations?

As the examples in section 44a indicate, public writing takes a wide range of forms, depending on the situation. The familiar categories of TOPIC, PURPOSE, AUDIENCE, **role**, and context and special requirements are especially important for understanding your options and requirements (1b).

Much public writing has the purpose of informing or persuading, and our earlier advice applies. One thing to keep in mind is that, unlike an instructor or someone in a work setting, public audiences aren't usually obligated to read your work. This means that you have to take particular care as you write for them, especially when you're writing for an audience that you don't know personally. Among other things, this means analyzing your readers and establishing your credibility for them.

"Establishing credibility" means convincing your readers that they need or want to listen to you. Create a strong ETHOS by being accurate and honest and by explaining your connection with the readers. What do you have in common with them?

For example, if you're writing a letter to the editor of your local newspaper, you'll gain credibility if you begin by establishing yourself as a member of your audience's community. That will help you convey that you have a sincere and long-standing interest in the welfare of that community.

Establishing credibility in public writing can also come through your style and ingenuity. After all, another common purpose of this writing is to entertain. Newspapers and magazines are full of feature stories that inform, certainly, but that are also enjoyable to read.

People also write for the public for the pleasure of expressing themselves. Social networking sites like Facebook or MySpace (46h) are prime examples, as are certain blogs and the online comment sections maintained by many newspapers. However, expressing yourself doesn't give you licence to be insulting, irresponsible, or inflammatory—at least if you expect anyone to pay attention. And what's the point of publishing your writing if you don't want readers?

((•

AUDIO
LESSON
Section 1: Big
Ideas—Using
Language Well
and Addressing
Your Audience

((•

AUDIO
LESSON
Section 2:
Practice
Questions—
Using Language
Well and
Addressing
Your Audience

((•

AUDIO
LESSON
Section 3:
Rapid Review—
Using Language
Well and
Addressing
Your Audience

44c How do I write reports for the public?

Reports for the public vary in length, format, and content. An action brief from a political organization might consist of a few pages detailing recent developments on an issue of concern, such as a proposed law. Often these are published on websites or distributed through e-mail messages.

Write your material in an evenhanded TONE so that your credibility is supported by your fairness. If you want to criticize something, be sure your argument is well reasoned and supported—and that it lacks BIAS or malice toward any person(s) or specific idea(s). This doesn't mean that your writing needs to be limp. Indeed, you can choose writing that's spirited, enthusiastic, and even stirring.

44c.1 Public reports

To write a public report, follow the guidelines in Quick Reference 44.1. Long reports sometimes begin with an executive summary, which is a brief overview of its main points.

QUICK REFERENCE 44.1

Writing a public report

- Decide your purpose. Will you only inform, or will you also analyze the information you present? Or—going one step further—will you make a recommendation based on the information and your analysis?
- State your findings objectively. Though you may later bring in your opinion by recommending a course of action, your credibility depends on your first reporting accurately.
- Organize a formal report using the following sections. Depending on the purpose of your report, however, you might combine or expand any of the sections.
  - **Executive summary:** Provides a very brief summary of the entire report, including conclusions or recommendations.
  - **Introduction:** Explains the purpose of the report, describes the problem studied, and often describes or outlines the organization of the entire report.
  - **Methods:** Describes how the data were gathered.
  - **Results:** Presents the findings of the report.
  - **Discussion:** States the implications of your findings.
  - **Conclusion:** Makes recommendations or simply summarizes the findings.

44c.2 Policy briefs

A policy brief is a concise public report in which experts put technical information into a form that non-experts and decision makers can understand. Most of these are published on the Internet. The usual purpose of policy briefs is to persuade people with facts and analysis that support a specific decision. Your readers need to perceive you as objective and careful, basing your position on logic and evidence. If you use a policy brief in a research paper, carefully analyze the quality of the source (34m). Figure 44.1 shows a news release summarizing a policy brief.

For immediate distribution–June 22, 2010

NEWS RELEASE

Multiple citizenship benefits Canada

Institute for Research on Public Policy

Institute de recherche en politiques publiques

Study says global trend in accepting dual citizenship is irreversible

Montreal – Canadian policy should not discourage multiple citizenship. Indeed, Canada has been at the forefront of the global trend toward the recognition and acceptance of multiple citizenship and is a model for the rest of the world, according to a new study published by the Institute for Research on Public Policy (IRPP).

"Multiple citizenship is here to stay. It reflects the growing diversity of our populations, as well as the changing nature of identity," says author Audrey Macklin, "It may also be an asset for the country in terms of better understanding the world and being able to maintain strong trade and cultural links with numerous other countries."

The study. "Multiple Citizenship, Identity and Entitlement in Canada," which Macklin co-wrote with François Crépeau, examines recent instances of popular anxiety in Canada around multiple citizenship. It maintains that settler societies have operated on the rationale that immigrants will be more likely to naturalize and integrate into the Canadian mainstream if doing so doesn't require severing connections to their past. "Multiple citizenship does not undermine Canadian citizenship and, as a matter of public policy and legal regulation, should not be restricted," says Macklin.

Figure 44.1 A news release summarizing a policy brief

EXERCISE 44-1   Using your Internet browser, enter "policy brief" (in quotation marks so that you search for this specific phrase) and the following terms (one at a time): food, health, energy, crime, or other terms that interest you. List the policy briefs you find for each, and evaluate their quality.

44d   How do I write to my community or decision makers?

Report 11: Position Paper (Interactive)

People can influence public opinion or actions by decision makers by writing persuasive arguments. Perhaps you want to endorse a new public project or react to a proposal, or support a law under consideration.

44d.1   Letters to the editor

When you respond to a piece of writing in a publication, always begin by referring precisely to the source, giving its title, section, and date, if possible.

Many letters to the editor (most often sent as e-mails) propose solutions to a community problem. These letters aim to persuade other readers that a problem exists and that a particular solution is the most advantageous of all the possible alternatives. Follow the general guidelines for writing ARGUMENTS (see Chapter 5). Use the format for a business letter or e-mail, and keep the following guidelines in mind when writing to propose a solution:

- Explain briefly the specific problem you're attempting to solve.
- Tell how your solution will solve all elements of the problem.
- Address briefly the possible objections or alternatives to your proposed solution.
- State why your solution offers the most advantages of all the alternatives.

In the letter in Figure 44.2, a citizen argues for preserving a city park in its present form.

To the Editor:

Re "Parking Plan Threatens Green Space" (news article, May 14):

For well over a century, Claremont Park has provided a welcome oasis in downtown Exeter. In this park, office workers eat lunches, schoolchildren play on the way home, and evening concerts and other events unite the community.

It is very shortsighted, then, that the City Council now considers converting a third of the park into additional parking.

I acknowledge that parking downtown has gotten difficult. As the manager of a small shop, I know that our customers sometimes have trouble finding a parking place. However, the park itself is one of the reasons our downtown has become more popular in the past decade.

Ironically, destroying the park's attractive green space will reduce the need for more parking, by hurting business.

A better solution is for the city to purchase the vacant property at the corner of Queen and Elm Streets and build a multi-storey garage. No doubt this option is more expensive than using the park. However, the land would be available cheaply, a garage would provide more parking than the park land, and a preserved park would bolster business, thereby increasing tax revenues. I'm sure most citizens would prefer to leave future generations a legacy of trees and grass rather than a debt of sterile concrete.

Joel C. Bradway
Exeter, May 17, 2013

Figure 44.2 A letter reprinted from a community newspaper

44d.2 Editorials, op-ed pieces, and reviews

Editorials are fairly short arguments that appear in newspapers and magazines. So are *op-ed* pieces (short for "opposite editorial," in reference to where they were usually published in newspapers—on the right-hand page, opposite the newspaper's editorials). They are also called "commentaries" or "opinion pieces." *Reviews* discuss movies, books, plays, music, and so on, explaining and summarizing them for readers and commenting on their quality. All are common forms of public writing.

44e What other types of public writing exist?

Many people write simply to express themselves or to entertain others. The most obvious examples are fiction, poetry, plays, film scripts, journals, and scrapbooks. In addition, many people produce newsletters, brochures, or similar documents, using not only words, but also graphic designs and images (Chapter 45).

COLUMNS

Columns are a series of pieces written by one author, usually appearing on a regular basis. Columnists tend to focus on a particular topic: sports, relationships, politics, food, and so on.

WEBSITES

Writing for the Internet is perhaps the broadest form of public writing, in the sense that anything you post there is available to any reader with online access. You might post book reviews on a bookseller's website or a message about an upcoming concert to a newsgroup. You might create a website about your talents, interests, or accomplishments, or a site for an organization, a social cause, or a special interest group. Chapter 46 discusses writing for the Web in detail.

BLOGS

One form of public writing is the BLOG (Web log), an online journal that a writer updates on a fairly regular basis. Some writers focus their blogs on a single topic or a narrow range of topics. Others record the events of their lives, as in a diary open for the world to read. We explain how to write blogs in 46e.

Chapter 45

DOCUMENT AND VISUAL DESIGN

((•·
AUDIO
LESSON
Section 3:
Rapid Review—
Technology and
Document
Design

45a What is visual design?

Visual design refers to the appearance of a document (how it looks), as opposed to its content (what it says). We're using the term *document* to refer to all kinds of texts, including papers, reports, letters, brochures, flyers, posters, PowerPoint slides, and webpages. Designing documents includes everything from choosing typefaces and heading styles to determining the use of colour, to selecting and placing photographs, illustrations, or other graphics.

Chapter 4 explained how to analyze visual images, and the advice there can help you choose images for your own documents. However, visual design involves the relationship between words and images. A well-designed document shows that you respect your readers and have spent time formatting your work so that it's attractive and helps achieve your PURPOSE.

Some documents follow formats that are fairly standardized, such as letters, memos, and e-mail messages (Chapter 43). Papers you write in academic settings usually follow guidelines established by the Modern Language Association (Chapter 36); the American Psychological Association (Chapter 37); the *Chicago Manual of Style;* the Council of Science Editors; or the IEEE (all three in Chapter 38). Check with your instructor about which style to use. Some instructors encourage—or even require—design elements such as photos, illustrations, and diagrams. However, before spending time and effort incorporating design elements into academic work, ask your instructor whether they are wanted.

Other document types invite more design creativity. Consider the public service announcement in Figure 45.1. Flyers, brochures, annual reports, reports on special projects, programs for concerts or plays, and so on give you considerable room for originality. Overall, the best design is always the one appropriate to the PURPOSE and writing situation at hand.

You don't have to be a graphic artist to produce well-designed documents. With a few tools and a little knowledge, you can produce visually effective documents. Word-processing programs such as Microsoft Word, Corel WordPerfect, and the freely available OpenOffice are sufficient for designing most basic documents. Graphic design software such as Adobe Photoshop or freely available GIMP allows you to edit photos, create other complex images, and format them to place into your word-processed document.

45b What are basic principles of design?

Brochure 2

The basic principles of design—whether for a chair, a car, a painting, a written document, or a webpage—are unity, variety, balance, and emphasis. **Unity** results from repetition and consistency. **Variety** comes from a logical, appropriate break from unity that adds interest. **Balance** refers to a sense of harmony or equilibrium. **Emphasis** directs the eye to what is most important. Quick Reference 45.1 (p. 634) describes how to check for these principles.

Compelling visual image creates a shock effect when seen with text

Images and text are balanced on page

Different typeface sizes help highlight most important text

Large typeface helps readers focus on text

Space around text enhances readability

Figure 45.1 A public service message showing various design elements

Checklist for document design

- **Unity:** Do all elements in my document work together visually? Is there a consistent use of bitmap or vector images? Does similar content have a consistent font?
- **Variety:** Have I introduced design elements, where appropriate, that break up monotony, such as headings that add to clarity or images that add to content?
- **Balance:** Are the elements of my document in proportion to each other in size, design, and placement?
- **Emphasis:** Does my document design draw attention to key information?

The flyer that a student produced for the Nature Club in Figure 45.2 reflects the four design principles. **Unity** results from similar parts of the flyer sharing the same features. All of the headings in this example (except the title) use the same font and colour, and all of the body text uses a separate font. In addition, dates for the speakers and events are displayed in a matching indented format. Unity also emerges from the colours of the headings and the image. **Variety** in the flyer comes from the use of a graphic to complement the

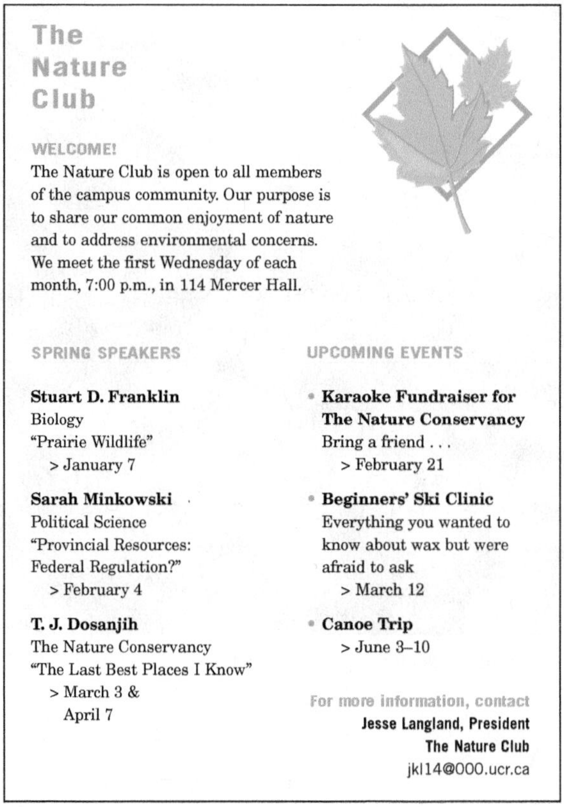

The Nature Club

WELCOME!
The Nature Club is open to all members of the campus community. Our purpose is to share our common enjoyment of nature and to address environmental concerns. We meet the first Wednesday of each month, 7:00 p.m., in 114 Mercer Hall.

SPRING SPEAKERS

Stuart D. Franklin
Biology
"Prairie Wildlife"
> January 7

Sarah Minkowski
Political Science
"Provincial Resources: Federal Regulation?"
> February 4

T. J. Dosanjih
The Nature Conservancy
"The Last Best Places I Know"
> March 3 & April 7

UPCOMING EVENTS

• **Karaoke Fundraiser for The Nature Conservancy**
Bring a friend . . .
> February 21

• **Beginners' Ski Clinic**
Everything you wanted to know about wax but were afraid to ask
> March 12

• **Canoe Trip**
> June 3–10

For more information, contact
Jesse Langland, President
The Nature Club
jkl14@000.ucr.ca

Figure 45.2 A flyer illustrating four key design principles

text. Heading, colour, and font sizes are different from the main text. Variety is also one way to create **emphasis**. For example, the title of the organization is the largest text on the page. Headings signal different types of information, and the ample use of white space allows information to stand out clearly. The contact information is in a typeface that is different from the preceding text, and its position at the lower right makes it stand out.

Finally, the page demonstrates **balance** in many ways. Each side of the flyer contains three elements, with space between them: On one side are the title, welcome, and speakers' names; on the other, picture, events, and contact information. The information about speakers and events is similar in format.

EXERCISE 45-1   Figures 45.3 and 45.4 are two alternative versions of the flyer for the Nature Club. Each of the two has problems with unity, variety, balance, or emphasis—or a combination of all four. Work alone or in groups to identify the problems in each design.

Figure 45.3 A poorly designed flyer

Figure 45.4 A poorly designed flyer

❋ 45c How do I design with text?

To format text, you need to decide which typeface—a particular style of type, such as Verdana or New Century Schoolbook—you'll use. Typefaces (also called fonts, in desktop publishing) come in two major categories. **Serif** typefaces have little extensions at the top and bottom of each letter; **sans serif** don't have them. Times New Roman is serif; Arial is sans serif. The serifs at the bottom of each letter help guide readers' eyes through lines of text; therefore, when you're writing longer segments of text, use a serif typeface. Reserve sans serif for short, isolated lines such as headings and captions.

Remember that a typeface can set a tone, so avoid using a playful one (Comic Sans MS) or one that simulates handwriting (*Kaufmann*) in academic and business writing. Fonts are different sizes of a single typeface, or variations on a typeface such as boldface and italic, and are measured in "points." For body text in longer documents, use 10- to 12-point serif typefaces.

8 point   12 point   16 point   24 point

45c.1 Highlighting text

Highlighting draws attention to key words or elements of a document. You can highlight in various ways, but in all cases, use moderation.

BOLDFACE, ITALICS, AND UNDERLINING

Italics and <u>underlining</u>—they serve the same purpose—have special functions in writing (for example, to indicate titles of certain works, as we discuss in 30f and Chapters 36–38), but they're also useful for emphasis and for headings. **Boldface** font is reserved for heavy emphasis.

BULLETED AND NUMBERED LISTS

You can use bulleted and numbered lists when you discuss a series of items or steps in a complex process or when you want to summarize key points or guidelines. A bulleted list identifies items with small dots, squares, or other shapes and symbols. Lists provide your reader with a way to think of the whole idea you're communicating. For this reason, they work particularly well as summaries.

COLOUR

Adding colour to a document can change it dramatically. In addition to including colourful visuals or BORDERS (45e), you can also change the font colour or use a coloured background for certain words or sections. Take time, however, to think about your reasons for adding colour to your text. How does colour suit the type of document? How will it help you accomplish your purpose? Use colour sparingly for variety and emphasis.

JUSTIFYING

When you make your text lines even in relation to the left or right margin, you're **justifying** them. There are four kinds of justification, or ways to line up text lines on margins: left, right, centred, and full.

Left justified text (text aligns on the left)

Right justified text (text aligns on the right)

Centre justified text (text aligns in the centre)

Full justified text (both left and right justified to full length, or measure, of the line of type)

Most academic and business documents are left justified, which means that the right ends of the lines are unjustified, or *ragged*. Centre, right, and full justification are useful for designing shorter documents (flyers, posters, and so on) because they can attract attention.

INDENTATION

When you move text toward the right margin, you are **indenting**. Using the ruler line in your word-processing program to control indentations makes it easier to make global changes in your indentation. The top arrow of the bar sets the paragraph indentation, while the bottom arrow sets the indentation for everything else in the paragraph. MLA-style Works Cited pages and APA References pages use hanging indentations in which the first line of an entry aligns at the left margin and every following line is indented. Indent bulleted and numbered lists to make them stand out, as in the list in 45d.

SETTING MARGINS

Margins are the boundaries of a page, which means the white space or blank areas at the top, bottom, and sides of a paper or screen. Narrow margins allow you to fit more information on a page but also decrease the amount of white space available. This can make a page appear cluttered, dense, and difficult to read. Essays, research papers, and most BUSINESS WRITING call for one inch, or about 2.5 cm, of space on all sides.

45d How do I use headings?

Headings clarify how you've organized your material and tell your readers what to expect in each section. Longer documents, including handbooks (like ours), reports, brochures, and webpages use headings to break content into chunks that are easier to digest and understand. In academic writing, APA style favours headings, whereas MLA tends to discourage them. Following are some guidelines for writing and formatting headings.

- **Create headings in a slightly larger type than the type size in the body of your text.** You can use the same or a contrasting typeface, as long as it coordinates visually and is easy to read.
- **Keep headings brief and informative.** Your readers can use them as cues.
- **Change the format for headings of different levels.** Think of levels in headings the way you think of items in an outline (see 2f). Level one headings show the main divisions of a document. Level two headings divide material that appears under level one headings, and

637

so on. Changing the format for different levels of headings creates a clear outline for the reader. You can do this in various ways: You can centre heads or left justify them; you can use a different font or type size; you can highlight using boldface, italics, or underlining; or you can use various combinations of capitals and lowercase letters. Always be consistent in the style you use within each document.

Level one heading (most important)	**First-Level Head**
Level two heading	<u>Second-Level Head</u>
Level three heading	*Third-level head*

- **Use parallel structure.** All headings at the same level should be similar in kind. For example, you might make all first-level heads questions and all second-level heads noun phrases. Quick Reference 45.2 presents common types of headings, with examples showing parallel structure.

QUICK REFERENCE 45.2

Common types of headings

- **NOUN PHRASES can cover a variety of topics.**
  Federal Government Responsibilities
  Provincial Government Responsibilities

- **Questions can evoke reader interest.**
  Can the Federal Government Overrule Provincial Laws?
  What Is the "Notwithstanding Clause"?

- **GERUNDS and *-ing* phrases can explain instructions or solve problems.**
  Submitting the Federal Budget
  Debating the Federal Budget

- **Imperative sentences can give advice or directions.**
  Consult Interest Groups
  Introduce a Bill in Parliament

45e How do I use borders?

Borders are lines used to set apart sections of text. They can take a number of forms, from single lines of varying thickness to patterns. A single rule (a simple straight line, horizontal or vertical) can emphasize breaks between major sections of a long report. Borders around text serve to set off information, as in a table or chart.

45f How should I incorporate graphics?

Informational Graphics

The Sleep of Reasoning (PowerPoint Presentation)

Graphics, also called *images* or *visuals,* can enhance document design when used appropriately. A visual can condense, compare, and display information more effectively than words, but only if its content is suitable. A graph showing how sales increased over a period of time, for example, makes the point more quickly and clearly than an explanation.

CHARTS, GRAPHS, AND TABLES

Business and scientific reports rely heavily on charts and graphs, as do some research papers. They're compact ways to present large amounts of information. Figures 45.5–45.8 illustrate these elements.

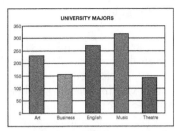

Figure 45.5 **Bar graphs** compare values, such as the number of different majors at a university, as shown in this graph.

Figure 45.6 **Line graphs** indicate changes over time. For example, advertising revenue is shown over an eight-month period in this graph.

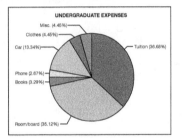

Figure 45.7 **Pie charts** show the relationship of each part to a whole, such as a typical budget for an undergraduate student, as shown in this chart.

Table 42.1 Total Number of Computer Lab Users by Semester		
Semester	Number of Users	Percentage (%) of Student Population
Spring 2013	2321	25.8
Summer 2013	592	6.6
Fall 2013	3425	38.1

Figure 45.8 **Tables** present data in list form, as shown here, allowing readers to grasp a lot of information at a glance.

   In academic or business documents, especially lengthy ones, number figures and tables, if you use more than one, and number them sequentially. If possible, choose only one term in a relatively short piece of writing: *Table 1, Table 2*; or *Figure 1, Figure 2*, and so forth.

CLIP ART

Clip art refers to pictures, sketches, and other graphics available on some word-processing programs. It can also be downloaded from the Internet, sometimes from free sites and sometimes for a small fee. Although clip art is rarely, if ever, appropriate in academic writing and business writing, it can add interest to flyers, posters, newsletters, and brochures designed for certain audiences.

PHOTOGRAPHS

In an age of digital cameras, not to mention an age when cell phones have the capacity to take pictures and send them around the world, **photographs** are everywhere. Because you can easily download photographs from a digital camera, you can place them into documents with equal ease. You can also scan photographs from printed photos or from books and articles. The Internet is another source of images; several websites (including many at libraries) offer thousands of photographs for free. Most images online, however, are copyrighted, and thus you need to gain permission to use images for any type of publication. Quick Reference 45.3 contains terms and special considerations when using images found on the Web.

Considerations when using visuals from the Web

Always observe copyrights. Images, just like text, are copyrighted as soon as they are fixed in any medium. In other words, most images online are owned by somebody, even if you can find them and display them on your screen for free. Although the copyright law is fairly generous in allowing students to use found images for projects done strictly for courses, you should document the source of the image. If you're using an image in a project for a wider audience, including any Web-based project, you need to get permission from the photographer or the rights-owner. Here are some important terms to understand.

- Rights-managed—When an image is rights-managed, it means that the owner of the image charges you, the user, according to how you will use the image. Many stock-photo websites such as Illustration Source <http://www.images.com> offer pricing options for use of photos.

- Royalty-free—This does not mean the image is free. Instead, the author of the image is selling a one-time use of the photo for a flat fee and doesn't expect royalties from your use of the image. Websites such as iStock <http://www.istockphoto.com> offer many royalty-free photos.

- Creative commons—Creative commons is a copyright alternative that allows authors to control how others may or may not use their works without the added issue of asking permission. There are many such options available at Creative Commons <http://creativecommons.org/>. A number of photos at Flickr <http://www.flickr.com/creativecommons/> have a creative commons licence.

- Public domain—Works in the public domain are free to use in whatever fashion a user wants without obtaining permission first. (The Canadian government copyrights its publications and images but allows non-commercial use of most of these. No permission is needed.)

Once a photograph is in your computer, you can place it in your document, usually with an "Insert" or "Import" command. A software feature such as the pictures toolbar within Microsoft Word can help you adjust a photograph by cropping it (trimming the top, bottom, or sides), rotating it, or making it larger or smaller. A powerful program like Adobe Photoshop lets you modify colours and create special effects.

For additional help in using visuals, follow the guidelines in Quick Reference 45.4.

Guidelines for using visuals

- **Design all visuals to be simple and uncluttered.**
- **Use the highest resolution and best images possible.** Small images stretched to fit a large space do not look professional. It's always best to use large pictures and then reduce the size later. Reducing the size of a picture will not harm the resolution.
- **Include a heading or title for each visual.** Doing so helps readers quickly understand what they're seeing.
- **Never use unnecessary visuals.** Make sure all visuals clearly contribute to your PURPOSE. Putting cute clip art on the pages of your writing won't make your reader think your work is well done. However, including a chart that summarizes your findings might.
- **Consider your audience and their sensibilities.** You don't want to offend your readers, nor do you want them to be confused.
- **Credit your source if a visual isn't your own.** Always avoid plagiarism by crediting your source using DOCUMENTATION. If you're using a visual (including a photograph) for a public purpose other than for a class project, you need written permission to use it in your work.

45g   What is page layout?

Layout is the arrangement of text, visuals, colour, and space on a page. You'll want to arrange these elements so that you follow the basic principles of design (45b). Experiment with ideas for layout by creating mock-up pages on a computer or by sketching possibilities by hand.

You might also see if any suitable **templates** are available. A template is a professionally designed form that shows you where to place visuals in relation to text; it has predefined typefaces, heading styles, margins, and so on. Page layout software and most word-processing software have a variety of templates for brochures, flyers, newsletters, and many other types of documents. Several websites offer them, too.

Quick Reference 45.5 explains how to position texts and visuals.

Guidelines for positioning text and visuals

- Consider the size of visuals in placing them so that they don't cluster at the top or the bottom of a page. That is, avoid creating a page that's top-heavy or bottom-heavy.
- To create balance in a document, imagine it as divided into halves, quarters, or eighths. As you position text or images in the spaces, see which look full, which look empty, and whether the effect seems visually balanced.

continued ➤

- Use the "Table" feature of your word-processing program to position text and visuals exactly where you want them. Turn off the grid lines when you're done so that the printed copy shows only the text and visuals.

- Avoid splitting a chart or table between one page and the next. If possible, fit the entire chart or table on a single page. If it runs slightly more than a page, look for ways to adjust spacing or cut text. If you have no choice but to split a chart or table, then on the second page, repeat the title and add the word "continued" at the top.

- Use the "Print Preview" feature to see what each printed version will look like, which will help you revise before completing your final document.

- Print copies of your various layouts and look at them from different distances. Ask others to look at your layouts and tell you what they like best and least about each.

You have many options for placing images in relation to text. Figure 45.9 shows one standard kind of placement, the image centred above the words. In contrast, Figure 45.10 shows the text wrapped around the picture, which creates a better sense of connection between the two. Finally, Figure 45.11 illustrates that words can also wrap elements other than graphics, in this case a list enclosed in borders forming a box.

USING WHITE SPACE

White space, the part of your document that has neither text nor visuals, allows readers to read your document more easily and to absorb information in chunks rather than in one big block. White space indicates breaks between ideas and thereby focuses attention on the key features of your document.

Traditionally, academic writing includes relatively little white space, except sometimes between sections of a document. Use double-spacing in your assignments unless your instructor requests otherwise; double-spacing leaves space for comments in response to your writing. Business writing usually calls for single-spaced lines, with an added line of white space between paragraphs.

However, our research shows that students who are involved in a volunteer project actually achieve better grades than those who are not. One possible reason is that having too much free time actually encourages people to waste it; being busier forces them to be more organized.

Figure 45.9 An image centred above text

However, our research shows that students who are involved in a volunteer project actually achieve better grades than those who are not. One possible reason is that having too much free time actually encourages people to waste it; being busier forces them to be more organized. A more interesting reason is that volunteering for a meaningful project gives people a sense of purpose that carries over into other phases of their lives. Students who are concerned about the state of the environment, for example, draw energy from working with others who share their passion.

Figure 45.10 Text wrapped around the image

However, our research shows that students who are involved in a volunteer project actually achieve better grades than those who are not. One possible reason is that having too much free time actually encourages people to waste it; being busier forces them to be more organized. A more interesting reason is that volunteering for a meaningful

Successful volunteers
-Follow their passions
-Budget their time
-Have positive outlooks
-Seek like-minded others

project gives people a sense of purpose that carries over into other phases of their lives.

Figure 45.11 Text wrapped around a box

Flyers, brochures, posters, reports, webpages, and similar documents tend to make extensive and varied use of white space because they rely heavily on graphics. Styles change over time, but most current professional designers prefer an uncluttered look with lots of white space.

Chapter 46

MULTIMODAL TEXTS AND WRITING FOR THE WEB

46a What are multimodal texts?

Multimodal texts communicate through multiple (MULTI-) means, materials, and modes (-MODAL). They combine words with images or even sound and video. As a result, while some multimodal texts are meant for print, others exist only in digital form. Examples include posters and flyers, PowerPoint presentations, websites, movies, videogames, and podcasts. Chapter 45 explained how a document's design contributes to its meaning, but the mode of a text also influences its meaning. Because new technologies give writers many options concerning the look and delivery of their communications, understanding how to design in multiple modes can make you a more sophisticated writer and communicator, both in your studies and beyond.

In academic settings, an instructor may assign a specific kind of text: a traditional paper, a poster, a website (46d), a blog (46e), a wiki (46f) a podcast (46g), and so on. We explain each below. On other occasions, however, the choice may be up to you.

Keep in mind that your writing situation must guide that choice. Sometimes a visual or audio presentation doesn't work as well as text alone. Also recognize that as you increase the complexity of your message by adding various media, you also increase the chance that your readers will get distracted or confused. In other words, multimodal writing often requires more attention and work than you may have planned.

46b What do I need to know about creating multimodal projects?

All elements within a multimodal text should effectively engage an AUDIENCE and clearly contribute to the overall PURPOSE of the piece. Also, a visual or audio presentation must have unity and coherent development and flow. When people read, hear, or watch an example of each mode, they expect it to follow certain conventions. Just as with traditional writing, the best way to learn these conventions is to read, listen, or watch many of them, analyzing them to see how they work. As you compose multimodal projects, apply the strategies of generating, planning, and organizing.

46c What is writing for the Web?

Writing for the Web means producing documents that are designed specifically to be read online. The World Wide Web consists of millions of sites (one or many connected pages) and billions of pages (a document within a site). Of course, many of the documents that appear on the Web were actually written for print publication. This includes articles in library databases (34c–d), online versions of newspapers and magazines, and even papers placed on the Web as Word documents and PDF (Portable Document Format) files.

As you know, webpages are common in academic, business, and public settings. They inform, entertain, and persuade through text, images, colour, and often sound and video. Because websites allow readers to jump from page to page to find information within a site and beyond, they provide exceptional flexibility. When you design a website you need to consider not only how a page looks but also how it relates to others, both pages you've created and those already online. Writing for the Web means that you can freely and easily change the content of your pages.

Figure 46.1 shows the home page of the Nature Club, a campus organization whose flyer appears in Figure 45.2. Notice that links combining graphics and text appear prominently under the logo that welcomes visitors to this home page. The clean design, making good use of white space, recalls the organization's message. Visitors to this home page can tell at a glance what kinds of information the site contains and go directly to the pages that interest them.

EXERCISE 46-1 Discuss how the webpage in Figure 46.1 differs from the flyer in Figure 45.2. How do the purposes of the two modes shape these differences?

46d How do I create a website?

The **Web writing process** has five parts: (1) writing the content, (2) creating the structure of the content, (3) designing the layout of the material on the computer screen, (4) checking whether the Web material is usable, and (5) loading the website on a **server**, a computer that is always online and available to Internet users.

Website 1:
Red Cross
Homepage
(Interactive)

Website 2:
Haven House
Website

Website 3:
S@fetyNET
Website
(Interactive)

Figure 46.1 The home page of the Nature Club

46d.1 How do I plan content for my website?

The Web differs from other media in distinct ways that affect your writing.

- Web writing calls for smaller blocks of text than print writing. Web readers prefer not to scroll down long sections of information.
- Web writing highlights the connections or links between related websites.
- Web writing emphasizes visual elements such as colour and pictures.

As you plan, ask yourself these questions:

- What is the purpose of my site? Is it to inform, to persuade, or to entertain?
- Who will my readers be? What knowledge and expectations will they have? How can I help them navigate—that is, move—from one document to another?
- What is the size of my Web writing project? How many pages will I want and how much content will I include in each?
- Should I include links to other websites? Which sites will support my purpose, perhaps with an illustration, an explanation, or a reference?

46d.2 How do I create a structure for my website?

Web structure is the organization of the content and documents that site creators include in a Web project. Almost all websites have a **home page** that introduces the site and provides links to the other pages that the site contains. The home page functions like a table of contents in print or, perhaps, the entryway to a building. It should be appealing and give visitors to the home page clear directions for navigating from page to page. Here are some guidelines for creating a site's structure.

- Determine all of the pages your site might contain and whether these pages should be grouped into **categories** (groups of pages all on the same topic).
- Generate a list of categories. You might use the planning techniques of BRAINSTORMING, FREEWRITING, and CLUSTERING discussed in Chapter 2.
- Plan a Web structure by drawing a map of all of your separate documents and the best way they connect to one another. Figure 46.2 shows two possible structures.
- Plan **hyperlinks**, which are direct electronic connections between two pages. Combinations of hyperlinks are the glue that holds Web writings together.

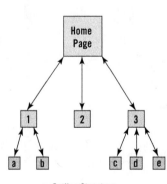

Outline Structure

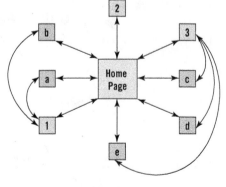

Cluster Structure

Figure 46.2 Two possible website structures

46d.3   How do I design webpages?

Once you've drafted a map of your website, you begin designing and creating your individual webpages. Generally, all the pages within a site need to have the same basic design and similar navigation features to ensure that the site is unified and that users have an easy, pleasant experience. Most guidelines and principles that contribute to good design in printed documents apply equally to Web design. Use the basic design principles of unity, variety, balance, and emphasis discussed in Chapter 45.

Begin by planning a webpage's general appearance. Make decisions about the placement of texts and graphics, the use of colour and white space, and what you want to emphasize. Early in your planning process, you might look at some websites that seem similar to what you have in mind. Figures 46.3 and 46.4 show two popular designs. In these figures, A is a *banner* showing the title of the organization or site. B is a menu of links to pages in the website, C is the main section for content, and D is for offsite or additional links.

Quick Reference 46.1 contains some general advice about designing webpages.

QUICK REFERENCE   **46.1**

General advice for designing webpages

- **Choose an appropriate title.** Make sure your page has a title that tells readers exactly what they'll find there.
- **Keep backgrounds and texts simple.** Like professional Web designers, strive for a clean, uncluttered look. Dark text on a plain light background is easiest to read, with white being the preferred background. In contrast to print documents. SANS SERIF fonts tend to be easier to read on computer screens than SERIF fonts. avoid multiple typefaces, sizes, and colours, multiple images and graphics, and busy backgrounds.
- **Use images to attract attention to important elements and to please the reader.** Readers will tend to look first at pictures and graphics on a page, so choose and then position them to reinforce your page's content.

continued ➤

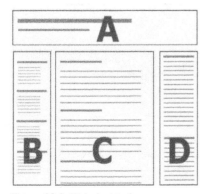

Figure 46.3 Web design 1

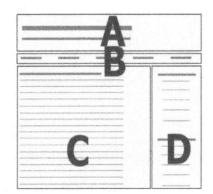

Figure 46.4 Web design 2

- **Unify the pages in your site.** Keep the overall appearance of pages within one site consistent in terms of typefaces, graphics, and colour. Your HTML editor's style sheet (46d.4) can ensure that pages share common features: the same basic layout, font, colour scheme, and header or **navigation bar** (the set of links on every webpage that allows users to get back to the site's home page and to major parts of the site).

- **Provide identifying information.** Generally, the bottom of a page includes the date the page is updated, or added to, along with contact information for the site's creator or administrator.

46d.4   How do I use Web writing software?

Webpages are written in a computer program language called HTML, for **H**yper**T**ext **M**arkup **L**anguage. Although it's possible to create webpages directly using HTML, it's easier to use an HTML editor—a program that generates tags, or codes, in much the same way that word-processing programs generate boldface type or other formatting.

USING STYLE SHEETS AND TABLES

Most contemporary Web designs use CSS (**C**ascading **S**tyle **S**heets). These let you define what particular elements, such as headings, links, and block text, will look like. You just need to define the elements and apply the style sheet.

Tables allow you to use HTML editors to place text and images accurately. Unlike designing with pen and paper or with computer drawing software, HTML editors don't allow you to position materials immediately at different points on the screen. Instead, a table divides the screen into a grid of spaces. You can then change the size of different rows, columns, or cells in the table to place blocks of text, images, links, and so on exactly where you want them. Figure 46.5 shows the basic table design underlying the Nature Club home page.

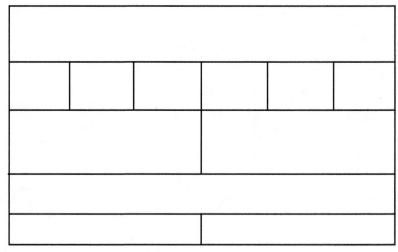

Figure 46.5 Table design of the Nature Club home page

46d.5 How do I incorporate images into webpages?

Webpages can include many different kinds of graphics. For example, bullets can mark off a list of items, as they do in print documents. Borders or rule lines can divide the page. You can also use photographs imported from a digital camera, scanned from print, or downloaded from the Internet, along with clip art and other graphics. Quick Reference 46.2 covers ways to use graphics effectively.

QUICK REFERENCE 46.2

Using graphics effectively on the Web

- **Use only images that enhance your message or design.** Most images require lots of digital storage space and loading time.
- **Resize or crop images using graphic design software.** Although you should use the largest, highest resolution digital images possible, you should size the images and set the resolution at 72 ppi (pixels per inch) before you insert them into your design.
- **Save images in a compressed format.** The two most popular formats for images on the Web are Graphical Interchange Format (GIF) and Joint Photographic Experts Group (JPEG). If you have a button, small piece of clip art, or a black and white picture, GIF is an ideal format since these types of graphics only use a few colours. JPEG uses 16.7 million colours and compresses the file size of the picture by getting rid of empty space and blending colours. This process can leave little imperfections in solid colour images, especially if you repeatedly save or rework the image.

EXERCISE 46-2 Working alone or in a group, choose one or more websites and print out a page from each. Analyze the use of images on the page(s). For help, consult the discussions of images in Chapter 4 and visual design in Chapter 45.

Be careful and respectful using any images that you haven't created yourself, especially when copying images from the Internet. E-mail the site's creator to ask permission. Quick Reference 45.3 discussed copyright issues connected to the use of images. For the correct DOCUMENTATION format for your graphic sources, see Chapter 36 for MLA style and Chapter 37 for APA style.

46d.6 How do I edit my page and test usability?

Before you publish your webpage (that is, before you upload it to a server), edit and proofread it as carefully as you would a print document. The key difference between editing a webpage and a print document is that you also need to check that all of the interactive parts of your webpage are working properly. Before you finalize your webpage, use the following checklist:

- **Are any images broken?** Broken images show up as small icons instead of the pictures you want. The usual cause of broken images is mistyping the file name or failing to upload the image.
- **Do all the links work?** For each link to a page on your own site, be sure a file with that exact name exists on the server. Mistyped or mislabelled files can cause broken links.

- **Is the website user-friendly?** Ask your friends, classmates, or colleagues to report any sections in which information is unclear or difficult to find. They can also provide feedback about content.

46d.7 How do I display my webpage?

After you've created and tested a webpage, you're ready to display it on the Web. To do this, you need two things: First, you need space on a **web server**, a centralized computer always online and primarily dedicated to storing and making webpages available. Second, you need the ability to load all of your files to that server, including the page(s) you've made and any associated graphics that you've included.

FINDING SPACE ON THE WEB

If you have a commercial Internet service provider (ISP), you may be able to use it to post your website. Your college or university may offer Web space to its students, so check with your computing service office. Some services on the Internet offer free Web space as well as help in building webpages. Try searching for "free Web hosting." Note that if you use "free" Web space, the provider may insert advertising on your page.

You'll also need some kind of File Transfer Protocol (FTP) program to upload the HTML files to your Web server. The host of your space should be able to advise you on the best way to upload files and which FTP program to use.

PUBLISHING YOUR PAGE

Posting a webpage is a form of publishing. Like all original writings, your website is automatically copyrighted. If you want to make this clear to users (to discourage PLAGIARISM, for example) include a copyright notice by typing the word *copyright*, the copyright symbol ©, the year of publication, and your name. If you want feedback, include your e-mail address. If you use material from SOURCES, credit them fully by using DOCUMENTATION; you might include a link titled "Works Cited," "References," or "Sources" that takes your readers to a separate page. Always ask for permission to use someone else's work on your website. Plagiarism is plagiarism (35b), whether the medium is print or electronic.

46e How do I write in a blog?

A BLOG (Web log) is a type of website that displays a series of posts, or items, usually diary-like entries or observations, but also images, videos, audio files, and links.

Some instructors have students keep blogs as a course requirement. This follows the tradition of having students keep journals as a regular way of writing about course content. The twist is that others can easily read and comment on each person's postings. If you're assigned to produce a course blog, your instructor will provide specific directions. Figure 1.2 shows how one blog integrates text and design.

If you'd like to create your own blog, decide on a type and purpose. Some blogs collect links and ask others to comment on those links. Others invite much longer response posts about current news stories or happenings. Still other blogs provide original material or refer to the events of the blogger's life.

Next, you'll want to figure out how much control you want over your blog's appearance. Some software allows you to start blogging almost immediately. However, if you would like to have more control, you may need to buy server space and set up the software yourself. CMS (Content Management Software) such as Movable Type and Drupal are powerful programs that let you design, write, and maintain your own blog.

You need to find an AUDIENCE that cares about your perspective. You might participate in blogs and network with others, eventually finding correspondents who are interested in what you have to say. Most important is to have something interesting to say. Not all blogs have to be public, but if you want to take advantage of the technology for sharing your ideas and experiences, you should make these entertaining, persuasive, and enlightening. Quick Reference 46.3 contains some guidelines.

QUICK REFERENCE   46.3

Guidelines for writing in a blog

- **Pick a unique title for your blog.** People and Internet search engines will recognize your blog if it has a good title.

- **Decide whether to use your own name or a username.** You can protect your privacy to some degree if you have a *pseudonym* or *username*. Especially if you're writing about controversial topics or taking controversial positions, you might not want employers, instructors, or even relatives to know your identity. Of course, an anonymous username doesn't give you licence to be irresponsible or unethical. The advantage of your real name, in contrast, is that you get credit for your writings. Think carefully about this decision.

- **Observe netiquette.** NETIQUETTE refers to etiquette in online environments. Remember, the Internet is available around the world to many people in many cultures and of many ages. What might seem normal in your life isn't necessarily normal to someone else online. So be respectful in your posts, avoid vulgar language or SHOUTING (typing in all capital letters), and, if you disagree with somebody, try to find common ground or evidence to the contrary rather than resorting to *ad hominem* (4i) attacks.

- **Link, show, and share.** Use the Web and its multimodality in your posts. Include links in your posts to other posts or items from the Web. Post images, videos, or audio files, but do respect copyrights. And share your posts and blog with others through the use of a blogroll or by participating in other blogs. Blogging is about sharing your ideas and experiences with others so that they share their ideas and experiences with you.

46f   How do I write in a wiki?

A wiki is a technology that allows anybody to change the content of a webpage without using special software. *Wiki* is a Hawaiian word meaning "fast," and the name refers to how quickly people using this technology can collaborate and revise information. One of the more popular wiki applications is the online encyclopedia, Wikipedia.

The technology behind wikis is similar to that in blogs; both use software that runs in the background and organizes the content. Wikis, however, are designed to allow collaborative writing and presentation rather than individual commentary and response. A wiki entry, or node, is updated and displayed immediately as the content of a website. Whatever was written at a particular node before it was edited is deleted, and the new content replaces it. In some ways, a wiki is more temporary than any other type of multimodal writing because many people can change it.

Wikis can be useful tools for collaborative writing projects because they keep a draft in front of all group members all the time. Individuals can easily make contributions and changes. However, as you can imagine, this can also lead to complications. If you're using a wiki for an academic project, you'll want to review strategies in Chapter 6 for writing with others.

There is usually no need to create a wiki if one already exists to serve a particular purpose. Contributing to the existing wiki is usually time better spent. However, if you want to create a wiki for an unmet need, such as providing information for an upcoming election, creating a collaborative space for a business, or designing a study aid for a course, setting one up is fairly easy. Simple software like PBworks <http://pbworks.com/> will allow you quickly to start creating your own wiki without worrying about server space. However, if you need more control, you will have to install specialized software such as TikiWiki, MediaWiki, or SnipSnap on a dedicated Web server. In either case, you should observe the guidelines in Quick Reference 46.4 for writing or revising a wiki node.

QUICK REFERENCE **46.4**

Guidelines for writing in a wiki

- **Revise with respect for others.** When revising a node, always consider ways to preserve what it originally contained before deleting what another person has written. The strength of a wiki is its ability to allow people to collaborate, so try to retain what others have said. In some cases, you might post on a wiki and find you totally disagree with what is written. Instead of deleting what's there, consider adding another section to the node entitled "opposing arguments" (see 5l).

- **Cite your sources whenever possible.** Much of the controversy concerning Wikipedia in recent years has to do with the fact that some entries do not have cited references. Whenever possible, you should cite your sources and find corroborating sources. Any addition to a wiki node that contains reference to reputable sources is less likely to be deleted or revised later.

- **Remember that a wiki is multimodal.** Just as with a blog, use the Web and its multimodality in your node edits. Include links and references from other sources on the Web. Post images, videos, or audio files, respecting copyrights in every case. The Web is suited to multimodal presentation, so take advantage of this capability when revising or writing in a wiki.

EXERCISE 46-3   Considering what you know about blogs, wikis, and multimodal writing, what are the benefits of using Wikipedia? What are the drawbacks?

46g How do I create podcasts or videos?

Podcasts are short audio or video files (as on YouTube, for example) that are distributed via the Internet. People can view or listen to them directly online (called "streaming") or as downloads to their computers or a digital player. (Not every podcast can be downloaded.) Audio podcasts are oral presentations, and serious ones need to be carefully planned and written so that listeners can easily follow them, just as they would a speech. Video podcasts often imitate formats that appear on television, although the production is usually not as elaborate. A podcast might be a useful source for a paper. Take care to evaluate and cite it as you would any source, and follow the appropriate documentation styles (Chapters 36–38).

Although you can create advanced Web designs or flyers with standard computer software and hardware, creating a professional audio or video presentation or podcast can require more specialized and expensive equipment. However, you should still be able to produce effective podcasts if you observe the guidelines in Quick Reference 46.5. Plan, draft, revise, and edit a podcast just as you would any other writing project.

QUICK REFERENCE **46.5**

Guidelines for producing a podcast

- **Consider the benefits of the mode.** Besides thinking about your AUDIENCE and PURPOSE, you need to also consider whether audio or video is an effective mode for your situation. Producing audio or video requires far more time than any other type of multimodal writing. Additionally, audio and video are both linear formats, which is to say that a good podcast has a beginning, a middle, and an end, and listeners or viewers can't easily skip around.

- **Create and practise a script.** You should write out a script that contains what you intend to say and that details how you will say particular passages, what might be appearing on the camera during a particular section, and gives cues for music or sound effects. Once the script is written, practise the script often by reading it aloud.

- **Create a storyboard for video projects.** A storyboard is a series of rough sketches (you can use "stick" people, for example) that show the major scenes or elements in your video. It helps you plan the sequence and keep track of what shots you need to make.

- **Find an appropriate place to record.** When recording audio or video, you should always be aware that microphones and cameras record more than you might have intended. Background sounds that you normally don't notice will be obvious in your recording. Many universities have practice rooms in the music departments that are designed to dampen noise, but at least look for a quiet place with good acoustics to record any audio.

- **Use the best equipment available to you.** Although many digital cameras have record-to-video functions, you will get better footage from a dedicated video camera. Similarly, although a laptop might have a built-in microphone, a dedicated microphone will produce the best results.

46h   What do I need to know about writing in social networking sites?

Social networking websites like MySpace and Facebook allow you to share your experiences, interests, and writing with other people of similar interests. Designing in these sites is limited by the software that each company uses, but you can still make your website interesting and effective. Most of the visual design elements that have been discussed in this chapter are applicable to setting up your space on a social networking site. Consider Quick Reference 46.1 and 46.3 when designing and writing on a social networking site.

Remember that even if you have made your page private, a friend of a friend or even a future employer could easily end up viewing it. People have lost jobs and job opportunities because of what employers have seen on their pages. Always assume that anything you post is public and permanent. Only post images, text, or music that you are confident are appropriate and that represent you well.

Because of the powerful social networking capability, an effectively designed page might attract potential employers or professional contacts more easily than a traditional resumé or website. Make sure, then, to represent yourself well for multiple audiences. Because viewers can often link to your friends' pages as well, make sure you accept friends who reflect well on you. Additionally, although you might think that private information such as your address or phone number is safe from others if you are listed as private, this information still can be leaked. You're not as anonymous as you might think. These concerns shouldn't scare you away from creating a presence on a social networking site that you and others can enjoy. Just be cautious and only post personal information when absolutely necessary.

Chapter 47

CREATING A WRITING PORTFOLIO

47a What is a writing portfolio?

A portfolio is a collection of your writings that you present to others to show what you are capable of. You might be familiar with artists or graphic artists who make portfolios of their work in order to show gallery owners or prospective employers. Writing portfolios are similar collections of best works. Students may need to submit them at the end of a course. Some students are required to submit a portfolio of work at the end of their major or program to demonstrate what they've accomplished over their years of study. Portfolios can even be part of the hiring process for some jobs.

As we explain in this chapter, portfolios can exist in paper formats or they can exist electronically, in digital versions. There are four key steps in making a successful portfolio: collecting all of your writings; selecting the works to include in a given portfolio; writing an introduction to, or analysis of, those works; and designing the presentation format. We explain each step below.

47b What do I need to collect for a portfolio?

To put it simply, save everything you write. Save every paper and project, every exam or lab report, even every draft. You can't put together a good portfolio if you don't have plenty of works to choose from, including plenty of works to ignore. Because computer storage is so cheap and plentiful, it's easy to keep electronic copies of everything. It's a good idea to keep paper copies, too, especially when they have an instructor's comments or grades; some portfolios, such as those submitted for awards or graduate school admissions, often require instructors' comments.

47c How do I choose works to include in a portfolio?

Selection is crucial to an effective portfolio. Rather than including everything you've written, you need to choose your best pieces that satisfy the requirements of the portfolio. One obvious thing you need to do is to meet any requirements for the number of works or pages to include. If you're asked to select three pieces, don't include two or four. If you're asked to submit a total of 20–25 pages, don't turn in 17 or 29. Beyond those requirements, you need to pay attention to specific things requested in a particular situation.

47c.1 Portfolios that demonstrate your general writing ability

Consider this kind of assignment: "Present three works that best display your strengths as a writer." Clearly, you're going to choose your best writing. However, you might additionally judge whether to choose pieces that show a range of your abilities. For example, if you're choosing from six papers, and three of them are all the same kind of writing, you might choose at least one different kind of paper that allows you to show how versatile you are. (Of course, if the other papers are considerably weaker than the three similar ones, go with your strengths.)

47c.2 Portfolios that demonstrate a particular quality or set of qualities

Consider another kind of situation: "One goal in this course was to improve your skill at writing for different situations. Create a portfolio of three works that demonstrate how you're able to write for different audiences and purposes and in different roles." In this case, you need to choose works that reflect different writing situations. Choosing becomes a little more like putting together a puzzle, as you look for the right combination of writings that allows you to meet the requirement. Occasionally, this means that a strong work gets omitted. Often, you need to choose works that satisfy multiple requirements. For example, you might choose papers A and B to illustrate different audiences, papers A and C to show different purposes, and B and C to show different roles.

47c.3 Portfolios that demonstrate improvement

Consider a third kind of portfolio: "Select four examples of your writing from this semester that demonstrate how your writing has developed." In this case, your instructor wants to see your improvement. One way to do this is to choose writings from the beginning, middle, and end of the course. Another way is to choose both early drafts and late, revised drafts of the same paper. In this kind of portfolio, as well as the others, an introductory or analytic statement will be valuable.

47d How do I write a portfolio introduction, reflection, or analysis?

A statement or essay in which you introduce or explain the works you're presenting is an important part of most portfolios. This statement, which may range from a few paragraphs to several pages, can go by several names: introduction, reflection, analysis, reflective introduction, reflective analysis, and so on. The basic elements are always the same: You want to introduce yourself as a writer; you want to introduce the works that follow (perhaps with a one- or two-sentence summary of each of them); and you want to make some points about them, especially how they satisfy your purpose.

It's helpful to think of the reflective introduction as a kind of argument. You're making claims about your work, and you're providing support for those claims. For example, if you say, "These pieces show my ability to adjust my writing for academic and popular audiences," then you need to "prove" your assertion. In this case, your evidence is one or more of the papers in the portfolio, and you'll want to summarize, paraphrase, or quote the appropriate passage. You'll need to explain how the evidence fits your claim. A helpful basic structure is the following:

1. Claim about your writing.
2. Summaries, paraphrases, or quotations from papers in the portfolio that support the claim.
3. Discussion of how the summary, paraphrase, or quotations support your claim.

Repeat this pattern for as many claims as you have about your portfolio. The following example illustrates weak and strong sections from reflective introductions.

EXAMPLE

Weak and Strong Sections from a Reflective Introduction

[The following paragraph is common to all three examples that follow.]

During the 2012 spring semester, I completed five papers in English 101, revising each of them several times with response from my peers and feedback from my instructor. At times the process was frustrating; I came into the course feeling confident in my writing, but I learned that there's always room for improvement. As I reflect back on my experiences, I'm especially satisfied with new strategies I learned for making effective arguments and with the skills I acquired in writing different kinds of academic papers. This portfolio includes three papers I've chosen to represent my current strengths as a writer.

Weak [Same introduction as above]

One quality apparent in these papers is my ability to adjust writings for different audiences, both academic and general. For example, "Analyzing the Merits of Organic Produce" addresses an academic readership. In contrast, "Is That Organic Apple Really Worth It?" is aimed at a more general audience.

Better [Same introduction as above]

One quality apparent in these papers is my ability to adjust writings for different audiences, both academic and general. For example, "Analyzing the Merits of Organic Produce" addresses an academic readership. This can be seen in my consistent use of APA citation style and a scholarly tone suitable for experts, as in my opening sentence, "Research on the health values of organic produce over nonorganic reveals that this issue remains unresolved" (Akule, 2007; Johnson, 2006).

In contrast, my paper "Is That Organic Apple Really Worth It?" is aimed at a more general audience. That paper uses scenes and examples designed to engage readers with a friendly tone. This is clear in my opening sentence, "As sticker shock in the grocery checkout line continues to worsen, consumers have to judge whether everything in their carts belongs there."

Strong [Same introduction as above]

One quality apparent in these papers is my ability to adjust writings for different audiences, both academic and general. For example, "Analyzing the Merits of Organic Produce" addresses an academic readership, specifically members of the scientific community looking for a review of the literature. This can be seen in my consistent use of APA citation style and a scholarly tone suitable for experts. One example is my opening sentence, "Research on the health values of organic produce over nonorganic reveals that this issue remains unresolved" (Akule, 2007; Johnson, 2006). The paper begins bluntly and directly because I decided scholars would require little orientation and would value my getting right to the point. Stressing what "research . . . reveals" emphasizes my ethos as a careful scholar, a quality reinforced by my including two citations. Academic readers will value this ethos more than they would an opinionated or informal one. The objective and cautious tone of "remains unresolved" differs from a more casual phrase like "is messy."

In contrast, my paper "Is That Organic Apple Really Worth It?" is aimed at a more general audience, such as readers of a weekly news magazine. That paper uses scenes and examples designed to engage readers with a friendly tone. On pages seven and eight, for example, I include an interview with organic grower Jane Treadway in which I narrate the setting. The way I reach out to general readers is clear even in my opening sentence, "As sticker shock at the grocery check out continues to get scarier, all of us have to judge whether everything in our carts belongs there." I've chosen a common experience and referred inclusively to "all of us," trying to show readers that I'm one of them. The phrase "sticker shock" and the reference to prices getting "scarier" both inject a common touch.

The first (weak) example simply makes a claim and points readers generally to a couple of examples. The second (better) example goes into more detail, referring to specific parts of the papers to illustrate the claim. However, that example lacks the discussion of the final (strong) example. Notice how that last one comments on the elements that are quoted or paraphrased, so that readers can see just how they're connected to the claim.

47e How do I present a paper portfolio?

Paper portfolios can come in several formats, from a set of papers stapled or clipped together to items included in a folder or a binder. It's important that you follow any specific directions from your instructor. You should ask whether you're to revise and reprint your writings or whether the portfolio should contain only the original works, perhaps with your instructor's comments. It's useful to number all the pages in the portfolio, as a whole. Generally, your portfolio will contain the elements identified in Quick Reference 47.1.

QUICK REFERENCE 47.1

Items to include in a portfolio

Cover page: Include a title, your name and contact information, the course, and the date. The cover page may include some images or other graphical elements, if appropriate.

Contents: List all of the pieces included in the portfolio, beginning with the reflective introduction, along with their page numbers.

Reflective introduction: See section 47d.

Writing 1. [Optional, if required, draft for Writing 1]

Writing 2. [Optional, if required, draft for Writing 2]

And so on, for as many writings as you include in the portfolio.

47f How do I create a digital portfolio?

Digital portfolios have the same elements as paper ones, with the important difference that they're made to be viewed on a computer, often online. As a result, digital portfolios offer versatility that paper portfolios can't. Digital portfolios can include sound files and videos as well as papers. They can allow different kinds of MULTIMODAL texts. They have the advantage of being portable and easily revised, and you can export works from a digital portfolio into other settings—for example, from a course portfolio into one you might compile for your major. Once again, you need to follow your instructor's specific directions, including directions regarding format or design.

Figure 47.1 Opening screen of a student's digital portfolio

Digital portfolios can take several forms. In the simplest ones, you just upload your work into an online course management program, such as BlackBoard. Another simple digital portfolio requires you to place your work into an online template. Don't worry; your instructor will provide specific directions for these kinds of portfolios.

More sophisticated digital portfolios take advantage of the computer's powerful ability to create links between files. You can do this with a word-processing program.

The most highly developed digital portfolios have an opening page that allows readers to understand all of the elements in the portfolio. From the opening page, which combines the functions performed by the cover and contents pages of a paper portfolio, readers can link to any of the components in the portfolio. All the elements of visual design are important in a digital portfolio. Figure 47.1 shows one example.

My CanadianCompLab

Visit MyCanadianCompLab at
mycanadiancomplab.ca for

- Diagnostic tests
- Grammar exercises
- Grammar video tutorials
- Other resources, including an eText version of this book

A Message to Multilingual Writers

If you ever worry about your English writing, you have much in common with us and many college and university students. Still, we recognize that because you're a multilingual writer, you face special challenges. In becoming a skilled writer in English, you need to concentrate on almost every word, phrase, sentence, and paragraph in ways native speakers of English do not.

The good news is that errors you make demonstrate that you're moving normally through the stages of second-language development. As with your progress in speaking, listening, and reading in a new language, developing writing skills takes time. The process of learning to write English is like learning to play a musical instrument. Few people can play fluently without first making many errors.

What can help you advance as quickly as possible from one writing stage to another? We recommend that you start by thinking about school writing in your first language. Recall how you were taught to present ideas in your written native language, especially when explaining information, giving specific details, and arguing logically about a topic. Then compare it to how writing Canadian English works. Making yourself aware of the differences will help you learn English strategies more easily.

Most college and university writing in Canada is direct in tone and straightforward in structure. Typically, the THESIS STATEMENT* (the central message of the piece) is in the first paragraph or, in a longer piece of writing, the second paragraph. Each paragraph that follows relates in content directly to the essay's thesis statement. Also, each paragraph after the thesis statement needs to begin with a TOPIC SENTENCE that contains the main point of the paragraph; the rest of the paragraph supports the point made in the topic sentence. The final paragraph brings the writing to a logical conclusion.

As you continue writing in English, you might look for interesting ways to blend the traditions and structures of writing in your first language with Canadian conventions of academic writing. Always honour the writing traditions of your own culture, for they reflect the richness of your heritage. At the same time, try to adapt to and practise the academic writing style characteristic of English-speaking Canada. The *Simon & Schuster Handbook* offers three special features that we've designed specifically for you as a multilingual learner. Chapters 8 through 31 focus on the most challenging grammar issues that you face as you learn to write English. In other chapters throughout the book, ESL Tips offer you more helpful hints about possible cultural references and grammar issues. Finally, in Chapter 49, we've provided an "English Errors Transferred from Other Languages" chart. In this chart, you'll find information about trouble spots that commonly occur when speakers of certain languages (Spanish, Russian, and so on) speak, read, or write in English.

Distinctive variations in school writing styles among people of different cultures and language groups have interested researchers for the past thirty years. As individuals, we greatly enjoy discovering the rich variations in the writing traditions of our students from many cultures of the world. As writing teachers, however, our responsibilities call for us to explain what you need to do as writers in this culture. If you were in one of our classes, we would say "Welcome!" and ask you to teach us about writing in your first language. Using that knowledge, we then would respectfully teach you the approach to writing that is used here so that we could do our best to help you succeed as a writer and learner in a North American academic program.

Lynn Quitman Troyka
Doug Hesse

*Words printed in SMALL CAPITAL LETTERS are discussed elsewhere in the text and are defined in the Terms Glossary at the back of this book.

Chapter 48

MULTILINGUAL STUDENTS WRITING IN CANADIAN COLLEGES AND UNIVERSITIES

48a How is writing taught in Canada?

Multilingual students who went to high school outside North America may find that teachers and students here behave differently from teachers and students in their home countries. If you're one of these students, you might be surprised by the seemingly informal interaction you find between teachers and students. No matter how you interpret what you might see, rest assured that the casual teacher-student relationship is based on respect. Instructors still expect students to pay attention, obey class rules, and meet all assignment deadlines.

In North America, teachers usually expect students to participate in class discussions. This can be challenging for multilingual students if they aren't used to this style of classroom interaction, especially if they don't feel confident about speaking English. If this is the case with you, do your best to make as many contributions to class discussion as you possibly can. The more you try, the easier it will become.

When your instructors assign work, they may show you model papers. It can be very helpful to examine the parts of these sample papers to see how the authors have organized information, presented main points, and supported those main points. This is especially true if the assignment is a new type of writing for you. When you look at examples, be sure you know which aspects of the papers your teacher thinks are strong, and which aspects he or she thinks need improvement. Chapter 7 explains some distinct types of academic writing. Of course, when you analyze sample papers, you're doing so only to learn which writing techniques work well. Remember: Don't copy phrases, ideas, content, or images from them. In Canada, copying someone else's work is called PLAGIARISM, and it's ethically and legally wrong. For a detailed discussion about plagiarism, see Chapter 35.

Just as classroom expectations and writing assignments differ from culture to culture, the way that writing is taught also varies. In writing classes in Canada, many instructors teach a process approach to writing. This approach emphasizes the steps that writers go through as they compose assignments for themselves, for their classes, and for work. The basic steps are planning, drafting, revising, editing, and proofreading. For more specific details, read Chapter 2 of this handbook.

Sometimes multilingual students become so concerned about making grammar mistakes that they neglect taking enough time to think about the ideas in their paper. Always remember that writing is about communicating ideas. To ensure you're conveying your own ideas and fulfilling the requirements of your assignments, spend as much time thinking about the content of your paper as you do working on your grammar. For help in working on thinking of ideas and expressing them, review sections 2b–f, of this handbook, which describe activities to help you come up with interesting material for your writing.

48b How does my past writing experience affect my writing in English?

Thinking about your own writing experiences and learning about others' can help you set goals for improving your writing. Exercise 48-1 can help you do both.

EXERCISE 48-1 Think about the following sentences. For each sentence, write "True," "False," or "I'm not sure." If invited, share your answers with your instructor so he or she can learn more about your previous writing experiences. Next, write your thoughts about all or some of the statements; these can give you insight into yourself as a writer in English. Outside of class, you might also discuss your answers with one or more of your multilingual classmates or friends.

1. I am better at writing in another language than I am at writing in English.
2. I have more experience writing in another language than I do in English.
3. I feel confident about writing in English.
4. I received all of my secondary (high school) education outside Canada.
5. When I write in English, I have trouble finding the appropriate vocabulary.
6. When I write in English, I use a dictionary that translates words between English and my first language.
7. When I write in English, I use an English-English dictionary.
8. When I write in English, I use a computer spell-check program.
9. When I write in English, I use a computer grammar-check program.
10. In the past, I have written many different kinds of papers in English.
11. When I write in English, I can write fairly quickly.
12. I think I will need to write a lot for my major.
13. I think I will need to write a lot in English for my future career.
14. When I write in English, I sometimes have trouble generating ideas.
15. A serious problem I have with writing in English is writing correct sentences.

((• 48c How can I know what my instructor expects in my writing?

AUDIO LESSON Section 1: Big Ideas—Using Language Well and Addressing Your Audience

Your past writing experiences influence the way you approach writing assignments. In the next passage, a bilingual student illustrates how her past experiences influenced her interpretation of writing assignments in North America. (Note: The original draft has been edited to improve readability.)

((•

AUDIO LESSON Section 2: Practice Questions— Using Language Well and Addressing Your Audience

When I studied here, I felt puzzled with different types of writing assignments. When I wrote my first term paper, I really did not know what my professor did expect from me and how to construct my paper. My previous training in my first and second language writing taught me little about how to handle writing assignments by using composing strategies. Since language teaching in my country is exam-oriented, I learned to write in Chinese and in English basically in the same way. Under the guidance of my professor, I read a sample paper, analyzed its content and structure, and tried to apply its strengths to my own writing. Writing was not a creative process to express myself but something that was to be copied for the purpose of taking exams. As a result, when I don't have a sample for my assignments, I really don't know how to start.

Like this student, you may have difficulty understanding what your instructor expects you to do when completing a specific writing assignment. Your instructor may expect you to take a clear position on your topic. He or she may want you to use examples from your personal experience to support your ideas, use quotations and specific ideas from an assigned reading, use outside sources, or use all three. Do not hesitate to ask your instructor questions about the assignment to make sure you understand exactly what he or she expects.

EXERCISE 48-2   Have you ever had trouble figuring out what an instructor expected from you when he or she assigned a writing exercise? Have you ever written a paper and later found out that what you wrote was not at all what your instructor expected? Write a paragraph or two describing your experiences.

When your instructor gives you a writing assignment, you may not know how to start because you don't know much about the topic. This might be especially true if the topic that your instructor asks students to write about relates to aspects of Canadian culture that you're not very familiar with. If this is the case, you might need to talk to your instructor about the situation and try to find more information about the topic in newspapers or magazines or by discussing the topic with other students. Similarly, if you're writing about your own culture or about your home country, keep in mind that your instructor and classmates may not know very much about your culture. This means you may need to explain information for them in more detail than you would if you were writing a paper for people who share your cultural background.

EXERCISE 48-3   Have you ever written or read something that didn't make sense because it didn't include the necessary cultural background information? Write a paragraph or two describing your experiences and explaining the source of miscommunication. Before you begin, read the following passage by a student who describes the importance of providing background information in writing. (Note: This excerpt has been edited for readability.)

> If I were writing in Chinese to Chinese readers and wanted to quote a story in Chinese history as evidence, I would simply have to mention the name of the people involved in the historic event or briefly introduce the story. However, when I am writing in English to tell the readers the same story, I have to tell the whole story in detail, even though I might only want to use a small part of it in my essay. Otherwise, the readers will surely get lost.

48d How do I organize my writing?

As part of the writing process, many instructors ask students to write an OUTLINE and a THESIS STATEMENT for their papers (2d). Some writers from other countries have observed that readers here expect papers to have a standardized organization and communicate their purpose in a clear, obvious way. In some cases, this rigid structure poses challenges. For example, one bilingual student wrote that when he writes in his first language, he can use a "flexible organization" and can place his thesis "at the beginning, middle, or end of the essay" or "simply leave the thesis out and the let the reader draw the conclusion to show respect for the reader's intelligence." He explains that he finds it challenging writing in English because he must follow a "restricted organization" that presents a thesis in the first paragraph and then supporting subtopics and detailed examples.

AUDIO LESSON Section 3: Rapid Review—Using Language Well and Addressing Your Audience

Office Hours: Prewriting

About the Audio Lessons for Before You Write, Organize

AUDIO LESSON Section 1: Big Ideas— Before You Write, Organize

AUDIO LESSON Section 2: Practice Questions— Before You Write, Organize

AUDIO LESSON Section 3: Rapid Review— Before You Write, Organize

EXERCISE 48-4   Are there differences between how you were taught to organize your writing in the past and how your instructors expect you to organize it now? Describe the differences in a paragraph or two, and, if you can, draw a picture that illustrates the differences. Before you begin, think back to the paragraph in Exercise 48-3 and what the student wrote about the differences organizing his papers in Chinese and English. Also, consider the following descriptions of organization in writing. (Note: Both of these examples have been edited for readability.)

> **EXAMPLE 1** Russian composition is not about composing supportive arguments around your own personal opinion, but instead is about composing a hierarchy of others' opinions on a certain topic. The process is very much like making a chain: You pick a citation and link it to another citation and so on.

> **EXAMPLE 2** From my TOEFL [Test of English as a Foreign Language] preparation class, I learned the basic framework for English writing: introduction plus body paragraphs plus conclusion, with topic sentences in the body paragraphs. I was impressed by the great difference between writing in my first language and English writing. For example, in a persuasive essay, writers from my country usually prefer to explain the problem first and then come up with their opinion. But for English writing, writers may be more likely to express the opinion at the very beginning and then give reasons to support the idea.

48e How can I use other writers' work to improve my writing?

AUDIO
LESSON
Section 1:
Big Ideas—
Becoming a
Critical
Reader and a
Better Writer

AUDIO
LESSON
Section 2:
Practice
Questions—
Becoming a
Critical
Reader and a
Better Writer

Office Hours:
Citing Sources

Office Hours:
Avoiding
Plagiarism

If you are writing a paper based on other texts that you have read, such as a text your teacher has given you or sources you have found for a research project, it is important to understand how directly your teacher wants you to draw on the text(s). He or she may want you to read the text and simply use it as a springboard for your own ideas; however, you may be expected to read and analyze the text closely and refer to specific ideas and sentences in the source text when you write your paper. It can be especially difficult for ESL students to analyze a text closely and write about it without relying too heavily on the author's wording and sentence structure. However, in Canadian colleges and universities, using another author's words, sentence structure, or even ideas without giving the author credit is considered to be a serious offence called PLAGIARISM, or stealing something that belongs to someone else. In contrast, in some cultures, reliance on the author's wording is not a problem, and may even be seen as a way of complimenting the author. As one bilingual student said, "When you are writing in my first language, you can always feel free to copy good sentences from other articles or writing pieces. But here, it is a violation of copyright. When you are writing in English, you cannot use someone else's work without citing it."

Chapter 35 of this handbook provides detailed information about how to document sources and avoid plagiarism.

48f What kind of dictionary should I use?

Although it can be helpful to use a dictionary that translates words from your native language into English, sometimes such dictionaries are not adequate. One ESL student, who has problems with word choice, says that dictionaries "don't always work" because some terms are "translated literally." She goes on to explain that when she uses dictionaries, she doesn't accept just any definition. The student learns how to use vocabulary in a "real English way" and whether it is "appropriate to use in a certain context."

If you realize that you need a dictionary that does more than translate words between your first language and English, you might try an English-English dictionary, especially one that was written for non-native learners of English.

48g What should I do with my classmates' and instructor's comments?

As part of the writing process, you and your classmates may participate in peer response, sometimes called peer review or peer editing. (See Chapter 6.) You might exchange papers or sit together and read your paper to the students in your group. The purpose of peer response is to offer your classmates advice about how to improve their writing and to receive their advice in turn. This type of group work may be uncomfortable for you if teachers in your home country did not assign group work or expect students to critique each other's work, or if you prefer working individually. Here are some strategies to help make peer response successful for you and your classmates:

- Let your group members know you really do want them to give you advice on your paper so that you can improve its quality before you turn it in for a grade.
- Ask your group members specific questions about your writing.
- Provide other group members with specific, tactful advice about their writing.
- Talk to your instructor if you don't know whether you should follow a specific piece of advice from a classmate.
- See Chapter 6 for more information about peer response.

In addition to receiving feedback from your classmates, try to get feedback from your instructor before he or she gives your paper a grade. Instructors expect to see significant changes based on their comments. If you have questions about how to revise your writing in response to what your teacher has told you, you should talk to your instructor or a tutor.

AUDIO LESSON Section 1: Big Ideas— Revising, Editing, and Proofreading

48h Where can I find strategies for editing my work?

When you are satisfied with the content, organization, and development of the ideas in your paper, you should focus on language-related concerns in your writing. Chapter 49 outlines strategies for proofreading your papers.

AUDIO LESSON Section 2: Practice Questions— Revising, Editing, and Proofreading

48i How can I set long-term goals for my writing?

Improving your writing can take a long time, whether you are writing in your first language or in a second language. Some students find it helpful to set long-term goals for writing to help them focus on what to improve. You may want to talk to a professor in your major (or in a subject you are thinking about majoring in) so that you can ask him or her what kinds of writing you might be expected to do later, both in your courses and in the workplace (if you plan to work in an English-speaking environment or in a context where English is used).

AUDIO LESSON Section 3: Rapid Review— Revising, Editing, and Proofreading

EXERCISE 48-5   Interview a professor in your major (or in a subject you are thinking about majoring in). Ask him or her the following questions, and write a report about the answers you receive. Compare your report with that of a classmate.

1. What kinds of writing do you assign to students in your classes?
2. How do students learn how to write these assignments?
3. (Choose one or two types of writing assignments that the professor mentions.) What are the important parts of this assignment? What steps should students go through to complete this kind of assignment?
4. When you grade student writing, what aspects are most important to you?
5. What kinds of writing do graduates in this major usually do in the workplace?
6. Can you show me some examples of student writing from your courses?

Chapter 49

HANDLING SENTENCE-LEVEL ISSUES IN ENGLISH

49a How can I improve the grammar and vocabulary in my writing?

AUDIO
LESSON
Section 1:
Big Ideas—
Writing Well
in College

The best way to improve your English-language writing, including your grammar and vocabulary, is by writing. Many students also find it helpful to read as much as they can in English to see how other authors organize their writing, use vocabulary, and structure their sentences. Improving your writing in a second language—or a first language, for that matter—takes time. You will probably find that your ability to communicate with readers improves dramatically if you work on the ideas outlined in the previous chapter, including understanding the writing assignment and improving the organization and ideas in your writing. Sometimes, though, readers may find it hard to understand your ideas because of problems with grammar or word choice in your sentences. In other cases, readers may become distracted from your ideas because you have a great many technical errors. We have designed this chapter to help you improve in these areas.

49b How can I improve my sentence structure?

Sometimes students write sentences that are hard to understand because of problems with overall sentence structure or length. For example, one student wrote the following sentence. Here it is, uncorrected.

> When the school started, my first English class was English 1020 as a grammar class, I started learning the basics of grammar, and at the same time the basic of writing, I worked hard in that class, taking by the teacher advice, try to memorize a lot of grammar rules and at the same time memorize some words I could use them to make an essay point.

The student needs to do several things. She needs to break the sentence into several shorter sentences (Chapter 20) and revise the result so that the sentences clearly connect to each other. She also needs to work on her verb tenses, which means she needs to ask for extra help at the writing centre or from her instructor. After patient study and work, her revision might look like this:

> When school started, my first English class, English 1020, was a grammar class, where I started learning the basics of grammar. At the same time, I learned the basics of writing. I worked hard in that class, taking the teacher's advice and memorizing a lot of grammar rules. In addition, I memorized some words I could use in my essays to make my points.

EXERCISE 49-1 Many different revisions of the previous example of a student's uncorrected sentence are possible. Write a different revision of that student's sentence.

EXERCISE 49-2 A student wrote the following passage in a paper about his experiences learning English. Rewrite the passage, improving the student's sentence structure and punctuation. In your revision of this passage, correct any errors that you see in grammar or spelling. Afterward, compare your revision with a classmate's. Then examine a piece of your own writing to see if you need to revise any of your sentences because of problems with sentence structure. (While you are doing this, if you have any questions about correct word order in English, see Chapter 52.)

> I went to school in my country since I was three years old, I was in Arabic and French school, and that's was my dad choice because his second language is French. So my second language at that time was French. In my elementary school I started to learn how to make an essay in French and Arabic. I learned the rules and it is too deferent from English. But later on when I was in my high school I had two choices between English class and science class so I choose the science because that's was my major. After I graduate I went to North American university and I start studying English and my first class was remedial English for people doesn't know anything about this language. I went to this class about two months and then I have moved to a new place and I start from the beginning as an ESL student.

49c How can I improve my word choice (vocabulary)?

An important aspect of writing in a second language is having enough vocabulary to express your ideas. Many students enjoy learning more and more words to be able to communicate precise meanings. For example, one ESL student explains that she has improved her writing by using "words as tools." She also says that by using "different words every time" she "refreshes" her writing and "eliminates the routine" from it. You, too, can experiment in your writing with new words that you hear and read in other contexts. To help make sure you're using a new word in the right way, consult the *American Heritage English as a Second Language Dictionary*, the *Oxford ESL Dictionary*, or the *Longman Dictionary of Contemporary English*. These can ease your way with English words and expressions.

49d How can I find and correct errors in my own writing?

Some multilingual writers find it easiest to find and correct their grammar errors by reading their writing aloud and listening for mistakes. This method is often preferred by students who feel their spoken English is better than their written English. Other writers like to ask a friend who is a native speaker of English to check their writing for grammatical mistakes. Still other multilingual writers prefer to circle each place where they think they've made an error and then use their handbook to check for possible errors.

Many multilingual writers like to keep a list of the types of grammar errors they make so that they can become especially sensitive to errors when proofreading their papers. The best system is to make a master list of the errors in categories so that the checking can be as efficient as possible.

(((•
AUDIO
LESSON
Section 1:
Big Ideas—
Verbs

(((•
AUDIO
LESSON
Section 2:
Practice
Questions—
Verbs

(((•
AUDIO
LESSON
Section 3:
Rapid
Review—
Verbs

49e How can I correct verb form (tense) errors in my writing?

Many multilingual writers consider verb-form errors the most difficult to correct. They want to be sure that their verb forms express the appropriate time frame for the event or situation they're describing. For a detailed discussion of verb forms, see 15b–f.

EXERCISE 49-3 Read the following passage in which a student describes her experience learning to write in English. The student's instructor has underlined errors related to time frames expressed by the verbs. Correct the underlined verbs, changing them to the correct time frames.

I must have started writing when I was nine years old. I remember my father used to give us papers and watercolours and let us draw as much as we <u>want</u>. At the end, he made sure that we <u>write</u> comments about why we <u>have</u> sketched the way we did. The only written thing that I <u>find</u> dating to that period was a kind of comment about a picture which I <u>have</u> sketched of a village enveloped in water.

I don't remember much about the kind of writing assignments we <u>have</u> at school, whether in my native language Arabic, or in my second languages, at that time, English and French. That period is a little bit hazy in my mind. However, I remember that whenever we had the chance to go to school, we made sure that we <u>fill</u> the playgrounds with creative farewell sentences indicating that we <u>have</u> been there. It <u>is</u> our little game against the witchcraft of war and against the will of the principal, who <u>forgive</u> us easily once we <u>have</u> recited the multiplication table or <u>sing</u> the national anthem.

((•
AUDIO LESSON Section 1: Big Ideas—Correcting Common Errors: Subject-Verb Agreement and Parallel Structure

49f How can I correct my errors in subject-verb agreement?

Subject-verb agreement means that a subject (a noun or a pronoun) and its verb must agree in number and in person. In the following two sentences, notice the difference in the way the subjects and the verbs that describe their actions agree: *Carolina runs charity marathons. They give her a sense of accomplishment.*

For more information about subject-verb agreement, review Chapter 17. To help you put subject-verb agreement rules into practice, try the next exercise.

((•
AUDIO LESSON Section 2: Practice Questions—Correcting Common Errors: Subject-Verb Agreement and Parallel Structure

EXERCISE 49-4 Examine the following student's description of his experiences learning English. The student's instructor has underlined verbs that do not agree with their subjects. Correct the underlined verb forms, changing them to agree with their subjects.

I describe the way I learned English as a natural way, where one first <u>learn</u> how to speak and communicate with others, before learning the grammar rules that <u>supports</u> a language. When I arrived here, I <u>works</u> hard to improve my communications skills in English, trying to speak even when the people <u>does</u> not understand me. Also, making friends with native speakers <u>help</u> a person learn the language. One can learn from them every single minute that one <u>spend</u> with them.

Do you have similar problems with subject-verb agreement in your own writing? Examine something you've written recently to check whether your subjects and verbs agree.

((•
AUDIO LESSON Section 3: Key Terms—Correcting Common Errors: Subject-Verb Agreement and Parallel Structure

49g How can I correct my singular/plural errors?

In English, if you're referring to more than one noun that is a count noun, you must make that noun plural, often by adding an *-s* ending. If you would like more information on this topic, see Chapter 50. To help you recognize when necessary plural forms are missing, try the next exercise.

EXERCISE 49-5   In the following passage, a student comments on the differences between writing in English and in Chinese. The student's instructor has underlined only the first two nouns that need to be plural. Read the passage, correct the two underlined nouns, and then find and correct the other nouns in the passage that need to be plural.

> English and Chinese have many <u>similarity</u>. They both have <u>paragraph</u>, sentence, and punctuation mark, like comma, full stops, and question marks. The biggest difference is that English has an alphabet with letter, while Chinese uses symbol for writing. My mother told me that about two thousand year ago, people in China used picture to draw what they wanted to say on turtle shells. Day after day, the pictures changed and turned into the Chinese character.

Examine a piece of your own writing and make sure that you have used plural words correctly.

49h   How can I correct my preposition errors?

Prepositions are words such as *in, on, for, over,* and *about,* which usually show where, how, or when. For example, in the sentence *She received flowers from her friend for her birthday,* the prepositions are *from* and *for.* English has many prepositions, and knowing which one to use can be very difficult. You can find information about using prepositions in section 14h and in Chapter 53. To practise finding and correcting preposition errors in your own writing, complete the next exercise.

EXERCISE 49-6   In the following passage about one student's learning experiences as a second-language learner, the student's instructor has underlined problems with preposition use. Try to correct the preposition errors. In some cases, more than one answer may be correct. If you can't find the information you need from Chapter 53 or in a dictionary, you might ask a native English speaker for help.

> I've always wanted to learn languages other than my first language. I started taking English and French lessons <u>of</u> school and I liked the idea of becoming fluent <u>for</u> at least one language. I thought English would help me a lot <u>to</u> the future because it could help me communicate <u>to</u> people from all over the world.

49i   What other kinds of errors might I make?

Depending on your language background and your prior experience with writing in English, you may make errors related to the use of articles (*a, an, the*), word order (including where to place adjectives and adverbs in sentences), and various verb forms and noun forms (for example, problems with noncount nouns and helping verbs). The next sentence has a problem with one article and the order of an adjective: *The downtown Vancouver is a place exciting.* The corrected sentence is *Downtown Vancouver is an exciting place.*

Chapters 50 through 55 address grammar errors that are often made by multilingual writers. Try to keep track of your most common errors and refer to the relevant sections of this handbook for help.

49j   How can I keep track of my most common errors?

Office Hours:
Revising

One way of becoming more aware of the types of errors you make is to keep track of the errors you often make in the papers you write. You can ask your instructor or a tutor to help you identify such errors, and you can make a list of them that you update regularly.

Remember the passage from Exercise 49-3 about a student's experiences learning to write? After the student examined the teacher's comments on her paper, she made a list of her errors and included a correction and a note about the error type for each. After making this list of her errors, the student writer realized that many of her errors related to verb form.

Specific Error	Correction	Type of Error
as much as we <u>want</u>	wanted	verb form
that we <u>write</u> comments	wrote	verb form
about why we <u>have</u> sketched	had	verb form
which I <u>have</u> sketched	had	verb form
we <u>fill</u> the playground	filled	verb form
that we <u>have</u> been there	had	verb form
once we <u>have</u> recited	had	verb form

EXERCISE 49-7 Using one or more pieces of your writing, make an error list similar to the one that goes with Exercise 49-3. (You could make this list on a sheet of paper or in an electronic file.) Examine the list. What are the most common types of errors that you make? Once you have identified your common error types, refer to the relevant proofreading exercises in the previous sections of this chapter and to the relevant ones in Chapters 50 through 55. Also, remember to keep your common errors in mind when you proofread your future writing assignments.

49k How can I improve my proofreading skills?

The most effective way to improve your proofreading skills is to practise frequently. Proofread your own writing and, after you have done so, ask your instructor, a tutor, or a friend who is a native English speaker to point out errors that you did not see on your own. If you know you often make a particular kind of error, such as errors with subject-verb agreement (Chapter 17), ask the person helping you to check for these specific problems. When you know which errors you've made, try to correct the errors without help. Finally, have your instructor or tutor check your corrections.

Another effective way to improve your proofreading skills is to exchange your writing with a partner. You can check for errors in his or her writing and he or she can check for errors in yours. Try Exercises 49-8 and 49-9 for more proofreading practice.

EXERCISE 49-8 The following passage was written by a student about her experiences learning to write in English. After you read it, rewrite it, correcting the linguistic errors you find.

I've always faced some problem in writing in English as it took me some time to get used to it. Facing these complexities encourage me to developed my skills in English writing. My first class in English was about grammar, spelling, and writing. I realize later that grammar is hard to learn, so I knew I have to put in a lot of effort to understand it perfectly and use it properly. I also had some difficulties for vocabulary, as it was hard to understand the meaning of some word.

Another thing that helped me with my English was when my mother enroll me in an English learning centre that specialize in teach writing skills. After a month of taking

AUDIO LESSON Section 1: Big Ideas—Revising, Editing, and Proofreading

AUDIO LESSON Section 2: Practice Questions—Revising, Editing, and Proofreading

AUDIO LESSON Section 3: Rapid Review—Revising, Editing, and Proofreading

classes, my teacher saw some improvement in my grammar and vocabulary. To test me, she asked me to write an essay on how to be successful. I was really excite of it and started write it immediately. After I finish my essay and my teacher check it, my teacher suggested that I take a few more classes for her. She taught me how to organized my ideas. After finishing these classes I realize that my writing was getting much better with time.

EXERCISE 49-9   In the following paragraph, a student describes the study of English at private schools in Japan. After you read the paragraph, rewrite it, correcting the errors that you find.

Recently, the number of private language schools are increased in Japan. These schools put special emphasize on oral communication skills. In them, student takes not only grammars and reading classes, which help them pass school examinations, but also speaking, listening classes. They can also study English for six year, which is same period as in public schools. Some of the teacher in these school are native speaker of English. Since these teachers do not use Japanese in the class, the students have to use the English to participate it. They have the opportunity to use the English in their class more than public school students. It is said that the students who took English in private schools can speak English better than those student who go to public schools.

The following chart contains information about errors that may be caused by a difference between your native language and English. The chart does not include all languages or all possible errors. Instead, it focuses on languages commonly spoken by ESL students in North America and it includes errors that often cause significant difficulties for students.

ENGLISH ERRORS TRANSFERRED FROM OTHER LANGUAGES

Languages	Error Topic	Sample Errors	Corrected Errors
Singulars and Plurals (Ch. 50)			
Chinese, Japanese, Korean, Thai	no (or optional) plural forms of nouns, including numbers	NO: She wrote many good **essay**. NO: She typed two **paper**.	YES: She wrote many good **essays**. YES: She typed two **papers**.
Hebrew, Italian, Japanese, Spanish	use of plural with embedded plurals	NO: We cared for five **childrens**.	YES: We cared for five **children**.
Italian, Spanish	adjectives carry plural	NO: They are **Canadians** students.	YES: They are **Canadian** students.
Articles (Ch. 51)			
Chinese, Japanese, Hindi, Korean, Russian, Swahili, Thai, Turkish, Urdu	no article (*a, an, the*), but can depend on whether article is definite/indefinite	NO: He ate sandwich.	YES: He ate **a** sandwich.
Word Order (Ch. 52)			
Arabic, Hebrew, Russian, Spanish, Tagalog	verb before subject	NO: **Questioned** Avi the teenagers.	YES: **Avi questioned** the teenagers.
Chinese, Japanese, Hindi, Thai	inverted word order confused in questions	NO: **The book was** it heavy?	YES: **Was the book** heavy?

continued ➤

Languages	Error Topic	Sample Errors	Corrected Errors
Word Order (Ch. 52) continued			
Chinese, Japanese, Russian, Thai	sentence adverb misplaced	NO: We will go home **possibly** now.	YES: **Possibly,** we will go home now.
Gerunds, Infinitives, and Participles (Ch. 54)			
French, German, Greek, Hindi, Russian, Urdu	no progressive forms or overuse of progressive forms with infinitive	NO: They **talk** while she **talk**. NO: They **are wanting** to talk now.	YES: They **are talking** while she **is talking.** YES: They **want** to talk now.
Arabic, Chinese, Farsi, Russian	omit forms of *be*	NO: She happy.	YES: She **is** happy.
Chinese, Japanese, Korean, Russian, Thai	no verb ending changes for person & number	NO: She **talk** loudly.	YES: She **talks** loudly.
Arabic, Chinese, Farsi, French, Thai, Vietnamese	no or nonstandard verb-tense markers	NO: He **laugh** yesterday. NO: They **has arrived** yesterday.	YES: He **laughed** yesterday. YES: They **arrived** yesterday.
Japanese, Korean, Russian, Thai, Vietnamese	nonstandard passives	NO: A car accident **was happened.**	YES: A car accident **was caused by the icy roads.**

675

Chapter 50

SINGULARS AND PLURALS

50a What are count and noncount nouns?

Count nouns name items that can be counted: *a radio* or *radios, a street* or *streets, an idea* or *ideas, a fingernail* or *fingernails.* Count nouns can be SINGULAR or PLURAL.

Noncount nouns name things that are thought of as a whole and not split into separate, countable parts: *rice, knowledge, traffic.* There are two important rules to remember about noncount nouns: (1) They're never preceded by *a* or *an,* and (2) they are never plural. Here are several categories of uncountable items, with examples in each category.

GROUPS OF SIMILAR ITEMS	clothing, equipment, furniture, jewellery, junk, luggage, mail, money, stuff, traffic, vocabulary
ABSTRACTIONS	advice, equality, fun, health, ignorance, information, knowledge, news, peace, pollution, respect
LIQUIDS	blood, coffee, gasoline, water
GASES	air, helium, oxygen, smog, smoke, steam
MATERIALS	aluminum, cloth, cotton, ice, wood
FOOD	beef, bread, butter, macaroni, meat, pork
PARTICLES OR GRAINS	dirt, dust, hair, rice, salt, wheat
SPORTS, GAMES, ACTIVITIES	chess, homework, housework, reading, sailing, soccer
LANGUAGES	Arabic, Chinese, Japanese, Spanish
FIELDS OF STUDY	biology, computer science, history, literature, math
EVENTS IN NATURE	electricity, heat, humidity, moonlight, rain, snow, sunshine, thunder, weather

Some nouns can be countable or uncountable, depending on their meaning in a sentence. Most of these nouns name things that can be meant either individually or as "wholes" made up of individual parts.

COUNT	You have **a hair** on your sleeve. [In this sentence, *hair* is meant as an individual, countable item.]
NONCOUNT	Kioko has black **hair**. [In this sentence, all the strands of *hair* are referred to as a whole.]
COUNT	**The rains** were late last year. [In this sentence, *rains* is meant as individual, countable occurrences of rain.]
NONCOUNT	**The rain** is soaking the garden. [In this sentence, all the droplets of *rain* are referred to as a whole.]

When you are editing your writing (see Chapter 2), be sure that you have not added a plural *-s* to any noncount nouns, for they are always singular in form.

❶ ALERT: Be sure to use a singular verb with any noncount noun that functions as a SUBJECT in a CLAUSE. ●

To check whether a noun is count or noncount, look it up in a dictionary that makes the distinction. For example, the *Dictionary of American English* (Heinle and Heinle) indicates count nouns with [C] and noncount nouns with [U] (for "uncountable"). Nouns that have both count and noncount meanings are marked [C;U].

50b   How do I use determiners with singular and plural nouns?

Determiners, also called *expressions of quantity,* are used to tell how much or how many with reference to NOUNS, or whether a noun is general (*a* tree) or specific (*the* tree) Other names for determiners include *limiting adjectives, noun markers,* and ARTICLES. (For information about articles—the words *a, an,* and *the*—see Chapter 51.)

Choosing the right determiner with a noun can depend on whether the noun is NONCOUNT or COUNT (see 50a). For count nouns, you must also decide whether the noun is singular or plural. Quick Reference 50.1 lists many determiners and the kinds of nouns that they can accompany.

QUICK REFERENCE | **50.1**

Determiners to use with count and noncount nouns

GROUP 1: DETERMINERS FOR SINGULAR COUNT NOUNS

With every **singular count noun,** always use one of the determiners listed in Group 1.

a, an, the	**a house**	**an egg**	**the car**
one, any, some,	**any house**	**each egg**	**another car**
every, each, either,			
neither, another,			
the other			
my, our, your, his,	**your house**	**its egg**	**Connie's car**
her, its, their,			
nouns with 's or s'			
this, that	**this house**	**that egg**	**this car**
one, no, the first,	**one house**	**no egg**	**the fifth car**
the second, etc.			

GROUP 2: DETERMINERS FOR PLURAL COUNT NOUNS

All the determiners listed in Group 2 can be used with **plural count nouns.** Plural count nouns can also be used without determiners, as discussed in section 51b.

the	**the bicycles**	**the rooms**	**the ideas**
some, any, both,	**some bicycles**	**many rooms**	**all ideas**
many, more, most,			
few, fewer, the			
fewest, a lot of, a			
number of, other,			
several, all, all the			

continued ➤

my, our, your, his, her, its, their, nouns with *'s* or *s'*	our bicycles	her rooms	student's ideas
these, those	these bicycles	those rooms	these ideas
no, two, three, etc.; *the first, the second, the third,* etc.	no bicycles	four rooms	the first ideas

GROUP 3: DETERMINERS FOR NONCOUNT NOUNS

All the determiners listed in Group 3 can be used with **noncount nouns** (always singular). Noncount nouns can also be used without determiners, as discussed in section 51b.

the	the rice	the rain	the pride
some, any, much, more, most, other, the other, little, less, the least, enough, all, all the, a lot of	enough rice	a lot of rain	more pride
my, our, your, his, her, its, their, nouns with *'s* or *s'*	their rice	India's rain	your pride
this, that	this rice	that rain	this pride
no, the first, the second, the third, etc.	no rice	the first rain	no pride

❶ ALERT: The phrases *a few* and *a little* convey the meaning "some": *I have **a few** rare books* means "I have *some* rare books." *They are worth **a little** money* means "They are worth *some* money."

Without the word *a*, the words *few* and *little* convey the meaning "almost none": *I have **few** [or **very few**] books* means "I have *almost no* books." *They are worth [very] **little** money* means "They are worth *almost no* money." ●

50c How do I use *one of*, nouns as adjectives, and *states* in names or titles?

ONE OF CONSTRUCTIONS

One of constructions include *one of the* and a NOUN or *one of* followed by a DETERMINER-noun combination (*one of my hats, one of those ideas*) or an ADJECTIVE-noun combination (*one of the red roses*). Always use a plural noun as the OBJECT when you use *one of the* or *one of* with these combinations.

NO   *One of the **reason** to live here is the beach.*

YES   *One of the **reasons** to live here is the beach.*

NO   *One of her best **friend** has moved away.*

YES   *One of her best **friends** has moved away.*

The VERB in these constructions is always singular because it agrees with the singular *one,* not with the plural noun: ***One** of the most important inventions of the twentieth century **is** [not are] television.*

For advice about verb forms that go with *one of the . . . who* constructions, see 171.

NOUNS USED AS ADJECTIVES

ADJECTIVES in English do not have plural forms. When you use an adjective with a PLURAL NOUN, make the noun plural but not the adjective: *the **green** [not greens] leaves.* Be especially careful when you use a word as a MODIFIER that can also function as a noun.

The bird's wingspan is 25 centimetres. [*Centimetres* is functioning as a noun.]

The bird has a 25-centimetre wingspan. [*Centimetre* is functioning as a modifier.]

Do not add *-s* (or *-es*) to the adjective even when it is modifying a plural noun or pronoun.

NO   Many **Canadians** students are hockey fans.

YES   Many **Canadian** students are hockey fans.

NAMES OR TITLES THAT INCLUDE THE WORD *STATES*

States is a plural word. However, names such as *United States* or *Organization of American States* refer to singular entities—one country and one organization, even though made up of many states. When *states* is part of a name or title referring to one thing, the name is a SINGULAR NOUN and therefore requires a SINGULAR VERB.

NO   The **United States have** a large entertainment industry.

NO   The **United State has** a large entertainment industry.

YES   The **United States has** a large entertainment industry.

50d   How do I use nouns with irregular plurals?

Some English nouns have irregularly spelled plurals. In addition to those discussed in section 31c, here are others that often cause difficulties.

PLURALS OF FOREIGN NOUNS AND OTHER IRREGULAR NOUNS

Whenever you are unsure whether a noun is plural, look it up in a dictionary. If no plural is given for a singular noun, add *-s* to form the plural.

Many nouns from other languages that are used unchanged in English have only one plural. If two plurals are listed in the dictionary, look carefully for differences in meaning. Some words, for example, keep the plural form from the original language for scientific usage and have another, English-form plural for nonscientific contexts: *formula, formulae, formulas; appendix, appendices, appendixes; index, indices, indexes; medium, media, mediums; cactus, cacti, cactuses; fungus, fungi, funguses.*

Words from Latin or Greek that end in *-is* in their singular form become plural by substituting *-es: parenthesis, parentheses; thesis, theses; oasis, oases.*

OTHER WORDS

Medical terms for diseases involving an inflammation end in *-itis: tonsillitis, appendicitis.* They are always singular.

The word *news,* although it ends in *s,* is always singular: *The **news is** encouraging.* The words *people, police,* and *clergy* are always plural even though they do not end in *s: The **police are** prepared.*

EXERCISE 50-1 Consulting all sections of this chapter, select the correct choice from the words in parentheses and write it in the blank.

> **EXAMPLE** Statistics Canada has been monitoring Canadians' (spending, spendings) <u>spending</u> in the postindustrial economy.

1. As people's (spendings, spending) _____ power increases, they devote a changing proportion of their (wealth, wealths) _____ to different categories of purchases.

2. The necessities of life—food, clothing, and shelter—took up more than half of (Canadian, Canadians) _____ consumers' spending in 1961, but today they take up only 40 percent.

3. Anyone who looks will see instantly that this is not because Canadians eat less (food, foods) _____ than in 1961 or that (much, many) people are paying less rent than before.

4. Some may argue that we wear worse (clothings, clothing) than in 1961, but those people are not referring to the number of shirts hanging in our closets or to the (qualities, quality) _____ of the fabrics; they are criticizing our taste.

5. One of the main (reason, reasons) _____ for the change in our spending is the simple fact that we now have more (moneys, money) _____ and therefore we have more opportunity to spend on luxuries, especially (consumer, consumers) _____ electronics and entertainment.

Chapter 51

ARTICLES

51a **How do I use *a, an,* or *the* with singular count nouns?**

The words *a* and *an* are called **indefinite articles**. The word *the* is the DEFINITE ARTICLE. Articles are one type of DETERMINER. (For more on determiners, see 14f; for other determiners, see Quick Reference 50.1 in 50b.) Articles signal that a NOUN will follow and that any MODIFIERS between the article and the noun refer to that noun.

a chair	**the** computer
a brown chair	**the** teacher's computer
a cold, metal chair	**the** lightning-fast computer

Every time you use a singular count noun, a COMMON NOUN that names one countable item, the noun requires some kind of determiner; see Group 1 in Quick Reference 50.1 (in 50b) for a list. To choose between *a* or *an* and *the,* you need to determine whether the noun is **specific** or **nonspecific**. A noun is considered specific when anyone who reads your writing can understand exactly and specifically to what item the noun is referring. If the noun refers to any of a number of identical items, it is nonspecific.

For nonspecific singular count nouns, use *a* (or *an*). When the singular noun is specific, use *the* or some other determiner. Quick Reference 51.1 can help you decide when a singular count noun is specific and therefore requires *the.*

QUICK REFERENCE 51.1

When a singular count noun is specific and requires *the*

- **Rule 1: A noun is specific and requires *the* when it names something unique or generally and unambiguously known.**

    The sun has risen above **the horizon.** [Because there is only one *sun* and only one *horizon*, these nouns are specific in the context of this sentence.]

- **Rule 2: A noun is specific and requires *the* when it names something used in a representative or abstract sense.**

    I would like to know who chose **the unicorn** to be **the symbolic animal** on Canada's coat of arms. [Because *unicorn* and *symbolic animal* are representative references rather than references to a particular unicorn or animal, they are specific nouns in the context of this sentence.]

continued ➤

- **Rule 3: A noun is specific and requires *the* when it names something defined elsewhere in the same sentence or in an earlier sentence.**

  The ship *St. Roch* was the first vessel to navigate the Northwest Passage in both directions. [The name *St. Roch* denotes a specific ship.]

  The carpet in my bedroom is new. [*In my bedroom* defines exactly which carpet is meant, so *carpet* is a specific noun in this context.]

  I have **a scanner** and **a fax machine.** I've nearly forgotten how to use **the fax machine.** [*Fax machine* is introduced as nonspecific in the first sentence, so it uses *a*. *Fax machine* has been made specific by the first sentence, so the second sentence uses *the* to refer to the same noun.]

- **Rule 4: A noun is specific and requires *the* when it names something that can be inferred from the context.**

  In my paperless office, I hardly ever need to use **the older device.** [If you read this sentence after the one about the fax machine in Rule 3, you understand that *older device* refers to the fax machine, and so it is specific in this context. Here the word *the* is similar to the word *this*.]

ALERT: Use *an* before words that begin with a vowel sound. Use *a* before words that begin with a consonant sound. Go by the sound, not the spelling. For example, words that begin with *h* or *u* can have either a vowel or a consonant sound. Make the choice based on the sound of the first word after the article, even if that word is not the noun.

an idea	**a g**ood idea
an umbrella	**a u**seful umbrella
an honour	**a h**istory book ●

One common exception affects Rule 3 in Quick Reference 51.1. A noun may still require *a* (or *an*) after the first use if more information is added between the article and the noun: *I bought **a sweater** today. It was **a** (not the) **red sweater**.* (Your audience has been introduced to *a sweater* but not *a red sweater,* so *red sweater* is not yet specific in this context and cannot take *the*.) Other information may make the noun specific so that *the* is correct. For example, *It was **the red sweater that I saw in the store yesterday*** uses *the* because the *that* CLAUSE makes specific which red sweater the writer means.

51b How do I use articles with plural nouns and with noncount nouns?

With plural nouns and NONCOUNT NOUNS, you must decide whether to use *the* or to use no article at all. (For guidelines about using DETERMINERS other than articles with nouns, see Quick Reference 50.1 in 50b.) What you learned in 51a about NONSPECIFIC and SPECIFIC NOUNS can help you choose between using *the* or using no article. Quick Reference 51.1 explains when a singular count noun's meaning is specific and calls for *the.* Plural nouns and noncount nouns with specific meanings usually use *the* in the same circumstances. However, a plural noun or a noncount noun with a general or nonspecific meaning usually does not use *the*.

> Geraldo grows **flowers** but not **vegetables** in his garden. He is thinking about planting **corn** sometime. [three nonspecific nouns]

PLURAL NOUNS

A plural noun's meaning may be specific because it is widely known.

> **The oceans** are being damaged by pollution. [Because there is only one possible meaning for *oceans*—the oceans on the Earth—it is correct to use *the*. This example is related to Rule 1 in Quick Reference 51.1.]

A plural noun's meaning may also be made specific by a word, PHRASE, or CLAUSE in the same sentence.

> Geraldo sold **the daisies from last year's garden** to the florist. [Because the phrase *from last year's garden* makes *daisies* specific, *the* is correct. This example is related to Rule 3 in Quick Reference 51.1.]

A plural noun's meaning usually becomes specific by its use in an earlier sentence.

> Geraldo planted **tulips** this year. **The tulips** will bloom in May. [*Tulips* is used in a general sense in the first sentence, without *the*. Because the first sentence makes *tulips* specific, the *tulips* is correct in the second sentence. This example is related to Rule 3 in Quick Reference 51.1.]

A plural noun's meaning may be made specific by the context.

> Geraldo fertilized **the bulbs** when he planted them last October. [In the context of the sentences about tulips, *bulbs* is understood as a synonym for *tulips*, which makes it specific and calls for *the*. This example is related to Rule 4 in Quick Reference 51.1.]

NONCOUNT NOUNS

Noncount nouns are always singular in form (see 50a). Like plural nouns, noncount nouns use either *the* or no article. When a noncount noun's meaning is specific, use *the* before it. If its meaning is general or nonspecific, do not use *the*.

> Kalinda served us **rice**. She flavoured **the rice** with curry. [*Rice* is a noncount noun. By the second sentence, *rice* has become specific, so *the* is used. This example is related to Rule 3 in Quick Reference 51.1.]

> Kalinda served us **the rice that she had flavoured with curry**. [*Rice* is a noncount noun. *Rice* is made specific by the clause *that she had flavoured with curry*, so *the* is used. This example is related to Rule 3 in Quick Reference 51.1.]

GENERALIZATIONS WITH PLURAL OR NONCOUNT NOUNS

Rule 2 in Quick Reference 51.1 tells you to use *the* with singular count nouns that carry general meaning. With GENERALIZATIONS using plural or noncount nouns, omit *the*.

> NO **The tulips** are **the flowers** that grow from **the bulbs.**
>
> YES **Tulips** are **flowers** that grow from **bulbs.**
>
> NO **The dogs** require more care than **the cats** do.
>
> YES **Dogs** require more care than **cats** do.

51c How do I use *the* with proper nouns and with gerunds?

PROPER NOUNS

PROPER NOUNS name specific people, places, or things (see 14b). Most proper nouns do not require ARTICLES: *We visited **Lake Rossignol** with **Asha** and **Larry**.* As shown in Quick Reference 51.2, however, certain types of proper nouns do require *the*.

QUICK REFERENCE 51.2

Proper nouns that use *the*

- **Nouns with the pattern *the . . . of . . .***

  the Dominion **of** Canada   **the** eleventh **of** November

  the Republic **of** Mexico   **the** University **of** Paris

- **Plural proper nouns**

  the United Arab Emirates

  the Johnsons

  the Rocky Mountains [*but* Mount Fuji]

  the Vancouver Canucks

  the Falkland Islands [*but* Baffin Island]

  the Great Lakes [*but* Lake Superior]

- **Collective proper nouns (nouns that name a group)**

  the Modern Language Association

  the Society of Friends

- **Some (but not all) geographical features and regions**

  the Amazon   **the** Gobi Desert   **the** Indian Ocean

  the Beauce   **the** Gaspé

- **A few countries and cities**

  the Congo   **the** Sudan   **the** Netherlands

  The Pas   **the** Hague   **the** Czech Republic

GERUNDS

GERUNDS, which look exactly like PRESENT PARTICIPLES (the *-ing* form of VERBS), are verb forms that are used as nouns: ***Skating** is challenging.* Gerunds are usually not preceded by *the*.

> NO **The constructing** new bridges is necessary to improve traffic flow.

> YES **Constructing** new bridges is necessary to improve traffic flow.

Use *the* before a gerund when two conditions are met: (1) The gerund is used in a specific sense (see 51a), and (2) the gerund does not have a DIRECT OBJECT.

NO   **The designing fabric** is a fine art. [*Fabric* is a direct object of *designing*, so *the* should not be used.]

YES   **Designing** fabric is a fine art. [*Designing* is a gerund, so *the* is not used.]

YES   **The designing of** fabric is a fine art. [*The* is used because *fabric* is the object of the preposition *of* and *designing* is meant in a specific sense.]

EXERCISE 51-1   Consulting all sections of this chapter, decide which of the words in parentheses is correct and write it in the blank. If no article is needed, leave the blank empty.

> **EXAMPLE**   If you are (a, an, the) a student from (a, an, the) a foreign country, what can you do to learn about (a, an, the) the Canadian way of life?

1. Some people say that (a, an, the) _____ best thing (a, an, the) _____ newcomer can do to discover (a, an, the) _____ new culture is to watch (a, an, the) _____ local television programs.

2. (A, An, The) _____ entertainment that Canadians like to watch on television reveals much about (a, an, the) _____ culture in this country.

3. News and public affairs are also important, which is why it is (a, an, the) _____ good idea to subscribe to (a, an, the) _____ newspaper or (a, an, the) magazine.

4. (A, An, The) _____ student who wants to learn more about Canada may also consider finding (a, an, the) _____ activities to do outside (a, an, the) _____ walls of (a, an, the) _____ campus—tutoring or volunteering, perhaps.

5. Finally, (a, an, the) _____ excellent way to soak up (a, an, the) _____ culture is to live with (a, an, the) _____ local family, as long as (a, an, the) _____ family involves (a, an, the) _____ student in its activities.

Chapter 52

WORD ORDER

Subjects and Verbs

52a How do I understand standard and inverted word order in sentences?

Subject-Object Agreement and Subject-Complement Agreement

Copular Verbs (Linking Verbs)

In **standard word order,** the most common pattern for DECLARATIVE SENTENCES in English, the SUBJECT comes before the VERB. (To understand these concepts more fully, review 14l through 14p.)

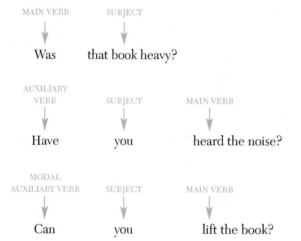

SUBJECT	VERB
That book	was heavy.

With **inverted word order,** the MAIN VERB or an AUXILIARY VERB comes before the subject. The most common use of inverted word order in English is in forming DIRECT QUESTIONS. Questions that can be answered with a yes or no begin with a form of *be* used as a main verb, with an auxiliary verb (*be, do, have*), or with a MODAL AUXILIARY (*can, should, will,* and others; see Chapter 55).

QUESTIONS THAT CAN BE ANSWERED WITH A YES OR NO

MAIN VERB	SUBJECT	
Was	that book heavy?	

AUXILIARY VERB	SUBJECT	MAIN VERB
Have	you	heard the noise?

MODAL AUXILIARY VERB	SUBJECT	MAIN VERB
Can	you	lift the book?

To form a yes-or-no question with a verb other than *be* as the main verb and when there is no auxiliary or modal as part of a VERB PHRASE, use the appropriate form of the auxiliary verb *do.*

AUXILIARY VERB	SUBJECT	MAIN VERB
Do	you	want me to put the book away?

A question that begins with a question-forming word such as *why, when, where,* or *how* cannot be answered with a yes or no: **Why** *did the book fall?* Some kind of information must be provided to answer such a question; the answer cannot be simply yes or no because the question is not *"Did* the book fall?" Information on *why* it fell is needed: for example, *It was too heavy for me.*

INFORMATION QUESTIONS: INVERTED ORDER

Most information questions follow the same rules of inverted word order as yes-or-no questions.

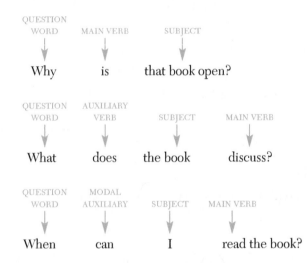

QUESTION WORD	MAIN VERB	SUBJECT	
Why	is	that book open?	

QUESTION WORD	AUXILIARY VERB	SUBJECT	MAIN VERB
What	does	the book	discuss?

QUESTION WORD	MODAL AUXILIARY	SUBJECT	MAIN VERB
When	can	I	read the book?

INFORMATION QUESTIONS: STANDARD ORDER

When *who* or *what* functions as the subject in a question, use standard word order.

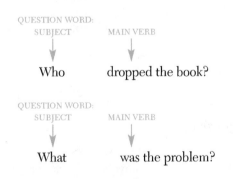

QUESTION WORD: SUBJECT	MAIN VERB
Who	dropped the book?

QUESTION WORD: SUBJECT	MAIN VERB
What	was the problem?

ALERT: When a question has more than one auxiliary verb, put the subject after the first auxiliary verb. ●

FIRST AUXILIARY	SUBJECT	SECOND AUXILIARY	MAIN VERB
↓	↓	↓	↓
Would	you	have	replaced the book?

The same rules apply to emphatic exclamations: *Was that book heavy! Did she enjoy that book!*

NEGATIVES

When you use negatives such as *never, hardly ever, seldom, rarely, not only,* or *nor* to start a CLAUSE, use inverted order. These sentence pairs show the differences, first in standard order and then in inverted order.

I have never seen a more exciting movie. [standard order]

Never have I seen a more exciting movie. [inverted order]

She is not only a talented artist **but also** an excellent musician.

Not only is she a talented artist, **but she is also** an excellent musician.

I didn't like the book, and **my husband didn't either**.

I didn't like the book, and **neither did my husband**.

ALERTS: (1) With INDIRECT QUESTIONS, use standard word order.

NO   She asked **how did I drop** the book.

YES   She asked **how I dropped** the book.

(2) Word order deliberately inverted can be effective, when used sparingly, to create emphasis in a sentence that is neither a question nor an exclamation (also see 9r). ●

52b How can I understand the placement of adjectives?

ADJECTIVES modify—describe or limit—NOUNS, PRONOUNS, and word groups that function as nouns (see 14f). In English, an adjective comes directly before the noun it describes. However, when more than one adjective describes the same noun, several sequences may be possible. Quick Reference 52.1 shows the most common order for positioning several adjectives.

QUICK REFERENCE   52.1

Word order for more than one adjective

1. **Determiners, if any:** *a, an, the, my, you, that, these, those,* and so on
2. **Expressions of order, including ordinal numbers, if any:** *first, second, third, next, last, final,* and so on

continued ➤

3. **Expressions of quantity, including cardinal (counting) numbers, if any:** *one, two, few, each, every, some,* and so on

4. **Adjectives of judgment or opinion, if any:** *pretty, happy, ugly, sad, interesting, boring,* and so on

5. **Adjectives of size or shape, if any:** *big, small, short, round, square,* and so on

6. **Adjectives of age or condition, if any:** *new, young, broken, dirty, shiny,* and so on

7. **Adjectives of colour, if any:** *red, green, blue,* and so on

8. **Adjectives that can also be used as nouns, or adjectives of group identity, if any:** *French, Protestant, metal, cotton,* and so on

9. **The noun**

1	2	3	4	5	6	7	8	9
a		few		tiny		red		ants
the	last	six					Thai	carvings
my			fine		old		oak	table

52c How can I understand the placement of adverbs?

ADVERBS modify—describe or limit—VERBS, ADJECTIVES, other adverbs, or entire sentences (see 14g). Adverbs may be positioned first, in the middle, or last in CLAUSES. Quick Reference 52.2 summarizes adverb types, what they tell about the words they modify, and where each type can be placed.

Common Grammar Errors: 12. Adjective-Adverb Confusion

ALERT: Do not let an adverb separate a verb from its DIRECT OBJECT or INDIRECT OBJECT. ●

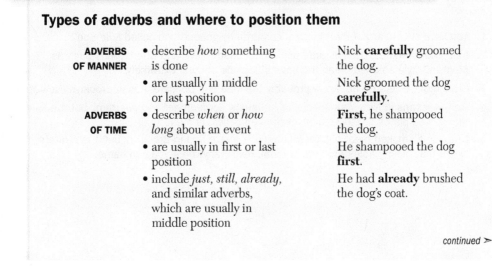

QUICK REFERENCE **52.2**

Types of adverbs and where to position them

ADVERBS OF MANNER	• describe *how* something is done	Nick **carefully** groomed the dog.
	• are usually in middle or last position	Nick groomed the dog **carefully**.
ADVERBS OF TIME	• describe *when* or *how long* about an event	**First**, he shampooed the dog.
	• are usually in first or last position	He shampooed the dog **first**.
	• include *just, still, already,* and similar adverbs, which are usually in middle position	He had **already** brushed the dog's coat.

continued ➤

ADVERBS OF FREQUENCY	• describe *how often* an event takes place	Nick has **never** been bitten by a dog.
	• are usually in middle position	
	• are in first position when they modify an entire sentence (see "Sentence adverbs" below)	**Occasionally**, he is scratched while shampooing a cat.
ADVERBS OF DEGREE OR EMPHASIS	• describe *how much* or *to what extent* about other modifiers	Nick is **extremely** calm around animals. [*Extremely* modifies *calm*.]
	• are directly before the word they modify	
	• include *only*, which is easy to misplace (see 21a)	
SENTENCE ADVERBS	• modify the entire sentence rather than just one word or a few words	**Incredibly**, he was once asked to groom a rat.
	• include transitional words and expressions (see 3g.1), as well as such expressions as *maybe, probably, possibly, fortunately, unfortunately,* and *incredibly*	
	• are in first position	

EXERCISE 52-1   Consulting all sections of this chapter, find and correct any errors in word order.

1. You have ever heard of the Montreal colourful neighbourhood called Mile End?

2. Mile End is where a Jewish large population used to live and where foods such as Montreal-style smoked meat and bagels became popular extremely.

3. Most Montrealers do not know probably the Mile End Delicatessen in Brooklyn, New York.

4. Delicatessens in New York specialize in usually corned beef and pastrami, but the Mile End serves plates of Montreal-style smoked delicious meat.

5. Not only a smoked meat big, fat sandwich is a rare find in Brooklyn, but it is a rare event to eat that much cholesterol in one meal, nearly anywhere you can name.

Chapter 53

PREPOSITIONS

Prepositions function with other words in PREPOSITIONAL PHRASES (14o). Prepositional phrases usually indicate *where* (direction or location), *how* (by what means or in what way), or *when* (at what time or how long) about the words they modify.

This chapter can help you with several uses of prepositions, which function in combination with other words in ways that are often idiomatic—that is, peculiar to the language. The meaning of an IDIOM differs from the literal meaning of each individual word. For example, the word *break* usually refers to shattering, but the sentence *Yao-Ming* **broke into** *a smile* means that a smile appeared on Yao-Ming's face. Knowing which preposition to use in a specific context takes much experience in reading, listening to, and speaking the language. A dictionary like the *Dictionary of American English* (Heinle and Heinle) or the *Oxford Advanced Learner's Dictionary* can be especially helpful when you need to find the correct preposition to use in cases not covered by this chapter.

53a | How can I recognize prepositions?

Quick Reference 53.1 lists many common prepositions.

Common
Grammar
Errors: 20.
Preposition
Problems

QUICK REFERENCE | 53.1

Common prepositions

about	before	except for	near	through
above	behind	excepting	next	throughout
according to	below	for	of	till
across	beneath	from	off	to
after	beside	in	on	toward
against	between	in addition to	onto	under
along	beyond	in back of	on top of	underneath
along with	but	in case of	out	unlike
among	by	in front of	out of	until
apart from	by means of	in place of	outside	up
around	concerning	inside	over	upon
as	despite	in spite of	past	up to
as for	down	instead of	regarding	with
at	during	into	round	within
because of	except	like	since	without

53b How do I use prepositions with expressions of time and place?

Quick Reference 53.2 shows how to use the prepositions *in, at,* and *on* to deliver some common kinds of information about time and place. The Quick Reference, however, does not cover every preposition that indicates time or place, nor does it cover all uses of *in, at,* and *on.* Also, it does not include expressions that operate outside the general rules. (Both these sentences are correct: *You ride in the car* and *You ride on the bus.*)

QUICK REFERENCE 53.2

Using *in, at,* and *on* to show time and place

TIME

- *in* **a year or a month** (*during* is also correct but less common)

  in 1995   **in** May

- *in* **a period of time**

  in a few months (seconds, days, years)

- *in* **a period of the day**

  in the morning (afternoon, evening)

  in the daytime (morning, evening) *but* **at** night

- *at* **a specific time or period of time**

  at noon   **at** 2:00   **at** dawn   **at** nightfall

  at takeoff (the time a plane leaves)

  at breakfast (the time a specific meal takes place)

- *on* **a specific day**

  on Friday   **on** my birthday

PLACE

- *in* **a location surrounded by something else**

  in Alberta   **in** the kitchen

  in Utah   **in** the apartment

  in downtown Mumbai   **in** the bathtub

- *at* **a specific location**

  at your house   **at** the bank

  at the corner of Maple Avenue and King Street

continued ➤

- *on a surface*

  on page 20

  on the second floor *but* **in** the attic *or* **in** the basement

  on Wellington Street (**in** Wellington Street is common outside North America)

  on the mezzanine

  on the highway

53c How do I use prepositions in phrasal verbs?

Phrasal verbs, also called *two-word verbs* and *three-word verbs,* are VERBS that combine with PREPOSITIONS to deliver their meaning. In some phrasal verbs, the verb and the preposition should not be separated by other words: ***Look at** the moon* [not ***Look** the moon **at**]. In **separable phrasal verbs**, other words in the sentence can separate the verb and the preposition without interfering with meaning: *I **threw away** my homework* is as correct as *I **threw** my homework **away**.

Here is a list of some common phrasal verbs. The ones that cannot be separated are marked with an asterisk (*).

SELECTED PHRASAL VERBS

ask out	get along with*	look out for*
break down	get back	look over
bring about	get off* (as an	make up
call back	INTRANSITIVE)	run across*
call off	go over*	speak to*
call up	hand in	speak with*
drop off	keep up with*	throw away
figure out	leave out	throw out
fill out	look after*	turn down
fill up	look around*	
find out	look into*	

Position a PRONOUN OBJECT between the words of a separable phrasal verb: *I threw **it** away.* Also, you can position an object PHRASE of several words between the parts of a separable phrasal verb: *I threw **my research paper** away.* However, when the object is a CLAUSE, do not let it separate the parts of the phrasal verb: *I threw away **all the papers that I wrote last year**.*

Many phrasal verbs are informal and are used more in speaking than in writing. For ACADEMIC WRITING, a more formal verb is usually more appropriate than a phrasal verb. In a research paper, for example, *propose* or *suggest* might be a better choice than *come up with.* For academic writing, acceptable phrasal verbs include *believe in, benefit from, concentrate on, consist of, depend on, dream of* (or *dream about*), *insist on, participate in, prepare for,* and *stare at.* None of these phrasal verbs can be separated.

EXERCISE 53-1 Consulting the preceding sections of this chapter and using the list of phrasal verbs in 53c, write a one- or two-paragraph description of a typical day at work or school in which you use at least five phrasal verbs. After checking a dictionary, revise your writing, substituting for the phrasal verbs any more formal verbs that might be more appropriate for academic writing.

53d How do I use prepositions with past participles?

PAST PARTICIPLES are verb forms that function as ADJECTIVES (54f). Past participles end in either *-ed* or *-d,* or in an equivalent irregular form (15d). When past participles follow the LINKING VERB *be,* it is easy to confuse them with PASSIVE VERBS (15n), which have the same endings. Passive verbs describe actions. Past participles, because they act as adjectives, modify NOUNS and PRONOUNS and often describe situations and conditions. Passive verbs follow the pattern *be* + past participle + *by: The child was frightened by a snake.* An expression containing a past participle, however, can use either *be* or another linking verb, and it can be followed by either *by* or a different preposition.

- The child **seemed frightened by** snakes.
- The child **is frightened of** all snakes.

Here is a list of expressions containing past participles and the prepositions that often follow them. Look in a dictionary for others. (See 54b on using GERUNDS after some of these expressions.)

SELECTED PAST PARTICIPLE PHRASES + PREPOSITIONS

be accustomed to	be interested in
be acquainted with	be known for
be composed of	be located in
be concerned/worried about	be made of (*or* from)
be disappointed with (*or* in)	be married to
be discriminated against	be pleased/satisfied with
be divorced from	be prepared for
be excited about	be tired of (*or* from)
be finished/done with	

53e How do I use prepositions in expressions?

In many common expressions, different PREPOSITIONS convey great differences in meaning. For example, four prepositions can be used with the verb *agree* to create five different meanings.

agree to means "to give consent": *Tony and I cannot **agree to** my buying you a new car.*

agree about means "to arrive at a satisfactory understanding": *We certainly **agree about** your needing a car.*

agree on means "to concur": *You and the seller must **agree on** a price for the car.*

agree with means "to have the same opinion": *I **agree with** you that you need a car.*

agree with also means "to be suitable or healthful": *The idea of having such a major expense does not **agree with** me.*

You can find entire books filled with English expressions that include prepositions. The following list shows a few that you're likely to use often.

SELECTED EXPRESSIONS WITH PREPOSITIONS

ability in	different from	involved with *[someone]*
access to	faith in	knowledge of
accustomed to	familiar with	made of
afraid of	famous for	married to
angry with *or* at	frightened by	opposed to
authority on	happy with	patient with
aware of	in charge of	proud of
based on	independent of	reason for
capable of	in favour of	related to
certain of	influence on *or* over	suspicious of
confidence in	interested in	time for
dependent on	involved in *[something]*	tired of

Chapter 54

GERUNDS, INFINITIVES, AND PARTICIPLES

Participles are verb forms (see 15b). A verb's *-ing* form is its PRESENT PARTICIPLE. The *-ed* form of a regular verb is its PAST PARTICIPLE; IRREGULAR VERBS form their past participles in various ways (for example, *bend, bent; eat, eaten; think, thought*—for a complete list, see Quick Reference 15.4 in 15d). Participles can function as ADJECTIVES (*a **smiling** face, a **closed** book*).

A verb's *-ing* form can also function as a NOUN (***Sneezing** spreads colds*), which is called a GERUND. Another verb form, the INFINITIVE, can also function as a noun. An infinitive is a verb's SIMPLE or BASE FORM, usually preceded by the word *to* (*We want everyone **to** smile*). Verb forms—participles, gerunds, and infinitives—functioning as nouns or MODIFIERS are called VERBALS, as explained in 14e. This chapter can help you make the right choices among verbals.

54a   How can I use gerunds and infinitives as subjects?

Gerunds are used more commonly than infinitives as subjects. Sometimes, however, either is acceptable.

Choosing the right health club is important.

To choose the right health club is important.

! ALERT: When a gerund or an infinitive is used alone as a subject, it is SINGULAR and requires a singular verb. When two or more gerunds or infinitives create a COMPOUND SUBJECT, they require a plural verb. (See 14l and 17e.) ●

54b   What verbs use a gerund, not an infinitive, as an object?

Some VERBS must be followed by GERUNDS used as DIRECT OBJECTS. Other verbs must be followed by INFINITIVES. Still other verbs can be followed by either a gerund or an infinitive. (A few verbs change meaning depending on whether they are followed by a gerund or an infinitive; see 54d.) Quick Reference 54.1 lists common verbs that must be followed by gerunds.

Verbs that use gerund objects

acknowledge	detest	mind
admit	discuss	object to
advise	dislike	postpone
anticipate	dream about	practise
appreciate	enjoy	put off
avoid	escape	quit
cannot bear	evade	recall
cannot help	favour	recommend
cannot resist	finish	regret
complain about	give up	resent
consider	have trouble	resist
consist of	imagine	risk
contemplate	include	suggest
delay	insist on	talk about
deny	keep (on)	tolerate
deter from	mention	understand

Yuri **considered *calling*** [not *to call*] the mayor.

He **was having trouble *getting*** [not *to get*] a work permit.

Yuri's boss **recommended *taking*** [not *to take*] an interpreter to the permit agency.

GERUND AFTER *GO*

The word *go* is usually followed by an infinitive: *We can* **go** *to* **see** [not *go seeing*] *a movie tonight.* Sometimes, however, *go* is followed by a gerund in phrases such as *go swimming, go fishing, go shopping,* and *go driving: I will* **go** ***shopping*** [not *go to shop*] *after work.*

GERUND AFTER *BE* + COMPLEMENT + PREPOSITION

Many common expressions use a form of the verb *be* plus a COMPLEMENT plus a PREPOSITION. In such expressions, use a gerund, not an infinitive, after the preposition. Here is a list of some of the most frequently used expressions in this pattern.

SELECTED EXPRESSIONS USING BE + COMPLEMENT + PREPOSITION

be (get) accustomed to	be interested in
be angry about	be prepared for
be bored with	be responsible for
be capable of	be tired of (*or* from)
be committed to	be (get) used to
be excited about	be worried about

We **are excited about** *voting* [not to vote] in the next election.

They were **interested in** *hearing* [not to hear] the candidates' debate.

ALERT: Always use a gerund, not an infinitive, as the object of a preposition. Be especially careful when the word *to* is functioning as a preposition in a PHRASAL VERB (see 53c): *We are committed to changing* [not to change] *the rules.* ●

54c What verbs use an infinitive, not a gerund, as an object?

Quick Reference 54.2 lists selected common verbs and expressions that must be followed by INFINITIVES, not GERUNDS, as OBJECTS.

She **wanted** *to go* [not wanted going] to the lecture.

Only three people **decided** *to question* [not decided questioning] the speaker.

QUICK REFERENCE 54.2

Verbs that use infinitive objects

afford	consent	intend	promise
agree	decide	know how	refuse
aim	decline	learn	require
appear	demand	like	seem
arrange	deserve	manage	struggle
ask	do not care	mean	tend
attempt	expect	need	threaten
be left	fail	offer	volunteer
beg	force	plan	vote
cannot afford	give permission	prefer	wait
care	hesitate	prepare	want
claim	hope	pretend	would like

INFINITIVE AFTER *BE* + SOME COMPLEMENTS

Gerunds are common in constructions that use a form of the verb *be* plus a COMPLEMENT and a PREPOSITION (see 54b). However, use an infinitive, not a gerund, when *be* plus a complement is not followed by a preposition.

We **are eager** *to go* [not going] camping.

I **am ready** *to sleep* [not sleeping] in a tent.

INFINITIVE TO INDICATE PURPOSE

Use an infinitive in expressions that indicate purpose: *I read a book* **to learn** *more about Mayan culture.* This sentence means "I read a book for the purpose of learning more about Mayan culture."

INFINITIVE WITH *THE FIRST, THE LAST, THE ONE*

Use an infinitive after the expressions *the first, the last,* and *the one: Nina is the first* **to arrive** [not *arriving*] *and the last* **to leave** [not *leaving*] *every day. She's always the one* **to do** *the most.*

UNMARKED INFINITIVES

Infinitives used without the word *to* are called **unmarked infinitives**, or sometimes *bare infinitives.* An unmarked infinitive may be hard to recognize because it is not preceded by *to.* Some common verbs followed by unmarked infinitives are *feel, have, hear, let, listen to, look at, make* (meaning "compel"), *notice, see,* and *watch.*

> Please let me **take** [not *to take*] you to lunch. [unmarked infinitive]
>
> I want **to take** you to lunch. [marked infinitive]
>
> I can have Kara **drive** [not *to drive*] us. [unmarked infinitive]
>
> I will ask Kara **to drive** us. [marked infinitive]

The verb *help* can be followed by a marked or an unmarked infinitive. Either is correct: *Help me* **put** [or **to put**] *this box in the car.*

ALERT: Be careful to use parallel structure (see Chapter 10) correctly when you use two or more gerunds or infinitives after verbs. If two or more verbal objects follow one verb, put the verbals into the same form.

> NO   We went **sailing** and **to scuba dive**.
>
> YES   We went **sailing** and **scuba diving**.
>
> NO   We heard the wind **blow** and the waves **crashing**.
>
> YES   We heard the wind **blow** and the waves **crash**.
>
> YES   We heard the wind **blowing** and the waves **crashing**.

Conversely, if you are using verbal objects with COMPOUND PREDICATES, be sure to use the kind of verbal that each verb requires.

> NO   We enjoyed **scuba diving** but do not plan **sailing** again. [*Enjoyed* requires a gerund object, and *plan* requires an infinitive object; see Quick References 54.1 and 54.2 in this chapter.]
>
> YES   We enjoyed **scuba diving** but do not plan **to sail** again. ●

54d   How does meaning change when certain verbs are followed by a gerund or an infinitive?

WITH *STOP*

The VERB *stop* followed by a GERUND means "finish, quit." *Stop* followed by an INFINITIVE means "interrupt one activity to begin another."

> We **stopped** *eating*. [We finished our meal.]
>
> We **stopped** *to eat*. [We stopped another activity, such as driving, to eat.]

WITH *REMEMBER* AND *FORGET*

The verb *remember* followed by an infinitive means "not to forget to do something": *I must* **remember to talk** *with Isa. Remember* followed by a gerund means "recall a memory": *I* **remember talking** *in my sleep last night.*

The verb *forget* followed by an infinitive means "fail to do something": *If you* **forget to put** *a stamp on that letter, it will be returned. Forget* followed by a gerund means "do something and not recall it": *I* **forget having put** *the stamps in the refrigerator.*

WITH *TRY*

The verb *try* followed by an infinitive means "make an effort": *I* **tried to find** *your jacket.* Followed by a gerund, *try* means "experiment with": *I* **tried jogging** *but found it too difficult.*

54e Why is the meaning unchanged whether a gerund or an infinitive follows sense verbs?

Sense VERBS include words such as *see, notice, hear, observe, watch, feel, listen to,* and *look at.* The meaning of these verbs is usually not affected by whether a GERUND or an INFINITIVE follows as the OBJECT. *I* **saw** *the water* **rise** and *I* **saw** *the water* **rising** both have the same meaning.

EXERCISE 54-1 Write the correct form of the verbal object (either a gerund or an infinitive) for each verb in parentheses. For help, consult 54b through 54e.

> **EXAMPLE** On some campuses, it seems as if nearly every student wants (find) <u>to find</u> a better apartment or dormitory room.

1. Often, students become as anxious over (find) _____ a suitable apartment as they do over (write) _____ a final exam.

2. In many places, senior undergraduates and graduate students tend (avoid) _____ dormitories.

3. Some students consider (live) _____ off campus a sign of maturity and independence.

4. Others just seem (need) _____ the extra physical and mental space.

5. In later life, people who were able (share) _____ a big, roomy house with school friends often remember the experience fondly.

6. We rarely see students (come) _____ up with an ideal solution, though, if they have left their search to the last minute.

7. The idea is to plan ahead and actively try (find) _____ a place that suits you; otherwise, you may be forced to try (sleep) _____ on your friend's couch for a few weeks.

8. The housing problem at one large Ontario university became known after a student acknowledged (live) _____ hidden in a campus stairwell.

9. (Explain) _____ this situation was a huge embarrassment for university officials, even after social workers attempted (blame) _____ this student's predicament on personal problems.

54f How do I choose between *-ing* and *-ed* forms of adjectives?

Deciding whether to use the *-ing* form (PRESENT PARTICIPLE) or the *-ed* form (PAST PARTICIPLE of a regular VERB) as an ADJECTIVE in a specific sentence can be difficult. For example, *I am* **amused** and *I am* **amusing** are both correct in English, but their meanings are very different. To make the right choice, decide whether the modified NOUN or PRONOUN is causing or experiencing what the participle describes.

Use a present participle (*-ing*) to modify a noun or pronoun that is the agent or the cause of the action.

Micah described your **interesting** plan. [The noun *plan* causes interest, so *interesting* is correct.]

I find your plan **exciting.** [The noun *plan* causes excitement, so *exciting* is correct.]

Use a past participle (*-ed* in regular verbs) to modify a noun or pronoun that experiences or receives whatever the modifier describes.

An **interested** committee wants to hear your plan. [The noun *committee* experiences interest, so *interested,* is correct.]

Excited by your plan, they called a board meeting. [The pronoun *they* experiences excitement, so *excited* is correct.]

Here are frequently used participles that convey very different meanings, depending on whether the *-ed* or the *-ing* form is used.

amused, amusing	frightened, frightening
annoyed, annoying	insulted, insulting
appalled, appalling	offended, offending
bored, boring	overwhelmed, overwhelming
confused, confusing	pleased, pleasing
depressed, depressing	reassured, reassuring
disgusted, disgusting	satisfied, satisfying
fascinated, fascinating	shocked, shocking

EXERCISE 54-2   Choose the correct participle from each pair in parentheses. For help, consult 54f.

> **EXAMPLE** Learning about the career of a favourite actor is always an (interested, interesting) <u>interesting</u> exercise.

1. Jim Carrey is an actor/comedian with a (fascinated, fascinating) _____ history.

2. (Raised, Raising) _____ by his parents in southern Ontario, Carrey grew up in one of the most media-rich areas in North America.

3. Biographies of Carrey reveal the (surprised, surprising) _____ news that this bright and talented student dropped out of school in grade ten.

4. After relocating to Los Angeles in the 1980s, a (disappointed, disappointing) _____ Carrey discovered the difficulties of acting after his first (cancelled, cancelling) _____ TV series left him briefly out of work.

5. Carrey's career skyrocketed with his (amused, amusing) _____ appearances on *In Living Color,* a TV show that led to numerous box office hits: *Ace Ventura: Pet Detective; The Mask; The Truman Show; Liar, Liar;* and *Bruce Almighty.*

Chapter 55

MODAL AUXILIARY VERBS

AUXILIARY VERBS are known as *helping verbs* because adding an auxiliary verb to a MAIN VERB helps the main verb convey additional information (see 15e). For example, the auxiliary verb *do* is important in turning sentences into questions. *You have to sleep* becomes a question when *do* is added: *Do you have to sleep?* The most common auxiliary verbs are forms of *be, have,* and *do.* Quick References 15.6 and 15.7 in section 15e list the forms of these three verbs.

MODAL AUXILIARY VERBS are one type of auxiliary verb. They include *can, could, may, might, should, had better, must, will, would,* and others discussed in this chapter. Modals differ from *be, have,* and *do* used as auxiliary verbs in the specific ways discussed in Quick Reference 55.1. This chapter can help you use modals to convey shades of meaning.

Modals and their differences from other auxiliary verbs

- Modals in the present or future are always followed by the SIMPLE FORM of a main verb: *I **might go** tomorrow.*

- One-word modals have no *-s* ending in the THIRD-PERSON SINGULAR: *She **could** go with me; he **could** go with me; they **could** go with me.* (The two-word modal *have to* changes form to agree with its subject: *I **have to** leave; she **has to** leave.*) Auxiliary verbs other than modals usually change form for third-person singular: *I **do** want to go; he **does** want to go.*

- Some modals change form in the past. Others (*should, would, must,* which convey probability, and *ought to*) use *have* + a PAST PARTICIPLE. *I **can do** it* becomes *I **could do** it* in PAST-TENSE CLAUSES about ability. *I **could do** it* becomes *I **could have done** it* in clauses about possibility.

- Modals convey meaning about ability, necessity, advisability, possibility, and other conditions: For example, *I **can** go* means "I am able to go." Modals do not describe actual occurrences.

((•
AUDIO
LESSON
Section 1:
Big Ideas—
Verbs

55a How do I convey ability, necessity, advisability, possibility, and probability with modals?

CONVEYING ABILITY

The modal *can* conveys ability now (in the present), and *could* conveys ability before (in the past). These words deliver the meaning "able to." For the future, use *will be able to.*

We **can** work late tonight. [*Can* conveys present ability.]

I **could** work late last night, too. [*Could* conveys past ability.]

I **will be able to** work late next Monday. [*Will be able* is the future tense; *will* here is not a modal.]

AUDIO
LESSON
Section 2:
Practice
Questions—
Verbs

Adding *not* between a modal and the MAIN VERB makes the CLAUSE negative: *We* **cannot** *work late tonight;* I **could** **not** *work late last night;* I **will** **not** **be able to** *work late next Monday.*

AUDIO
LESSON
Section 3:
Rapid
Review—
Verbs

ALERT: You will often see negative forms of modals turned into CONTRACTIONS: *can't, couldn't, won't, wouldn't,* and others. Because contractions are considered informal usage by some instructors, you will never be wrong if you avoid them in ACADEMIC WRITING, except when you are reproducing spoken words. ●

CONVEYING NECESSITY

The modals *must* and *have to* convey a need to do something. Both *must* and *have to* are followed by the simple form of the main verb. In the present tense, *have to* changes form to agree with its subject.

You **must** leave before midnight.

She **has to** leave when I leave.

In the past tense, *must* is never used to express necessity. Instead, use *had to.*

PRESENT TENSE We **must** study today. We **have to** study today.

PAST TENSE We **had to** [not *must*] take a test yesterday.

The negative forms of *must* and *have to* also have different meanings. *Must not* conveys that something is forbidden; *do not have to* conveys that something is not necessary.

You **must not** sit there. [Sitting there is forbidden.]

You **do not have to** sit there. [Sitting there is not necessary.]

CONVEYING ADVISABILITY OR THE NOTION OF A GOOD IDEA

The modals *should* and *ought to* express the idea that doing the action of the main verb is advisable or is a good idea.

You **should** go to class tomorrow morning.

In the past tense, *should* and *ought to* convey regret or knowing something through hindsight. They mean that good advice was not taken.

You **should have** gone to class yesterday.

I **ought to have** called my sister yesterday.

The modal *had better* delivers the meaning of good advice or warning or threat. It does not change form for tense.

You **had better** see the doctor before your cough gets worse.

Need to is often used to express strong advice, too. Its past-tense form is *needed to.*

You **need to** take better care of yourself. You **needed to** listen.

CONVEYING POSSIBILITY

The modals *may, might,* and *could* can be used to convey an idea of possibility or likelihood.

> We **may** become hungry before long.

> We **could** eat lunch at the diner next door.

For the past-tense form, use *may, might,* and *could,* followed by *have* and the past participle of the main verb.

> I **could have studied** German in high school, but I studied Spanish instead.

CONVEYING PROBABILITY

In addition to conveying the idea of necessity, the modal *must* can also convey probability or likelihood. It means that a well-informed guess is being made.

> Marisa **must** be a talented actress. She has been chosen to play the lead role in the school play.

When *must* conveys probability, the past tense is *must have* plus the past participle of the main verb.

> I did not see Boris at the party; he **must have left** early.

EXERCISE 55-1   Fill in each blank with the past-tense modal auxiliary that expresses the meaning given in parentheses. For help, consult 55a.

> **EXAMPLE**   We (advisability) <u>had better</u> finish that research we were planning to do before reading week.

1. I think you (advisability) _____ looked at the latest report from Statistics Canada on consumer spending patterns.

2. Given your specialization in economics, you (probability) _____ find those reports essential to your research.

3. You (making a guess) _____ not _____ been thinking when you let your online subscription to *Perspectives on Labour and Income* expire, then.

4. If I had looked at that issue before my midterms, I (ability) _____ aced the question on economic structures and population change.

5. I'd take more pleasure in reading about how little of their spending Canadians now (necessity) _____ devote to the necessities of life, though, if I (ability) _____ find a decent part-time job.

55b   **How do I convey preferences, plans, and past habits with modals?**

CONVEYING PREFERENCES

The modal *would rather* expresses a preference. *Would rather,* the PRESENT TENSE, is used with the SIMPLE FORM of the MAIN VERB, and *would rather have,* the PAST TENSE, is used with the PAST PARTICIPLE of the main verb.

We **would rather see** a comedy than a mystery.

Carlos **would rather have stayed** home last night.

CONVEYING PLAN OR OBLIGATION

A form of *be* followed by *supposed to* and the simple form of a main verb delivers a meaning of something planned or of an obligation.

I **was supposed to meet** them at the bus stop.

CONVEYING PAST HABIT

The modals *used to* and *would* express the idea that something happened repeatedly in the past.

I **used to** hate going to the dentist.

I **would** dread every single visit.

ALERT: Both *used to* and *would* can be used to express repeated actions in the past, but *would* cannot be used for a situation that lasted for a period of time in the past.

NO   I **would** live in Corner Brook.

YES   I **used** to live in Corner Brook. ●

55c   How can I recognize modals in the passive voice?

Modals use the ACTIVE VOICE, as shown in sections 55a and 55b. In the active voice, the subject does the action expressed in the MAIN VERB (see 15n and 15o).

Modals can also use the PASSIVE VOICE (15p). In the passive voice, the doer of the main verb's action is either unexpressed or expressed as an OBJECT in a PREPOSITIONAL PHRASE starting with the word *by*.

PASSIVE   The waterfront **can be seen** from my window.

ACTIVE   **I can see** the waterfront from my window.

PASSIVE   The tax form **must be signed** by the person who fills it out.

ACTIVE   The person who fills out the tax form **must sign** it.

EXERCISE 55-2   Select the correct choice from the words in parentheses and write it in the blank. For help, consult 55a through 55c.

> **EXAMPLE** I (should, should have) <u>should have</u> taken kayaking lessons my first summer in British Columbia.

1. I (would, used to) _____ live far from the ocean and the mountains.
2. In those days I (can, could) _____ only dream of kayaking down the coast where the Rocky Mountains meet the Pacific.
3. Sometimes I think I (must be come, must have come) _____ to the world's most beautiful landscape.
4. My move to the West Coast (should not have been, should not have) _____ put off for so long.
5. If you have a dream, you (cannot, should not) _____ leave it unfulfilled.

EXERCISE 55-3   Select the correct choice from the words in parentheses and write it in the blank. For help, consult 55a through 55c.

> **EXAMPLE** I (should have, should) <u>should have</u> looked at the newest tablet devices as well as the laptops.

1. Although I (used to, had to) _____ buy a new device, I could not find the time to consider all the offerings.

2. I (should have, must have) _____ started my search earlier, but instead I left it to the last moment.

3. Even after I finally finished my exams, I (must, could) _____ not take time off because of the demands of my work-study internship.

4. I (could have, could have been) _____ done better than I did, passing over the latest technology for an older machine.

5. When I came home with my new laptop, my roommates teased me, "Julie, you (should not have, would not have) _____ forgotten your resolution to be seen with only the coolest toys!"

Terms Glossary

This glossary defines important terms used in this handbook, including the ones that are printed in small capital letters. Many of these glossary entries end with parenthetical references to the handbook section(s) or chapter(s) where the specific term is fully discussed.

absolute phrase A phrase containing a subject and a participle that modifies an entire sentence. (14o) *The semester [subject] **being** [present participle of be] over, the campus looks deserted.*

abstract A very short summary that presents all the important ideas of a longer piece of writing. Sometimes appears before the main writing, as in APA style. (37d)

abstract noun A noun that names something not knowable through the five senses: *idea, respect.* (14b)

academic writing Writing you do for college or university classes, usually intended to inform or to persuade. (1d)

action verbs Strong verbs that increase the impact of your language and reduce wordiness. *Weak verbs,* such as *be* or *have,* increase wordiness. (11e)

active voice An attribute of verbs showing that the action or condition expressed in the verb is done by the subject, in contrast with the *passive voice,* which conveys that the action or condition of the verb is done to the subject. (15n, 15o)

adjective A word that describes or limits (modifies) a noun, a pronoun, or a word group functioning as a noun: *silly, three.* (14f, Chapter 18)

adjective clause A dependent clause, also known as a *relative clause.* An adjective clause modifies a preceding noun or pronoun and begins with a relative word (such as *who, which, that,* or *where*) that relates the clause to the noun or pronoun it modifies. Also see *clause.* (14p)

adverb A word that describes or limits (modifies) verbs, adjectives, other adverbs, phrases, or clauses: *loudly, very, nevertheless, there.* (14g, Chapter 18)

adverb clause A dependent clause beginning with a subordinating conjunction that establishes the relationship in meaning between the adverb clause and its independent clause. An adverb clause modifies the independent clause's verb or the entire independent clause. Also see *clause, conjunction.* (14p)

agreement The required match of number and person between a subject and verb or a pronoun and antecedent. A pronoun that expresses gender must match its antecedent in gender also. (Chapter 17)

analogy An explanation of the unfamiliar in terms of the familiar. Unlike a simile, an analogy does not use *like* or *as* in making the comparison. Analogy is also a rhetorical strategy for developing paragraphs. (3i, 12c)

analysis A process of critical thinking that divides a whole into its component parts in order to understand how the parts interrelate. Sometimes called *division,* analysis is also a rhetorical strategy for developing paragraphs. (3i, 4b, 40g, 41c)

analytic frameworks Systematic ways of investigating a work. (40c)

antecedent The noun or pronoun to which a pronoun refers. (16l–16s, 17o–17t)

APA style See *documentation style.*

appeals to reason Tools a writer uses to convince the reader that the reasoning in an argument is sound and effective; there are three types—logical, emotional, and ethical appeals. (5g–5j)

appositive A word or group of words that renames a preceding noun or noun phrase: *my favourite month, **October.*** (14n)

argument A rhetorical attempt to persuade others to agree with a position about a topic open to debate. (1c, Chapter 5)

articles Also called *determiners* or *noun markers,* articles are the words *a, an,* and *the. A* and *an* are indefinite articles, and *the* is a definite article; also see *determiner.* (14f, Chapter 51)

assertion A statement. In a thesis statement, an assertion expresses a point of view about a topic; in an argument, an assertion states the position you want to argue. (2d, 5d)

assessing reasoning processes Judging whether claims and conclusions are justified by the evidence, reasons, explanations, and analysis presented.

audience The readers to whom a piece of writing is directed; the three types include *general audience, peer audience,* and *specialist audience.* (1d)

auxiliary verb Also known as a *helping verb,* an auxiliary verb is a form of *be, do, have, can, may, will,* or certain other verbs that combines with a main verb to help it express tense, mood, and voice. Also see *modal auxiliary verb.* (15e)

balanced sentence A sentence composed of two parallel structures, usually two independent clauses, that present contrasting content. (10b)

base form See *simple form.*

bias In writing, a distortion or inaccuracy caused by a dislike or hatred of individuals, groups of people, or ideas. (4e.2)

bibliographic notes In a note system of documentation, a *footnote* or *endnote* gives the bibliographic information the first time a source is cited. (35f, 36d.2, Chapter 38)

bibliography A list of sources used or consulted for research writing. (Chapters 36–38)

block style Style used in writing business letters. Block style uses no indents, single spacing within paragraphs, and double spacing between paragraphs. All lines start flush left, which means at the left margin. (43f) "Block style" also refers to indented block quotations. (36c, 37c)

blog Shortened form of "**Web log,**" a kind of online journal. (46e)

body paragraphs Paragraphs that provide the substance of your message in a sequence that makes sense. (3d)

Boolean expressions In a search engine, symbols or words such as And, Or, and Not that let you create keyword combinations that narrow and refine your search. (34l)

borders Lines used to set apart sections of text. (45e)

brainstorming Listing all ideas that come to mind on a topic and then grouping the ideas by patterns that emerge. (2c.3)

bureaucratic language Sometimes called *bureaucratese;* language that is overblown or overly complex. (12l)

business writing Writing designed for business, including letters, memos, resumés, job application letters, and e-mail messages. (1d, 3b, Chapter 43)

case The form of a noun or pronoun in a specific context that shows whether it is functioning as a subject, an object, or a possessive. In modern English, nouns change form in the possessive case only (city = form for subjective and objective cases; city's = possessive-case form). Also see *pronoun case.* (16a–16k)

cause and effect The relationship between outcomes (effects) and the reasons for them (causes). Cause-and-effect analysis is a rhetorical strategy for developing paragraphs. (3i, 4h, 4j)

chronological order Also called *time order,* an arrangement of information according to time sequence; an organizing strategy for sentences, paragraphs, and longer pieces of writing. (3h)

citation Information that identifies a source quoted, paraphrased, summarized, or referred to in a piece of writing; *in-text citations* appear within sentences or as *parenthetical references.* Also see *documentation.* (Chapters 34 and 35)

civic writing Writing done to influence public opinion or to advance causes. (44d)

claim An element of argument stating an issue and taking a position on a debatable topic. A claim is supported with evidence and reasons, moving from broad reasons to specific data and details. (5d)

classical argument An argument with a six-part structure consisting of introduction, thesis statement, background, evidence and reasoning, response to opposing views, and conclusion. (5e)

classification A rhetorical strategy for paragraph development that organizes information by grouping items according to underlying shared characteristics. (3i)

clause A group of words containing a subject and a predicate. A clause that delivers full meaning is called an *independent* (or *main*) *clause.* A clause that lacks full meaning by itself is called a *dependent* (or *subordinate*) *clause.* Also see *adjective clause, adverb clause, nonrestrictive element, noun clause, restrictive element.* (14p)

cliché An overused, worn-out phrase that has lost its capacity to communicate effectively: *ripe old age.* (12i)

climactic order Sometimes called *emphatic order,* an arrangement of ideas or other kinds of information from least important to most important. (3h, 5e)

clip art Pictures, sketches, and other graphics available for reuse on some word-processing programs. (45f) clustering See *mapping.*

coherence The clear progression from one idea to another using transitional expressions, pronouns, selective repetition, or parallelism to make connections between ideas. (3g)

collaborative writing Writing a paper together with other students. (Chapter 6)

collective noun A noun that names a group of people or things: *family, committee.* Also see *noncount noun.* (14b, 17j, 17t)

colloquial language Casual or conversational language. (12h)

comma fault See *comma splice.*

comma splice The error that occurs when only a comma connects two independent clauses; also called a *comma fault.* (Chapter 20)

common noun A noun that names a general group, place, person, or thing: *dog, house.* (14b)

comparative form The form of a descriptive adjective or adverb that shows a different degree of intensity between two things: *bluer, less blue; more easily, less easily.* Also see *positive form, superlative form.* (18e)

comparison and contrast A rhetorical strategy for organizing and developing paragraphs by discussing similarities (*comparison*) and differences (*contrast*). It has two patterns: *point-by-point* and *block organization.* (3i)

complement An element after a verb that completes the predicate, such as a direct object after a transitive verb or a noun or adjective after a linking verb. Also see *object complement, predicate adjective, predicate nominative, subject complement.* (14n)

complete predicate See *predicate.*

complete subject See *subject.*

complex sentence See *sentence types.*

compound-complex sentence See *sentence types.*

compound construction A group of nouns or pronouns connected with a coordinating conjunction. (16d)

compound noun See *subject.*

compound predicate See *predicate.*

compound sentence See *coordinate sentence, sentence types.*

compound subject See *subject.* (14l, 17e)

compound word Two or more words placed together to express one concept. (31g)

conciseness An attribute of writing that is direct and to the point. (Chapter 11)

concrete noun A noun naming something that can be seen, touched, heard, smelled, or tasted: *smoke, sidewalk.* (14b)

conjunction A word that connects or otherwise establishes a relationship between two or more words, phrases, or clauses. Also see *coordinating conjunction, correlative conjunction, subordinating conjunction.* (14i)

conjunctive adverb An adverb, such as *therefore* or *meanwhile,* that communicates a logical connection in meaning. (14g)

connotation An idea implied by a word, involving associations and emotional overtones that go beyond the word's dictionary definition. (12d)

context The circumstances in which readers encounter writing. (1b)

contraction A word where an apostrophe takes the place of one or more omitted letters. (27d)

coordinate adjectives Two or more adjectives of equal weight that modify a noun. (24e)

coordinate sentence Two or more independent clauses joined by either a semicolon or a comma with coordinating conjunction showing their relationship; also called a *compound sentence.* Also see *coordination.* (9d)

coordinating conjunction A conjunction that joins two or more grammatically equivalent structures: *and, or, for, nor, but, so, yet.* (9f–9h, 14i, 20b)

coordination The use of grammatically equivalent forms to show a balance or sequence of ideas. (9d–9h)

correlative conjunction A pair of words that joins equivalent grammatical structures, including *both . . . and, either . . . or, neither . . . nor, not only . . . but* (or *but also*). (14i)

count noun A noun that names an item or items that can be counted: *radio, streets, idea, fingernails.* (14b, 50a)

critical reading A parallel process to critical thinking where you comprehend, analyze, infer, synthesize, and evaluate as you read. (4c–4g)

critical response Formally, an essay summarizing a source's central point or main idea. It includes a *transitional statement* that bridges this summary and the writer's synthesized reactions in response. (7f.2)

critical thinking A form of thinking where you take control of your conscious thought processes. (4a, 4b, 40f)

cumulative adjectives Adjectives that build meaning from word to word: *distinctive musical style.* (24e)

cumulative sentence The most common structure for a sentence, with the subject and verb first, followed by modifiers adding details; also called a *loose sentence.* (9o)

dangling modifier A modifier that attaches its meaning illogically, either because it is closer to another noun or pronoun than to its true subject or because its true subject is not expressed in the sentence. (21d–21e)

declarative sentence A sentence that makes a statement: *Skydiving is exciting.* Also see *exclamatory sentence, imperative sentence, interrogative sentence.* (14k)

deduction, deductive reasoning The process of reasoning from general claims to a specific instance. (4i)

definite article See *articles.*

definition A rhetorical strategy in which you define or give the meaning of words or ideas. Includes *extended definition.* (3i)

demonstrative pronoun A pronoun that points out the antecedent: *this, these; that, those.* (14c, 14f)

denotation The dictionary definition of a word. (12d.1)

dependent clause A clause that cannot stand alone as an independent grammatical unit. Also see *adjective clause, adverb clause, noun clause.* (9j, 14p, 19b)

description A rhetorical strategy that appeals to a reader's senses—sight, sound, smell, taste, and touch. (3i)

descriptive adjective An adjective that names the condition or properties of the noun it modifies and (except for a very few, such as *dead* and *unique*) has comparative and superlative forms: *flat, flatter, flattest.* (14f)

descriptive adverb An adverb that names the condition or properties of whatever it modifies and that has comparative and superlative forms: *happily, more happily, most happily.* (14g)

determiner A word or word group, traditionally identified as an adjective, that limits a noun by telling how much or how many about it. Also called *expression of quantity, limiting adjective,* or *noun marker.* (14f, 50b, Chapter 51)

diction Word choice. (12e)

digital portfolio A collection of several texts in electronic format that you've chosen to represent the range of your skills and abilities. (1f)

direct address Words naming a person or group being spoken to. Written words of direct address are set off by commas. (24g) *The answer,* **my friends***, lies with you. Go with them,* **Gene***.*

direct discourse In writing, words that repeat speech or conversation exactly and so are enclosed in quotation marks. (22e, 24g, 28b)

direct object A noun or pronoun or group of words functioning as a noun that receives the action (completes the meaning) of a transitive verb. (14m)

direct question A sentence that asks a question and ends with a question mark: *Are you going?* (23a, 23c)

direct quotation See *quotation.*

direct title A title that tells exactly what the essay will be about. (2i)

discovery draft A first draft developed from focused freewriting. (2g)

disclaimer A statement appended to the top or bottom of e-mails designed to protect the company from legal liability. (43d)

documentation The acknowledgment of someone else's words and ideas used in any piece of writing by giving full and accurate information about the person whose words were used and where those words were found. For example, for a print source, docmentation usually includes names of all authors, title of the source, place and date of publication, and related information. (35a–35k, Chapters 36–38)

documentation style A system for providing information about the source of words, information, and ideas quoted, paraphrased, or summarized from some source other than the writer. Documentation styles discussed in this handbook are MLA, APA, CM, CSE, and IEEE. (33h, Chapters 36–38)

document design A term for the placement of tables, graphs, and other illustrations on printed and online material. (Chapter 45)

double negative A nonstandard negation using two negative modifiers rather than one. (18c)

drafting A part of the writing process in which writers compose ideas in sentences and paragraphs. *Drafts* are versions—*first* or *rough, revised,* and *final*—of one piece of writing. (2g)

edited Canadian English English language usage that conforms to established rules of grammar, sentence structure, punctuation, and spelling in Canada; a variety of *standard English.* (12b)

editing A part of the writing process in which writers check the technical correctness of grammar, spelling, punctuation, and mechanics. (2j)

elliptical construction The deliberate omission of one or more words in order to achieve conciseness in a sentence. (11d.3, 14p, 22h)

emotional appeal A rhetorical strategy employing descriptive language and concrete details or examples to create a mental picture for readers. The Greek name is *pathos.* (5g)

essential element See *restrictive element.*

ethical appeal A rhetorical strategy intended to reassure readers that the writer is authoritative, honest, fair, likeable, and so on. The Greek name is *ethos.* (5g)

ethnography A research method that involves careful observation of a group of people or a setting, often over a period of time. Ethnography also refers to the written work that results from this research. (7d.5)

ethos See *ethical appeal.*

euphemism Language that attempts to blunt certain realities by speaking of them in "nice" or "tactful" words. (12k)

evaluation A step in the critical thinking process where a person makes judgments of quality. (Chapter 4)

evidence Facts, data, examples, and opinions of others used to support assertions and conclusions. Also see *sources.* (4g)

exclamatory sentence A sentence often beginning with *What* or *How* that expresses strong feeling: *What a ridiculous statement!* (14k)

expletive The phrase *there is (are), there was (were), it is,* or *it was* at the beginning of a clause, changing structure and postponing the subject: *It is Mars that we hope to reach.* [Compare: *We hope to reach Mars.*] (11c)

expository writing See *informative writing.*

expressive writing Writing that reflects personal thoughts and feelings. (1c.1)

faulty parallelism Grammatically incorrect writing that results from nonmatching grammatical forms. (10d)

faulty predication A grammatically illogical combination of subject and predicate. (22g)

field research Primary research that involves going into real-life situations to observe, survey, interview, or participate in some activity. (32c)

figurative language Words that make connections and comparisons and draw on one image to explain another and enhance meaning. (12c)

finite verb A verb form that shows tense, mood, voice, person, and number while expressing an action, occurrence, or state of being. (Chapter 15)

first person See *person.*

focused freewriting A technique that may start with a set topic or may build on one sentence taken from earlier freewriting. (2g)

formal outline An outline that lays out the topic levels of generalities or hierarchies by marking them with Roman numerals, letters, and numbers indented in a prescribed fashion. (2f)

frames Areas of a webpage that function independently of the other areas of the page.

freewriting Writing nonstop for a period of time to generate ideas by free association of thoughts. Also see *discovery draft.* (2g)

fused sentence The error that consists of running independent clauses into each other without the required punctuation that marks them as complete units; also called a *run-on sentence* or *run-together sentence.* (Chapter 20)

future perfect progressive tense The form of the future perfect tense that describes an action or condition ongoing until some specific future time: *I will have been talking.* (15j)

future perfect tense The tense indicating that an action will have been completed or a condition will have ended by a specified point in the future: *I will have talked.* (15i)

future progressive tense The form of the future tense showing that a future action will continue for some time: *I will be talking.* (15j)

future tense The form of a verb, made with the simple form and either *shall* or *will,* expressing an action yet to be taken or a condition not yet experienced: *I will talk.* (15g)

gender The classification of words as masculine, feminine, or neutral. (12f, 17s)

gender-free language See *gender-neutral language.*

gender-neutral language Also called *gender-free language* or *nonsexist language,* it uses terms that do not unnecessarily say whether a person is male or female, as with *police officer* instead of *policeman.* (17s)

generalization A broad statement that is not supported by details. (1c.3)

gerund A verb form that functions as a noun: *Walking is good exercise.* Also see *verbal.* (14e, 51c, Chapter 54)

helping verb See *auxiliary verb.*

homonyms Words spelled differently that sound alike: *to, too, two.* (31f)

home page The opening main page of a website that provides access to other pages on the site. (46d)

HTML (**H**yper**T**ext **M**arkup **L**anguage) A computer program language used for webpages. (46d)

hyperbole See *overstatement.*

hyperlink Online connection from one digital document to another. (46d)

idiom, idiomatic expression A word, phrase, or other construction that has a different meaning from its literal meaning: *He lost his head. She hit the ceiling.* (Chapter 53)

illogical predication See *faulty predication.*

imperative mood The mood that expresses commands and direct requests, using the simple form of the verb and often implying but not expressing the subject, you: *Go.* (15l)

imperative sentence A sentence that gives a command: *Go to the corner to buy me a newspaper.* (15k, 19b.3)

incubation The prewriting technique of giving ideas time to develop and clarify. (2c.8)

indefinite article See *articles, determiner.*

indefinite pronoun A pronoun, such as *all, anyone, each,* and *others,* that refers to a nonspecific person or thing. (14c, 14f, 17i)

independent clause A clause that can stand alone as an independent grammatical unit. (14p)

indicative mood The mood of verbs used for statements about real things or highly likely ones: *I think Kofi is arriving today.* (15l, 22d)

indirect discourse Reported speech or conversation that does not use the exact structure of the original and so is not enclosed in quotation marks. (22e, 24h)

indirect title Title that hints at an essay's topic; sparks interest by presenting a puzzle that can be solved by reading the essay. (2i.3)

indirect object A noun or pronoun or group of words functioning as a noun that tells to whom or for whom the action expressed by a transitive verb was done. (14m)

indirect question A sentence that reports a question and ends with a period: *I asked if you are leaving.* (23a, 23c, 52a)

indirect quotation See *quotation.*

induction The reasoning process of arriving at general principles from particular facts or instances. (4h)

inductive reasoning A form of reasoning that moves from particular facts or instances to general principles. (4h)

inference What a reader or listener understands to be implied but not stated. (4e)

infinitive A verbal made of the simple form of a verb and usually, but not always, *to* that functions as a noun, adjective, or adverb. Infinitives without the word *to* are called *unmarked* (or *bare*) *infinitives.* (14e, 15k, Chapter 54)

infinitive phrase An infinitive, with its modifiers and object, that functions as a noun, adjective, or adverb. Also see *verbal phrase.* (14e)

informal language Word choice that creates a tone appropriate for casual writing or speaking. (1d, 12h)

informal outline Non-traditional outline that doesn't follow the rules of a *formal outline.* (2f)

informative writing Writing that gives information and, when necessary, explains it; also known as *expository writing.* (1c.2)

intensive pronoun A pronoun that ends in *-self* and emphasizes its antecedent. Also called *reflexive pronoun: Vida* **himself** *argued against it.* (14c)

interjection An emotion-conveying word that is treated as a sentence, starting with a capital letter and ending with an exclamation point or a period: *Oh! Ouch!* (14j, 24c)

interrogative pronoun A pronoun, such as *whose* or *what,* that implies a question: **Who** *called?* (14c, 19b.1)

interrogative sentence A sentence that asks a direct question: *Did you see that?* (14k)

in-text citation Source information placed in parentheses within the body of a research paper. Also see *citation, parenthetical reference.* (36b, 37b)

intransitive verb A verb that does not take a direct object. (15f)

invention techniques Ways of gathering ideas for writing. Also see *planning.* (2c–2g)

inverted word order Order in which the main verb or an auxiliary verb comes before the subject, in contrast to standard order. Most questions and some exclamations use inverted word order. (17h, 9r, Chapter 52)

irony Use of words to imply the opposite of their usual meaning. (12c)

irregular verb A verb that forms the past tense and past participle in some way other than by adding *-ed* or *-d.* (15d)

jargon A particular field's or group's specialized vocabulary that a general reader is unlikely to understand. (12j)

journalist's questions Who? What? When? Where? Why? How? Traditionally, news stories answer these questions.

justify When used as a design term, it refers to aligning text evenly along both the left and right margins. (45c)

key terms In an essay, the words central to its topic and its message. (3c, 3k, 4c, 5e, 5l)

keywords The main words in a source's title or the words that the author or editor has identified as central to that source. Use keywords in searching for sources online or in library databases. (34d)

layout The arrangement of text, visuals, colour, and space on a page. (45g)

levels of formality Word choices and sentence structures reflecting various degrees of formality of language. A formal level is used for ceremonial and other occasions when stylistic flourishes are appropriate. A medium level, neither too formal nor too casual, is acceptable for most academic writing. (12b)

levels of generality Degrees of generality used to group or organize information or ideas as you write, as when moving from the most general to the most specific. See also *levels of specificity.* (2e)

levels of specificity Degrees of specificity used to group or organize information or ideas as you write, as when moving from the most specific to the most general. See also *levels of generality.* (2e)

limiting adjective See *determiner.*

linking verb A main verb that links a subject with a subject complement that renames or describes the subject. Linking verbs, sometimes called *copulative verbs,* convey a state of being, relate to the senses, or indicate a condition. (15a, 15c)

logical appeal Rhetorical strategy that relies on formal reasoning, including providing evidence and drawing conclusions from premises. Greek name is *logos.* (5g)

logical fallacies Flaws in reasoning that lead to illogical statements. (4i)

main clause See *independent clause.*

main verb A verb that expresses action, occurrence, or state of being and that shows mood, tense, voice, number, and person. (14d, 15b)

mapping An invention technique based on thinking about a topic and its increasingly specific subdivisions; also known as *clustering* or *webbing.* (2c)

margins The boundaries of a page, which means the white space or blank areas at the top, bottom, and sides of a paper or screen. (45c)

mechanics Conventions governing matters such as the use of capital letters, italics, abbreviations, and numbers. (Part Four)

memo or memorandum A brief form of business correspondence with a format that is headed with lines for "To," "From," and "Subject." (43e)

metaphor A comparison implying similarity between two things. A metaphor does not use words such as *like* or *as,* which are used in a simile and which make a comparison explicit: *a mop of hair* (compare the simile *hair like a mop*). (12c)

misplaced modifier Describing or limiting words that are wrongly positioned in a sentence so that their message is either illogical or relates to the wrong word or words. Also see *squinting modifier.* (21a)

mixed metaphors Incongruously combined images. (12c)

mixed sentence A sentence that unintentionally changes from one grammatical structure to another, incompatible one, so that the meaning is garbled. (22f); also called *mixed construction.*

MLA style See *documentation style, parenthetical reference.*

modal auxiliary verb One of a group of nine auxiliary verbs that add information such as a sense of needing, wanting, or having to do something or a sense of possibility, likelihood, obligation, permission, or ability. (15e, Chapter 55)

modified block style An alternative to block style. In modified block style the lines for the inside address and the body begin flush left but the heading, closing, and signature begin about halfway across the page. (43f)

modifier, modify A word or group of words functioning as an adjective or adverb to describe or limit another word or word group. Also see *misplaced modifier.* (9p, 14n, Chapter 18)

mood The attribute of verbs showing a speaker's or writer's attitude toward the action by the way verbs are used. Also see *imperative mood, indicative mood, subjunctive mood.* (15l, 15m)

multimodal Combining words, images, sound, and video. (4l, Chapter 46)

narrative A rhetorical strategy that tells a story; a narrative deals with what is or what has happened. (3i)

navigation bar The set of links on every webpage that allows users to get back to the site's home page and to major parts of the site. (46c–46d)

netiquette Coined from the word *etiquette,* netiquette is good manners when using e-mail, the Internet, and online sites such as bulletin boards, chatrooms, etc. (43d)

noncount noun A noun that names a thing that cannot be counted: *water, time.* Also see *collective noun.* (14b, Chapters 50 and 51)

nonessential element See *nonrestrictive element.*

nonrestrictive clause See *nonrestrictive element.*

nonrestrictive element A descriptive word, phrase, or dependent clause that provides information not essential to understanding the basic message of the element it modifies and so is set off by commas. Also see *restrictive element.* (24f)

nonsexist language See *gender-neutral language.*

nonspecific noun A noun that refers to any of a number of identical items; it takes the indefinite articles *a, an.* (51a)

nonstandard English Language usage other than what is called *edited English.* (12b)

noun A word that names a person, place, thing, or idea. Nouns function as subjects, objects, or complements. (14b)

noun clause A clause that functions as a subject, object, or complement. (14p)

noun complement See *complement.*

noun determiner See *determiner.*

noun phrase A noun and its modifiers functioning as a subject, object, or complement. (14o)

number The attribute of some words indicating whether they refer to one (*singular*) or more than one (*plural*). (15a, 17b, 22b, Chapter 50)

object A noun, pronoun, or group of words functioning as a noun or pronoun that receives the action of a verb (*direct object*); tells to whom or for whom something is done (*indirect object*); or completes the meaning of a preposition (*object of a preposition*). (14m)

object complement A noun or adjective renaming or describing a direct object after verbs such as *call, consider, name, elect,* and *think: I call the most obsessive joggers **fanatics**.* (14n)

objective case The case of a noun or pronoun functioning as a direct or indirect object or the object of a preposition or of a verbal. A few pronouns change form to show case (*him, her, whom*). Also see *case.* (Chapter 16)

outline Technique for laying out ideas for writing. An outline can be formal or informal. (2f)

overstatement Deliberate exaggeration for emphasis; also called *hyperbole.* (12c)

paragraph A group of sentences that work together to develop a unit of thought. They are the structured elements of an essay, which is composed of an *introductory paragraph, body paragraphs,* and a *concluding paragraph.* Also see *shaping.* (Chapter 3)

paragraph arrangement The arrangement of sentences using specific techniques to communicate a paragraph's message. (3h)

paragraph development The use of specific, concrete details (RENNS) to support a generalization in a paragraph; rhetorical strategies or patterns for organizing ideas in paragraphs. (3f, 3i)

parallelism The use of equivalent grammatical forms or matching sentence structures to express equivalent ideas and develop coherence. (3g.4, Chapter 10)

paraphrase A restatement of someone else's ideas in language and sentence structure different from those of the original. (35i)

parenthetical reference Information enclosed in parentheses following quoted, paraphrased, or summarized material from a source to alert readers to the use of material from a specific source. Parenthetical references, also called *in-text citations*, function together with a list of bibliographic information about each source used in a paper to document the writer's use of sources. Also see *citation*. (36b)

participial phrase A phrase that contains a present or a past participle and any modifiers and that functions as an adjective. Also see *verbal phrase*. (14o)

participle See *past participle, present participle, present perfect participle*.

passive construction See *passive voice*.

passive voice The form of a verb in which the subject is acted on; if the subject is mentioned in the sentence, it usually appears as the object of the preposition *by*: *I was frightened by the thunder.* [Compare the active voice: *The thunder frightened me.*] The passive voice emphasizes the action, in contrast to the *active voice*, which emphasizes the doer of the action. (15n–15p)

past participle The third principal part of a verb, formed in regular verbs, like the past tense, by adding *-d* or *-ed* to the simple form. In irregular verbs, it often differs from the simple form and the past tense: *break, broke, broken.* (14e, 15b, 54f)

past perfect progressive tense The past perfect tense form that describes an ongoing condition in the past that has been ended by something stated in the sentence: *I had been talking.* (15j)

past perfect tense The tense that describes a condition or action that started in the past, continued for a while, and then ended in the past: *I had talked.* (15g, 15i)

past progressive tense The tense that shows the continuing nature of a past action: *I was talking.* (15j)

past subjunctive The simple past tense in the subjunctive mood. (15m)

past tense The tense that tells of an action completed or a condition ended. (15g)

past-tense form The second principal part of a verb, in regular verbs formed by adding *-d* or *-ed* to the simple form. In irregular verbs, the past tense may change in several ways from the simple form. (15b, 15d)

peer-response group A group of students formed to give each other feedback on writing. (Chapter 6)

perfect infinitive Also called *present perfect participle*, a tense used to describe an action that occurs before the action in the main verb. (15k)

perfect tenses The three tenses—the present perfect (*I have talked*), the past perfect (*I had talked*), and the future perfect (*I will have talked*)—that help show complex time relationships between two clauses. (15g, 15i)

periodic sentence A sentence that begins with modifiers and ends with the independent clause, thus postponing the main idea—and the emphasis—for the end; also called a *climactic sentence*. (9o)

periodical A publication such as a newspaper, magazine, or journal that is published at a regular interval. (2c.7, 34f)

person The attribute of nouns and pronouns showing who or what acts or experiences an action. *First person* is the one speaking (*I, we*); *second person* is the one being spoken to (*you, you*); and *third person* is the person or thing being spoken about (*he, she, it, they*). All nouns are third person. (15a, 17b)

personal pronoun A pronoun that refers to people or things, such as *I, you, them, it*. (14c, 16n)

persuasive appeal Rhetorical strategy that appeals to the emotions, logic, or ethics of readers. (5g)

persuasive writing Writing that seeks to convince the reader about a matter of opinion. It is also known as *argumentative writing*. (1c.3, Chapter 5)

phrasal verb A verb that combines with one or more prepositions to deliver its meaning: *ask out, look into*. (53c)

phrase A group of related words that does not contain both a subject and a predicate and thus cannot stand alone as an independent grammatical unit. A phrase functions as a noun, verb, or modifier. (14o)

plagiarism A writer's presenting another person's words or ideas without giving credit to that person. Documentation systems allow writers to give proper credit to sources in ways recognized by scholarly communities. Plagiarism is a serious offence, a form of intellectual dishonesty that can lead to course failure or expulsion. (Chapter 35)

715

planning An early part of the writing process in which writers gather ideas. Along with shaping, planning is sometimes called *prewriting.* (Chapter 2)

plural See *number.*

podcast A brief sound file shared over the Internet, somewhat like an online radio broadcast. (1f, 46g).

positive form The form of an adjective or adverb when no comparison is being expressed: *blue, easily.* Also see *comparative form, superlative form.* (18e)

possessive case The case of a noun or pronoun that shows ownership or possession: *my, your, their,* and so on. Also see *case, pronoun case.* (Chapter 16, 27a–27c)

predicate The part of a sentence that contains the verb and tells what the subject is doing or experiencing or what is being done to the subject. A *simple predicate* contains only the main verb and any auxiliary verbs. A *complete predicate* contains the verb, its modifiers, objects, and other related words. A *compound predicate* contains two or more verbs and their objects and modifiers, if any. (14l)

predicate adjective An adjective used as a subject complement: *That tree is **leafy**.* (14n)

predicate nominative A noun or pronoun used as a subject complement: *That tree is a **maple**.* (14n)

prediction A major activity of the *reading process,* in which the reader guesses what comes next. (4c)

premises In a deductive argument expressed as a syllogism, statements presenting the conditions of the argument from which the conclusion must follow. (4h)

preposition A word that conveys a relationship, often of space or time, between the noun or pronoun following it and other words in the sentence. The noun or pronoun following a preposition is called its *object.* (14h, Chapter 53)

prepositional phrase A preposition and the word it modifies. Also see *phrase, preposition.* (14h, 14o)

presentation style The way you deliver what you have to say. Memorization, reading, mapping, and speaking with notes are different types of presentation styles. (42h)

present infinitive Names or describes an activity or occurrence coming together either at the same time or after the time expressed in the main verb. (15k)

present participle A verb's *-ing* form. Used with auxiliary verbs, present participles function as main verbs. Used without auxiliary verbs, present participles function as nouns or adjectives. (14e, 15b, 54f)

present perfect participle See *perfect infinitive.*

present perfect progressive tense The present perfect tense form that describes something ongoing in the past that is likely to continue into the future: *I have been talking.* (15j)

present perfect tense The tense indicating that an action or its effects, begun or perhaps completed in the past, continue into the present: *I have talked.* (15g, 15i)

present progressive tense The present-tense form of the verb that indicates something taking place at the time it is written or spoken about: *I am talking.* (15j)

present subjunctive The simple form of the verb for all persons and numbers in the subjunctive mood. (15m)

present tense The tense that describes what is happening, what is true at the moment, and what is consistently true. It uses the simple form (*I talk*) and the *-s* form in the third-person singular (*he, she, it talks*). (15g, 15h)

prewriting All activities in the writing process before drafting. Also see *planning, shaping.* (Chapter 2)

primary sources Firsthand work: write-ups of experiments and observations by the researchers who conducted them; taped accounts, interviews, and newspaper accounts by direct observers; autobiographies, diaries, and journals; expressive works (poems, plays, fiction, essays). Also known as *primary evidence.* Also see *secondary source.* (4d.2, 32a, 32d)

process A rhetorical strategy in writing that reports a sequence of actions by which something is done or made. (3i)

progressive forms Verb forms made in all tenses with the present participle and forms of the verb *be* as an auxiliary. Progressive forms show that an action, occurrence, or state of being is ongoing. (15g, 15j)

pronoun A word that takes the place of a noun and functions in the same ways that nouns do. Types of pronouns are *demonstrative, indefinite, intensive, interrogative, personal, reciprocal, reflexive,* and *relative.* The word (or words) a pronoun replaces is called its *antecedent*. (14c, Chapter 16)

pronoun-antecedent agreement The match in expressing number and person—and for personal pronouns, gender as well—required between a pronoun and its antecedent. (17o–17t)

pronoun case The way a pronoun changes form to reflect its use as the agent of action (*subjective case*), the thing being acted upon (*objective case*), or the thing showing ownership (*possessive case*). (16a–16k)

pronoun reference The relationship between a pronoun and its antecedent. (16l–16s)

proofreading The act of reading a final draft to find and correct any spelling or mechanics mistakes, typing errors, or handwriting illegibility; the final step of the writing process. (2k)

proper adjective An adjective formed from a proper noun: *Victorian, American*. (30e)

proper noun A noun that names specific people, places, or things and is always capitalized: *Moose Jaw, Buick*. (14b, 30e, 51c)

public writing Writing intended for readers outside of academic and work settings. (Chapter 44)

purpose The goal or aim of a piece of writing: to express oneself, to provide information, to persuade, or to create a literary work. (1c)

quotation Repeating or reporting another person's words. *Direct quotation* repeats another's words exactly and encloses them in quotation marks. *Indirect quotation* reports another's words without quotation marks except around any words repeated exactly from the source. Both *direct* and *indirect quotation* require *documentation* of the *source* to avoid *plagiarism*. Also see *direct discourse, indirect discourse*. (Chapter 28, 35h)

readers Readers are the audiences for writing; readers process material they read on the literal, inferential, and evaluative levels. (1c–1d)

reading process Critical reading that requires the reader to read for *literal meaning*, to draw *inferences*, and to *evaluate*. (4c–4g)

reciprocal pronoun The pronouns *each other* and *one another* referring to individual parts of a plural antecedent: *We respect each other*. (14c)

References In many documentation styles, including APA, the title of a list of sources cited in a research paper or other written work. (33h, 33i, 34c, Chapters 37 and 38)

reflexive pronoun A pronoun that ends in *-self* and that refers back to its antecedent: *They claim to support themselves*. (14c)

regional language Also called *dialectal language*; words and expressions specific to certain geographical areas. (12h)

regular verb A verb that forms its past tense and past participle by adding *-ed* or *-d* to the simple form. Most English verbs are regular. (15b, 15d)

relative adverb An adverb that introduces an adjective clause: *The lot where I usually park my car was full*. (14g)

relative pronoun A pronoun, such as *who, which, that, whom*, or *whoever*, that introduces an adjective clause or sometimes a noun clause. (9j, 14c)

RENNS Test See *paragraph development*. (3f)

research question The controlling question that drives research. (33e)

research writing Also called *source-based writing*, a process in three steps: conducting research, understanding and evaluating the results of the research, and writing the research paper with accurate documentation. (Chapter 33)

restrictive clause See *restrictive element*.

restrictive element A word, phrase, or dependent clause that contains information that is essential for a sentence to deliver its message. Do not set off with commas. (24f)

revising, revision A part of the writing process in which writers evaluate their rough drafts and, based on their assessments, rewrite by adding, cutting, replacing, moving, and often totally recasting material. (2i)

rhetoric The area of discourse that focuses on the arrangement of ideas and choice of words as a reflection of both the writer's purpose and the writer's sense of audience. (Chapter 3)

rhetorical strategies In writing, various techniques for presenting ideas to deliver a writer's intended message with clarity and impact. Reflecting typical patterns of human thought, rhetorical strategies include arrangements such as chronological and climactic order; stylistic techniques such as parallelism and planned repetition; and patterns for organizing and developing writing such as description and definition. (3i)

Rogerian argument A technique of argument adapted from the principles of communication developed by the psychologist Carl Rogers. (5j) role The position the writer is emphasizing for a given task—for example, student, client, taxpayer, supervisor. (1b)

run-on sentence See *fused sentence.*

sans serif Font types that do not have little "feet" or finishing lines at the top and bottom of each letter. (45c)

search engine An Internet-specific software program that can look through all files at Internet sites. (34l)

secondary source A source that reports, analyzes, discusses, reviews, or otherwise deals with the work of someone else, as opposed to a primary source, which is someone's original work or firsthand report. A reliable secondary source should be the work of a person with appropriate credentials, should appear in a respected publication or other medium, should be current, and should be well reasoned. (4d.2, 32d, Chapter 34)

second person See *person.*

sentence See *sentence types.*

sentence fragment A portion of a sentence that is punctuated as though it were a complete sentence. (Chapter 19)

sentence outline Type of outline in which each element is a sentence. (2f)

sentence types A grammatical classification of sentences by the kinds of clauses they contain. A *simple sentence* consists of one independent clause. A *complex sentence* contains one independent clause and one or more dependent clauses. A *compound-complex sentence* contains at least two independent clauses and one or more dependent clauses. A *compound* or *coordinate sentence* contains two or more independent clauses joined by a coordinating conjunction. Sentences are also classified by their grammatical function; see *declarative sentence, exclamatory sentence, imperative sentence, interrogative sentence.* (9f, 14k, 14q)

sentence variety A result of using various lengths and structures in writing sentences; see *coordinate sentence, cumulative sentence, periodic sentence, sentence types.* (Chapter 9)

serif Font types that are characterized by little "feet" or finishing lines at the top and bottom of each letter. (45c)

server A computer that is always online and available to Internet users. (46b)

sexist language Language that unnecessarily communicates that a person is male or female or that assigns characteristics based on gender. For example, *fireman* implies that only males fight fires; *fire fighter* includes males and females. (12f, 17s)

shaping An early part of the writing process in which writers consider ways to organize their material. Along with planning, shaping is sometimes called *prewriting.* (Chapters 2 and 3)

shift Within a sentence, an unnecessary abrupt change in *person, number, subject, voice, tense, mood,* or *direct* or *indirect discourse.* (22a–22c)

simile A comparison, using *like* or *as,* of otherwise dissimilar things. (12c)

simple form The form of the verb that shows action, occurrence, or state of being in the present. It is also the first principal part of a verb. The simple form is also known as the *dictionary form* or *base form.* (15b)

simple predicate See *predicate.*

simple sentence See *sentence types.*

simple subject See *subject.*

simple tenses The present, past, and future tenses, which divide time into present, past, and future. (15g, 15h)

singular See *number.*

slanted language Language that tries to manipulate the reader with distorted facts. (12g)

source-based writing See *research writing.*

sources Books, articles, print or Internet documents, other works, and persons providing credible information. In *research writing,* often called *outside sources.* (4d.2, 32d, Chapters 34 and 35)

spatial order An arrangement of information according to location in space; an organizing strategy for sentences, paragraphs, and longer pieces of writing. (3h)

specific noun A noun understood to be exactly and specifically referred to; uses the definite article *the.* (51a)

split infinitive One or more words coming between the two words of an infinitive. (21b)

squinting modifier A modifier that is considered misplaced because it is not clear whether it describes the word that comes before it or the word that follows it. (21a)

standard English English as used by educated people throughout the world that conforms to established rules of grammar, sentence structure, and punctuation. (12b)

standard word order The most common order for words in English sentences: The subject comes before the predicate. Also see *inverted word order.* (9r, Chapter 52)

stereotype A kind of hasty generalization (a *logical fallacy*) in which a sweeping claim is made about all members of a particular ethnic, racial, religious, gender, age, or political group. (4i)

subject The word or group of words in a sentence that acts, is acted upon, or is described by the verb. A *simple subject* includes only the noun or pronoun. A *complete subject* includes the noun or pronoun and all its modifiers. A *compound subject* includes two or more nouns or pronouns and their modifiers. (14l)

subject complement A noun or adjective that follows a linking verb, renaming or describing the subject of the sentence; also called a *predicate nominative.* (14n)

subjective case The case of the noun or pronoun functioning as a subject. Also see *case, pronoun case.* (Chapter 16)

subject tree Shows you visually whether you have sufficient content, at varying levels of generality or specificity, to start a first draft of your writing. A subject tree also visually demonstrates whether you have a good balance of general ideas and specific details. (2e)

subject-verb agreement The required match between a subject and a verb in expressing number and person. (17b–17n)

subjunctive mood A verb mood that expresses wishes, recommendations, indirect requests, speculations, and conditional statements. *I wish you **were** here.* (15l, 15m)

subordinate clause See *dependent clause.*

subordinating conjunction A conjunction that introduces an adverb clause and expresses a relationship between the idea in it and the idea in the independent clause. (9j, 14i, 14p, 20c.4)

subordination The use of grammatical structures to reflect the relative importance of ideas. A sentence with logically subordinated information expresses the most important information in the independent clause and less important information in dependent clauses or phrases. (Chapter 9)

summary A brief version of the main message or central point of a passage or other discourse; a critical thinking activity preceding synthesis. (4b, 35j)

superlative form The form of an adjective or adverb that expresses comparison among three or more things: *bluest, least blue; most easily, least easily.* (18e)

syllogism The structure of a deductive argument expressed in two *premises* and a *conclusion.* The first premise is a generalized assumption or statement of fact. The second premise is a different assumption or statement of fact based on evidence. The conclusion is also a specific instance that follows logically from the premises. (4h)

synonym A word that is very close in meaning to another word: *cold* and *icy.* (12d)

synthesis A component of critical thinking in which material that has been summarized, analyzed, and interpreted is connected to what is already known (one's prior knowledge) or to what has been learned from other authorities. (4b, 4f)

tag question An inverted verb-pronoun combination added to the end of a sentence, creating a question that asks the audience to agree with the assertion in the first part of the sentence. A tag question is set off from the rest of the sentence with a comma: *You know what a tag question is, **don't you?*** (24g)

tense The time at which the action of the verb occurs: the present, the past, or the future. Also see *perfect tenses, simple tenses.* (15g–15k)

tense sequence In sentences that have more than one clause, the accurate matching of verbs to reflect logical time relationships. (15k)

thesis statement A statement of an essay's central theme that makes clear the main idea, the writer's purpose, the focus of the topic, and perhaps the organizational pattern. (2d)

third person See *person.*

title The part of an essay that clarifies the overall point of the piece of writing. It can be *direct* or *indirect.* (2i)

tone The writer's attitude toward his or her material and reader, especially as reflected by word choice. (1b, Chapter 8)

topic The subject of discourse. (1b)

topic sentence The sentence that expresses the main idea of a paragraph. A topic sentence may be implied, not stated. (3e)

Toulmin model A model that defines the essential parts of an argument as the *claim* (or *main point*), the *support* (or *evidence*), and the *warrants* (or *assumptions behind the main point*). (5h)

transition The connection of one idea to another in discourse. Useful strategies within a paragraph for creating transitions include transitional

719

expressions, parallelism, and the planned repetition of key terms and phrases. In a long piece of writing, a *transitional paragraph* is the bridge between discussion of two separate topics. Also see *critical response*. (3g.1, 3j)

transitional expressions Words and phrases that signal connections among ideas and create coherence. (3g.1)

transitive verb A verb that must be followed by a direct object. (15f)

understatement Figurative language in which the writer uses deliberate restraint for emphasis. (12c)

unity The clear and logical relationship between the main idea of a paragraph and the evidence supporting the main idea. (3d, 3e)

unstated assumptions Premises that are implied but not stated. (4h)

usage A customary way of using language. (Chapter 13)

valid Correctly and rationally derived; applied to a deductive argument whose conclusion follows logically from the premises. Validity applies to the structure of an argument, not its truth. (4h)

verb Any word that shows action or occurrence or describes a state of being. Verbs change form to convey time (*tense*), attitude (*mood*), and role of the subject (*voice,* either *active* or *passive*). Verbs occur in the predicate of a clause and can be in verb phrases, which may consist of a main verb, auxiliary verbs, and modifiers. Verbs can be described as *transitive* or *intransitive,* depending on whether they take a direct object. Also see *voice*. (Chapter 15)

verbal A verb part functioning as a noun, adjective, or adverb. Verbals include *infinitives, present participles* (functioning as adjectives), *gerunds* (present participles functioning as nouns), and *past participles*. (14e, Chapter 54)

verbal phrase A group of words that contains a verbal (an infinitive, participle, or gerund) and its modifiers. (14o)

verb phrase A main verb, any auxiliary verbs, and any modifiers. (14o)

verb tense Verbs show tense (time) by changing form. English has six verb tenses. (15g)

visual design Refers to the appearance of a document (how it looks), as opposed to its content (what it says). (45a)

voice An attribute of verbs showing whether the subject acts (*active voice*) or is acted on (*passive voice*). (15n–15p)

warrants One of three key terms in the *Toulmin model* for argument; refers to implied or inferred assumptions. They are based on *authority, substance,* and *motivation*. (5h)

Web See *World Wide Web*.

webbing See *mapping*.

webpage On the Internet, a file of information. Such a file is not related in length to a printed page, as it may be a paragraph or many screens long. (46c)

website A page or a collection of linked pages organized under a domain name and often including a home page. (46c)

Web structure The organization of the content and documents that site creators include in a Web project. (46d)

white space The part of a document that has neither text nor visuals. (45g)

wiki A website that allows readers to change its content. (1f, 46f)

wordiness An attribute of writing that is full of empty words and phrases that do not contribute to meaning. The opposite of *conciseness*. (Chapter 11)

word order See *standard word order, inverted word order*.

World Wide Web The *Web*, a user-friendly computer network allowing access to information in the form of text, graphics, and sound on the Internet. (Chapter 46)

working bibliography A preliminary list of useful sources in research writing. (33i)

Works Cited In MLA documentation style, the title of a list of all sources cited in a research paper or other written work. (36a)

writer's block The desire to start writing, but not doing so. (2h)

writing process Stages of writing in which a writer gathers and shapes ideas, organizes material, expresses those ideas in a rough draft, evaluates the draft and revises it, edits the writing for technical errors, and proofreads it for typographical accuracy and legibility. The stages often overlap; see *planning, shaping, drafting, revising, editing, proofreading*. (Chapters 1 and 2)

writing situation The beginning of the writing process for each writing assignment as defined by four elements: topic, purpose, audience, special requirements. (1b)

List of Quick Reference Features

Credits

PHOTOGRAPHS

Hemera / Thinkstock (page 80)

Alan Haynes / Alamy (page 98)

Scott Cunningham / Merrill Education (page 100 top)

Stockbyte / Getty Images (page 100 bottom)

Paul Conklin / Taxi / Getty Images (page 101)

Copyright © Greenpeace. Reproduced with permission of Greenpeace Canada. (page 102)

Copyright © World Wildlife Fund. Reproduced with permission of WWF. (page 103)

Bob Mahoney / The Image Works (page 121)

Jeremy Gilbert (page 584)

iStockphoto.com (page 659)

TEXT/ART

Steve Truelove, "Journey of Hope - Day 10 - Kili Climb, TrueKawz Productions blog. http://web .me.com/journeyofhope2011/Journey_of_Hope_2011/Blog/Entries/2011/1/29_Journey_ of_Hope_-_Day_10_-_Kili_Climb.html. Used with permission of Steve Truelove. (page 6)

Richard B. Manchester, "Diamonds" from *Mammoth Book of Fascinating Information*, 1980, A&W Visual Books. (page 7)

Janice Gross Stein, excerpt from *The Cult of Efficiency*. Toronto: House of Anansi Press, 2003. (page 7)

James S. Trefil, "Concentric Clues from Growth Rings Unlock the Past" from *Trees are Living Archives*, Smithsonian, July 1985, pp 46–54. Copyright © 1985. (page 8)

Sharon Butala, excerpt from "Rural Saskatchewan: Creating the Garden" from *Voices: Essays on Canadian Families*, Edited by Marian Lynn. Toronto: Nelson Canada. Copyright ©1995 Sharon Butala. With permission of the author. (page 8)

Microsoft Word Screens. Copyright Microsoft Corporation. All rights reserved. (page 13) © Google (page 27)

Daniel Goleman, "Researchers Trace Empathy's Roots to Infancy" from *Working with Emotional Intelligence*. New York: Bantam Books, 1998. (page 57)

Gerald Secor Couzens, "If Lightning Strikes" from *House Calls: How Doctors Treat Themselves and Their Own Families for Common Illnesses and Injuries*. New York: Simon & Schuster, 1993. (page 57)

Abigail Haworth, "Nothing About These Women is Real," *Marie Claire*, July 2005. Copyright © 2005. (page 58)

Jeremy Yudkin, excerpt from "Composers and Patrons in the Classic Era" in *Understanding Music*, 3rd edition. Copyright © 2002. (page 59)

Robert Lanz, "A New Theory of the Universe", *The American Scholar*, Spring 2007. (page 59)

C.M. Millward, "The Arrival of the English" from *A Biography of the English Language* 2nd edition. Copyright © 1996. (page 59)

David Mamet, excerpt from *Three Uses of the Knife: On the Nature and Purpose of Drama*. Copyright © 1998 by Columbia University Press. (page 59)

Wendy Thomas, excerpt from *Getting Started on a Great Canadian Garden*, p. 47. © Bookmark Publishing Group. Reprinted with permission of Pearson Canada. (page 60)

Bruce Mau, excerpt from "Imagining the Future", *The Walrus*, March 1, 2011. Reproduced with permission of the author. (page 60)

Terry Bullick, excerpt from "When is a Grizzly not a Grizzly?" *Equinox*, December 1993. (page 61)

Dr. Henry Benson, *The Relaxation Response*. New York: HarperCollins, 2001. (page 62)

Geoff Pevere and Greig Dymond, excerpt from *Mondo Canuck*. Toronto: Prentice Hall Canada, 1996. By permission of Pearson Canada. (page 64)

Sara Wilson, "Clean House: Getting Laid off from his Job Gave this Franchisee a Fresh Start", *Entrepreneur*, August 2005. Copyright © 2005. (page 64)

Nancy Bonvillain, excerpt from *Cultural Anthropology*, 2nd edition. Copyright © 2009. Reprinted by permission of Pearson Education, Upper Saddle River, NJ. (page 64)

Margaret Mead and Rhoda Metraux, excerpt from "New Superstitions for Old", *Redbook Magazine*, 126 No. 3, January 1966. (page 65)

Richard Gwyn, excerpt from *The 49th Paradox*. Copyright © 1985 by R. & A. Gwyn Associates Ltd. Published by McClelland & Stewart. Used with permission of the author and the publisher. (page 65)

Ward McBurney, excerpt from "Bathurst Street Bridge" from *Sky Train and Other Ward Stories*, reprinted with permission from the Dundurn Group. Copyright 2001. (page 66)

Randolph H. Manning, "Fighting Racism with Inclusion." (page 66)

Tony Hillerman, *Hillerman Country*. New York: HarperCollins, 1991. (page 66)

Robert Bringhurst, excerpt from *The Solid Form of Language*. Copyright © Robert Bringhurst, 2004, and reproduced with permission of Gaspereau Press. (page 67)

William Least Heat-Moon, excerpt from *Blue Highway: A Journey into America*. Little, Brown and Company, 1982. (page 67)

Wayne Grady, excerpt from *Chasing the Chinook*. Toronto: Penguin Books, 1999. Reproduced by permission of Bella Pomer Agency. (page 68)

Arthur Andrew, excerpt from *The Rise and Fall of Middle Power*. Toronto: James Lorimer & Company Ltd. (page 68)

Linda Weltner, "Stripping Down to Bare Happiness." (page 69)

Edwin Bliss, *Getting Things Done: The ABCs of Time Management*. New York: Charles Scribner's Sons, 1976. (page 69)

Marie Hart, "Sport: Women Sit in the Back of the Bus" in *Psychology Today*, October 1971. Copyright © 1971 by Sussex Publishers, Inc. (page 70)

Carol Tavris, "Old Age Isn't What it Used to Be." (page 70)

Jim Doherty, "The Hobby That Challenges You to Think Like a Bee." (page 70)

Douglas Goold and Andrew Willis, *The Bre-X Fraud*. Copyright © 1997. Published by McClelland & Stewart Ltd. Used with permission of the authors and the publisher. (page 71)

Gretel Ehrlich, "Other Lives" from *The Solace of Open Spaces*. New York: Penguin Books, 1986. (page 72)

Ruth Mehrtens Galvin, "Sybarite to Some, Sinful to Others, but How Sweet it Is!" *Smithsonian*, February, 1986. (page 72)

Lori de Mori, "Making Olive Oil" from *Florence: Authentic Recipes for Celebrating the Foods of the World*. Copyright © 2004 by Weldon Owe Inc. and Williams-Sonoma Inc. (page 72)

Banesh Hoffman, "My Friend, Albert Einstein" from *Albert Einstein: Creator and Rebel*. New York: Penguin Group. Copyright © 1972 by Helen Dukas and Banesh Hoffman. (page 73)

John Arrend Timm, *General Chemistry*, 3rd edition. New York: McGraw-Hilly Companies, 1956. (page 73)

D. Kern Holoman, "Jazz" from *Masterworks: A Musical Discovery*, 1st edition. Coyright © 1998. Pearson Education, Upper Saddle River, NJ. (page 73)

Warren Bennis, excerpt from "Time to Hang Up the Old Sports Cliches" from *The New York Times*, July 1987. (page 75)

Alison Lurie, excerpt from *The Langugae of Clothes*. Copyright © 1981 by Alison Lurie. (page 75)

Tamara Holt, "The Science of Yummy," *Popular Science*, 2007. (page 76)

Deborah Tannen, excerpt from *You Just Don't Understand*. Copyright © 1990 by Deborah Tannen. New York: HarperCollins Publishers. (page 76)

Michael Ignatieff, excerpt from *Blood and Belonging*. Toronto: Penguin Books, 2006. (page 76)

James Gorman, "Gadgets." (page 76)

Wayne Grady, excerpt from *Chasing the Chinook*. Toronto: Penguin Books, 1999. Reproduced by permission of Bella Pomer Agency. (page 76)

Jane Brody, "A Hoarder's Life: Filling the Cache—and Finding It" from *The New York Times*, November 19, 1991. (page 77)

Mark Kingwell, "The Voice of the Pundit is Heard in the Land" from *Marginalia: A Cultural Reader*. Toronto: Penguin Books, 1999. (77)

Ovide Mercredi, "Self-Government as a Way to Heal" from *In the Rapids: Navigating the Future of First Nations*. Copyright © 1993 Ovide Mercredi and Mary Ellen Turpel. Toronto: Penguin Group. (page 78)

Mordecai Richler, excerpt from *Oh Canada! Oh Quebec! Requiem for a Divided Country*. Toronto: Knopf Canada, 1992. (84)

Jean Vanier, excerpt from *Becoming Human*. Copyright © 1998, Paulist Press, Inc., New York/Mahwah, NJ. Used with permission of Paulist Press. (page 91)

© Dr. Paul De Palma (page 91)

Copyright © MEDECINS SANS FRONTIERES / DOCOTRS WITHOUT BORDERS (MSF), Inc. (page 111)

Statistics Canada. "University Degrees, Diplomas and Certificates Awarded." *The Daily*, 14 July 2010, http://www.statcan.gc.ca/daily-quotidien/100714/t100714b1-eng.htm. (page 142)

Statistics Canada, Canadian Social Trends, 11-008-XPE, Fall 1997, no 46, http://www.statcan.gc.ca/bsolc/olc-cel/olc-cel?catno=11-008-X19970023180&lang=eng. (page 143)

Julia Whitty and Robert Knoth, excerpt from "Sea Change," *Mother Jones*, October 2007. (page 152)

John Browne, excerpt from "Beyond Kyoto," *Foreign Affairs*, July/August 2004. (page 152)

Ronni Sandoff, excerpt from "Too Many Choices" from *Consumer Reports on Health*. (page 153)

Joshua Green, excerpt from "Google's Tar Pit," *The Atlantic*, December 2007. (page 159)

Laura C. Johnson, Jean Andrey and Susan M. Shaw, excerpt from "Mr Dithers Comes to Dinner: Telework and the merging of women's work and home domains in Canada." *Gender, Place & Culture*, 14 (2):141–161, 2007. (page 160)

Elise Geraghty, excerpt from *In the Name of the Father: Self Naming in the Face of Institutional Patriarchy*. (160)

ArticleFirst Advanced Search search engine, copyright © OCLC Online Computer Library Center, Inc. Reprinted by permission. FirstSearch and WorldCat are registered trademarks of OCLC Online Computer Library Center, Inc. (page 434)

PsychINFO search, reprinted with permission of the American Psychological Association, publisher of the PsychINFO ® database. Copyright © APA, all rights reserved. (page 439)

PsychINFO search, reprinted with permission of the American Psychological Association, publisher of the PsychINFO ® database. Copyright © APA, all rights reserved. (page 440)

Malcolm Gladwell, *Outliers: The Story of Success*. New York: Little, Brown & Company, 2008. (page 459)

Mark Kingwell, "The Voice of the Pundit is Heard in the Land" from *Marginalia: A Cultural Reader*. Toronto: Penguin Books, 1999. (460)

ESL Index

731

Index

Index